James W. Neville
May 1975

ARISTOPHANES

ECCLESIAZUSAE

ARISTOPHANES
ECCLESIAZUSAE

EDITED WITH
INTRODUCTION AND COMMENTARY
BY

R. G. USSHER
SENIOR LECTURER IN GREEK AND LATIN
NEW UNIVERSITY OF ULSTER

OXFORD
AT THE CLARENDON PRESS
1973

Oxford University Press, Ely House, London W. 1

GLASGOW   NEW YORK   TORONTO   MELBOURNE   WELLINGTON
CAPE TOWN   IBADAN   NAIROBI   DAR ES SALAAM   LUSAKA   ADDIS ABABA
DELHI   BOMBAY   CALCUTTA   MADRAS   KARACHI   LAHORE   DACCA
KUALA LUMPUR   SINGAPORE   HONG KONG   TOKYO

Printed in Great Britain
at the University Press, Oxford
by Vivian Ridler
Printer to the University

PREFACE

In presenting this edition of *Ecclesiazusae*, I am conscious of debts to many friends and colleagues. Professor J. P. Barron and Professor G. L. Huxley read and commented on the work at early stages, and the final version has profited greatly from their helpful references and suggestions. Professor Huxley has added to his kindness by reading minutely through the proofs.

Inevitably, when working at a distance from large libraries, one makes heavy demands on the resources of the library of one's own institution. I should like to express my gratitude to library colleagues, past and present, in both Londonderry and Coleraine, for their patient and invaluable help.

The Clarendon Press have shown courteous attention: in particular, I have greatly appreciated the comments and suggestions of the Printer's reader, as well as his salutary queries.

My greatest debt is to Professor K. J. Dover, for his painstaking interest in and rigorous criticism of the work.

R. G. USSHER

Magee University College
Londonderry
April 1972

CONTENTS

ABBREVIATIONS

I

Aristophanes (plays and fragments) has been cited from the Oxford Classical Text of Hall and Geldart, other comic writers from Edmonds (*CAF*) or Demiańczuk, *Supplementum Comicum* (D). Tragic fragments (where not otherwise stated) are from Nauck (*TGF²*), fragments of historians from Jacoby (*FGrH*) or (if missing there) from Müller (*FHG*). Jacoby references are given in the form 'Philochorus 328 F 148'. Lyric fragments are from Diehl (D², ³).

II

Abbreviations of the names of ancient authors and their works are those used in Liddell, H. G., and Scott, R., *A Greek–English Lexicon*⁹ (revised by Sir Henry Stuart Jones and R. McKenzie), Oxford, 1940, and in the *Oxford Latin Dictionary*, fasc. i, Oxford, 1968. An exception is the 'Plaut.' for Plautus: 'Pl.' here stands for Plato.

Abbreviations of periodicals are those used in *L'Année philologique*.

The following, however, may be noted:

CML	*Corpus Medicorum Latinorum.*
D–K	*Die Fragmente der Vorsokratiker* (ed. H. Diels, rev. W. Kranz, Zürich/Berlin, 11. Auflage, 1964).
FJCP	*Fleckeisen's Jahrbücher für classische Philologie.*
GLP	*Greek Literary Papyri* (ed. D. L. Page, London, 1942–).
GP	*The Greek Particles*² (J. D. Denniston, Oxford, 1954).
KB	Kühner, R., *Ausführliche Grammatik der griechischen Sprache*, Part i, ed. 3 (rev. F. Blass, Hanover, 1890–2).
KG	id., Part ii, ed. 3 (rev. B. Gerth, Hanover, 1898–1904).
L–P	*Poetarum Lesbiorum Fragmenta* (ed. E. Lobel and D. Page, Oxford, 1955).
NJL	*Neue Jahrbücher für das klassische Altertum, Geschichte, und deutsche Literatur.*
NTF	*Nordisk Tidsskrift for Filologi.*
PA	*Prosopographia Attica*² (J. E. Kirchner, supp. S. Lauffer, Berlin, 1966).
PG	*Corpus Paroemiographorum Graecorum* (ed. E. L. von Leutsch and F. G. Schneidewin, Göttingen, 1839–51).
PMG	*Poetae Melici Graeci* (ed. D. L. Page, Oxford, 1962).

III

Editions and commentaries are referred to by editor's or commentator's name alone. Books and articles are cited by full titles at first reference.

x   ABBREVIATIONS

The following are thereafter referred to by author's name alone or by the short title shown in square brackets.

ABRAHAMS, E. B., *Greek Dress* (London, 1908), repr. in M. Johnson (ed.), *Ancient Greek Dress* (Chicago, 1964).

ADAM, J., *The Republic of Plato*,[2] i (London, 1963, 345–55).

ANTI, C., *Teatri greci arcaici da Minosse a Pericle* (Padua, 1947).

BARRY, E., 'The *Ecclesiazusae* as a Political Satire' (University of Chicago dissertation, 1942).

BENTON, S., 'The Evolution of the Tripod-Lebes' (*ABSA* xxxv [1934–5], 74–130).

BIEBER, M., *Griechische Kleidung* (Berlin–Leipzig, 1928). [*GK*]

—— *The History of the Greek and Roman Theater*[2] (Princeton, N.J., 1961). [*HT*]

BOUDREAUX, P., *Le Texte d'Aristophane et ses commentateurs* (Paris, 1919).

BURCKHARDT, A., *Spuren der athenischen Volksrede in der alten attischen Komödie* (Basle, 1924).

COULON, V., *Essai sur la méthode de la critique conjecturale appliquée au texte d'Aristophane* (Paris, 1933).

—— (with Van Daele, H.), *Aristophane V. L'Assemblée des femmes, Ploutus*[3] (Paris, 1963). [Coulon]

DALE, A. M., *The Lyric Metres of Greek Drama*[2] (London, 1968).

DENNISTON, J. D., *The Greek Particles*[2] (Oxford, 1954).

DEUBNER, L., *Attische Feste*[2] rev. B. Doer (Berlin, 1966).

EHRENBERG, V., *The People of Aristophanes. A Sociology of Old Attic Comedy*[2] (Oxford, 1951).

EVANS, M. M., *Chapters on Greek Dress* (London and New York, 1893), repr. in M. Johnson (ed.), *Ancient Greek Dress* (Chicago, 1964).

FRAENKEL, E., 'Dramaturgical Problems in the *Ecclesiazusae*', in *Greek Poetry and Life, Essays presented to Gilbert Murray* (Oxford, 1936), 257–76. Reprinted as: *Kleine Beiträge zur klassischen Philologie*, (Rome, 1964), i. 469–86.

HÄNDEL, P., *Formen und Darstellungsweisen in der aristophanischen Komödie* (Heidelberg, 1963).

HESS, W. H., 'Studies in the *Ecclesiazusae* of Aristophanes' (Princeton dissertation, 1963).

HIGNETT, C., *A History of the Athenian Constitution to the end of the Fifth Century B.C.* (Oxford, 1952, repr. 1958).

JACKSON, J., *Marginalia Scaenica* (Oxford, 1955).

JOHNSON, M. (ed.), *Ancient Greek Dress* (Chicago, 1964).

JONES, A. H. M., *Athenian Democracy* (Oxford, 1957, repr. 1960).

KAIBEL, G., 'Aristophanes' (*RE* ii. 1–2 [Stuttgart, 1895], 971–94).

KASSIES, W., *Aristophanes' Traditionalisme* (Amsterdam, 1963).

KIRCHNER, J. E., *Prosopographia Attica*[2] (supp. S. Lauffer, Berlin, 1966).

KRAUS, W., 'Testimonia Aristophanea cum scholiorum lectionibus' (*AAWW* lxx. 2 [1931], 49–50). ['Testimonia']

ABBREVIATIONS   xi

LOTTICH, O., *De sermone vulgari Atticorum maxime ex Aristophanis fabulis cognoscendo* (Halle, 1881).

LOWE, J. C. B., 'The manuscript evidence for changes of speaker in Aristophanes' (*BICS* ix [1962], 27–42).

MAAS, P., *Greek Metre*, tr. H. Lloyd-Jones (Oxford, 1962).

MEDER, A., *Der athenische Demos zur Zeit des Peloponnesischen Krieges im Lichte zeitgenössischer Quellen* (Munich, 1938).

MILNE, M. J., see Richter.

MOONEY, W. W., *The House-Door on the Ancient Stage* (Baltimore, Maryland, 1914).

MURRAY, G. G. A., *Aristophanes: A Study* (Oxford, 1933).

NORWOOD, G., *Greek Comedy* (London, 1931).

OERI, H. G., *Der Typ der komischen Alten in der griechischen Komödie* (Basle, 1948).

PEPPLER, C. W., 'The Termination -κός, as used by Aristophanes for Comic Effect' (*AJP* xxxi [1910], 428–44). [Peppler]

PICKARD-CAMBRIDGE, SIR A., *The Theatre of Dionysus in Athens* (Oxford, 1946). [*TDA*]
—— *The Dramatic Festivals of Athens²*, rev. John Gould and D. M. Lewis (Oxford, 1968). [*DFA*]

POULTNEY, J. W., *The Syntax of the Genitive Case in Aristophanes* (Baltimore, Maryland, 1956). [Poultney]
—— *Studies in the Syntax of Attic Comedy* (*AJP* lxxxiv [1963], 359–76). [*Syntax*]

PRITCHETT, W. K., 'The Attic Stelai II' (*Hesperia* xxv [1956], 178–328).

RAU, P., *Paratragodia* (Munich, 1967).

RAVEN, D. S., *An Introduction to Greek Metre²* (London, 1968).

RICHTER, G. M. A., *A Handbook of Greek Art⁶* (London, 1969). [*Handbook*]
—— (with Milne, M. J.), *Shapes and Names of Athenian Vases* (New York, 1935).

ROBINSON, D. M., *Excavations at Olynthus* (Baltimore, Maryland, 1929–). [*Excavations*]

ROGERS, B. B., *The Ecclesiazusae of Aristophanes* (London, 1902).

ROOS, E., 'De exodi Ecclesiazusarum fabulae ratione et consilio' (*Eranos* xlix [1951], 5–15).

RUSSO, C. F., 'I due teatri di Aristofane' (*RAL* xi [1956], 14–27). [*Russo*]
—— *Aristofane autore di teatro* (Florence, 1962). [*Aristofane*]

TAILLARDAT, J., *Les Images d'Aristophane²* (Paris, 1965). [*Images*]

TURYN, A., *The Byzantine Manuscript Tradition of the Tragedies of Euripides* (Urbana, Ill., 1957).

WEBSTER, T. B. L., 'The Masks of Greek Comedy' (*BJRL* xxxii [1949–50], 97–133). ['Masks']
—— *Studies in Later Greek Comedy* (Manchester, 1953).
—— *Greek Theatre Production²* (London, 1970). [*GTP*]

WEBSTER, T. B. L., *Monuments illustrating Old and Middle Comedy*² (*BICS* Supp. 23, 1969). [*Monuments*]

WHITE, J. W., *The Verse of Greek Comedy* (London, 1912). [*VGC*]

VON WILAMOWITZ-MOELLENDORFF, U., *Aristophanes Lysistrate, Beilage Ekklesiazusen* (Berlin, 1927, repr. 1958). [*Lysistrate*]

—— *Griechische Verskunst*² (Darmstadt, 1958). [*GV*]

WILLEMS, A., *Aristophane* III (Paris–Brussels, 1919).

INTRODUCTION

I

'I want to make a small suggestion to the judges . . .' (1154).

WE do not know with what success (if any) Aristophanes
put out his 'small suggestion': his *Ecclesiazusae*, it is certain,
has won very little favour since. It is seldom referred to in
antiquity,[1] and only three manuscripts transmit the text in
full.[2] Scholars and critics are, with few exceptions,[3] hostile:
they relegate the play to Middle Comedy[4] (justifiably, indeed,
if one looks at form and structure) or 'the literature of fatigue'
(the phrase is Murray's).[5] But impartial reading[6] shows that
in spirit and in content the play stands well within Old
Comedy's traditions,[7] and that Aristophanes, while indubi-
tably older, does not suffer from concomitant exhaustion.

But first (since the play is unfamiliar) a few words on
the plot may be in place. The women, despairing of their
men-folk as agents of σωτηρία for Athens, plan to pack the
Assembly—disguised of course as men—and have it hand

[1] The ancient references and quotations are assembled by W. Kraus,
'Testimonia Aristophanea cum scholiorum lectionibus', *AAWW*, Ph.-
Hist. Kl. lxx. 2 (1931), 49–50. Of course, the mere fact of its survival (if
the extant plays are a deliberate selection) may be proof of an original
high standing. Eustathius' 'unaccustomed comedy' is perhaps this play
(1169 n.): otherwise, he cites it only twice. See Harold W. Miller,
'A Note on ὁ κωμικός in Eustathius', *TAPhA* lxxiii (1942), 353–7.

[2] For details of the manuscripts see § V.

[3] Notably T. B. L. Webster, *Studies in Later Greek Comedy* (1953), 14,
and (to a lesser extent) E. Fraenkel, 'Dramaturgical Problems in the
Ecclesiazusae', in *Greek Poetry and Life* (1936), 276.

[4] On this vaguely used classification see K. Lever, *The Art of Greek
Comedy* (1956), 160–85.

[5] Gilbert Murray, *Aristophanes* (1933), 197.

[6] That is, by a reader not committed to the view that comedy changed
completely in 400.

[7] So, rightly, E. Barry, 'The *Ecclesiazusae* as a political Satire' (University of Chicago dissertation, 1942), 1 ff.

things over to themselves. But only Praxagora, their leader, who has lived there for a while and heard the speakers (243–4), knows much about procedure on the Pnyx. So rehearsal is essential: the would-be orators, however, fall ludicrously short of what is needed, and finally it is Praxagora herself who has to assume the role of spokesman (169–70). The arguments of this strange pale youth (427–8) in the Assembly (whose meeting is reported, not enacted) persuade a crowded house to pass his motion. Praxagora, returning, meets her husband (520), who has heard of the Assembly's resolution: he has not been able to attend the Pnyx himself, prevented by lack of clothes (Praxagora had borrowed them) as well as by the pressing calls of nature. Praxagora receives his news with simulated ignorance, and sketches the bill that in fact she has already (as ἡ στρατηγός, 491) been charged with putting into operation (583 ff.). The discussion of her communistic programme is succeeded by two scenes which show it put in practice: an honest citizen, Chremes, is clearing out his house to deposit his belongings with the State (730–833), while three old women, standing on their rights in the new polity—which grants the aged and ugly of both sexes priority in sexual attention—detain a youthful lover from his sweetheart, demanding such attention for themselves (877–1111). A heraldess had earlier (834 ff.) proclaimed a public banquet, and to this in the final scene all hasten, accompanied by revelry and dancing (1151–83).

These are the bare bones of the comedy: the Commentary (see also § III below) will show how Aristophanes has clothed them. Its first main theme is the decision (reported by Chremes, 455) to accept the 'monstrous regiment of women'. This idea (γυναικοκρατία) has novelty—a claim that Aristophanes makes elsewhere for his writing (578 n., *Nu.* 547, *V.* 1053)—without such absurd, though delightful, fantasy as Dicaeopolis' private peace. For it is, in fact, a logical extension of women's position in the home. Socrates held that State and household management were different only in degree,[1]

_____
[1] He also believed in the equality of women (X. *Symp.* ii. 9). Cf. id.

and this is Praxagora's position (211 n.). Her women, once
in office, will carry on as usual (599). So far, Aristophanes
(despite his claim of novelty) perhaps built on a comic
predecessor: for it looks as if γυναικοκρατία was the theme
of Pherecrates' *Tyrannis*[1] (cf. 210, 835 nn.). But Praxagora
takes a further step—no slight one—for which there is no evidence in Pherecrates' gynaecocracy, and one which Blepyrus
and Chremes, in discussing the new government, could hardly
be expected to foresee. For Praxagora's programme as στρατηγός (491), which she outlines with some fears on account of
its boldness (583–5), is one that allows not just for common
property, but also for common wives and children. Here
is the second theme, and one that is by no means predictably
dependent on the other, since women (if Praxagora's
assessment is correct, see 214–28) are little inclined to
innovation, and communism is of all creeds least likely to
appeal to them as rulers.[2] But Praxagora knows too that
desperate situations require drastic measures to correct them,
and in fact the last hope of σωτηρία for Athens is reversal of the
whole existing order, the turning upside-down of *all* accepted
attitudes, towards sex or economics or the State.

The communist or 'natural' society was not a new idea
at the time. Herodotus had written of the Scythians and
Libyans (iv. 104, 180. 5):[3] in Greece, the theory was mooted in
Euripides,[4] and the practice had been allowed for by Lycurgus
(Plu. *Lyc.* 15. 6 ff.).[5] Yet one is surprised to discover that

Oec. vii. 11 ff., Pl. *R.* 455 d, 456 a. Their emancipation was perhaps a
current talking-point: cf. I. Bruns, *Frauenemancipation in Athen* (Kiel,
1900), 14: '. . . die Frauenfrage ein Problem war, welches die damalige
Gesellschaft in hohem Grade beschäftigte.'

[1] As it was of the later plays by Amphis (fr. 8) and Alexis (fr. 41).

[2] Except perhaps in one aspect (228): this predilection (*Lys.* 715, *Th.*
487 ff.) will have full scope in the communist regime.

[3] For Egyptian communistic practice see Isoc. xi. 18.

[4] Fr. 402 νόμοι γυναικῶν οὐ καλῶς κεῖνται πέρι· | χρῆν γὰρ τὸν εὐτυχοῦνθ'
ὅτι πλείστας ἔχειν | γυναῖκας . . ., fr. 653 κοινὸν γὰρ εἶναι χρῆν γυναικεῖον
λέχος.

[5] Cf. Plb. xii. 66. 8. So in the fabulous southern island (of Ceylon?),
D.S. ii. 58. 2.

Praxagora has so fully thought out its implications: that she has, indeed, found common ground with Plato. The inter-relationship of poet and philosopher has been long debated, inconclusively:[1] does Aristophanes here guy the views of Plato?[2] does Plato build (with reproaches for his levity) on principles put forward by the playwright?[3]

Neither alternative convinces. The parallel of Praxagora's ideas with Plato's in Book v of the *Republic* is too remarkable to be neglected: but it should not be exaggerated either.[4] Their common topics—community of wives, of children, and of property, absence of lawsuits, and founding of συσσίτια (detailed comparison in 590–673 nn.)—may well be regarded as the stock-in-trade of current intellectual discussion, since communism (there is reason to believe) was at this time much in the air.[5] Similarities of language and expression, although close (see 590 ff. with notes),[6] are not such as lead to a belief that Aristophanes is basing himself on Plato's book: and the play itself has no allusion to suggest that Plato's thought or writing underlie it (571, 647, 995 nn.).[7]

[1] For a history of the discussion since Bizet (1608), see J. Adam, *The Republic of Plato*[2], i (1963), 345 ff., H. Kesters, 'Platoon's Staat en Aristophanes' Ekklesiazusai', *PS* iii (1931–2), 105 ff. The literature is large: it is also, for the most part, repetitive, and references here have been restricted.

[2] B. B. Rogers, *The Ecclesiazusae of Aristophanes* (1902), p. xxiv. Cf. Gilbert Norwood, *Greek Comedy* (1931), 269, Murray, 187 ff., id. *Greek Studies* (1946), 37.

[3] Adam, 355.   [4] As Rogers, xxiv.

[5] Cf. Adam, 354, A. Meder, *Der athenische Demos zur Zeit des Peloponnesischen Krieges im Lichte zeitgenössischer Quellen* (Munich, 1938), 81 n. 213. But I favour a different theory (below).

[6] The resemblances are listed conveniently in Adam, 350.

[7] That Plato is not named (like Socrates or Cleon) is ascribed to the two men's (unproven) friendship: so G. Zuccante, 'Aristofane e Platone', *RIL* lxii (1929), 380, Murray, 188. The former (385) adds the decree of Syracosius: but this very shadowy legislation (see Meder, 21, Max Radin, 'Freedom of Speech in Ancient Athens', *AJP* xlviii (1927), 219 ff.) presumably would have precluded reference to others (such as Agyrrhius) as well. A simple explanation might be that Plato at this time was still little known.

Chronology, in any case, makes this view very difficult: the
Republic, though its dating is uncertain, can hardly have
appeared before the play.[1] Of course, there *may* have been
an earlier edition,[2] or part *may* have been issued in advance.[3]
But such hypotheses evince determination to establish a
relationship at all costs: they serve the purpose equally of
those who think that the poet laughs at Plato, and those who
would have it (still more strangely) that Plato is referring to
the play.[4] Book v is an answer (it is argued) to its travesty of
Plato's already known views (*R.* 415 d, 423 e):[5] and Plato
refers to Aristophanes in speaking of the man 'who plucks the
unripe fruit of laughter' ἀτελῆ τοῦ γελοίου δρέπων καρπόν (v.
457 b). But neither this, nor other places quoted from Book v,[6]

[1] Dates suggested are: 387— ('at least soon after Plato was forty'),
A. E. Taylor, *Plato, the Man and his Work*[4] (1934, repr. 1960), 20;
'somewhere about 375', G. C. Field, *Plato and his Contemporaries* (1930),
71; 374 or shortly after, U. von Wilamowitz-Moellendorff, *Platon, sein
Leben und seine Werke*[5] (Berlin, 1959), 308; after 366, G. Ryle, *Plato's
Progress* (1966), 244 ff. Ryle's date refers to a conflation (in an eight-book
edition) of material written earlier, 'in the late 370's or the very early
360's' (249): the ten-book version was still later.

[2] Cf. M. Pohlenz, *Aus Platos Werdezeit* (Berlin, 1913), 227–8.

[3] Gell. xiv. 3. 3, Rogers, xxii. See, however, Wilamowitz, *Platon,
Beilagen und Textkritik*[3] (Berlin, 1962), 181. Or Plato's views may have
been already formed (some twenty years before their publication) and
widely circulated through his teaching: so A. Chiapelli, 'Le Ecclesiazusae di Aristofane e la Repubblica di Platone', *RF* xi (1883), 209, F.
Ueberweg–K. Praechter, *Die Philosophie des Altertums*[12], i (Berlin, 1926,
repr. Basle, 1960), 208: cf. G. R. Nielsen, 'Om forholdet mellem Aristophanes' "Ekklesiazusai" og Platons "Stat"', *NTF* xi (1902), 58.
Wilamowitz justifiably dismisses 'der unglückliche Gedanke dass Aristophanes platonische Gedanken (die der noch gar nicht hatte) verspotte',
Aristophanes Lysistrate, Beilage Ekklesiazusen (Berlin, 1927, repr. Zürich,
1958), 204 n. 1, cf. *Platon, Beilagen und Textkritik*, 200.

[4] One agrees here with Ueberweg–Praechter, 207, 'Abhängigkeit des
Philosophen in einem Hauptpunkte seines philosophischen Bekennt-
nisses von einem gelegentlichen Scherz des Komikers wird schwerlich
jemand glaubhaft finden.'

[5] This opinion goes back at least to A. Boeckh, *De simultate quam
Plato cum Xenophonte exercuisse fertur* (Berlin, 1811), 26: it is revived by
Zuccante, 380, cf. Nielsen, 73, Kesters, 112.

[6] 450 b, e, 451 b, c, d, 454 e, 455 a, 464 b, 473 e.

need have reference to comedy at all—even if it did, the *Ecclesiazusae* is evidently not the play in question. When Plato does take Aristophanes to task (as in vii. 529 b) his allusion (to the *Clouds*)[1] is very clear, and the language is not of the intemperate variety he uses against his target here: language which contrasts so very strongly with his tribute (if the tribute *is* Plato's) to the playwright.[2] We need not doubt that the philosopher maintained his communistic views with great conviction, but we may doubt (despite the report of his reaction to Xenophon's *Cyropaedia*, Gell. xiv. 3. 4) that a current play provoked him to the point of forcing him to write Book v in answer. His own words (in this same book) provide the aptest comment: the fear of being laughed at would be childish (v. 450 e).

Theories concerned to link playwright and philosopher directly may be properly abandoned.[3] Yet their common themes do call for explanation—it is not sufficient to fall back on the belief that 'les beaux esprits se rencontrent.'[4] Do they, in fact, reflect a common source? This idea, although mooted, has never been seriously treated:[5] for Aristotle says that Plato was the first to propose community of wives and children (*Pol.* 1266ᵃ34),[6] and that this, with community of property,

[1] ἐάν τέ τις ἄνω κεχηνὼς ἢ κάτω συμμεμυκὼς τῶν αἰσθητῶν τι ἐπιχειρῇ μανθάνειν. Cf. V. 636 ff., Pl. *Mx.* 235 c.

[2] Αἱ Χάριτες, τέμενός τι λαβεῖν ὅπερ οὐχὶ πεσεῖται ζητοῦσαι, ψυχὴν ηὗρον Ἀριστοφάνους (fr. 14D).

For the treatment of Aristophanes (which some have thought disparaging) in Plato's *Symposium* see G. Daux, 'Sur Quelques Passages du "Banquet" de Platon', *REG* lv (1942), 237–58.

[3] As by most modern writers: (for example) D. Comparetti, in A. Franchetti, *Le Donne a Parlamento di Aristofane* (Città di Castello, 1901), xxiii; Meder, 79; Barry, 29 ff.; W. J. W. Koster, *Naar Aanleiding van het communisme bij Aristophanes en Plato* (Groningen, 1955), 22; S. I. Sobolewski, *BCO* v (1960), 27.

[4] Comparetti, who believes (op. cit. xxiii ff.) similarities are fortuitous or arise from identity of theme.

[5] See Nielsen, 67; Adam, 352; Meder, 79 n. 210.

[6] He means, of course, the first *philosopher*, whether or not he knew the play.

distinguished his (Plato's) πολιτεία (ibid. 1274ᵇ9).[1] This is
a clearly worded and authoritative statement, which perhaps
makes further speculation futile. Yet one should not overlook its context. Aristotle is speaking of those who have put
forward opinions περὶ πολιτείας: he claims to have mentioned
almost all those private citizens with anything noteworthy
about them (περὶ ὧν εἴ τι ἀξιόλογον, εἴρηται σχεδὸν περὶ πάντων,
Pol. 1273ᵇ30). That he does not name an earlier communistic theorist is no proof that none such had existed—rather,
Aristotle may in retrospect regard him as an unimportant
amateur in statecraft (ibid. 1266ᵃ31),[2] whose Πολιτεία (if it
glanced at these disparate ideas in passing) did not follow them
up and combine them in a fully worked-out system, as did
Plato. Communist theory, by Aristotle's time, was not a novelty
(ibid. 1264ᵃ2), and his chief concern is not the attribution of
its various details to their proposers, but rather the rebuttal
of the total social system proposed in the *Republic* and the *Laws*.

A predecessor for Plato, then, is possible, but scholarship is
rash that tries to *name* him. Protagoras affords a clear
temptation.[3] Resemblances between the two were noted in
antiquity: Porphyrion was struck by similarities in arguments put forward by Protagoras and Plato, and felt that,
had more of Protagoras survived, Plato's plagiarism would be
clearer.[4] But the statement (attributed to Aristoxenus and
Favorinus) that Plato's *Republic* 'is found almost entire' in

---

[1] A certain amount of common land was allowed for by Hippodamus
(1267ᵇ35): proposals for *equality* of property are ascribed to Phaleas of
Chalcedon, date unknown (1266ᵃ39, 1274ᵇ9).

[2] εἰσὶ δέ τινες πολιτεῖαι καὶ ἄλλαι, αἱ μὲν ἰδιωτῶν . . .

[3] Cf. (for example) Gilbert Murray, *The Rise of the Greek Epic*⁴ (1934,
repr. 1960), 19 n. 1.

[4] H. Diels–W. Kranz, *Die Fragmente der Vorsokratiker*¹¹ (Zürich–Berlin,
1964), ii. 264. 12. For Plato's possible debt in the *Republic* to Protagoras
see C. Frick, 'Die sozialhygienischen Bestimmungen in Platons Staat und
in der Lykurgischen Grundschrift in ihrem Verhältnis zu den Antilogia
des Protagoras' *WKP* xxix (1912), 809. His influence has been found
in the debate on constitutions in Herodotus iii. 80–2: W. Aly, 'Form-
probleme der frühen griechischen Prosa', *Ph.* Supp. Band xxi. 3 (1929),
102.

Protagoras' *Antilogika*[1] is one that we have now no means of testing. On the surface it certainly suggests exaggeration on the part of an anti-Plato party,[2] and Aristotle's silence on the eminent philosopher precludes us from supposing him a model for Plato's constitutional ideas.[3] That model is rather some now unknown thinker, prominent at the period (see below) of the play, but later ignored (as not 'noteworthy' among others of his kind) by Aristotle.

No ancient reader has remarked on the resemblances between Aristophanes and Plato. This may be chance: or it may be that the fact seemed too well known or obvious for mention. Or perhaps, while certain ancient writings still survived, there was no need of further explanation. If Plato did find his tenets in an other (albeit in a less developed form), and if Aristophanes' play was meant to parody[4] those same tenets found in the same source, the reason for their common themes is clear. In our present state of knowledge any answer will be tentative. But that Aristophanes parodies Plato is (if not quite impossible) unlikely; that Plato copies Aristophanes (or even refers to him) much more so. That both rely on an earlier philosopher is not only likely, but attractive.

II

The *Ecclesiazusae*, like the *Thesmophoriazusae*, has no didascalia extant, and belief that the play is a 'send-up' of an

---

[1] D.L. iii. 37 (Aristoxenus fr. 67 Wehrli), and 57 Πολιτείας . . . ἦν καὶ εὑρίσκεσθαι σχέδον ὅλην παρὰ Πρωταγόρᾳ ἐν τοῖς Ἀντιλογικοῖς φησι Φαβωρῖνος ἐν Παντοδαπῆς ἱστορίας δευτέρῳ (D–K ii. 265. 10).

[2] For Aristoxenus' hostility to Plato see frs. 61–8 (with Wehrli).

[3] For which one might have thought Protagoras' *Politeia* (D.L. ix. 55, D–K ii. 267. 8) a likelier source than his *Antilogika*.

[4] As suggested by K. Ziegler, 'Menschen- und Weltenswerden', *NJL* xxx (1913), 549 n. 1. Cf. Murray, loc. cit. H. Müller-Strübing, 'Protagorea, zu den Vögeln des Aristophanes' (*FJCP* xxvi [1880], 81) sees a reference to Protagoras in *Av.* 1073 (reading Διαγόραν τὸν Τήϊον), cf. Eup. fr. 146a. Cf. *Nu.* 112 ff., 658 ff. (D–K ii. 260. 5, 262. 14). C. M. Bowra (*Landmarks in Greek Literature*, 1966, 208) suggests (without discussion) that Antisthenes (366 n.) is the underlying model (he wrote περὶ νόμου ἢ περὶ πολιτείας, D.L. vi. 16).

earlier philosopher gives no help in determining its date. Dating rests (a) on Praxagora's allusions to the current situation in the city, (b) on a scholium purporting to explain what she means by 'this alliance' (193).[1] The scholiast (to take the second point up first) quotes Philochorus: an alliance had been struck between the Spartans and Boeotians two years before the staging of the play. No such alliance is recorded: even if it were, it would hardly fit the context, for clearly Praxagora is speaking of a partnership to which the Athenians are a party. Most writers (since Petit) assume a blunder by either scholiast or Philochorus: Λακεδαιμονίων is changed to Ἀθηναίων,[2] and reference found to the Spartan League of the archonship of Diophantus (395/4, D.S. xiv. 82). The *Ecclesiazusae*, if the scholiast is credible in *this* part of his comment, may then be dated to Demostratus' archonship (393/2, D.S. xiv. 90).[3] Does this square with Praxagora's allusions to contemporary happenings in Athens?

Her allusions are, unhappily, exceedingly obscure,[4] and a

[1] περὶ δὲ τοῦ συμμαχικοῦ Φιλόχορος ἱστορεῖ ὅτι πρὸ δύο ἐτῶν ἐγένετο συμμαχία Λακεδαιμονίων καὶ Βοιωτῶν (see next note).

[2] S. Petit, *Miscellanea* (Paris, 1630), 1. iv. 53: so printed in Philoch. 328 F 148. The need for change is unconvincingly disputed: R. J. Walker, *An Essay on the Date of Aristophanes' Ecclesiazusae viewed in the Light both of Greek History and of the Aristophanic Catalogue* (Monaco, 1925), 16, A. Rostagni, *RFIC* iv (1926), 229, W. H. Hess, 'Studies in the Ecclesiazusae of Aristophanes' (Princeton dissertation, 1963), 74. For corruption arising from familiar proper names see (for example) Th. vi. 95. 2, where Θηβαίων (B, correctly) is corrupted to Ἀθηναίων (cett.).

[3] So most modern editors and writers: see (for example) J. van Leeuwen, *Aristophanis Ecclesiazusae* (Leyden, 1905), *Prolegomena* xviii, Wilamowitz, *Lysistrate*, 203, Koster, 4. Other datings: 391, J. Kirchner, *Prosopographia Attica* (Berlin, 1901), 143, P. Geissler, *Chronologie der altattischen Komödie* (Berlin, 1925), 73, Barry, 6 ff., *Oxford Classical Dictionary* (2nd edn., 1970), 113; 390/89, Walker, 14, Rostagni, 230; 389, G. Goetz, *De temporibus Ecclesiazuson Aristophanis commentatio* (Leipzig, 1874), 365 ff. For details of the various dates proposed and their supporters see Barry, 13 n. 2, P. Moraux, 'Trois vers d'Aristophane (Assemblée des Femmes, 201–203)', *Mélanges Henri Grégoire*, iv (1952), 326.

[4] Cf. A. Briel, *De Callistrato et Philonide* (Berlin, 1887), 65: 'iam ex his, quae diximus, cognoscitur, quam sit quaestio [the dating of this play] implicata et difficilis, quapropter hoc loco eam diiudicare non audeo.'

number of questions seek an answer. We shall ask, and try to answer them, as they crop up in the course of her address.

1. τῶν δὲ ῥητόρων | ὁ τοῦτ' ἀναπείσας εὐθὺς ἀποδρὰς ᾤχετο (195–6). Who is the speaker who persuaded the Athenians to join in an anti-Spartan compact and then was compelled to take to flight? Conon, says the scholiast, but this cannot be right. Praxagora—if the meaning of the noun is to be taken as 'one of those who spoke on the occasion' (195 n.)—could not describe that general as 'rhetor': for Conon had not been in the city at the time the alliance was proposed (X. *HG* i. 5. 18, ii. 1. 29, iv. 8. 9). Epicrates might fill the bill as rhetor (71 n.), but otherwise his claims are very slender.[1] He was said, it is true, to have taken bribes from Persia to keep up hostilities with Sparta (*Hell. Oxy.* ii. 2, Paus. iii. 9. 8: but see X. *HG* iii. 5. 2), and a client of Lysias denounced him (Lys. xxvii. 16). The date of that speech, however, is unknown. A date in 394 could well suit denunciation of someone who had left the city εὐθύς (sc. after a debate in 395). But strong arguments have also been advanced for 391 and 389:[2] and it scarcely matters, since Epicrates' flight has no evident relation to the context.[3] To whom, then, is Praxagora referring? The candid answer is, we do not know. There were many who supported an alliance: but Xenophon, who says so (*HG* iii. 5. 16), has singled none out for special mention.

2. Κορινθίοις ἄχθεσθε, κἀκεῖνοί γέ σοι (199). Why is there this mutual bad feeling? Many editors (with Reiske) read ἤχθεσθε: the reference is then to Corinth's attitude towards

---

[1] They are put by M. Gigante, 'Echi di vita politica nelle "Ecclesiazusae" di Aristofane', *Dioniso*, xi (1948), 147–51. Cf. his *Lisia, Contro Epicrate*[2] (Naples, 1960), 21. But K. J. Dover points out that 71 is then a joke 'against a man no longer on the political scene' (*Lustrum*, ii [1957], 101).

[2] Writers who support these dates are (for example): 394, P. Treves, 'Note sulla guerra corinzia', *RFIC* xv (1937), 128 n. 2; 391, F. Levy, *SIFC* iii (1923), 63 ff.; 389, Ziegler, art. cit. n. 54. Gigante (believing Epicrates referred to at 195) proposes 392/1 (*Contro Epicrate*, 22).

[3] See Didymus (quoting Philochorus), *in Demosthenem* x. 34, col. 7, 11 ff.: H. Diels and W. Schubart, *Didymos Kommentar zu Demosthenes* (Papyrus 9780), Berliner Klassikertexte i (Berlin, 1904).

Athens at the close (as indeed at the beginning) of the Peloponnesian War (X. *HG* ii. 2. 19, Th. i. 103. 4).[1] But the
manuscripts' ἄχθεσθε gives good sense, whether taken (below)
of a historical occasion or (see under (3)) of a consequent
(but temporary) viewpoint. After the success of Thebes and
Athens against Pausanias at Haliartus (X. *HG* iii. 5. 18, D.S.
xiv. 81. 2), many other states (among them Corinth) had
joined in an anti-Spartan League (D.S. xiv. 82. 1). But
defeat at Nemea (X. *HG* iv. 2. 11 ff., D.S. xiv. 83. 1) and an
indecisive contest at Coronea (summer 394, X. *HG* iv. 3. 16,
D.S. xiv. 84) was followed by a campaign of attrition around
Corinth (which ultimately became absorbed in Argos as the
outcome of a bloody revolution, X. *HG* iv. 4. 2, D.S. xiv. 86,
92). Events at Corinth—in earlier times not noted for her
friendliness to Athens—no doubt brought some disenchant-
ment (195): and Corinth, whose territory had seen most of
the fighting, might well hold a similar opinion: in fact,
Xenophon expressly says so (*HG* iv. 4. 1).

3. νῦν εἰσὶ χρηστοί (200). When could Praxagora so speak
of the Corinthians? The answer is again, we do not know.
But νῦν here need not mean 'at this moment' (the time of the
production of the play): rather it indicates *one* temporary
view in contrast to another (199). '(At one moment) you're
fed-up with the Corinthians, (then at the next) you think
them fine chaps, and the whole cry is "Be you decent too." '
(200 n., 'Let's not be beastly to the Germans.') The Athenians are seen, in other words, as μετάβουλοι (cf. Woman *B*'s
husband later, 797 n.): and this is expressed in a style of
'jerky' vividness which brings to mind New Comedy technique (cf. e.g. Menander, *Dyscolus* 58–68).

4. Ἀργεῖος ἀμαθής, ἀλλ' Ἱερώνυμος σοφός (201). What is
the point of these remarks, if any? If any, because Aristophanes will sometimes (in case he should appear to grow too
earnest) throw off an idle line in some such way. The words

[1] The emendation is not needed to support a theory (which is probable, see below) that Praxagora satirizes the capriciousness of Athens in
her public change of attitude towards Corinth (Moraux, 334).

are a sample of Athenian opinion, quickly formed and as
speedily abandoned: '(At one moment) you think the
Argives nitwits, while Hieronymus is *wise*.' The Argives had
been vehement opponents of a peace[1] which Hieronymus (it
seems) supported.[2] 'Yet when peace (σωτηρία, 202) *does* pop its
head out, you again demonstrate your indecisiveness by failing
to call on Thrasybulus' (Praxagora's *own* recipe for 'salvation').

5. σωτηρία παρέκυψεν, ἀλλ' ὀργίζεται | Θρασύβουλος αὐτὸς
οὐχὶ παρακαλούμενος (202–3). The final question then is: to
what prospects of peace does Praxagora refer? And what was
the role of Thrasybulus? The aorist is used by way of varying
the set of vivid presents that precede it ('from time to time we
caught a glimpse of safety'). Such glimpses (we may think)
were allowed on three occasions: the possibilities are (*a*) the
talks at Sardis, when deputations from both Sparta and the
allies appeared in front of Tiribazus (X. *HG* iv. 8. 12); (*b*)
those at Sparta when Andocides was present and urged that
Spartan terms should be accepted (And. iii *passim*). The
order of these two discussions is not clear:[3] the point for our
purpose is, first, they were abortive (which clearly fits well
with παρέκυψεν), secondly, they fall within the period of
393–391. There remains (*c*) the victory at Cnidus (in early
August 394), when Conon, along with Pharnabazus, crushed
a Spartan fleet commanded by Pisander (X. *HG* iv. 3. 11,
D.S. xiv. 83. 5).[4] To Aristophanes—for whom σωτηρία
means peace, but assuredly also peace with honour[5]—this

---

[1] And. iii. 24–32. The Corinthians, who had also (ibid. 41) opposed
it, perhaps had second thoughts: hence the approving words (200).
Moraux, 333, finds difficulty in a view that excludes them from the blame
cast on the Argives.

[2] It seems unlikely that the reference here is to Conon's admiral (D.S.
xiv. 81. 4): though Treves, 134, sees an indirect compliment to Conon.

[3] For opinions see Moraux, 329–30.

[4] Plato (*Mx.* 245 a) says that Athens' part was unofficial: but cf.
Isoc. iv. 142.

[5] For peace and patriotism as Aristophanes' ideals see V. Paronzini,
'L'ideale politico d'Aristofane', *Dioniso*, xi (1948), 1, 26–42. The idea of
σωτηρία is studied by V. Frey, 'Zur Komödie des Aristophanes', *MH* v
(1948), 168–77.

might well have seemed an opportunity of gaining that desirable end. The words in 197 ('suppose we must launch ships') could hardly have been used when such a launching was quite inconceivable for Athens: they suggest a period of renewed faith in her sea power (a natural reaction after Cnidus).[1] In all this we know at least a little of the part that Thrasybulus played. He had warned against Athenian involvement (*Hell. Oxy.* i. 2), and supported a Thebes–Athens partnership with caution (X. *HG* iii. 5. 16). We know, too, that Aristophanes admired him (*Pl.* 550):[2] and this (we may suppose) is what Praxagora is saying (by way of climax) here.[3] 'There *was* a chance (after Cnidus) of σωτηρία: it has lapsed, because Thrasybulus, your former great σωτήρ, is not being called in to assist you.'[4]

If this view is tenable, the play could have appeared as early as the spring of 393. The common date (we saw) is 392. But this rests on a misinterpretation.[5] Praxagora's 'alliance' (193) is not the League formed after Haliartus, but rather the original pact of Thebes and Athens, which clearly preceded that engagement (Lys. xvi. 13).[6] The reference then is to the archonship of Phormio (396/5),[7] which dates the play again to 393.[8] Its author is a few years short of sixty.[9]

---

[1] Cf. Isoc. ix. 56 ἡ δὲ πόλις ἡμῶν τῆς παλαιᾶς δόξης μέρος τι πάλιν ἀνέλαβε καὶ τῶν συμμάχων ἡγεμὼν κατέστη, id. vii. 12.

[2] ὑμεῖς γ' οἵπερ καὶ Θρασυβούλῳ Διονύσιον εἶναι ὅμοιον (sc. φατέ).

[3] It is possible, of course, but less effective (inasmuch as it anticipates the climax, 202) to read 201 in the same manner: i.e. to assume that Aristophanes is speaking, through the mouth of Praxagora, for peace.

[4] Reading ὀργίζεται (Hermann) in 202 (n.).

[5] As Rogers, xx, saw.

[6] ὅτε τὴν συμμαχίαν ἐποιήσασθε πρὸς τοὺς Βοιωτοὺς καὶ εἰς Ἁλίαρτον ἔδει βοηθεῖν. Cf. And. iii. 25, *IG* ii². 14.

[7] D.S. xiv. 81. 2, cf. X. *HG* iii. 5. 16. See too F. Jacoby, *FGrH* IIIb 519, who (although believing Diodorus incorrect) takes the scholiast's calculation as exclusive.

[8] Further than this one cannot go with safety. We are not (for example) to argue on the basis of a recent celebration of the Skira (referred to in 18 and 59). See, however, 415 n.

[9] Assuming his birth around 450. But our only clue (*Nu.* 528 ff.) could indicate dates earlier or later (c. 460–445). Cf. K. J. Dover,

III

His finely bawdy comedy shows little loss of vigour with the years. The rehearsal scene, the scene of Blepyrus at stool, the entrances and exits of the chorus, have opportunities for comic exploitation that Aristophanes would not have missed.[1] Moreover, his wit is no less mordant: it is pitiless to physical distinctions (the great beards of Epicrates and Pronomus (71, 102 nn.), the snub-nose of Lysicrates (630 n.), the bleary eyes of Neoclides (254 n.)), to personal habits (as Lamius is noted for his σκύταλον and πορδή, 76–8, Antisthenes for his constant constipation, 366, 806, and Smoius for what Greeks called merely 'labda', 846, 920), to perverts like Epigonus (the sight of whom misleads Woman *B* to suppose that her audience are women, 167–8) or Agyrrhius (though here, for once, the feeling may be personal: Agyrrhius had cut the poets' pay, 103, 184 n.). There are old butts of long standing like Cinesias, whose lapse apparently is still remembered (330 n.), new ones like Aristyllus (647 n.: does *any*body still believe this last nasty fellow intended to conceal a tilt at Plato?[2]) and Cephalus, the inefficient potter (248 n.). The old jokes, too, are here: the husbands' meanness (they keep cupboards under lock and key, 14 n.), the women's flair for gossip (120), drink (14, 227), and sex (225, 228). But these jokes, though old, are subtly interwoven in the

Aristophanes Clouds (1968), xviii ff. and 528 n. Biographical material is scanty. See (for example) V. Coulon and H. Van Daele, *Aristophane I* (Paris, 1934), i, W. Schmid and O. Stählin, *Geschichte der griechischen Literatur* I. iv. 2, 1 (Munich, 1946), 175. The ancient sources for his life and work are assembled by R. Cantarella, *Aristofane, Le Commedie*, i (Milan, 1949), 135.

[1] Cf. H. Steiger, 'Die Groteske und die Burleske bei Aristophanes', *Ph.* N.F. xliii (1934), 419, 'Wer so prächtige Szenen feiner und derber Art zu schaffen verstand, der war als Dichter noch nicht alt geworden.'

[2] The idea was first (it seems) put forward by A. Bergk, *Commentationum de reliquiis Comediae Atticae antiquae duo libri* (Leipzig, 1838), 403 n.: 'obiterque etiam Aristophanes Platonis notavit libidines in Ecclesiazusis v. 994 . . . sed hic Platonem intelligi, pariter atque v. 647 et in Pluto v. 314 alias ostendam.'

context, not dragged in to titillate the groundlings (although there is plenty for them too), and seem, in their new context, almost new (e.g. αἴρειν τὼ σκέλει, 265 n.). An actor who muffs his lines is still good for a reference, 21–23 nn. (like Hegelochus twelve years before in *Frogs*), but the dead Euripides ποιητής is displaced (though not for adverse comment) by another Euripides πορριστής (825 n.). Attacks on politicians and officials are still trenchant. The State (says Praxagora) has προστάται πονηροί: if one of them, for a single day, is χρηστός, he resumes his πονηρία for ten (177–8). The people fear those who wish them well (like Thrasybulus), and woo those (like Agyrrhius) who would harm them (181–2). *His* current popularity arises from his grant of increased pay for attending the Assembly: before that they *knew* him for a rascal (184–5). Every man is out for his own pocket (206–7), and the State meanwhile (like Aesimus) goes reeling (208 n.). Praxagora's speech takes the place of a παράβασις (the chorus here, as in *Lysistrata*, are closely integrated in the action, and do not lay aside their masks for comment):[1] and the views expressed are supplemented by the comments of her hearers, as reported. How can Neoclides—who cannot cure himself—presume to heal the troubles of the city?[2]

The mention of the chorus may justify, at this point, some further remarks upon its role. In two places (729, 876) our earliest manuscript (R, see § V below) has handed down an enigmatic χοροῦ. Does this mean either (*a*) that Aristophanes wrote no further choral part himself, but left the chorus to improvise a song at these points in the play or merely dance (cf. the ἐμβόλιμα attributed to Agathon, Aristotle, *Po.* 1456a29), or (*b*) that he *did* write a song, but it has vanished, as has that in the first version of *Clouds* at 888, where V denotes its absence in the extant play (because of incomplete

[1] On the absence of παράβασις see Barry, 25 ff.

[2] 400–2. In view of these passages (and 195–203) it is misleading to assert that Aristophanes loses interest in politics after the *Lysistrata* (W. Kassies, *Aristophanes' Traditionalisme* [Amsterdam, 1963], 20). Cf. R. Cantarella, 'L'ultimo Aristofane', *Dioniso*, xl (1966), 36.

revision) by inserting χοροῦ in the margin: perhaps here the
choral song was *deliberately* 'cut' at some stage in editions
meant for reading, or (*c*) (as the ancient *Life* asserts about the
Plutus) that after choruses had ceased to be supplied he
wrote in χοροῦ in his manuscript to let the actors rest and
change their masks? It is difficult (to take the last suggestion
first) to see how χοροῦ might achieve this purpose: in any
case, there *is* a chorus in *Plutus* as in *Ecclesiazusae*, and no
change of mask (whatever of *Pl.* 1096) is needed here. With
(*a*) one asks why the dramatist decided to write no further
choral odes at *this* point, with (*b*) why an editor has chosen
these lines in particular for 'cutting'. It seems best to suppose
that later editors and readers, familiar with New Comedy
conventions (cf. Menander, *Dyscolus* 232) inserted this note
when they observed the 'stage' was empty (as here after
Chremes has gone indoors: cf. *Pl.* 626, 770) or thought of an
act or scene as ending: though it *could* mark a choral performance (cf. *Pl.* 321),[1] and something of this kind may have
been added in later productions of the play. But no lapse of
time whether actual (cf. scholiast *Pl.* 850, 1042) or dramatic
(*Pl.* 253, with scholiast ad init.) is necessary in either place
where manuscripts have χοροῦ, and *Aristophanes*' chorus,
having called on Praxagora to introduce her project, fall
silent till their boisterous dance in the finale: their role is
essentially an actor's, and complete when the new Republic
is in being.[2] It is still, however, even in this late play, a *vital*
role: the comic chorus's decline and disappearance was less
swift than is sometimes represented.[3]

[1] E. W. Handley, '*XOPOY* in the Plutus', *CQ* N.S. iii (1953), 59–60.

[2] Cf. C. F. Russo, *Aristofane autore di teatro* (Florence, 1962), 346. For
further discussion see K. J. Maidment, 'The Later Comic Chorus', *CQ*
xxix (1935), 11 ff., W. Beare, 'The Meaning of *XOPOY*', *Hermathena*,
lxxxiv (1954), 93–103, W. J. W. Koster, *Autour d'un manuscrit d'Aristophane écrit par Démétrius Triclinius* (Groningen–Djakarta, 1957), 117 ff.,
P. Händel, *Formen und Darstellungsweisen in der aristophanischen Komödie*
(Heidelberg, 1963), 126–39.

[3] See C. Ferrari, 'Il frammento del papiro Berlinense 1171 e la
trasformazione del coro da Aristofane a Menandro', *Dioniso*, xi (1948),
177–87.

To return to the political allusions: it would here (as else-where) be mistaken to cast Aristophanes κωμῳδοποιός as political theorist or thinker.[1] He performs the very healthy function of a satirist, but offers no solution of his own. And in fact there are signs in these years (as we have seen) of a growing if not new (473 n.) disillusion with the city. The Assembly voted for the women not because they thought the women would be better, but because this was the one thing not yet tried (456 n.). There is no dream of escape now—even for an Aristophanic hero—to an ideal city in the clouds, no solace in poetry or music. For underlying the γέλοια and the comedy are certainly σπουδαῖα and distress.[2] The background of poverty is patent. It is true that the farmers have recovered from the war, and are coupled (198) with the rich. But this only makes the more distasteful their attitude towards the city-dwellers, who never (they say, 300 ff.) rushed to sit in the Assembly before the present payment of three obols. There is, indeed, great emphasis on being there in time to get the money (282, 290 ff.; Chremes is too late, 381): but this theme, however it is used for comic purposes, betrays not cupidity but need. Euaeon proposed in the Assembly (408 ff.) that in winter the fullers and tanners should offer clothes and sleeping-room (the comic invention again has sober undertones), and men will go on shipboard for the wages (197). Praxagora, when told of the decision to hand the city over to the women, foresaw the disappearance of the poor man (566), and her communistic programme may have seemed to her the way to that desirable goal. At least (like the γυναικοκρατία itself) it had not been tried before and might be worth it. But Aristophanes is not concerned to comment (for praise or blame) on this creed in the abstract.

---

[1] True, he 'has had his share in the madness of philosophy' (Pl. *Smp.* 218 b): cf. Douglas J. Stewart, 'Aristophanes and the Pleasures of Anarchy', *AR* (spring 1965), 189. But his own speech gives no proof of that remark of Alcibiades: see K. J. Dover, 'Aristophanes' Speech in Plato's Symposium', *JHS* lxxxvi (1966), 47.

[2] Cf. *Ra.* 391   καὶ πολλὰ μὲν γέλοιά μ' εἰ-
πεῖν, πολλὰ δὲ σπουδαῖα . . .

He does not present it as a serious solution, nor does he, on the other hand, condemn it.[1] For public ridicule is not by any means the same thing as private condemnation—Aristophanes is playing for the laughs. This is a simple truth: to fail to grasp it is to misread the last scenes of the play. Mis*read*, for they have at times been treated as if so many chapters in a textbook.[2]

The interest of the final scenes lies elsewhere. Two questions, one of staging, the other of identity, deserve some investigation here. Where are the girl and the hag standing as they bandy (884) reproaches and abuse, and who is the unnamed 'master' (1125) whom the servant comes to summon to the banquet?

The first of these questions is connected with the larger one of comic convention as to staging: particularly, did the back-stage have *two* entrance-doors or only one? It is commonly agreed that two *houses* are required as background in *Ecclesiazusae*:[3] on the other hand (it is argued) a single *door* will satisfy the action. This view I believe to be mistaken.

Miss Dale, in presenting it,[4] has singled out two passages as lending it particular support. The first is the scene (327)

[1] Even indirectly, 'ohne selbst dabei irgendeine direkte Kritik auszusprechen' (Meder, 82, cf. Steiger, 416).

[2] Cf. (for example) E. Roos, 'De exodi Ecclesiazusarum fabulae ratione et consilio', *Eranos*, xlix (1951), 5–15: who finds in each of these three scenes a practical refutation of Praxagora's three communistic bases (set out by van Leeuwen, xvii). See the notes at 746, 877, 1148, 1176. Similarly, Paronzini, 35 ff.: Aristophanes rejects her programme (cf. his praise of Poverty in *Plutus*). The view expressed here agrees with (for example) M. Croiset, *Aristophane et les partis à Athènes* (Paris, 1906), 290 ff.: 'la série de scènes qui terminent la pièce ne doivent pas être prises pour une réfutation à proprement parler. Ce sont ... des inventions fantaisistes, qui visent surtout à faire rire.' Cf. Dover, *Lustrum*, ii. 101–2.

[3] So (for example) P. Mazon, *Essai sur la composition des comédies d'Aristophane* (Paris, 1904), 151, van Leeuwen, 3 n. 1, Wilamowitz, 206. Others believe *three* houses represented (Rogers, 1, Murray, 189), or even *four* (C. Anti, *Teatri greci arcaici* [Padua, 1947], 227).

[4] A. M. Dale, 'An Interpretation of Ar. *Vesp.* 136–210 and its Consequences for the Stage of Aristophanes', *JHS* lxxvii (1957), 205–11 (= *Collected Papers of A. M. Dale*, 1969, 103–18).

where a neighbour (Woman *B*'s husband) comes upon Blepyrus, who is struggling with his troubles *in the dark*. Now, none will disagree that 'comic technique jumps from one assumption to the other, according to the immediate requirements.'[1] But is an audience's understanding of the action not made difficult, if six lines after Blepyrus has told us it is night-time (321), his neighbour can observe him from a window and remark (329) on the colour he is wearing? This is a jump neither natural nor needed, for the whole conversation suggests strongly a personal and face-to-face encounter—the neighbour has emerged in order to investigate (see 327 n.) from *his* house. Nor does one understand why Woman *B*'s husband should talk to Blepyrus from his window to avoid appearing incompletely dressed.[1] The scene, in short, is *possible*, but very *improbable*, with one door : certainly it falls far short of proving that only one stage-door was in existence.

The same is true of the other passage cited in support of that belief (976 n.). In this scene, the boy, having called upon his sweetheart to run down (961) and admit him, takes to knocking with impatience on her door. What happens? The hag appears, with a resulting 'confrontation παρὰ προσδοκίαν at the (only) door'.[1] Is there not, perhaps, a better explanation? When the boy says ἀποθάνοιμ' ἄρα (i.e. in effect 'I damned well didn't'), is he not very likely speaking truth? For the hag, who has not been far away (see 946), is pretending she has heard a knock at *her* door, to which she now comes running and accosts him. Her words are no more than those of Woman *B*'s husband completely convincing proof of *one* door.[2]

We assume, then, a setting with two houses—each boasting its own door—in the background. Their occupants, at the opening of the play, are Praxagora and her neighbour, Woman *B*, afterwards Blepyrus and Woman *B*'s husband (see above), then Blepyrus and Chremes (477, 730). Their

---

[1] Ibid. 209.

[2] This interpretation (independently arrived at) now finds support in K. J. Dover, 'The Skene in Aristophanes', *PCPS* xii (1966), 16.

final tenants are the old hag and the girl. Throughout this scene the girl remains upstairs (see 961), either (like Philocleon, *Wasps* 317 *b*) at her window, or possibly (like Dicaeopolis' wife, *Acharnians* 262) upon the roof. But the hag, in rushing to her door (976) is returning to her post at the beginning: it was there that 'lonely' women (884 n.) took their stand, and there that her brightly coloured dress (879) would be shown at full length to best advantage. That *she* should half hide herself behind a window is unlikely:[1] that *both* are on the roof is even more so.[2]

And so to the last scene of the play. Near one of the background doors the chorus are assembled, when a tipsy servant comes to seek her master. She is told that if she waits here she will see him, that is (see 1127 n.) he is bound to come back home at *some* time: and in fact soon spies him, emerging from the right (282 n.),[3] and accompanied on each side by a dancer. Of the thirty thousand citizens, he alone has not yet dined, and she passes on from *his wife* (1137), *her mistress* (1113), a message to hurry to the banquet. Accordingly, he goes off dancing (1166), along with his girl-friends and the chorus.

Who is the 'master' thus depicted? He must, in the first place, be a character the audience will recognize at once. That Aristophanes should at this late stage introduce a

[1] Most commentators (since Bothe) have assumed that both hag and girl are at their windows. So (for example) Wilamowitz, 215, Van Daele, 56, Coulon, *RhM* cv (1962), 21, Dale, 28, Russo, *Aristofane*, 348. Both Dale and Fraenkel (261) speak wrongly, by the way, of 'courtesans' (the women are citizens, 877 n.). So also C. Robert, 'Aphoristische Bemerkungen zu den Ecclesiazusen des Aristophanes', *Hermes* lvii (1922), 334, E. Droysen, *Quaestiones de Aristophanis re scenica* (Bonn, 1868), 78, 'Itemque factum esse, ut inde a versu 877 usque ad versum 1111 in Ceramico vel ἐν Πειραιεῖ παρὰ ταῖς πόρναις rem agi sciant spectatores, facile intelligimus', H. G. Oeri, *Der Typ der komischen Alten in der griechischen Komödie* (Basle, 1948), 29. Droysen had rightly been refuted by J. Nieiahr, *Quaestiones Aristophaneae Scaenicae* (Greifswald, 1877), 33.

[2] Fraenkel, 265.

[3] Not from his house: as Wilamowitz noted (219), we should then expect ἐξέρχεται (48 n.).

completely new *persona*, who will head the ἔξοδος (1166), has
no parallel and is unlikely. Moreover, his wife is clearly not
just a nonentity (the anonymous wife of an anonymous
Athenian),[1] but one who is μακαριωτάτη (1113) and able to
issue invitations to the banquet, not only to her husband but
to others (1137–43). We may well suspect that the woman is
Praxagora: if the 'servant' is in fact the κηρύκαινα (834)—
which would obviate the (trivial) objection that Praxagora
earlier (593 n.) had no servant—spectators will identify her
'mistress' straight away, and eagerly await the reappearance
of her master, the old buffoon Blepyrus.[2] That the unnamed
master *is* Blepyrus, there cannot (I think) be any doubt. His
interests, we recollect, are twofold, food (359 n., 717) and sex
—he is quick to see snags in Praxagora's proposals (611, 615,
623), and *had* been known on occasions (668 n.) to sleep away
from home. The second interest was briefly uppermost: he
had gone off, determined (726 n.) to bask in his wife's
reflected glory, but had been deflected (one supposes, for
Praxagora knows his doings, 1138) from his purpose on
encountering the girls.[3] But he was already making for the
banquet (1128, 1135) when Praxagora's servant met him
with the message. And the chorus pay tribute to his gastro-
nomic interests with their menu-card (1168).

[1] U. von Wilamowitz-Moellendorff, 'Der Schluss der Ekklesiazusen
des Aristophanes', *SPAW* i (1903), 451. He later confessed himself
mistaken and recognized the 'master' as Blepyrus (*Lysistrate*, 219).

[2] For Blepyrus βωμολόχος see 583 n. His apparently final exit (727)
does not preclude his reappearance here (Wilamowitz, *Lysistrate*, 219
n. 3). Cf.—though admittedly the interval is shorter—the old woman's
sudden reappearance in *Pl.* 1197 (van Leeuwen, 2 n. 3). The 'inconsistency' weighed heavily with O. Bachmann, who thought the whole
scene 1112–81 an addition when the true scene had been lost, *Conjectu-*
rarum Observationumque Aristophanearum Specimen, i (Göttingen, 1878), 119.
Cf. Comparetti, xl.

[3] This interpretation (independently arrived at) is similar to (but
more specific than) C. Beer, *Über die Zahl der Schauspieler bei Aristophanes*
(Leipzig, 1844), 111. Roos, 10 (with approval from W. Süss, *RhM*
xcvii [1954], 292), believes she was too busy up till now with affairs of
state to think about her husband.

The scene has been read as representing the reward of the solid and patriotic Chremes: he has carefully bestowed his belongings (730 ff.) upon the city, and is thus late (1136).[1] But apart from the fact that the play is not intended to inculcate any kind of message,[2] the solid qualities of Chremes are exactly the wrong ones for the context. For although he will do his *duty* (471 n.) by the ladies, there is no hint whatever that to *his* mind 'reward' would mean a dancing-girl and dinner. No, what we want here is the classical buffoon, a Philocleon (*Wasps* 1484) or Trygaeus (*Peace* 1305), and for this role Aristophanes casts Blepyrus.[3]

So ends the *Ecclesiazusae*: with a scene which is neither a kind of loose appendage to enable the play to be completed,[4] nor a descent from a communist Utopia to the hard facts of everyday existence (see 1148 n.). The first belief does Aristophanes small credit, the second treats a commonplace of comedy (ἢν ἀπίωσιν οἴκαδε, 1148 n.) with an unjustifiable respect. It is easy to pick holes in the structure of this scene,[5] as of others in the play: to deplore the emphasis on farce and crude γέλοια, to mourn the loss of music in the chorus. Yet this is to see it from the study. One feels that in spectators seated on the hillside and viewing the events in the orchestra, these critical stirrings would be stilled. And after the finale when Blepyrus with his 'torch' (1150 n.) and the young girl dancers and the chorus trooped off in their spectacular

[1] Fraenkel, 270 ff.

[2] See above, p. xxx n. 2. One differs here (for example) from A. Croiset, *De Personis apud Aristophanem* (Paris, 1873), 12: 'In Pluto denique et in Feminarum concione, repetitis exemplis explicat Aristophanes quae bona malave vel ex mutatis legibus vel ex divitiis aliter inter homines distributis oritura sint.'

[3] The identification of the 'master' with Blepyrus was originally made by J. H. Voss.

[4] Wilamowitz, *SPAW* i (1903), 455: 'Gefühlt hat A. ganz wohl, dass sein Drama am Ende bedenklich abfiel, dass er der Handlung keinen Schluss geben konnte, sondern nur diesen Mangel verbergen.'

[5] Its defence, on the other hand, should not be pressed unduly: looseness of structure and 'weak' ending are a feature (cf. *Wasps*) of the ancient comic drama.

departure, would we not perhaps say (like Woman *A* earlier)
εὖ γ᾽ εὖ γε νὴ Δί᾽ εὖ γε. For this is the old Aristophanes we
knew.

IV

The effort to visualize the final scene confronts us (in a more
acute and more important manner) with a problem that
recurs throughout the play. Manuscripts, the Ravennas in
particular, are careless when it comes to naming speakers:
moreover, their judgement—or in greater fairness to the
seemingly painstaking scribe of R, the judgement of the text
that lay before him—in marking *change* of speaker is often
arbitrary and erratic.[1] For although the earlier texts in fact
did give such indications, Hellenistic and later commentators
(as is evidenced by plays with copious scholia, like the
Clouds) showed no unwillingness to alter or adapt them in
accordance with their own view of (*a*) the author's practice
and (*b*) the action of the play. Thus (for example) the
Ravennas (when the scribe encounters οὐκοῦν) wrongly
interrupts Praxagora (95 n.). The manuscripts, in fact, on
this point have no authority: how then do we discover who is
speaking?

Quot homines, tot sententiae: the answer here will largely be
subjective. Praxagora's role in the opening scenes is reason-
ably easy to establish, the roles of Women *A* and *B* less so.
The reference to Lamius (77) seems certainly to come from
Woman *A*: for Lamius is presumably her husband, whom so
far she alone has not yet mentioned. There is some help too
in characterization. I see Woman *A* (from her first appearance, 30) as somewhat magisterial in manner (thus 43, 86,
279 will suit her): she is foremost in answering Praxagora
(60, 70), in offering her services (131) as orator, and ful-
somely applauding (189, 213, 241) her leader's oratorical
attainments. Woman *B*, on the other hand, is simple: her
mind is clearly more at home with wool and cuttlefish (88,

---

[1] For full discussion see J. C. B. Lowe, 'The Manuscript Evidence for
Changes of Speaker in Aristophanes', *BICS* ix (1962), 27–42.

126) than with problems of government and statecraft (though she *has* heard the name of Neoclides). She is no fool, however, as a rhetor (as Praxagora admits, 159), and to mark her out (cf. 120 n.) as 'l'interlocutrice buffonne'[1] is to separate her comic role too sharply from that of her companion Woman *A*. A clearer distinction *is* possible (I think) between the parts of Chremes and Blepyrus, who question Praxagora closely on her programme (583–729). Some of the questions are important, others sadly lower the tone of the discussion. These last, which Aristotle would have classed as βωμολοχία, will issue from Blepyrus βωμολόχος. But Chremes is a genuinely interested citizen (cf. 564, 568): if the serious questions (as they should be) are ascribed to him, the scene gains from his full participation (583–729 nn.). I cannot believe that he emerges from his house to stand, a tongue-tied figure, in the background.

For an audience, of course, any question of identity is settled by the actor's mask and costume. A good deal is known (from both Pollux and the monuments) of the stock masks of the later comic drama, and some of these may have survived from the Old Comedy (for which monumental evidence is slighter).[2] Blepyrus and Chremes are *both* old men (323, 465), but their masks must have in some way been distinguished: perhaps these are the *First* and *Second Old Men* (Poll. iv. 143).[3] For the most part, a reader of the *Ecclesiazusae* must make his own deductions from the play. Thus Woman *B*'s husband, to judge from his wife's report (37–9), is younger (his appearance must be sufficiently distinctive to allow us to identify him later as the dissident citizen, 746), and the 'young man' (938) a very stripling, with attractive curls (955). His mask may be plausibly

[1] V. Coulon, 'Notes sur l'Assemblée des femmes d'Aristophane', *REG* xxxvi (1923), 374.

[2] T. B. L. Webster, 'The Masks of Greek Comedy', *BJRL* xxxii (1949–50), 111, cf. id. *Greek Theatre Production*[2] (1970), 55. For the need to interpret this evidence with caution see Sir A. Pickard-Cambridge, *The Dramatic Festivals of Athens*[2] (1968), 179.

[3] Cf. Pickard-Cambridge, *DFA*, 223.

identified as that of the (beardless) *Second Youth with Wavy Hair* (Poll. iv. 147).[1] Of the women, Praxagora is younger than her husband—she looks like a 'handsome youth' to Chremes (427). He is also struck, however, by her pallor (428), and she and the other women of the chorus (presumably near her own age and differing little in appearance) will have white beardless masks at the beginning. Women *A* and *B* are differentiated (I suggest) by their physical proportions, 'the long and the short of it' in terms of the old music-hall (with which Aristophanic comedy has more than a little common ground).[2] The girl and the hag will form a striking contrast: the former fresh-cheeked and blooming (a mere youngster),[3] the latter with plucked eyebrows (904 n.) and 'plastered with white lead' (878). She and her two 'weird sisters' must have offered the spectator (even if not the boy) a hearty horse-laugh—the masks of Old Comedy were fashioned (says Pollux, iv. 143)[4] for the maximum of laughter. The second hag is 'an Empusa', with the fiery bright face of that bogy (1057 n.), the third (in strong contrast) is 'chock-full of white lead', an old woman risen from the tomb. It may be that here we ought to recognize the three *Old Woman* masks of Pollux (iv. 150–1):[5] more likely,

[1] Poll. iv. 147 (ἐπισείονται αἱ τρίχες) ὥσπερ καὶ τῷ δευτέρῳ ἐπισείστῳ, ἁπαλωτέρῳ ὄντι καὶ ξανθῷ τὴν κόμην. For a possible illustration see Webster, *Monuments illustrating Old and Middle Comedy*[2], *BICS* Supp. 23 (1969), pl. IV d, Pickard-Cambridge, *DFA*, fig. 110.

[2] Cf. (for example) E. Scribe and Anon. [A. F. Varner], *Les Comices d'Athènes*, ou *les femmes orateurs*, comédie-vaudeville en un acte, traduit [*sic*] du grec d'Aristophane (Paris, 1817).

[3] Perhaps, like Juliet, she 'hath not yet seen the change of fourteen years'. Though she is not a courtesan (877 n.) her mask may have been something like those seen in M. Bieber, *History of the Greek and Roman Theater*[2] (Princeton, N.J., 1961), figs. 361, 362: cf. Pickard-Cambridge, *DFA*, figs. 132–9.

[4] τὰ δὲ κωμικὰ πρόσωπα τὰ μὲν τῆς παλαιᾶς κωμῳδίας ὡς τὸ πολὺ τοῖς προσώποις ὧν ἐκωμῴδουν ἀπεικάζετο ἢ ἐπὶ τὸ γελοιότερον ἐσχημάτιστο.

[5] τὰ δὲ γυναικῶν πρόσωπα εἴη τοιαῦτα· γρᾴδιον ἰσχνὸν ἢ λυκαίνιον, γραῦς παχεῖα, γρᾴδιον οἰκουρὸν ἢ οἰκετικὸν ἢ ὀξύ. Cf. Webster, 'Masks', 117 ff., *Monuments*, 10. Possible illustrations, Bieber, figs. 348–52: cf. Pickard-Cambridge, *DFA*, figs. 128–30.

they were specially commissioned by Aristophanes for this occasion.[1]

So much for *masks*: what conclusions are possible concerning actors' *costume*? The evidence indicates that (some at least) male characters[2] appeared with grotesquely padded bodies,[3] in close-fitting tights[4] with a crudely dangling phallus (sometimes a red-tipped one 'to give the boys a laugh', *Clouds* 539).[5] It is true that Aristophanes (there and elsewhere) disclaims such βωμολοχία for *his* plays: we need not take the claim too much to heart (see 313, 579 nn.). It would certainly surprise one if Blepyrus the buffoon (who appears in his wife's κροκωτίδιον, 318 n.) was not also demonstrably phallic. The play gives no specific indication, unless his fears for his performance as an old man (cf. 468, 619) are thought to be in keeping with his costume. It may be, too, that Woman *B*'s husband is seen (as well as stated) to be virile. But one doubts whether Chremes (the conventional Athenian) is other than conventionally dressed: and all in all it seems more likely that the padding and the phallus are reserved for the buffoon.[6] The chorus too (from 514 n.) appear in their ordinary chitons: none of them (nor Praxa-

---

[1] A similar mask to the snub-nosed 'little housekeeper' (τὸ δ᾽ οἰκουρὸν γρᾴδιον σιμόν, Poll. iv. 151) would justify the lad's reluctance (939) διασποδῆσαι ἀνάσιμον.

[2] The words 'some' and 'male' here are important: see W. Beare, 'Actor's Costume in Aristophanic Comedy', *CQ* iv (1954), 75, id. 'Aristophanic Costume Again', *CQ* vii (1957), 184.

[3] T. B. L. Webster, 'South Italian Vases and Attic Drama', *CQ* xlii (1948), 19, id. *JHS* lxxi (1951), 229, *BJRL* xxxvi (1953–4), 563 (cf. *GTP* 29), *AE* 1953–4 B[1], 193 ff., *WS* lxix (1956), 110, Pickard-Cambridge, *Dithyramb, Tragedy and Comedy*[2] (Oxford, 1962), 169 ff. See *Nu.* 1237, *Ra.* 200, Bieber, figs. 481–502.

[4] σωμάτιον ἡ τῶν ὑποκριτῶν σκευή (Poll. ii. 235, iv. 115). See Webster, *CQ* v (1955), 95, id. *WS* lxix. 111, Bieber, 39, 332 n., Pickard-Cambridge, *DFA* 222.

[5] For phallic costume see Pickard-Cambridge, *DFA*, 220–2.

[6] Cf. E. Wüst, *PhW* lxii (1942), 460, 'ausser dem βωμολόχος wird ihn (den Phallos) kaum jemand in der ganzen aristophanischen Komödie getragen haben.'

gora) is padded. Praxagora is λεπτή (her own word, 539):
she may be joking, but is Chremes, who describes her as
εὐπρεπὴς νεανίας (427)? The audience *knows* that he is
speaking of Praxagora: if they have just before this seen her
padded, his description is less funny than confusing.

Praxagora (in man's ἱμάτιον and ἐμβάδες), Blepyrus (in
woman's κροκωτίδιον and κοθόρνω), the first old hag (in her
κροκωτός)—these are the patent facts of costume.[1] The rest
(as Blepyrus' appearance in 520 n.) depends on supposition
and conjecture. Both facts and suppositions—despite some
help from monuments—are ultimately based upon the text.

v

The text is preserved (in whole or part) in seven manuscripts,
referred to summarily as follows:[2]

R	Ravennas 429 (formerly 137 4A)
A	Parisinus inter Regios 2712
Γ	Laurentianus plut. 31. 15 (Leidensis Voss Gr. F 52)
B	Parisinus inter Regios 2715
Mu1	Monacensis 137
Λ	Perusinus H 56
Vb1	Barberinianus I 45

The last two—both of the fifteenth century, with scholia,
Vb1 ending at 1135—have not previously been collated (to
the best of my belief) for the *Ecclesiazusae*. They do not add
greatly to our knowledge. Vb1—allowing for small errors
in transcription—appears to be an apograph of Γ: Λ (a
finely written manuscript) has close affinities with Mu1. Vb1

[1] The distinction of characters by different-coloured clothing (for
example, old women wearing green or blue, Poll. iv. 119) is clearly
inapplicable here.

[2] The nomenclature for the most part follows that of J. W. White, 'The
Manuscripts of Aristophanes', *CP* i (1906), 9 ff. I have collated the
MSS. from microfilm and the facsimile (see following note) of R:
the descriptions are based on A. von Velsen, *Aristophanis Ecclesiazusae*
(Leipzig, 1883), v–viii and (for A and Γ) on A. Turyn, *The Byzantine
Manuscript Tradition of the Tragedies of Euripides* (Urbana, 1957), 89 ff.,
335 ff.: cf. D. M. Jones in *CQ* ii (1952), 168.

contains, in 2, the interesting reading ἐξηρτημένον (proposed in emendation by Le Paulmier).

By reason of its early date most authority resides in the great tenth-century codex in Ravenna:[1] it is the only manuscript of the play that antedates the Crusaders' sack of Constantinople. This parchment manuscript, some of whose one hundred and ninety-one leaves exhibit damp-stains, contains the eleven plays surviving. A second hand, of similar date, has added scholia (in small uncials)[2] and corrections. R, Mu1, and Λ alone transmit the full text of the play: in R it is placed second last, before *Lysistrata*, and following *Thesmophoriazusae*. There is much use of paragraphus and double point, but speakers (see apparatus criticus) are rarely named or otherwise identified.

The codex which modern editors designate as A (Parisinus 2712, in the Bibliothèque Nationale) contains, in three hundred and twenty pages, seven comedies, of which the *Ecclesiazusae* (preserved as far as 282) comes last. This codex (parchment, fourteenth century[3]), which is known to have been in Venice in 1506 (A. Turyn, *Studies in the Manuscript Tradition of the Tragedies of Sophocles*, Urbana, 1952, 190), includes the Sophoclean corpus and six plays of Euripides as well. The tragedies, written in a different hand from that which transcribed the comic dramas, are set out in three columns to the page: the comedies, however, are written out in two, with some forty verses to the column. *Notae personarum*

[1] Reproduced in facsimile by J. van Leeuwen (Leyden, 1904).

[2] Edited in part by W. G. Rutherford, *Scholia Aristophanica*, 1896. The Aristophanic scholia can still be adequately read only in F. Dübner, *Scholia Graeca in Aristophanem* (Paris, 1842). A new edition (D. Holwerda, W. J. W. Koster, L. Massa Positano, Leiden) has not yet reached the *Ecclesiazusae*. For scholia in the papyri and their source see G. Zuntz in *Byzantion*, xiii (1938), 631–90.

[3] This former dating (displaced for a time in favour of the thirteenth century) has now been reinstated. See W. J. W. Koster, 'De Codicis Par. Gr. 2712 aetate' (*Mn.* 4S xii [1959], 135): contrast his earlier description of this manuscript (*REG* lxvi [1953], 30). The date is supported by the Moschopulean elements, and cannot be earlier than 1300 (Turyn, 89 n. 146).

are in red: and the same hand has acted as corrector. The work of a later corrector can also be detected here and there. There are no scholia for *Ecclesiazusae*.

Γ, a paper codex, written probably in Thessalonica, *c.* 1325, is extant in two separated sections, one in Leiden, one in Florence (Laurentianus, see above).[1] The latter, with four of Euripides', has six of Aristophanes' plays. Of these, only two are preserved in their entirety: the *Ecclesiazusae*, standing second in the order, breaks off at 1135. The manuscript's one hundred and sixty-nine pages have seemingly been shared between two writers,[2] and two correctors' hands can be distinguished. Scholia, though frequent elsewhere, are scanty for *Ecclesiazusae*.

B, also paper (sixteenth century), contains six of the comedies in full. The *Ecclesiazusae* (second last, before the *Peace*) again ends at 1135. This manuscript shows the hand of a corrector, but offers neither scholia, nor, for the last two plays, *notae personarum*. Change of speaker is marked, not by paragraphus or double point, but by leaving a space of a few letters.

Finally, four of the plays are found in Mu1 (N, von Velsen: paper, fifteenth century, in Munich). The *Ecclesiazusae* (last in order) has been marked by the inks of two different correctors—the red is more frequent than the black. There are no scholia, but the codex (of one hundred and twenty-seven pages) is completed by the Περιήγησις τῆς γῆς of Dionysius Periegetes, in a hand which also has corrected the text of Aristophanes in places. *Notae personarum* (in this manuscript convincing) are not found after 906, but are replaced by spaces (cf. B). A subscription identifies the copyist as Michael Apostoles, a Byzantine, who πενίᾳ συζῶν

---

[1] Their unity is demonstrated by von Velsen, *Über den codex Urbinas der Lysistrata und der Thesmophoriazusen des Aristophanes* (Halle, 1871), 53. A similar situation is noted by D. Holwerda, 'De duobus codicibus Aristophaneis, quorum alter consilio, alter casu divisus' (*Mn.* 4S viii [1955], 298–300). For the date and provenance of *Γ* (D in Euripides) see Turyn, 336.

[2] Cf. F. W. Hall, *A Companion to Classical Texts* (1913), 85.

(after his 'holy fatherland' was taken) καὶ τόδε τὸ βιβλίον ἐξέγραψεν, οὐκ ἄνευ μέντοι μισθοῦ.[1] The earliest printed edition of our play (Venice, 1498)[2] is possibly based partly on his codex.[3]

This last manuscript (as has been stated) is closely allied to Λ. Both share many readings with R (here, as elsewhere in this paragraph, a few examples only can be quoted: cf. 3, 8, 23, 101, 140, 150, 175, 188, 207, 297, 317, 332, 414, 527, 684, 783, 796, 868, 881, 911, 946, 987, 1026, 1068, 1095, 1127) and may perhaps derive from it: if so, however, they have been collated against other manuscripts *en route* (cf. 72, 118, 609, 896, 1177) and edited at least to the extent of having *notae personarum* added. A, Γ, and B are related: apart from common readings (cf. especially 23, 175, 188, 200) they display the same omissions (24–6, 81, 141, 198), though A at times agrees with R and/or Λ and Mu1 (11, 44, 72, 98, 118, 131, 142, 147, 189) against the others. A alone has the true reading in 9 (perhaps by conjectural correction). When A fails (after 282) B continues to exhibit the same close relationship to Γ (shared omissions and lacunae, 357, 359, 360, 361, 363, 365, 398, 559–61, 594, 616, 628, 638, 658, 661, 668, 673, 742, 800–1, 802, 894, 988): it attempts, however, at times throughout the play to correct Γ's reading by conjecture (cf. 195, 609, 792). Conjecture or simple correction in B has not infrequently produced true readings, either shared with R and/or Λ and Mu1 (54, 282, 355, 473, 619, 635, 638, 664, 673, 678, 688, 692, 781, 794, 825, 832, 931, 978, 987, 1079, 1102, 1123) or found in B alone (29, 183, 226, 261, 335, 366, 459, 474, 652, 758, 832, 857, 1056, 1067).

---

[1] On Michael Apostoles (1422–80), the manuscripts that carry his subscription, and its forms, see M. Vogel and V. Gardthausen, *Die griechischen Schreiber des Mittelalters und der Renaissance* (Leipzig, 1909, repr. Hildesheim, 1960), 305.

[2] Prepared for Aldus (hence 'Aldine') by 'Marcus Musurus the Cretan'. For description and contents see J. W. White, *The Scholia on the Aves of Aristophanes* (1914), ci.

[3] Hess, Appendix, 151. The Aldine elsewhere displays a close relationship to Triclinius (p. xliii n. 1).

All the manuscripts (apart from R) have been subjected to
Byzantine scholars' emendation: and some late Byzantines
(of the twelfth to fifteenth centuries), treated their texts too
cavalierly. Most famous is Demetrius Triclinius (early
fourteenth century), whose edition of Aristophanes (eight
plays but not *Ecclesiazusae*) is now known from the manuscript L (early fifteenth century, Bodleian) which is closely
related to the Aldine.[1] Parisinus Supp. Gr. 463 is identified
as being (either wholly or partly) from his hand:[2] and his
textual work is recognized in B.[3] Another figure known
from Aristophanic scholia is Manuel Moschopoulos, whose
influence is possibly discernible (and clearly so in three of the
Sophoclean plays) in A. The studies of his elder contemporary,
Planudes, may also have left their mark in places.[4]

The manuscripts derive from an original in minuscules,
ninth century in date.[5] They represent a Byzantine tradition
of that period (the era of Photius and Arethas),[6] itself based

[1] See N. G. Wilson, 'The Triclinian edition of Aristophanes', *CQ*
N.S. xii (1962), 32–47.

[2] Wholly, Koster, op. cit. n. 122. See, however, Turyn, 33 n. 49,
G. Zuntz, *An Inquiry into the Transmission of the Plays of Euripides* (1965),
204.

[3] V. Coulon, *Aristophane*, i² (Paris, 1934), xviii n. 3. He unjustifiably
disregards B as a 'manuscript' (cf. J. van Leeuwen, *Aristophanis Ecclesiazusae* [Leyden, 1905], xxii).

[4] For the work of these scholars see W. J. W. Koster and D. Holwerda,
'De Eustathio, Tzetza, Moschopoulo, Planude Aristophanis commen-
tatoribus' I (*Mn.* 4S vii [1954], 136–56), II (*Mn.* 4S viii [1955], 196–
206), Koster, *REG* lxxvi (1963), 381–96. For Moschopulean elements in
A see Turyn, *Sophocles*, 190.

[5] See (for example) G. Zuntz, 'Die Aristophanes-Scholien der
Papyri III', *Byzantion*, xiv (1939), 601–5 (who argues further that that
archetype depends on several uncial manuscripts which survived from a
date in late antiquity). There is evidence, however, for other sources
also: W. J. W. Koster, 'Aristophane dans la tradition byzantine' (*REG*
lxxvi [1963], 383). Cf. in general N. G. Wilson, 'A Chapter in the
History of Scholia' (*CQ* N.S. xvii [1967], 244–56).

[6] Photius (*c.* 810–91) and Arethas (*c.* 860–*c.* 939, Vogel–Gardthausen,
39) led a literary revival in the East. Their work is well summarized in
L. D. Reynolds and N. G. Wilson, *Scribes and Scholars* (1968), 53–7. For

apparently on the text used by Symmachus, who was writing his Aristophanic commentary in the late first or early second century.[1] Symmachus has been credited with selecting the eleven plays surviving.[2] But there is prima facie evidence against this in the scholia (*Lys.* 722, *Pl.* 1011), and it may be that he merely annotated a selection (including *The Merchant-men*) of comedies 'devenues classiques'.[3] The commentary which he added was but one—among others that of Didymus, a century earlier, merits mention[4]—in a scholarly line going back to Alexandria and the early third century B.C.[5] Here the great library afforded the materials for studying the ancient comic drama,[6] and texts were sifted, catalogued,[7] and corrected. Aristophanes (as might have been expected) attracted particular attention,[8] and his namesake of Byzan-

---

Photius' quotations from our play see Kraus's 'Testimonia' (p. xiii n. 1). Arethas' library perhaps produced the archetype (Zuntz, *Byzantion*, xiv. 604 n. 1).

[1] On Symmachus see White, *Scholia Aves*, xlix, P. Boudreaux, *Le Texte d'Aristophane et ses commentateurs* (Paris, 1919), 144. There are no fragments of his commentary found in the scholia to *Ec.* (ibid. 151).

[2] So (for example) U. von Wilamowitz-Moellendorff, *Euripides Herakles*, i (*Einleitung in die griechische Tragödie*)⁴ (Bad Homburg, 1959) 180 ff. (cf. Zuntz, *Byzantion*, xiii. 657).

[3] Boudreaux, 145. The comedies originally numbered forty-four: for the ancient catalogues see ibid. 14, Cantarella, i. 142, 152.

[4] For this 'commentateur passionné' (hence called Χαλκέντερος, διὰ τὴν περὶ τὰ βιβλία ἐπιμονήν, *Suda* s.v. Δίδυμος Διδύμου) see Boudreaux, 91. He is named sixty-four times in the scholia (but not for *Ec.*). The vulgate text of Aristophanes of Byzantium (see below) was probably his basis: and Symmachus drew largely on him (Boudreaux, 153).

[5] On Alexandria's contribution to the scholarship of comedy see White, *Scholia Aves*, xiv, on the general history of text and exegesis Cantarella, ii. 29–73.

[6] Eratosthenes (for example) wrote περὶ τῆς ἀρχαίας κωμῳδίας (D.L. vii. 5).

[7] The first catalogue was completed by Callimachus, πίνακες τῶν ἐν πάσῃ παιδείᾳ διαλαμψάντων καὶ ὧν συνέγραψαν ἐν βιβλίοις κ' καὶ ρ' (*Suda* s.v. Καλλίμαχος).

[8] First from Euphronius ἐν ὑπομνήμασι (Ath. 495 c), scholiast *Av.* 1403. Cf. C. Strecker, *De Lycophrone, Euphronio, Eratosthene comicorum*

tium emerges as the first real Aristophanic scholar.[1] His
work (the basis of most succeeding scholarship) consisted not
only in collation: he gave much time to matters of ortho-
graphy and metre (our modern colometry seems to be derived
from him),[2] and to him are attributed the metrical hypotheses (as that of *Ecclesiazusae*).[3]

The text from an early period was protected by scholia and
learned annotation,[4] and between the Alexandrians and our
archetype suffered little irreversible corruption.[5] But despite

interpretibus (Greifswald, 1884). For similar activities in Pergamum
(scholiast *Av.* 1508, ἐν τοῖς Ἀτταλίοις εὗρον σκιάδιον καὶ ἐν τῷ παλαιῷ τῷ
ἐμῷ) see White, *Scholia Aves*, xxxvii, Boudreaux, 79.

[1] *Suda* s.v. Ἀριστοφάνης Βυζάντιος, Wilamowitz, *Herakles*, i. 138.
Boudreaux, 25–47. Commentaries followed from Callistratus (scholiast
Av. 1337) and the celebrated Aristarchus (scholiast *Ra.* 1437). Neither
writer is mentioned in the scholia to *Ec.*

[2] Wilamowitz, *Herakles*, i. 142. He thus anticipates metricians like
Heliodorus (mid first century), for whom see J. W. White, *The Verse of
Greek Comedy* (1912), 384 ff., D. Holwerda, 'De Heliodori commentario
metrico in Aristophanem', *Mn.* xvii (1964), 113–39.

[3] See W. J. W. Koster, 'De Aristophane Byzantio argumentorum
metricorum auctore' (*Charisteria F. Novotný*, Prague, 1962), 45–8. But his
authorship is justifiably denied by (for example) A. Nauck, *Aristophanis
Byzantii Grammatici Alexandrini Fragmenta* (Halle, 1848, repr. Hildesheim,
1963), 256, and J. N. Gröbl, *Die ältesten Hypotheseis zu Aristophanes*
(Dillingen, 1889–90), 12–13, on grounds (a) of content (b) of metre (cf.
Boudreaux, 31). The *prose* hypotheses also have ancient elements (perhaps Alexandrian, Gröbl, 10: he seems to except, however, the one
prefixed to *Ec.*), cf. Boudreaux, 32.

[4] A distinction must be made between old, valuable scholia (the
corpus perhaps dates from the fourth century, White, *Scholia Aves*, lxvi,
J. Irigoin, *Histoire du texte de Pindare* [Paris, 1952], 97) and later Byzantine
(often worthless). For protection of texts (verse in particular) by scholia
see Hall, 46–52. The ancient corpus was ascribed to Phaeinus (p. xlvi
n. 4) by Wilamowitz, *Herakles* i. 183. But this view is untenable
(Boudreaux, 176), cf. T. Gelzer, *Gnomon*, xxxiii (1961), 28. On the
composition of collections of scholia and their date see now Wilson art.
cit. (p. xliii n. 5).

[5] For errors (easily detected for the most part) that might arise, for
instance, from minuscule confusion, see V. Coulon, *Essai sur la méthode de
la critique conjecturale appliquée au texte d'Aristophane* (Paris, 1953), 11. On

devoted scholarship gross errors would survive from the
period succeeding the production. An ancient playwright
looked for only one performance :[1] the fame of his play would
then depend on readers,[2] and on copies which gave readers
small assistance. Punctuation, metrical division, even identity of speakers, were left to their private understanding.
Copying, if texts were wanted urgently, might well be as-
signed to different writers : the form of the old Attic alphabet
perhaps still existed alongside the new Ionic, and undivided
lines of capitals were open to erroneous division.[3] A knowledge of the ills that texts were heir to must inspire both
surprise at their relative correctness and gratitude to those
whose toil attained it.

The scholars who built upon the work of Alexandria
(many, unhappily, mere names among the scholia)[4] have
elsewhere left a rich storehouse of knowledge, but their
comments on *Ecclesiazusae* (except in R) are relatively
scanty. This is true also of the 'indirect' tradition (quotations, that is, in lexicographers and others), for even the *Suda*,
which quotes the plays extensively, has very few citations
drawn from this one.[5] Clearly, its readers, in contrast with
those of *Plutus*, *Clouds*, or *Frogs*[6] were few. And after the first

the whole question of mistakes and their correction see Coulon *passim*,
Hall, 150.

[1] Cf. Webster, *GTP* xi, 'runs were unknown' (ibid. 1). And a second
production within the author's lifetime (as alleged of *Frogs*, see *Hypotheses* I, III, by Dicaearchus) presumably would be uncommon.

[2] Cf. *Ra.* 52, καὶ δῆτ' ἐπὶ τῆς νεὼς ἀναγιγνώσκοντί μοι | τὴν Ἀνδρομέδαν
πρὸς ἐμαυτὸν ἐξαίφνης πόθος | τὴν καρδίαν ἐπάταξε.

[3] Coulon, *Essai*, 7–8.

[4] Notably Phaeinus (of uncertain date, but pre-Byzantine), whose
work (based on Symmachus) is quoted in the scholia to *Eq.* See Boudreaux, 161–4. White regards him as merely 'some shallow local cele-
brity of the day' (*Scholia Aves*, lxix).

[5] Kraus, 'Testimonia' (p. xiii n. 1). For the *Suda* as a textual authority
see (for example) White, lxxviii.

[6] The 'Byzantine triad' which, with notes by Thomas Magister (early
fourteenth century), became a school-book. For Thomas's methods see
T. Hopfner, *SAWW* clxxii. 3 (1912), 4–30, 54–9.

performance (until modern times) there would presumably be *no* spectators.[1]

---

[1] For this or for any of the plays. *Ecclesiazusae* has been presented (in translation) in recent times in Athens and New York. See F. M. Pontani, 'Sopravvivenza di Aristofane in Grecia', *Dioniso*, xxxix (1965), 386, Bieber, *HT*, 261.

SIGLA

For descriptions of the manuscripts see Introduction § V

R	Ravennas 429 (X vel XI)
A	Parisinus inter Regios 2712 (XIV); vv. 1–282
Γ	Laurentianus pluteus 31. 15 (Leidensis Voss Gr. F 52) (XIV); vv. 1–1135
Λ	Perusinus H 56 (XV)

a	consensus codicum R(A)(Γ)Λ

Mu1	Monacensis 137 (XV); non nisi lectio (quod perraro) a Λ differt citatus est
x	unus vel alter vel uterque e codicibus Parisino inter Regios 2715 (B) et Vaticano Barberiniano I 45 (Vb1)

Σ	scholium
*	abscissa charta
†	spatium quod uni litterae sufficit
dic.	dicolon
par.	paragraphus

Notae adscriptae (e.g. R_1, $Mu1^{ac}$, $^\lambda\Sigma^R$)

ac	ante correctionem
i	in linea
mg	in margine
pc	post correctionem
s	supra lineam
λ	in lemmate scholii
1	ipsius scribae manus
2	una et altera e manibus recentioribus

Sigla quae ad testimonia tantum pertinent

S	Suda
Sch.	scholium apud testem
§	fabulam non nominat testis
§§	nec fabulam nec poetam nominat testis
†	verba fabulae adeo transposuit omisit corrupit testis ut nullius pretii sit omnia memorare
‡	verba quae in Ecclesiazusis legimus alii fabulae tribuit testis

ΥΠΟΘΕΣΕΙΣ

Argumenta duo: quorum I in codicibus RA invenimus, II I (sic disposita) in codicibus ΓΛ.

I

Αἱ γυναῖκες συνέθεντο πάντα μηχανήσασθαι εἰς τὸ δόξαι ἄνδρες
εἶναι καὶ ἐκκλησιάσασαι πεῖσαι παραδοῦναι σφίσι τὴν πόλιν,
δημηγορησάσης μιᾶς ἐξ αὐτῶν. αἱ δὲ μηχαναὶ τοῦ δόξαι αὐτὰς
ἄνδρας εἶναι τοιαῦται. πώγωνας περιθέτους καὶ ἀνδρείαν
ἀναλαμβάνουσι στολήν, προνοήσασαι καὶ προασκήσασαι τὸ 5
σῶμα αὑτῶν, ὡς ὅτι μάλιστα ἀνδρικὸν εἶναι δόξαι· μία δὴ ἐξ
αὐτῶν Πραξαγόρα λύχνον ἔχουσα προέρχεται κατὰ τὰς συνθήκας
καὶ φησίν "ὦ λαμπρὸν ὄμμα".

Hypoth. I a   1 ἄνδρας ΑΓ   2 ἐκκλησιάσασθαι Γ   3 δημη-
γορήσεις Γ   4 ἄνδρας εἶναι om. ΑΓ   περιθέτους ποιοῦνται· καὶ ΑΓΛ
(-ται,)   5 ἀναλαμβάνονται ΑΓ   προνο- καὶ προασ- Brunck: προασ- καὶ
προνο- a   6 αὑτῶν Kuster: αὐ- a   δὴ] δὲ Α: δ' Γ   8 φησὶ Γ

II

Ἐν τοῖς Σκίροις τὰ γύναι' ἔκρινεν ⟨ἐν⟩ στολαῖς
ἀνδρῶν προκαθίζειν γενομένης ἐκκλησίας
περιθέμεναι πώγωνας ἀλλοτρίων τριχῶν.
ἐποίησαν οὕτως. ὑστεροῦντες οὖν στολαῖς
ἄνδρες γυναικῶν ἐκάθισαν· καὶ δὴ μία   5
δημηγορεῖ περὶ τοῦ λαβούσας τῶν ὅλων
τὴν ἐπιτροπὴν βέλτιον ἄρξειν μυρίῳ.

Hypoth. II ΓΛ: om. RA   1 ἔκρινεν ⟨ἐν⟩ Port: ἔκρινε ΓΛ
2 ἀνδρῶν Nauck: ἀνέρων ΓΛ   προκαθίζειν Bergk: προκαθέζοντα Γ:
προκαθίζοντα Λ   3 περιθέμεναι Ald.: παραθέμεναι Λ: παραθέμενα Γ
5 ἄνδρες Coulon: ἀν- ΓΛ   6 ὅλων Λ   7 μυρίῳ Le Febvre:
μυρίων ΓΛ

ἐκέλευσέ τ' εἰς κοινὸν φέρειν τὰ χρήματα
καὶ χρῆσθ' ἄπασιν ἐξ ἴσου ταῖς οὐσίαις,
καὶ ταῖς γυναιξὶ μετατίθεσθαι τοὺς νόμους.   10

8 τε *Γ*   φέρον *Γ*   9 χρῆσθ' Dindorf: χρῆσθαι *ΓΛ*   ἐξίσου *Λ*
10 τοῖς *Γ*

ΤΑ ΤΟΥ ΔΡΑΜΑΤΟΣ ΠΡΟΣΩΠΑ

Πραξαγόρα
Γυναῖκες Α Β
Χορὸς γυναικῶν
Βλέπυρος ἀνὴρ τῆς Πραξαγόρας
Ἀνὴρ γυναικὸς Β   5
Χρέμης
Κῆρυξ
Γρᾶες Α Β Γ
Νεᾶνις
Νεανίας   10
Θεράπαινα

Σίκων καὶ Παρμένων   } κωφὰ πρόσωπα
Ὀρχηστρίδες δύο

Index personarum deest in RΑΓ

1 Πραξαγόρα Ald.: γυνὴ τὶς πραξαγόρα Λ   2 Γυναῖκες Α Β Ussher
(cf. Rogers): ἑτέρα γυνὴ Λ   3 Χορὸς γυναικῶν Ald.: χορὸς Λ
4 Βλέπυρος ἀνὴρ τῆς Πραξαγόρας Ald.: ἀνὴρ τις Λ   5 Ἀνὴρ γυναικὸς Β
Rogers: ἕτερος ἀνὴρ Βλέπυρος Λ   6 Χρέμης Ald.: ἕτερος ἀνὴρ ἀπὸ
ἐκκλησίας χρέμης, post 6 add. ἄλλος ἀνὴρ φειδωλὸς Λ   7 Κῆ-
ρυξ] Κηρύκαινα Le Febvre   8 Γρᾶες Α Β Γ Ussher (cf. Rogers):
γραῦς Λ   9 Νεᾶνις Tyrwhitt: ἑτέρα νέα Λ   10 Νεανίας Brunck:
om. Λ   12 Σίκων καὶ Παρμένων Ussher (cf. van Leeuwen, 833, 867):
om. Λ   13 Ὀρχηστρίδες δύο Ussher: om. Λ

ΕΚΚΛΗΣΙΑΖΟΥΣΑΙ

ΠΡΑΞΑΓΟΡΑ

Ὦ λαμπρὸν ὄμμα τοῦ τροχηλάτου λύχνου,
κάλλιστ' ἐν εὐστόχοισιν ἐξηυρημένον—
γονάς τε γὰρ σὰς καὶ τύχας δηλώσομεν·
τροχῷ γὰρ ἐλαθεὶς κεραμικῆς ῥύμης ἄπο
μυκτῆρσι λαμπρὰς ἡλίου τιμὰς ἔχεις—   5
ὄρμα φλογὸς σημεῖα τὰ ξυγκείμενα.
σοὶ γὰρ μόνῳ δηλοῦμεν εἰκότως, ἐπεὶ
κἂν τοῖσι δωματίοισιν Ἀφροδίτης τρόπων
πειρωμέναισι πλησίον παραστατεῖς,
λορδουμένων τε σωμάτων ἐπιστάτην   10
ὀφθαλμὸν οὐδεὶς τὸν σὸν ἐξείργει δόμων.
μόνος δὲ μηρῶν εἰς ἀπορρήτους μυχοὺς
λάμπεις ἀφεύων τὴν ἐπανθοῦσαν τρίχα·
στοάς τε καρποῦ Βακχίου τε νάματος
πλήρεις ὑποιγνύσαισι συμπαραστατεῖς·   15
καὶ ταῦτα συνδρῶν οὐ λαλεῖς τοῖς πλησίον.
ἀνθ' ὧν συνείσει καὶ τὰ νῦν βουλεύματα
ὅσα Σκίροις ἔδοξε ταῖς ἐμαῖς φίλαις.
ἀλλ' οὐδεμία πάρεστιν ἃς ἥκειν ἐχρῆν.
καίτοι πρὸς ὄρθρον γ' ἐστίν, ἡ δ' ἐκκλησία   20

4 (κε- . . .) § S ρ 294   10 § S λ 681   14 § S σ 1126

---

1 Πραξαγόρα A (ut vid.) Λ: par. R: om. Γ   ὦ om. Γ: ὅ Λ
τραχηλάτου Γ   2 εὐσκόποισιν ΑΓΛ   ἐξηυρημένον Meineke: ἐξητη-
μένον a: ἐξηρτημένον x   3 σὰς] δισσὰς ΑΓ   4 καιραμικης Rac
ὕπο Kuster   6 ὄρμα R   8 τοῖς ΑΓ   δοματίοισιν R   τρόπω ΑΓ
9 πλησίως R: πλησίος ΓΛ   12 ante 11 R₁   11 ὀφθαλμὸς
ΑΓ   ἐξείρ δόμῳ Γ   14 Βακχείου R₂   15 πλήρης
ΑΓΛ   16 λαλοῖς Γ   17 ἀνθῶν Γ   συνείσει Biset: συνοίσει a
18 ἔδοξεν R

αὐτίκα μάλ' ἔσται· καταλαβεῖν δ' ἡμᾶς ἕδρας
δεῖ τὰς ἑταίρας κῶλά θ' ἱζομένας λαθεῖν,   23
ἃς Φυρόμαχός ποτ' εἶπεν, εἰ μέμνησθ' ἔτι.   22
τί δῆτ' ἂν εἴη; πότερον οὐκ ἐρραμμένους
ἔχουσι τοὺς πώγωνας, οὓς εἴρητ' ἔχειν;   25
ἢ θαἰμάτια τἀνδρεῖα κλεψάσαις λαθεῖν
ἦν χαλεπὸν αὐταῖς; ἀλλ' ὁρῶ τονδὶ λύχνον
προσιόντα. φέρε νυν ἐπαναχωρήσω πάλιν,
μὴ καί τις ὢν ἀνὴρ ὁ προσιὼν τυγχάνῃ.

ΓΥΝΗ Α

ὥρα βαδίζειν, ὡς ὁ κῆρυξ ἀρτίως   30
ἡμῶν προσιόντων δεύτερον κεκόκκυκεν.

Πρ. ἐγὼ δέ γ' ὑμᾶς προσδοκῶσ' ἐγρηγόρη
τὴν νύκτα πᾶσαν. ἀλλὰ φέρε τὴν γείτονα
τήνδ' ἐκκαλέσωμαι θρυγανῶσα τὴν θύραν.
δεῖ γὰρ τὸν ἄνδρ' αὐτῆς λαθεῖν.

ΓΥΝΗ Β

                         ἤκουσά τοι   35
ὑποδουμένη τὸ κνῦμά σου τῶν δακτύλων,
ἅτ' οὐ καταδαρθοῦσ'. ὁ γὰρ ἀνήρ, ὦ φιλτάτη,

34 (τρυ-...) § S τ 1095   35–6 §§ S κ 1892   36 (κν- δακ-) §
Hdn. in Eust. 1746. 8

21 δ' om. Γ   22 et 23 tr. Dover   23 ἑτέρας ed. Junt.
(1515)   κῶλά θ' ἱζομένας Coulon: κωλαθιζομένας R: καθαγιαζομένας
ΑΓ: κἀγαθιζομένας Λ   πῶς post -ρας RΛ: πως post -νας ΑΓ
22 ἃς R   σφυρόμαχός ΑΓΛ: κλεόμαχος ᵛΣᴿ   24–6 om. ΑΓx
25 τὰς R   26 ἢ θαἰμάτια Ald.: εἴθ' αἱμάτια (cf. ᵛΣᴿ) R: ἦσθ'
αἱμάτια Λ   27 ὁρᾷ R   28 νυν Bekker: νῦν a   29 τυγχάνεις a
30 Γυ. Α Brunck: par. R: γυνή τις ΑΛ: om. Γ: μία τῶν ἐρχομένων
γυναικῶν Σᴿ   31 προσιουσῶν Le Febvre   32 Πρ.] par. R:
om. Γ   γ' om. ΑΓ   ἐγρηγόρη Porson: -ρεῖν a   33 φέ Rᵃᶜ
34 ἐκκαλέσομαι ΑΓ   θρυγανῶσα Bentley (cf. Hsch. s.v. θρυγανᾷ): -γυν-
RΛ (Muiᵖᶜ): τρυγανῶσα Α: τρυγονῶσα Γ (cf. ᵛΣᴿ): θρυγωνῶσα Muiᵃᶜ
35 Γυ. Β Brunck: dic. R: γυνὴ ΓΛ: om. Α   37 καταθοῦσ Γ

Σαλαμίνιος γάρ ἐστιν ᾧ ξύνειμ' ἐγώ,
τὴν νύχθ' ὅλην ἤλαυνέ μ' ἐν τοῖς στρώμασιν,
ὥστ' ἄρτι τουτὶ θοἰμάτιον αὐτοῦ 'λαβον.   40

Πρ.   καὶ μὴν ὁρῶ καὶ Κλειναρέτην καὶ Σωστράτην
προσιοῦσαν ἤδη τήνδε καὶ Φιλαινέτην.

Γυ.ᵃ   οὔκουν ἐπείξεσθ'; ὡς Γλύκη κατώμοσεν
τὴν ὑστάτην ἤκουσαν οἴνου τρεῖς χοᾶς
ἡμῶν ἀποτείσειν κἀρεβίνθων χοίνικα.   45

Γυ.ᵝ   τὴν Σμικυθίωνος δ' οὐχ ὁρᾷς Μελιστίχην
σπεύδουσαν ἐν ταῖς ἐμβάσιν; Γυ.ᵃ καί μοι δοκεῖ
κατὰ σχολὴν παρὰ τἀνδρὸς ἐξελθεῖν μόνη.

Γυ.ᵝ   τὴν τοῦ καπήλου δ' οὐχ ὁρᾷς Γευσιστράτην
ἔχουσαν ἐν τῇ δεξιᾷ τὴν λαμπάδα;   50

Γυ.ᵃ   καὶ τὴν Φιλοδωρήτου τε καὶ Χαιρητάδου
ὁρῶ προσιούσας χἀτέρας πολλὰς πάνυ
γυναῖκας, ὅ τι πέρ ἐστ' ὄφελος ἐν τῇ πόλει.

---

38 cf. Phot. s.v. Σαλ-   43–4 §§ S χ 362   44–5 § Σ Ach. 961
48 §§ S κ 809; cf. Phot. s.v. κατὰ σχολήν   52–3 S § † (1) o 995;
(ὅ τι . . .) § (2) o 738

---

39 στρώμασι Γ   40 αὐτοῦ 'λαβον Velsen: αὐτοῦ λαβών (-ών Γ)
R₁ΑΓΛ: αὐτ' οὔλαβον R₂   41 Πρ. Reiske: γυνὴ Α: om. RΓΛ
42 προσιοῦσαν Ald.: παροῦσαν a   Φιλαινέτην] φιλαινεκάτην R₁ (ut vid.)
43 om. Γ   Γυ.ᵃ Ussher: par. R: πραξ ΑΛ   οὔκουν in ras. Α
κατώμοσε Α   44 ἤκουσαν R   45 ἡμῶν in ras. Α   κἀρεβίνθου Γ
46 Γυ.ᵝ van Leeuwen: om. a   σιμικυθίωνος Rᵃᶜ   δ' om. ΑΓΛ
μελιστιάχην Γ: μὲ λεστίχην Λ (μὲ λι- Μυι)   47 τοῖς Γ   ἐμβάσι ΑΓ
Γυ.ᵃ Ussher: om. a   καί μοι] ἐμοι Γ: καίτοι Cobet   48 κατασχολὴν
RΓΛ   49 Γυ.ᵝ Brunck: par. R: γυνὴ Λ: om. ΑΓ   51 Γυ.ᵃ
Ussher: par. R: om. ΑΓΛ   Φιλοδωρίτου RΓΛ   Χαρητάδου Λ
52 in. πραξ Λ   53 ἐστιν S (1) (2)

ΧΟΡΟΣ

καὶ πάνυ ταλαιπώρως ἔγωγ᾽, ὦ φιλτάτη,
ἐκδρᾶσα παρέδυν. ὁ γὰρ ἀνὴρ τὴν νύχθ᾽ ὅλην   55
ἔβηττε τριχίδων ἑσπέρας ἐμπλήμενος.

Πρ.   κάθησθε τοίνυν, ὡς ⟨ἂν⟩ ἀνέρωμαι τάδε
        ὑμᾶς, ἐπειδὴ συλλελεγμένας ὁρῶ,
        ὅσα Σκίροις ἔδοξεν εἰ δεδράκατε.

Γυ.ᵃ   ἔγωγε. πρῶτον μέν γ᾽ ἔχω τὰς μασχάλας   60
        λόχμης δασυτέρας, καθάπερ ἦν ξυγκείμενον.
        ἔπειθ᾽ ὁπόθ᾽ ἀνὴρ εἰς ἀγορὰν οἴχοιτό μου
        ἀλειψαμένη τὸ σῶμ᾽ ὅλον δι᾽ ἡμέρας
        ἐχραινόμην ἑστῶσα πρὸς τὸν ἥλιον.

Γυ.ᵝ   κἄγωγε· τὸ ξυρὸν δέ γ᾽ ἐκ τῆς οἰκίας   65
        ἔρριψα πρῶτον, ἵνα δασυνθείην ὅλη
        καὶ μηδὲν εἴην ἔτι γυναικὶ προσφερής.

Πρ.   ἔχετε δὲ τοὺς πώγωνας, οὓς εἴρητ᾽ ἔχειν
        πάσαισιν ὑμῖν, ὁπότε συλλεγοίμεθα;

Γυ.ᵃ   νὴ τὴν Ἑκάτην, καλόν γ᾽ ἔγωγε τουτονί.   70

Γυ.ᵝ   κἄγωγ᾽ Ἐπικράτους οὐκ ὀλίγῳ καλλίονα.

55–6 § † Σ Eq. 662 ; S § † (1) ε 1028 ; § † (2) τ 1038   60–1 (ἐχ-...)
§ S λ 713   63–4 § S λ 713   71 S § (1) π 2150 ; §§ (2) ε 2417 ('Ε...)

54 ΧΟΡΟΣ Ussher (cf. Rogers) : par. RA : γυνὴ Λ : om. Γ   -ρως
γ᾽ ἔγωγ᾽ ΑΓ : -ρῶ ἔγωγ᾽ Λ   55 ἐκδρᾶσαι Γ : -ράσ- Α   56 ἐμπε-
πλησμένος ΑΓ : ἐμπλησμένος Λ : πεπλησμένος S (2)   57 Πρ.] par. RA :
om. Γ   τόνυν R : τοὶ νῦν A   ⟨ἂν⟩ ἀνέρωμαι Dawes : ἀνείρωμαι RΛ : ἂν
εἴρωμαι ΑΓ   58 συλλελαγμένας Α   60 Γυ.ᵃ Bergk : par. R :
γυνὴ Λ : om. ΑΓ   61 λόχμης R₂ (cf. ᐸΣᴿᵖᶜ) S : λόγχμης R₁
(cf. ᐸΣᴿᵃᶜ) : λό+χμης Α : λόγχης Γ : λόγμης Λ   ὥσπερ S   ξυγκείμενος Α
62 ὁπόθ᾽ ἀνὴρ Dawes : ὁπόθ᾽ ἀνὴρ R : ὁπότ᾽ ἀνὴρ ΑΓΛ   64 ἐχραινόμην
Bergk : ἐχλιαινόμην a : ἐχλιαίνετο S   65 Γυ.ᵝ Bergk : par. R : ἑτέρα
γυνή Λ : om. ΑΓ   τὸ] τὸν Λ   66 ἔρριψεν Γ : ἔριψα Λ   68 Πρ.]
om. RΑΓ   δὲ] δὴ R   69 πάσαισι Γ   ἡμῖν ΑΓ   ὅππὀτε Γ
70 Γυ.ᵃ Bergk : par. RA : γυνὴ Λ : om. Γ   ἑκάτην R   γ᾽ om. ΑΓΛ
71 Γυ.ᵝ Bergk : par. R : ἑτέρα γυνὴ Λ : om. ΑΓ   ἐπὶ κράτους RΓΛ
καλλίονα πώγων᾽ ἔχω S (-εις S (2))

Πρ. ὑμεῖς δὲ τί φατε; Γυ.ᵃ φασί· κατανεύουσι γοῦν.

Πρ. καὶ μὴν τά γ᾽ ἀλλ᾽ ὑμῖν ὁρῶ πεπραγμένα.
     Λακωνικὰς γὰρ ἔχετε καὶ βακτηρίας
     καὶ θαἰμάτια τἀνδρεῖα, καθάπερ εἴπομεν.   75

Γυ.ᵃ ἔγωγέ τοι τὸ σκύταλον ἐξηνεγκάμην
     τὸ τοῦ Λαμίου τουτὶ καθεύδοντος λάθρᾳ.

Γυ.ᵝ τοῦτ᾽ ἔστ᾽ ἐκείνου τὸ σκύταλον, ὃς πέρδεται.

Πρ. νὴ τὸν Δία τὸν σωτῆρ᾽ ἐπιτήδειός γ᾽ ἂν ἦν
     τὴν τοῦ πανόπτου διφθέραν ἐνημμένος   80
     εἴπερ τις ἄλλος βουκολεῖν τὸν δήμιον.
     ἀλλ᾽ ἄγεθ᾽ ὅπως καὶ τἀπὶ τούτοις δράσομεν,
     ἕως ἔτ᾽ ἐστὶν ἄστρα κατὰ τὸν οὐρανόν·
     ἡκκλησία δ᾽, εἰς ἣν παρεσκευάσμεθα
     ἡμεῖς βαδίζειν, ἐξ ἕω γενήσεται.   85

Γυ.ᵃ νὴ τὸν Δί᾽, ὥστε δεῖ σε καταλαβεῖν ἕδρας
     ὑπὸ τῷ λίθῳ τῶν πρυτάνεων καταντικρύ.

Γυ.ᵝ ταυτί γέ τοι νὴ τὸν Δί᾽ ἐφερόμην, ἵνα
     πληρουμένης ξαίνοιμι τῆς ἐκκλησίας.

76 §§ S σ 721   76–7 (τὸ . . . -μίου) § S σ 721   78 § S σ 721
80 §§ S ε 1312; (δι- . . . -νος) §§ Zonar. 747

72 Πρ.] par. R: om. ΑΓ   Γυ.ᵃ Bergk: γυνὴ Λ: om. ΡΑΓ
κατάνευσι R: κατανεῦσαι Γ   γοῦν RΛ: γὰρ ΑΓ   73 Πρ.] par. R:
om. ΑΓ   τἄλλα γ᾽ Α   75 τἀνδρεῖα om. R₁   εἴπαμεν RΓ:
εἴπωμεν Λ   76 Γυ.ᵃ Bergk: par. RA: γυνὴ Λ: om. Γ   78 Γυ.ᵝ
Meineke: par. R: πραξ Λ: om. ΑΓ   τουτέστιν S   ἐκείνου τὸ
σκύταλον ὃς Ussher: ἐκεῖνο (-νων S) τῶν σκυτάλων ὧν aS: ἐκεῖνο τὸ σκύταλον ᾧ Bothe   79 Πρ. Dindorf: par. R: om. ΑΓΛ   80 πανέ-
πτου ΑΓᵃᶜ (ut vid.): πανόπου Λ   81 ἄλλος om. ΑΓ   post βουκολεῖν
add. ἐθέλει × τὸν δημήμιον R: τὸ δήμιον Bothe: τὴν Δημιὼ Velsen
82 in. γυνὴ R₂Λ: par. Α   ἀλλ᾽ ἄγεθ᾽ Dindorf: +γέθ᾽ R: λέγεθ᾽ ΑΓΛ
δράσαμεν Μui   85 om. Γ   ἐξέω R   86 Γυ.ᵃ Brunck: par.
RA: πραξ Λ: om. Γ   ἕδρας Γ   87 τῶ πρυτάνεων Α: τῷ τρυτάνεω Γ
κατ᾽ ἀντικρύ RᵃᶜΑΓ: κατ᾽ ἀντικὼ Λ   88 Γυ.ᵝ Bergk: ἄλλη R₂Λ:
om. R₁ΑΓ   δία Γ   89 ξαίνοι Rᵃᶜ

Πρ.   πληρουμένης τάλαινα; Γυ.^β νὴ τὴν Ἄρτεμιν   90
       ἔγωγε. τί γὰρ ἂν χεῖρον ἀκροώμην ἄρα
       ξαίνουσα; γυμνὰ δ᾽ ἐστί μου τὰ παιδία.

Πρ.   ἰδού γέ σε ξαίνουσαν, ἦν τοῦ σώματος
       οὐδὲν παραφῆναι τοῖς καθημένοις ἔδει.
       οὐκοῦν καλά γ᾽ ἂν πάθοιμεν, εἰ πλήρης τύχοι   95
       ὁ δῆμος ὢν κἄπειθ᾽ ὑπερβαίνουσά τις
       ἀναβαλλομένη δείξειε τὸν Φορμίσιον.
       ἢν δ᾽ ἐγκαθεζώμεσθα πρότεραι, λήσομεν
       ξυστειλάμεναι θαἰμάτια· τὸν πώγωνά τε
       ὅταν καθῶμεν ὃν περιδησόμεσθ᾽ ἐκεῖ,   100
       τίς οὐκ ἂν ἡμᾶς ἄνδρας ἡγήσαιθ᾽ ὁρῶν;
       Ἀγύρριος γοῦν τὸν Προνόμου πώγων᾽ ἔχων
       λέληθε· καίτοι πρότερον ἦν οὗτος γυνή.
       νυνὶ δ᾽, ὁρᾷς, πράττει τὰ μέγιστ᾽ ἐν τῇ πόλει.
       τούτου γέ τοι, νὴ τὴν ἐπιοῦσαν ἡμέραν,   105
       τόλμημα τολμῶμεν τοσοῦτον οὕνεκα,
       ἤν πως παραλαβεῖν τῆς πόλεως τὰ πράγματα
       δυνώμεθ᾽ ὥστ᾽ ἀγαθόν τι πρᾶξαι τὴν πόλιν.
       νῦν μὲν γὰρ οὔτε θέομεν οὔτ᾽ ἐλαύνομεν.

Γυ.^α   καὶ πῶς γυναικῶν θηλύφρων ξυνουσία   110
       δημηγορήσει; Πρ. πολὺ μὲν οὖν ἄριστά που.

97 §§ S φ 605   102–3 (...-θεν) S §§ (1) a 385; (Πρ-... ἐλάνθανε)
§§ (2) π 2527; (...-θεν) §§ Zonar. 21   109 § S θ 304

90 Πρ.] par. RA: om. Γ   Γυ.^β Bergk: dic. RΓ: γυνὴ Λ: om. A
92 γυμὰ Α^{ac} (ut vid.): γ+νὰ Λ (-υμ- in lac. duarum fere litterarum
Mul₂)   μοι R   93 Πρ.] par. RA: om. Γ   ἦν ΓΛ   94 παραφανῆναι
Γ   ἴδει Λ   95 in. par. R₂   οὐκοῦν Λ: οὐκ οὖν R: οὐκ ἂν ΑΓ   πλή̄+ Γ
96 τις] τε Λ   97 δείξειεν RΓ: δείξει S   τὴν ΑΓS   98 ἐγκαθε-
ζώμεσθα Dindorf: -θι- RAΛ: ἐκαθεζόμεσθα Γ   πότερα λήσομεν Γ
99 om. R₁   συ- Γ   100 περ δησόμεσθ᾽ Λ   101 ἡγήσεθ᾽ RΛ
102 in. par. RA   πρὸ νόμου Mul   103 λέληθεν ΛS (1): ἐλάνθανε
S (2)   πρότερον καίτοι Γ   ἦν R   104 δορᾷς Λ   τὰ om. Mul
105 in. par. R   107 ἦν R   109 θέαμεν Γ   ἐλαύνομεν in ras. A
110 Γυ.^α Bergk: par. R: γυνὴ Λ: om. ΑΓ   ἐξουσία Λ   111 Πρ.]
dic. R: om. ΑΓ   οὖν om. A   ἄριστά που in ras. A

λέγουσι γὰρ καὶ τῶν νεανίσκων ὅσοι
πλεῖστα σποδοῦνται, δεινοτάτους εἶναι λέγειν.
ἡμῖν δ᾽ ὑπάρχει τοῦτο κατὰ τύχην τινά.

Γυ.ᵃ   οὐκ οἶδα. δεινὸν δ᾽ ἐστὶν ἡ μὴ 'μπειρία.   115

Πρ.   οὔκουν ἐπίτηδες ξυνελέγημεν ἐνθάδε,
ὅπως προμελετήσωμεν ἀκεῖ δεῖ λέγειν;
οὐκ ἂν φθάνοις τὸ γένειον ἂν περιδουμένη
ἄλλαι θ᾽ ὅσαι λαλεῖν μεμελετήκασί που.

Γυ.ᵃ   τίς δ᾽ ὦ μέλ᾽ ἡμῶν οὐ λαλεῖν ἐπίσταται;   120

Πρ.   ἴθι δὴ σὺ περιδοῦ καὶ ταχέως ἀνὴρ γενοῦ.
ἐγὼ δὲ θεῖσα τοὺς στεφάνους περιδήσομαι
καὐτὴ μεθ᾽ ὑμῶν, ἤν τί μοι δόξῃ λέγειν.

Γυ.ᵝ   δεῦρ᾽ ὦ γλυκυτάτη Πραξαγόρα, σκέψαι τάλαν
ὡς καὶ καταγέλαστον τὸ πρᾶγμα φαίνεται.   125

Πρ.   πῶς καταγέλαστον; Γυ.ᵝ ὥσπερ εἴ τις σηπίαις
πώγωνα περιδήσειεν ἐσταθευμέναις.

Πρ.   ὁ περιστίαρχος, περιφέρειν χρὴ τὴν γαλῆν.
πάριτ᾽ ἐς τὸ πρόσθεν. Ἀρίφραδες, παῦσαι λαλῶν.
κάθιζε παριών. τίς ἀγορεύειν βούλεται;   130

---

113 cf. Phot.s.v. σποδοῦν   115 (δει-...) §Sη319   116 (οὔ-...
-μεν) §§ S ε 2680   121 § S π 1101; (πε-...) §§ Σᴬˡᵈ· *Eq.* 791
126–7 (ὥσ-...) §§ S ε 3197   129 (Ἀ-...) § S α 3940

115 Γυ.ᵃ Bergk: par. R: γυνὴ Λ: om. ΑΓ   δ᾽ om. ΑΓ   μὴ
'μπειρία x S: 'μη 'μπειρία RΛ: μημ 'πειρία ΑΓ   116 Πρ.] par. RA:
om. Γ   οὔκουν Λ   συν- Α (-ελέ- in ras.)   117 προμελετήσαιμεν
Kidd   ἀκεῖ] ἆ Γ   118 in. par. RA   περιδομένη R: περιδυμένη Γ
119 ἄλλαι Meineke   μεμετήκασί R₁   120 Γυ.ᵃ Bergk: par. R:
γυνὴ Λ: om. ΑΓ   121 Πρ.] par. RA: om. Γ   περιδοῦ x:
περίδου aS   123 ἡμῶν Λ   μοι] μὴ Γ   δόξει R   λέξειν in ras. R₂
124 Γυ.ᵝ Hermann: par. A: γυνὴ Λ: om. ΑΓ   125 ΑΓ   λάλαν Muιᵃᶜ
126 Πρ.] par. R: om. ΑΓ   Γυ.ᵝ Hermann: γυνὴ Λ: om. RΑΓ
127 ἐστ- Γ   128 Πρ.] par. A: om. RΓ   φέρειν ΑΓ   γαλήν RΑΓ
129 πάριτ᾽ Rᵃᶜ   ληρῶν S

Γυ.ᵃ   ἐγώ. Πρ. περίθου δὴ τὸν στέφανον τύχἀγαθῇ.

Γυ.ᵃ   ἰδού. Πρ. λέγοις ἄν. Γυ.ᵃ εἶτα πρὶν πιεῖν λέγω;

Πρ.   ἰδοὺ πιεῖν. Γυ.ᵃ τί γὰρ ὦ μέλ' ἐστεφανωσάμην;

Πρ.   ἄπιθ' ἐκποδών· τοιαῦτ' ἂν ἡμᾶς ἠργάσω
κἀκεῖ. Γυ.ᵃ τί δ'; οὐ πίνουσι κἂν τἠκκλησίᾳ;   135

Πρ.   ἰδού γε σοὶ πίνουσι. Γυ.ᵃ νὴ τὴν Ἄρτεμιν,
καὶ ταῦτά γ' εὔζωρον. τὰ γοῦν βουλεύματα
αὐτῶν, ὅσ' ἂν πράξωσιν ἐνθυμουμένοις,
ὥσπερ μεθυόντων ἐστὶ παραπεπληγμένα.
καὶ νὴ Δία σπένδουσί γ'· ἢ τίνος χάριν   140
τοσαῦτ' ἂν ηὔχοντ', εἴπερ οἶνος μὴ παρῆν;
καὶ λοιδοροῦνταί γ' ὥσπερ ἐμπεπωκότες,
καὶ τὸν παροινοῦντ' ἐκφέρουσ' οἱ τοξόται.

Πρ.   σὺ μὲν βάδιζε καὶ κάθησ'· οὐδὲν γὰρ εἶ.

Γυ.ᵃ   νὴ τὸν Δί', ἦ μοι μὴ γενειᾶν κρεῖττον ἦν·   145
δίψῃ γάρ, ὡς ἔοικ', ἀφαυανθήσομαι.

Πρ.   ἔσθ' ἥτις ἑτέρα βούλεται λέγειν; Γυ.ᵝ ἐγώ.

138–9 (ὅσ'...) §§ S π 406   146 ἀ- cf. Eust. 1387. 3, Zonar. 357

131–45 Γυ.ᵃ Bergk   131 Γυ.ᵃ] par. RA: γυνὴ Λ: om. Γ   Πρ.]
dic. R: par. A: om. Γ   παράθου ΓΛ   132 Γυ.ᵃ] par. A: γυνὴ Λ: om.
RΓ   Πρ.] par. R: dic. Γ: om. A   Γυ.ᵃ] par. RA: γυνὴ Λ: om. Γ
133 Πρ] par. R: om. AΓ   Γυ.ᵃ] dic. A: γυνὴ Λ: om. RΓ   134 Πρ.]
par. RA: om. Γ   ἄπιθ' Γ   ἐκποδών x: -δῶν a   εἰργάσω RΓ (ἐρ-) Λ
135 Γυ.ᵃ] dic. AΓ: γυνὴ Λ: om. R   πίνουσιν ἀν Γ   136 Πρ.]
par. R: om. AΓ   πίνουσι (-σι; A) AΓ: -σιν RΛ   Γυ.ᵃ] dic. RAΓ: γυνὴ Λ
138 ὅσοι ἂν Λ   εὐθυμουμένοις A   139 ἐστὶν Γ   140 σπεύδουσί
AΓ   τίνας Rᵃᶜ   141 τοσαῦτ' ἂν Hermann: τοσαῦτά γ' R: -τα γ' A:
τοσαῦτ' ΓΛ   ηὔχοντ' Meineke: εὔχοντο R: εὔχονται AΓ: ἔχοντ' Λ
οἶνος... ὥσπερ (142) om. AΓ   142 ἐμπεπωκότες Ald.: ἐκ- R:
ἐμπεπτωκότες AΛ: ἐκ- Γ   143 ἐκφέρουσιν AΓ   144 Πρ.] par.
RA: om. Γ   βάδιζε] κάθιζε AΓ: κάθιζ' Λ   145 Γυ.ᵃ] par. RA:
γυνὴ Λ: om. Γ   146 δίψῃ x: δίψει a   ἔοικε AΓ   ἀφαυανθήσομαι R₁:
φαυανθήσομαι ΑΓΛ   147–67 Γυ.ᵝ Bergk   147 Πρ.] par. R:
om. AΓ   Γυ.ᵝ] dic. RAΓ: γυνὴ Λ

Πρ.   ἴθι δὴ στεφανοῦ· καὶ γὰρ τὸ χρῆμ' ἐργάζεται.
       ἄγε νυν ὅπως ἀνδριστὶ καὶ καλῶς ἐρεῖς
       διερεισαμένη τὸ σχῆμα τῇ βακτηρίᾳ.   150

Γυ.ᵝ   ἐβουλόμην μὲν ἕτερον ἂν τῶν ἠθάδων
       λέγειν τὰ βέλτισθ', ἵν' ἐκαθήμην ἥσυχος.
       νῦν δ' οὐκ ἐάσω, κατά γε τὴν ἐμὴν μίαν,
       ἐν τοῖς καπηλείοισι λάκκους ἐμποιεῖν
       ὕδατος. ἐμοὶ μὲν οὐ δοκεῖ, μὰ τὼ θεώ.   155

Πρ.   μὰ τὼ θεώ; τάλαινα, ποῦ τὸν νοῦν ἔχεις;

Γυ.ᵝ   τί δ' ἔστιν; οὐ γὰρ δὴ πιεῖν γ' ᾔτησά σε.

Πρ.   μὰ Δί' ἀλλ' ἀνὴρ ὢν τὼ θεὼ κατώμοσας,
       καίτοι τά γ' ἄλλ' εἰποῦσα δεξιώτατα.

Γυ.ᵝ   ὢ νὴ τὸν Ἀπόλλω. Πρ. παῦε τοίνυν, ὡς ἐγὼ   160
       ἐκκλησιάσουσ' οὐκ ἂν προβαίην τὸν πόδα
       τὸν ἕτερον, εἰ μὴ ταῦτ' ἀκριβωθήσεται.

Γυ.ᵝ   φέρε τὸν στέφανον· ἐγὼ γὰρ αὖ λέξω πάλιν.
       οἶμαι γὰρ ἤδη μεμελετηκέναι καλῶς.
       ἐμοὶ γάρ, ὦ γυναῖκες αἱ καθήμεναι,—   165

154 cf. Phot. s.v. λάκκος (2)   161–2 (οὐδ-...) § S a 982; (οὐδ-...)
§ Zonar. 114

---

148 Πρ.] par. R: om. ΑΓ   149 in. par. R   νυν Bekker: νῦν **a**
150 διερεισαμένη Schaefer (cf. Σᴿ): διερείσ μὲν ἡ Rᵃᶜ: διερεισμένη
RᵖᶜΑΓΛ   τῆς βακτηρίας ΑΓ   151 Γυ.ᵝ] par. A: γυνὴ Λ: om. RΓ
ἂν τὸν ἕτερον ΑΓ: ἑτέρων ἂν Λ   152 ἵν'] ἦν R   153 νυν R
154 τοῖσι RΛ   155 μὰ τὼ] μετὰ Rᵃᶜ   156 Πρ.] par. RA: om. Γ
post τάλαινα dic. R   τον νοῦν] τὸνᵒᵘ A   post 156 del. τί γὰρ δὴ π R₁
157 Γυ.ᵝ] γυνὴ Λ: om. RΑΓ   158 om. A* (cf. 160, 162, 164, 166,
168) Πρ.] par. R: om. Γ   τὼ] τῶν Rᵃᶜ: τῶ in ras. Rᵖᶜ   159 ἀλλ' A:
om. R₁: ἀλλ' R₂ˢ: αλλ' Γ: ἄλλα Λ   εἶπας σὺ Blaydes   160 om. A*
Γυ.ᵝ] γυνὴ Λ: om. RΓ   ὢ RΛ   ἀπόλλωνα Γ   Πρ.] dic. R: om. ΓΛ
161 ἐκκλησιάσουσ' Bentley: ἐκκλησιάζουμπρο Rᵃᶜ: ἐκκλησιάζουσ' RᵖᶜΓΛ:
ἐκκληζιάζουσ' A   οὐκ] οὐδ' S   162 om. A*   ἕτερα Rᵃᶜ
ἀκριβωθῆσαι R₁: -σαιται R₂ (ut vid.)   163 Γυ.ᵝ] par. RA: ἡ
προτέρα γυνὴ Λ: om. Γ   164 om. A*   μεμελημεμωκέναι Rᵃᶜ
165 καθημένη R

Πρ.   γυναῖκας αὖ, δύστηνε, τοὺς ἄνδρας λέγεις;

Γυ.ᵝ   δι' Ἐπίγονόν γ' ἐκεῖνον· ἐπιβλέψασα γὰρ
       ἐκεῖσε πρὸς γυναῖκας ᾠόμην λέγειν.

Πρ.   ἄπερρε καὶ σὺ καὶ κάθησ' ἐντευθενί.
       αὐτὴ γὰρ ὑμῶν γ' ἕνεκά μοι λέξειν δοκῶ   170
       τονδὶ λαβοῦσα. τοῖς θεοῖς μὲν εὔχομαι
       τυχεῖν κατορθώσασα τὰ βεβουλευμένα.
       ἐμοὶ δ' ἴσον μὲν τῆσδε τῆς χώρας μέτα
       ὅσονπερ ὑμῖν· ἄχθομαι δὲ καὶ φέρω
       τὰ τῆς πόλεως ἅπαντα βαρέως πράγματα.   175
       ὁρῶ γὰρ αὐτὴν προστάταισι χρωμένην
       ἀεὶ πονηροῖς. κἄν τις ἡμέραν μίαν
       χρηστὸς γένηται, δέκα πονηρὸς γίγνεται.
       ἐπέτρεψας ἑτέρῳ· πλείον' ἔτι δράσει κακά.
       χαλεπὸν μὲν οὖν ἄνδρας δυσαρέστους νουθετεῖν,   180
       οἳ τοὺς φιλεῖν μὲν βουλομένους δεδοίκατε,
       τοὺς δ' οὐκ ἐθέλοντας ἀντιβολεῖθ' ἑκάστοτε.
       ἐκκλησίαισιν ἦν ὅτ' οὐκ ἐχρώμεθα
       οὐδὲν τὸ παράπαν· ἀλλὰ τόν γ' Ἀγύρριον
       πονηρὸν ἡγούμεσθα. νῦν δὲ χρωμένων   185
       ὁ μὲν λαβὼν ἀργύριον ὑπερεπήνεσεν,
       ὁ δ' οὐ λαβὼν εἶναι θανάτου φῆσ' ἀξίους
       τοὺς μισθοφορεῖν ζητοῦντας ἐν τἠκκλησίᾳ.

167–8 (ἐπιβ-...) § S ε 2268   173–8 §§ S (1) π 2809   173–5 §§
(2) μ 678   180 §§ S δ 1596   181–2 (τοὺς ...) S §§ (1) ε 357;
(εἰ τοὺς ...) §§ (2) δ 1596   182 §§ Zonar. 680

166 om. A*   Πρ.] par. R: om. Γ   αὖ] ὦ Γ   167 Γυ.ᵝ]
par. RA: γυνὴ Λ: om. Γ   διεπίγονον Γ   εἴ τι βλέψασα RᵃᶜΛ: ἐπι
βλέψασα Rᵖᶜ: ἐπιβλέψας S   168 om. A*   ᾠόμη R   169 Πρ.]
par. RA: om. Γ   ἔπερρε Γ   κάθησθ' ΑΓΛ   ἐντευνί R₁   170 γ'...
δοκῶ om. A*: γ' om. R   171 τὸν δὴ R   172 κατορθώσας ΑΓ
173 χώρας+ R   174 ὅσο+περ Γ: ὅσον παρ' Λ   175 πράγματα
βαρέως ΑΓS (1)   180 δυσαρέτους Λ   182 ἀντιβολεῖτ' ἐ- Λ
183 ἦν x: ἦν RΑΓ: ἦν Λ   184 τό] γε Μu1   185 ἡγούμεθα ΑΓ
187 ἄξιος Α   188 μισθοφορεῖν ζητοῦντας] μισθοφοροῦντας ΑΓ

Γυ.ᵃ   νὴ τὴν Ἀφροδίτην εὖ γε ταυταγὶ λέγεις.

Πρ.   τάλαιν᾽ Ἀφροδίτην ὤμοσας; χαρίεντά γ᾽ ἂν   190
       ἔδρασας, εἰ τοῦτ᾽ εἶπας ἐν τἠκκλησίᾳ.

Γυ.ᵃ   ἀλλ᾽ οὐκ ἂν εἶπον. Πρ. μηδ᾽ ἐθίζου νῦν λέγειν.
       τὸ συμμαχικὸν αὖ τοῦθ᾽, ὅτ᾽ ἐσκοπούμεθα,
       εἰ μὴ γένοιτ᾽, ἀπολεῖν ἔφασκον τὴν πόλιν.
       ὅτε δὴ δ᾽ ἐγένετ᾽, ἤχθοντο, τῶν δὲ ῥητόρων   195
       ὁ τοῦτ᾽ ἀναπείσας εὐθὺς ἀποδρὰς ᾤχετο.
       ναῦς δεῖ καθέλκειν· τῷ πένητι μὲν δοκεῖ,
       τοῖς πλουσίοις δὲ καὶ γεωργοῖς οὐ δοκεῖ.
       Κορινθίοις ἄχθεσθε, κἀκεῖνοί γέ σοι·
       νῦν εἰσὶ χρηστοί, καὶ σύ νυν χρηστὸς γενοῦ.   200
       Ἀργεῖος ἀμαθής, ἀλλ᾽ Ἱερώνυμος σοφός.
       σωτηρία παρέκυψεν, ἀλλ᾽ ὀργίζεται
       Θρασύβουλος αὐτὸς οὐχὶ παρακαλούμενος.

Γυ.ᵃ   ὡς ξυνετὸς ἀνήρ. Πρ. νῦν καλῶς ἐπήνεσας.
       ὑμεῖς γάρ ἐστ᾽, ὦ δῆμε, τούτων αἴτιοι.   205
       τὰ δημόσια γὰρ μισθοφοροῦντες χρήματα
       ἰδίᾳ σκοπεῖσθ᾽ ἕκαστος ὅ τι τις κερδανεῖ,

206-8 §§ Stob. iii. 10. 9   207-8 (σκο-...) § S αι 320

---

189 et 192 Γυ.ᵃ Brunck   189 Γυ.ᵃ] par. RA: γυνὴ Λ: om. Γ
ταυτασί Λ   190 Πρ.] par. RA: om. Γ   ὤμοσας Dobree: ὠνόμασας
RAΛ: γ᾽ ὠ- Γ   191 ἔδρασας εἰ τοῦτ᾽ in ras. A   192 Γυ.ᵃ]
par. R: γυνὴ Λ: om. AΓ   Πρ.] dic. Γ: om. RA   νῦν] ναῦ Γ
193 in. par. R   195 mg Γ   δ᾽] γ᾽ RΛ   ἤσθοντο A: ἤ+χθοντο Γ
τῶν δερητόρων R: τῶν ῥητόρων Γ   197 mg Γ   δεῖ] δὲ AΓ: δὴ Λ
καθέλκει Λ   τοῖς πένησι x   μέν σοι δοκεῖ AΓ   198 καὶ om. AΓ
199 mg Γ   ἄχθεσθαι RMu₁ᵃᶜ: ἤχθεσθε Γ   κἀκεῖνο Γ   200 νυν
Cobet: νῦν a   γενοῦ χρηστὸς AΓ (σ γεν in ras. R₂)   201 Ἀργεῖος
van Leeuwen: ἀ- a   202 ὀργίζεται Hermann: ὀρειζεται R: οὐχ᾽
ὁρίζεται AΓ: ὁρίζεται Λ   204 Γυ.ᵃ Brunck: par. A: γυνὴ Λ: om.
RΓ   ἀνήρ Dindorf: ἀ- a   Πρ. om. RAΓ   205 γ᾽ ἄρ᾽ Λ   ἐστ᾽]
ὥστ᾽ A   τοῦτ᾽ in ras. A   206 τὰ δημ in ras. A   μισθοφο in ras. A
207 σκοπιεῖς AΓ   ὅ τι τί A (τί in ras.) Γ   κερδανεῖς A

τὸ δὲ κοινὸν ὥσπερ Αἴσιμος κυλίνδεται.
ἢν οὖν ἐμοὶ πείθησθε, σωθήσεσθ᾽ ἔτι.
ταῖς γὰρ γυναιξὶ φημὶ χρῆναι τὴν πόλιν   210
ἡμᾶς παραδοῦναι. καὶ γὰρ ἐν ταῖς οἰκίαις
ταύταις ἐπιτρόποις καὶ ταμίαισι χρώμεθα.

*Γυ.*ᵃ   εὖ γ᾽ εὖ γε νὴ Δί᾽, εὖ γε. *Γυ.*ᵝ λέγε, λέγ᾽ ὦγαθέ.

Πρ.   ὡς δ᾽ εἰσὶν ἡμῶν τοὺς τρόπους βελτίονες
ἐγὼ διδάξω. πρῶτα μὲν γὰρ τἄρια   215
βάπτουσι θερμῷ κατὰ τὸν ἀρχαῖον νόμον
ἁπαξάπασαι, κοὐχὶ μεταπειρωμένας
ἴδοις ἂν αὐτάς. ἡ δ᾽ Ἀθηναίων πόλις,
εἰ τοῦτο χρηστῶς εἶχεν, οὐκ ἂν ἐσῴζετο,
εἰ μή τι καινὸν ἄλλο περιηργάζετο.   220
καθήμεναι φρύγουσιν ὥσπερ καὶ πρὸ τοῦ.
ἐπὶ τῆς κεφαλῆς φέρουσιν ὥσπερ καὶ πρὸ τοῦ.
τὰ Θεσμοφόρι᾽ ἄγουσιν ὥσπερ καὶ πρὸ τοῦ.   223a
πέττουσι τοὺς πλακοῦντας ὥσπερ καὶ πρὸ τοῦ.   223b
τοὺς ἄνδρας ἐπιτρίβουσιν ὥσπερ καὶ πρὸ τοῦ.
μοιχοὺς ἔχουσιν ἔνδον ὥσπερ καὶ πρὸ τοῦ.   225
αὐταῖς παροψωνοῦσιν ὥσπερ καὶ πρὸ τοῦ.

208 § Zonar. 72   209 §S ε 3312; §Zonar. 896   215–16 (πρ-...)
§ S β 98; (πρ- ...) § Zonar. 378   218–20 (ἡ ...) §S χ 517

208 τὸ δὲ in ras. A   ἄσιμος Rᵃᶜ: ιμος κυ in ras. A   209 ἢν R
πείθεσθε Λ: πέπεισθε S   σωθήσεσθ᾽] θήσε in ras. A   210 ταῖς
in ras. A   χρῆναι τὴν in ras. A   211 γὰρ ἐν in ras. A   212 ταύτ
in ras. A   ταμίαις Γ   213 Γυ.ᵃ Bergk: par. RA: γυνὴ Λ: om. Γ
γ᾽] γε ΑΓ   Γυ.ᵝ Bergk: om. a   214 Πρ.] par. RA: om. Γ   ὡς δ᾽
in ras. A   βελ in ras. A   βελτίωνες Λ   215 μὲν in ras. A   μήτ᾽
ἄρια S   216 βλάπτουσι Λ   ἀρχαῖον in ras. A   218 ων in ras. A
219 εἰ τοῦτο] εἴ πού τι Dobree   ἀνεσώζετο Λ   220 κακὸν Γ   ἄλλο]
ἀλλότριον R₁   περιηργάζετο incertum quis primus: -ερ- A (γάζ in ras.) :
-ειρ- RΓΛ   221 πρὸ τοῦ x: προτου a (sim. 223a, 224, 225, 226,
227, 228)   222 πρὸ τοῦ R: προτου ΑΓΛ   223a om. R₁: mg R₂
θεσμοφόρ Γ   223b om. ΑΓΛ   226 αὐταῖς x: αὐ- a   παρο (in
ras.) +ψωνοῦσιν Γ

οἶνον φιλοῦσ' εὔζωρον ὥσπερ καὶ πρὸ τοῦ.
βινούμεναι χαίρουσιν ὥσπερ καὶ πρὸ τοῦ.
ταύταισιν οὖν ὧνδρες παραδόντες τὴν πόλιν
μὴ περιλαλῶμεν, μηδὲ πυνθανώμεθα   230
τί ποτ' ἄρα δρᾶν μέλλουσιν, ἀλλ' ἁπλῷ τρόπῳ
ἐῶμεν ἄρχειν, σκεψάμενοι ταυτὶ μόνα,
ὡς τοὺς στρατιώτας πρῶτον οὖσαι μητέρες
σῴζειν ἐπιθυμήσουσιν· εἶτα σιτία
τίς τῆς τεκούσης θᾶττον ἐπιπέμψειεν ἄν;   235
χρήματα πορίζειν εὐπορώτατον γυνή,
ἄρχουσά τ' οὐκ ἂν ἐξαπατηθείη ποτέ·
αὐταὶ γάρ εἰσιν ἐξαπατᾶν εἰθισμέναι.
τὰ δ' ἄλλ' ἐάσω. ταῦτ' ἐὰν πείθησθέ μοι,
εὐδαιμονοῦντες τὸν βίον διάξετε.   240

Γυ.ᵃ   εὖ γ' ὦ γλυκυτάτη Πραξαγόρα καὶ δεξιῶς.
        πόθεν, ὦ τάλαινα, ταῦτ' ἔμαθες οὕτω καλῶς;

Πρ.   ἐν ταῖς φυγαῖς μετὰ τἀνδρὸς ᾤκησ' ἐν πυκνί.
        ἔπειτ' ἀκούουσ' ἐξέμαθον τῶν ῥητόρων.

Γυ.ᵃ   οὐκ ἐτὸς ἄρ' ὦ μέλ' ἦσθα δεινὴ καὶ σοφή.   245
        καί σε στρατηγὸν αἱ γυναῖκες αὐτόθεν

234-5 (τὰ σι- . . .) §§ S θ 63

---

227 οἶνον φιλοῦσ' εὔζωρον Hanow: τὸν οἶνον εὔζωρον (εὔ- R) φιλοῦσ'
(-σιν ΑΓ) a   229 παραδοῦντες Λ   230 μεθα in ras. A
231 ἆρα R   ἀλλ' ἁπλῷ] ἀλλὰ τῷ Α (-ῶ) Γ   232 μόνα] διώνα Γ
234 σώζουσιν ΑΓ   ἐπιθυμοῦσιν ΑΓΛ   εἰ τὰ σιτία Α: εἰ τὰ σιτία τε Γ
235 om. Α* ut 158 (cf. 237, 239, 241, 243, 245, 247, 249)   τίς om. ΓS
θᾶττον S: μᾶλλον a   ἐπιπέμψειας Γ   237 om. Α*   238 αὗται
ΑΓ   239 om. Α*   ταῦτ' ἐὰν Bergk: ταῦτα κἂν (κἂν R) RΛ: κἂν Γ
μου Γ   240 διέξετε Λ   241 om. Α*   Γυ.ᵃ Brunck: par. R:
γυνὴ Λ: om. Γ   243 om. Α*   Πρ.] par. R: om. Γ   μετ' ἀνδρὸς
R₁: μετὰ τ' ἀνδρὸς R₂ (-τα) Λ   ᾤκισ' Γ   πνυκί Γ   244 ἡτόρων
in ras. A   245 om. Α*   Γυ.ᵃ Brunck: par. R: γυνὴ Λ: om. Γ
οὐκετὸς ἄρ' R   καὶ δεινὴ καὶ Γ   246 στρατηγεῖν ΑΓ   αὐτῶνθεν
Rᵃᶜ (ut vid.)

αἱρούμεθ᾽, ἢν ταῦθ᾽ ἀπινοεῖς κατεργάσῃ.
ἀτὰρ ἢν Κέφαλός σοι λοιδορῆται προσφθαρείς,
πῶς ἀντερεῖς πρὸς αὐτὸν ἐν τῇκκλησίᾳ;

Πρ.   φήσω παραφρονεῖν αὐτόν. Γυ.ᵃ ἀλλὰ τοῦτό γε   250
    ἴσασι πάντες. Πρ. ἀλλὰ καὶ μελαγχολᾶν.

Γυ.ᵃ   καὶ τοῦτ᾽ ἴσασιν. Πρ. ἀλλὰ καὶ τὰ τρύβλια
    κακῶς κεραμεύειν, τὴν δὲ πόλιν εὖ καὶ καλῶς.

Γυ.ᵝ   τί δ᾽ ἢν Νεοκλείδης ὁ γλάμων σε λοιδορῇ;

Πρ.   τοῦτον μὲν εἶπον ἐς κυνὸς πυγὴν ὁρᾶν.   255

Γυ.ᵝ   τί δ᾽ ἢν ὑποκρούωσίν σε; Πρ. προσκινήσομαι
    ἅτ᾽ οὐκ ἄπειρος οὖσα πολλῶν κρουμάτων.

Γυ.ᵃ   ἐκεῖνο μόνον ἄσκεπτον, ἤν σ᾽ οἱ τοξόται
    ἕλκωσιν, ὅ τι δράσεις ποτ᾽. Πρ. ἐξαγκωνιῶ
    ὡδί· μέση γὰρ οὐδέποτε ληφθήσομαι.   260

Χο.   ἡμεῖς δέ γ᾽, ἢν αἴρωσ᾽, ἐᾶν κελεύσομεν.

Γυ.ᵃ   ταυτὶ μὲν ἡμῖν ἐντεθύμηται καλῶς.
    ἐκεῖνο δ᾽ οὐ πεφροντίκαμεν, ὅτῳ τρόπῳ

255 Σ Ach. 863; (ἐς . . .) S π 3110; cf. Apostol. vi. 84   256-7 §
S υ 529

247 om. A* αἱρούμεθ᾽ Λ ἢν Γ ταῦθας Λ ἃ ᾽πινοεῖς Γ : πινοεῖς Λ
κατεργάσει R 248 ἀτὰρ ΑΓ λοιδορεῖται R προσφθαρεῖς Rᵖᶜ :
προφθαρεῖς Γ 249 om. A* προσαυτὸν R 250 Πρ.] par. R : om.
ΑΓ Γυ.ᵃ Brunck : par. A : dic. Γ : γυνὴ Λ : om. R τοῦτόν γ᾽ A : καὶ
τοῦτόν γ᾽ Γ 251 Πρ.] dic. Γ : om. RA μελασχολᾶν Γ
252 Γυ.ᵃ Brunck : par. A : γυνὴ Λ : om. RΓ τοῦστ᾽ ἴσασεν Rᵃᶜ : τοῦτ᾽
ἴσασι Λ Πρ.] par. R : dic. ΑΓ 253 in. par. R εὖ καὶ om. R
254 Γυ.ᵝ Ussher : par. RA : γυνὴ Λ : om. Γ λοιδορεῖ Γ 255 Πρ.]
par. R : om. ΑΓ τοῦτον Ussher : τούτῳ a εἴποιμ᾽ x 256 Γυ.ᵝ
Ussher : par. R : γυνὴ Λ : om. ΑΓ τίνδ᾽ ἢν R ὑποκρούωσσί(ν)
ΑΓΛ Πρ.] dic. ΑΓ : om. R 257 ἅτ᾽ οὐκ in ras. A : ἅτ᾽ οὐκ RΛ
258 Γυ.ᵃ Brunck : par. RA : γυνὴ Λ : om. Γ σ᾽ οἱ] σε ΑΓ : σοι Λ
259 Πρ.] dic. RΓ : dic. et par. A 260 in. par. R 261 Χο.
Ussher (cf. Rogers) : par. RA : γυνὴ Λ : om. Γ ἠναίρως R ἐᾶν x :
ἐᾶν a κελεύσωμεν RΓ 262 Γυ.ᵃ Blaydes (auct. Bergk) : par. R :
πραξ Λ : om. ΑΓ ἦμιν RΓΛ 263 in. γυνὴ Λ τρόπῳ] τρώπῳ Rᵃᶜ

τὰς χεῖρας αἴρειν μνημονεύσομεν τότε.
εἰθισμέναι γάρ ἐσμεν αἴρειν τὼ σκέλει. 265

Πρ. χαλεπὸν τὸ πρᾶγμ'· ὅμως δὲ χειροτονητέον
ἐξωμισάσαις τὸν ἕτερον βραχίονα.
ἄγε νυν ἀναστέλλεσθ' ἄνω τὰ χιτώνια·
ὑποδεῖσθε δ' ὡς τάχιστα τὰς Λακωνικάς,
ὥσπερ τὸν ἄνδρ' ἐθεᾶσθ', ὅτ' εἰς ἐκκλησίαν 270
μέλλοι βαδίζειν ἢ θύραζ' ἑκάστοτε.
ἔπειτ' ἐπειδὰν ταῦτα πάντ' ἔχῃ καλῶς,
περιδεῖσθε τοὺς πώγωνας. ἡνίκ' ἂν δέ γε
τούτους ἀκριβώσητε περιηρμοσμέναι,
καὶ θαἰμάτια τἀνδρεῖ' ἅπερ γ' ἐκλέψατε 275
ἐπαναβάλησθε, κᾆτα ταῖς βακτηρίαις
ἐπερειδόμεναι βαδίζετ' ᾄδουσαι μέλος
πρεσβυτικόν τι, τὸν τρόπον μιμούμεναι
τὸν τῶν ἀγροίκων. Χο. εὖ λέγεις. Γυ.ᵃ ἡμεῖς δέ γε
προΐωμεν αὐτῶν. καὶ γὰρ ἑτέρας οἴομαι 280
ἐκ τῶν ἀγρῶν ἐς τὴν πύκν' ἥξειν ἄντικρυς
γυναῖκας. Πρ. ἀλλὰ σπεύσαθ' ὡς εἴωθ' ἐκεῖ

266-7 (χει- . . .) S § (1) ε 1839; § (2) χ 262   269 §§ S υ 480
275-6 §§ † S ε 1953; (ἱμάτια . . . -λεσθε) §§ Zonar. 819

264 αἱρεῖν Mu1   265 εἰθισμέναι] μέν in ras. A   ἐσμὲν R : εἰς
μεν Λ   ειν in ras. A   τὼ] τὰ Λ   266 Πρ.] par. R : om. Γ
ὅμως A   δὲ (in ras. A) post -τέον Γ   267 ἐξωμιάσαις ΑΓ
268 νυν Bekker : νῦν a   νια in ras. A   269 ὑποδ in ras. A   δ'] μ' R
a τὰς in ras. A   270 ἄνδρ' ἐθεᾶσθε ΑΓ : ἄνδρα θεᾶσθ' Λ   ἐκκλησίαν
in ras. A   271 μέλλει A (μέλλε in ras.) : μέλοι Γ   ύραζ in ras. A
272 ἔπειτα A   ἔχει R : ἔχη in ras. A   273 ἶσθε τ in ras. R₂
274 ἀκριβώσειτε Γ   275 θαιτάτια R₁ : θαιμά- R₂ΓΛ : θοιμά- A
(θοιμ in ras.)   τἀνδρεῖ' ἅπερ γ' Elmsley : τἀνδρεῖα τ' ἅπερ RΓ (τ' ἅπ-)
Λ (τάπ-) : τἀνδρεῖα γ' ἅπερ A   276 ἐπαναβάλησθε Denniston :
ἐπ' ἀναβάλλεσθε R : ἐπανα- ΑΓ : ἐπανε- Λ : ἐπαναβάλεσθε xS   κᾶτα R :
κατὰ Γ   277 ζετ in ras. A : βαδίζουσ' Γ   ᾄδουσαι x : ᾅδουσαι R : ἄδ-
ΑΛ : ἄδου Γ   279 τὸν om. R   Χο. Ussher : dic. RΓ : γυνὴ Λ : om. A
λέγ in ras. A   Γυ.ᵃ Ussher : om. a   ἡμεῖς bis Rᵃᶜ   280 αὐτῶ
ΑΓˢ : αὐτὸν Γⁱ   281 εἰς ΑΓΛ   πνύκ' R : πνύχ' ΑΓ   282 Πρ.
Brunck : om. a   σπεύσασθ' ΑΓΛ   ωσείωθ' R   hic desinit A

τοῖς μὴ παροῦσιν ὀρθρίοις ἐς τὴν πύκνα
ὑπαποτρέχειν ἔχουσι μηδὲ πάτταλον.

Χο.   ὥρα προβαίνειν ὦνδρες ἡμῖν ἐστι· τοῦτο γὰρ χρὴ   285
μεμνημένας ἀεὶ λέγειν, ὡς μήποτ' ἐξολίσθῃ,
ἡμᾶς. ὁ κίνδυνος γὰρ οὐχὶ μικρός, ἢν ἁλῶμεν
ἐνδυόμεναι κατὰ σκότον τόλμημα τηλικοῦτον.

χωρῶμεν εἰς ἐκκλησίαν ὦνδρες· ἠπείλησε γὰρ   [στρ. 289/90
ὁ θεσμοθέτης, ὃς ἂν   291a
μὴ πρῳ πάνυ τοῦ κνέφους
ἥκῃ κεκονιμένος,   291b
στέργων σκοροδάλμῃ   292a
βλέπων ὑπότριμμα, μὴ   292b
δώσειν τὸ τριώβολον.
ἀλλ', ὦ Χαριτιμίδη   293a
καὶ Σμίκυθε καὶ Δράκης,   293b
ἕπου κατεπείγων,   294
σαυτῷ προσέχων ὅπως   295a
μηδὲν παραχορδιεῖς
ὧν δεῖ σ' ἀποδεῖξαι·   295b
ὅπως δὲ τὸ σύμβολον   296

283–4 S § (1) υ 154   284 (ἔχ- ...) §§ (2) υ 131; §§ S (3) π 775
286–7 (... -ᾶς) §§ S ε 1787   291a–b (ὃς ...) S § (1) π 2940; §§
(2) κ 1254   291a κνέφους Eust. 1354. 1   292a–b (βλ-....-μῃ) §
S υ 616   294 §§ S ε 2820   295a–b §§ S π 490; cf. AB 113. 2
296–7 (τὸ ... -δούμενοι) §§ S σ 1375

---

283 μὴ om. R₁   ὀρθίοις R: ὀρθρίσιν Γ¹   πνύκα Γ   285 Χο.]
par. R : om. Γ   288 ἐνδυόμεναι Le Febvre : ἐνδούμεναι a   290 ἐπεί-
λησε Γ : ἠπή- Λ   291a ὅσαν R : ὡς ἂν Λ   πρῶτα S (2)   291b ἥκει Λ
292a–b στέργων ... ὑπότριμμα Porson : βλέπων ὑπότριμμα στέργων σκοροδάλμῃ aS   292b τὸ om. Λ   293a Χαριτιμίδη Bentley : χάρι
τιμία (-ια R) ἢ a   295a παραχορδιῆς ΓΛ   296 σύμολον R

λαβόντες ἔπειτα πλη-   297
σίοι καθεδούμεθ', ὡς
ἂν χειροτονῶμεν
ἅπανθ' ὁπόσ' ἂν δέῃ   298
τὰς ἡμετέρας φίλας—   299
καίτοι τί λέγω; φίλους
γὰρ χρῆν μ' ὀνομάζειν.

ὅρα δ' ὅπως ὠθήσομεν τούσδε τοὺς ἐξ ἄστεως   [ἀντ. 300/1
ἥκοντας, ὅσοι πρὸ τοῦ   302a
μέν, ἡνίκ' ἔδει λαβεῖν
ἐλθόντ' ὀβολὸν μόνον,   302b
καθῆντο λαλοῦντες   303a
ἐν τοῖς στεφανώμασιν,   303b
νυνὶ δ' ἐνοχλοῦσ' ἄγαν.

ἀλλ' οὐχί, Μυρωνίδης   304a
ὅτ' ἦρχεν ὁ γεννάδας,   304b
οὐδεὶς ἂν ἐτόλμα   305a
τὰ τῆς πόλεως διοι-   305b
κεῖν ἀργύριον φέρων·
ἀλλ' ἧκεν ἕκαστος   306
ἐν ἀσκιδίῳ φέρων   307
πιεῖν ἅμα τ' ἄρτον αὑ-   308
τῷ καὶ δύο κρομμύω
καὶ τρεῖς ἂν ἐλάας.

307 ἀσ- cf. Poll. x. 71

297 πλησία Γ : πληθίοι Λ   καθεδοῦμεν Γ : -ούμενοι S   298 ὅπως Γ
298–9 δέῃ τὰς] δέκτας Λ   300 in. par. R : in. ἕτερος χορὸς Λ   ὅπω
Γ   ὠθήσομαι Λ   301 ἐξ ἄστεος Λ : ξένους Γ   302a ὅσου R₂
πρὸ τοῦ χ : προτοῦ a   302a–b ἔδει λαβεῖν ἐλθόντ' Dawes : ἐλθόνα δεῖ
λαβεῖν R₁ᵃᶜ : ἐλθόντα δεῖ λαβεῖν R₁ᵖᶜ : ἐλθόντ' ἔδει λαβεῖν R₂Λ : ἐλθόντες ἔδει
λαβεῖν Γ   302b ὀβολὸν R   303a κάθητο R   λαλοῦσαι Γ
303b ἐν τοῖς στεφανώμασιν om. ΓΛ   304b γενάδας Λ   306–7 (ἀλλ'
... φέρων) et 308 (πιεῖν ... κρομμύω) tr. Γ : corr. Γ mg   308 αὑτῷ
von Velsen: αὖ Λ : αὐ R : om. Γ   κρομμύω R

νυνὶ δὲ τριώβολον   309
ζητοῦσι λαβεῖν, ὅταν   310
    πράττωσί τι κοινὸν ὥσ-
    περ πηλοφοροῦντες.

ΒΛΕΠΥΡΟΣ

τί τὸ πρᾶγμα; ποῖ ποθ' ἡ γυνὴ φρούδη 'στί μοι;
ἐπεὶ πρὸς ἔω νῦν γ' ἔστιν, ἡ δ' οὐ φαίνεται.
ἐγὼ δὲ κατάκειμαι πάλαι χεζητιῶν,
τὰς ἐμβάδας ζητῶν λαβεῖν ἐν τῷ σκότῳ
καὶ θοἰμάτιον. ὅτε δὴ δ' ἐκεῖνο ψηλαφῶν   315
οὐκ ἐδυνάμην εὑρεῖν, ὁ δ' ἤδη τὴν θύραν
ἐπεῖχε κρούων ὁ κοπρεαῖος, λαμβάνω
τουτὶ τὸ τῆς γυναικὸς ἡμιδιπλοίδιον,
καὶ τὰς ἐκείνης Περσικὰς ὑφέλκομαι.
ἀλλ' ἐν καθαρῷ ποῦ ποῦ τις ἂν χέσας τύχοι;   320
ἢ πανταχοῦ τοι νυκτός ἐστιν ἐν καλῷ;
οὐ γάρ με νῦν χέζοντά γ' οὐδεὶς ὄψεται.
οἴμοι κακοδαίμων, ὅτι γέρων ὢν ἠγόμην
γυναῖχ'· ὅσας εἴμ' ἄξιος πληγὰς λαβεῖν.
οὐ γάρ ποθ' ὑγιὲς οὐδὲν ἐξελήλυθεν   325
δράσουσ'. ὅμως δ' οὖν ἐστιν ἀποπατητέον.

ΑΝΗΡ

τίς ἔστιν; οὐ δήπου Βλέπυρος ὁ γειτνιῶν;

Βλ.   νὴ τὸν Δί' αὐτὸς δῆτ' ἐκεῖνος. Αν. εἰπέ μοι,

318 cf. Phot. s.v. ἡμι-

309 τριόβολον Λ   310 post πηλοφοροῦντες add. ὡς χειροτέχναι
καὶ μισθωτοί Λ (cf. Σᴿ)   311 Βλ. Ald.: ἀνήρ τις Σᴿ: ἀνήρ τις
βλέπυρος Λ: om. ΡΓ   πρᾶγμ' Γ   312 προσέω Ρ   ἠδ' Ρ (ἠ-) Γ
313 ζη in ras. Ρ₂   316 ὁ δ' Kuster: ὅδ' a   θύρα Ρ
317 κοπραῖος Γ   319 ἀφέλκομαι Γ   320 τίς ΡΓ   ἀνχεσας
Ρ   322 νῦν οὐδεὶς χέζοντά γ' οὐδεὶς Γ   323 in. Βλ. Ρ₂   ὅτε Γ
ὢν Ρ   324 εἴμ' x: εἴμ' ΡΓ: εἰμ' Λ   325 λαβεῖν οὐδὲν Ρᵃᶜ
327 Αν. om. Γ   328 Βλ.] par. Ρ: om. Γ   Αν. om. ΡΓ

τί τοῦτό σοι τὸ πυρρόν ἐστιν; οὔτι που
Κινησίας σου κατατετίληκέν ποθεν;   330

Βλ. οὔκ, ἀλλὰ τῆς γυναικὸς ἐξελήλυθα
τὸ κροκωτίδιον ἀμπισχόμενος οὐνδύεται.

Αν. τὸ δ᾽ ἱμάτιόν σου ποῦ 'στιν; Βλ. οὐκ ἔχω φράσαι.
ζητῶν γὰρ αὔτ᾽ οὐχ ηὗρον ἐν τοῖς στρώμασιν.

Αν. εἶτ᾽ οὐδὲ τὴν γυναῖκ᾽ ἐκέλευσάς σοι φράσαι;   335

Βλ. μὰ τὸν Δί᾽ οὐ γὰρ ἔνδον οὖσα τυγχάνει,
ἀλλ᾽ ἐκτετρύπηκεν λαθοῦσά μ᾽ ἔνδοθεν.
ὃ καὶ δέδοικα μή τι δρᾷ νεώτερον.

Αν. νὴ τὸν Ποσειδῶ ταὐτὰ τοίνυν ἄντικρυς
ἐμοὶ πέπονθας· καὶ γὰρ ᾗ ξύνειμ᾽ ἐγὼ   340
φρούδη 'στ᾽ ἔχουσα θοἰμάτιον οὑγὼ 'φόρουν.
κοὔ τοῦτο λυπεῖ μ᾽, ἀλλὰ καὶ τὰς ἐμβάδας.
οὔκουν λαβεῖν γ᾽ αὐτὰς ἐδυνάμην οὐδαμοῦ.

Βλ. μὰ τὸν Διόνυσον, οὐδ᾽ ἐγὼ γὰρ τὰς ἐμὰς
Λακωνικάς, ἀλλ᾽ ὡς ἔτυχον χεζητιῶν,   345
ἐς τὼ κοθόρνω τὼ πόδ᾽ ἐνθεὶς ἵεμαι,
ἵνα μὴ 'γχέσαιμ᾽ ἐς τὴν σισύραν· φανὴ γὰρ ἦν.
τί δῆτ᾽ ἂν εἴη; μῶν ἐπ᾽ ἄριστον γυνὴ

329–30 (. . . -κεν) §§ S τ 693   347 § S φ 71

---

330 κατατετίληκέν ποθεν; Brunck: -κεν ποθεν R (dic. ante π-) Γ: -λικεν;
Βλ. πόθεν ΛΜυι₁: -λικεν; Βλ. πόθεν Μυι₂   331 Βλ. Brunck: om. a
332 κροκωτίδιον Arnald: κροκώτιον R: κροκώπιον ΓΛ   ἀμπεσχόμενος Γ
οὐ 'νδ- Γ: ὃ ὑνδύεται Λ   333 Αν.] par. R: om. Γ σοι Γ Βλ.] dic. R:
om. Γ   334 αὔτ᾽ x : αὖτ᾽ a   ηὗρον Dindorf: εὗρον a   335 Αν.]
par. R: om. Γ   ἐκέλευσάς x: -σά a   336 Βλ. om. RΓ
337 μύνδοθεν Λ   338 δρᾶν Γ   339 Αν.] par. R: om. Γ
ταῦτα RΓ   340 ξύνεμι᾽ R: ξύνειμι Λ   341 οὐ 'γὼ 'φο- Γ: οὐγὼ
φόρουν Λ   342 τοῦτο πο R₁: τοῦτό πω ΓΛ   343 γ᾽ om. Γ
ἠδυνάμην Γ   344 Βλ.] par. R: om. Γ   345 Λακωνικῶς Γ
ἔτυχε Λ   346 ἐς] ἐν Γ   τω κοθόρνωι R: τὸ κοθόρνω Λ   ἵεμαι ΓΛ:
ἵεμε R   347 'νχέσαιμ᾽ R₁ (ut vid.)   σισσύραν Λ   φανῆ RΓ
348 in. ἀνὴρ Λ

κέκληκεν αὐτὴν τῶν φίλων; Αν. γνώμην γ' ἐμήν.
οὔκουν πονηρά γ' ἐστὶν ὅ τι κἄμ' εἰδέναι.   350
ἀλλὰ σὺ μὲν ἱμονιάν τιν' ἀποπατεῖς, ἐμοὶ ⟨δ'⟩
ὥρα βαδίζειν ἐστὶν εἰς ἐκκλησίαν,
ἤνπερ λάβω θοἰμάτιον, ὅπερ ἦν μοι μόνον.

Βλ. κἄγωγ', ἐπειδὰν ἀποπατήσω· νῦν δέ μοι
ἀχράς τις ἐγκλῄσασ' ἔχει τὰ σιτία.   355

Αν. μῶν ἦν Θρασύβουλος εἶπε τοῖς Λακωνικοῖς;

Βλ. νὴ τὸν Διόνυσον ἐνέχεται γοῦν μοι σφόδρα.
ἀτὰρ τί δράσω; καὶ γὰρ οὐδὲ τοῦτό με
μόνον τὸ λυποῦν ἐστιν, ἀλλ' ὅταν φάγω,
ὅποι βαδιεῖταί μοι τὸ λοιπὸν ἡ κόπρος.   360
νῦν μὲν γὰρ οὗτος βεβαλάνωκε τὴν θύραν,
ὅστις ποτ' ἔσθ' ἄνθρωπος ἀχραδούσιος.
τίς ἂν οὖν ἰατρόν μοι μετέλθοι καὶ τίνα;
τίς τῶν καταπρώκτων δεινός ἐστι τὴν τέχνην;
ἆρ' οἶδ' Ἀμύνων; ἀλλ' ἴσως ἀρνήσεται.   365
Ἀντισθένη τις καλεσάτω πάσῃ τέχνῃ·
οὗτος γὰρ ἀνὴρ ἕνεκά γε στεναγμάτων
οἶδεν τί πρωκτὸς βούλεται χεζητιῶν.

349 γν- . . . ἐ- cf. Phryn. PS 58. 5, Greg. Cor. 31, Zonar. 444
350 §§ S o 374   355 cf. Lex. Bachm. 176. 12   355–6 § S a 4713
361–2 St. Byz. 153. 2   366–8 S § (1) π 2950; § (2) χ 182

349 αὐτὴ Γ   Αν. Ussher: dic. R : Βλ. Λ : om. Γ   350 par. R : in.
ἀνὴρ Λ   351 ⟨δ'⟩ incertum quis primus   354 Βλ.] par. R : om. Γ
νῦν x : νυνὶ a   μοι Meineke : μου a   355 in. ἀνὴρ Λ   ἀχραστις
Γ : ἀχρά τι σ' Λ   ἐγκλείσας RΓ: -κλείσασ' S   356 Αν. Brunck:
par. R : om. ΓΛ   ἦν x : ἦν R : ἢ ΓΛ   Θρυσύβουλος R   ἀλκωμανικοῖς
R₁ : λακωμα- R₂   357 Βλ.] par. R : om. Γ   τὸν δι+++++ Γ
361 οὗτος . . . θύραν in lac. om. Γ   362 πόθ' R   ἔσθ' ἄνθρωπος
Blaydes: ἐστ' ἄνθρωπος (ε- R, -ἰν Γ) a   ἀχραδούσιος Dindorf: ἀχ- a
363 οὖν] εἶναι Γ   μοι . . . τίνα in lac. om. Γ   364 κατὰ πρώκτων
ΓMuiᵃᶜ   365 ἆρ' ΓΛ: ἀλλ' Meineke   μύνων . . . ἀρνήσεται
in lac. om. Γ   366 Ἀντισθένη x :-νην a   τίς a   367 ἀνὴρ Reisig:
ἀ- a   368 πρωκτ ++'εται χεζητιῶ Λ

ΕΚΚΛΗΣΙΑΖΟΥΣΑΙ

ὦ πότνι' Εἰλείθυια μή με περιίδῃς
διαρραγέντα μηδὲ βεβαλανωμένον,   370
ἵνα μὴ γένωμαι σκωραμὶς κωμῳδική.

ΧΡΕΜΗΣ

οὗτος, τί ποιεῖς; οὔτι που χέζεις; Βλ. ἐγώ;
οὐ δῆτ' ἔτι γε μὰ τὸν Δί', ἀλλ' ἀνίσταμαι.

Χρ.   τὸ τῆς γυναικὸς δ' ἀμπέχει χιτώνιον;

Βλ.   ἐν τῷ σκότῳ γὰρ τοῦτ' ἔτυχον ἔνδον λαβών.   375
       ἀτὰρ πόθεν ἥκεις ἐτεόν; Χρ. ἐξ ἐκκλησίας.

Βλ.   ἤδη λέλυται γάρ; Χρ. νὴ Δί' ὄρθριον μὲν οὖν.
       καὶ δῆτα πολὺν ἡ μίλτος, ὦ Ζεῦ φίλτατε,
       γέλων παρέσχεν, ἣν προσέρραινον κύκλῳ.

Βλ.   τὸ τριώβολον δῆτ' ἔλαβες; Χρ. εἰ γὰρ ὤφελον.   380
       ἀλλ' ὕστερος νῦν ἦλθον, ὥστ' αἰσχύνομαι.

Βλ.   μὰ τὸν Δί' οὐδέν' ἄλλον ἢ τὸν θύλακον.
       τὸ δ' αἴτιον τί; Χρ. πλεῖστος ἀνθρώπων ὄχλος,
       ὅσος οὐδεπώποτ' ἦλθ' ἀθρόος ἐς τὴν πύκνα.
       καὶ δῆτα πάντας σκυτοτόμοις ἠκάζομεν   385
       ὁρῶντες αὐτούς· οὐ γὰρ ἀλλ' ὑπερφυῶς

369-70 S § (1) π 2950; (μή . . .) § (2) β 214   371 §§ S σ 692
378-9 §§ S μ 1071   385 § S σ 727   386-7 (οὐ...) S ‡ (1) ο
768; (ἀλλ' . . .) § (2) σ 727

---

369 Εἰλείθυι' R₁   371 σκόραμις Γ   372 in. ἀνὴρ χρέμης ἀπὸ
ἐκκλησίας Λ : par. R : om. Γ   Βλ.] dic. R : om. Γ   373 ἔτι γε] ἔγνως Γ
374 Χρ. om. RΓ   τριβώνιον ΓΛ   375 Βλ. om. RΓ   376 αὐτὰρ Γ
Χρ.] par. R : dic. Γ   377 Βλ. Brunck : om. a   Χρ. Brunck : dic.
RΓ : Βλ. Λ   νὴ τὸν δί' Λ   378 in. par. R : in. Χρ. Λ   379 καὶ
γέλων Γ   ἣν R : ἢν Γ   προσαίραινον Rᵃᶜ   380 Βλ.] par. R : om. Γ
Χρ.] dic. R : om. Γ   381 ὕστερον Μυιᵃᶜ   νῦν] νὴ δί' R : νυνὶ Λ
382 Βλ. Ussher : om. a   οὐδὲν ἄλλο x   383 in. Βλ. Λ   Χρ.] dic. RΓ
384 ἦλθ' x : ἦλθεν a   ἀθρόος Meineke : ἀθρόως R : -ος ΓΛ   πνύκα Γ
385 πάντες σκυτοτόμοι ΓΛ   386 ἀλλ' R₂

ὡς λευκοπληθὴς ἦν ἰδεῖν ἡκκλησία.
ὥστ᾽ οὐκ ἔλαβον οὔτ᾽ αὐτὸς οὔτ᾽ ἄλλοι συχνοί.

Βλ.　οὐδ᾽ ἄρ᾽ ἂν ἐγὼ λάβοιμι νῦν ἐλθών; Χρ. πόθεν;
οὐδ᾽ εἰ μὰ Δία τότ᾽ ἦλθες ὅτε τὸ δεύτερον　　　　390
ἀλεκτρυὼν ἐφθέγγετ᾽. Βλ. οἴμοι δείλαιος.
Ἀντίλοχ᾽, ἀποίμωξόν με τοῦ τριωβόλου
τὸν ζῶντα μᾶλλον· τἀμὰ γὰρ διοίχεται.
ἀτὰρ τί τὸ πρᾶγμ᾽ ἦν, ὅτι τοσοῦτον χρῆμ᾽ ὄχλου
οὕτως ἐν ὥρᾳ ξυνελέγη; Χρ. τί δ᾽ ἄλλο γ᾽ ἢ　　　395
ἔδοξε τοῖς πρυτάνεσι περὶ σωτηρίας
γνώμας καθεῖναι τῆς πόλεως; κᾷτ᾽ εὐθέως
πρῶτος Νεοκλείδης ὁ γλάμων παρείρπυσεν.
κἄπειθ᾽ ὁ δῆμος ἀναβοᾷ πόσον δοκεῖς,
"οὐ δεινὰ τολμᾶν τουτονὶ δημηγορεῖν,　　　　　400
καὶ ταῦτα περὶ σωτηρίας προκειμένου,
ὃς αὐτὸς αὑτῷ βλεφαρίδ᾽ οὐκ ἐσώσατο;"
ὁ δ᾽ ἀναβοήσας καὶ περιβλέψας ἔφη
"τί δαί με χρὴ δρᾶν;" Βλ. "σκόροδ᾽ ὁμοῦ τρίψαντ᾽
ὀπῷ
τιθύμαλλον ἐμβαλόντα τοῦ Λακωνικοῦ　　　　　405
σαυτοῦ παραλείφειν τὰ βλέφαρα τῆς ἑσπέρας",
ἔγωγ᾽ ἂν εἶπον, εἰ παρὼν ἐτύγχανον.

392-3 (ἀ-...) §§ S a 3715　　398 §§ S π 599　　404-6 (σκο-...)
S §§ (1) γ 277; (σκο-... -μάλλῳ) § (2) τ 582

387 λευκοπληθὲς Λ　　389 Βλ.] par. R: om. Γ　　ἄρα ΓΛ　　Χρ.]
dic. R: om. Γ　　391 ἀλεκτρυὼν Dindorf: ἀ- a　　ἐφθέγγετ᾽ Bekker:
ἐφθέγγετο a　　Βλ.] dic. R: om. Γ　　392 ἀντίχολ᾽ R₁ (ut vid.)
ἀποίμωζόν RΓ　　393 τὰ μὰ RΓ ('μὰ)　　οἴχεται Γ　　394 αὐτὰρ
Γ　　ὅτε ΓΛ　　ὄχλος Γ　　395 συνελέγη Γ　　395-404 Χρ. et
Βλ.] dic. R: om. Γ　　397 προθεῖναι Schoemann　　κατευθέως Γ
398 πρῶτος Νεοκλείδης om. in lac. Γ　　παρέρπυσεν Γ　　399 πόθον Λ
400 οὐ om. Γ　　402 ὅς] ὡς Λ　　αὐτῷ x: αὐ- R: σαυτῶ Λ: αὐτῷ ΓMu1
φλεβαρίδ᾽ Γ: τὰ βλέφαρα Λ　　403 ὁ δ᾽ Kuster: ὅδ᾽ a　　404 χρῆν Λ
405 τιθύμαλλον a: -μάλλῳ (om. ὀπῷ) S (2)　　ἐκβαλόντα Γᵃᶜ: ἐκβαλόντα
Γᵖᶜ　　406 σαυτῶ ΓΛ

Χρ.   μετὰ τοῦτον Εὐαίων ὁ δεξιώτατος
παρῆλθε γυμνός, ὡς ἐδόκει τοῖς πλείοσιν—
αὐτός γε μέντοὔφασκεν ἱμάτιον ἔχειν—   410
κᾆπειτ' ἔλεξε δημοτικωτάτους λόγους·
"ὁρᾶτε μέν με δεόμενον σωτηρίας
τετραστατήρου καὐτόν· ἀλλ' ὅμως ἐρῶ
ὡς τὴν πόλιν καὶ τοὺς πολίτας σώσετε.
ἢν γὰρ παρέχωσι τοῖς δεομένοις οἱ κναφῆς   415
χλαίνας, ἐπειδὰν πρῶτον ἥλιος τραπῇ,
πλευρῖτις ἡμῶν οὐδέν' ἂν λάβοι ποτέ.
ὅσοις δὲ κλίνη μή 'στι μηδὲ στρώματα,
ἴεναι καθευδήσοντας ἀπονενιμμένους
ἐς τῶν σκυλοδεψῶν· ἢν δ' ἀποκλῄῃ τῇ θύρᾳ   420
χειμῶνος ὄντος, τρεῖς σισύρας ὀφειλέτω."

Βλ.   νὴ τὸν Διόνυσον χρηστά γ'. εἰ δ' ἐκεῖνά γε
προσέθηκεν, οὐδεὶς ἀντεχειροτόνησεν ἄν,
τοὺς ἀλφιταμοιβοὺς τοῖς ἀπόροις τρεῖς χοίνικας
δεῖπνον παρέχειν ἅπασιν ἢ κλάειν μακρά,   425
ἵνα τοῦτ' ἀπέλαυσαν Ναυσικύδους τἀγαθόν.

Χρ.   μετὰ τοῦτο τοίνυν εὐπρεπὴς νεανίας

408–9 (*Εὐ-*...*-νός*) § S τ 406   411 cf. Zonar. 502   411–13 § S (1)
τ 405   411–12 (ὁ δὲ ἔ-...*-νον*) S §§ (2) δ 467   412–13 (ὁ-...
-ρου) S § (3) σ 1009; (σω-...*-ρου*) § † Poll. ix. 58   415–17 S § (1)
κ 1855; § (2) τ 406   418–21 § S τ 406   418–20 (...*-ψῶν*) S
§§ (2) σ 708   420 (ἢν...*-ραν*) S § (2) α 1453   421 § Σ Ra.
1459; S § (2) σ 487   422–3 (εἰ...) §§ S α 2643   424–5 S § (1)
α 1453; (...*-έχειν*) § (2) τ 406   426 cf. Phot. s.v. Ν-

408 Χρ. om. RΓ   410 μὲν τοὔφασκεν R: μέντ' οὔ 'φασκεν Γ
411 κᾆπειτ' a: ὁ δὲ S (2)   ἔλεγξε Λ   414 σώσητε Γ   415 ἢν R
κναφεῖς S (1) et (2)   417 -τις ἂν ἡμῶν R   οὐδένα βλάψοι S (1)
418 μῆστι R   419 ἀπονεμιμμένους R: ἀπονενιμμένους Γ: ἀπονενημ-
μένους S (2)   420 κυλοδεψῶν ΓΛ   ἀποκλῄῃ Dindorf: ἀποκλίνη (-νηι
R) a   τὴν θύραν S (2)   421 ὀφείλεται Γ: ἀφείλετο S (2)   422 Βλ.
om. RΓ   424 ἀλφιταμοιβὰς Λ   τοῖς] τοὺς R₁   ἀπόρροις Mui
425 μακρά] μακρὰν παρέχειν Γ   426 ναυσιμήδης x   427 Χρ. om.
RΓ   τοίνυν] νῦν Γ   εὐτρεπὴς Γ

λευκός τις ἀνεπήδησ' ὅμοιος Νικίᾳ
δημηγορήσων, κἀπεχείρησεν λέγειν
ὡς χρὴ παραδοῦναι ταῖς γυναιξὶ τὴν πόλιν.   430
εἶτ' ἐθορύβησαν κἀνέκραγον ὡς εὖ λέγοι,
τὸ σκυτοτομικὸν πλῆθος, οἱ δ' ἐκ τῶν ἀγρῶν
ἀνεβορβόρυξαν. Βλ. νοῦν γὰρ εἶχον, νὴ Δία.

Χρ. ἀλλ' ἦσαν ἥττους· ὁ δὲ κατεῖχε τῇ βοῇ,
     τὰς μὲν γυναῖκας πόλλ' ἀγαθὰ λέγων, σὲ δὲ   435
     πολλὰ κακά. Βλ. καὶ τί εἶπε; Χρ. πρῶτον μέν σ' ἔφη
     εἶναι πανοῦργον. Βλ. καὶ σέ; Χρ. μή πω τοῦτ' ἔρῃ.
     κἄπειτα κλέπτην. Βλ. ἐμὲ μόνον; Χρ. καὶ νὴ Δία
     καὶ συκοφάντην. Βλ. ἐμὲ μόνον; Χρ. καὶ νὴ Δία
     τωνδὶ τὸ πλῆθος. Βλ. τίς δὲ τοῦτ' ἄλλως λέγει;   440

Χρ. γυναῖκα δ' εἶναι πρᾶγμ' ἔφη νουβυστικὸν
     καὶ χρηματοποιόν. κοὔτε τἀπόρρητ' ἔφη
     ἐκ Θεσμοφόροιν ἑκάστοτ' αὐτὰς ἐκφέρειν,
     σὲ δὲ κἀμὲ βουλεύοντε τοῦτο δρᾶν ἀεί.

Βλ. καὶ νὴ τὸν Ἑρμῆν τοῦτό γ' οὐκ ἐψεύσατο.   445

Χρ. ἔπειτα συμβάλλειν πρὸς ἀλλήλας ἔφη
     ἱμάτια χρυσί' ἀργύριον ἐκπώματα
     μόνας μόναις, οὐ μαρτύρων ἐναντίον,
     καὶ ταῦτ' ἀποφέρειν πάντα κοὐκ ἀποστερεῖν,
     ἡμῶν δὲ τοὺς πολλοὺς ἔφασκε τοῦτο δρᾶν.   450

428 §§ S λ 326   441 §§ S ν 511; cf. Σ V. 1294, Phot. s.v. νου-
446–8 §§ S σ 1355   449 § S α 3632

428 λευκή S   τίς Γ   ἀνεπέδησεν Γ   429 κἀπεχείρησε ΓΛ
431 ἐθορυβήθησαν Γ   λέγει Rᵃᶜ   433 Βλ.] dic. R: om. Γ
434 Χρ. om. Γ   435 λέγων om. Γ   436–8 Βλ. et Χρ.] dic. RΓ
437 καὶ om. Γ   439 om. R₁: mg R₂   Βλ. et Χρ. om. R₂Γ
440 Βλ.] dic. RΓ   441 Χρ.] par. R: dic. Γ   ἔφη πρᾶγμ' εἶναι ΓΛ
νοῦ βυστικὸν R: νοῦ βαστιζὸν Γ: νουβαστικὸν Λ   442 κοὔτ' ΓΛ
ἀπόρρητ' ΓΛ   443 θεσμοφόρων Γ   444 βουλεύοντε ed. Junt.²
(1525): -ονται R: δουλεύοντε ΓΛ   445–6 Βλ. et Χρ. om. RΓ   νὴ
om. Γ   446 ἀλλήλους Γ   447 χρυσία Γ: -σίον S   448 γ' οὐ Γ
γ' ἐναντίον R (ε-) ΛS

Βλ. νὴ τὸν Ποσειδῶ μαρτύρων γ' ἐναντίον.

Χρ. ἕτερά τε πλεῖστα τὰς γυναῖκας ηὐλόγει· 454
οὐ συκοφαντεῖν, οὐ διώκειν, οὐδὲ τὸν 452
δῆμον καταλύειν, ἄλλα πολλὰ κἀγαθά.

Βλ. τί δῆτ' ἔδοξεν; Χρ. ἐπιτρέπειν γε τὴν πόλιν 455
ταύταις· ἐδόκει γὰρ τοῦτο μόνον ἐν τῇ πόλει
οὔπω γεγενῆσθαι. Βλ. καὶ δέδοκται; Χρ. φήμ' ἐγώ.

Βλ. ἅπαντά τ' αὐταῖς ἐστι προστεταγμένα
ἃ τοῖσιν ἀστοῖς ἔμελεν; Χρ. οὕτω ταῦτ' ἔχει.

Βλ. οὐδ' ἐς δικαστήριον ἄρ' εἶμ', ἀλλ' ἡ γυνή; 460

Χρ. οὐδ' ἔτι σὺ θρέψεις οὓς ἔχεις ἀλλ' ἡ γυνή.

Βλ. οὐδὲ στένειν τὸν ὄρθρον ἔτι πρᾶγμ' ἀρά μοι;

Χρ. μὰ Δί' ἀλλὰ ταῖς γυναιξὶ ταῦτ' ἤδη μέλει·
σὺ δ' ἀστενακτὶ περδόμενος οἴκοι μενεῖς.

Βλ. ἐκεῖνο δεινὸν τοῖσιν ἡλίκοισι νῶν, 465
μὴ παραλαβοῦσαι τῆς πόλεως τὰς ἡνίας
ἔπειτ' ἀναγκάζωσι πρὸς βίαν— Χρ. τί δρᾶν;

Βλ. κινεῖν ἑαυτάς. Χρ. ἢν δὲ μὴ δυνώμεθα;

Βλ. ἄριστον οὐ δώσουσι. Χρ. σὺ δέ γε νὴ Δία
δρᾶ ταῦθ', ἵν' ἀριστᾷς τε καὶ κινῇς ἅμα. 470

464 § S a 4230; cf. Zonar. 328

451 Βλ. om. ΡΓ   454 tr. Bachmann   Χρ. Ussher: om. a   ηὐλόγει
Meineke: εὐλόγει (-εῖ R) a   452 in. Χρ. Λ   453 ἄλλα Ussher:
ἀλλὰ a: κἄλλα Bachmann   πολλά τε κἀ- Λ   ad fin. βλάπτειν add. Γ
455 Βλ.] par. R: om. Γ   Χρ.] dic. ΡΓ   γε χ: σε a   457 Βλ. et
Χρ.] dic. ΡΓ   458 Βλ. om. ΡΓ   θ' ΡΛ   459 ἔμελεν χ: ἔμελλεν
R: τ' ἔμελλεν ΓΛ   Χρ.] dic. ΡΓ   οὔπω Γ   460–5 Βλ. et Χρ. om.
ΡΓ   460 εἶμ' ΓΛ   461 om. Γ   οὐδὲ τί Λ   462 στέγειν Μυι
ἀρά Kuster: ἄρα ΡΓ: ἀρά Λ   463 μέλλει Λ   464 ἀστενακτεὶ Λ
μενεῖς] μ + + Λ   466 ἡνίας Λ   467 ἀναγκάζουσι Γ   Χρ.] dic. ΡΓ
468–9 Βλ. om. ΡΓ   Χρ.] dic. ΡΓ   469 δώσουσιν Γ   470 ἀριστᾶ
ΓΛ   κινεῖς ΡᵃᶜΓΛ

Βλ.   τὸ πρὸς βίαν δεινότατον. Χρ. ἀλλ' εἰ τῇ πόλει
       τοῦτο ξυνοίσει, ταῦτα χρὴ πάντ' ἄνδρα δρᾶν.

Βλ.   λόγος γέ τοί τις ἔστι τῶν γεραιτέρων,
       ἀνόηθ' ὅσ' ἂν καὶ μῶρα βουλευσώμεθα,
       ἅπαντ' ἐπὶ τὸ βέλτιον ἡμῖν ξυμφέρειν.   475

Χρ.   καὶ ξυμφέροι γ', ὦ πότνια Παλλὰς καὶ θεοί.
       ἀλλ' εἶμι· σὺ δ' ὑγίαινε. Βλ. καὶ σύ γ', ὦ Χρέμης.

Χο.   ἔμβα χώρει.
       ἆρ' ἔστι τῶν ἀνδρῶν τις ἡμῖν ὅστις ἐπακολουθεῖ;
       στρέφου, σκόπει,   480
       φύλαττε σαυτὴν ἀσφαλῶς, πολλοὶ γὰρ οἱ πανοῦργοι,
       μή πού τις ἐκ τοὔπισθεν ὢν τὸ σχῆμα καταφυλάξῃ.

       ἀλλ' ὡς μάλιστα τοῖν ποδοῖν ἐπικτυπῶν βάδιζε.   [στρ.
       ἡμῖν δ' ἂν αἰσχύνην φέροι
       πάσαισι παρὰ τοῖς ἀνδράσιν τὸ πρᾶγμα τοῦτ' ἐλεγχθέν.
       πρὸς ταῦτα συστέλλου σεαυ-   486
           τὴν καὶ περισκοπουμένη
       ⟨ἄθρει κύκλῳ⟩ κἀκεῖσε καὶ
       τἀκ δεξιᾶς, μὴ συμφορὰ γενήσεται τὸ πρᾶγμα.
       ἀλλ' ἐγκονῶμεν· τοῦ τόπου γὰρ ἐγγύς ἐσμεν ἤδη,
       ὅθενπερ εἰς ἐκκλησίαν ὡρμώμεθ' ἡνίκ' ᾖμεν.   490

473-5 S §§ † (1) γ 195; §§ † (2) μ 1337

---

471 Βλ.] par. R : om. Γ   Χρ.] par. R : dic. Γ   εἰ] ἢ Γ   473 Βλ.
Meineke : om. a   γε S cod. G : τε a   γηραιτέρων ΓΛ   474 ἀνόηθ'
ὅσ' ἂν καὶ μῶρα x : ὃς ἂν ἀνόητα χ' ἢ μῶρα RS (1) : ὅσ' ἂν ἀνόητα καὶ
μῶρα Γ (-ρὰ) Λ   476 Χρ. om. ΓΛ   477 ὑγίαινες Λ   Βλ.] par.
R : om. Γ   478 Χο.] dic. Γ   479 ἄρ' ΡΓ   481 φύλασσε
σεαυτὸν Γ   482 φυλάξῃ Γ   483 ὡς] ὦ Γ   484 ἂν om. ΓΛ
485 ἀνδράσιν Brunck : ἀνδράσι a   τοῦτο Γ   487 ⟨ἄθρει κύκλῳ⟩ e.g.
Ussher   τἀκεῖσε Le Febvre   488 τἀκ' R : τά τ' ἐκ ΓΛ (τὰ)
490 ὅθενπερ R   ὡρμώμεθ' Port : ὁρ- a

τὴν δ' οἰκίαν ἔξεσθ' ὁρᾶν, ὅθενπερ ἡ στρατηγὸς
ἔσθ' ἡ τὸ πρᾶγμ' εὑροῦσ' ὃ νῦν ἔδοξε τοῖς πολίταις.

ὥστ' εἰκὸς ἡμᾶς μὴ βραδύνειν ἔστ' ἐπαναμενούσας [ἀντ.
πώγωνας ἐξηρτημένας,
μὴ καί τις ὄψεθ' ἡμέρας χἠμῶν ἴσως κατείπῃ.   495
ἀλλ' εἶα δεῦρ' ἐπὶ σκιᾶς
    ἐλθοῦσα πρὸς τὸ τειχίον,
παραβλέπουσα θατέρῳ,   498
πάλιν μετασκεύαζε σαυτὴν αὖθις ἥπερ ἦσθα,
καὶ μὴ βράδυν'· ὡς τήνδε καὶ δὴ τὴν στρατηγὸν ἡμῶν 500
χωροῦσαν ἐξ ἐκκλησίας ὁρῶμεν. ἀλλ' ἐπείγου
ἅπασα καὶ μίσει σάκον πρὸς τοῖν γναθοῖν ἔχουσα·
χαῦται γὰρ ἄκουσαι πάλαι τὸ σχῆμα τοῦτ' ἔχουσιν.

Πρ.   ταυτὶ μὲν ἡμῖν, ὦ γυναῖκες, εὐτυχῶς
τὰ πράγματ' ἐκβέβηκεν ἀβουλεύσαμεν.   505
ἀλλ' ὡς τάχιστα, πρίν τιν' ἀνθρώπων ἰδεῖν,
ῥιπτεῖτε χλαίνας, ἐμβὰς ἐκποδὼν ἴτω—
χάλα συναπτοὺς ἡνίας Λακωνικάς—
βακτηρίας ἄφεσθε. καὶ μέντοι σὺ μὲν
ταύτας κατευτρέπιζ', ἐγὼ δὲ βούλομαι   510
εἴσω παρερπύσασα πρὶν τὸν ἄνδρα με
ἰδεῖν, καταθέσθαι θοἰμάτιον αὐτοῦ πάλιν
ὅθενπερ ἔλαβον, τἄλλα θ' ἁξηνεγκάμην.

511–12 (... ἰδεῖν) §§ S π 565

---

492 πρᾶγμα Γ   εὑροῦσ' x : εὑροῦσα (ευ- R) a   493 ἡμᾶς om. Γ
495 καί] κε R   ὄψεθ' R : ὄψαιτο Γ   ἡμέρας von Blumenthal: ἡμᾶς a
ἴσω κατέπτη ΓΛ   496 ἐπὶ] ὑπὸ Bachmann   499 ἥπερ Γ
500 βράδυν' Ald. : βράδυννε a   502 τοῖν Cobet : ταῖν a   503 ἄκουσαι Ussher: ἥκουσιν a   ἔχουσιν Ussher: -σαι a   504 Πρ. om. Γ
ὦ γυναῖκες ἡμῖν R   505 ἀβουλεύσαμεν R: ἃ 'βουλεύσαμεν ΓΛ
507 ἐκποδὼν x : -δῶν a   ἴτω R   508 συνάπτους' R₁ : -τοῦσ' R₂
510 κατευτρέπιζε Γ   513 ἃ ξυνέγκαμεν Γ: ἃ 'ξηνέγκαμεν Λ

Χο.   κεῖται ⟨καὶ⟩ δὴ πάνθ' ἅπερ εἶπας, σὸν δ' ἔργον τἄλλα
       διδάσκειν,
       ὅ τί σοι δρῶσαι ξύμφορον ἡμεῖς δόξομεν ὀρθῶς ὑπακούειν.
       οὐδεμιᾷ γὰρ δεινοτέρᾳ σου ξυμμείξασ' οἶδα γυναικί. 516

Πρ.   περιμείνατέ νυν, ἵνα τῆς ἀρχῆς ἣν ἄρτι κεχειροτόνημαι,
       ξυμβούλοισιν πάσαις ὑμῖν χρήσωμαι. καὶ γὰρ ἐκεῖ μοι
       ἐν τῷ θορύβῳ καὶ τοῖς δεινοῖς ἀνδρειόταται γεγένησθε.

Βλ.   αὕτη, πόθεν ἥκεις, Πραξαγόρα; Πρ. τί δ', ὦ μέλε, 520
       σοὶ τοῦθ'; Βλ. ὅ τί μοι τοῦτ' ἔστιν; ὡς εὐηθικῶς.

Πρ.   οὗτοι παρὰ τοῦ μοιχοῦ γε φήσεις. Βλ. οὐκ ἴσως
       ἑνός γε. Πρ. καὶ μὴν βασανίσαι τουτί γέ σοι
       ἔξεστι. Βλ. πῶς; Πρ. εἰ τῆς κεφαλῆς ὄζω μύρου.

Βλ.   τί δ'; οὐχὶ βινεῖται γυνὴ κἄνευ μύρου;   525

Πρ.   οὐ δὴ τάλαιν' ἔγωγε. Βλ. πῶς οὖν ὄρθριον
       ᾤχου σιωπῇ θοἰμάτιον λαβοῦσά μου;

Πρ.   γυνή μέ τις νύκτωρ ἑταίρα καὶ φίλη
       μετεπέμψατ' ὠδίνουσα. Βλ. κᾆτ' οὐκ ἦν ἐμοὶ
       φράσασαν ἰέναι; Πρ. τῆς λεχοῦς δ' οὐ φροντίσαι   530

516 §§ S ξ 106

514 Χο. om. Γ ⟨καὶ⟩ Dobree   515 ξύμφερον Γ   516 ξυμμίξας
Γ: ξυμμίξασ' Λ: ξυμμίξασ' S   οἰδαννακί Λ   517 Πρ. om. RΓ
περιμείνατέ νυν incertum quis primus: περιμείνατε νῦν RΛ: παραμείνατε
νῦν Γ   518 ἀπάσαις ΓΛ   ἡμῖν Λ   χρήσομαι Λ   520–62 Βλ.
Brunck   520 Βλ.] ὁ ἀνὴρ Λ: par. R: om. Γ   Πρ.] dic. RΓ
521 τοῦθ' Ald.: τοῦτο a   Βλ.] dic. Γ: ἀνὴρ Λ: om. R   ὡς] Πρ. ὡς Λ
522 Πρ. Brunck: par. R: om. Γ   του Brunck   μοιχοῦ] μοι R₁   Βλ.]
dic. R: om. Γ: ἀνὴρ Λ   523 ἑνός om. Λ   Πρ.] dic. RΓ   βασανίσι
Λ (Μυιᵖᶜ): βασανεστι Μυιᵃᶜ (ut vid.)   524 Βλ.] dic. RΓ: ἀνὴρ Λ
525 ἄνευ Γ   μοίρου R₂   526 Πρ.] par. R: dic. Γ   οὐ δῆτα, τάλαν,
Reiske   Βλ.] par. R: dic. Γ: ἀνὴρ Λ   527 σιπῇ Γ   μοι ΓΛ
528 Πρ.] par. R: dic. Γ   529 Βλ.] par. R: om. Γ: ἀνὴρ Λ   ἦν Γ
530 φράσουσαν Λ   Πρ.] par. R: dic. Γ

οὕτως ἐχούσης, ὦνερ; Βλ. εἰποῦσάν γέ μοι.
ἀλλ᾽ ἔστιν ἐνταῦθά τι κακόν. Πρ. μὰ τὼ θεὼ
ἀλλ᾽ ὥσπερ εἶχον ᾠχόμην· ἐδεῖτο δὲ
ἥπερ μεθῆκέ μ᾽ ἐξιέναι πάσῃ τέχνῃ.

Βλ.   εἶτ᾽ οὐ τὸ σαυτῆς ἱμάτιον ἐχρῆν σ᾽ ἔχειν;   535
      ἀλλ᾽ ἔμ᾽ ἀποδύσασ᾽ ἐπιβαλοῦσα τοὐγκυκλον
      ᾤχου καταλιποῦσ᾽ ὡσπερεὶ προκείμενον,
      μόνον οὐ στεφανώσασ᾽ οὐδ᾽ ἐπιθεῖσα λήκυθον.

Πρ.   ψῦχος γὰρ ἦν, ἐγὼ δὲ λεπτὴ κἀσθενής·
      ἔπειθ᾽ ἵν᾽ ἀλεαίνοιμι τοῦτ᾽ ἠμπεσχόμην.   540
      σὲ δ᾽ ἐν ἀλέᾳ κατακείμενον καὶ στρώμασιν
      κατέλιπον, ὦνερ. Βλ. αἱ δὲ δὴ Λακωνικαὶ
      ᾤχοντο μετὰ σοῦ κατὰ τί χἠ βακτηρία;

Πρ.   ἵνα θοἰμάτιον σώσαιμι, μεθυπεδησάμην
      μιμουμένη σε καὶ κτυποῦσα τοῖν ποδοῖν   545
      καὶ τοὺς λίθους παίουσα τῇ βακτηρίᾳ.

Βλ.   οἶσθ᾽ οὖν ἀπολωλεκυῖα πυρῶν ἑκτέα,
      ὃν χρῆν ἔμ᾽ ἐξ ἐκκλησίας εἰληφέναι;

Πρ.   μὴ φροντίσῃς· ἄρρεν γὰρ ἔτεκε παιδίον.

537-8 §§ S ω 285   540 § S a 1109; § Zonar. 135; § AB 381. 25;
§ Lex. Bachm. 73. 8; cf. Phryn. PS 23. 9, S a 1147, Phot. B 73. 11
547 § S ε 644; §§ Zonar. 653

531 Βλ.] par. R: dic. Γ: ἀνὴρ Λ   532 Πρ.] par. R: dic. Γ
534 ἥπερ R   535 Βλ.] ὁ ἀνὴρ R: ἀνὴρ Λ: om. Γ   σ᾽ ἐχρῆν ἔχειν
Γ   536 ἀποδύσας R: -δύσασά σ᾽ Λ   ἐπιλαβοῦσα Λ   τοῦ κύκλον Γ
537 καταλιποῦσα Μυ1ᵃᶜ (ut vid.)   538 λύκηθον Λ   539 Πρ.]
par. R: om. Γ   540 ἔπειθ᾽] οὐκοῦν Lex. Bachm.   ἵνα λεαίνοιμι Λ
ἠμπεσχόμην AB Lex. Bachm.: ημπισχόμην R: ἠμ- ΛS: ἠμπισχημένον Γ
542 κατέλειπον R   Βλ.] par. R: dic. Γ: ἀνὴρ Λ   543 κᾆστι χ᾽ ἡ
Γ: κατίσχ᾽ ἡ Λ   544 Πρ.] par. R: om. Γ   547-52 om. Λ
547 Βλ.] par. R: om. Γ: ἀνὴρ Μυ1   ἑκτέα Μυ1   548 ἐμὲ 'ξ
ἐκ- Μυ1   549 Πρ. Μυ1: par. R: om. Γ   ἔτεκεν R

34　　　　　　*ΕΚΚΛΗΣΙΑΖΟΥΣΑΙ*

Βλ.　ἠκκλησία; Πρ. μὰ Δί᾽ ἀλλ᾽ ἐφ᾽ ἣν ἐγᾠχόμην.　　　550
　　　ἀτὰρ γεγένηται; Βλ. ναὶ μὰ Δί᾽. οὐκ ᾔδησθά με
　　　φράσαντά σοι χθές; Πρ. ἄρτι γ᾽ ἀναμιμνῄσκομαι.

Βλ.　οὐδ᾽ ἄρα τὰ δόξαντ᾽ οἶσθα; Πρ. μὰ Δί᾽ ἐγὼ μὲν οὔ.

Βλ.　κάθησο τοίνυν σηπίας μασωμένη.
　　　ὑμῖν δέ φασι παραδεδόσθαι τὴν πόλιν.　　　555

Πρ.　τί δρᾶν; ὑφαίνειν; Βλ. οὐ μὰ Δί᾽ ἀλλ᾽ ἄρχειν. Πρ. τίνων;

Βλ.　ἁπαξαπάντων τῶν κατὰ πόλιν πραγμάτων.

Πρ.　νὴ τὴν Ἀφροδίτην μακαρία γ᾽ ἄρ᾽ ἡ πόλις
　　　ἔσται τὸ λοιπόν. Βλ. κατὰ τί; Πρ. πολλῶν οὔνεκα.
　　　οὐ γὰρ ἔτι τοῖς τολμῶσιν αὐτὴν αἰσχρὰ δρᾶν　　　560
　　　ἔσται τὸ λοιπόν. οὐδαμοῦ δὲ μαρτυρεῖν,
　　　οὐ συκοφαντεῖν— Βλ. μηδαμῶς πρὸς τῶν θεῶν
　　　τουτὶ ποιήσῃς μηδ᾽ ἀφέλῃ μου τὸν βίον.

Χρ.　ὦ δαιμόνι᾽ ἀνδρῶν, τὴν γυναῖκ᾽ ἔα λέγειν.

Πρ.　μὴ λωποδυτῆσαι, μὴ φθονεῖν τοῖς πλησίον,　　　565
　　　μὴ γυμνὸν εἶναι μὴ πένητα μηδένα,
　　　μὴ λοιδορεῖσθαι, μὴ 'νεχυραζόμενον φέρειν.

554 § S σ 332

550 Βλ.] par. R : ἀνὴρ Μυι : οm. Γ　　ἡ ἐκ- Γ : ἡ 'κ Μυι　　Πρ. Μυι :
par. R : om. Γ　　ἔγωγ᾽ ᾠχ- ΓΜυι　　551 αὐτὰρ Γ　Βλ.] par. R :
dic. Γ : ἀνὴρ Μυι　　ᾔδησθά Brunck : ᾔδεισθά ΡΜυι : ᾔδεισθα Γ
552 Πρ. Μυι : par. R : om. Γ　　553 Βλ.] par. R : ἀνὴρ Λ : om. Γ
τὴν δόξαν τῶν Γ　　Πρ.] par. R : dic. Γ　　554 Βλ.] par. R : ἀνὴρ
Λ : om. Γ　　555 παραδιδόσθαι Λ　　556 Πρ.] par. R : om. Γ
τι R　Βλ.] par. R : dic. Γ : ἀνὴρ Λ　Πρ.] par. R : om. Γ　τίνος Λ
557 Βλ.] par. R : ἀνὴρ Λ : om. Γ　　558 Πρ.] par. R : om. Γ　γὰρ
ΓΛ　　559 Βλ.] par. R : ἀνὴρ Λ : om. Γ　　κατὰ . . . λοιπόν (561)
om. Γ　Πρ.] par. R　οὔνεκα Λ　　561 λοιπόν. οὐδαμοῦ Μυι : -πὸν
-μοῦ RΛ　　562 Βλ.] par. R : ἀνὴρ Λ : ἄλλος βλέπυρος ἐλθών Σᴿ
563 μήδ᾽ ἀφέλῃς Λ　　564 Χρ. Rogers : ὁ ἀνὴρ π̅ρ̅ R : πρὰξ Λ : om. Γ
δαιμόνιε Γ　　565 Πρ. Brunck : par. R : om. ΓΛ　　567 μὴ
'νευυραζόμενον Rᵃᶜ : μήτ᾽ ἐνχυραζόμενον Γ

Χρ.   νὴ τὸν Ποσειδῶ μεγάλα γ᾽, εἰ μὴ ψεύσεται.

Πρ.   ἀλλ᾽ ἀποφανῶ τοῦθ᾽, ὥστε σέ τέ μοι μαρτυρεῖν
      καὶ τοῦτον αὐτὸν μηδὲν ἀντειπεῖν ἐμοί.   570

Χο.   νῦν δὴ δεῖ σε πυκνὴν φρένα καὶ φιλόσοφον ἐγείρειν
          φροντίδ᾽ ἐπισταμένην
      ταῖσι φίλαισιν ἀμύνειν.
      κοινῇ γὰρ ἐπ᾽ εὐτυχίαισιν
      ἔρχεται γλώττης ἐπίνοια πολίτην
      δῆμον ἐπαγλαϊοῦσα   575
      μυρίαισιν ὠφελίαισι βίου· δηλοῦν ⟨δ᾽⟩ ὅ τί περ δύναται
          καιρός.
      δεῖται γάρ τοι σοφοῦ τινος ἐξευρήματος ἡ πόλις ἡμῶν.
      ἀλλὰ πέραινε μόνον
      μήτε δεδραμένα μήτ᾽ εἰρημένα πω πρότερον.
      μισοῦσι γὰρ ἢν τὰ παλαιὰ πολλάκις θεῶνται.   580

      ἀλλ᾽ οὐ μέλλειν, ἀλλ᾽ ἅπτεσθαι καὶ δὴ χρῆν ταῖς διανοίαις,
      ὡς τὸ ταχύνειν χαρίτων μετέχει πλεῖστον παρὰ τοῖσι
          θεαταῖς.

Πρ.   καὶ μὴν ὅτι μὲν χρηστὰ διδάξω πιστεύω· τοὺς δὲ θεατάς,
      εἰ καινοτομεῖν ἐθελήσουσιν καὶ μὴ τοῖς ἠθάσι λίαν
      τοῖς τ᾽ ἀρχαίοις ἐνδιατρίβειν, τοῦτ᾽ ἔσθ᾽ ὃ μάλιστα
          δέδοικα.   585

Βλ.   περὶ μὲν τοίνυν τοῦ καινοτομεῖν μὴ δείσῃς· τοῦτο γὰρ
          ἡμῖν
      δρᾶν ἀντ᾽ ἄλλης ἀρχῆς ἐστιν, τῶν δ᾽ ἀρχαίων ἀμελῆσαι.

586-7 (τοῦ- ... ἐστι) S § (1) κ 1177; §§ † (2) a 2607

568 Χρ. Rogers: ὁ αλλος R: ὁ ἄλλος ἀνὴρ Λ (ὁ om. Mu1): om. Γ
μεγάλ᾽ εἰ Γ   569 Πρ. om. RΓ   ὥστε σέ τέ Cobet: ὥστέ σε γέ R:
ὅστις γε ΓΛ   570 ἐμοί] ἔχειν Nauck   571 Χο. om. Γ   σε] γε x
πυκνὰν Λ   573 κοινῇ RΓ   574 γνώμης Markland   576 εὐτυ-
χίαισι(ν) ΓΛ   ⟨δ᾽⟩ Voss: om. a   582 πλείστων Rac   583 Πρ.
om. Γ   584 ἐθελήσουσι Γ   585 τ᾽ om. Γ   τοῦθ᾽ Λ   586 Βλ.]
par. R: dic. Γ   587 ἀρχῆς] ἀρετῆς Bergk

Πρ.   μή νυν πρότερον μηδεὶς ὑμῶν ἀντείπῃ μηδ' ὑποκρούσῃ,
     πρὶν ἐπίστασθαι τὴν ἐπίνοιαν καὶ τοῦ φράζοντος ἀκοῦ-
     σαι.
     κοινωνεῖν γὰρ πάντας φήσω χρῆναι πάντων μετέχον-
     τας   590
     κἀκ ταὐτοῦ ζῆν, καὶ μὴ τὸν μὲν πλουτεῖν, τὸν δ' ἄθλιον
     εἶναι,
     μηδὲ γεωργεῖν τὸν μὲν πολλήν, τῷ δ' εἶναι μηδὲ ταφῆναι,
     μηδ' ἀνδραπόδοις τὸν μὲν χρῆσθαι πολλοῖς, τὸν δ' οὐδ'
     ἀκολούθῳ.
     ἀλλ' ἕνα ποιῶ κοινὸν πᾶσιν βίοτον, καὶ τοῦτον ὅμοιον.

Βλ.   πῶς οὖν ἔσται κοινὸς ἅπασιν;   Πρ. κατέδει πέλεθον
     πρότερός μου.   595

Βλ.   καὶ τῶν πελέθων κοινωνοῦμεν;   Πρ. μὰ Δί' ἀλλ' ἔφθης
     μ' ὑποκρούσας.
     τοῦτο γὰρ ἤμελλον ἐγὼ λέξειν· τὴν γῆν πρώτιστα ποιήσω
     κοινὴν πάντων καὶ τἀργύριον καὶ τἄλλ' ὁπός' ἐστὶν
     ἑκάστῳ.
     εἶτ' ἀπὸ τούτων κοινῶν ὄντων ἡμεῖς βοσκήσομεν ὑμᾶς
     ταμιευόμεναι καὶ φειδόμεναι καὶ τὴν γνώμην προσ-
     έχουσαι.   600

Χρ.   πῶς οὖν ὅστις μὴ κέκτηται γῆν ἡμῶν, ἀργύριον δὲ
     καὶ Δαρεικούς, ἀφανῆ πλοῦτον;   Πρ. τοῦτ' ἐς τὸ μέσον
     καταθήσει.
     καὶ μὴ καταθεὶς ψευδορκήσει.   Βλ. κἀκτήσατο γὰρ διὰ
     τοῦτο.

588 Πρ.] par. R: om. Γ   νυν Bekker: νῦν a   ἀποκρούσῃ RΓ
590 μετέχοντες Λ   592 μηδὲ (1)] καὶ μὴ Γ   593 τόνδ' RΓ   οὐδ'
om. Λ   ἀλούθω Γ   594 ποῶ Γ   κοινὸν om. Γ   πᾶσιν Kuster: -σι
a   595–6 Βλ. et Πρ.] dic. Γ: om. R   595 κατέδει Brunck: -δεῖ a
πέλεθον Bothe: σπε- a   596 πελέθων Bothe: σπε- a   597 ποήσω Γ
599 κοινῶν] καὶ τῶν Λ   600 ταμιευόμαι Mu1   προέχουσαι Rac
601 Χρ. Ussher: Βλ. Λ: om. RΓ   602–3 Πρ. et Βλ.] dic. Γ:
om. R

Πρ. ἀλλ᾽ οὐδέν τοι χρήσιμον ἔσται πάντως αὐτῷ. Χρ. κατὰ
δὴ τί;

Πρ. οὐδεὶς οὐδὲν πενίᾳ δράσει· πάντα γὰρ ἕξουσιν ἅπαντες,
ἄρτους, τεμάχη, μάζας, χλαίνας, οἶνον, στεφάνους, ἐρεβίνθους.   606
ὥστε τί κέρδος μὴ καταθεῖναι; σὺ γὰρ ἐξευρὼν
ἀπόδειξον.

Χρ. οὔκουν καὶ νῦν οὗτοι μᾶλλον κλέπτουσ᾽ οἷς ταῦτα
πάρεστιν;

Πρ. πρότερόν γ᾽, ὦταῖρ᾽, ὅτε τοῖσι νόμοις διεχρώμεθα τοῖς
προτέροισιν·
νῦν δ᾽ ἔσται γὰρ βίος ἐκ κοινοῦ, τί τὸ κέρδος μὴ καταθεῖναι;   610

Βλ. ἢν μείρακ᾽ ἰδὼν ἐπιθυμήσῃ καὶ βούληται σκαλαθῦραι,
ἕξει τούτων ἀφελὼν δοῦναι, τῶν ἐκ κοινοῦ δὲ μεθέξει
ξυγκαταδαρθών. Πρ. ἀλλ᾽ ἐξέσται προῖκ᾽ αὐτῷ ξυγκαταδαρθεῖν.
καὶ ταύτας γὰρ κοινὰς ποιῶ τοῖς ἀνδράσι συγκατακεῖσθαι
καὶ παιδοποιεῖν τῷ βουλομένῳ. Βλ. πῶς οὖν οὐ πάντες
ἴασιν   615
ἐπὶ τὴν ὡραιοτάτην αὐτῶν καὶ ζητήσουσιν ἐρείδειν;

611 § S σ 521

604–5 Πρ.] par. R : om. Γ   604 Χρ. Ussher : dic. R : Βλ. Λ : om.
Γ   κᾱτα Γ   605 οὐδ᾽ ἐν R : οὐδ᾽ ἐν Λ   πενίᾳ] πνεύματι Γ   608 Χρ.
Ussher : Βλ. Λ : om. ΡΓ   κλέπτους Λ   πάρεστιν; χ : -στι a
609–11 Πρ. et Βλ. om. ΡΓ   609 πρό͞τ Γ : πρώτερον Μυι   ὦτέρ᾽ R :
ὦ ᾽ταῖρο Γ (ut vid.)   ὅτε τοῖσι] τούτοισι Γ (ut vid.)   611 βούληται
χ : βούλει ταῖ R : βούλεται ΓΛ   τοῦτον ante σκα- ΓΛ   612 μεθέξειν Γ
613 ξυγκαταδαρθών Λ : -δραθών ΡΓ (-ων)   Πρ.] dic. ΡΓ (ante ξυγ-)
προῖκα Γ   αὐτῷ om. Γ   καταδαρθεῖν Γ   614 in. Βλ. Λ   ποῶ Γ
συγκατακεῖσθαι Brunck : ξυν- ΡΛ : ξυγκαταδαρθεῖν Γ   615 Βλ.
Brunck : dic. R : om. ΓΛ   οὐ om. Γ   ἴσασιν Γ   616 καὶ om. Γ
ζητοῦσιν ΓΛ

Πρ.　αἱ φαυλότεραι καὶ σιμότεραι παρὰ τὰς σεμνὰς καθ-
　　　εδοῦνται.
　　　κᾆτ' ἢν ταύτης ἐπιθυμήσῃ, τὴν αἰσχρὰν πρῶθ' ὑπο-
　　　κρούσει.

Βλ.　καὶ πῶς ἡμᾶς τοὺς πρεσβύτας, ἢν ταῖς αἰσχραῖσι
　　　συνῶμεν,
　　　οὐκ ἐπιλείψει τὸ πέος πρότερον πρὶν ἐκεῖσ' οἷ φῂς
　　　ἀφικέσθαι;　　　　　　　　　　　　　　　620

Πρ.　οὐχὶ μαχοῦνται περὶ σοῦ· θάρρει, μὴ δείσῃς· οὐχὶ μα-
　　　χοῦνται.

Βλ.　περὶ τοῦ; Πρ. τοῦ μὴ ξυγκαταδαρθεῖν. καὶ σοὶ τοιοῦτον
　　　ὑπάρχει.

Βλ.　τὸ μὲν ὑμέτερον γνώμην τιν' ἔχει· προβεβούλευται γὰρ
　　　ὅπως ἂν
　　　μηδεμιᾶς ᾖ τρύπημα κενόν· τὸ δὲ τῶν ἀνδρῶν τί ποιήσει;
　　　φεύξονται γὰρ τοὺς αἰσχίους, ἐπὶ τοὺς δὲ καλοὺς βαδι-
　　　οῦνται.　　　　　　　　　　　　　　　625

Πρ.　ἀλλὰ φυλάξουσ' οἱ φαυλότεροι τοὺς καλλίους ἀπιόντας
　　　ἀπὸ τοῦ δείπνου καὶ τηρήσουσ' ἐπὶ τοῖσιν δημοσίοισιν.
　　　κοὐκ ἐξέσται παρὰ τοῖσι καλοῖς ⟨καὶ τοῖς μεγάλοις⟩
　　　καταδαρθεῖν
　　　ταῖσι γυναιξὶν πρὶν τοῖς αἰσχροῖς καὶ τοῖς μικροῖς
　　　χαρίσωνται.

Βλ.　ἡ Λυσικράτους ἄρα νυνὶ ῥὶς ἴσα τοῖσι καλοῖσι φρονή-
　　　σει;　　　　　　　　　　　　　　　　630

630 § S λ 860

617–19 Πρ. et Βλ. om. RΓ　　617 καθευδοῦνται Λ　　619 ξυνῶμεν
ΓΛ　　620 ἐπιλήψει Rᵃᶜ　　φῂς Rᵃᶜ　　621 Πρ. om. RΓ　　θάρρ' εἰ Γ
ante οὐχί (2) dic. RΓ: Βλ. Λ　　622 Βλ. ed. Junt.: om. a　　Πρ.]
dic. RΓ　　ante καὶ in. dic. RΓ: in. Βλ. Λ　　τοιούτων Λ　　ὑπάρξει Λ
623 Βλ. om. RΓ　　ἡμέτερον Λ　　624 ᾖ] ᾖ R₁: ᾖ Γ　　ποήσει R
625 ἐπὶ δὲ τοὺς ΓΛ　　626–631 Πρ. et Βλ. om. RΓ　　627 τοῖσι
ΓΛ　　628 om. Γ　　⟨καὶ τοῖς μεγάλοις⟩ Tyrwhitt　　629 ταῖς ΓΛ
μικροῖσιν Γ　　χαρίσονται R: χαρί Γ　　630 τοῖς καλοῖς Γ

Πρ.   νὴ τὸν Ἀπόλλω καὶ δημοτική γ' ἡ γνώμη καὶ καταχήνη
      τῶν σεμνοτέρων ἔσται πολλὴ καὶ τῶν σφραγῖδας ἐχόν-
      των,
      ὅταν ἐμβάδ' ἔχων εἴπῃ πρότερος, "παραχώρει κᾆτ' ἐπι-
      τήρει,
      ὅταν ἤδη 'γὼ διαπραξάμενος παραδῶ σοι δευτεριάζειν."

Χρ.   πῶς οὖν οὕτω ζώντων ἡμῶν τοὺς αὑτοῦ παῖδας ἕκαστος
      ἔσται δυνατὸς διαγιγνώσκειν; Πρ. τί δὲ δεῖ; πατέρας
      ⟨γὰρ⟩ ἅπαντας   636
      τοὺς πρεσβυτέρους αὐτῶν εἶναι τοῖσι χρόνοισιν νομι-
      οῦσιν.

Βλ.   οὐκοῦν ἄγξουσ' εὖ καὶ χρηστῶς ἑξῆς τὸν πάντα γέροντα
      διὰ τὴν ἄγνοιαν, ἐπεὶ καὶ νῦν γιγνώσκοντες πατέρ' ὄντα
      ἄγχουσι. τί δῆθ' ὅταν ἀγνὼς ᾖ; πῶς οὐ τότε κἀπι-
      χεσοῦνται;   640

Πρ.   ἀλλ' ὁ παρεστὼς οὐκ ἐπιτρέψει· τότε δ' αὐτοῖς οὐκ ἔμελ'
      οὐδὲν
      τῶν ἀλλοτρίων, ὅστις τύπτοι, νῦν δ' ἢν πληγέντος
      ἀκούσῃ,
      μὴ αὐτὸν ἐκεῖνον τύπτει δεδιὼς τοῖς δρῶσιν τοῦτο μα-
      χεῖται.

Βλ.   τὰ μὲν ἄλλα λέγεις οὐδὲν σκαιῶς· εἰ δὲ προσελθὼν
      Ἐπίκουρος

631-2 (δη- . . .) § S κ 868   631 cf. Poll. ii. 97   634 (ἐγὼ
ἤδη . . .) §§ S δ 294; (ἐγὼ ἤδη . . .) §§ Zonar. 491

631 ἀπόλλω' R   δημοτικὴν ἡ Γ   632 σφραγίδας Λ   633 om. Γ
ἔχων om. Λ   634 ἐγὼ ἤδη S   παραπραξάμενος Γ   635 Χρ.
Ussher: Βλ. Λ: om. RΓ   αὐτοῦ ΓΛ   636 διαγινώσκειν ΓΛ   Πρ.]
dic. RΓ   δὲ] δαὶ Γ   πατέρας] πρᾶσαν Λ   ⟨γὰρ⟩ Le Febvre
637 αὐτῶν R (ut vid.): αὐ- ΓΛ   τοῖς χρόνοισι Γ   638-44 Βλ. et
Πρ. om. RΓ   638 οὐκοῦν R^pc: οὔκουν ΓΛ   ἄγξωσ' R   ἑξῆς om.
Γ   639 ἐόντα Λ   640 κἀπιχενοῦνται Γ   641 ἐπιτρίψει RΓ
ἔμελλ' ΓΛ   642 τύπτει Mu1^ac (ut vid.)   643 τύπτῃ ΓΛ   δρῶσιν
Kuster: -σι a

ἢ Λευκόλοφος "πάππαν" με καλεῖ, τοῦτ' ἤδη δεινὸν
ἀκοῦσαι.   645

Πρ.   πολὺ μέντοι δεινότερον τούτου τοῦ πράγματός ἐστι—
Βλ. τὸ ποῖον;

Πρ.   εἴ σε φιλήσειεν Ἀρίστυλλος φάσκων αὐτοῦ πατέρ' εἶναι.

Βλ.   οἰμώζοι γ' ἂν καὶ κωκύοι. Πρ. σὺ δέ γ' ὄζοις ἂν καλα-
μίνθης.
ἀλλ' οὗτος μὲν πρότερον γέγονεν πρὶν τὸ ψήφισμα
γενέσθαι,
ὥστ' οὐχὶ δέος μή σε φιλήσῃ. Βλ. δεινὸν μέντἂν ἐπε-
πόνθειν.   650

Χρ.   τὴν γῆν δὲ τίς ἔσθ' ὁ γεωργήσων; Πρ. οἱ δοῦλοι. σοὶ δὲ
μελήσει,
ὅταν ᾖ δεκάπουν τὸ στοιχεῖον, λιπαρὸν χωρεῖν ἐπὶ
δεῖπνον.

Χρ.   περὶ δ' ἱματίων τίς πόρος ἔσται; καὶ γὰρ τοῦτ' ἔστιν
ἐρέσθαι.

Πρ.   τὰ μὲν ὄνθ' ὑμῖν πρῶτον ὑπάρξει, τὰ δὲ λοίφ' ἡμεῖς
ὑφανοῦμεν.

645 (τοῦ- . . .) § S α 3938   647 § S α 3938; cf. Σ Pl. 314, EM
142. 55   648 (σὺ . . .) § S κ 196   651–2 (σοὶ . . .) § S δ 178
652 cf. Apostol. v. 92

645 Λευκόλοφος Reiske: -λόφος R: -λόφας ΓΛ   πάππαν Brunck:
πάπαν a   καλῇ Λ   646–7 Πρ. om. RΓ   646 Βλ.] par. R: dic. Γ
647 φιλήσει Γ   Ἀρίστυλος S   αὐτοῦ Kuster: αὐ- a   648 Βλ. om.
RΓ   μ' ἂν Λ   Πρ.] dic. Γ: om. R   649 οὗτο R₁   μὲν τὸ
πρότερον Γ   γέγονε ΓΛ   πρὶν] πρὸς Γ   650 μή] οὐ μὴ Γ   Βλ.]
dic. R: om. Γ   ἐπεπόνθην Λ   651 Χρ. Ussher: om. a   τίς] τῆς
Λ   Πρ.] dic. R: om. (dic. ante σοὶ) Γ   σοὶ] σὺ R   μελήσηι Rᵃᶜ
652 λιπαρὸν x: -ρῶς aS   653 Χρ. Ussher: Βλ. Λ: om. RΓ   δ' x:
δὲ RΛ: om. Γ   654 Πρ. om. RΓ   τὰ δελοὶ φ' R   φανοῦμεν Γ

Χρ. ἐν ἔτι ζητῶ. πῶς ἦν τις ὄφλῃ παρὰ τοῖς ἄρχουσι δίκην
  τῳ, 655
  πόθεν ἐκτείσει ταύτην; οὐ γὰρ τῶν κοινῶν γ᾽ ἐστὶ
  δίκαιον.

Πρ. ἀλλ᾽ οὐδὲ δίκαι πρῶτον ἔσονται. Βλ. τουτὶ τοὖπος σ᾽
  ἐπιτρίψει.

Χρ. κἀγὼ ταύτην γνώμην ἐθέμην. Πρ. τοῦ γὰρ τάλαν οὕνεκ᾽
  ἔσονται;

Βλ. πολλῶν οὕνεκα, νὴ τὸν Ἀπόλλω· πρῶτον δ᾽ ἑνὸς οὕνεκα
  δήπου,
  ἤν τις ὀφείλων ἐξαρνῆται. Πρ. πόθεν οὖν ἐδάνεισ᾽ ὁ
  δανείσας, 660
  ἐν τῷ κοινῷ πάντων ὄντων; κλέπτων δήπου ᾽στ᾽ ἐπί-
  δηλος.

Χρ. νὴ τὴν Δήμητρ᾽ εὖ γε διδάσκεις. Βλ. τουτὶ τοίνυν φρασάτω μοι,
  τῆς αἰκείας οἱ τύπτοντες πόθεν ἐκτείσουσιν, ἐπειδὰν
  εὐωχηθέντες ὑβρίζωσιν; τοῦτο γὰρ οἶμαί σ᾽ ἀπορήσειν.

Πρ. ἀπὸ τῆς μάζης ἧς σιτεῖται· ταύτης γὰρ ὅταν τις ἀφ-
  αιρῇ, 665
  οὐχ ὑβριεῖται φαύλως οὕτως αὖθις τῇ γαστρὶ κολασθείς.

658 (...-μην) § S ε 314

---

655 Χρ. Ussher: Βλ. Λ: om. ΡΓ   ἤν τις R₂: ἤν τι R₁: ἥτις Γ:
εἴ τις Λ   τῳ] τῶν Γ: τῶ Λ   656 ἐκτείσει van Leeuwen: κτίσῃ R:
ἐκτίσει ΓΛ   657 Πρ.] par. R: om. Γ   δίκαια Γ   Βλ.] Χο. ΡΓ
τοὖπος σ᾽ Hansing: τ᾽ οὖπος R: πόσσ ΓΛ   658 Χρ. Rogers: par.
R: Βλ. Γ: om. Λ   Πρ. τοῦ ... ἔσονται om. in lac. Γ   Πρ.] par. R
659 Βλ. om. ΡΓ   οὕνεκα Meineke: ἔνεκεν ΡΓ (-κε) Λ (οὔ- Μυι)
ἀπόλλω᾽ R   δ᾽ om. R   660 ἐξαρνεῖται R   Πρ.] dic. R: om. Γ
661 ὄντων om. Γ   662 Χρ. Rogers: Χο. a   Βλ.] dic. R
663 αἰκίας ΓΛ   ἐκτείσουσιν van Leeuwen: κτίσουσιν R: ἐκτίσουσιν ΓΛ
664 ὑβρίζουσι Γ   665 Πρ. om. ΡΓ   ταύτην ΓΛ   666 φ᾽+αυλως
Λ   αὖθις R: om. Γ

42 ΕΚΚΛΗΣΙΑΖΟΥΣΑΙ

Βλ.   οὐδ' αὖ κλέπτης οὐδεὶς ἔσται; Πρ. πῶς γὰρ κλέψει
      μετὸν αὐτῷ;

Βλ.   οὐδ' ἀποδύσουσ' ἄρα τῶν νυκτῶν; Πρ. οὐκ ἦν οἴκοι γε
      καθεύδῃς·
      οὐδ' ἤν γε θύραζ' ὥσπερ πρότερον· βίοτος γὰρ πᾶσιν
      ὑπάρξει.
      ἢν δ' ἀποδύῃ γ' αὐτὸς δώσει· τί γὰρ αὐτῷ πρᾶγμα μά-
      χεσθαι;   670
      ἕτερον γὰρ ἰὼν ἐκ τοῦ κοινοῦ κρεῖττον ἐκείνου κομι-
      εῖται.

Βλ.   οὐδὲ κυβεύσουσ' ἄρ' ἄνθρωποι; Πρ. περὶ τοῦ γὰρ τοῦτο
      ποιήσει;

Βλ.   τὴν δὲ δίαιταν τίνα ποιήσεις; Πρ. κοινὴν πᾶσιν. τὸ γὰρ
      ἄστυ
      μίαν οἴκησίν φημι ποιήσειν συρρήξασ' εἰς ἓν ἄπαντα,
      ὥστε βαδίζειν ὡς ἀλλήλους. Βλ. τὸ δὲ δεῖπνον ποῦ
      παραθήσεις;   675

Πρ.   τὰ δικαστήρια καὶ τὰς στοιὰς ἀνδρῶνας πάντα ποιήσω.

Βλ.   τὸ δὲ βῆμα τί σοι χρήσιμον ἔσται; Πρ. τοὺς κρατῆρας
      καταθήσω
      καὶ τὰς ὑδρίας, καὶ ῥαψῳδεῖν ἔσται τοῖς παιδαρίοισιν
      τοὺς ἀνδρείους ἐν τῷ πολέμῳ, κεἴ τις δειλὸς γεγένηται,

667 S § (1) μ 794; (οὐ με- ...) ‡ (2) ο 918   668–9 (οὐκ ἀπο- ...
-ρον) §§ ο 855   672 (τοῦ ...) §§ S τ 811   676 § S α 2194
677–8 (... -δρίας) § S β 257   678–80 (ῥα- ...-νοι) § S ρ 68

667 Βλ. om. ΡΓ   οὐδ'] ὁδ' Λ   Πρ.] dic. Γ: om. R   κλέψει Brunck:
κλέψαι aS   668 Βλ. om. ΡΓ   οὐκ ἀποδύσῃ S   ἄρα R: om. S
Πρ.] dic. R: om. Γ   γε om. Γ   669 om. Λ   γε] σε x   θύραζε Γ
671 κομιεῖται ἐκείνου Λ   672–3 Βλ. om. ΡΓ   Πρ.] dic. ΡΓ
672 ἄρ' Bekker: ἄρ' a   673 δὲ om. Γ   πᾶσι ΓΛ   674 συρρήξας Γ
675 ὡς] εἰς R   Βλ.] dic. Γ: om. R   676 Πρ. om. ΡΓ   τὰ δὲ δι-
Γ   δισκατήρια R   στοὰς ΓS   677 Βλ. om. ΡΓ   Πρ.] dic. ΡΓ
678 ὕδρας R₁   παιδαρίοισι ΓΛ

ἵνα μὴ δειπνῶσ᾽ αἰσχυνόμενοι. Βλ. νὴ τὸν Ἀπόλλω

χάριέν γε.   680

τὰ δὲ κληρωτήρια ποῖ τρέψεις; Πρ. εἰς τὴν ἀγορὰν

κ α τ α θ ή σ ω.

κᾆτα στήσασα παρ᾽ Ἁρμοδίῳ κληρώσω πάντας, ἕως ἂν

εἰδὼς ὁ λαχὼν ἀπίῃ χαίρων ἐν ὁποίῳ γράμματι δειπνεῖ.

καὶ κηρύξει τοὺς ἐκ τοῦ βῆτ᾽ ἐπὶ τὴν στοιὰν ἀκολουθεῖν

τὴν βασίλειον δειπνήσοντας, τὸ δὲ θῆτ᾽ ἐς τὴν παρὰ

ταύτην,   685

τοὺς δ᾽ ἐκ τοῦ κάππ᾽ ἐς τὴν στοιὰν χωρεῖν τὴν ἀλφιτόπωλιν.

Βλ.   ἵνα κάπτωσιν; Πρ. μὰ Δί᾽ ἀλλ᾽ ἵν᾽ ἐκεῖ δειπνῶσιν.

Βλ. ὅτῳ δὲ τὸ γράμμα

μὴ 'ξελκυσθῇ καθ᾽ ὃ δειπνήσει, τούτους ἀπελῶσιν ἅπαν-

τες.

Πρ.   ἀλλ᾽ οὐκ ἔσται τοῦτο παρ᾽ ἡμῖν·

πᾶσι γὰρ ἄφθονα πάντα παρέξομεν,   690

ὥστε μεθυσθεὶς αὐτῷ στεφάνῳ

πᾶς τις ἄπεισιν τὴν δᾷδα λαβών.

αἱ δὲ γυναῖκες κατὰ τὰς διόδους

προσπίπτουσαι τοῖς ἀπὸ δείπνου

τάδε λέξουσιν· "δεῦρο παρ᾽ ἡμᾶς,   695

ἐνθάδε μεῖράξ ἐσθ᾽ ὡραία."

681–92 § S κ 1786   691–2 S §§ (2) α 4539   693–6 § S δ 1153
693–4 (κατὰ ...) S §§ (2) π 2788

---

680 Βλ.] dic. RΓ   Ἀπόλλω᾽ R   γε] τε Λ   681 Πρ.] dic. R :
om. Γ   καθήσω R   682 στήσα R₁ : στήσασ᾽ R₂   ἁρμοδίῳ Λ
683 ἀπῄει RS   ποίῳ S   684 κήρυξε Γ   βῆτα RS   καὶ επι Rᵃᶜ
στοὰν ΓS   685 ἐς τὴν] ἐστι Γ   παρ᾽ αὐτὴν Γ   686 στοὰν ΓS
687 Βλ. Bentley : om. a   κάπτωσι ΓS   Πρ. Bentley : dic. RΓ : Βλ. Λ
Βλ. Bentley : om. a   ὅτο R : οὕτω S   688 μὴ ἐξ- ΓΛS   καθὸ ΓΛS
τούτοισ R   ἀμπελῶσιν Γ : ἐξελῶσιν S   689 Πρ.] dic. Γ : om. R
οὐκ ἔστι ΓΛS   692 ἄπεισι ΓS (1) et (2) : ἄπισι R   693 κατα-
διόδους Γ   694 ἀπὸ τοῦ δείπνου R : ἀποδείπνων Λⁱ   695 λέξουσι ΓS
696 μείρεξ Λ   ἐσθ᾽ Bekker : ἔσθ᾽ a

"παρ' ἐμοὶ δ' ", ἑτέρα
φήσει τις ἄνωθ' ἐξ ὑπερῴου,
"καὶ καλλίστη καὶ λευκοτάτη·
πρότερον μέντοι δεῖ σε καθεύδειν   700
αὐτῆς παρ' ἐμοί."

τοῖς εὐπρεπέσιν δ' ἀκολουθοῦντες   702a
καὶ μειρακίοις οἱ φαυλότεροι   702b
τοιάδ' ἐροῦσιν· "ποῖ θεῖς οὗτος;   703
πάντως οὐδὲν δράσεις ἐλθών.

τοῖς γὰρ σιμοῖς καὶ τοῖς αἰσχροῖς   705
ἐψήφισται προτέροις βινεῖν,
ὑμᾶς δὲ τέως θρῖα λαβόντας
   διφόρου συκῆς
   ἐν τοῖς προθύροισι δέφεσθαι."

φέρε νυν φράσον μοι, ταῦτ' ἀρέσκει σφῷν; Βλ. πάνυ. 710

Πρ. βαδιστέον τἄρ' ἐστὶν εἰς ἀγορὰν ἐμοί,
   ἵν' ἀποδέχωμαι τὰ προσιόντα χρήματα,
   λαβοῦσα κηρύκαιναν εὔφωνόν τινα.
   ἐμὲ γὰρ ἀνάγκη ταῦτα δρᾶν ᾑρημένην
   ἄρχειν, καταστῆσαί τε τὰ ξυσσίτια,   715
   ὅπως ἂν εὐωχῆσθε πρῶτον τήμερον.

Βλ. ἤδη γὰρ εὐωχησόμεσθα; Πρ. φήμ' ἐγώ.
   ἔπειτα τὰς πόρνας καταπαῦσαι βούλομαι
   ἁπαξαπάσας. Βλ. ἵνα τί; Πρ. δῆλον τουτογί·

707-8 Ath. 77 d   707-9 § S δ 296

---

697 ἑτέρα Μυι[ac]   700 πότερον Γ   702a εὐπρεπέσιν δ' Bentley :
δ' εὐπρεπέσιν a   702b μειρακίοισι Ρ[ac]Γ   703 ἐροῦσι Γ   θεὸς Γ
706 ἐψίφισται Μυι   πρὸ͂ Γ   κινεῖν Γ   707 λαβούσας Γ
709 ἐν τοῖς] ἐντὸς R₁   710 in. Πρ. R   νυν incertum quis primus :
νῦν a   ἀρέσκειν Λ   Βλ.] dic. R : om. Γ   711 Πρ.] par. R : om. Γ
ἄρ' ΓΛ   714 ἀνάγκην Γ   716 εὐωχεῖσθε R   τήμερον Brunck :
σή- a   717 Βλ. om. RΓ   εὐοήχησόμεθα Γ   Πρ.] dic. RΓ
719 Βλ.] dic. R : Βλ. Χρ. Μυι : om. Γ   Πρ.] dic. RΓ   τουτογί Bentley :
τουτοτί R : τοῦτο τι ΓΛ

ἵνα τῶν νέων ἔχωσιν αὗται τὰς ἀκμάς.   720
καὶ τάς γε δούλας οὐχὶ δεῖ κοσμουμένας
τὴν τῶν ἐλευθέρων ὑφαρπάζειν Κύπριν,
ἀλλὰ παρὰ τοῖς δούλοισι κοιμᾶσθαι μόνον,
κατωνάκην τὸν χοῖρον ἀποτετιλμένας.

Βλ.   φέρε νυν ἐγώ σοι παρακολουθῶ πλησίον,   725
ἵν᾽ ἀποβλέπωμαι καὶ λέγωσιν ἐμὲ ταδί,
"τὸν τῆς στρατηγοῦ τοῦτον οὐ θαυμάζετε;"

Χρ.   ἐγὼ δ᾽ ἵν᾽ εἰς ἀγοράν γε τὰ σκεύη φέρω,
προχειριοῦμαι κἀξετάσω τὴν οὐσίαν.

χώρει σὺ δεῦρο, κιναχύρα, καλὴ καλῶς   730
τῶν χρημάτων θύραζε πρώτη τῶν ἐμῶν,
ὅπως ἂν ἐντετριμμένη κανηφορῇς,
πολλοὺς κάτω δὴ θυλάκους στρέψασ᾽ ἐμούς.
ποῦ ᾽σθ᾽ ἡ διφροφόρος; ἡ χύτρα, δεῦρ᾽ ἔξιθι·
νὴ Δία μέλαινά γ᾽· οὐδ᾽ ἂν εἰ τὸ φάρμακον   735
ἕψουσ᾽ ἔτυχες ᾧ Λυσικράτης μελαίνεται—
ἴστω παρ᾽ αὐτήν· δεῦρ᾽ ἴθ᾽, ἡ κομμώτρια.
φέρε δεῦρο ταύτην τὴν ὑδρίαν, ὑδριαφόρε,
ἐνταῦθα. σὺ δὲ δεῦρ᾽, ἡ κιθαρῳδός, ἔξιθι,

724 §§ S κ 1115; cf. Moerim 201. 6 [Bekker]   732-3 §§ S ε 1466
732 §§ Zonar. 751; cf. Phryn. PS 71. 15   735-6 (οὐδ᾽ . . .)
S § (1) λ 860; (οὐδ᾽ . . .) § (2) φ 103   737 §§ S ι 702   738 cf. Poll.
iii. 55, Phot. s.v. ὑδριαφόροι

720 ἔχωσι Γ   αὐταὶ Scaliger   721 in. par. R   724 κατωνάκην Dobree: -κη a: -κη S   725 Βλ.] ὁ ἀνὴρ R: Πρ. Γ   νυν
Bekker: νῦν a   παρακολουθῶν Γ   726 λέγωσιν ἐμὲ Willems: -σί
μοι RΓ: -σί με Λ   727 θαυμάζεται Λ (cf. 757)   728-869 Χρ.
Rogers   728 Χρ.] Πρ. Λ: om. RΓ   γε] τε Λ   729 προχειροῦμαι Γ
post h. v. χοροῦ R   730 in. αλλος ανηρ R: ἀνὴρ Λ   σὺ om. Γ
733 στρέψας Γ: -ασα ΛS   734 δεῦρο Γ   735 μέλαινά γ᾽· Jackson:
μέλαινά γ᾽ a   ὡς ἂν Halbertsma: οὐδὲν Jackson   εἰς Λ: εἰ Jackson
736 ἕψουσ᾽ om. S (2)   μελαίνεται— Ussher   737 ἴστω Γ   ἴθι κομ- S
κομμότρια Γ   738 φέρω Γ

πολλάκις ἀναστήσασά μ' εἰς ἐκκλησίαν 740
ἀωρὶ νύκτωρ διὰ τὸν ὄρθριον νόμον.
ὁ τὴν σκάφην λαβών, προῖτω· τὰ κηρία
κόμιζε, τοὺς θαλλοὺς καθίστη πλησίον,
καὶ τὼ τρίποδ' ἐξένεγκε καὶ τὴν λήκυθον.
τὰ χυτρίδι' ἤδη καὶ τὸν ὄχλον ἀφίετε. 745

Αν.   ἐγὼ καταθήσω τἀμά; κακοδαίμων ἄρα
ἀνὴρ ἔσομαι καὶ νοῦν ὀλίγον κεκτημένος.
μὰ τὸν Ποσειδῶ γ' οὐδέποτ', ἀλλὰ βασανιῶ
πρώτιστον αὐτὰ πολλάκις καὶ σκέψομαι.
οὐ γὰρ τὸν ἐμὸν ἱδρῶτα καὶ φειδωλίαν 750
οὐδὲν πρὸς ἔπος οὕτως ἀνοήτως ἐκβαλῶ,
πρὶν ἐκπύθωμαι πᾶν τὸ πρᾶγμ' ὅπως ἔχει.
οὗτος, τί τὰ σκευάρια ταυτὶ βούλεται;
πότερον μετοικιζόμενος ἐξενήνοχας
αὔτ' ἢ φέρεις ἐνέχυρα θήσων; Χρ. οὐδαμῶς. 755

Αν.   τί δῆτ' ἐπὶ στοίχου 'στὶν οὕτως; οὔ τι μὴν
Ἱέρωνι τῷ κήρυκι πομπὴν πέμπετε;

Χρ.   μὰ Δί' ἀλλ' ἀποφέρειν αὐτὰ μέλλω τῇ πόλει
ἐς τὴν ἀγορὰν κατὰ τοὺς δεδογμένους νόμους.

740-1 § S o 585   744 Poll. x. 80   751 S §§ (1) o 805;
(οὔ- . . .) §§ (2) o 975; cf. Greg. Cypr. iv. 72, Apostol. xiii. 15 b
752 §§ S o 805   756-7 (τί δή ποτε ἐπὶ . . .) Priscian. xviii. 258

741 ἄωρι νύκτωρ RS: ἀωρὶ νυκτῶν Γ: ἀωρινυκτῶν Λ   ὀρθοίον Rac (ut
vid.)   742 ὁ om. Γ   744 τῷ τρίδ' Λ   746-872 Αν. Rogers
746 Αν.] par. R₁: ἄλλος φειδωλὸς R₂Γ: ἀνὴρ φειδωλὸς Λ   748 -δῶ
οὐδέποτέ γ' Porson   751 οὕτως om. ΓΛ   752 ἐκπύθωμαι Λ
755 αὔτ' RΛ   Χρ.] dic. RΓ: ἀνὴρ Λ   756-84 Αν. et Χρ.] φειδωλὸς
(om. in 767) et ἀνὴρ Λ   756-60 Αν. et Χρ. om. RΓ   756 μὴν
Ussher: μὴ a: που Dobree   757 πέμπεται Λ (cf. 727)   758 ἀλλ'
ἀποφέρειν x: ἀλλὰ φέρειν (-λα R₁) a   759 δεδιδαγμένου ςΓ

Αν. μέλλεις ἀποφέρειν; Χρ. πάνυ γε. Αν. κακοδαίμων ἄρ'
εἶ, 760
νὴ τὸν Δία τὸν σωτῆρα. Χρ. πῶς; Αν. πῶς; ῥᾳδίως.

Χρ. τί δ'; οὐχὶ πειθαρχεῖν με τοῖς νόμοισι δεῖ;

Αν. ποίοισιν, ὦ δύστηνε; Χρ. τοῖς δεδογμένοις.

Αν. δεδογμένοισιν; ὡς ἀνόητος ἦσθ' ἄρα.

Χρ. ἀνόητος; Αν. οὐ γάρ; ἠλιθιώτατος μὲν οὖν 765
ἀπαξαπάντων. Χρ. ὅτι τὸ ταττόμενον ποιῶ;

Αν. τὸ ταττόμενον γὰρ δεῖ ποιεῖν τὸν σώφρονα;

Χρ. μάλιστα πάντων. Αν. τὸν μὲν οὖν ἀβέλτερον.

Χρ. σὺ δ' οὐ καταθεῖναι διανοεῖ; Αν. φυλάξομαι,
πρὶν ἄν γ' ἴδω τὸ πλῆθος ὅ τι βουλεύεται. 770

Χρ. τί γὰρ ἄλλο γ' ἢ φέρειν παρεσκευασμένοι
τὰ χρήματ' εἰσίν; Αν. ἀλλ' ἰδὼν ἐπειθόμην.

Χρ. λέγουσι γοῦν ἐν ταῖς ὁδοῖς. Αν. λέξουσι γάρ.

Χρ. καί φασιν οἴσειν ἀράμενοι. Αν. φήσουσι γάρ.

Χρ. ἀπολεῖς ἀπιστῶν πάντ'. Αν. ἀπιστήσουσι γάρ. 775

Χρ. ὁ Ζεύς σέ γ' ἐπιτρίψειεν. Αν. ἐπιτρίψουσι γάρ.
οἴσειν δοκεῖς τιν' ὅστις αὐτῶν νοῦν ἔχει;
οὐ γὰρ πάτριον τοῦτ' ἐστίν, ἀλλὰ λαμβάνειν

760–1 Χρ. et Αν.] dic. RΓ 761 πῶς ῥᾳ- RΓ 762 Χρ.] par. R :
om. Γ δ'; οὐχὶ Invernizi: δ' οὐ R : δ' οὐχὶ ΓΛ με om. Γ 763 Αν.]
par. R : om. Γ Χρ.] dic. RΓ 764 Αν. om. RΓ 765 Χρ.] par.
R : om. Γ Αν.] dic. RΓ 766 Χρ.] dic. RΓ ταττόμον Λ ποῶ
RΓ 767 Αν.] par. R : om. ΓΛ ποιεῖν χ : ποεῖν a : πο+εῖν Μυι
768 Χρ.] par. R : om. Γ Αν.] dic. RΓ 769 Χρ.] par. R : dic.
Γ οὐ] οὐδε R Αν.] dic. RΓ 770 πρίν γ' ἀν Γ βούλεται Γ
771–3 Χρ. om. RΓ Αν.] dic. RΓ 773 λέξουσι Ald. : λέγουσι a
774 Χρ. et Αν.] dic. R : om. Γ 775 Χρ.] dic. Γ: om. R πάντ'
Ald. : πάντα RΛ: om. Γ Αν.] dic. R : om. Γ 776 Χρ.] dic. R :
om. Γ Αν.] dic. RΓ 777 in. dic. et par. R τίν' ΓΛ φειδωλὸς
ante ὅστις Λ

ἡμᾶς μόνον δεῖ νὴ Δία· καὶ γὰρ οἱ θεοί.

γνώσει δ᾽ ἀπὸ τῶν χειρῶν γε τῶν ἀγαλμάτων·   780
ὅταν γὰρ εὐχώμεσθα διδόναι τἀγαθά,
ἔστηκεν ἐκτείνοντα τὴν χεῖρ᾽ ὑπτίαν,
οὐχ ὥς τι δώσοντ᾽ ἀλλ᾽ ὅπως τι λήψεται.

Χρ.   ὦ δαιμόνι᾽ ἀνδρῶν, ἔα με τῶν προὖργου τι δρᾶν.
ταυτὶ γάρ ἐστι συνδετέα. ποῦ μοῦσθ᾽ ἱμάς;   785

Αν.   ὄντως γὰρ οἴσεις; Χρ. ναὶ μὰ Δία, καὶ δὴ μὲν οὖν
τωδὶ ξυνάπτω τὼ τρίποδε. Αν. τῆς μωρίας,
τὸ μηδὲ περιμείναντα τοὺς ἄλλους ὅ τι
δράσουσιν εἶτα τηνικαῦτ᾽ ἤδη— Χρ. τί δρᾶν;

Αν.   ἐπαναμένειν, ἔπειτα διατρίβειν ἔτι.   790

Χρ.   ἵνα δὴ τί; Αν. σεισμὸς εἰ γένοιτο πολλάκις,
ἢ πῦρ ἀπότροπον, ἢ διᾴξειεν γαλῆ,
παύσαιντ᾽ ἂν ἐσφέροντες, ὦμβρόντητε σύ.

Χρ.   χαρίεντα γοῦν πάθοιμ᾽ ἄν, εἰ μὴ ᾽χοιμ᾽ ὅποι
ταῦτα καταθείην. Αν. μὴ γὰρ οὐ λάβοις ὅποι;   795
θάρρει, καταθήσεις, κἂν ἕνης ἔλθῃς. Χρ. τιή;

791-2 (σει- . . .) §§ S σ 1372   796-8 § S ε 1295

779 νὴ δί᾽ R : dic. νὴ δία Γ : φειδωλὸς νὴ δί᾽ Λ   οἱ x : om. a   780 γε Reiske: τε R : τε καὶ ΓΛ (-έ)   τῶν ἀγαλμάτων R : τἀγάλματα Γ : om. Λ   781 εὐχώμεθα ΓΛ   782 χεῖρας Γ   783 δώσοντες Γ   τι x : τί RΓ : τις Λ   784 Χρ.] ἀνὴρ ὁ θέλων καταθεῖναι ΛΣ^R : om. RΓ   ὦ] ὃ Γ   με ε om. Γ   τῶν προύγου Γ : τὸν προῦργου Λ   785 -δοτέα RΛ   ᾽μας Λ : ἤμας Λ : 786-852 Αν. et Χρ.] φειδωλὸς et ἀνὴρ (om. in 831) Λ   786 Αν. om. RΓ   Χρ. dic. RΓ   787 Αν.] dic. RΓ   788 παραμείναντα Γ   789 Χρ.] dic. RΓ   δρᾶς Λ   790 Αν.] par. R : om. Γ   791 Χρ.] par. R : om. Γ   Αν.] dic. Γ : om. R   γένηται Γ   792 διᾴξειεν Γ : δείξειεν Λ   793 ἂν] ἄρ᾽ R   ὦ ᾽μβρότητε Γ   794 Χρ. om. RΓ   πύθοιμ᾽ ΓΛ   μὴ ᾽χοιμ᾽ Bentley: μήχοιμ᾽ RΛ (μῆ-): μήχ᾽ οἴμ᾽ Γ   795 καταθείην Brunck: -θείμην a : -θοίμην x   Αν.] dic. RΓ   λάβῃς Heindorf   ὅποι; Glypheus: ὅποι a: -αι Mu1   796 χαρρ᾽ εἱ Γ   κατατεύξῃ S   Χρ.] dic. RΓ

Αν.   ἐγῷδα τούτους χειροτονοῦντας μὲν ταχύ,
ἅττ' ἂν δὲ δόξῃ ταῦτα πάλιν ἀρνουμένους.

Χρ.   οἴσουσιν, ὦ τᾶν. Αν. ἢν δὲ μὴ κομίσωσι, τί;

Χρ.   ἀμέλει, κομιοῦσιν. Αν. ἢν δὲ μὴ κομίσωσι, τί;   800

Χρ.   μαχούμεθ' αὐτοῖς. Αν. ἢν δὲ κρείττους ὦσι, τί;

Χρ.   ἄπειμ' ἐάσας. Αν. ἢν δὲ πωλῶσ' αὐτά, τί;

Χρ.   διαρραγείης. Αν. ἢν διαρραγῶ δέ, τί;

Χρ.   καλῶς ποιήσεις. Αν. σὺ δ' ἐπιθυμήσεις φέρειν;

Χρ.   ἔγωγε· καὶ γὰρ τοὺς ἐμαυτοῦ γείτονας   805
ὁρῶ φέροντας. Αν. πάνυ γ' ἂν οὖν Ἀντισθένης
αὕτ' εἰσενέγκοι· πολὺ γὰρ ἐμμελέστερον
πρότερον χέσαι πλεῖν ἢ τριάκονθ' ἡμέρας.

Χρ.   οἴμωζε. Αν. Καλλίμαχος δ' ὁ χοροδιδάσκαλος
αὐτοῖσιν εἰσοίσει τι; Χρ. πλείω Καλλίου.   810

Αν.   ἄνθρωπος οὗτος ἀποβαλεῖ τὴν οὐσίαν.

Χρ.   δεινά γε λέγεις. Αν. τί δεινόν; ὥσπερ οὐχ ὁρῶν
ἀεὶ τοιαῦτα γιγνόμενα ψηφίσματα.
οὐκ οἶσθ' ἐκεῖν' οὔδοξε τὸ περὶ τῶν ἁλῶν;

807-8 (πο- . . .) § S π 1732

---

797 Αν.] dic. R : om. Γ   οἶδα γὰρ S   τούτοις Λ   ταχεῖς ΓΛ
798 ἅττ' R   δόξει R   σαῦτα Μυιᵃᶜ   799 Χρ. om. ΡΓ   Αν.]
dic. ΡΓ   800 Χρ.] par. R   Αν.] dic. R   800 ἢν . . . 801
αὐτοῖς om. Γ   801 Χρ. om. R   μαχούμεθα τοῖς Λ   Αν.] dic. R :
om. Γ   802 om. Γ   Χρ.] par. R   ἄπει μ' ἐάσας Μυι (ut vid.)
Αν.] dic. R   803 Χρ.] par. R : om. Γ   Αν.] dic. ΡΓ   804 Χρ.]
par. R : om. Γ   ποήσεις R   Αν.] dic. ΡΓ   805 Χρ.] par. R : om. Γ
806 Αν.] dic. R : om. Γ   808 πλεῖς Γ   809 Χρ.] par. ΡΓ   Αν.
om. ΡΓ   810 τί ΡΛ   Χρ.] dic. R : om. Γ   πλεῖον Γᵖᶜ   κάλλιον Γ
811 Αν. om. ΡΓ   ἄνθρωπος Dindorf: ὤν- a   812 Χρ. om. ΡΓ
δεινά γε] δεινὸν Cobet   Αν.] dic. ΡΓ   813 αἰεὶ ΓΛ   γινόμενα ΓΛ
814 ἐκεῖνα Γ   οὔδοξε Λ

50   ΕΚΚΛΗΣΙΑΖΟΥΣΑΙ

Χρ   ἔγωγε. Ἀν. τοὺς χαλκοῦς δ' ἐκείνους ἡνίκα   815
      ἐψηφισάμεθ', οὐκ οἶσθα; Χρ. καὶ κακόν γέ μοι
      τὸ κόμμ' ἐγένετ' ἐκεῖνο. πωλῶν γὰρ βότρυς
      μεστὴν ἀπῆρα τὴν γνάθον χαλκῶν ἔχων,
      κἄπειτ' ἐχώρουν εἰς ἀγορὰν ἐπ' ἄλφιτα.
      ἔπειθ' ὑπέχοντος ἄρτι μου τὸν θύλακον,   820
      ἀνέκραγ' ὁ κῆρυξ μὴ δέχεσθαι μηδένα
      χαλκοῦν τὸ λοιπόν· "ἀργύρῳ γὰρ χρώμεθα."

Ἀν.   τὸ δ' ἔναγχος οὐχ ἅπαντες ἡμεῖς ὤμνυμεν
      τάλαντ' ἔσεσθαι πεντακόσια τῇ πόλει
      τῆς τετταρακοστῆς, ἣν ἐπόρισ' Εὐριπίδης;   825
      κεὐθὺς κατεχρύσου πᾶς ἀνὴρ Εὐριπίδην.
      ὅτε δὴ δ' ἀνασκοπουμένοις ἐφαίνετο
      ὁ Διὸς Κόρινθος καὶ τὸ πρᾶγμ' οὐκ ἤρκεσεν,
      πάλιν κατεπίττου πᾶς ἀνὴρ Εὐριπίδην.

Χρ.   οὐ ταὐτόν, ὦ τᾶν. τότε μὲν ἡμεῖς ἤρχομεν,   830
      νῦν δ' αἱ γυναῖκες. Ἀν. ἃς ἐγὼ φυλάξομαι,
      νὴ τὸν Ποσειδῶ, μὴ κατουρήσωσί μου.

Χρ.   οὐκ οἶδ' ὅ τι ληρεῖς. φέρε σὺ τἀνάφορον, ὁ παῖς.

818 Poll. ix. 92; cf. Phryn. PS 7. 10, Phot. B 155. 2   819–20 § S
v 406   821–2 Poll. ix. 93; § S v 406   833 (φε-...) § S a 2126;
(φε- ...) Zonar. 189; cf. Lex. Vind. a 62

815 Χρ. om. ΡΓ   Ἀν.] dic. ΡΓ   816 ἐψηφισάμεθ' x : -μεσθ'
ΡΛ : -μεθα Γ   Χρ.] dic. ΡΓ   818 ἀπῆιρα Ρ   γλιάθον Λ
χακῶν Γ   820 ἔπειτ' Γ   μου ἄρτι S   821 ἀνέκα' γ' Ρac:
ἐνέκραγε Γ   ὁ om. Γ   822 χαλκὸν Pollux   823 Ἀν. om. ΡΓ
825 τετταρακοστῆς Brunck : τεσσαρα- (-σε- R) a   εὐπόρισ' ΓΛ
826 κεὐθὺς Kuster : καὐθὺς a   εὐριπίδης Λ   827 δ'] θ' R
ἐμφαίνεται Γ   829 κατεπίπτου ΓΛ   830 Χρ. om. ΡΓ   οὐ
ταὐτόν x : οὐτ' αὐτὸν R : οὐ ταυτὸν ΓΛ   831 Ἀν.] dic. R : om. ΓΛ
ἅς γ' ἐγὼ ΓΛ   832 κατουρήσωσί x : -σουσί a   833 Χρ.] dic.
R : om. Γ   τἀνόφορον Γ : τἀνάφαρον Λ

ΚΗΡΥΞ

ὦ πάντες ἀστοί, νῦν γὰρ οὕτω ταῦτ' ἔχει,
χωρεῖτ', ἐπείγεσθ' εὐθὺ τῆς στρατηγίδος,   835
ὅπως ἂν ὑμῖν ἡ τύχη κληρουμένοις
φράσῃ καθ' ἕκαστον ἄνδρ' ὅποι δειπνήσετε.
ὡς αἱ τράπεζαί γ' εἰσὶν ἐπινενησμέναι
ἀγαθῶν ἁπάντων καὶ παρεσκευασμέναι,
κλῖναί τε σισυρῶν καὶ δαπίδων νενησμέναι·   840
κρατῆρας ἐγκιρνᾶσιν, αἱ μυροπώλιδες
ἑστᾶσ' ἐφεξῆς· τὰ τεμάχη ῥιπίζεται,
λαγῷ' ἀναπηγνύασι, πόπανα πέττεται,
στέφανοι πλέκονται, φρύγεται τραγήματα·
χύτρας ἔτνους ἕψουσιν αἱ νεώταται,   845
Σμοῖος δ' ἐν αὐταῖς ἱππικὴν στολὴν ἔχων
τὰ τῶν γυναικῶν διακαθαίρει τρύβλια.
Γέρων δὲ χωρεῖ χλανίδα καὶ κονίποδα
ἔχων, καχάζων μεθ' ἑτέρου νεανίου,
ἐμβὰς δὲ κεῖται καὶ τρίβων ἐρριμμένος.   850
πρὸς ταῦτα χωρεῖθ', ὡς ὁ τὴν μᾶζαν φέρων
ἕστηκεν· ἀλλὰ τὰς γνάθους διοίγνυτε.

Αν.   οὐκοῦν βαδιοῦμαι δῆτα. τί γὰρ ἕστηκ' ἔχων
ἐνταῦθ', ἐπειδὴ ταῦτα τῇ πόλει δοκεῖ;

Χρ.   καὶ ποῖ βαδιεῖ σὺ μὴ καταθεὶς τὴν οὐσίαν;   855

838–9 §§ † Phryn. PS 21. 6; (αἱ . . .) § S ε 2483; § Zonar. 840
842 (τὰ . . .) § S ρ 181   843 Ath. 110 a   846–7 §§ S σ 748
853 cf. Phryn. PS 54. 9

834 Κῆρυξ om. Γ   835 εὐθὺς Λ^{ac}   836 ὑμῖν Le Febvre:
ἡμῖν a   εἰ τύχοι R   837 φράσει R   καθέκαστον ΡΓΛ^{pc}
838 ἐπινενησμέναι Brunck : -νασ- aS   840 νενησμέναι Brunck : -νασ- a
841 κρατῆρας ἐγκιρνᾶσιν Dawes : κρατῆρα συγ- R (συν-R^{ac}) : κρατῖνα συγ-
ΓΛ   842 ἑστῶσ' Λ   843 λαγῷ' Ald. : λαγῷ R : λαγὼ Γ : λαχῷ' Λ
844 φρύγονται ΓΛ   τρυγήματα Λ   845 ἕψουσιν ΡΓ   846 Σμοῖος
Brunck : σμοιὸς ΡΛ(-οῖ-) : σμυὸς Γ   848 κονίποδε Dindorf   849 νεα-
νίδου Γ   850 ἐριμμένος ΡΛ   852 διοίγνετε Ρ^{ac}ΓΛ : διοίγετε Σ^R
853–72 Αν. et Χρ. Rogers : ὁ μὴ καταθεὶς et κῆρυξ Λ   853–5 Αν. et
Χρ.] par. R : om. Γ   853 οὔκουν Γ   855 καὶ ποιεῖ σὺ R₁

Αν.   ἐπὶ δεῖπνον. Χρ. οὐ δῆτ᾽, ἤν γ᾽ ἐκείναις νοῦς ἐνῇ,
      πρίν γ᾽ ἂν ἀπενέγκῃς. Αν. ἀλλ᾽ ἀποίσω. Χρ. πηνίκα;

Αν.   οὐ τοὐμόν, ὦ τᾶν, ἐμποδὼν ἔσται. Χρ. τί δή;

Αν.   ἑτέρους ἀποίσειν φήμ᾽ ἔθ᾽ ὑστέρους ἐμοῦ.

Χρ.   βαδιεῖ δὲ δειπνήσων ὅμως; Αν. τί γὰρ πάθω;   860
      τὰ δυνατὰ γὰρ δεῖ τῇ πόλει ξυλλαμβάνειν
      τοὺς εὖ φρονοῦντας. Χρ. ἢν δὲ κωλύσωσι, τί;

Αν.   ὁμόσ᾽ εἶμι κύψας. Χρ. ἢν δὲ μαστιγῶσι, τί;

Αν.   καλούμεθ᾽ αὐτάς. Χρ. ἢν δὲ καταγελῶσι, τί;

Αν.   ἐπὶ ταῖς θύραις ἕστως— Χρ. τί δράσεις; εἰπέ μοι.   865

Αν.   τῶν ἐσφερόντων ἁρπάσομαι τὰ σιτία.

Χρ.   βάδιζε τοίνυν ὕστερος· σὺ δ᾽, ὦ Σίκων
      καὶ Παρμένων αἴρεσθε τὴν παμπησίαν.

Αν.   φέρε νυν ἐγώ σοι ξυμφέρω. Χρ. μὴ μηδαμῶς.
      δέδοικα γὰρ μὴ καὶ παρὰ τῇ στρατηγίδι,   870
      ὅταν κατατιθῶ, προσποιῇ τῶν χρημάτων.

Αν.   νὴ τὸν Δία, δεῖ γοῦν μηχανήματός τινος,
      ὅπως τὰ μὲν ὄντα χρήμαθ᾽ ἕξω, τοῖσδέ τε

867-8 (σὺ...) §§ S π 129   868 παμ- Poll. x. 12   869 (... -ρω)
§§ S ξ 109

856 Αν.] par. R : om. Γ   Χρ.] dic. Γ: om. R   857 πρίν γ᾽ ἂν x :
πρίν γ᾽ a : πρὶν ἂν γ᾽ Porson   ἀπὸ νίκης Γ: ἀπενείκης Λ   Αν. et
Χρ.] dic. RΓ   ὁπηνίκα ΓΛ   858 Αν. om. RΓ   ἐμποδὼν x :
-δῶν a   Χρ.] dic. RΓ   859 Αν. om. RΓ   εἰθ᾽ R   860 Χρ.]
par. R : dic. Γ   ὅπως Λ   Αν.] dic. RΓ   861 ξυλαμ- Λ   862 Χρ.]
dic. RΓ   κωλύωσι x   863 Αν. om. RΓ   Χρ.] dic. RΓ   μαστιγώσῃ Γ
864 Αν.] par. R : dic. Γ   καλούμεθα Γ   Χρ.] dic. RΓ   865 Αν.]
par. R : om. Γ   Χρ.] dic. RΓ   866 Αν.] par. R : dic. Γ   εἰσφερόντων Γ
σιτα Γ   867 Χρ.] par. R : ὁ καταθείς Σ^R : om. Γ   868 Παρμένων]
Ξενόφαντες S   πομπησίαν Γ   869 Αν. om. RΓ   νυν Bekker : νῦν a
Χρ.] dic. RΓ   μὴ] σὺ x : om. Γ   872 Αν. om. RΓ   δεῖ] δὴ R^ac
873 μένοντα R   τοῖσδέ τε Ussher : τοῖσδέ γε RΓ : τοῖς δέ γε Λ : τοισδεδὶ
Bergk

τῶν ματτομένων κοινῇ μεθέξω πως ἐγώ.
ὀρθῶς, ἔμοιγε φαίνεται· βαδιστέον 875
ὁμόσ' ἐστὶ δειπνήσοντα κοὐ μελλητέον.

ΓΡΑΥΣ Α

τί ποθ' ἄνδρες οὐχ ἥκουσιν; ὥρα δ' ἦν πάλαι.
ἐγὼ δὲ καταπεπλασμένη ψιμυθίῳ
ἕστηκα καὶ κροκωτὸν ἠμφιεσμένη
ἀργός, μινυρομένη τι πρὸς ἐμαυτὴν μέλος, 880
παίζουσ' ὅπως ἂν περιλάβοιμ' αὐτῶν τινὰ
παριόντα. Μοῦσαι, δεῦρ' ἴτ' ἐπὶ τοὐμὸν στόμα,
μελύδριον εὑροῦσαί τι τῶν Ἰωνικῶν.

ΝΕΑΝΙΣ

νῦν μέν με παρακύψασα προὔφθης, ὦ σαπρά.
ᾤου δ' ἐρήμας οὐ παρούσης ἐνθάδε 885
ἐμοῦ τρυγήσειν καὶ προσάξεσθαί τινα
ᾄδουσ'· ἐγὼ δ' ἢν τοῦτο δρᾷς ἀντᾴσομαι.
κεἰ γὰρ δι' ὄχλου τοῦτ' ἐστὶ τοῖς θεωμένοις,
ὅμως ἔχει τερπνόν τι καὶ κωμῳδικόν.

Γρ.ᵃ τούτῳ διαλέγου κἀποχώρησον· σὺ δέ, 890
φιλοττάριον αὐλητά, τοὺς αὐλοὺς λαβὼν
ἄξιον ἐμοῦ καὶ σοῦ προσαύλησον μέλος.

882-3 (δεῦ-...) § S μ 543   888-9 § S δ 1220

---

874 πῶς RΓ   876 ὁ 'μός Γ   δειπνήσωντα Rᵃᶜ   μελητέον RΛ
post h. v. χοροῦ R (cf. 729)   877-918 Γρ. A Brunck   877 Γρ.ᵃ]
γραῦς a   ἄνδρες Dindorf: ἄν- a   ἥκουσιν Brunck: ἥξουσι(ν) a
878 ψιμυθίων Γ   880 τι Ald.: τί a   881 παίζουσ' ὅμως Γ:
παίζουσα. πῶς Dobree   παραλάβοιμ' Γ   882 ἴτε Γ   στέμμα S
883 μελίδρυον Γ   τί RΓ   884-911 Νεᾶνις Tyrwhitt: ἀλλ(η) νέα
RΛ: om. Γ   885 δὲ ῥήμας Γ   886 προσάξασθαι Γ
887 ἄδουσα Γ   δ'] δὲ Γ   δρᾷς ἀντάσομαι Port: δράσαντ' αἴσομαι R:
δράσαντ' ἄσομαι ΓΛ   888 γὰρ om. S   διόχλου RΛ   τοῦτό Γ
889 τι τερπνόν S   890 Γρ.ᵃ] par. R: γρᾶ Λ: γραῦς Mui: om. Γ
κἀπιχώρησον ΓΛ   891 αὐλούς] αὐλητὰς Γ

εἴ τις ἀγαθὸν βούλεται πα-
θεῖν τι, παρ' ἐμοὶ χρὴ καθεύδειν.
οὐ γὰρ ἐν νέαις τὸ σοφὸν ἔν-   895
εστιν, ἀλλ' ἐν ταῖς πεπείροις.
οὐδέ τοι στέργειν ἂν ἐθέλοι
μᾶλλον ἢ 'γὼ τὸν φίλον ᾧπερ ξυνείην,
ἀλλ' ἐφ' ἕτερον ἂν πέτοιτο.

Νε^{ιs}.   μὴ φθόνει ταῖσιν νέαισι·   900
τὸ τρυφερὸν γὰρ ἐμπέφυκε
τοῖς ἁπαλοῖσι μηροῖς,
κἀπὶ τοῖς μήλοις ἐπαν-
θεῖ· σὺ δ', ὦ γραῦ, παραλέλεξαι κἀντέτριψαι
τῷ θανάτῳ μέλημα.   905

Γρ.^α   ἐκπέσοι σου τὸ τρῆμα
τό τ' ἐπίκλιντρον ἀποβάλοις
βουλομένη σποδεῖσθαι.
κἀπὶ τῆς κλίνης ὄφιν προσελκύσαιο
βουλομένη φιλῆσαι.   910

Νε^{ιs}.   αἰαῖ, τί ποτε πείσομαι;
οὐχ ἥκει μοὐταῖρος
μόνη δ' αὐτοῦ λείπομ'· ἡ
γάρ μοι μήτηρ ἄλλῃ βέβηκεν.

895-8 (. . . φίλον) § S π 997   904 cf. Phot. s.v. παραλέγειν
907 §§ S ε 2392 (τοῦτ' . . . -βάλλον); §§ Zonar. 811; cf. Poll. vi. 9

893 in. ᾄδει η γραυς mg R₂: γραῦς Γ: ἡ γραῦς ᾄδει Λ   894 τί R
χρὴ καθεύδειν om. Γ   895 ἔν ἐστιν ΓΛ   896 πεπείροις S: -ραις
R: ἐμπείροις Γ: πεπείροισι Λ   897 τοι] τις x   898 ἡ νέα ante
ᾧπερ Λ   899 ἀφ' ἕτερον Γ   πέποτο Γ   900 Νε^{ιs}.] par. R:
ἀντᾴδει ἡ νέα τῇ γραΐ Σ^R   ταῖσι ΓΛ   902 ἁπαλοῖσι R: ἁπαλοῖς ΓΛ
μηρίοις RΛ   906 Γρ.^α] par. R: γραῦς ΓΛ   907 ἀποβάλοιο
Bothe   908 βολομένη Λ   909 ὄφιν Wilamowitz: ὄφιν εὔροις καὶ
R: ὄφιν εὔροις ΓΛ   προσελκύσαι Γ   910 βολομένη Λ   911 Νε^{ιs}.]
ἡ νεα RΓ (-έ-): om. Λ   αἰαῖ Dindorf: αῖ αῖ R: αῖ αῖ ΓΛ   πειράσομαι Γ
912 μοὐταῖρος Reiske: μ' ουτ' αῖρος R: μου τοὔρος ΓΛ   913 βέβηκε R

καὶ τἄλλα ⟨μ'⟩ οὐδὲν ⟨τὰ⟩ μετὰ ταῦτα δεῖ λέγειν.
ἀλλ', ὦ μαῖ', ἱκετεύομαι, κά-   915
λει τὸν Ὀρθαγόραν, ὅπως
σαυτῆς ⟨ἂν⟩ κατόναι' ἀντιβολῶ σε.

*Γρ.*ᵃ   ἤδη τὸν ἀπ' Ἰωνίας
τρόπον, τάλαινα, κνησιᾷς.
δοκεῖς δέ μοι καὶ λάβδα κατὰ τοὺς Λεσβίους.   920
ἀλλ' οὐκ ἄν ποθ' ὑφαρπάσαιο
τἀμὰ παίγνια· τὴν δ' ἐμὴν
ὥραν οὐκ ἀπολεῖς οὐδ' ἀπολήψει.

Νεˡˢ.   ᾆδ' ὁπόσα βούλει καὶ παράκυφθ' ὥσπερ γαλῆ.

*Γρ.*ᵃ   οὐδεὶς γὰρ ὡς σὲ πρότερον εἴσεισ' ἀντ' ἐμοῦ.   925

Νεˡˢ.   οὔκουν ἐπ' ἐκφοράν γε· καινόν γ', ὦ σαπρά.

*Γρ.*ᵃ   οὐ δῆτα. *Νεˡˢ.* τί γὰρ ἂν γραῖ καινά τις λέγοι;

*Γρ.*ᵃ   οὐ τοὐμὸν ὀδυνήσει σε γῆρας. *Νεˡˢ.* ἀλλὰ τί;
ἤγχουσα μᾶλλον καὶ τὸ σὸν ψιμύθιον;

*Γρ.*ᵃ   τί μοι διαλέγει; *Νεˡˢ.* σὺ δὲ τί διακύπτεις; *Γρ.*ᵃ ἐγώ;
ᾄδω πρὸς ἐμαυτὴν Ἐπιγένει τὠμῷ φίλῳ.   931

Νεˡˢ.   σοὶ γὰρ φίλος τίς ἐστιν ἄλλος ἢ Γέρης;

928–9 §§ † S a 416; §§ † Zonar. 29   932 § S γ 197

914 τἄλλ' ⟨μ'⟩ οὐδὲν Dobree: τἆλλ' οὐδὲν (τἆλλ' Λ) **a**   ⟨τὰ⟩ μετὰ
ταῦτα Dobree: μετὰ ταῦτα RΓ: με ταῦτα Λ   δεῖ λέγειν om. Γ
917 ⟨ἂν⟩ κατόναι' Hermann: κατόναι' (-αι Γ) **a**   918 *Γρ.*ᵃ] ἡ γραῦς
R: γραῦς Γ: om. Λ   ἀπὸ ΓΛ   920 καὶ] κἂν Blaydes   λάμβδα
R: λαύδα Γ: λαβδᾶν Agar   924 *Νεˡˢ.* Brunck: par. et ἡ νεα R:
om. ΓΛ   παράκυφθ' Γ: -κυφρ' Λ   ὥσπερ] ὡς Γ   925 *Γρ.*ᵃ
Ussher: om. **a**   926 *Νεˡˢ.* Bentley: dic. Λ: om. RΓ   ante καινόν
par. R: dic. ΓΛ   γ' om. Γ   927 *Γρ.*ᵃ et *Νεˡˢ.* Brunck
*Γρ.*ᵃ] par. R: om. ΓΛ   *Νεˡˢ.*] dic. R: om. ΓΛ   γραῖ Bekker: γραῖ
R: γρᾶ ΓΛ   928 *Γρ.*ᵃ Brunck: par. R: om. ΓΛ   γέρας Γ
Νεˡˢ. Brunck: dic. **a**   929 in. par. R   ἤγχουσα Bentley: ἤγ- RΛ:
ηὔ- Γ   μᾶλλον bis Λ   ψιμμύθιον Λ   930 *Γρ.*ᵃ Bentley: par. R:
om. ΓΛ   *Νεˡˢ.* et *Γρ.*ᵃ Bentley: dic. **a**   931 ἐπὶ γένει ΓΛ
932 *Νεˡˢ.* Brunck: par. R: om. ΓΛ   σοὶ] σὺ R   γὰρ] δὲ S

*Γρ.*ᵃ   δείξει γε καὶ σοί. τάχα γὰρ εἶσιν ὡς ἐμέ.

*Νε*ⁱˢ.   ὁδὶ γὰρ αὐτός ἐστιν. *Γρ.*ᵃ οὐ σοῦ γ᾽, ὦλεθρε,
      δεόμενος οὐδέν. *Νε*ⁱˢ. νὴ Δί᾽, ὦ φθίνυλλα σύ,   935
      δείξει τάχ᾽ αὐτός, ὡς ἔγωγ᾽ ἀπέρχομαι.

*Γρ.*ᵃ   κἄγωγ᾽, ἵνα γνῷς ὡς πολύ σου μεῖζον φρονῶ.

ΝΕΑΝΙΑΣ

      εἴθ᾽ ἐξῆν παρὰ τῇ νέᾳ καθεύδειν,
      καὶ μὴ ᾽δει πρότερον διασποδῆσαι
      ἀνάσιμον ἢ πρεσβυτέραν·   940
      οὐ γὰρ ἀνασχετὸν τοῦτό γ᾽ ἐλευθέρῳ.

*Γρ.*ᵃ   οἰμώζων ἄρα, νὴ Δία, σποδήσεις.
      οὐ γὰρ τἀπὶ Χαριξένης τάδ᾽ ἐστίν.
      κατὰ τὸν νόμον ταῦτα ποιεῖν
      ἔστι δίκαιον, εἰ δημοκρατούμεθα.   945

      ἀλλ᾽ εἶμι τηρήσουσ᾽ ὅ τι καὶ δράσεις ποτέ.

*Νε*ᵃˢ.   εἴθ᾽, ὦ θεοί, λάβοιμι τὴν καλὴν μόνην,
      ἐφ᾽ ἣν πεπωκὼς ἔρχομαι πάλαι ποθῶν.

*Νε*ⁱˢ.   ἐξηπάτησα τὸ κατάρατον γρᾴδιον.

939–41 §§ S a 2067   943 § S χ 116; (τἀπὶ . . .) Eust. 326. 45;
(τὰ . . . -νης) §§ *EM* 367. 26

933 *Γρ.*ᵃ Brunck: dic. *ΓΛ*: om. R   δείξει Ald.: δόξει R*Γ*: δόξῃ *Λ*
εἰσὶν R   934 *Νε*ⁱˢ. Ussher: *Γρ.*ᵃ cont. **a**   *Γρ.*ᵃ Bergk: dic. R:
om. *ΓΛ*   935 *Νε*ⁱˢ. Bergk: dic. R₁: ἡ νεωτέρᾳ mg R₂: νέα *Γ*:
om. *Λ*   936 ante ὡς dic. R   938–60 *Νεανίας* Brunck
938 *Νε*ᵃˢ.] νεος τίς R: dic. *Λ*: om. *Γ*   ἐξῆν *Λ*   939 μὴ ᾽δει
Elmsley: μηδὲν **aS**   ἀνασποδῆσαι S   940 πρεσβυτέραν Bothe:
-ρον **aS**   942 *Γρ.*ᵃ Bergk: ἡ γραῦς R: dic. *Λ*: om. *Γ*   ἄρα R
943 τάδε γ᾽ ἐστί S   944 ποιεῖν R   946 εἶμι] εἰ μὴ *Γ*   δράσοι
Γ: δράσει Brunck   947 *Νε*ᵃˢ. Brunck: ἄλλος ἀνὴρ R: ἀνὴρ *Γ*: dic. *Λ*
948 πεπτωκὼς *Γ*   ποθῶν πάλιν *Γ*   949 *Νε*ⁱˢ. Brunck: ὁ νέος R:
νέος *Γ*: om. *Λ*

φρούδη γάρ ἐστιν οἰομένη μ' ἔνδον μένειν.   950
ἀλλ' οὑτοσὶ γὰρ αὐτὸς οὗ 'μεμνήμεθα.

δεῦρο δή, δεῦρο δή,   952a
φίλον ἐμόν, δεῦρό μοι   952b
πρόσελθε καὶ ξύνευνέ μοι
τὴν εὐφρόνην ὅπως ἔσει.   954a
πάνυ γάρ τις ἔρως με δονεῖ   954b
τῶνδε τῶν σῶν βοστρύχων.   955
ἄτοπος δ' ἔγκειταί μοί τις πόθος,
ὅς με διακναίσας ἔχει.
μέθες, ἱκνοῦμαί σ', Ἔρως,
καὶ ποίησον τόνδ' ἐς εὐνὴν   959a
τὴν ἐμὴν ἱκέσθαι.   959b

Νε^{as}. δεῦρο δή, δεῦρο δή,   960
φίλον ⟨ἐμόν⟩, καὶ σύ μοι
καταδραμοῦσα τὴν θύραν
ἄνοιξον τήνδ'· εἰ δὲ μή, καταπεσὼν κείσομαι.
ἀλλ' ἐν τῷ σῷ βούλομαι κόλπῳ
πληκτίζεσθαι μετὰ τῆς σῆς πυγῆς.   965
Κύπρι, τί μ' ἐκμαίνεις ἐπὶ ταύτῃ;

952 (δεῦ-₂ . . . -μόν) §§ S φ 390   954b-5 S § (1) β 403; § (2) δ
1361   956-7 S § (1) a 4374; § (2) δ 586

---

950 μενεῖν Dindorf   951 Νε^{ιs}. Bentley: ἡ νέα R : νέα Γ: dic.
Λ 'μεμνήμεθα Brunck : μεμ- a   952b ἐμόν] ἐμοὶ Γ   953 ξύνευνέ
Bergk: -νός a   954b γὰρ ⟨δεινὸς⟩ Dindorf   ἔρως ⟨δεινός⟩ Coulon
955 τῶν σῶν om. S (1) et (2)   956 ἄτοπος δὲ πόθος τις (Dindorf)
μοὔγκειται (Blaydes) Wilamowitz   958 μάθες Γ   959a ποίησον
χ : πο- a   τόν δέ σ' εὔνην Γ   960 Νε^{as}. Brunck : ὁ νεος R : dic. ΓΛ
961 φίλον (ex 964) ⟨ἐμόν⟩ Wilamowitz   963 τήνδ' del. Blaydes
964 ἀλλ' Wilamowitz: φίλον (-λον; Λ) ἀλλ' a cf. 961   τῷ del. Wilamowitz βούλομ' ἐγὼ Wilamowitz   965 τῆς del. Bentley

μέθες, ἱκνοῦμαί σ᾽, Ἔρως,
καὶ ποίησον τήνδ᾽ ἐς εὐνὴν   968a
τὴν ἐμὴν ἱκέσθαι.   968b

καὶ ταῦτα μέντοι μετρίως πρὸς τὴν ἐμὴν ἀνάγκην
εἰρημέν᾽ ἐστίν. σὺ δέ μοι, φίλτατον, ὦ ἱκετεύω,   970
ἄνοιξον, ἀσπάζου με.
διά τοι σὲ πόνους ἔχω.
ὦ χρυσοδαίδαλτον ἐμὸν μέλημα, Κύπριδος ἔρνος,   973a
μέλιττα Μούσης, Χαρίτων θρέμμα, Τρυφῆς πρόσωπον,
ἄνοιξον, ἀσπάζου με.   974
διά τοι σὲ πόνους ἔχω.   975

Γρ.^α   οὗτος, τί κόπτεις; μῶν ἐμὲ ζητεῖς; *Νε*^{ας}. πόθεν;

Γρ.^α   καὶ τὴν θύραν γ᾽ ἤραττες. *Νε*^{ας}. ἀποθάνοιμ᾽ ἄρα.

Γρ.^α.   τοῦ δαὶ δεόμενος δᾷδ᾽ ἔχων ἐλήλυθας;

Νε^{ας}.   Ἀναφλύστιον ζητῶν τιν᾽ ἄνθρωπον. *Γρ.*^α τίνα;

Νε^{ας}.   οὐ τὸν Σεβῖνον, ὃν σὺ προσδοκᾷς ἴσως.   980

Γρ.^α   νὴ τὴν Ἀφροδίτην, ἤν τε βούλῃ γ᾽ ἤν τε μή.

971–2 § S a 4197   973a–4 (. . . -ξον) § S θ 520   973a S §
(2) δ 108   973b (χα- θρύμμα) S §§ (2) χ 127

968a τήνδ᾽ x : τῆνδ᾽ R : τήνδε Γ : τὴν Λ   969 in. Νε^{ις}. Hermann
μέντοι] μέν μοι ΓΛ   971 ἄνελθε κἀσπάζου Velsen   με x : τε **a**
973b θρύμμα RS   976–1045 Γρ.^α et Νε^{ας}. Brunck   976 Γρ.^α]
par. R₁: ἡ γραῦς ἐξελθοῦσα R₂: γραῦς Γ: dic. Λ   Νε^{ας}.] par. R:
νέος Γ: om. Λ   πόθεν;] πόθος Γ   977 Γρ.^α] dic. Λ: om. RΓ
θύρ + +αν R   Νε^{ας}.] dic. RΓ: om. Λ   978 Γρ.^α] par. R:
dic. Λ: om. Γ   τοῦ] ποῦ ΓΛ   δαὶ] δὲ Γ   979 Νε^{ας}.]
Λ: om. RΓ   τίν᾽ RΓ   ἀνθρώπων Λ^{ac}   Γρ.^α] dic. **a**   980 Νε^{ας}.]
dic. Λ: om. RΓ   οὐ τὸν] αὐτὸν ΓΛ   Σεβῖνον Bentley: σὲ βινοῦνθ᾽
R : σε κι- Γ: σε βινῶνθ᾽ Λ   981 Γρ.^α] dic. Λ: om. RΓ   βούλει
Γ

Νε^{as}. ἀλλ' οὐχὶ νυνὶ τὰς ὑπερεξηκοντέτεις
εἰσάγομεν, ἀλλ' εἰσαῦθις ἀναβεβλήμεθα.
τὰς ἐντὸς εἴκοσιν γὰρ ἐκδικάζομεν.

Γρ.^a ἐπὶ τῆς προτέρας ἀρχῆς γε ταῦτ' ἦν, ὦ γλύκων· 985
νυνὶ δὲ πρῶτον εἰσάγειν ἡμᾶς δοκεῖ.

Νε^{as}. τῷ βουλομένῳ γε κατὰ τὸν ἐν πεττοῖς νόμον.

Γρ.^a ἀλλ' οὐδὲ δειπνεῖς κατὰ τὸν ἐν πεττοῖς νόμον.

Νε^{as}. οὐκ οἶδ' ὅ τι λέγεις· τηνδεδί μοι κρουστέον.

Γρ.^a ὅταν γε κρούσῃς τὴν ἐμὴν πρῶτον θύραν. 990

Νε^{as}. ἀλλ' οὐχὶ νυνὶ κρησέραν αἰτούμεθα.

Γρ.^a οἶδ' ὅτι φιλοῦμαι· νῦν δὲ θαυμάζεις ὅτι
θύρασί μ' ηὗρες. ἀλλὰ πρόσαγε τὸ στόμα.

Νε^{as}. ἀλλ', ὦ μέλ' ὀρρωδῶ τὸν ἐραστήν σου. Γρ.^a τίνα;

Νε^{as}. τὸν τῶν γραφέων ἄριστον. Γρ.^a οὗτος δ' ἐστὶ τίς; 995

Νε^{as}. ὃς τοῖς νεκροῖσι ζωγραφεῖ τὰς ληκύθους.
ἀλλ' ἄπιθ', ὅπως μή σ' ἐπὶ θύραισιν ὄψεται.

Γρ.^a οἶδ', οἶδ' ὅ τι βούλει. Νε^{as}. καὶ γὰρ ἐγώ σε, νὴ Δία.

Γρ.^a μὰ τὴν Ἀφροδίτην, ἥ μ' ἔλαχε κληρουμένη,
μὴ 'γώ σ' ἀφήσω. Νε^{as}. παραφρονεῖς, ὦ γρᾴδιον. 1000

---

991 § S κ 2398; cf. Phot. s.v. κρησέρα   996 S §§ (1) γ 436; §
(2) λ 439

982-7 Νε^{as}.] dic. Λ : om. ΡΓ   982 ὑπὲρ (ὑπερ Mu1) ἐξηκοντέστεις Λ
985 Γρ.^a] dic. Λ : om. ΡΓ   γε om. ΓΛ   987 πεττοῖς x : πετοῖς Γ:
παιτοῖς ΡΛ   988 om. Γ   Γρ.^a] par. Ρ : dic. Λ   οὐδ' ἐδείπνεις Bentley
παιτοῖς ΡΛ   989 Νε^{as}.] par. Ρ : om. ΓΛ   990 Γρ.^a] dic. Λ :
om. ΡΓ   991 Νε^{as}.] par. Ρ : dic. Λ : om. Γ   νῦν Γ   992 Γρ.^a]
dic. Λ : om. ΡΓ   993 εὗρες (εὖ- Ρ) a   πρός γε ΓΛ   994 Νε^{as}.]
νέος ΡΓ : dic. Λ   μέλε' Λ   Γρ.^a] par. Ρ : dic. ΓΛ   995 Νε^{as}.]
par. Ρ : dic. Λ : om. Γ   Γρ.^a] dic. Λ : om. ΡΓ   996 Νε^{as}.] par.
Ρ : dic. Λ : om. Γ   998 Γρ.^a] dic. Λ : om. ΡΓ   Νε^{as}.] dic. a
999 Γρ.^a] dic. Λ : om. ΡΓ   1000 in. par. Ρ   μη 'γώσ Ρ   Νε^{as}.]
dic. ΓΛ : om. Ρ

Γρ.ᵃ   ληρεῖς· ἐγὼ δ' ἄξω σ' ἐπὶ τἀμὰ στρώματα.

Νεᵃˢ.   τί δῆτα κρεάγρας τοῖς κάδοις ὠνούμεθα,
        ἐξὸν καθέντα γρᾴδιον τοιουτονὶ
        ἐκ τῶν φρεάτων τοὺς κάδους ξυλλαμβάνειν;

Γρ.ᵃ   μὴ σκῶπτέ μ', ὦ τάλαν, ἀλλ' ἔπου δεῦρ' ὡς ἐμέ.   1005

Νεᵃˢ.   ἀλλ' οὐκ ἀνάγκη μοὐστίν, εἰ μὴ τῶν ἐμῶν
        τὴν πεντακοσιοστὴν κατέθηκας τῇ πόλει.

Γρ.ᵃ   νὴ τὴν Ἀφροδίτην, δεῖ γε μέντοι σ'· ὡς ἐγὼ
        τοῖς τηλικούτοις ξυγκαθεύδουσ' ἥδομαι.

Νεᵃˢ.   ἐγὼ δὲ ταῖς γε τηλικαύταις ἄχθομαι,   1010
        κοὐκ ἂν πιθοίμην οὐδέποτ'. Γρ.ᵃ ἀλλά, νὴ Δία,
        ἀναγκάσει τουτί σε. Νεᵃˢ. τοῦτο δ' ἐστὶ τί;

Γρ.ᵃ   ψήφισμα, καθ' ὅ σε δεῖ βαδίζειν ὡς ἐμέ.

Νεᵃˢ.   λέγ' αὐτὸ τί ποτε κἄστι. Γρ.ᵃ καὶ δή σοι λέγω.
        ἔδοξε ταῖς γυναιξίν, ἢν ἀνὴρ νέος   1015
        νέας ἐπιθυμῇ, μὴ σποδεῖν αὐτὴν πρὶν ἂν
        τὴν γραῦν προκρούσῃ πρῶτον. ἢν δὲ μὴ 'θέλῃ
        πρότερον προκρούειν, ἀλλ' ἐπιθυμῇ τῆς νέας,
        ταῖς πρεσβυτέραις γυναιξὶν ἔστω τὸν νέον
        ἕλκειν ἀνατεὶ λαβομένας τοῦ παττάλου.   1020

1002 Poll. x. 31   1002–4 S §§ (1) ε 1800; §§ (2) κ 2360

1001 Γρ.ᵃ] par. R: dic. Λ: om. Γ   1002 Νεᵃˢ.] par. R: dic.
ΓΛ   ὠνούμεθα Cobet: ὠνοίμεθ' ἂν RS (2): ὠνοίμεθα ἂν Γ: ὠνήμεθ'
ἂν Λ: ὠνούμεθ' ἂν S (1)   1004 συλλαμβάνειν Γ: ξυλαμβάνειν Λ
1005–8 Γρ.ᵃ et Νεᵃˢ.] par. R: dic. Λ: om. Γ   1006 οὐκ] οὐδ' R
εἰ] η R   ἐμῶν] ἐτῶν Tyrwhitt   1008 γε om. Λ   1010 Νεᵃˢ.] dic.
ΓΛ: om. R   δὲ] δέ γ' Rᵃᶜ   ἥδομαι ΓΛ   1011 πυθοίμην
οὐδέποτε Γ   Γρ.ᵃ] dic. ΓΛ: om. R   1012 Νεᵃˢ.] dic. a
1013 Γρ.ᵃ] dic. Λ: om. RΓ   καθ' ὅ χ: καθό (ὅ R) a   δεῖ om. Γ
1014 Νεᵃˢ.] dic. Λ: om. RΓ   κἄστι χ: κἄστιν R: κἄστι ΓΛ   Γρ.ᵃ]
dic. a   1016 ἐπιθυμεῖν Λ   1017 'θέλῃ Bachmann: θέλη R:
θελήσῃ ΓΛ   1018 προσκρούειν R   1019 ἔστω R   1020 ἀνατεὶ
Brunck: ἀνατί RΛ: ἀνὰ τι Γ

Νε^{as}.   οἴμοι, Προκρούστης τήμερον γενήσομαι.

Γρ.^a   τοῖς γὰρ νόμοις τοῖς ἡμετέροισι πειστέον.

Νε^{as}.   τί δ᾽ ἦν ἀφαιρῆταί μ᾽ ἀνὴρ τῶν δημοτῶν
         ἢ τῶν φίλων ἐλθών τις; Γρ.^a ἀλλ᾽ οὐ κύριος
         ὑπὲρ μέδιμνόν ἐστ᾽ ἀνὴρ οὐδεὶς ἔτι.   1025

Νε^{as}.   ἐξωμοσία δ᾽ οὐκ ἔστιν; Γρ.^a οὐ γὰρ δεῖ στροφῆς.

Νε^{as}.   ἀλλ᾽ ἔμπορος εἶναι σκήψομαι. Γρ.^a κλάων γε σύ.

Νε^{as}.   τί δῆτα χρὴ δρᾶν; Γρ.^a δεῦρ᾽ ἀκολουθεῖν ὡς ἐμέ.

Νε^{as}.   καὶ ταῦτ᾽ ἀνάγκη μουστί; Γρ.^a Διομήδειά γε.

Νε^{as}.   ὑποστόρεσαί νυν πρῶτα τῆς ὀριγάνου,   1030
         καὶ κλήμαθ᾽ ὑπόθου συγκλάσασα τέτταρα,
         καὶ ταινίωσαι καὶ παράθου τὰς ληκύθους,
         ὕδατός τε κατάθου τοὔστρακον πρὸ τῆς θύρας.

Γρ.^a   ἦ μὴν ἔτ᾽ ὠνήσει σὺ καὶ στεφάνην ἐμοί.

Νε^{as}.   νὴ τὸν Δί᾽, ἤνπερ ᾖ γέ που τῶν κηρίνων.   1035
         οἶμαι γὰρ ἔνδον διαπεσεῖσθαί σ᾽ αὐτίκα.

Νε^{is}.   ποῖ τοῦτον ἕλκεις; Γρ.^a τόνδ᾽ ἐμαυτῆς εἰσάγω.

1029 cf. ‡ Sch. Pl., R. 493 d, ‡ Zen. iii. 8   1030 ὁ- fem. Phryn.
PS 97. 18; cf. S o 599, EM 630. 48, An. Par. iv. 12, 31   1032 (καὶ₂
...) §§ S λ 439   1033 (καὶ παρά- ...) § S τ 838

1021–3 Νε^{as}. et Γρ.^a] dic. Λ: om. RΓ   1021 προσκρούστης R
σήμερον Γ   1022 ἡμετέροις Λ   πιστέον R   1023 ἀφαίρηται (sic)
μ᾽ ἀνὴρ RΛ: ἀνὴρ ἀφαίρηταί μ᾽ Γ: ἀφέρηται μ᾽ ἀνὴρ Mui   1024 ἐλθών
τις] ἐλθόντες Λ   Γρ.^a] dic. RΛ: om. Γ   1026 Νε^{as}.] dic. Λ: om. RΓ
ἐξωμοσίᾳ Γ   στροφῇ Γ   1027 Νε^{as}.] par. R: dic. Λ: om. Γ
Γρ.^a] dic. RΛ: om. Γ   κλάγε σύ Γ: κλάε σὺ Λ   1028 Νε^{as}.] par.
R: dic. Λ: om. Γ   τι R   Γρ.^a] par. R: dic. ΓΛ   1029 Νε^{as}.]
par. R: dic. Λ: om. Γ   μουστί χ: μούστι(ν) a   Γρ.^a] dic. RΛ: om. Γ
γε] τε Λ   1030 Νε^{as}.] dic. Λ: om. RΓ   ὑποστόρισαι Λ   νυν
Bekker: νῦν a   πρῶτον R   1031 συγκλάσα R₁   1033 πρό] πρὸς Γ
1034 Γρ.^a] dic. Λ: om. RΓ   ἤ] ἦ RΓ   στεφώνην Λ(Mui^{ac})   1035 Νε^{as}.]
par. R: dic. Λ: om. Γ   Γρ.^a]   ἦν περί ΓΛ   1037 Νε^{is}. Brunck: νέα R:
dic. Λ: om. Γ   Γρ.^a] par. R: dic. ΓΛ   τόνδ᾽ Ussher: τὸν a: εἰς
Meineke   εἰσάγων Γ

Νε^{ις}.   οὐ σωφρονοῦσά γ'· οὐ γὰρ ἡλικίαν ἔχει
       παρὰ σοὶ καθεύδειν τηλικοῦτος ὤν, ἐπεὶ
       μήτηρ ἂν αὐτῷ μᾶλλον εἴης ἢ γυνή.   1040
       ὥστ' εἰ καταστήσεσθε τοῦτον τὸν νόμον,
       τὴν γῆν ἅπασαν Οἰδιπόδων ἐμπλήσετε.

Γρ.^α   ὦ παμβδελυρά, φθονοῦσα τόνδε τὸν λόγον
       ἐξηῦρες· ἀλλ' ἐγώ σε τιμωρήσομαι.

Νε^{ας}. νὴ τὸν Δία τὸν σωτῆρα, κεχάρισαί γέ μοι,   1045
       ὦ γλυκύτατον, τὴν γραῦν ἀπαλλάξασά μου.
       ὥστ' ἀντὶ τούτων τῶν ἀγαθῶν εἰς ἑσπέραν
       μεγάλην ἀποδώσω καὶ παχεῖάν σοι χάριν.

ΓΡΑΥΣ Β
       αὕτη σύ, ποῖ παραβᾶσα τόνδε τὸν νόμον
       ἕλκεις, παρ' ἐμοὶ τῶν γραμμάτων εἰρηκότων   1050
       πρότερον καθεύδειν αὐτόν; Νε^{ας}. οἴμοι δείλαιος.
       πόθεν ἐξέκυψας, ὦ κάκιστ' ἀπολουμένη;
       τοῦτο γὰρ ἐκείνου τὸ κακὸν ἐξωλέστερον.

Γρ.^β   βάδιζε δεῦρο. Νε^{ας}. μηδαμῶς με περιίδῃς
       ἑλκόμενον ὑπὸ τῆσδ', ἀντιβολῶ σ'. Γρ.^β ἀλλ' οὐκ ἐγώ,
       ἀλλ' ὁ νόμος ἕλκει σ'. Νε^{ας}. οὐκ ἐμέ γ', ἀλλ Ἔμπουσά
          τις,   1056
       ἐξ αἵματος φλύκταιναν ἠμφιεσμένη.

1053 cf. Phryn. PS 72. 9

_____

1038 Νε^{ις}.Brunck:dic.Λ:om.RΓ   1040 ἄνom.R   1043 Γρ.^α]
dic. ΓΛ: om. R   λόγον Le Febvre: νόμον a   1044 ἐξηῦρες
incertum quis primus: -εῦ- a   1045 Νε^{ας}.] ὁ νέος R: νέος Γ: dic. Λ
1047 in. ἑτέρα γραῦς x   εἰς om. R^{ac}: ἐς Λ   1048 ταχεῖάν Γ
1049–65 Γρ. B Brunck   1049 Γρ.^β] ἑτέρα γραῦς R₂Γ: dic. Λ
αὕτη Γ   τονδὶ παραβᾶσα Bothe   1051 Νε^{ας}.] dic. RΛ: νέος Γ
1054 Γρ.^β] par. R : γραῦς Γ: dic. Λ   Νε^{ας}.] dic. RΛ: νέος Γ: ὁ νεώτερος
Σ^R   1055 τῆς ΓΛ   Γρ.^β] dic. a   1056 in. par. R   ἕλκει σ'
x : ἕλκεισ RΛ : ἕλκει σε Γ   Νε^{ας}.] dic. RΛ: om. Γ   1057 φίκταιναν Γ
ἠμφιεσμένην Λ

Γρ.^β ἕπου, μαλακίων, δεῦρ᾽ ἀνύσας καὶ μὴ λάλει.

Νε^{as}. ἴθι νυν ἔασον εἰς ἄφοδον πρώτιστά με
ἐλθόντα θαρρῆσαι πρὸς ἐμαυτόν· εἰ δὲ μή,   1060
αὐτοῦ τι δρῶντα πυρρὸν ὄψει μ᾽ αὐτίκα
ὑπὸ τοῦ δέους. *Γρ.*^β θάρρει, βάδιζ᾽. ἔνδον χεσεῖ.

Νε^{as}. δέδοικα κἀγὼ μὴ πλέον γ᾽ ἢ βούλομαι.
ἀλλ᾽ ἐγγυητάς σοι καταστήσω δύο
ἀξιόχρεως. *Γρ.*^β μή μοι καθίστη.

ΓΡΑΥΣ Γ   ποῖ σὺ ποῖ   1065
χωρεῖς μετὰ ταύτης; *Νε*^{as}. οὐκ ἔγωγ᾽, ἀλλ᾽ ἕλκομαι.
ἀτὰρ ἥτις εἶ γε, πόλλ᾽ ἀγαθὰ γένοιτό σοι,
ὅτι μ᾽ οὐ περιεῖδες ἐπιτριβέντ᾽. ὦ Ἡράκλεις,
ὦ Πᾶνες, ὦ Κορύβαντες, ὦ Διοσκόρω,
τοῦτ᾽ αὖ πολὺ τούτου τὸ κακὸν ἐξωλέστερον.   1070
ἀτὰρ τί τὸ πρᾶγμ᾽ ἔστ᾽, ἀντιβολῶ, τουτί ποτε;
πότερον πίθηκος ἀνάπλεως ψιμυθίου,
ἢ γραῦς ἀνεστηκυῖα παρὰ τῶν πλειόνων;

Γρ.^γ μὴ σκῶπτέ μ᾽, ἀλλὰ δεῦρ᾽ ἕπου. *Γρ.*^β δευρὶ μὲν οὖν.

Γρ.^γ ὡς οὐκ ἀφήσω σ᾽ οὐδέποτ᾽. *Γρ.*^β οὐδὲ μὴν ἐγώ.   1075

1072 cf. Clem. Al. *Paed.* iii. 5. 3   1073 §§ S π 1735

1058 *Γρ.*^β] dic. Λ: om. RΓ   μαλλακίων Λ   1059 *Νε*^{as}.] dic.
Λ: om. RΓ   νυν Bekker: νῦν a   ἐς ΓΛ   1060 θερρῆσαι R₁
1061 τι x: τί a   1062 *Γρ.*^β] dic. a   βάδιζε Γ   χεσοῖ ΓΛ
1063 *Νε*^{as}.] par. R: dic. Λ: om. Γ   γ᾽ om. ΓΛ   1064 δύω R^{ac}
1065 *Γρ.*^β] dic. a   *Γρ.* Γ Brunck: dic. R₁Λ: ἄλλη γραῦς τρίτη πρὸς
τὸν νεώτερον R₂: ἄλλη γραῦς Γ   1066 μετ᾽ αὐτῆς ΓΛ   *Νε*^{as}.] dic.
RΛ: νέος Γ   ἔγωγε Γ   1067 αὐτὰρ Γ   ἥτις x: εἴ τις (εἴτις R) a
γε] σὺ Cobet   πολλὰ᾽ 'γαθὰ Λ   1068 μ᾽ οὐ] μου Λ   ἐπιτριβέντα
ὦ Γ   1069 διὸς κόρω R: διοσκόρῳ Γ   1070 τοῦτο Γ   αὖ] ἂν
ΓΛ   1071 αὐτὰρ Γ   πρᾶγμα ἐστὶν Γ   τουτί τί ποτε Γ
1073 ᾖ] ἢ Γ   1074–97 *Γρ.*^γ et *Γρ.*^β Bergk   1074 *Γρ.*^γ] par. R:
dic. Λ: om. Γ   *Γρ.*^β] dic. a   1075 *Γρ.*^γ om. a   σ᾽ οὐδέποτε ΓΛ:
οὐδέποτέ σ᾽ Dindorf   *Γρ.*^β] dic. a

Νε^{ας}. διασπάσεσθέ μ', ὦ κακῶς ἀπολούμεναι.

Γρ.^β ἐμοὶ γὰρ ἀκολουθεῖν σ' ἔδει κατὰ τὸν νόμον.

Γρ.^γ οὔκ, ἢν ἑτέρα γε γραῦς ἔτ' αἰσχίων φανῇ.

Νε^{ας}. ἢν οὖν ὑφ' ὑμῶν πρῶτον ἀπόλωμαι κακῶς,
φέρε πῶς ἐπ' ἐκείνην τὴν καλὴν ἀφίξομαι;   1080

Γρ.^γ αὐτὸς σκόπει σύ· τάδε δέ σοι ποιητέον.

Νε^{ας}. ποτέρας προτέρας οὖν κατελάσας ἀπαλλαγῶ;

Γρ.^β οὐκ οἶσθα; βαδιεῖ δεῦρ'. Νε^{ας}. ἀφέτω νύν μ' αὑτηί.

Γρ.^γ δευρὶ μὲν οὖν ἴθ' ὡς ἔμ'. Νε^{ας}. ἢν ἡδί μ' ἀφῇ.

Γρ.^β ἀλλ' οὐκ ἀφήσω μὰ Δία σ'. Γρ.^γ οὐδὲ μὴν ἐγώ.   1085

Νε^{ας}. χαλεπαί γ' ἂν ἦστε γενόμεναι πορθμῆς. Γρ.^β τιή;

Νε^{ας}. ἕλκοντε τοὺς πλωτῆρας ἂν ἀπεκναίετε.

Γρ.^β σιγῇ βάδιζε δεῦρο. Γρ.^γ μὰ Δί' ἀλλ' ὡς ἐμέ.

Νε^{ας}. τουτὶ τὸ πρᾶγμα κατὰ τὸ Καννωνοῦ σαφῶς
ψήφισμα, βινεῖν δεῖ με διαλελημμένον.   1090
πῶς οὖν δικωπεῖν ἀμφοτέρας δυνήσομαι;

1086-7 § S π 2071   1089-90 S §§ (1) ει 222; (καὶ βι- . . .) §§ (2)
β 288

1076-7 Νε^{ας}. et Γρ.^β] par. R₁ : dic. Λ : om. Γ   1076 Νε^{ας}.]
νέος R₂   διασπάσασθέ Γ   1077 Γρ.^β] par. R₁ : γραῦς R₂ : dic. Λ :
om. Γ   σε δεῖ Cobet   1078 Γρ.^γ] ἡ ἑτέρα R₂   οὔ R₁ : οὐκ' R₂ :
οὔκουν Γ   1079-82 Νε^{ας}. et Γρ.^γ] dic. Λ : om. RΓ   1079 ἡμῶν ΓΛ
1082 ποτέρας ποτέρας Λ   καλέσας Γ   1083 Γρ.^β] par. R : dic.
Λ : om. Γ   δεῦρ' x : -ρο a   Νε^{ας}.] dic. a   νύν Bekker : νῦν a   αὑτηί ΓΛ
1084 Γρ.^γ] par. R : dic. Λ : om. Γ   ἔμ' x : ἐμέ a   Νε^{ας}.] dic. ΓΛ :
om. R   1085 Γρ.^β] par. R : dic. ΓΛ   σ' x : σε a   Γρ.^γ] dic. a
1086 Νε^{ας}.] par. R : dic. Λ : om. Γ   γ' ἂν ἦστε Ald. : γ' ἂν ἦσται R : γ'
ἦστε Γ : γ' ἂν ἦστε Λ : γ' ἂν ἦτε S   πορθμεῖς S   Γρ.^β] dic. a   τιή
om. ΓΛ   1087 Νε^{ας}.] par. R : dic. Λ : om. Γ   ἕλκοντε R^{ac} :
ἕλκοντες ΓS   ἐπεκναίετε Γ   1088 Γρ.^β] dic. Λ : om. RΓ   Γρ.^γ]
dic. ΓΛ : om. R   1089 Νε^{ας}.] dic. ΓΛ : om. R   κατὰ τοῦ Γ   Καννωνοῦ
Dindorf : καννώνου R : κανόνου Γ : καννόνου Λ   1090 με δεῖ S (1) :
δεῖ om. S (2)

Γρ.^β καλῶς, ἐπειδὰν καταφάγῃς βολβῶν χύτραν.

Νε^{ας}. οἴμοι κακοδαίμων· ἐγγὺς ἤδη τῆς θύρας
ἑλκόμενός εἰμ'— Γρ.^γ ἀλλ' οὐδὲν ἔσται σοι πλέον.
ξυνεσπεσοῦμαι γὰρ μετὰ σοῦ. Νε^{ας}. μὴ πρὸς θεῶν· 1095
ἑνὶ γὰρ ξυνέχεσθαι κρεῖττον ἢ δυοῖν κακοῖν.

Γρ.^γ νὴ τὴν Ἑκάτην, ἐάν τε βούλῃ γ' ἤν τε μή.

Νε^{ας}. ὦ τρισκακοδαίμων, εἰ γυναῖκα δεῖ σαπρὰν
βινεῖν ὅλην τὴν νύκτα καὶ τὴν ἡμέραν,
κἄπειτ', ἐπειδὰν τῆσδ' ἀπαλλαγῶ, πάλιν   1100
Φρύνην ἔχουσαν λήκυθον πρὸς ταῖς γνάθοις.
ἆρ' οὐ κακοδαίμων εἰμί; βαρυδαίμων μὲν οὖν,
νὴ τὸν Δία τὸν σωτῆρ', ἀνὴρ καὶ δυστυχής,
ὅστις τοιούτοις θηρίοις συνείρξομαι.
ὅμως δ' ἐάν τι πολλὰ πολλάκις πάθω   1105
ὑπὸ τοῖνδε τοῖν κασαλβάδοιν δεῦρ' ἐσπλέων,
θάψαι μ' ἐπ' αὐτῷ τῷ στόματι τῆς ἐσβολῆς,
καὶ τήνδ' ἄνωθεν ἐπιπολῆς τοῦ σήματος
ζῶσαν καταπιττώσαντες εἶτα τὼ πόδε
μολυβδοχοήσαντες κύκλῳ περὶ τὰ σφυρὰ   1110
ἄνω 'πιθεῖναι πρόφασιν ἀντὶ ληκύθου.

1092 (κατα- . . .) § S β 361   1101 §§ S φ 760

1092 Γρ.^β] del. par. R₂ : dic. Λ : om. Γ   καταφαγὼν S   1093 Νε^{ας}.]
dic. Λ : om. RΓ   τί πέπονθα post -μων· Γ   1094 Γρ.^γ] dic. RΛ :
ἀλλη Γ   1095 ξυμπεσοῦμαι Γ   Νε^{ας}.] dic. a   1096 ἔνα Λ (ἐν Μυ1)
1097 Γρ.^γ] dic. Λ : om. RΓ   βούλει R : βουλούλη Λ   1098 Νε^{ας}.]
par. R : dic. Λ : om. Γ   ὦ Ussher : ὦ a   1101 Φρύνη S   ἔχουσα Γ
1102 ἆρ' ΓΛ   κακοδαίμον R   1103 σωτῆρα ΓΛ   1104 συνείρξομαι Bergk : συνείξομαι a   1105 ὅμως] ὑμᾶς Meineke   δὲ ἀν R
1106 τοῖνδε τοῖν Cobet : ταῖνδε (-δαι R) ταῖν a   1107 μ' ἐμαυτῷ ΓΛ
1108 τήνδ' Bergler : τῶν a   ἐπὶ πολλῆς Λ   1109 καταπιττώ-
σαντας RΛ   1110 μολυβδοχοήσαντες van Herwerden : -λιβ- Γ : -τας
RΓ : -τος Λ   1111 ἄνω 'πιθεῖναι Λ (ἄν 'ω Μυ1^{ac}) : ἂν ὠπιθῆναι
R : ἄνω 'πιτιθεῖναι Γ   post 1111 add. ΧΟΡΟΥ Bergk (cf. 729, 876)

ΘΕΡΑΠΑΙΝΑ

ὦ μακάριος μὲν δῆμος, εὐδαίμων δ' ἐγώ,
αὐτή τέ μοι δέσποινα μακαριωτάτη,
ὑμεῖς θ' ὅσαι παρέστατ' ἐπὶ ταῖσιν θύραις,
οἱ γείτονές τε πάντες οἵ τε δημόται,   1115
ἐγώ τε πρὸς τούτοισιν ἡ διάκονος,
ἥτις μεμύρισμαι τὴν κεφαλὴν μυρώμασιν,
ἀγαθοῖσιν, ὦ Ζεῦ. πολὺ δ' ὑπερπέπαικεν αὖ
τούτων ἁπάντων τὰ Θάσι' ἀμφορείδια.
ἐν τῇ κεφαλῇ γὰρ ἐμμένει πολὺν χρόνον,   1120
τὰ δ' ἄλλ' ἀπανθήσαντα πάντ' ἀπέπτατο,
ὥστ' ἐστὶ πολὺ βέλτιστα, πολὺ δῆτ' ὦ θεοί.
κέρασον ἄκρατον· εὐφρανεῖ τὴν νύχθ' ὅλην
ἐκλεγομένας ὅ τι ἂν μάλιστ' ὀσμὴν ἔχῃ.
ἀλλ', ὦ γυναῖκες, φράσατέ μοι τὸν δεσπότην,   1125
τὸν ἄνδρ', ὅπου 'στί, τῆς ἐμῆς κεκτημένης.

Χο.   αὐτοῦ μένουσ' ἡμῖν γ' ἂν ἐξευρεῖν δοκεῖς.

Θε.   μάλισθ'· ὁδὶ γὰρ ἐπὶ τὸ δεῖπνον ἔρχεται.
ὦ δέσποτ', ὦ μακάριε καὶ τρισόλβιε.

1113-16 (μα- . . .) §§ † S (1) a 2896; §§ † (2) μ 581   1117-18
(. . . -θοῖσιν) S § (1) a 2896; (. . . -θοῖς) § (2) μ 581   1117 Ath.
691 b   1118-19 (πο- . . .) S § (1) μ 581; (Θά- . . .) §§ (2) a 1785;
(τὰ . . .) ‡ Poll. x. 72   1120-1 § S a 2896   1126 § S κ 1274;
cf. Moerim 201. 9 [Bekker]

1112-36 Θεράπων Brunck   1112 Θε. Γ: par. R: dic. Λ: διακ. (ut
vid.) θερ Σᴿ   ὦ Ussher: ὦ a   δ' ἐγώ] δὲ γῇ Dobree   1113 αὐτή RΓ
1114 θ' Dindorf: δ' a   πάρεστ' ΓΛ   ταῖσι ΓΛ   1115 τε (1) om. ΓΛ
οἵ τε δημόται Brunck: οἱ τῶν δημοτῶν a   1117 μεμύρισμαι Ath.:
μεμύρωμαι RΛS (1) et (2): μύρωμαι Γ   1118 ὑπερπέπαικαν Λ
1119 τούτων] τῶν Γ: αὐτῶν S (2)   1121 ἀπανθήσασα Λ   πάντ' ἀπέπτατο S: πάντα πέπτατο a: πάντ' ἀπέπτετο Brunck   1123 ἄκατον ΓΛ
1124 μάλιστα Γ   ἔχοι Γ   1125 μου Γ   1126 ὅπο Rᵃᶜ 'στιν R
1127 χορὸς R: dic. Λ: om. Γ   αὐτοῦ μένουσ'] αἰτουμένης Γ   γ' ἂν
Brunck: γὰρ a   1128 Θε.] dic. Γ: om. RΛ

Βλ.　ἐγώ; Θε. σὺ μέντοι, νὴ Δί', ὥς γ' οὐδεὶς ἀνήρ.　1130
　　τίς γὰρ γένοιτ' ἂν μᾶλλον ὀλβιώτερος,
　　ὅστις πολιτῶν πλεῖον ἢ τρισμυρίων
　　ὄντων τὸ πλῆθος οὐ δεδείπνηκας μόνος;

Χο.　εὐδαιμονικόν γ' ἄνθρωπον εἴρηκας σαφῶς.

Θε.　ποῖ ποῖ βαδίζεις; Βλ. ἐπὶ τὸ δεῖπνον ἔρχομαι.　1135

Θε.　νὴ τὴν Ἀφροδίτην, πολύ γ' ἁπάντων ὕστατος.
　　ὅμως δ' ἐκέλευε συλλαβοῦσάν μ' ἡ γυνὴ
　　ἄγειν σε καὶ τασδὶ μετὰ σοῦ τὰς μείρακας.
　　οἶνος δὲ Χῖός ἐστι περιλελειμμένος
　　καὶ τἄλλ' ἀγαθά. πρὸς ταῦτα μὴ βραδύνετε,　1140
　　καὶ τῶν θεατῶν εἴ τις εὔνους τυγχάνει,
　　καὶ τῶν κριτῶν εἰ μή τις ἑτέρωσε βλέπει,
　　ἴτω μεθ' ἡμῶν· πάντα γὰρ παρέξομεν.

Βλ.　οὔκουν ἅπασι δῆτα γενναίως ἐρεῖς
　　καὶ μὴ παραλείψεις μηδέν', ἀλλ' ἐλευθέρως　1145
　　καλεῖς γέροντα, μειράκιον, παιδίσκον; ὡς
　　τὸ δεῖπνον αὐτοῖς ἐστ' ἐπεσκευασμένον
　　ἀπαξάπασιν—ἢν ἀπίωσιν οἴκαδε.
　　ἐγὼ δὲ πρὸς τὸ δεῖπνον ἤδη 'πείξομαι·
　　ἔχω δέ τοι καὶ δᾷδα ταυτηνὶ καλῶς.　1150

Χο.　τί δῆτα διατρίβεις ἔχων, ἀλλ' οὐκ ἄγεις
　　τασδὶ λαβών; ἐν ὅσῳ δὲ καταβαίνεις, ἐγὼ

1131 (τόδ' ἂν γέ-　. . . -ρον) § Thom. Mag. 238. 10

1130–5 Βλέπυρος Voss　1130 Βλ.] par. R : dic. ΓΛ　Θε.] dic. a
δία R　1131 τί Λ　1134 Χο.] dic. ΓΛ : om. in ras. R　1135 Θε.]
par. R : dic. Λ : om. Γ　βαδίσεις Μυ1ᵃᶜ (ut vid.)　Βλ.] dic. a : δεσπότης
Ald. hic desinunt Γx　1136 Θε.] par. R : dic. Λ　1137 συλλαβοῦσα
R　1138 τὰς δὴ Λ　1139 παραλελειμμένος R　1142 βλέπῃ Λ
1144 Βλ. Bothe : par. R : om. Λ　οὔκουν Λ　1145 μηδὲν Λ
1146 καλεῖς Cobet : καλεῖν a　1150 ἔχω δέ τοι R : om. ('' ' sic)
Λ　1151 Χο.] par. R : om. Λ : Θε. Wilamowitz　τι R　διατρίβης
Μυ1ᵃᶜ

ἐπᾴσομαι μέλος τι μελλοδειπνικόν.

σμικρὸν δ᾽ ὑποθέσθαι τοῖς κριταῖσι βούλομαι,   1154
τοῖς σοφοῖς μὲν τῶν σοφῶν μεμνημένοις κρίνειν ἐμέ,
τοῖς γελῶσι δ᾽ ἡδέως διὰ τὸν γέλων κρίνειν ἐμέ—
σχεδὸν ἅπαντας οὖν κελεύω δηλαδὴ κρίνειν ἐμέ—
μηδὲ τὸν κλῆρον γενέσθαι μηδὲν ἡμῖν αἴτιον,
ὅτι προείληχ᾽· ἀλλὰ πάντα ταῦτα χρὴ μεμνημένους
μὴ 'πιορκεῖν, ἀλλὰ κρίνειν τοὺς χοροὺς ὀρθῶς ἀεί,   1160
μηδὲ ταῖς κακαῖς ἑταίραις τὸν τρόπον προσεικέναι,
αἳ μόνον μνήμην ἔχουσι τῶν τελευταίων ἀεί.

ὦ, ὦ, ὥρα δή,
⟨ὦ⟩ φίλαι γυναῖκες, εἴπερ μέλλομεν τὸ χρῆμα δρᾶν,
ἐπὶ τὸ δεῖπνον ὑπανακινεῖν. Κρητικῶς οὖν τὼ πόδε   1165
καὶ σὺ κίνει. Βλ. τοῦτο δρῶ. Χο. καὶ τάσδε νῦν . . .
. . . . . . λαγαρὰς τοῖν σκελίσκοιν τὸν ῥυθμόν.

τάχα γὰρ ἔπεισι
λοπαδοτεμαχοσελαχογαλεο-
    κρανιολειψανοδριμυποτριμματο-   1170
    σιλφιολιπαρομελιτοκατακεχυμενο-
    κιχλεπικοσσυφοφαττοπεριστερα-

1153 (με- . . .) § S μ 536   1165 (ὑ- . . .) S § (1) κ 2410; § (2)
μ 536   1168–70 (. . . κρά) § S μ 536

1153 τί Λ   μελο- Λ   1154 ὑπερθέσθαι Λ   1155 σοφοῖς
Scaliger: σοφοῖσι a   μεμνημένος Λ   1156 τὸ γελᾶν Porson
1159 ἀλλ᾽ ἅπαντα Λ : ἀλλ᾽ ἅπαντας Dobree   1161 τὸν Brunck: τόν τε a
1163 in. ἡμιχ. R: in. Θε. Wilamowitz   1164 ⟨ὦ⟩ Dindorf: om.
a   1165 ὑπανακίνει S (2) : -απο- Cobet   κρητικὼ S (2)   οὖν om. S
1166 Βλ. Meineke: ἡμιχ. R: om. Λ: Θε. Wilamowitz   Χο.] ἡμιχ. R:
dic. Λ   1166–7 νῦν . . . λαγαρὰς] νῦν λαγαρὰς a: νῦν λαγαρὰς + +
Mui : νῦν ⟨τὰς μείρακας | δεικνύναι κέλευε⟩ λαγαρὰς van Leeuwen : λαγαρὰς
⟨ἄγαν | ταχὺ χορείας ὅρσον ὑπάγειν⟩ Coulon (auct. White): alii alia metri
causa   σκελίσκειν Mui   1169 λεπαδο- Le Febvre   -σελαγολαχο- Rᵃᶜ:
-σσ- Rᵖᶜ   1171 σιλφιολιπαρο- Ussher: σιλφιοπαραο- a   1172 κιχλ-
Le Febvre: κινκλ- a   κοσσυφοφαττο- Dindorf: κοσσυκοφατο- R:
κοσσυφαο- Λ

λεκτρυονοπτοπιφαλλι⟨δ⟩οκιγκλοπε-
λειολαγῳοσιραιοβαφητραγα-
νοπτερυγών. σὺ δὲ ταῦτ᾽ ἀκροασάμε-   1175
νος ταχὺ καὶ ταχέως λαβὲ τρύβλιον.
εἶτα λαβὼν κόνισαι
λέκιθον, ἵν᾽ ἐπιδειπνῇς.
ἀλλὰ λαιμάττουσί που.
αἵρεσθ᾽ ἄνω, ἰαί, εὐαί,   1180
δειπνήσομεν, εὐοῖ, εὐαί,
εὐαί, ὡς ἐπὶ νίκῃ.
εὐαί, εὐαί, εὐαί, εὐαί.

1177–8 §§ S ε 2291; §§ Zonar. 837   1180–3 S ε 2807

1173 λεκτριον- *Λ*   -οπτοπιφαλλιδο- Ussher: -οπτεγκεφαλλιο- **a**:
-οπτοκεφαλιο- Coulon   1174–5 τραγα-|νοπτερυγών Schneider: -γων
a: τραγαλο- Blaydes   1176 τρίβλιον *Λ*   1177 κόνισαι λαβὼν R
κόνισαι ἰσχυρῶς post -νῆς (1178) S   1179 in. ἥμιχ. R: in. *Βλ.*
Blaydes   1180 ἰαί εὐαί S: ἰενάι (-εύ- in ras.) εὐαί R: εὖ αἲ *Λ*
1181 εὖ οἶ εὖ αἲ *Λ*   1182 εὐαίως ἐπινίκῃ *Λ*   1183 εὖ αἲ quinquies
Λ: εὐαί, εὐαί, εὐά, εὐά S

COMMENTARY

THE background represents a street in Athens (33). A figure emerges from the back-stage (on the question of stage-doors, Introduction § III). It carries a lighted lamp, thus indicating darkness (near daybreak, 20, 83), in the other hand a stick (74). Its cloak is white, and decorated only at the edges (a *man's* cloak, 26, 75) : it is wearing men's shoes (74). How are we—the audience—to recognize this figure as a woman? The first verbal help is in 9 (πειρωμέναισι) : and male actors hardly employed sustained falsetto (whatever they might do on occasion, *Th.* 267). Probably Praxagora—not named till 124—has a white (64 n.) beardless mask, and first puts on a beard for the rehearsal (118–23). A female *coiffure* could be concealed when necessary (at 285) by drawing up the cloak a common way with women of covering the head, as vases and statuary show: cf. M. Bieber, *Griechische Kleidung*, [Berlin–Leipzig, 1928], pls. XXXI, XXXII).

1–29. *Praxagora's soliloquy*

Points to notice are (*a*) parody of the prayer-forms used in hymns (H. Kleinknecht, *Die Gebetsparodie in der Antike* [Stuttgart–Berlin, 1937, repr. Hildesheim, 1966]); (*b*) parody of tragic apostrophe and language (P. Rau, *Paratragodia* [Munich, 1967], 205). Euripides often provides the closest parallels, but this may be only accidental: cf. A. T. Murray, *On Parody and Paratragoedia in Aristophanes* (Berlin, 1891), 4. Euripides had been dead some thirteen years now: his plays (it is true) were widely read, but did Aristophanes continue to burlesque them? (*c*) comic eulogy of common objects like a lamp (possibly guying such encomia as those upon bumble-bees and salt, Isoc. x. 12, Pl. *Smp.* 177 b); (*d*) the allusions to existence of a plot (6, 7, 17, 19), with a vague hint at its nature (21). The women are planning (we gradually learn) a γυναικοκρατία for Athens: their aim is to hold a brief rehearsal before entering and speaking (dressed as men) in the Assembly.

The whole of this first scene has many similarities to that of the *Lysistrata* (q.v.): (*a*) the time (dawn), (*b*) the emergence of a youngish woman alone upon the stage, (*c*) her complaints about the non-arrival of the women who were told (*Lys.* 13) to meet there, (*d*) the eventual arrival of these women, individually or in groups, with their excuses.

1 ff. ὦ λαμπρὸν ὄμμα . . . : address to the lamp as to the Sun-god, E. *Ph.* 1 ὦ τὴν ἐν ἄστροις οὐρανοῦ τέμνων ὁδὸν | καὶ χρυσοκολλήτοισιν ἐμβεβὼς δί-φροις | ˝Ηλιε, θοαῖς ἵπποισιν εἱλίσσων φλόγα (2 perhaps breaks off abruptly

to suggest some similar elaborate address). Cf. *Cyc.* 599 Ἥφαιστ' ἄναξ
Αἰτναῖε, γείτονος κακοῦ | λαμπρὸν πυρώσας ὄμμ' ἀπαλλάχθηθ' ἅπαξ,
Heracl. 749 λαμπρόταται θεοῦ αὐγαί, *TGF*² 848.   **τροχήλατος** means
(a) 'whirling' (E. *IT* 82), (b) 'whirled' (on the potter's wheel, τροχῷ
ἐλαθείς, 4). Cf. τῆς τροχηλάτου κόρης (Xenarch. fr. **1.** 9).   **λύχνου**:
the ordinary Greek lamp of the period was a small round terracotta
object (very much more rarely stone or metal), normally without
decoration, and partly or wholly glazed in black: it might or might
not have a handle. A central opening admitted olive-oil, and one or
more nozzles at the side (μυκτῆρες, 5) held wicks (θρυαλλίδες, *Nu.* 59).
There Strepsiades protests against a thick one: for oil (*V.* 251) was
scarce in wartime. See J. Perlzweig, *Lamps from the Athenian Agora*
(Princeton, N.J., 1963), and for some fine fourth-century examples
D. M. Robinson, *Excavations at Olynthus*, ii (Baltimore, Md., 1930),
137-45.

2 κάλλιστ' . . . ἐξηυρημένον: cf. E. fr. 324. 1 ὦ χρυσέ, δεξίωμα κάλλιστον,
Heracl. 533 εὕρημα . . . κάλλιστον ηὕρηκ'. Superlative, as in tragic
hymn-prayer contexts, *Hipp.* 70, *IA* 553. The text is doubtful. ἡ ἔννοια
(says scholiast) . . . κάλλιστα τοῖς σοφοῖς εὑρημένον: I follow his lead
with hesitation. Perhaps *EΞHYPHMENON* was written *EΞHTPH-
MENON* (*T* and *Y* confused, as in papyri, cf. Herod. 3. 72), hence, by
'correction', *EΞHTHMENON* of MSS. (ἐξῃτημένον, 'whose help is
prayed for'?, a late use, *PMag. Par.* i. 434). ἐζητημένον (Bergler),
'invented' (hardly justified by *Th.* 439, but palaeographically good:
cf. E. *HF* 248, where οὐ μόνον στενάξετε is a necessary change for οὐ . . .
στενάζετε LP). ἐξηρτημένον (Vb1), 'suspended' (494), cf. Polem. Hist.
fr. 63 *FHG* iii. 134 τὸν λύχνον . . . τὸν ἐκ τῆς ὀροφῆς ἐξηρτημένον. This
last necessitates (see apparatus criticus) our reading εὐσκόποισιν, 'on
the heights', X. *Cyr.* vi. 3. 2. But where are we to think the lamp
suspended? For εὐστόχοισιν (R), 'aiming well', hence 'clever', 'skilful'
cf. Ephipp. fr. 14. 1 ἔπειτ' ἀναστὰς εὔστοχος νεανίας . . . | ἔλεξεν.

3 γὰρ: explaining the tone of the apostrophe, '(I address you in this
way as a god) for I intend to demonstrate your birth and fortune'
(i.e. to show you really are one). Cf. *Ach.* 588, S. *Tr.* 289.   **γονάς:**
(a) literal, 'your birth' (the plural of gods, as often in Old and Middle
Comedy: Ἀφροδίτης, Διονύσου Γοναί are play-titles from Nicophon,
Antiphanes, Polyzelus, and Philiscus); (b) 'your pedigree', 'your
stock' (S. *Aj.* 1094).   **τύχας:** the plural (used often of the ups and
downs of fortune, περιπετεῖς ἔχεις τύχας, E. *Andr.* 982) here means
'your *good* fortune', 'your success' (Pi. *P.* 8. 72: contrast δήλωσον
ἡμῖν . . . τύχας, S. *Aj.* 283). The γοναί/τύχαι antithesis is natural (and
though unparalleled was possibly a commonplace) in contexts of
encomia and hymns.

4-5 '(And I *can* make this contrast) for, whirled on the wheel' (τροχὸς
τῶν κεραμικῶν, X. *Smp.* vii. 2), 'born of the impulse set in motion by

the potter' (τροχοῦ ῥυμαῖσι τευκτὸν κοιλοσώματον κύτος, Antiph. fr.
52. 2), i.e. μηδὲν ὢν γοναῖσιν (S. *Aj.* 1094), 'you now have the bright
honours of the sun.'   ἄπο: so MSS., 'born from' (or 'after'?, *Av.*
489 with Kuster). Cf. E. *Alc.* 509 χαῖρ᾽ ὦ Διὸς παῖ, Περσέως τ᾽ ἀφ᾽
αἵματος. The phrase then elaborates in paratragic manner τροχῷ
ἐλαθεὶς (τροχήλατος, 1). ὕπο, Kuster: cf. *Nu.* 407 ὑπὸ τοῦ ῥοίβδου καὶ
τῆς ῥύμης αὐτὸς ἑαυτὸν κατακάων.   μυκτῆρσι: 'your nostrils' (see
1 ff.), cf. J. Taillardat, *Les Images d'Aristophane*[2] (Paris, 1965), 141.
There may be the suggestion of a fire-breathing monster (E. *Med.* 478,
S. fr. 336 Pearson) comically intermingling with the concept of the
λύχνος as a god. Such an effect would in fact have been achieved by the
lamp (shaped like a bull's head) illustrated by Perlzweig, op. cit. fig.
19.   ἡλίου τιμὰς: (*a*) 'the honours fitting for the sun-god' (S. *Ant.*
745 οὐ γὰρ σέβεις, τιμάς γε τῶν θεῶν πατῶν) ; (*b*) his 'prerogatives' or
'special functions' (A. *Eu.* 419, Athena : τιμάς γε μὲν δὴ τὰς ἐμὰς πεύσῃ
τάχα) : here (7 ff.) the right to be πανόπτης (καὶ τὸν πανόπτην κύκλον
ἡλίου καλῶ, id. *Pr.* 91). τιμὰς ἔχεις: in hymn contexts, (of the Dios-
curi) E. *El.* 993 τιμὰς σωτῆρας ἔχοντες, (of Dionysus) Orph. *H.*, *Prelude
to Musaeus*, 8 ὅς τε μεγίστας | τιμὰς ἐν μακάρεσσιν ἔχεις.

6 ὅρμα . . . ξυγκείμενα: the signal for the women to assemble is also, as
it were, a call to battle. Cf. Th. iv. 111. 1 ὅπως, ὁπότε πύλαι τινὲς
ἀνοιχθεῖεν καὶ τὸ σημεῖον ἀρθείη ὃ ξυνέκειτο, πρῶτοι ἐσδράμοιεν.
φλογὸς σημεῖα: the thought is of a beacon, A. *A.* 480 φλογὸς παραγ-
γέλμασιν.

7–9 γὰρ: either (*a*) in delayed reference to 5 (E. *HF* 1176, J. D. Denniston, *The Greek Particles*[2] [1954], 63) or (*b*) looking back to the idea of
arrangements implicit in 6 (see 17). (*b*) is better: these implied
arrangements will then be the object of δηλοῦμεν. Repeated γάρ (3, 4)
is typical of hymns, *Ra.* 405, *Pax* 780 σοὶ γὰρ τάδ᾽ ἐξ ἀρχῆς μέλει.
μόνῳ: in hymn-prayer contexts (12), Orph. *H.* 87. 8 (Abel) ἐν σοὶ γὰρ
μούνῳ πάντων τὸ κριθὲν τελοῦται, *Pax* 590 μόνη γὰρ ἡμᾶς ὠφέλεις.
ἐπεὶ: the lamp assists them (*a*) in sex-play (see below), (*b*) in depilation
(12–13), (*c*) in tippling (14–16).   κἂν . . . παραστατεῖς: 'you stand
by us also in' (κἂν, i.e. καὶ ἐν, by crasis, 'mixing') 'our rooms when we
make love' (in addition to your present help outside). Complicity
of lamps and lovers is a commonplace (*AP* v. 4, 8, 165), cf. O. Seel,
Aristophanes oder Versuch über Komödie (Stuttgart, 1960), 112 : they stay
lit during intercourse (as here). This was not necessarily a *preference*
(as found in the modern *male*, see A. C. Kinsey, W. B. Pomeroy, C. E.
Martin, *Sexual Behaviour in the Human Male* [Philadelphia–London,
1948], 581) : Greek lamps, once out, were difficult to light again (Lys.
i. 14).   δωματίοισιν: probably not 'houses' (as at *Ra.* 100, 311 αἰθέρα
Διὸς δωμάτιον) despite δόμων (11), but 'bedrooms' (as *Lys.* 160).
Bedrooms in a Greek house were normally upstairs (*Th.* 479 ff., Lys.
i. 9).   δωμάτιοισιν (synizesis, i.e. 'fusing together', as van Leeuwen)

would keep the tragic metre, but would itself be untragic (and see 4).
Ἀφροδίτης τρόπων: 'the turns of Love', i.e. σχήματα συνουσίας (so
Rogers). σχήματα, the 'postures' of an athlete (Isoc. xv. 183), directs
attention to the metaphor (athletics) that lies behind the passage (see
below). Cf. *Pax* 894–ς05. πειρωμέναισι: of entering upon athletic
contests, *Il*. xxiii. 707, *Od*. viii. 100. πλησίον: cf. E. *Ph*. 159,
ἐκεῖνος ἑπτὰ παρθένων τάφου πέλας | Νιόβης Ἀδράστῳ πλησίον παρα-
στατεῖ. Notice the three-word trimeter: cf. 15, A. *Eu*. 14. For this
Aeschylean feature see W. B. Stanford, *Aeschylus in his Style* (Dublin,
1942), 80.

10–11 λορδουμένων: 'curved', with head thrown back and body convex
(in front, contrast the sense of κύβδα, *Th*. 489), a σχηματισμὸν . . .
σώματος οὐ σεμνόν (Eust. 1524. 23). Cf. fr. 140 λορδοῦ κιγκλοβάταν
ῥυθμόν, Mnesim. fr. 4. 52 πᾶς δὲ κατ' οἴκους . . . | πίνει, σκιρτᾷ, λορδοῖ,
κεντεῖ. Coital postures are shown on the vases: and see (for example)
265, *Pax* 894 ff., *Lys*. 773. Λόρδων and Κύβδασος are named as deities
(by Aphrodite), Pl. Com. fr. 174. 17. τε: best translated independently, since καί . . . τε ('both . . . and') is very doubtful. The preceding καί (8) = 'also'. ἐπιστάτην: 'superintendent' of (a) public
boards in Athens (*Ath. Pol*. 44. 1), (b) public building operations (*IG* i.
322. 1, Aeschin. iii. 14), (c) (the present reference) athletics. Cf. Pl. *Lg*.
949 a καὶ γυμνικῶν τε καὶ ἱππικῶν ἄθλων ἐπιστάτας καὶ βραβέας, X.
Lac. 8. 4.

12–13 Depilation. Methods were plucking (ἀπο-, παρατίλλειν, *Lys*. 151)
and singeing off (ἀφεύειν) with a lamp. Cf. *Lys*. 827 ἀπεψιλωμένον τῷ
λύχνῳ, *Th*. 238 (the *locus classicus*); both methods, ibid. 590, Pl. Com.
fr. 174. 14. For the singeing operation see the cylix by Panaetius
(*JÖAI* xii [1909], 86). μόνος: see 7 n. μηρῶν . . . τρίχα:
a similar passage 902, *Lys*. 552. Cf. *AP* xii. 36. 2 μηροῖς ὄξυς ἔπεστι
χνόος. ἀπορρήτους: (a) 'hidden', 'secret' (expressing an implicit
sense of μύχος), Pl. *R*. 460 c ἐν ἀπορρήτῳ τε καὶ ἀδήλῳ; (b) 'contra-
band', 'forbidden' (442), τὰ μέρη τὰ ἀπόρρητα (Longin. 43. 5).
Perhaps the 'mysteries' of Love are glanced at (Pl. *Phd*. 62 b). The
word has overtones of 'not quite polite to speak of' (cf. D. xxi. 149).
μυχοὺς: a common tragic word, cf. (in hymn) *Th*. 324. ἀφεύων: *Th*.
216, 236, 590 (see above). τὴν ἐπανθοῦσαν τρίχα: X. *Cyn*. iv. 8
αἱ . . . πυρραὶ ἔχουσαι ἔστωσαν λευκὴν τρίχα ἐπανθοῦσαν περὶ τὰ μέτωπα,
cf. *V*. 1064. A similar context 903.

14–15 Filching food and secret drinking. Women managed household
expenses (211, *Lys*. 494), but doubtless some husbands curbed their
spending. Thus the Theophrastan ἀνελεύθερος (*Char*. 22. 10) will not
allow his wife to have a servant, and men are accused of reversing
former practice by keeping cupboards under lock and key, *Th*. 418.
The women 'pinch' food, ibid. 813. Their incessant eating is remarked
on by Semonides (fr. 7 D.² 46–7). They are also portrayed as secret

drinkers ('the fondness of women for wine is common knowledge', Ath. 440 e). Cf. (among numerous examples) 43, *Lys.* 114, *Th.* 347. A terracotta female figure from Olynthus is shown clinging tightly to a wine-jar (*Excavations*, iv. 83). στοάς: 'storehouses' (τὰ ταμιεῖα, scholiast), so called from similarity of shape (καὶ γὰρ παραμήκη, 'oblong'). Similarly Hsch. s.v., Poll. i. 78. Our main information on the classical Greek house is gained from excavations at Olynthus, which do not support this observation (*Excavations*, viii. 207–8). Nor does what can be inferred of a country house in Attica (J. E. Jones, L. H. Sackett, A. J. Graham, 'The Dema House in Attica', *ABSA* lvii [1962], 108 ff.). The 'Long Colonnade' in the Piraeus (Paus. i. 1. 3) served as both a corn-store and a market (ἡ ἀλφιτόπωλις στοά, 686 n.) : from this fact, more than from similarity of shape, the Athenian private larder took its name. καρποῦ: 'grain', cf. *Pl.* 515 καρπὸν Δηοῦς. Βακχίου: (*a*) adjectival, for Βακχείου (S. *Tr.* 219) ; (*b*) for Βάκχου synonymous with οἶνος (E. *IT* 953). Cf. (again in parody of tragedy) Antiph. fr. 237. 1 ἄλλοι δὲ καὶ δὴ Βακχίου παλαιγενοῦς | ἀφροσκίαστον χρυσοκόλλητον δέπας | . . . ἕλκουσι γναθοῖς. With Βακχίου . . . νάματος cf. νᾶμα Νυμφῶν ('water'), Men. *Dysc.* 947. ὑποιγνύσαισι: ὑπο- of furtiveness or secrecy, *Th.* 424 πρὸ τοῦ μὲν οὖν ἦν ἀλλ' ὑποῖξαι τὴν θύραν | ποιησαμέναισι δακτύλιον τριωβόλου, Alcimus 560 F 2 ἔτυχε δ' ἡ γυνὴ τοῦ τὴν οἰκίαν κεκτημένου πίθον οἴνου λαθραίως ὑποίξασα. συμπαρασтατεῖς: of the favouring presence of a god, *Ra.* 386 Δήμητερ ἁγνῶν ὀργίων | ἄνασσα συμπαραστάτει. Note the three-word trimeter (see 9).

16 καὶ ταῦτα συνδρῶν: E. *Or.* 1535 Πυλάδην τε τὸν τάδε ξυνδρῶντά μοι. οὐ λαλεῖς τοῖς πλησίον: 'you don't babble to anyone' (perhaps a stock expression), ὁ συνειδὼς καὶ μὴ φράζων (Pl. *Lg.* 742 b). λαλεῖς, of heedless chattering, the common sense in comedy (cf. the Theophrastan λάλος). οἱ πλησίον, (*a*) 'the neighbourhood' (Pl. *Tht.* 174 b ὁ μὲν πλησίον καὶ γείτων), (*b*) 'the next man', 'anyone' (565). Cf. in general *Ra.* 752.

17–18 συνείσει: i.e. 'you will share in my present plans as well.' The lamp, for its faithfulness in small things, is now to be allowed to know of great ones. I accept συνείσει (Biset) as better suiting ἀνθ' ὧν : confusion of ει, οι (συνοίσει, MSS.), arising from the fact that they were both pronounced as ι, is one of the commonest in Greek. The manuscripts' text is, however, not impossible, 'you will help me in my present plans' (accusative of relation) 'as well'. And it might be regarded as an Aeschylean echo (πιστοῖσι πιστὰ συμφέρων βουλεύματα, *Pers.* 528). ὅσα Σκίροις ἔδοξε: 59. Σκίροις, 'at the Skira' (for omission of the article see *Th.* 834). Cf. Διασίοις, *Nu.* 864, further examples KG i. 600. Details of this obscure women's celebration (*Th.* loc. cit.) may be found in L. Deubner, *Attische Feste²* (Berlin, 1966), 40.

19–21 The grandiloquent tone is now abandoned as Praxagora recalls that her friends (18) are absent. Cf. *Lys.* 4 νῦν δ᾽ οὐδεμία πάρεστιν ἐνταυθοῖ γυνή. The abrupt change here is worth a mention: it seemed for a moment that Praxagora (in the manner of certain tragic prologues) was going to reveal the total plot. Is Aristophanes mocking this convention? ἃς . . . ἐχρῆν: cf. E. *Ba.* 26 ἀδελφαὶ . . . ἃς ἥκιστα χρῆν (ἥκιστ᾽ ἐχρῆν, LP). Attraction (ὧν, Blaydes, van Leeuwen) would be commoner: but see (for example) *Hipp.* 1062 οὐ δῆτα. πάντως οὐ πίθοιμ᾽ ἂν οὓς (οἷς, P) με δεῖ. καίτοι . . . γ᾽: 'and yet' (*Ach.* 357, *Nu.* 921) 'it is getting on for morning.' πρὸς ὄρθρον: *Lys.* 1089, *V.* 772 κατ᾽ ὄρθρον. Cf. πρὸς ἔω, 312. ἡ . . . ἐκκλησία . . . ἔσται: cf. 84, 740 for dawn as the time of the Assembly. So *Ach.* 19 οὔσης . . . ἐκκλησίας | ἑωθινῆς ἔρημος ἡ πνὺξ αὑτηί, *Th.* 376. The Athenians kept early hours, *Av.* 489–92 ὁπόταν μόνον (sc. ὁ ἀλεκτρυών, 483) ὄρθριον ᾄσῃ | ἀναπηδῶσιν πάντες ἐπ᾽ ἔργον . . . αὐτίκα μάλ᾽: a common combination, cf. *Eq.* 746 καὶ μὴν ποιήσας αὐτίκα μάλ᾽ ἐκκλησίαν. It occurs ('forthwith') in decrees of the Assembly, cf. the near contemporary (394 B.C.) inscription, Ἑλέσθαι δὲ πρ]έσβεις αὐτίκα μάλ[α] τὴ[ν] βουλὴν δέκα ἄνδρ]ας (*IG* ii². 16. 10). ἔσται: alternatively, ἐκκλησία γενήσεται (85, see 551).

21–3 The strange arrangement of these lines in the MSS. is possibly a mark of deep corruption. Transposition of 22 and 23 gives some improvement: (*a*) τὰς ἑταίρας (adjectival, 'of ἑταῖραι') is nearer the word (ἕδρας) it refers to (surely not ἡμᾶς, 'wir, die verschworenen Genossinen' as C. Robert, 'Aphoristische Bemerkungen zu den Ekklesiazusen des Aristophanes', *Hermes*, lvii [1922], 341); (*b*) εἰ μέμνησθ᾽ ἔτι, coming at the end, allows time for audience reaction (cf. 365, 888 nn.), 'Do we *what*?' (On audience participation in general see V. Ehrenberg, *The People of Aristophanes*² [1951], 27 ff.) The concluding words permit a moment for her hearers to recollect the context of ἑταίρας: an actor's *lapsus linguae* (see below). καταλαβεῖν . . . ἕδρας: 86. Cf., of seats in the theatre, D. xxi. 178 θέαν τινὸς καταλαμβάνοντος ᾔατο. ἕδρα is (*a*) a seat, (*b*) the seat, i.e. the rump, *Nu.* 1507 (ambiguous, as here) τῆς σελήνης ἐσκοπεῖσθε τὴν ἕδραν. τὰς ἑταίρας: so MSS., correctly. The psychological slip is ascribed to one Phyromachus, whom scholiasts call (*a*) a politician, who decreed seats apart for the ἑταῖραι (but *no* woman ever attended the Assembly), (*b*) a tragic actor, who was mocked for his wrong pronunciation: καὶ φασὶ Κλεόμαχον (ΛΣᴿ) τραγικὸν ὑποκριτήν. οὗτος φαίνεται ὑποκρινόμενός ποτε εἰρηκέναι ἕδρας (for ἕδρας, Robert 342) ἐν δράματι καὶ ἐσκῶφθαι διά τι κακέμφατον. This view is basically right, although the error was clearly not in ἕδρας but ἑταίρας, a slip which suggested that ἕδρα had its *other* sense (above). Cf. the mockery of Hegelochus for his slip-up in a line of the *Orestes* (*Ra.* 303), and the wild reaction to Timarchus' unwitting *double entendre* in the Assembly (Aeschin. i. 80–4). V. Coulon combines both explanations (*REG* xxxvi [1923], 369): Cleomachus, an un-known politician—afterwards referred to, for his error, as Phyro-machus, from φύρειν, 'to jumble', 'to confuse'—said, instead of ἐτέρας, ἐταίρας (cf. A. Willems, *Aristophane* iii [Paris–Brussels, 1919], 253). **κῶλά θ' ἰζομένας:** 'settling our limbs' (see 98). This is an unparalleled expression: R's πῶς κωλαθιζομένας presumably preserves the query (which he then went on to answer) of an ancient commentator on the passage. Cf. (for example) scholiast *Th.* 80: τοῦτο τῶν ζητουμένων ἐστί, πῶς καὶ τρίτην καὶ μέσην εἶπεν . . . ἡ λύσις οὖν ἥδε. The scholiast (on 1) seems to hint at reminiscences of Agathon or Dicaeogenes, but his reading in 23 is uncertain. πως κἀγκαθεζομένας (Hall and Geldart), which rests upon his comment, is attractive: 98, *Th.* 184, ἐγκαθεζόμενος λάθρᾳ. But ἐτέρας, the metrically necessary change, is something very little short of nonsense: though note that ἐταίρ-/ἐτέρ-confusion occurs twice in a Bucharest manuscript of Theophrastus, *Char.* 12. 15, 17. 3 (T. Costa, 'De codicibus Theophrasti Bucarestinis duobus', *LF* xc [1967], 7, 8). **Φυρόμαχος:** the name (R's reading) recurs in Alex. fr. 221. 10, Euphron fr. 8. 6, and in two fifth-century inscriptions (*PA* 15052–3). See also the Athenian casualty list in *Hesperia*, xxv (1956), 377. Σφυρόμαχος (scholiast, all other manu-scripts) is not found elsewhere: perhaps from dittography of ϲ?

24–6 **τί δῆτ' ἂν εἴη;** 348, E. *Rh.* 577.   **δῆτ':** a particle much used in comic questions (cf. for example 455, 640). It always has 'a logical connective force' (*GP* 269): the connection of thought appears to be '(they know this) what then can be the matter?' Cf. *Lys.* 54 ἆρ' οὐ παρεῖναι τὰς γυναῖκας δῆτ' ἐχρῆν; Other uses, 328 n.   **οὓς εἴρητ' ἔχειν:** 68, sc. αὐτάς or αὐταῖς: cf. Hdt. vii. 26. 1 ἐνθαῦτα γὰρ εἴρητο συλλέγεσθαι πάντα τὸν . . . στρατόν, X. *An.* iii. 4. 4 καὶ εὐθὺς ἔθεον ὁμόσε οἷς εἴρητο. The imperative of direct speech is replaced by the infinitive with λέγω.   **θαἰμάτια:** crasis (8 n.) with aspiration, τὰ ἱμάτια, 75. So in the singular θοἰμάτιον, 40, 315.   **λαθεῖν:** cf. 23, 35. 24–6 are omitted in ΑΓΒVb1, an error doubtless due to this close repetition. Were change required, Brunck's λαβεῖν is attractive: cf. 314, 343, *Th.* 419.

27–9 **ἀλλ' ὁρῶ . . . προσιόντα:** for the formula cf. 41, 52.   **τονδί:** notice (as often in comedy in formulas which herald new arrivals on the scene) iota demonstrative or deictic. So 934, *V.* 1324 ὁδὶ δὲ καὶ δὴ σφαλλόμενος προσέρχεται. | ἀλλ' ἐκποδὼν ἄπειμι πρὶν πληγὰς λαβεῖν. It is used (a) when speakers can indicate, as here, the person or thing that they refer to; (b) for a gesture in the abstract (*Ra.* 139, with Stanford's note). The use is peculiarly comic and colloquial (cf. Pl. *Grg.* 489 b), and does not occur in tragedy at all.   **φέρε νυν ἐπανα-χωρήσω:** 725, 869. Similarly, *V.* 1516 φέρε νυν ἡμεῖς αὐτοῖς ὀλίγον ξυγχωρήσωμεν ἅπαντες. The verb is oftenest in military or quasi-military contexts, Th. vi. 49. 4, *Lys.* 461. She is thinking of 'beating a retreat'.   **καί:** 'in fact', 'actually', 495, 870.

30-56 Praxagora steps back to await the new arrival (recalling such similar withdrawals as Orestes', A. *Ch.* 20, E. *El.* 109). Cf. *Th.* 36. The newcomer is, in fact, a woman: her lamp (27) is apparently conducting a number of companions as well. Praxagora reproaches their delay, knocks up her neighbour, and questions the women, who from now on hurry in, about how they have prepared for the Assembly.

30-1 The words of Woman *A* (γυνή τις, *ΑΛ*Μυι) as she enters. To whom are they meant to be addressed? (*a*) to herself (so Rogers, most improbably), (*b*) to Praxagora (but she is still in hiding, presumably coming forward only on hearing Woman *A* start to speak), (*c*) (the most likely) to a group of other women, who follow her in as chorus members (cf. ὑμᾶς, 32). The methods of entry of a comic chorus vary (in the *Birds*, for example, they enter one by one) : here the majority (assuming that at this time the chorus numbered twenty-four) will be in the group with Woman *A*, the seven mentioned later (41-51) come running either singly or in pairs. See further on *Parodos*, 285 n.

ὥρα βαδίζειν: 352, cf. *Th.* 1189, 1228.   **ὁ κῆρυξ:** (1) 'the herald' who summoned the Assembly (*Th.* 295) : we then assume (*a*) at least two proclamations, (*b*) that κοκκύζω is a slang word. If so, however, the slang use could originate from (2) 'the cock' (so scholiast in R : cf. Herod. 4. 12, Headlam) whose second crowing (see 390) was a 'herald' of the close approach of day.   **κοκκύζω,** of cuckoos (Poll. v. 89) was frequently applied to roosters' crowing: cf. (for example) *Ra.* 1380, Pl. Com. fr. 209, E. K. Borthwick, *CQ* N.S. xv (1965), 261. Meaning (2) cannot be *proved* for Aristophanes: but surely he makes use of the ambiguity of κῆρυξ? The audience (remembering 20-1) would naturally think of meaning (1) : δεύτερον κεκόκκυκεν is then παρὰ προσδοκίαν—a 'contrary to expectation' joke.   **ἡμῶν προσιόντων:** the masculine participle (MSS.) may stand. Woman *A* and her friends are dressed as *men*. She wants not so much to act her part out fully (she is more absent-minded, 189) as to give the audience a chuckle.

32-3 δέ γ': 'in retorts and lively rejoinders' (*GP* 153). Cf. 261, 648. **ἐγρηγόρη:** so Porson. The manuscripts have -ειν, cf. 650. If the ἦ, ἦν variation is a parallel, the use of the -ειν form in 'indifferent' positions (i.e. before a consonant or at line-ends) is likely to be later than our play (see W. S. Barrett on E. *Hipp.* 700). Note (*a*) the absence of augment, cf. *Pl.* 744: but in neither place is it guaranteed by metre, and Hall and Geldart (silently) here print ἠ-; (*b*) the use as an imperfect, *Nu.* 1347, X. *Cyr.* i. 4. 20 καὶ ἅμα θαυμάζων ὡς καὶ ἐφρόνει καὶ ἐγρηγόρει.   **τὴν νύκτα πᾶσαν:** *Nu.* 1129. Praxagora exaggerates slightly (like others of her sex, see 92 n.).

33-4 φέρε: with aorist subjunctive, 28.   **ἐκκαλέσωμαι:** 'call out from the house' (cf. 76 n.), the usual Aristophanic meaning. So (for example) *V*. 221 οἷς ἐκκαλοῦνται τοῦτον. **θρυγανῶσα**: 'gently scratching', as the scholiast (ἡσύχως κνῶσα) understands it (θρυγανωσῶν τὰς μύλας, Pherecr. fr. 10. 4). Cf. *Th.* 481 οὗτος πόθῳ μου 'κνυεν ἐλθὼν τὴν θύραν. **τὴν θύραν**: indicated, with Praxagora's, behind (the article need not mean only *one* door in the back-stage), Introduction § III.

35–7 Woman *B* (γυνή, ΓΛΜυιΥβι) now emerges from her door: she closes it slowly and carefully behind her, so as not to rouse her husband by its creaking. (For this sound, giving rise to a suspicion of one's wife, see Lys. i. 14: cf. *Th.* 487). **τοι**: 'I heard, you know, as I was putting on my shoes' (i.e. don't think I was asleep). Similarly, 972, 1150, *Lys.* 16 (in 54 n.). **τὸ κνῦμα**: 'the scratching of your fingers' (cf. κνύω, *Th.* 481). Galen (*Glossarium*, xix. 12 Kühn) explains the word as onomatopoeic (ὠνοματοπεποίηται μιμήσει τοῦ ψόφου): whether so or not, a class of κν- words does have the connotation 'scratching', 'itching'. So (for example) κναίω (κνάω, κνήθω), κνίζω, κνησιάω (919). **ἄτ'**: *Th.* 456 ἄτ' ἐν ἀγρίοισι τοῖς λαχάνοις αὐτὸς τραφείς: elsewhere in Aristophanes (cf. 257) used with ὤν.

37–40 **γὰρ**: in successive lines (as often). Cf. 3, 163, *Ach.* 512, where the second γάρ anticipates, as here. **Σαλαμίνιος**: (*a*) a dweller on the island; (*b*) one who, from living there, has gained skill as an oarsman (Rogers explains of one accustomed to rowing between there and the mainland), *Ra.* 203–5 κᾆτα πῶς δυνήσομαι | ἄπειρος ἀθαλάττωτος ἀσαλαμίνιος | ὢν εἶτ' ἐλαύνειν; (*c*) possibly a crew-member (scholiast, comparing Παράλιος, Πάραλος) of the Σαλαμίνια (*Av.* 147, 1204). The natural meaning to an audience is (*a*): the islanders no doubt enlisted as oarsmen in large numbers. Reference to Salamis seems often to suggest obscene allusions (*Lys.* 59, 411, cf. *Eq.* 785). Translate here (see below) 'a sturdy oarsman'. **ᾧ ξύνειμ' ἐγώ**: 340, 898, see 619. **τὴν νύχθ' ὅλην**: 55, 1123. **ἤλαυνε**: *sensu obscaeno*, 109. Cf. Pl. Com. fr. 3. 4 ἡ μὲν ἐλαυνομένη λαθρίοις ἐρετμοῖς, ὁ δ' ἐλαύνων. ἐρέσσω, ἐρέτης have similar uses in erotics. **ἐν τοῖς στρώμασιν**: 334, fr. 695 ὅστις ἐν ἡδυόσμοις | στρώμασι παννυχίζων | τὴν δέσποιναν ἐρείδεις. **ἄρτι**: 'now and only now' (*nunc demum*), 552. Cf. *Lys.* 70 οὔ σ' ἐπαινῶ Μυρρίνη | ἤκουσαν ἄρτι περὶ τοιούτου πράγματος. **τουτὶ θοἰμάτιον**: 27, 26 nn. **αὐτοῦ 'λαβον**: for the prodelision, or aphaeresis, cf. 341, 1111. It is rarer in Aristophanes than in Aeschylus: and rarest in this play and the *Plutus*. M. Platnauer, 'Prodelision in Greek Drama', *CQ* N.s. x (1960), 140 credits Aristophanes with 92 examples of the collocation -ου ε-, but does not indicate his reading (see apparatus criticus) here.

41–2 **καὶ μὴν ὁρῶ**: 27, 51. The particles announce a new arrival (γυνή, A): cf. 73 n., *Ach.* 908, *Eq.* 691. But only rarely (*Av.* 1462) are they other than the first words of a speaker: this tells against the attribution of 35–42 to Woman *B* (as by P. Händel, *Formen und Dar-*

stellungsweisen in der aristophanischen Komödie [Heidelberg, 1963], 192
n. 4). Assignment of parts here is difficult: MSS. give very little help.
See J. C. B. Lowe, 'The Manuscript Evidence for Changes of Speaker
in Aristophanes', *BICS* ix (1962), 27-42.   προσιοῦσαν: Aldus,
followed by most editors. Cf. 28, 31, 52, *Pl.* 333. MSS.' παροῦσαν
might be taken (especially in Praxagora's mouth, cf. 19) to mean that
the women are here *now* (*Lys.* 69, 73). But it seems a not quite natural
expression. These and the other women named, along with those
already (see 30 n.) in the orchestra, form the chorus to whose leader
Bergk attributes 43-5. Cf. 293 ff. for the mention of individuals by
name. (K. K. Hulley, 'The Prologue of the Ecclesiazusae', *CW* xlvi. 9
[1953], 153, believes that lines should be distributed at least among
the seven women mentioned.) Despite a suggestion that Lysistrata
and Myrrhine are intended as real persons (D. M. Lewis, 'Notes on
Attic Inscriptions ii', *ABSA* l (1955), 1 ff.), the names here are typical,
not personal; for citizens' wives (despite Rogers on *Th.* 605) would
normally not be public figures: except Geusistrata (see 49 n.). For the
name Sostrate see *Nu.* 678, *V.* 1397, *Th.* 375 (a speaker in the Council
of the Women). It is well known from inscriptions (*PA* 13308 ff.,
13308a ff.).

43 οὔκουν ἐπείξεσθ'; the words may belong to (*a*) Praxagora (ΑΛΜui,
see *Th.* 783): rather more probably she next speaks at 57; (*b*) the
chorus leader (cf., with Rogers, *V.* 240): this view acquires strong
general support from the similar expression *Pax* 950; (*c*) (as I believe)
to Woman *A*, herself reproached for lateness, 32. οὔκουν, though it
need not (343), often coincides (1144) with change of speaker (similarly οὐκοῦν, 95 n.). Her seeming urgency gives way to comic bathos—
a further reference (14 n.) to Athenian housewives' love of wine. And
the *general* urgency is abandoned (88 n.) as they enter on a full-scale
dress rehearsal.   Γλύκη: not a member of the chorus. Possibly she is
the celebrated thief (*Ra.* 1344, 1362): but doubtless the name was
fairly common (*PA* 3039-41, 3038a, b). Robert (335) thinks that
Glyce is Praxagora, comparing Stilbonides (*Av.* 139), who later appears (in 644) as Pisthetaerus.   κατώμοσεν: 'has threatened and
confirmed her threat by oath'. The verb (like English 'swear') can
connote both threat and promise, *Av.* 630 ἐπηπείλησα καὶ κατώμοσα |
. . . μὴ πολὺν χρόνον | θεοὺς ἔτι σκῆπτρα τἀμὰ τρίψειν. See also 158. Cf.
the oath exacted by Lysistrata (*Lys.* 235): εἰ δὲ παραβαίην, ὕδατος
ἐμπλῇθ' ἡ κύλιξ.

44-5 τρεῖς χοᾶς: two gallons and a half, cf. *Eq.* 95 ἀλλ' ἐξένεγκέ μοι
ταχέως οἴνου χοᾶ.   ἡμῶν: slightly better in the mouth of Woman *A*
than in that of Praxagora (above), who tends (see 69 n.) to exclude
herself, as leader, from the rest. Note the position (translate with
ὑστάτην): the partitive genitive of unemphatic pronouns is sometimes
so postponed, 601, *Av.* 1084 κεἴ τις ὄρνιθας τρέφει | εἰργμένους ὑμῶν ἐν

αὐλῇ ... There is thus no substance in H. Richards's objection that the placing here is very awkward (*Aristophanes and Others* [1909], 54). **ἐρεβίνθων**: 'chick-peas' (*cicer arietinum*), still used for food in southern Europe. The ancient varieties are named by Theophrastus (*HP* viii. 5. 1), who says that the white forms are the sweetest. They were roasted (cf. *Pax* 1136, Pherecr. fr. 159) and eaten with wine as a dessert, πίνοντα γλυκὺν οἶνον, ὑποτρώγοντ' ἐρεβίνθους (Xenoph. fr. 22. 3). Hence the present collocation (606). See Pl. *R.* 372 c, Ath. 54 f. With the passage in general cf. *V.* 689 (of those who come late to the *law-courts*): ἥκειν εἴπῃ πρῲ κἂν ὥρᾳ δικάσονθ', ὡς ὅστις ἂν ὑμῶν | ὕστερος ἔλθῃ τοῦ σημείου, τὸ τριώβολον οὐ κομιεῖται.

46 τὴν Σμικυθίωνος: sc. γυναῖκα. So 49, 51, cf. τὴν Λάκωνος (*Lys.* 270). Sometimes the word understood is 'daughter', 'slave' (Headlam on Herod. 5. 3), ἑταίραν (Philetaer. fr. 9. 2). Smicython (cf. *V.* 401) is an Attic name well known from inscriptions: here he may be a contemporary citizen (see *PA* 12769 γραμματεὺς ἐπιστατῶν Ἐλευσῖνι, 407/6). If so, does the audience recognize in him a peevish aged husband (see below), unwilling to let his wife go out alone (μόνη, unaccompanied by servants)? κατὰ σχολὴν is then 'with difficulty' (ἀντὶ τοῦ μόλις ἢ ἀψοφητί, scholiast: πράως καὶ λάθρα, Phot. s.v.). But this is not an Aristophanic usage, and probably the phrase should be translated 'at her leisure' (cf. Pl. *Lg.* 951 a). The joke will then be that Smicython is impotent: Melistiche *alone* need not have hurried. It is weak to explain that her husband is only too glad to see her go (Händel, 192 n. 4). **Μελιστίχην**: the name is found in Crete, H. Collitz and F. Bechtel, *Sammlung der Griechisch Dialekt-Inschriften*, iii. 2 (Göttingen, 1905), 5008, ... [Μ]ελισ[τ]ίχα ... [παρι]όντος τῶ ἀπολαγασάντος | Ἐράσωνος τῶ Τηλεμνάστω.

47 σπεύδουσαν: she is running, like the rest, who, however, are carrying their shoes (74 n.). Melistiche, in her husband's footwear, cuts a comic figure (cf. *Eq.* 321 πρὶν γὰρ εἶναι Περγασῆσιν ἔνεον ἐν ταῖς ἐμβάσιν, Thphr. *Char.* 4. 1). **ἐμβάσιν**: these were the *shoes* (cf. *EM* s.v. ἀπὸ τοῦ ἐμβαίνειν τοὺς πόδας) of the ordinary citizen (ὁ ἐμβάδ' ἔχων, 633 n.) as distinct from the *sandal* (ὑπόδημα). The word is (*a*) a generic term for shoe (hence Λακωνικαί, sc. ἐμβάδες, 74), (*b*) used of *men's* shoes, especially of *old* men's (cf. 314, 850 n.), which suits the present passage (see above). For detailed discussion see A. A. Bryant, 'Greek Shoes in the Classical Period' (*HSPh* x [1899], 81). Monuments depicting footwear give no help in distinguishing the ἐμβάς (E. B. Abrahams, *Greek Dress*, 1908, repr. in *Ancient Greek Dress*, ed. M. Johnson [Chicago, 1964], 115–19, Bieber, *GK*, pl. LXIV).

47–8 καί μοι: correction of the MSS. to καίτοι (Cobet) is unnecessary. Woman *A* (who has not explained her own delay) implies that *Melistiche* has nothing to detain her (cf. 37–9), 'Yes, and to *my* mind ...' (καί connective). **ἐξελθεῖν**: 'left the house' (331, 734).

49–50 τὴν τοῦ καπήλου: 46 n. The wife of the keeper of the 'local' (ὁ κάπηλος οὐκ τῶν γειτόνων, Nicostr. Com. fr. 22. 1) would be better known (41 n.).   δ': position as in 46, 374. Γευσιστράτην: the nominal ending (41, cf. Λυσιστράτη, Φοβεσιστράτη, Eq. 1177) is prefaced by reference either (a) to γεύω (which well suits a tavernkeeper's wife: cf. Eub. fr. 138 οἶνον γάρ με Ψίθιον γεύσας | ἡδὺν ἄκρατον) or (b) to γεύομαι (sc. οἴνου, alluding to her fondness for her wares). Another meaning may be glanced at: cf. A. fr. 421 Mette ⟨νέας γυναικὸς⟩ οὔ με μὴ λάθηι φλέγων | ὀφθαλμός, ἥ τις ἀνδρὸς ἦι γεγευμένη. ἔχουσαν . . . λαμπάδα: the mere fact of carrying a light would not distinguish her (see 1, 27) from the rest. But her light is a λαμπάς (i.e. 'torch') and not a lamp: and some current story (as the article suggests) may underlie the mention of it here. Cf. (of a reveller) Philostr. Im. i. 2. 2 τὸ ἐν τῇ δεξιᾷ λαμπάδιον. But revellers (admitting that Geusistrata resembles one) would hardly carry torches in their *right* hand as a *rule* (any more than a Maenad did the thyrsus, E. Ba. 943 with Dodds), and it may be that some *double entendre* is intended (cf. Nu. 734). Note that innkeepers seemingly sold *torches* (Nicostr. Com. loc. cit.) as well as wine: and perhaps Geusistrata's is a symbol (1150 n.) of her profession(s).

51–3 καί . . . ὁρῶ προσιούσας: 27, 41 nn.   τὴν Φιλοδωρήτου . . . Χαιρητάδου: the second article (as commonly) omitted. So (for example) Nu. 622 ἡνίκ' ἂν πενθῶμεν ἢ τὸν Μέμνον' ἢ Σαρπηδόνα, Th. 491. Cf. Th. vii. 56. 4 τὴν Ἀθηναίων τε πόλιν καὶ Λακεδαιμονίων, Lucian, D. Deor. 20. 12 τὴν Φρυγίαν τε καὶ Λυδίαν. A. W. Gomme (CR xxxvi [1922], 163) remarks on the position of τε (γε, Meineke), which shows (in his view) that the two nouns are intended (as Lucian loc. cit.) to form one concept. ('We may imagine a well-known rumour of a *ménage à trois* or a single act of adultery condoned.') This is far-fetched: (a) it requires emendation (Gomme προσιοῦσαν 52), (b) apart from Th. loc. cit. (for which he suggests an explanation) the 'rule' admits of numerous exceptions (cf. Pax 35, Lys. 1244, Ra. 964).   χἀτέρας πολλὰς πάνυ: assuming that half the chorus (i.e. twelve, see 30 n.) has entered along with Woman A, the 'very many others' will be five. But they need not in fact appear at all (see 805). The main body enters (30), followed by the seven individually mentioned (41): finally the leader (54).   ὅ τι πέρ ἐστ' ὄφελος: 'all of any worth'. So often: as X. HG v. 3. 6, Lucian, Herod. 8 αὐτοί τε οὖν ἤδη συνεληλύθατε (i.e. you Macedonians) ὅ τι περ ὄφελος ἐξ ἑκάστης πόλεως. ἐν τῇ πόλει: as distinct from those ἐκ τῶν ἀγρῶν (281).

54–6 καὶ πάνυ ταλαιπώρως: cf. Calonice (Lys. 16), χαλεπή τοι γυναικῶν ἔξοδος ('it's hard, you know, for women to get out'). The speaker (γυνή, ΑΜui), who has had to nurse her husband (contrast 37–9), cannot be Woman B (Bergk). Identity is otherwise uncertain: (1) Woman A (van Leeuwen) is impossible: her late explanation comes

82 COMMENTARY

in oddly and at variance with what (on van Leeuwen's own suggestion) she says below (76); (2) a new arrival (Woman Γ) who does not appear to speak again (cf. the three-line appearance of the Reveller, *V*. 1332); (3) (best) the chorus leader (see above). **καὶ** is either (*a*) a 'particle of emphasis' (καὶ πάνυ *GP* 318), or (*b*) connective (in response to 52, which she hears as she enters the orchestra): i.e. '(Yes, I'm coming) and a very hard job I had to slip away' (47 n., S. *Aj*. 527 Jebb). Here (*a*) is, if less attractive, safer. **ἔγωγ'**: 'I for my part' (i.e. I can't speak for those already here). So 60, 65 (and often). **ὦ φιλτάτη**: to Praxagora (cf. 37). **ἐκδρᾶσα**: 'escaping' (cf. *V*. 126). **παρέδυν**: 'I made my way here secretly' (337). Cf. Pl. *R*. 421 e ὅπως μήποτε αὐτοὺς λήσει εἰς τὴν πόλιν παραδύντα. **ὁ γὰρ ἀνήρ**: 37. Cf. Calonice's explanation of delay (*Lys*. 17), ἡ μὲν γὰρ ἡμῶν περὶ τὸν ἄνδρ' ἐκύπτασεν . . . **τὴν νύχθ' ὅλην**: 39, 1123. **τριχίδων** . . . **ἐμπλήμενος**: cf. *Eq*. 935, *V*. 1127 ἐπανθρακίδων ἐμπλήμενος. τριχίδες, 'anchovies' (Arist. *HA* 569ᵇ25). For their popularity, cf. *Eq*. 662, where the Sausage-seller sways the Boule by the news of a very cheap supply. They were eaten boiled and pickled (fr. 416 ὦ κακοδαίμων, ὅστις ἐν ἅλμῃ πρῶτον τριχίδων ἀπεβάφθη): and their fine *hair*-bones (θρίξ, cf. Phot. s.v.) would cause the husband's trouble—'he kept coughing.'

57–9 κάθησθε τοίνυν: cf. 554 *Nu*. 254 κάθιζε τοίνυν ἐπὶ τὸν ἱερὸν σκίμποδα. The implication of the particle is partially explained in 58: 'Sit down then (since you all seem now, in spite of the delay, to have arrived).' It answers not the words but the attitude—half-apologetic, half-expectant—of the women towards Praxagora their chief. Cf. *GP* 569. The normal position is second word, as here (cf. 160, 554): see, however, 339. ⟨ἂν⟩ **ἀνέρωμαι**: most editors (with Dawes). Omission of ἂν would be easy (by haplography): Ionic forms (see apparatus criticus, cf. B. Speck, *De Aristophanis dialecto* [Breslau, 1878], 21) are hardly to be tolerated here. Cf. *Pax* 745 ἵν' ὁ σύνδουλος σκώψας αὐτοῦ τὰς πληγὰς εἶτ' ἀνέροιτο. **συλλελεγμένας**: the rarer participial form (cf. διαλελημμένον from διαλαμβάνω, 1090), if not merely metrical convenience, may lend a formal note to the address. The common form is συνειλεγμένος (D. x. 1), cf. *Av*. 294 (συνείλεκται). Note συλλέγω of convening an ecclesia (for which this is a rehearsal, 69). So Th. vi. 9. 1, X. *HG* iii. 3. 8 καὶ οὐδὲ τὴν μικρὰν καλουμένην ἐκκλησίαν συλλέξαντα. **ὅσα Σκίροις ἔδοξεν**: 18 n.

The women sit down at Praxagora's command, perhaps on the edge of a low platform in front of the skene (1152 n.): alternatively, they are seated (round the edge of the orchestra) on the ground. She herself remains standing near the altar (which represents the bema, 86 n.) and facing the spectators (129). When rehearsal starts (130), would-be speakers rise in turn, deliver their speeches at the altar, and return to their place when they have done (144, 169). This is the routine of the Assembly (408, 428). Compare and contrast the ecclesia portrayed in *Thesmophoriazusae* (295).

60–1 ἔγωγε: as commonly in answers (91, 1066).   **πρῶτον μέν** ...
ἔπειθ': 436, *Eq.* 1366 (contrast *V.* 1177).   **μέν γε:** introducing an example of how she has honoured the agreement. Cf. (for example) *Nu.* 1382, *V.* 564.   **λόχμης δασυτέρας:** Plu. *Moralia* 552 c χώραν ἰδὼν λόχμης ἔμπλεω δασείας, Hsch. s.v. λόχμη, σύμφυτος τόπος, ἢ κρύφιμος, δασεῖαν ὕλην ἔχων (cf. *Nu.* 325). See for the present use *Lys.* 800, Lucian, *Salt.* 5 ἔστ' ἂν δασύς τε εἴην, τὰ σκέλη καὶ τὸ γένειον ἀπαράτιλτος. Similarly δασύνω (66).   **καθάπερ ἦν ξυγκείμενον:** 'just as was agreed' (καθάπερ συνέκειτο, Th. iv. 23. 1). The conjunction (common in inscriptions) may lend a formal tone (*GP* 490 n. 1). A similar periphrastic form, *Av.* 1291 πολλοῖσιν ὀρνίθων ὀνόματ' ἦν κείμενα: see also 1094.

62 εἰς ἀγορὰν: (*a*) he had a shop, or other occupation, there; (*b*) he was a 'lounger' (ἀγοραῖος) who spent all his time around the market. (*a*) is better: and conceivably the phrase means simply 'to business' (anywhere). See *Th.* 457. Or if Woman *A*'s was a somewhat poorer household, her husband (like Chremes, 819 n.) may very well have done the shopping. For omission of the article (711, 728, 819) cf. *Eq.* 147 (Neil): contrast 681, 759.

63–4 ἀλειψαμένη ... ἐχραινόμην: 'I used to oil myself all over throughout the day' (*Nu.* 1053; cf. διὰ νυκτός, Th. ii. 4. 2) 'and try to get a suntan' (in order to look more like a man). The effort it appears, was unsuccessful (126, 387, 428). For the benefits of oil and sunlight to the male, compared with the cloistered woman's pallor, see Lucian, *Anach.* 25. Cf. E. *Ba.* 457 ff. λευκὴν δὲ χροιὰν ἐκ παρασκευῆς ἔχεις, | οὐχ ἡλίου βολαῖσιν, ἀλλ' ὑπὸ σκιᾶς, | τὴν Ἀφροδίτην καλλονῇ θηρώμενος. This whiteness of women is distinctive on many black-figure Attic vases: it was fostered (878 n.) by cosmetics. MSS. ἐχλιαινόμην ('I warmed myself'): but (*a*) the sense is feeble, (*b*) the short iota (Mel. *AP* v. 151. 6 and often, S. fr. 3 D² Ἥλιος ἦν, οὐ παῖς, Εὐριπίδη, ὅς με χλιαίνων | γυμνὸν ἐποίησεν) is not found in Attic comic writers (*Lys.* 386 οὐκοῦν ἐπειδὴ πῦρ ἔχεις, σὺ χλιανεῖς σεαυτόν, *Ach.* 975). For the present text (Bergk) see Lucian, *Bis Acc.* 6 τὸ σῶμα πρὸς τὸν ἥλιον εἰς τὸ Αἰθιοπικὸν ἐπιχράναντες, Phryn. *PS* (de Borries, 126) χραίνεσθαι πρὸς τὸν ἥλιον· τὸ λεγόμενον ὑπὸ τῶν πολλῶν ἐπικαίειν ἐν τῷ ἡλίῳ.   **πρὸς τὸν ἥλιον:** 'in the sun' (as often, see above), cf. *Nu.* 771. Similarly, French 'au soleil'.

65 τὸ ξυρὸν: an essential item of feminine equipment (see above and the list in fr. 320). The effeminate Agathon is asked to lend a razor (Ἀγάθων σὺ μέντοι ξυροφορεῖς ἑκάστοτε), *Th.* 218: he is pale (above) and shaven (ἐξυρημένος ἰδεῖν, ibid. 191).   **δέ γ':** 'and I threw away my razor, to begin with.' Possibly the particles are used as in 32 (n.), but seem best taken individually (i.e. γε emphasizes ξυρόν). Similarly

153, 780. Separation (as in these last) is a metrical convenience: it does not affect the sense (728 n.).

68–9 ἔχετε: cf. 74. They have not yet donned their beards (see 118). οὖς εἴρητ' ἔχειν: 25 n.   ὑμῖν: RΛMui, other manuscripts have ἡμῖν. Praxagora, possibly unconsciously, excludes herself, as leader, from the rest.   ὁπότε συλλεγοίμεθα: after εἴρητο (a secondary tense introducing indirect speech) the optative here represents ἄν with the subjunctive, as the form in which the order was conceived: i.e. the instructions were, ὁπόταν συλλεξώμεθα, ἔξετε τοὺς πώγωνας. Similarly, X. An. iii. 5. 18 παρήγγειλαν, ἐπειδὴ δειπνήσαιεν . . . πάντας ἀναπαύεσθαι.

70 νὴ τὴν Ἑκάτην: the worship of this goddess was popular (cf. V. 804) in Athens, particularly among women (Lys. 63, 700). The history of her cult in Greece is summarized in M. L. West, Hesiod Theogony (1966), 277. For the present oath in women's mouths cf. 1097, Th. 858 (otherwise νὴ τὴν Φωσφόρον, Lys. 738). So νὴ τὴν Ἄρτεμιν, μὰ τὼ θεώ (90, 155 nn.).   καλόν γ': 'a fine one' (exclamatory γε, in admiration, 422). A different connotation, 95 n.   τουτονί: 27 n. Women A and B each produce a long black beard from under their himatia (88 n.): carried perhaps in the pocket that was formed by the chiton pulled up above the girdle (A. Th. 1039, Hdt. vi. 125. 3).

71 Ἐπικράτους: a politician (Lys. xxvii, D. xix. 277, see also Introduction § II), whose facial hairiness was hymned by comic writers. Cf. Pl. Com. fr. 122 ἄναξ ὑπήνης Ἐπικράτης σακεσφόρος (for which epithet see 502 n. noting also the play on σάκος, 'shield'). For the brachylogy ('Ἐπικράτους = τοῦ Ἐπικράτους πώγωνος) cf. V. 1064 κύκνου τ' ⟨ἔτι⟩ πολιώτεραι δὴ | αἵδ' ἐπανθοῦσιν τρίχες. A big beard was an attribute of Spartans (Plu. Phoc. 10. 1).   οὐκ ὀλίγῳ: i.e. πολλῷ (by the figure of meiosis or litotes).

72 ὑμεῖς: the chorus, now seated (57 n.).   δέ: asking for further information. Cf. (among numerous examples) 799–803, 862–4.   φασί: 'they say "yes"', commoner in this sense in the mouth of the answerer himself, 457, Pl. 395. Cf. Av. 555 κἂν μὴ φῇ (i.e. 'if he says "no"'), S. OC 317.   κατανεύουσι: 'they are nodding their heads downwards' (in assent): cf. κατάνευσον, ἔασον (Th. 1020). Contrast ἀνανεύω, 'I nod upwards', expressing disapproval or dissent (Lys. 126). γοῦν: ΛMui (R has γ' οὖν). γάρ of other MSS. is weak. This is the use 'in part proof' (GP 451): 'they are nodding downwards (from which one may infer that they mean "yes").' So (for example) 102, Eq. 952. The information is perhaps for those spectators whose seats were remote from the orchestra, for whom a nod—unless much more emphatic than the present circumstances seem to warrant—would not be very easy to distinguish.

73 καὶ μὴν . . . γ': 'well, I see that you have carried out the rest.' The particles are (a) progressive, introducing a new point (583), (b) expressive of 'a generally favourable reaction' (GP 353) to the answers

LINES 68-77

of the women (523). For γε here (never used when καὶ μήν proclaims
a new arrival, 41 n.) see Neil's *Knights* (Appendix I, 193).

74-5 Λακωνικὰς: a type of man's shoe (sc. ἐμβάδας, 47 n.), 269, 345, *Th.*
142. They were normally red and originally Spartan (Poll. vii. 88).
Cf. Ἀμυκλᾶδες (fr. 978) with which Hsch. (s.v.) equates them, Περ-
σικαί (319). They were seemingly heavier (544 n.) as well as more
attractive (*V.* 1158) than the ordinary ἐμβάς (47). See Bryant, 82.
ἔχετε: not implying (cf. 68 n.) that *all* of them are actually *wearing*
shoes and cloaks (269, 268, 275 nn.). The later, more hurried arrivals
may have snatched up their husbands' himatia and run. Melistiche at
least (47) has her shoes on: but possibly only Praxagora—apart from
the beard—is fully dressed and ready. For shoelessness as a sign of
haste cf. A. *Pr.* 135 σύθην δ' ἀπέδιλος ὄχῳ πτερωτῷ, Theoc. 24. 36
ἄνοστα, μηδὲ πόδεσσι τεοῖς ὑπὸ σάνδαλα θείης.   **βακτηρίας:** 276, 509.
The Athenian's walking-stick (*V.* 1296) accompanied him to the
Assembly (150, *V.* 33). Though it could be carried (as vases show) by
citizens of *any* age, it was more especially a mark of (*a*) the old man
(*Ach.* 682), (*b*) those younger men who affected Spartan manners
(Thphr. *Char.* 5. 9). Extreme Laconomanes went further: σκυτάλι'
(i.e. small-scale Spartan σκύταλαι) ἐφόρουν (*Av.* 1283).   **καθάπερ
εἴπομεν:** Arist. *EN* 1099ᵃ32, 1100ᵇ33.   εἴπαμεν RVb1, but the first
person plural of the first aorist form is doubtful Attic. In Arist. *EN*
1100ᵇ9 the editors emend to second aorist -ομεν (cf. id. *Top.* 161ᵃ13).

76-7 ἔγωγέ τοι: '*I* have brought Lamius' stick at any rate' (i.e. if you
consider that as counting). Similarly, 473, S. *Tr.* 234 ἔγωγέ τοι σφ'
ἔλειπον ἰσχύοντά τε | καὶ ζῶντα . . . (*GP* 550).   **τὸ σκύταλον:** the
word is a handle for the joke (78 n.) and probably means nothing
more than 'stick'. But Woman *A* is carrying a big one (like the club
of Heracles, Pi. *O.* 9. 30) or possibly, indeed, a very small one (hence
Praxagora's *ironic* admiration, 79–81). The verb means (*a*) to bring
on stage from within (*Nu.* 634 and commonly), (*b*) to bring out (books
and papers, for example) from the place where they are regularly
kept (D. xlix. 43).   **τοῦ Λαμίου:** presumably her husband, of whom
she has not yet (in contrast to the other women) spoken. The name is
known from inscriptions (*PA* 8984–6): it may (*a*) refer to a contemporary citizen (otherwise Mnesitheus, Gnesitheus: Phot., Hsch. s.v.),
(*b*) recall the unpleasant trait of Lamia (*V.* 1177 ἡ Λάμι' ἀλοῦσ'
ἐπέρδετο, Crates Com. fr. 18 σκυτάλην ἔχουσ' ἐπέρδετο. Cf. *V.* 1035,
Pax 758, fr. 700b, Hsch., Phot. s.v.). Lamius—if he existed—was 'un
pétomane' (Van Daele) with a celebrated 'stick'. (These two facts
explain 78.) The scholiasts guess that (*a*) he was a poor man, who
made his livelihood by gathering wood (πένης καὶ ἀπὸ ξυλοφορίας ζῶν:
Λάμιος (-ας, Hsch.) was known as ὁ πέλεκυς, ὁ πρίων, (*b*) he is mocked
at as a gaoler (δεσμοφύλαξ, see below). But probably *anyone* called
Lamius (in view of the stories of Lamia, above) was liable to find

himself a target for jokes concerning σκύταλον and πορδή. Hence Woman *B*'s 'crack' (78). **τουτί**: 27 n. **καθεύδοντος**: directly contradicting 55–6 if the speaker there (see note) is Woman *A*.

78 τοῦτ' ... **πέρδεται**: most editors have followed the *Suda* (s.v. σκύτα-λον) : τοῦτ' ἔστ' ἐκείνων τῶν σκυτάλων ὧν πέρδεται. But ὧν (i.e. οἶς, by attraction) is nonsensical: 'one of those sticks (by means of which?)', as similarly Bothe's ἐκεῖνο (MSS.) τὸ σκύταλον ᾧ ... The present reading assumes *EKEINOYTO*, *Y* written much like *T* (see 2 n.) : it was then omitted (by haplography), thus causing the rest of the line to be emended. **ἐκείνου,** 'that well-known fellow' (*ille*). Cf. 167, *Nu.* 180 τί δῆτ' ἐκεῖνον τὸν Θαλῆν θαυμάζομεν;

79–80 νὴ τὸν Δία τὸν σωτῆρ': the oath by Zeus Soter (a common one, 1103) has no special meaning in the context (see 761, 1045 nn.), unless it is thought apt for Lamius as 'saviour' of the people (τὸ δήμιον, Bothe in 81, see under). **τοῦ πανόπτου**: i.e. Argus, the hundred-eyed guardian of Io (Ἄργου τινὸς πανόπτου, Aristid. xxvi. 6 Keil). Cf. A. *Supp.* 304 πανόπτην οἰοβουκόλον, E. *Ph.* 1115, Plaut. *Aul.* 555 and a vase described by P. Kretschmer, *Die Griechische Vasen-inschriften* (Gütersloh, 1894), 202, 185 on which the letters ΠΟΝΔΠ (i.e. πανοπ[written right to left) appear above the head of Argus. The scholiast refers to the *Inachos* of Sophocles (fr. 281 Pearson). **διφθέραν ἐνημμένος**: dressed, that is, in the goat-skin of the country-man (cf. *Nu.* 72). For διφθέρα in combination with σκυτάλιον cf. Nicophon fr. 2. The meaning *may* be that Lamius lacks vigilance (77 καθεύδοντος). By dressing like Argus he will gain it: and thus possess *all* traits essential for shepherds (political or real). So J. Taillardat, *RPh* xxxviii. 1 (1964), 41. But this is far-fetched, as is Rau's view (206, wrongly comparing *Ach.* 435) that Argus' dress, with holes for all his eyes (cf. πανόπτης) suits Lamius the poor man (see above).

81 τὸν δήμιον: 'the public executioner' (sc. δοῦλον, Lys. xiii. 56). Lamius (the subject of ἦν, 79), with Argus' διφθέρα and a σκύταλον of *that* size, could keep an eye on *him* (not merely Io). The παρὰ προσδοκίαν admittedly is weak: but Aristophanes does not always strike top form (much would depend, in any case, on knowing the current incumbent of the office) and no change proposed is an improvement (I include my own ὁ Λάμιος, *Hermes*, xciv. 3 [1966], 376). Rogers attributes the words to Woman *A*, explaining that the public executioner was 'doubtless' subordinate to Lamius the gaoler (cf. the scholiast above): the woman magnifies 'her own dexterity in escaping' (from the latter) 'unobserved'. But they rather belong to Praxagora, who (once she has expressed her wonder at Lamius' cudgel) returns to serious business (82) : and there seems to be no need to give **βουκολεῖν** its secondary sense of 'to deceive' (Men. *Sam.* 596). τὴν Δημιώ (δῆμος, Ἰώ), von Velsen, is ingenious: this strange creature may be thought of as a deity (βουκολεῖς Σαβάζιον, *V.* 10).

82-5 ἀλλ' ἄγεθ': all editors since Dindorf (see apparatus criticus). **ὅπως . . . δράσομεν:** 'see' (sc. ὅρα, 300) 'that we do', 296. Second person is more common (149) in this construction. **τἀπὶ τούτοις:** cf. *Pl.* 56 ἄγε δὴ σὺ πότερον σαυτὸν ὅστις εἶ φράσεις, | ἢ τἀπὶ τούτοις δρῶ; **ἕως . . . οὐρανόν:** 20, 31 n. **ἠκκλησία:** cf. for the crasis 387, 550, 135. **δ':** as not uncommonly, for γάρ. So (for example) 84, 115. **ἐξ ἕω γενήσεται:** 21 n., 551.

86-7 ὥστε δεῖ σε: referring directly to Praxagora (to whom the words are mistakenly attributed in *Λ*Mu i) but meaning in practice *all* the women. This suits the somewhat officious tone (see 30, 43) of Woman *A*. (Blaydes, ὡς ἐκεῖ γε, i.e. 'on the Pnyx', cf. 100). **καταλαβεῖν ἕδρας:** 21 n. The Assembly met seated (94). At an earlier period wooden seats are mentioned: the prytaneis (below) are represented as jostling each other for a front one (*Ach.* 25). But the people in general sat either on the rocks (*Eq.* 783) or on the ground (*V.* 31, 42). **ὑπὸ τῷ λίθῳ:** just underneath the platform (bema) used by orators addressing the Assembly. It is not clear if λίθος means a separate stone platform, or one shaped and hewn from the rock (λίθος and πέτρα are usually taken, in earlier plays, to mean the bema, *Eq.* 956, *Pax* 680: see, however, Allen, art. cit. below). The area is spoken of (admittedly in comic language) as big enough to 'run about on' (ἀναβὰς γὰρ ἐπὶ τὸ βῆμ' ὑλακτεῖ περιτρέχων, Eup. fr. 207. 3). **τῶν πρυτάνεων καταντικρύ:** the prytaneis were the presidents or chairmen appointed to preside at each Assembly (*Ach.* 173). A tribe (i.e. its fifty representative *bouleutai*) was allotted this task (Aeschin. i. 33): each of the ten tribes holding office for a period (πρυτανεία) that varied, to suit the lunar year, from thirty-six days to thirty-five (*Ath. Pol.* 43. 2). Part of their duty (see also 396 n.) lay in disciplining speakers (*Ach.* 56): they sat near the bema, confronting the Assembly, and looking down upon the Agora, from which the Pnyx was, by a gentle slope, approached. The women hope, by coming early, to install themselves in seats where they may 'catch the Speaker's eye'—the positions they adopt in the orchestra (57 n.) prefigure their place in the Assembly. See K. Kourouniotes and Homer A. Thompson, 'The Pnyx in Athens' (*Hesperia*, i [1932], 90-138), and (differing from them in certain details) J. T. Allen, 'Aristophanes and the Pnyx' (*UCPCP* xii. 2 [1936], 27-34).

88-9 ταυτί: 27 n. She seems to have brought wool for combing (see below), which presupposes wool-combs and a basket (*Lys.* 579). Where are the articles carried? The wool and combs, maybe, like the beards (see 70 n.) within the κόλπος, the basket in her hand beneath her cloak. (She can hardly have carried it openly, without exciting comment before now.) **ἐφερόμην:** (*a*) 'I was intending to bring *these* (to the Pnyx), you know' (as Praxagora affects to understand her, 93), (*b*) 'I was bringing *these* (but now I find them useless).' That is, she intended to work at her wool up till the very last moment (95) and then take her seat upon the Pnyx. But the need for hurry—implied by Woman *A*, though of course the whole rehearsal is to follow—makes her feel that she will not now have the time. Either way γε emphasizes ταυτί, τοι (35 n.) stands alone. (So *Th.* 887: κακῶς τἄρ' ἐξολοῖο κἄξολεῖ γέ τοι, 'hang him! and he will be hanged, you know.') For the use of the imperfect, cf. *Nu.* 57 οἴμοι· τί γάρ μοι τὸν πότην ἧπτες λύχνον; 'why did you light the thirsty lamp (which now proves to have used up all the oil)?' The middle implies' for my own purposes': her children are 'naked' (92 n.) and she means to improve the shining hour.   ξαίνοιμι: there are frequent allusions to women's work with wool, not only in writers but on vases. First they washed it (216 n.), then combed it off into a basket (καλαθίσκον, *Lys.* 536, 579) in order to provide fine strands for spinning (Lucian, *Fug.* 12). The operations of combing, spinning, weaving (ξαίνειν, κατάγειν, κερκίζειν, Pl. *Sph.* 226 b) are shown on a black-figure lekythos illustrated in Gisela M. A. Richter, *A Handbook of Greek Art*[6] (1969), 334, fig. 447.

90–2 πληρουμένης: repeating the other's word in indignation (93 n.): cf. 133, 136. '*Filling*, you wretch!' (when the point is, 98, to be there before it starts to fill at all). But before Praxagora can amplify her meaning, Woman *B* (following her own train of thought) speaks as if she had objected to ξαίνοιμι.   νὴ τὴν Ἄρτεμιν: so (for example) 136, *Th.* 517 νὴ τὴν Ἄρτεμιν | ἡμεῖς γε. Artemis (like Hecate, 70 n.) was particularly a woman's goddess.   τί . . . ἄρα: the particle after interrogatives lends liveliness (*GP* 39), 231. For the late position (more commonly it follows the interrogative directly) cf. *V.* 273 τί ποτ' οὐ πρὸ θυρῶν φαίνετ' ἄρ' ἡμῖν ὁ γέρων οὐδ' ὑπακούει; See also 460, 668. ἀκροῴμην: sc. ὑμῶν, i.e. as you rehearse. She wished only to be quiet (152). But Praxagora prefers to understand it of listening to the speakers on the Pnyx.   γυμνὰ: they haven't a stitch to their backs (she takes advantage of the latitude permitted to her sex).

93–4 ἰδού γε: here as 136 (cf. 133) in indignation. Normally (90 n., 136) the speaker's word is reproduced exactly, not as here worked into the construction (*Lys.* 851). See (for example) *Eq.* 87, *Th.* 206. ἦν . . . ἔδει: Praxagora fears that the woman may adopt an indecorous pose in the Assembly, like that of the wool-working woman on the cylix (Duris, Bieber, *GK* 1) who has tucked up her clothes and put a leg up (cf. ξαίνειν ξυζωσάμενος, *Lys.* 536). This is in jest: that she knows the woman's meaning is clear from 95–6.   παραφῆναι: (*a*) 'to give a view in passing' (96), (*b*) 'bring out from under cover and display' (cf. Philem. fr. 70, of a sword). So Hsch., s.v. Δωριάζειν· γυμνοῦσθαι· ἀπὸ τῶν ἐν Πελοποννήσῳ παρθένων, αἵτινες χορεύουσαι ἱματίδιον ἐπεπόρπηντο παραφαίνουσαι τὸ πολὺ τοῦ σώματος.

95–7 οὐκοῦν: R here indicates a change of speaker, as it tends to do with this word or οὔκουν (43 n.), 350, 1144.   καλά γ': the particle (ex-

clamatory, 70 n.) expresses irony (cf. 190, 794), i.e. 'fine things indeed!'
ὁ δῆμος: i.e. the Assembly, as in the formulaic prescript ἔδοξε τῶι
δήμωι in decrees, *IG* ii². 28. 2.   ὑπερβαίνουσα: (*a*) 'stepping over
those already assembled to her seat', (*b*) 'going up' (ἀναβαίνουσα) on
the bema (the scholiast's unlikely explanation).   ἀναβαλλομένη:
'with her clothes up'. So Thphr. *Char.* 4. 4 καὶ ἀναβεβλημένος ἄνω τοῦ
γόνατος καθιζάνειν, ὥστε τὰ γυμνὰ (αἰδοῖα, Schneider) αὐτοῦ φαίνεσθαι.
These participles do *not* explain ξαίνουσαν (F. Hauser, 'Aristophanes
und Vasenbilder', *JÖAI* xii [1909], 85).   τὸν Φορμίσιον: famed like
Epicrates (71 n.) for his hairiness, *Ra.* 965 with scholiast (μέγαν ἔχων
πώγωνα). Thus Hsch. s.v. Ἀριστόδημος: Φορμισίους δὲ (sc. οἱ κωμικοὶ
ἔλεγον) τὰ γυναικεῖα αἰδοῖα. This is true of at least the present passage
(from which perhaps his statement is derived). So the scholiast: δασὺς
ἦν. λέγει οὖν τὸ αἰδοῖον. Cf. the use of Θεόδωρος (πρωκτός, Hsch. s.v.).
98–101 ἦν . . . λήσομεν: this explains her indignation (90).   ἐγκαθ-
εζώμεθα: 23 n.   ξυστειλάμεναι θαἰμάτια: 'with our cloaks wrapped
tight round us' (486 n.).   Contrast the rustic girl in Sapph. fr. 57
L–P: τίς δ' ἀγροῖτωˢ θέλγει νόον . . . | ἀγροΐωτιν ἐπεμμένα σπόλαν . . . |
οὐκ ἐπισταμένα τὰ βράκε' ἔλκην ἐπὶ τῶν σφύρων;   πώγωνα . . . καθῶμεν:
cf. Ephipp. fr. 14. 7 εὖ δ' ὑποκαθιεὶς ἄτομα πώγωνος βάθη, Lucian,
Philops. 5 ἐκεῖνος οὕτω βαθὺν πώγωνα καθειμένος.   ὃν περιδησόμεσθ':
68 n.   ἐκεῖ: on the Pnyx, 86 n., 117.   τίς . . . ὁρῶν; doubtless,
but what of τις ἀκούων? They seem unconcerned about their voices
(and of course this is no problem for the *actors*). No doubt they will
shrink from conversation: they intend to sit together (296), and only
one or two of them (perhaps with mannish voices) mean to speak. In
the end it is only Praxagora herself (170, 427 n.) who addresses the
meeting on the Pnyx. See on ἀνδριστί, 149.
102–4 R and A have a paragraphus, and the words *could* belong to
Woman *A*. But after rhetorical questions γοῦν suggests continuity of
speaker (cf. *V.* 622): Praxagora herself is then adducing Agyrrhius'
case in her support (γοῦν 'in part proof', 72 n.). He was once a
'woman' (εὐρύπρωκτος, scholiast) and probably—she seems to hint—
still is. (A similar remark of Hegesandrus, Aeschin. i. 111.) But now
he successfully disguises his true nature by borrowing Pronomus'
beard, and is chief man in Athens (184 n.).   Προνόμου: the name
is a rare one (not cited in *PA*), but we need not suppose the man
referred to the same as the celebrated piper (Duris 76 F29). The
figure of the musician so named on the 'Pronomos' Vase (410 B.C.)
is beardless.   νυνὶ: 'at this very moment'. For the form see 27 n.,
Av. 800.   ὁρᾷς: cf. *Nu.* 355 καὶ νῦν γ' ὅτι Κλεισθένη εἶδον, ὁρᾷς,
διὰ τοῦτ' ἐγένοντο γυναῖκες.   πράττει τὰ μέγιστ': *Av.* 799 ἐξ οὐδενὸς |
μεγάλα πράττει.
105–9 Which is just (she goes on) the very reason why *they* must now
attempt to intervene. Cf. the very similar context, *Lys.* 522.

105–6 τούτου γέ τοι . . . οὕνεκα: 'it's because of *him*, you know' (see 88 n.). τούτου, depending on οὕνεκα (hyperbaton, E. W. Handley, *Menander Dyskolos* [1965], 171) : 658, S. *El.* 578 τούτου θανεῖν | χρῆν αὐτὸν οὕνεκ' ἐκ σέθεν; **νὴ τὴν ἐπιοῦσαν ἡμέραν:** a strange oath ('by the coming day', cf. E. *Ph.* 1637) but not to be emended. The coming day will, for them, be all-important. Similarly, Beatrice swears 'by this good day' (*Much Ado About Nothing*, v. iv. 94). **τόλμημα τολμῶμεν:** cf. *Pl.* 419 τόλμημα γὰρ τολμᾶτον.

107–8 ἤν πως . . . δύνωμεθ': 'in the hope of being able to take over', cf. (for example) *V.* 271, *Ach.* 1031 ἴθ' ἀντιβολῶ σ' (smear my eyes, 1029) ἤν πως κομίσωμαι τὼ βόε. **παρα-,** i.e. take over from the men. **τῆς πόλεως τὰ πράγματα:** 175, *Pl.* 919, Th. viii. 97. 1 ἐν ᾗπερ καὶ τοὺς τετρακοσίους καταπαύσαντες τοῖς πεντακισχιλίοις ἐψηφίσαντο τὰ πράγματα παραδοῦναι. Cobet proposed τὰς ἡνίας (466 n.).

109 μὲν: we must try to *benefit* the city (but note that in 108 τὴν πόλιν is subject of πρᾶξαι) for at present it is simply standing still. The μέν clause contrasts with the preceding (*GP* 377), 361. **οὔτε θέομεν οὔτ' ἐλαύνομεν:** a metaphor from sailing, 'we (citizens in general) are driven by neither sail nor oar.' Another sense is also possible: 'we (women) don't run races or row' (as 39 n.), i.e. we can't do the things that men do. θέω, of vessels that 'run' before the wind, *Lys.* 550 ἔτι γὰρ νῦν οὔρια θεῖτε: for the juxtaposition with ἐλαύνω see X. *HG* vi. 2. 29 εἰ μὲν αὖρα φέροι, θέοντες ἅμα ἀναπαύοντο· εἰ δὲ ἐλαύνειν δέοι, κατὰ μέρος τοὺς ναύτας ἀνέπαυεν. The phrase was proverbial, πάντα θεῖ κελαύνεται (Aristaenet. i. 14 Hercher). Cf. Men. fr. 241, Cic. *Flac.* 32 'utrum . . . cursu et remis . . . navigarit', L. Bauck, *De proverbiis aliisque locutionibus ex usu vitae communis petitis apud Aristophanem comicum* (Königsberg, 1880), 13.

110–11 καὶ . . . δημηγορήσει: paratragic, whether borrowed *in toto* (from a source now unknown) or composed. See *TGF²* 849. **θηλύφρων:** only here and in Vettius Valens (second century) 2. 32 (Kroll). Cf. γυναικόφρων (E. fr. 362. 34). **ξυνουσία:** *possibly* with *double entendre* (LSJ) of sexual intercourse intended. But we need not look beyond the common sense, 'a gathering' (*Th.* 21). **δημηγορήσει:** of addressing the Assembly, 400, 429.

111–13 μὲν οὖν: 'on the contrary', used as if in answer to a negative statement from Woman *A* ('women couldn't speak in the Assembly'). Cf. 765 n., *Av.* 1386 Πι. ἐκ τῶν νεφελῶν γὰρ ἄν τις ἀναβολὰς λάβοι; | Κι. κρέμαται μὲν οὖν ἐντεῦθεν ἡμῖν ἡ τέχνη. **που:** 'if I'm not mistaken'. Cf. (both for meaning and position) 119 n., 1179. Praxagora argues that even among orators (νεανίσκοι, of young upstart rhetors, cf. *Ach.* 680) the most 'womanly' are also the best speakers. *Real* women should thus be better still. Lucian reverses Aristophanes' argument, *Rh. Pr.* 23 ὁρᾷς ὡς λαλίστεραι αἱ γυναῖκες καὶ λοιδοροῦνται περίττως καὶ ὑπὲρ τοὺς ἄνδρας; εἰ δὴ τὰ ὅμοια πάσχοις, καὶ ταῦτα διοίσεις τῶν ἄλλων.

σποδοῦνται: i.e. βινοῦνται, 908, *Th.* 492. The literal meaning of the verb is 'crush' or 'pound' (*Lys.* 366). This same behaviour is attributed to orators (cf. Agyrrhius in 102) in *Eq.* 878–80, *Nu.* 1093, Pl. Com. fr. 186. Aristophanes in Pl. *Smp.* 192 a (repeating this traditional joke of comedy) remarks on the intimate connection of paederasty with public life.

114 ἡμῖν . . . **τινά**: 'and as good luck will have it this comes naturally to *us*.'   **ὑπάρχει,** 622 n., *Th.* 154 ἀνδρεῖα δ' ἦν ποιῇ τις, ἐν τῷ σώματι | ἔνεσθ' ὑπάρχον τοῦθ' (i.e. by nature).   **κατὰ τύχην τινά**: D. xlviii. 24. Similarly used is κατὰ θεόν, cf. *Eq.* 147, E. *IA* 411 Ἑλλὰς δὲ σὺν σοὶ κατὰ θεὸν νοσεῖ τινα.

115 οὐκ οἶδα: 'I'm not so sure: for inexperience' (despite nature, 114) 'is a great drawback.' So *Ra.* 30, where Xanthias' answer means: '*I*'m doing the carrying, by the feel of it.'   **δεινὸν**: 'a terrible thing', *V.* 27, 834 ὡς δεινὸν ἡ φιλοχωρία.   **δ'**: 84 n., *Ra.* loc. cit.   **ἡ μὴ 'μπειρία**: 'lack of experience'. Similarly Pl. *Lg.* 966c τὴν δὲ μὴ (Ast, μὴν MSS.) ἐπιτροπὴν εἶναι . . . 'exclusion from office consists in . . .' On the prodelision see 14 n., 418, 1160.

116–17 οὔκουν: 'isn't that just why we gathered here?' (to help our inexperience by practice). Praxagora wants to get things moving (82 n.): she therefore cuts short any possible discussion of nature *v.* experience in speaking. Cf. *Pl.* 916 οὔκουν δικαστὰς ἐξεπίτηδες ἡ πόλις | ἄρχειν καθίστησιν; ΒΛ and Aldus read οὐκοῦν (a confusion which recurs 638, 853, 1144).   **ξυνελέγημεν**: 58 n.   **προμελετήσωμεν**: the subjunctive may stand (προμελετήσαιμεν, Kidd) as expressing a continuing interest in the purpose. See J. W. Poultney, 'Studies in the Syntax of Attic Comedy', *AJP* lxxxiv (1963), 371.   **ἀκεῖ: ἐκεῖ**, the Pnyx (cf. 100).

118–19 οὐκ ἂν φθάνοις . . . **που**: 'you couldn't be too soon, I imagine' (111 n.), cf. *Pl.* 485 οὐκ ἂν φθάνοιτον τοῦτο πράττοντ'. For the double ἄν cf. *Pax* 321.   **τὸ γένειον**: 'the' beard that she brought out with a flourish (70 n.): now resting on her lap? (see 57 n.).

120 Woman *A* takes up **λαλεῖν** in its common sense of 'gossip', 'chatter idly' (see 16 n.). The word reassures her (after doubts in 115): '*chatter*—any woman can do *that*!' For this trait in women (a Euripidean slander, *Th.* 393) see Lucian, *Rh. Pr.* 23 (quoted in the note at 113). A garrulous woman is amusingly described, Men. fr. 66. 3 τὸ Δωδωναῖον ἄν τις χαλκίον | . . . καταπαύσαι θᾶττον ἢ | ταύτην λαλοῦσαν. νύκτα γὰρ προσλαμβάνει. Similarly, Plaut. *Aul.* 124, *Cistellaria* 120 (restricted to prostitutes, however), and Juvenal's female λογοποιός (*Sat.* 6. 408).   **ὦ μέλ'**: this masculine form, see 124 n., used at first by women only (if one believes the scholiast on Pl. *Tht.* 178 e) is in comedy addressed without distinction to men *and* women (133). Its use may imply (*a*) admiration (245), (*b*) strong remonstrance (520, 994), (*c*) disappointment, mingled with reproach, real (133) or playful

(here): 'now why didn't you say that in the first place?' Coulon
gives the line to Woman *B*, seeing her (after van Leeuwen) as 'l'interlocutrice buffonne' throughout (i.e. 57–284). Cf. H. G. Oeri, *Der
Typ der komischen Alten in der griechischen Komödie* (Basle, 1948), 32:
though one would surely hesitate to think of the speaker here as *old*.

121–3 ἴθι δή: 'come, then (since you feel so self-assured).' Praxagora
replies to Woman *A*'s comic confidence by calling on her to take
the floor. Cf. 148, *Pax* 405 ἴθι δὴ κάτειπ'. A similar usage, 131.
περιδοῦ: sc. τὸ γένειον. Praxagora points to the beard: the word itself
has therefore no need to be repeated. In 123 the words καὐτὴ μεθ'
ὑμῶν make the sense of περιδήσομαι clear. **θεῖσα τοὺς στεφάνους:**
apparently 'setting down the garlands', cf. *Ach.* 365 θεὶς δεῦρο τοὐπί-
ξηνον ἐγχείρει λέγειν. Praxagora has had a great deal to attend to. In
addition to her beard, stick, and lamp she has been carrying some
wreaths to be handed to the speakers (131, 148). Either she has had
them in her hand from the beginning, or now (at 118) produces them
from underneath her cloak. Or did slaves perhaps bring them on
when needed? The plural is odd, as *one* garland would be adequate.
But change (τὸν στέφανον, Cobet: the confusion is parallelled in *Pl.*
1041) would here be rash, and unsupported by 131, 163. (The sense
could not, I think, be putting on the garland', E. *Med.* 1160: for
(*a*) ἀμφὶ βοστρύχοις there clarifies the meaning, (*b*) Praxagora, though
putting her beard on along with the others, 123, lifts the garland only
later, 171.) *Two* garlands (τὼ στεφάνω?) could be used with good
effect here: 147–50 n. **μεθ' ὑμῶν:** i.e. those of you who mean to
speak. They need to practise not just speaking, but speaking with the
unaccustomed beard. (It is only would-be speakers who assume it
here: the others not till 273.) Thus Praxagora's **ἤν . . . λέγειν**, 'in case
I should decide to put a word in'.

Woman *A*—still seated—now dons her great black beard: the sight
of which (against her pale complexion, 64 n.) reduces Woman *B* to
a 'fit'. Praxagora, however (126) is not amused: she gives no answer to
Woman *B*'s nonsense, but, after tying on her own beard, proceeds
with the long-delayed rehearsal.

124–5 δεῦρ' . . . σκέψαι: 'look here, Praxagora' (cf. *Nu.* 91 δεῦρό νυν
ἀπόβλεπε) 'how *absurd* . . .' (cf. *Ra.* 1030 σκέψαι . . . | ὡς ὠφέλιμοι τῶν
ποιητῶν οἱ γενναῖοι γεγένηνται). σκέψαι, taken with both δεῦρ' and ὡς
(i.e. constructed ἀπὸ κοινοῦ). Alternatively punctuate δεῦρ'· (Coulon):
cf. *Nu.* 690 δεῦρο, δεῦρ' Ἀμυνία. **τάλαν:** 'my dear girl' (playfully,
contrast 1005). The masculine (or neuter, cf. English 'old thing')
used to women (120 n., *Ra.* 559), and always in Aristophanes used *by*
them (658, cf. Wilamowitz, *Das Schiedsgericht* [Berlin, 1925, repr. 1958],
74). **καὶ:** exclamatory and emphatic, *V.* 900 ὡς δὲ καὶ κλέπτον
βλέπει. **καταγέλαστον:** so of a face that is shaved on one side only,
Th. 226.

LINES 121–131 93

126–7 πῶς καταγέλαστον; 'what do you mean, absurd?' (as English likewise uses 'how'). Cf. *Pl.* 356 πῶς οὐδὲν ὑγιές; the last speaker's words (as here) repeated. **ὥσπερ . . . ἐσταθευμέναις:** her companion's light tan recalls the colour of fried cuttlefish (Alex. fr. 187). So Euelpides' appearance causes laughter and a simile (*Av.* 804, cf. *V.* 1309). σταθεύω (it seems) here means something like 'brown lightly' (scholiast, τὸ μὴ λίαν ὀπτῆσαι: cf. *Ach.* 1040). This comparison (the scholiast complains) is not to the point (ἀπρόσλογος). But the point surely is that Woman *B*, who aspires to a share in the government of Athens, has a mind that fails to rise above the kitchen. For fish as delicacies, 56 n.

Praxagora (standing near the altar, 57 n.) combines the roles of president and herald. Her notions of procedure are naturally vague (no women were admitted, 165 n.), but she realistically calls the house to order, and asks for any speaker to come forward. Woman *A* answers (131).

128–30 ὁ περιστίαρχος: nominative for vocative, 833. The περιστίαρχος was the officer who purified the place of the Assembly (Poll. viii. 104). But the animal he carried was a young *pig* (cf. Poll. loc. cit.) not a *cat* (Praxagora has taken things up wrongly). Doubtless the polecat, as a *house* pet (924 n.) would come to mind more readily for women. **πάριτ' ἐς τὸ πρόσθεν:** 'move forward', in order to be inside the purified area (τὸ κάθαρμα). So the herald says (*Ach.* 43) πάριτ' ἐς τὸ πρόσθεν, | πάριθ' ὡς ἂν ἐντὸς ἦτε τοῦ καθάρματος. The initial procedure at Assemblies is described by Aeschin. i. 23. These words (like the following imperatives) refer to a real Assembly (not to the present rehearsal): Praxagora is going through the motions. We need not suppose (*a*) that the women do come forward, (*b*) that παῦσαι λαλῶν ('stop chattering') is spoken to any of the group. Similarly, **κάθιζε παριών** (130) addresses an imagined late arrival (cf. 95–7): 'come forward and sit down in your seat.' **Ἀρίφραδες:** cf. *Pax* 883. But a reference to that notorious character (*Eq.* 1281, *V.* 1280) appears—apart from the mildness of the context—at this late date perhaps not very likely. Either this Ariphrades was noted for loquacity (in this respect resembling women, *Th.* 393) or else we have here just a typical Athenian name (see 41 n.). Inscriptional evidence is against the latter view (*PA* 2201–2).

130–1 τίς . . . βούλεται; the prescribed form to initiate debates in the Assembly. Cf. *Ach.* 45, Aeschin. i. 23. **περίθου . . . τύχἀγαθῇ:** '(well, since you wish to speak, δή, 121 n.) put on the garland: and grant that the outcome be auspicious.' The whole procedure is closely paralleled in *Th.* 379: Κη. τίς ἀγορεύειν βούλεται; | Γυ. Α. ἐγώ. Κη. περίθου νυν τόνδε πρῶτον πρὶν λέγειν. **τὸν στέφανον:** the singular (see 122 n.) suggests 'the garland that is worn on these occasions'. Public speakers wore one (*Eq.* 1227, *Av.* 463). But so did sacrificial victims (hence Strepsiades' fear, *Nu.* 256), and banqueters and revellers (691, 844: hence Woman *A*'s question, 132). **τύχἀγαθῇ**: cf. *Av.* 435 ἄγε δὴ σὺ καὶ σὺ τὴν πανοπλίαν μὲν πάλιν | ταύτην λαβόντε κρεμάσατον τύχἀγαθῇ | ἐς τὸν ὕπνον εἴσω πλησίον τοὐπιστάτου. The translation (above) attempts to render the solemnity of τύχηι ἀγαθῆι (ἀγαθῆι τύχηι) as often found in treaties and decrees: ὅ[τι] δο|[κεῖ τῆ]ι βουλῆι δέχεσθαι τὴν συμμαχία[ν] π|[αρὰ τῶν] Χαλκιδ[έω]ν τύχηι ἀγαθῆι . . . (*IG* ii². 44. 12).

132–3 ἰδού: 'there!' Woman *A* has risen as she answers (131): and moving over towards the bema (57 n.) puts on the wreath Praxagora holds out.   **λέγοις ἄν**: 'please speak', a polite form of imperative, cf. *Ra.* 1401 λέγοιτ' ἂν ὡς αὕτη 'στὶ λοιπὴ σφῷν στάσις.   **εἶτα . . . λέγω**; 'am I to speak' (deliberative subjunctive, *Ra.* 1) 'before I *drink*, then?', 535. Euelpides likewise misunderstands a garland (see last note) to signify a dinner (δειπνήσειν μέλλομεν; *Av.* 464).   **πιεῖν**: she shows herself a woman (see 14 n.).

133 ἰδοὺ πιεῖν: 90, 93 nn.   **τί γὰρ**: '(I ask this) for why . . .' (if not for drinking). For similar ellipsis cf. *Nu.* 403 τί γάρ ἐστιν δῆθ' ὁ κεραυνός; (i.e. if it doesn't come from Zeus).

133–43 The reproachful question (**ὦ μέλ'**, cf. 120 n.) reveals Woman *A* as a dullard. Praxagora rejects her as a speaker out of hand: but finds she cannot shake her off so lightly. For Woman *A* is keen to show that 'drink' is not irrelevant to the Assembly. She argues that (*a*) its decrees are inexplicable, unless one assumes the members drunk, (*b*) their procedure includes prayers, which mean libations (*V.* 863, *Pax* 431), and these of course in turn require wine, (*c*) they brawl like drunks and are removed by the police.

135 κἀκεῖ: 'there too', in the real Assembly on the Pnyx (100 n.).   **τί δ'**; 'what!' The particle here implies surprise (as 525) and indignation (157 n.).   **ἐν τἠκκλησίᾳ**: so always with the article in crasis (188, 191, 249), doubtless for metrical purposes. Contrast ἐν πυκνί (243 n.), εἰς ἐκκλησίαν (270), ἐξ ἐκκλησίας (376).

136–9 ἰδού γε σοὶ πίνουσι: 'just listen to you—"drink"!' (see 93 n.). The curious syntax (though not the sense) of σοί is paralleled in *Ach.* 470: perhaps the usage here comes closest to our (sarcastic) 'well, good for *you*.'   **νὴ τὴν Ἄρτεμιν**: 90 n.   **καὶ ταῦτά γ'**: 'and good strong stuff at that' (401). The women themselves are alleged (227) to like their wine εὔζωρος ('neat'). γε may be seen here (cf. 140, 142) as 'feminine underlining' (Tucker, *Ra.* 564).   **γοῦν**: 72 n.   **ὅσ' . . . ἐνθυμουμένοις**: 'when one reflects' either (*a*) 'upon their actions' or (*b*) 'on their deliberations', cf. *Ach.* 755 ἄνδρες πρόβουλοι τοῦτ' ἔπραττον τᾷ πόλει, | ὅπως τάχιστα καὶ κάκιστ' ἀπολοίμεθα. The second sense seems better here.   **ὥσπερ μεθυόντων**: an opposite sentiment, *Lys.* 1228.   **παραπεπληγμένα**: 'struck at the side', then 'palsied', 'mad' (cf. παράπληκτος, παραπλήξ). The word is more natural of *persons*, *Lys.*

831, Plu. *Aem.* 24. 1 παραπεπληγμένῳ . . . τὸν λογισμόν. It is, however, elsewhere used of laughter: E. *HF* 935.

140–1 καὶ . . . γ': 'yes, and further . . .', commoner with *one* word intervening, 142, 199. **τοσαῦτ' ἂν ηὔχοντ'**: Hermann–Meineke (see apparatus criticus), i.e. 'would they pray such lengthy prayers?' Cf. *V.* 461 and (for Attic augment ηὐ-) *Av.* 72. For preliminary prayer at the Assembly see Aeschin. i. 23 ἐπειδὰν . . . ὁ κῆρυξ τὰς πατρίους εὐχὰς εὔξηται. The 'heraldess' gives some idea of their content (*Th.* 295).

142–3 καὶ λοιδοροῦνται: the verb (both in active and in middle) of interrupting speeches in the 'House' (248, *Ach.* 38). But the meaning here is rather 'they brawl among themselves' (567). **ὥσπερ ἐμπεπωκότες**: 'like people in their cups', *Pax* 1156 ὡς ἂν ἐμπίῃ μεθ' ἡμῶν (*Pax* 1143). **τὸν παροινοῦντ'**: 'the man who has got out of hand through drink', παροινήσας οὖν καὶ ὀργισθεὶς . . . ἀποσφάττει αὐτόν (Pl. *Euthphr.* 4 c). Hermogenes defines the state (παροινία) in X. *Smp.* 6. 2 : τὸ τοίνυν παρ' οἶνον λυπεῖν τοὺς συνόντας, τοῦτ' ἐγὼ κρίνω παροινίαν (cf. *V.* 1300). **ἐκφέρουσ' οἱ τοξόται**: 'the archers carry out . . .', as they would have to, a member too far gone in drink to walk (cf. *Ach.* 1224). Amphitheus (*Ach.* 55) makes verbal protest: elsewhere we hear of 'dragging' an offender (258, *Eq.* 665, Pl. *Prt.* 319 c). Perhaps as well the verb suggests precautions (by knocking him out stiff like a corpse, see 926 n.) to make the drunk man easier to handle. 'The archers' are the Scythians (*Lys.* 451) employed as policemen in the city: a body of three hundred had been purchased at some date following 450 (Aeschin. ii. 173).

144–6 Praxagora by now is out of patience, and orders Woman *A* to her seat. The woman (still garlanded) retires: explaining (as she pulls off her beard) that it has tickled her, and thirstiness has turned her thoughts to drink.

144 μὲν: 'go *you* at least' (whatever of the others). The so-called '*μέν* solitarium*', 155, *Av.* 12 σὺ μὲν ὦ τᾶν τὴν ὁδὸν ταύτην ἴθι. **οὐδὲν γὰρ εἶ**: *Ach.* 681, *V.* 1504 ἐν τῷ ῥυθμῷ γὰρ οὐδέν ἐστ'. For this use, which 'belongs essentially to serious literature', see A. C. Moorhouse, *CQ* N.S. xv (1965), 32.

145–6 ἦ . . . ἦν: 'I wish I'd never got a beard.' Cf. (for example) *V.* 478 νὴ Δί' ἦ μοι κρεῖττον ἐκστῆναι τὸ παράπαν τοῦ πατρός. **δίψη . . . ἀφαυανθήσομαι**: see above. Her thirst was doubtless not lessened (132 n.) by the wearing of a garland on her head: ὥσπερ Κοννᾶς, στέφανον μὲν ἔχων αὖον δίψῃ δ' ἀπολωλώς (*Eq.* 534). Notice the αὐ- form (cf. fr. 613), used commonly in this and other compounds: it does not appear (despite LSJ s.v.) more particularly Attic than αὐαίνω (αὐαίνου MSS. *Ra.* 194).

147–50 Praxagora calls for other speakers, and Woman *B* rises and comes forward. She is given a *second* wreath (the *first* one is still being worn by Woman *A*, cf. 144–6) and exhorted to speak out 'like a man'.

147 130–1 nn.

148–50 ἴθι δὴ στεφανοῦ: 121, 131 nn.   καὶ γὰρ . . . ἐργάζεται: 'for
the business in fact' (cf. 211) 'is at work', i.e. is in progress, under way.
She means (I think) not that time is passing (as scholiast and editors
explain it) but rather 'the project has been started': εἴπερ μέλλομεν τὸ
χρῆμα δρᾶν (1164) we cannot abandon our plans now. (One is
sorely tempted to do so, she implies, after Woman *A*'s nonsense about
drink.) Cf. in general Thphr. *CP* vi. 18. 11: καὶ γὰρ διὰ τὴν ὑγρότητα
καὶ γλισχρότητα οὐχ ὁμοίως ἐργάσεται τὸ θερμόν. ἐργαστέον, van
Leeuwen: cf. A. *Ch.* 298, E. *Med.* 791.   ἄγε νυν ὅπως: 'come now,
see that . . .', 82 n., *Nu.* 489.   ἀνδριστὶ: 'in a man's voice' (ironical,
101 n.): ἀνδριστὶ μιμεῖσθαι φωνήν (Crates Com. fr. 3 D.). Cf. *Th.* 267.
διερεισαμένη . . . τῇ βακτηρίᾳ: 74 n., 276. Cf. Ephipp. fr. 14. 11 (of
a speaker) σχῆμ' . . . ἐπικαθεὶς βακτηρίᾳ.

The scene could of course be so arranged that Woman *A* becomes
the *second* speaker, not the *first*: in which case (as seemingly van
Leeuwen) she is leaning on Lamius' stick (76 n.). But (*a*) that joke is
long over, (*b*) the play was written for seeing, not for reading: if
Lamius' stick is in evidence, it does not need a mention in the text.
Praxagora (I think) here gives a demonstration of how Woman *B* is to
stand.

151–5 Woman *B* takes up her position. She starts with a fine oratorical
prooemium: begins to propose legislation (very warmly approved by
Praxagora, 159) to banish water-tanks from public houses: but is
carried away by her feelings on the subject and employs a woman's
oath to emphasize them.

151–2 ἐβουλόμην . . . ἄν: 'I should have liked one of the customary
speakers . . .' (τῶν εἰωθότων, D. iv. 1). The opening move there is
similar: cf. Thrasym. B 1 (D–K ii. 322), Isoc. vi. 2. See E. Fraenkel,
Beobachtungen zu Aristophanes (Rome, 1962), 138. Further parody of
rhetoric 171 ff., 412, 504, 588 nn. For Aristophanes' knowledge and
use of its techniques see Charles T. Murphy, 'Aristophanes and the
Art of Rhetoric', *HSPh* xlix (1938), 69–113.   τῶν ἠθάδων: *Av.* 271.
λέγειν τὰ βέλτισθ': cf. D. iii. 11 ἐπειδὰν . . . τὴν τοῦ βέλτιστα λέγειν ὁδὸν
παράσχητ' ἀσφαλῆ, D. iii. 12, 13.   ἵν' ἐκαθήμην ἥσυχος: 'in which
case (ἵνα) I would have sat silent.' Cf. (for construction) 426, *V.* 961,
Lys. iv. 3 ἐβουλόμην δ' ἄν μὴ ἀπολαχεῖν αὐτὸν κριτὴν Διονυσίοις, ἵν'
ὑμῖν φανερὸς ἐγένετο ἐμοὶ διηλλαγμένος, (for meaning) D. iv. 1 ἡσυχίαν
ἄν ἦγον.

153–5 νῦν: 992 n.   κατά γε τὴν ἐμὴν μίαν: sc. ψῆφον, 'as far as *my*
one vote goes, anyway' (Pl. *Phlb.* 57 a ἔγωγ' ἄν δύο κατὰ τὴν ἐμὴν
ψῆφον τιθείην ἑκατέραν τούτων). The noun is omitted (1) as in κατὰ τὴν
ἐμήν (sc. γνώμην), i.e. 'in my opinion'. This common idiom (Pl. *Plt.*
277 a νῦν δὲ κατά γε τὴν ἐμήν) at first sight is very tempting here: but it
must be thought at least strange with ἐάσω; (2) as elsewhere after μία,

when the context suggests the missing noun (*Eq.* 50, *Ra.* 693 τοὺς ναυμαχήσαντας μίαν, sc. μάχην). The present is a more extreme example: but change seems unjustified and rash. κατά γε τὴν παροιμίαν (cf. Pl. Com., fr. 174. 3), E. Romagnoli, *SIFC* vi (1898), 64. **λάκκους:** 'pits' for wine storage (X. *An.* iv. 2. 22) such as doubtless were found in any 'local'. (Their existence is well known from Olynthus: *Excavations*, xii. 204, 305-7.) She means to forbid their use —for water! Her παρὰ προσδοκίαν joke in 155 is eased by the fact that λάκκος can mean 'cistern' (Apollod. Gel. fr. 1, Anaxil. fr. 3 ὕδατός τε λακκαίου). The tilt is at the women's dislike of watered wine (227), not at fraudulent suppliers (*Th.* 348, *Pl.* 436, Thphr. *Char.* 30. 5). For other overtones of λάκκος see *Nu.* 1330, Aeschin. i. 84.

155 μὲν: 144 n.   **οὐ δοκεῖ:** she utters the 'non placet' of an ecclesiast dissenting from a motion (198).   **μὰ τὼ θεώ:** in Athens the 'two gods' are Demeter and Persephone (for Sparta see *Lys.* 81, for Boeotia *Ach.* 905): the oath characterized Athenian *women* (532, *Lys.* 148). It escapes Woman *B* in her zeal.

156-68 Praxagora's anger at the speaker's indiscretion is heightened (159) by disappointment. She pulls the garland away from Woman *B* (as she had not, 144, from Woman *A*). The woman reclaims it (163) and attempts to improve on her performance. But she catches sight (as she explains it) of Epigonus, and this makes her stumble once again.

156 μὰ τὼ θεώ: 90, 93 nn.   **τάλαινα:** reproachfully (90, 190), 242 n. Contrast the tone of τάλαν (124).   **ποῦ ... ἔχεις;** literally, 'where have you your mind?' The sense is not 'where have your wits gone?' (ποῦ ποτ' εἶ φρένων; S. *El.* 390) but 'what are you thinking of?' (ποῦ; = πρὸς τί;). Cf. (for example) Pl. *Grg.* 504 d πρὸς τοῦτο ἀεὶ τὸν νοῦν ἔχων. Her mind has been wandering (οἴκοι δὲ τὸν νοῦν ἔσχον, ἐνθάδ' οὖσά που, E. *Ion* 251).

157 τί δ' ἔστιν; 'what's wrong?', the fuller form (*Ach.* 178) of τί δ'; (135 n.).   **οὐ γὰρ δὴ ... γ':** '(I say this) for (133 n.) I certainly didn't ask you to *drink*' (like Woman *A*, 132). A similar use, *Nu.* 402 τί μαθών; (does Zeus strike down the oaks with lightning) οὐ γὰρ δὴ δρῦς γ' ἐπιορκεῖ. γ' there is missing in good manuscripts (see apparatus criticus in K. J. Dover, *Aristophanes Clouds*, 1968), but has won editorial acceptance.

158-9 μὰ ... : 'no, but ...', 463, 550.   **κατώμοσας:** 'you swore by', cf. *Ra.* 305 Δι. κατόμοσον. Ξ. νὴ τὸν Δία. Contrast the use in 43 n. **καίτοι ... εἰποῦσα:** this construction only here in Aristophanes (elsewhere 20, 103, the finite verb). Cf. *Lys.* xxxi. 34 καίτοι πολλά γε παραλιπών. G. M. Bolling (who emends there and in Pl. *R.* 511 d) believed it only a post-classical usage (*AJP* xxiii [1902], 319-21). But it is found in Aristotle, as he later (reviewing *GP*) admitted (*Language*, xi [1935] 261): and we need not suppose (despite the existence of 'women's language' in some cultures) that 'either Praxagora is praising her follower's speech in sub-standard language . . . or her syntax reveals her sex, just as much as did the other woman's oath μὰ τὼ θεώ to which Praxagora is taking exception' (ibid., 261–2).

160–2 νὴ τὸν Ἀπόλλω: expressing dismayed recognition of her error ('Oh yes, by Apollo, so I did!') and making amends, at the same time, by employing an oath which is chiefly used by *men* (659, 680: cf., however, 631). It elsewhere denotes (*a*) strong agreement or approval (631, 680), (*b*) strong denial or refusal (*Ach.* 59, *Av.* 263).   **παῦε τοίνυν:** 'stop' (παῦε intransitive, cf. *Ra.* 843) 'then, in that case' (τοίνυν, 339, i.e. since you realize your error).   **ἐκκλησιάσουσ':** MSS. ἐκκλησιάζουσ'. For the *future* participle (Bentley) see *Th.* 90 (ἐς Θεσμοφοροῖν ἐλθεῖν) ἐκκλησιάσοντ' ἐν ταῖς γυναιξί.   **οὐκ ἂν προβαίην . . . ἕτερον:** 'I wouldn't take another step.' Cf. Lucian, *Hist. Conscr.* 29 οὐδὲ τὸν ἕτερον πόδα ἐκ Κορίνθου πώποτε προβεβηκώς. Similar expressions, Thgn. 283, E. *Ph.* 1412, Din. i. 82 οὐκ ἂν ἔφασκεν ἐκ τῆς πόλεως ἐξελθεῖν οὐδὲ τὸν ἕτερον πόδα. Cf. also 267.

163 φέρε τὸν στέφανον: somewhat peremptory (cf. *Av.* 463). She reaches for the garland, dons it quickly, and starts on her oration (165).   **αὖ . . . πάλιν:** *Nu.* 975, *Lys.* 977. The pleonasm is commoner in tragedy, E. *Hel.* 528 ἥδ' αὖ τάφου τοῦδ' εἰς ἕδρας ἐγὼ πάλιν | στείχω.

164 οἶμαι . . . καλῶς: (*a*) 'I think I have practised well by this time' (μελετάω, to practise, sc. λαλεῖν 119): but the sense here is less funny than absurd, (*b*) 'I think I've trained myself (i.e. I've got the right idea) now.' For the absolute (though more literal) use of μελετάω cf. *Th.* i. 80. 4 εἰ μελετήσομεν . . . χρόνος ἐνέσται.

165 γάρ: for the particle here (remark its use in three successive clauses, *Pl.* 1172) see Pl. *Phd.* 86 e Λέγω δή, ἦ δ' ὃς ὁ Κέβης. ἐμοὶ γὰρ φαίνεται . . .   **ὦ γυναῖκες:** Woman B forgets herself again. She addresses herself to her companions (who are seated, 57 n.): ignoring the fact that her hearers on the Pnyx will be (270–1) and here in the theatre (probably) are *men*. The sight of Epigonus misled her. The joke, though self-contained, is pointed if only men attended at the plays (440, 1144 nn.). But evidence on this is indecisive, and women's presence seems to be attested (at any rate, in the fourth century, at tragedy) by Pl. *Grg.* 502 b–d. If women did attend, their seats would (one imagines) be nearer to the back than to the front (cf. *Pax* 962–7). For discussion see Rogers, xxix–xxxv, Ehrenberg, 27 n. 2, and Sir Arthur Pickard-Cambridge, *The Dramatic Festivals of Athens*², rev. John Gould and D. M. Lewis (1968), 264.

166 αὖ: the word here serves to point the *contrast* between γυναῖκας and τοὺς ἄνδρας. 'You wretch' (*Lys.* 426) 'are you calling men *women*?' Cf. X. *HG* ii. 3. 28 ὅπως αὐτὸς μὲν αὖ ἐν τῷ ἀσφαλεῖ καταστῇ, ἡμεῖς δὲ δίκην δῶμεν. ὦ (ΓVb₁B, cf. 763) is specious.

167–8 δι' ... ἐκεῖνον: 'it was' (a) 'that well-known [78 n.] Epigonus',
(b) 'Epigonus there [pointing] who's to blame'. In sense (b) ἐκεινονί
(Elmsley, 27 n.) would be good. But ἐπιβλέψασα (which thus loses its
prefix) is pointed, 'my eye lit on him there.' Compare ἐφοράω in Hdt.
i. 10. 2 and Thphr. *Char.* 16. 14. Epigonus is not elsewhere named in
Aristophanes (*Ἐπιγένη*, Beloch, 931). The joke is the old one (102 n.):
with its context here cf. *Nu.* 355 καὶ νῦν γ' ὅτι Κλεισθένη εἶδον, ὁρᾷς,
διὰ τοῦτ' ἐγένοντο γυναῖκες. For mention of a member of the audience
by name see 129, for actual pointing to him *V.* 74 Ἀμυνίας μὲν ὁ
Προνάπους φῆσ' οὑτοσὶ | εἶναι φιλόκυβον αὐτόν (cf. *Pl.* 800).   **ἐκεῖσε**:
i.e. in his direction. Was Epigonus currently a member of the boule?
If so, his seat was ἐν βουλευτικῷ (*Av.* 794), a section of the theatre
reserved for the bouleutai (scholiast *Av.* ad loc.).

169–240 Praxagora at last realizes that she herself will have to be the
speaker. She dismisses Woman *B*, takes the crown (171), and starts
on her speech (173 n.). Her remarks fall into four divisions: (1)
173–88, (2) 192–203, (3) 205–12, (4) 214–40. These four parts are
punctuated by expressions of admiration from the women.
    The first section (a) attacks demagogues in general, (b) taunts the
citizens who fear those who would help them while fawning upon
those who will not. Agyrrhius exemplifies these last.

169–71 καὶ σύ: as well as Woman *A* (144).   **ἄπερρε** is a strong word
of contemptuous dismissal (cf. *Nu.* 783).   **ἐντευθενί**: from the bema
(57 n.). Note the separation of ἄπερρε from ἐντευθενί: cf. 105, 490,
1049 nn.   **αὐτή ... λαβοῦσα**: 'for as far as *you* people are concerned
at any rate' (i.e. from what I have seen of your ability) 'I think I'll
take this crown and speak myself.'   **ὑμῶν γ' ἔνεκα**, 367 n. γε is
idiomatic in this type of expression (*Ach.* 387): to translate 'for your
sake' (i.e. 'on your behalf', cf. *Pl.* 177) deprives the particle of meaning.   **μοι δοκῶ**: cf. (for example) *V.* 250 οὔκ, ἀλλὰ τῳδί μοι δοκῶ τὸν
λύχνον προβύσειν.   **τονδί**: 27 n., sc. τὸν στέφανον (cf. *Th.* 380).

171–2 τοῖς θεοῖς ... βεβουλευμένα: the Sausage-seller and Euripides
(*Eq.* 634, *Ra.* 892) invoke their private deities before launching forth
upon a speech, and this was also Pericles' custom (Plut. *Per.* 8. 4). But
though Praxagora's speech proper begins in 173 (n.), the prefatory
prayer that she employs here is standard oratorical convention: cf. D.
xviii. 1 πρῶτον μέν, ὦ ἄνδρες Ἀθηναῖοι, τοῖς θεοῖς εὔχομαι πᾶσι καὶ πάσαις.
μέν: 'solitarium' (144 n.). Her meaning is, 'I pray to the *gods* (for I see
little chance of *human* help).' There is no need to read a 'pious μόνον'
(J. Jackson, *Marginalia Scaenica* [Oxford, 1955], 162 ff.: S. *Ph.* 528).
τύχειν κατορθώσασα: cf. in general *Pax* 939 ὡς πάνθ' ὅσ' ἂν θεὸς θέλῃ
χἠ τύχη κατορθοῖ, | χωρεῖ κατὰ νοῦν.

173–4 ἐμοὶ δ' ... ὑμῖν: δέ has an idiomatic use in tragedy, to mark
the *real* beginning of a speech: S. *Ant.* 1196, E. *Med.* 526. But here
(where paratragedy can hardly be intended) it merely answers μέν

(171). For analysis of her speech in terms of rhetoric see Murphy, 109–10. **μέτα**: i.e. μέτεστι, as anaphora, or moving back of normal accent, shows. She is not (I think) expressing 'dass nicht Stolz sie reden heisse' (A. Burckhardt, *Spuren der athenischen Volksrede in der alten Komödie* [Basle, 1924], 34, cf. *Th.* 383): at least the word-order seems against it. Rather, her claim here echoes Creon's (S. *OT* 630), κἀμοὶ πόλεως μέτεστιν, οὐχὶ σοὶ μόνῳ.

174–5 ἄχθομαι: *Pax* 683 (next note). **τὰ τῆς πόλεως . . . πράγματα:** 107. The distortion of the natural word-order recalls (for example) 169 (n.). **ἄπαντα:** the manuscript text should not be changed. Jackson rejects it (and Palmer's σαπέντα), *Marginalia*, loc. cit.: 'would the Pnyx have been favourably impressed by an unknown speaker, mounting the rostrum for the first time in order to announce that he disapproved of everything?' Perhaps not: but this is a fictional situation, and Praxagora is saying what she means—the state needs saving (209) because the men have made a total mess. It must be handed over to the women. She need not, of course, have expressed herself (cf. 429–56) in quite the same manner on the Pnyx.

176–8 προστάταισι: the word means (*a*) patron (of μέτοικοι, cf. *Ra.* 569), (*b*) leader (especially in democratic government, Pl. *R.* 565 d), (*c*) statesman, in general (as here). Cf. *Eq.* 1128. She means Agyrrhius (see 184). **χρωμένην . . . πονηροῖς:** *mots justes* in such a context, cf. *Ra.* 731 καὶ πονηροῖς κἀκ πονηρῶν εἰς ἄπαντα χρώμεθα. Similarly, *Pax* 683 ἀχθεσθεῖσ' ὅτι | αὑτῷ πονηρὸν προστάτην ἐπεγράψατο (cf. Pl. 920), D. iii. 27. Thucydides saw the Sicilian disaster and the origin of civil strife in Athens as due to the squabbles of Pericles' successors περὶ τῆς τοῦ δήμου προστασίας (ii. 65. 11). **κἄν τις . . . γίγνεται:** cf. Pl. Com. fr. 186 ἦν γὰρ ἀποθάνῃ | εἷς τις πονηρός, δύ' ἀνέφυσαν ῥήτορες. **ἡμέραν μίαν:** 'for one whole day'. Cf. *Nu.* 1200 διὰ τοῦτο προὐτένθευσαν ἡμέρᾳ μιᾷ. **χρηστὸς:** the regular opposite of πονηρός, cf. *Ra.* 1455. The whole of that passage is an admirable parallel to what Praxagora is saying here: she is trying to find an answer to Aeschylus' pessimistic question, πῶς οὖν τις ἂν σώσειε τοιαύτην πόλιν . . . ; (*Ra.* 1458). On the moral, social, and political antithesis χρηστός/πονηρός see Neil's *Knights* (Appendix II, 206).

179 ἐπέτρεψας: perhaps intransitive (cf. *Ra.* 811) or sc. αὐτήν, τὴν πόλιν (455). 'You have handed (it) over' (i.e. suppose you do): 197 n., *Av.* 78 ἔτνους δ' ἐπιθυμεῖ, δεῖ τορύνης καὶ χύτρας. The second person singular (199, 200) implies 'you, the average Athenian' as representative of Athens.

180–2 χαλεπὸν μὲν οὖν: 'now' (οὖν, *Th.* 67) 'it's *hard*' (μέν 'solitarium', 144 n.) 'to give advice to peevish people' (but nevertheless I must attempt it). An oratorical formula (see Lys. xix. 12): cf. ῥᾴδιον μὲν οὖν (ibid. 24). **τοὺς φιλεῖν . . . βουλομένους:** i.e. if you allow them (she means Thrasybulus, 203 n.). **τοὺς δ' οὐκ ἐθέλοντας:** i.e. even

if you give them the chance to (as you do: she means Agyrrhius, 184).
For βούλομαι/ἐθέλω implying desire/consent, see LSJ s.vv.

183–4 ἦν ὅτ': before the fee was raised for our attendance (292 n.,
where they hurry not to lose it). This was a measure which Agyrrhius
had sponsored (*Ath. Pol.* 41. 3): hence his present reputation (186).
W. H. Hess, 'Studies in the Ecclesiazusae of Aristophanes' (Princeton
dissertation, 1963), 49, sees this enactment as occasioning the play.
But even if they *didn't* come to meetings (says Praxagora) they knew
Agyrrhius for what he was.   **οὐδὲν τὸ παράπαν:** *Pl.* 1182 νῦν δ'
οὐδὲ εἷς | θύει τὸ παράπαν οὐδὲν οὐδ' εἰσέρχεται.

184–5 ἀλλὰ . . . γ': 'but we did think Agyrrhius a rogue' (177 n.). The
meaning seems to be 'Agyrrhius at least' (whatever our ignorance of
others): if so, perhaps read εἰ τότ' (183), 'if in times past' (*Pl.* 1117) in
contrast to νῦν δέ (185). Cf. Pl. *La.* 183 a εἰ δὲ ἐκείνους ἐλελήθει, ἀλλ' οὐ
τούτους γε τοὺς διδασκάλους αὐτοῦ λέληθεν αὐτὸ τοῦτο. Agyrrhius had
been convicted of embezzlement (D. xxiv. 135: cf. And. i. 133). But
he currently enjoyed great reputation: and on Thrasybulus' murder
(some years later than this play) was sent to replace him in the
Hellespont (X. *HG* iv. 8. 31). Demosthenes (loc. cit.) calls him χρηστός
(178) and eager for the welfare of the people: and Aristophanes'
judgement may be coloured, not so much by his sentence (or his vices,
102) as by his lowering of the comic poets' payment (*Ra.* 367, with
scholiast, Pl. Com. fr. 133). His career is reconstructed by Hess, 17 ff.,
who sees him (very unconvincingly) as 'the focal point of the political
satire of the *Ecclesiazusae*' (a latter-day substitute for Cleon).

185–8 χρωμένων: sc. ἡμῶν (ἐκκλησιάσαισιν). So X. *An.* v. 4. 16 οἱ δὲ
πολέμιοι προσιόντων (sc. τῶν Ἑλλήνων mentioned earlier) τέως μὲν
ἡσύχαζον.   **ὁ . . . λαβὼν ἀργύριον:** 183 n., cf. 380.   **ὑπερεπήνεσεν:**
'praises to the skies' (see *Eq.* 680).   **ὁ δ' οὐ λαβὼν:** there is no
suggestion of a *legal* disability. The words do, however, imply that
some Athenians (apart from those who came late on any one occasion)
could not, for private reasons, get to meetings. Their chagrin revealed
itself in strong denunciation of their luckier fellows, and the system.
μισθοφορεῖν: intransitive, *Ach.* 608 . . . ὑμᾶς μὲν ἀεὶ μισθοφορεῖν ἀμη-
γέπῃ, contrast 206, *Ach.* 602.

189 νὴ τὴν Ἀφροδίτην: this line may belong to Woman B, whose admiration leads her to an indiscreet woman's oath again (cf. 155, 160).
See 558, 981. But it rather suits Woman A, whose self-control
(31 n.) here breaks down. Hence her piqued ἀλλ' οὐκ ἂν εἶπον (192).
ταυταγὶ: i.e. demonstrative ταυτί (27 n.) with intervening γε (719).
Cf. *Av.* 171 νὴ τὸν Διόνυσον εὖ γε μωμᾷ ταυταγί.

190–1 ὤμοσας: Dobree's emendation (see apparatus criticus), cf. *Nu.* 825
ὤμοσας νυνὶ Δία.   **χαρίεντά γ':** 95 n., 680.   **εἶπας:** this first-
aorist form of the second person singular is preferred by Attic writers
(514): who always, however, write εἶπον (192, 255), 75 n.

193–203 The second part of Praxagora's address. The people were eager for the Anti-Spartan League: when they got it, they turned against its author. They cannot, moreover, agree on any policy—they should meet Corinthian overtures half-way. Their judgement on political leaders is erratic: there had been chances of salvation (202), but Thrasybulus now is out of favour.

For full commentary and discussion, see Introduction § II.

193–6 τὸ συμμαχικὸν . . . τοῦθ': the *original* Anti-Spartan League of 395 (consisting of Athens, Thebes, and Locris), not the later, larger combination. For the relevance of this point to the dating of the play, see Introduction § II.   **αὖ**: adding a further point, 'again' (667, *Ra.* 1069).   **ὅτε δὴ δ'**: 'but when finally' (315, 827). Note postponed δέ, illustrating 'the completeness with which the particle' (δή) 'sometimes fuses with the relative' (*GP* 220). Cf. ἐπεί + δή > ἐπειδή. **ἤχθοντο**: 'they showed vexation' (199).   **τῶν δὲ ῥητόρων | ὁ . . . ἀναπείσας**: the speaker referred to is unknown. τῶν ῥητόρων, i.e. those who spoke on the occasion (cf. *Ach.* 38), not implying a regular speaker like (presumably) Epicrates (71 n., Introduction § II). ἀναπείσας suggests persuasion either (*a*) against their will (τὸν υἱὸν τουτονὶ | ἄκοντ' ἀναπείσας, *Nu.* 868) or (*b*) against their current judgement (ὅτιὴ ζητεῖς τοῦτ' ἀναπείθειν ἡμᾶς, ὡς ἔστιν ἄμεινον | Πενία Πλούτου, *Pl.* 573).

197–8 ναῦς δεῖ καθέλκειν: either (*a*) 'suppose we must' (179 n.) or (*b*) '(at one moment) we must launch ships' (which is better, see Introduction § II). Cf. D. l. 4 ἐκκλησίας γενομένης . . . ἐψηφίσασθε τὰς ναῦς καθέλκειν τοὺς τριηράρχους.   **τῷ πένητι . . . δοκεῖ**: 'the poor man' (i.e. poor townsman, Ehrenberg, 80) 'votes in favour' (155 n.), since he might earn steady wages as an oarsman (cf. *Pl.* 172). The rate before the Sicilian disaster was a drachma a day, though halved thereafter (Th. vi. 31. 3, viii. 45. 2). But (because of ἡ τριηραρχία, a service imposed on them at Athens) the extra money needed to acquire a good man (cf. Th. vi. 31. 3) as well as the cost of fitting out and keeping up a trireme, would come from the pocket of the rich (*Eq.* 912, Lys. xxi. 6, D. l. 7 ff.). And farmers—apart from any natural aversion to service as sailors—always suffered from enemy inroads on their land (*Ach.* 183, *Pax* 628). Hence these two classes (whom ps.-Xenophon combines in a similar context, *Ath.* ii. 14) would naturally vote against the measure. For policy division based onec onomic interest cf. *Hell. Oxy.* i. 2–3, D.S. xviii. 10. 1.

199–200 ἄχθεσθε: for the present tense, and its proposed interpretation, see Introduction § II.   **καὶ . . . γε**: 'and what is more'. Cf. 140.   **σοι**: i.e. the demos (179 n., 205).   **νῦν**: no contrast is intended with the Corinthians' behaviour at the time of the Peloponnesian War. See again Introduction § II. We might have (on any view) expected νῦν δέ (185). But Praxagora's style (p. xxiii) is crisp and paratactic.

καὶ σύ νυν . . . γενοῦ: I read this as a typical exhortation to the demos at a time when the Corinthians are χρηστοί. Praxagora's delivery could ape the tone and gestures of some capricious politician. For the form of expression cf. καὶ σύ νυν φέρε (*Eq.* 971).

201 Ἀργεῖος . . . σοφός: the line is best read in van Leeuwen's emendation (Ἀργεῖος, MSS., X. *HG* vii. 1. 33) as a momentary popular opinion, 'the Argives' (who opposed a peace) 'are dunces.' See further Introduction § II.

202-3 σωτηρία: the great theme of the subsequent debate in the Assembly (394 ff., cf. 209). Aristophanes' concept is studied by V. Frey, 'Zur Komödie des Aristophanes', *MH* v (1948), 168–77. παρέκυψεν: 'popped her head out' (slily, and withdrew it, 884 n.) as Peace is requested not to do (*Pax* 979–85). ὀργίζεται . . . παρακαλούμενος: 'Thrasybulus himself' (like us in the Assembly, his supporters) 'is angry at not being called to your assistance' (181 n.). I print and so explain (without complete conviction) ὀργίζεται (Hermann: ὁρίζεται ΛΜυι) : cf. ὀργιζόμενος/ὁριζόμενος in scholiast V *Nu.* 5. ὁρίζεται is possibly just explicable as (*a*) 'is having limits put on him', 'is restricted', or (*b*) (as Rogers) 'is banished' (from your counsels). But both seem unnatural and strained. Thrasybulus (356 n.) was at this time out of favour (or at least could be sneered at by opponents with impunity if the same Thrasybulus is referred to in Lys. xvi. 15). But *Pl.* 550, while illustrating this, shows Aristophanes' own opinion, ὑμεῖς γ' οἵπερ καὶ Θρασυβούλῳ Διονύσιον εἶναι ὅμοιον (φατέ), and here Praxagora is saying in effect (like Euripides, *Ra.* 1446), εἰ τῶν πολιτῶν οἷσι νῦν πιστεύομεν | τούτοις ἀπιστήσαιμεν, οἷς δ' οὐ χρώμεθα, | τούτοισι χρησαίμεσθ', ἴσως σωθεῖμεν ἄν. παρακαλούμενος, 'called in', as an adviser (X. *An.* i. 6. 5). See further Introduction § II.

204 καλῶς: in the right way (by speaking of ὁ ἀνήρ). Woman *A* this time (189 n.) goes out of her way to be correct.

205-12 The third (and crucial) section of Praxagora's address. She blames the demos for its mercenary attitude: everyone is out for his own pocket (a stock charge, repeated in 778), and the state (τὸ κοινόν, *V.* 917) goes reeling. Then comes her own revolutionary recipe. Deliverance (σωτηρία) will only be achieved if the state is handed over (209, 210 nn.) to the women, to manage as they manage their own houses.

205-8 ὑμεῖς . . . αἴτιοι: a charge brought often by the orators, as Cleon (Th. iii. 38. 4), αἴτιοι δ' ὑμεῖς . . . οἵτινες εἰώθατε θεαταὶ μὲν τῶν λόγων γίγνεσθαι, ἀκροαταὶ δὲ τῶν ἔργων . . . See further Burckhardt, 58. ὦ δῆμε: cf. σοί, σύ (199, 200). μισθοφοροῦντες: 188 n. ὥσπερ Αἴσιμος: Aesimus is seemingly a symbol of unsteadiness. Scholiasts say (*a*) that he was lame, (*b*) that he was ἀμαθής, ἄτιμος. These two adjectives do not describe the Aesimus who stood (with Thrasybulus and Anytus, 203 n.) against the advocates of war with Sparta (cf. Lys.

xiii. 80–2). But clearly enough they are mere guesses, and he may well be the man intended here. See also 248 n. Perhaps (as van Leeuwen's note implies) a recent accident had made him currently a comic figure. Or had he (from the poet's standpoint) 'wavered' in his view by the time of the production of the play?

209 ἦν οὖν . . . σωθήσεσθ': *Lys.* 497, 527 (*Λυ.*) ἦν οὖν ἡμῶν χρηστὰ λεγουσῶν ἐθελήσητ' ἀντακροᾶσθαι | . . . ἐπανορθώσαιμεν ἂν ὑμᾶς. Her words again recall the technique of the orators: cf. D. viii. 71 ὑμεῖς δ', εἰ πείσεσθέ μοι, μείζους ἂν εἴητε.

210–12 ταῖς . . . γυναιξὶ . . . παραδοῦναι: the reception given to Praxagora's suggestion is described by Chremes (431). This idea (γυναικοκρατία) was also used by Amphis and Alexis, who each wrote a play under that title (Ath. 336 c, 125 b): and see Pherecr. fr. 141A. **καὶ γὰρ . . . χρώμεθα:** 'for in fact (148) we employ them . . .' For the fact see 14 n., for the argument *Lys.* 494, for its practical application 599. Cf. X. *Mem.* iii. 4. 12 ἡ . . . τῶν ἰδίων ἐπιμέλεια πλήθει μόνον διαφέρει τῆς τῶν κοινῶν. **ἐπιτρόποις καὶ ταμίαισι:** 'stewards and treasurers' (ἐν ταῖς οἰκίαις, Hdt. iii. 63. 2) but applicable to *public* office also (*Pax* 686, Hdt. viii. 51. 2). The words combined again, fr. 294.

213 εὖ γ' εὖ γε: *Eq.* 470, *Pax* 285. **ὦγαθέ:** emphatically masculine, for Woman *B* too (cf. 204 n.) has learnt her lesson. The passage shows (since this is now a *serious* rehearsal) that interruption (256 n.) either for praise (204, 431, *Eq.* 651) or blame (399, *Ach.* 56) was a regular feature of Assemblies. ῥήτορες who so behaved were subject to a penalty (Aeschin. i. 35): but the law there quoted is of doubtful authenticity, and seems to extend the sense of ῥήτωρ (195 n.) to anyone who tried to get a word in.

214–40 Praxagora supports her plan with reasons. Women are conservative (215–28). They are mothers and will naturally want to save their sons (233–4) and will take good care to send those sons their rations (234–5). Women are very resourceful (236) and could not be cheated when in office (237–8). For their perspicacity in affairs cf. *Lys.* 507 ff., 650.
  She ends (as Woman *A* started, 151 n.) with a rhetorician's flourish (239 n.).

214 τοὺς τρόπους βελτίονες: 'better in their ways', cf. *Pl.* 104 οὐ γὰρ εὑρήσεις ἐμοῦ | ζητῶν ἔτ' ἄνδρα τοὺς τρόπους βελτίονα. For a detailed comparison (by women) of the vices and virtues of the sexes, see *Th.* 802, for the claim made here *Th.* 810 οὕτως ἡμεῖς πολὺ βελτίους τῶν ἀνδρῶν εὐχόμεθ' εἶναι.

215–17 πρῶτα μὲν: μέν 'solitarium' (144 n.). Praxagora's line of thought is broken by the parenthetic 218–20: she therefore resumes at 221 without (for example) εἶτα δέ (cf. *Av.* 712) expressed. A similar use, *Eq.* 774. **τἄρια | βάπτουσι:** though wool shops existed, their owners could be rascally (cf. *Ra.* 1386) and women sometimes washed a fleece themselves (cf. *Lys.* 574). But here the reference is to dyeing (*Eq.* 523, *Lys.* 51). Cf. Pl. *R.* 429 d (with Adam) βάψαι ἔρια ὥστ᾽ εἶναι ἁλουργά, Thphr. *HP* iv. 6. 8 χρήσιμον δὲ ἡ δρῦς εἰς βαφὴν ἐρίων ταῖς γυναιξίν. What is known of Greek textiles and their colouring is conveniently summed up (with illustrations) in Richter, *Handbook*, 380.

θερμῷ: sc. ὕδατι, cf. *Nu.* 1044 ὅστις σε θερμῷ φησι λοῦσθαι πρῶτον οὐκ ἐάσειν. Similarly ψυχρῷ (Hdt. ii. 37. 3). An astringent was added to the water in order to produce a faster dye (Arist. *Pr.* 931ª13).

ἁπαξάπασαι: 'every single one of them' (710, 1148). There are no progressives among women.   **μεταπειρωμένας:** 'introducing novelties' (μετα-, as commonly, of change). The word is (ironically) ἅπαξ λεγόμενον: and Praxagora's election manifesto (588) is a far from reactionary programme.

218–20 ἡ . . . περιηργάζετο: 'but Athens, if this' (the old way) 'were all right' (as it is)'would not be content to find salvation' (literally, 'would not be for being saved', cf. for the imperfect 323 n., *Nu.* 63, 65) 'unless she were meddling in some new way' (586). This takes (1) τοῦτο as a comprehensive reference to everything ἀρχαῖος νόμος stands for, (2) χρηστῶς ἔχειν (here only) as καλῶς ἔχειν (272). Most editors adopt Dobree's εἴ πού τι: the further change to χρηστόν would improve it.   **καινὸν ἄλλο:** the Athenians of later times were noted for an eagerness for seeing and hearing 'some new thing' (Acts 17 : 21). καινόν, of 'innovations' (X. *Mem.* i. 1. 3), ἄλλο, not just 'different', but (like καινόν) suggesting 'bad', 'unworthy' (LSJ s.v. III. 4). **περιηργάζετο:** περι- of excess, officiousness, cf. the Theophrastan περίεργος ('the over-doer', *Char.* 13). So Pl. *Ap.* 19 b (of Socrates), περιεργάζεται, ζητῶν τά τε ὑπὸ γῆς καὶ οὐράνια.

221 καθήμεναι φρύγουσιν: (1) sc. τραγήματα (844), scholiast τρίχας (κριθάς, Dobree: Th. vi. 22) (2) absolute, i.e. they do the cooking, Hdt. viii. 96. 2 Κωλιάδες δὲ γυναῖκες ἐρετμοῖσι φρύξουσι. Cf. Pherecr. fr. 22 ἡ γυνὴ δ᾽ ἡμῶν ἑκάστῳ λέκιθον ἕψουσ᾽ ἢ φακῆν | ἀναμένει καὶ σμικρὸν ὀπτῶσ᾽ ὀρφανὸν ταρίχιον. In richer families (cf. *Ra.* 517) or for banquets (cf. *Av.* 1637) a cook might be specially employed. An early fifth-century terracotta shows women *squatting* (καθήμεναι, Hdt. ii. 35. 3, cf. Pherecr. fr. 75) making loaves (Ehrenberg, pl. XI, 125). **ὥσπερ καὶ πρὸ τοῦ:** *Th.* 398 δρᾶσαι δ᾽ ἔθ᾽ ἡμῖν οὐδὲν ὥσπερ καὶ πρὸ τοῦ | ἔξεστι. The humorous repetition (cf. *Av.* 114 ὥσπερ νὼ ποτέ, 773 n.) helps to stress their resistance to all change.

222 ἐπὶ τῆς κεφαλῆς φέρουσιν: for this style of carrying by women, see Pl. 1198 (τὰς χύτρας) λαβοῦσ᾽ ἐπὶ τῆς κεφαλῆς φέρε. There a religious procession is in question (cf. *Ach.* 253): an everyday instance is the woman with the bowl (Richter, *Handbook*, 200). Men carried burdens on a pole (*Ra.* 8) or on their shoulders (Ehrenberg, pl. XIV, 172), and Herodotus (ii. 35. 3) notes the different Egyptian convention, τὰ ἄχθεα οἱ μὲν ἄνδρες ἐπὶ τῶν κεφαλέων φορέουσι, αἱ δὲ γυναῖκες ἐπὶ τῶν ὤμων.

223a τὰ Θεσμοφόρι' ἄγουσιν: for this women's festival (the subject of Aristophanes' play of 411) see Deubner, 50.

223b πέττουσι τοὺς πλακοῦντας: *Pax* 869 ὁ πλακοῦς πέπεπται, *Pl.* 1126. These 'flat' cakes (πλακόεις, see *Ach.* 1126) are frequently referred to in the plays. They are named as specialities (*a*) of Paros (Alex. fr. 22), (*b*) of Samos (Sopat. fr. 4), (*c*) of Athens (Archestr. fr. 62. 15). These last were flavoured with honey (cf. Antiph. fr. 52): cheese and sesame were also used (*Ach.* 1125, 1092). The word covers many types of baking (Ath. 643 e). There is no valid reason for rejecting this line, which manuscripts except R have omitted.

224 τοὺς ἄνδρας ἐπιτρίβουσιν: 'they're the death of their husbands' as Strepsiades complains (*Nu.* 438) about his marriage, διὰ . . . τὸν γάμον, ὅς μ' ἐπέτριψεν. But Praxagora's meaning is more specialized: they exhaust their husbands (*a*) by raising (unfulfilled) desire (*Lys.* 888, 1090) or (*b*) by insatiable sexual demands. Either explanation suits what follows: (*a*) their husbands are denied, but lovers are granted favours freely, (*b*) they not only drain their husbands, but require lovers' services as well.

225 μοιχοὺς ἔχουσιν ἔνδον: the taking of lovers is regarded as a common-place (*Lys.* 212, fr. 187), and women submit themselves to slaves and muleteers if no other lover is to hand (*Th.* 491, cf. Semon. fr. 7 D.² 49). Mnesilochus is appealing (*Th.* loc. cit.) for honesty in facing up to facts, after protests in the Assembly (ibid. 392) against the Euripidean slanders which have made wives suspected by their husbands, ὥστ' εὐθὺς εἰσιόντες ἀπὸ τῶν ἰκρίων | ὑποβλέπουσ' ἡμᾶς σκοποῦνταί τ' εὐθέως | μὴ μοιχὸς ἔνδον ᾖ τις ἀποκεκρυμμένος (ibid. 395–7). See also 522, 884 nn. ἔνδον, 'in the house', as often (336).

226 παροψωνοῦσιν: (*a*) 'they buy little extras' (παρα-, 'in addition' παροψίς fr. 187), (*b*) 'they buy on the side' (λάθρα, scholiast: παρερπύσασα, 511). Shopping was often done either by a slave (ἀγοραστής, X. *Mem.* i. 5. 2) or by men (*Lys.* 560): Herodotus again (222 n.) notes the opposite Egyptian convention. But women could sell goods in the agora (cf. *Ra.* 1349), and no doubt could purchase there as well. The passage hints again at husbands' meanness (see 14 n.), which forces wives to purchase on the sly.

227 οἶνον . . . εὔζωρον: the old joke (14 n.) once again. Cf. 137 n., ἄκρατον (1123).

228 βινούμεναι χαίρουσιν: a comic theme, expanded and exemplified in *Th.* 473–519. Compare the trouble (a special case, admittedly) in keeping the women to their oath (*Lys.* 715): βινητιῶμεν, ᾗ βράχιστον τοῦ λόγου. Notice the climactic sexual joke to clinch the argument: cf. (for example) *Av.* 793–6. The structure in both passages permits an actor's pausing till the audience's laughter has subsided.

With the assonance in 221–8 cf. 773–6.

229-34 παραδόντες τὴν πόλιν: 211, 430, 555.   **μὴ περιλαλῶμεν:**
'let's not waste time in chatter' (like Euripides' plays, fr. 376). περι-,
of excess (220 n.). Or possibly 'talk round the point' (like περιλέγω,
περίλεξις, *Nu.* 318).   **τί ποτ':** 'what in the world', 'what ever' (259)
with ἄρα adding liveliness (91 n.). Cf. E. *Rh.* 134 (τί γὰρ ἄμεινον ἢ) . . .
κατόππαν μολεῖν . . . ὅ τί ποτ' ἄρα . . . δαίεται;   **ἁπλῷ τρόπῳ:** probably
best taken as synonymous with ἁπλῶς, and translated 'simply' (with
ἐῶμεν) i.e. without any further questions (D. xviii. 308). This has the
advantage that it brings out the contrast implied in περι-, ἁπλῷ.
Other implications are not thereby excluded: (*a*) 'absolutely' (with
ἄρχειν), i.e. without qualification (Th. vii. 34. 5), (*b*) 'in an open,
simple manner' (cf. ἁπλοῖ τρόποι, *Pl.* 1158) in contrast to the policies of
men (whom, according to Chremes' report in 437, she called πανοῦρ-
γοι in the Assembly).   **ὡς . . . ἐπιθυμήσουσιν:** presumably by
refusing (as far as possible) to commit their government to war.

234-5 σιτία . . . ἐπιπέμψειεν ἄν; 'send them additional (ἐπι-) rations',
when their three-day supply had been exhausted. This was the
regulation quantity for servicemen departing on campaign (*Ach.* 197,
V. 243, *Pax* 312). Cf. Th. i. 48. 1 ἐπειδὴ δὲ παρεσκεύαστο τοῖς Κορινθίοις, λαβόντες τριῶν ἡμερῶν σιτία ἀνήγοντο, (for ἐπιπέμπειν) id. vii. 15.
   1.   **θᾶττον** (*Suda*, see apparatus criticus) gives better sense than
μᾶλλον: men in office would send the extra *sometime*: *mothers* in power
would send it *quicker*. For a mother's view of military service see *Lys.*
588.

236-8 χρήματα πορίζειν: 'raising money' for public operations, 825,
Th. i. 142. 1 μέγιστον δέ, τῇ τῶν χρημάτων σπάνει κωλύσονται, ὅταν
σχολῇ αὐτὰ ποριζόμενοι διαμέλλωσι. Chremes expresses the idea by
χρηματοποιός (442).   **εὐπορώτατον γυνή:** the thought recalls E.
Andr. 85 πολλὰς ἂν εὕροις μηχανάς· γυνὴ γὰρ εἶ. For the neuter cf. E.
Med. 928 γυνὴ δὲ θῆλυ κἀπὶ δακρύοις ἔφυ. Cf., in general, *Eq.* 759.
οὐκ ἂν ἐξαπατηθείη: like the male population in Assembly (*Ach.* 114,
636). On the other hand, they were quick to call out 'trickery' when
genuine peace moves came from Sparta (*Pax* 215-19).   **ἐξαπατᾶν
εἰθισμέναι:** cf. E. *IT* 1298 ὁρᾶτ' ἄπιστον ὡς γυναικεῖον γένος, A. *A.* 1636.
239-40 τὰ δ' ἄλλ' ἐάσω: 'I will pass over the other points', cf. D. xxv. 9,
Aeschin. i. 81 τὰ . . . πολλὰ καὶ παλαιὰ ἐάσω.   **εὐδαιμονοῦντες . . .
διάξετε:** cf. *Nu.* 464 ζηλωτότατον βίον ἀνθρώπων διάξεις. The whole
is reminiscent of a typical speech-ending: Lys. xxiii. 16, xxxi. 34, D. xiv.
41 ἵνα δ', ὦ ἄνδρες Ἀθηναῖοι, μὴ μακρὰ λίαν λέγων ἐνοχλῶ, τὰ κεφάλαι'
. . . φράσας ἄπειμι . . . κἂν ταῦτα ποιῆτε, καὶ ὑμῖν αὐτοῖς καὶ τοῖς τἀναντία
πείθουσι συμφέροντα πράξετε. Cf. in general *Pl.* R. 621 b-d.
241-84 The rehearsal is over and Praxagora (amid congratulations)
doffs her garland. But a few points remain to be discussed. Suppose
Cephalus or Neoclides interrupts her (248-57): suppose the archers
remove her (258): and how will women (who raise their legs at other

times) remember to raise their *arms* for *voting*? (263–5). These problems settled, they see to their disguises, and set off singing for the Pnyx.

241–2 εὖ γ' . . . δεξιῶς: sc. εἶπας ταῦτα. Cf. 213, *Av.* 1511 εὖ γ' ἐπενόησας αὐτὸ καὶ προμηθικῶς. **ὦ τάλαινα:** here in admiration (cf. the use of μέλε, 245).

243–4 ἐν ταῖς φυγαῖς: any time in the period from 413 to 405 will suit her use of this expression, which may well mean 'among the refugees' (τὸν συλλέξαντα τὰς φυγάς, Pl. *Lg.* 682 e). Reference has been seen (1) to the proscriptions of the Thirty (scholiast, Isoc. viii. 123 τὰς φυγὰς καὶ τὰς ὑπὸ τῶν τυράννων καὶ τὰς ἐπὶ τῶν τριάκοντα γενομένας). But the Pnyx seems an improbable asylum; (2) to the flight of the farmers into Athens in the opening stages of the war (Th. ii. 14). But that was forty years ago, a long time for her schooling to mature: and how old is Praxagora at present? (she can pass for 'a handsome youth' still, 427); (3) to the flight before Lysander (X. *HG* ii. 2. 2). **ᾤκησ' ἐν πυκνί:** for the houses there see Aeschin. i. 81, and for archaeological evidence H. A. Thompson and R. L. Scranton, 'Stoas and City Walls on the Pnyx', *Hesperia*, xii (1943), 361. The article omitted only here in Aristophanes: but the use is later standard. So D. xviii. 55 ἀνειπεῖν . . . ἐν πυκνὶ τῇ ἐκκλησίᾳ, Aeschin. iii. 34. Cf. 270, 376 nn. **ἐξέμαθον:** 'I learned by heart, learned fully' (sc. ταῦτα, 242), cf. *V.* 1387. There may be implicit a suggestion that the speeches were all very much the same.

245 οὐκ ἐτὸς ἄρ': 'it's no wonder, then, that you were clever' (i.e. in the speech you made just now). Cf. *Pl.* 404 οὐκ ἐτὸς ἄρ' ὡς ἔμ' ἦλθεν οὐδεπώποτε. ἄρ', 'in that event (as I now see)', *Ra.* 921 ὦ παμπόνηρος, οἷ' ἄρ' ἐφενακιζόμην ὑπ' αὐτοῦ. See also 558, 711 nn. **ὦ μέλ':** in admiration, 120 n. For similar praise of a would-be woman orator, see *Th.* 433 οὔπω ταύτης ἤκουσα | πολυπλοκωτέρας γυναικὸς | οὐδὲ δεινότερον λεγούσης, cf. in general *V.* 631. **δεινὴ καὶ σοφή:** possibly a stock phrase used of sophists, cf. D. xix. 126 ὁ σοφὸς καὶ δεινὸς οὗτος καὶ εὔφωνος. Praxagora is in the enlightened tradition of Aspasia, Pl. *Mx.* 236 b (though see Wilamowitz, 'Lesefrüchte', *Hermes*, xxxv [1900], 551).

246–7 σε στρατηγὸν . . . αἱρούμεθ': RΛMui cf. *Nu.* 581 Παφλαγόνα | ἡνίχ' ἡρεῖσθε στρατηγόν, and Praxagora is later so described (491, 500, 727). στρατηγεῖν (ΑΓVbiB) is equally permissible: ἐμὲ . . . ᾑρημένην | ἄρχειν (714). **αὐτόθεν:** 'here and now', 'on the spot' (*Eq.* 330).

248–9 ἀτὰρ ἦν: 'but supposing' (ἀτάρ marking the fact of a fresh thought having struck her), *Nu.* 187 ἀτὰρ τί ποτ' ἐς τὴν γῆν βλέπουσιν οὗτοί; **Κέφαλος:** this distinguished orator and democrat (D. xviii. 219, Aeschin. iii. 194, *PA* 8277) and less distinguished potter (253) was said (like Epicrates, 71 n.) to have taken bribes from the Persians (Paus. iii. 9. 8). He later appears as an ambassador to Chios (*IG* ii². 34.

LINES 241-253   109

35) in company with Aesimus (208 n.). The scholiast (apparently
because of λοιδορῆται) says οὐχ ὃν λέγει Δημοσθένης, ἀλλὰ λοίδορος.
There seem to be no grounds for the distinction.   **σοι λοιδορῆται**
προσφθαρείς: σοι is perhaps to be taken ἀπὸ κοινοῦ with both *middle*
λοιδορῆται (*Eq.* 1400, *Pl.* 456 σὺ δ' ὦ κάκιστ' ἀπολουμένη τί λοιδορεῖ |
ἡμῖν προσελθοῦσ'..., contrast σε λοιδορῇ in 254, and note the later
construction of middle and *accusative* in Aelian, loc. cit. under) and
προσφθαρείς, 'meeting you, to your misfortune' (cf. Alciphr. iv. 5. 1
τάλαινα γυνὴ τῆς ἀνοίας, ἥτις τῷ τοιούτῳ θηρίῳ προσέφθαρσαι). For λοι-
δορέω of abusive interruption in the 'House' see 142 n., 254, for the
use of προσφθαρείς Ael. *VH* 14. 26 Ἀρκεσίλαον τὸν ἐξ Ἀκαδημείας Ἀντα-
γόρας ὁ ποιητὴς ἐλοιδορεῖτο προσφθαρεὶς αὐτῷ. The word has a force of
imprecation (i.e. 'curse him'): cf. *Pl.* 456 (above).   **ἀντερεῖς πρὸς**
αὐτόν: cf. *Nu.* 1079. The verb occurs more commonly with dative (570,
Nu. 998).

250-1 **παραφρονεῖν**: 'he is beside himself' (παρα-): so 1000.   **ἀλλὰ**
καί: meanings are (*a*) '(not only that) but also' (Pl. *Phdr.* 233 b),
(*b*) 'further', 'what is more' (*Eq.* 985), (*c*) (ἀλλὰ by itself) of an alternative suggestion (*Ra.* 56, so *GP* 9). (*b*), the 'progressive' sense,
seems best here (cf. 252), since Praxagora is building to a climax.
μελαγχολᾶν: 'is totally deranged', a stronger word (this context
suggests) than παραφρονεῖν.   For their juxtaposition see D. xlviii. 56
παραφρονῶν ὡς οὐδεὶς πώποτε παρεφρόνησεν ἀνθρώπων (explaining
μελαγχολᾶν preceding). Cf. *Av.* 14, *Pl.* 11 ἰατρὸς ὤν... σοφὸς | μελαγ-
χολῶντ' ἀπέπεμψέ μου τὸν δεσπότην, a passage which illustrates the
word's medical overtones (μελαγχολία in the Hippocratic Corpus is
a 'biliousness' resulting from excess μελαίνη χολή). See 1057 n., and
further in H. W. Miller, 'Aristophanes and Medical Language',
TAPhA lxxvi (1945), 74–84, Hellmut Flashar, *Melancholie und Melan-
choliker in den medizinischen Theorie der Antike* (Berlin, 1966), 38.

252-3 **τὰ τρύβλια**: these were saucer-shaped vessels, rather larger than
the type (ὀξύβαφον) that vinegar was kept in (scholiast *Av.* 361 : his
note here is εἶδος ὀξυβάφου). For illustrations of such pottery see
G. M. A. Richter and M. J. Milne, *Shapes and Names of Athenian Vases*
(New York, 1935), figs. 152–66. They were all-purpose vessels, used as
cups (*Ach.* 278, *Eq.* 905), for serving sprats (*Av.* 77) and mixing food
in (*Pl.* 1108). H. Van Effenterre, 'Trublion' (*RPh* xxxvii [1963],
41–6) sees τρύβλιον as a pot in which one stored in vinegar commodities
that needed to be 'kept'. Another meaning, 847 n.   **κακῶς**
κεραμεύειν: Cephalus thus combines his politics with pottery, as Cleon
(*Pax* 270 ὁ βυρσοπώλης, ὃς ἐκύκα τὴν Ἑλλάδα) his tanning, or Aristoxenus (*Pl.* 175) his trade in needles. His craft (his father's, scholiast) is
shown (for example) on a hydria (fifth-century Attic) in Milan
(Richter, *Handbook*, 318). The verb, in two senses, is best translated
'mould' (cf. R's reading in *Av.* 1538), καὶ ἐὰν... τὸν κεραμέα κεραμεύῃ

(Pl. *Euthd.* 301 d). I assume that Woman *A* was about to interrupt, with
another objection: 'but they know this.' But she cannot (and does
not) make this answer when Praxagora continues τὴν δὲ πόλιν ... For
stronger comment on Cephalus see Pl. Com. fr. 185 βόσκει δυσώδη
Κέφαλον, αἰσχίστην νόσον.   εὖ καὶ καλῶς: 'in fine style', Alex. fr. 133.
5 τῷ σιλφίῳ μάστιξον εὖ τε καὶ καλῶς. Cf. 638, εὖ κἀνδρικῶς (*V.* 153).

254 **Νεοκλείδης ὁ γλάμων**: 398 n., *Pl.* 665 εἷς μέν γε Νεοκλείδης, ὅς ἐστι
μὲν τυφλός (cf. *Pl.* 747), | κλέπτων δὲ τοὺς βλέποντας ὑπερηκόντικεν.
Scholiasts here and *Pl.* (locc. citt.) describe him also as συκοφάντης,
ξένος, ῥήτωρ: Hess (55, with great improbability, in view of the comic
poet's frankness) supposes that he stands for Heraclides (*Ath.
Pol.* 41. 3). His eyes (like Archedemus', *Ra.* 588) are μεστοὶ ἀκαθαρ-
σίας (as the scholiast explains ὁ γλάμων here). Physical peculiarities
or defects are often so mocked (46, 630 n.).   **λοιδορῇ**: 248 n.

255 **τοῦτον ... εἶπον**: 'I bid him' (here and now, hence aorist εἶπον).
Editors, desiring a future sense (cf. 250, 256) have altered (with
Brunck) to ἂν εἴποιμ'. But Praxagora (in paratragic language) is pro-
claiming an edict, as it were, on Neoclides. Cf. E. *Med.* 271 σὲ τὴν
σκυθρωπὸν καὶ πόσει θυμουμένην, | Μήδειαν, εἶπον τῆσδε γῆς ἔξω περᾶν
... and the common use of εἶπεν in decrees. On this analogy I venture
to alter the τούτῳ of MSS. to τοῦτον: forms of οὗτος are frequently
confused, A. *Pers.* 738. The dative was retained here the more readily,
in view of its common use with εἶπον elsewhere (as E. *El.* 1276). But
this place (and most of those which Blaydes quotes) only doubtfully
exemplifies his 'aoristus praesens'.   **μέν**: 144 n. She can offer this
advice to *him*, at least. What the advice means (apart from the fact
that it aims to be offensive) is obscure: nor (despite the scholiast
there) can one see a connection with *Ach.* 863 τοῖς ὀστίνοις φυσῆτε τὸν
πρωκτὸν κυνός. A glance at the backside of a dog (and of three foxes,
which the scholiast here adds to the expression) is an unlikely remedy
for blindness.

There is some evidence for dogs as healing agents of Asclepius at
Epidaurus (Collitz, 3339. 125): Οὗ[τος] (παῖς ἀϊδής) ὕπαρ ὑπὸ κυνὸς
τῶν κατὰ τὸ ἱαρὸν θ[εραπ]ευόμενος τοὺς ὀπτίλλους ὑ[γιὴ]ς ἀπῆλθε. But
probably the healing (as in Irish belief) was there brought about by
licking (cf. *Pl.* 736): it is hard to believe that dogs were kept for the
purpose indicated by the proverb. Παροιμία παιδική (says scholiast)
ἐπὶ τῶν ὀφθαλμιώντων: and but for the addition of the foxes (see
above) we might suppose his words a mere deduction. The phrase
would seem to have been either (*a*) a synonym or (*b*) advice for the
short-sighted, and Praxagora means either 'I proclaim him as a
bleary-eye' (who sees no further than one would up 'a dog's arse') or
'I bid him look up . . .', a popular retort (as Professor Dover thinks),
i.e. 'Try looking up . . . ,' to complaints that 'I can't *see* it *any*where.'
In either sense, the phrase is unexplained.

256–7 ὑποκρούωσιν: 'have a go at you' (a) by way of interruption (588, Ach. 38 βοᾶν ὑποκρούειν λοιδορεῖν τοὺς ῥήτορας), (b) by way of sexual assault (618), the sense in which Praxagora understands it (cf. κρούω, 989, 990). She knows all about κρούματα (Aristophanes' pun on the meaning of the noun is not found elsewhere). So προσκινήσομαι i.e. 'I'll not be backward.' Cf. the women's oath (Lys. 227), (ἐὰν δέ μ' ἄκουσαν βιάζηται βίᾳ) | κακῶς παρέξω κοὐχὶ προσκινήσομαι. ἄτ': 37 n. 258–60 ἦν... ἔλκωσιν: 143 n. ὅ τι δράσεις ποτ': 946 n. ἐξαγκωνιῶ | ὡδί: 'I'll square up in front of them, like this.' Praxagora strikes a pose of readiness for combat in the most approved style of the palaestra (or at least what she supposes it to be). So O. Lendle, Hermes, lxxxv (1957), 493–5. This preliminary wrestler's stance (see under) may be seen in E. N. Gardiner, Greek Athletic Sports and Festivals (1910), 379. For similar athletic gestures (ὡδί, 27 n.) cf. Pax 34–6 ὥσπερ παλαιστής, παραβαλὼν τοὺς γομφίους, | καὶ ταῦτα τὴν κεφάλην τε καὶ τὼ χεῖρέ πως | ὡδὶ περιάγων . . . , for the sense of the verb here Arist. Rh. 1416ᵃ2 οὐδὲν γὰρ προεξαγκωνίσας (i.e. without prooemium) οὐδὲ προανακινήσας (sc. ὁ Γοργίας) εὐθὺς ἄρχεται Ἧλις πόλις εὐδαίμων. μέση . . . ληφθήσομαι: 'be seized around the waist', as in a wrestling-bout, cf. Nu. 1047 εὐθὺς γάρ σ' ἔχω μέσον λαβὼν ἄφυκτον, Gardiner, 386, H. A. Harris, Greek Athletes and Athletics (1964), pl. 13B. So ἀμεσολάβητος in inscriptions (BCH xvi [1892], 455, 94. 12): and μέσος ἔχομαι is similarly used (Ach. 571, Ra. 469). But the sense here looks back to ὑποκρούω in its second meaning (256 n.): Ach. 274(below).
261 ἡμεῖς: the speaker is (I think) the coryphaeus, not (as usually stated) Woman A. The chorus seem to promise prodigies of valour (δέ γ' in 'lively rejoinders', 32 n.) but finish with 'we'll bid them let you be.' Is the παρὰ προσδοκίαν (31 n.) meant to parody the similar passivity displayed by tragic choruses (A. A. 1347, E. Hipp. 782)? ἢν αἴρωσ': 'if they lift you' (like a wrestler, see above). The double meaning is made clear by Dicaeopolis (Ach. 273): τὴν Στρυμοδώρου Θρᾷτταν . . . | μέσην λαβόντ' ἄραντα κατα-|βαλόντα καταγιγαρτίσ' ὦ | Φαλῆς Φαλῆς.
264–5 τὰς χεῖρας αἴρειν: i.e. in voting (χειροτονητέον, 266). The direct vote for certain state offices (the archonship, for example) was abolished in 487 B.C. and replaced by a lottery (Ath. Pol. 22. 5), the system of κλήρωσις ἐκ προκρίτων (ibid. 8. 1, Arist. Pol. 1298ᵇ9). For Athenian voting procedure see A. L. Boegehold in Hesperia, xxxii (1963), 366–74. But στρατηγοί (the position to be occupied by Praxagora, 246) were still elected in the old way (517, cf. Ach. 598), and voting by hand would be natural of course in policy matters like the present (297, 797): ἀράτω τὰς χεῖρας, ὅτῳ ταῦτα δοκεῖ (scholiast on A. Supp. 607). See further 267 n. τότε: 'then', i.e. in the Assembly (ἐκεῖ, 100), rather strange. She means (I think) to emphasize (the word is emphatic by position) the fact that they can all remember now: but will

they when they get on to the Pnyx? Or ποτε 'how ever' (259)? For this confusion cf. (for example) E. *El.* 42.　**αἴρειν τὼ σκέλει**: the women swear (*Lys.* 229) οὐ πρὸς τὸν ὄροφον ἀνατενῶ τὰ Περσικά. So *Pax* 889 ὥστ' εὐθέως ἄραντας ὑμᾶς τὼ σκέλει | ταύτης μετέωρα καταγαγεῖν ἀνάρρυσιν (cf. *Av.* 1254). οἰκία . . . τὰ σκέλη ἠρκυῖα is a brothel (Thphr. *Char.* 28. 3). Similarly Latin 'pedem tollo' (Cic. *Att.* ii. 1. 5, Mart. x. 81. 4).

266–7 χαλεπὸν τὸ πρᾶγμ': to remember (264) to raise their hands. But she means, I think, also to suggest the difficulty of remembering that they are dressed as *men*. For in voting they will have to raise the *right* arm (A. *Supp.* 607 πανδημίᾳ γὰρ χερσὶ δεξιωνύμοις | ἔφριξεν αἰθὴρ τόνδε κραινόντων λόγον), the one that (though methods of draping the himation, as monuments show, could vary greatly) was normally by *men* (276 n.) left unimpeded. Hence **ἐξωμισάσαις**, as though wearing an ἐξωμίς (*Lys.* 662), a tunic which left one shoulder bare. The sense then is 'baring to the shoulder'.　**τὸν ἕτερον βραχίονα**: 'one arm' (the right one, see above). Cf. in general 161.

268 ἄγε νυν: 149. While Praxagora gives her final orders, the women bustle round her to obey them: doubtless providing a good deal of comic entertainment in the process.　**ἀναστέλλεσθ' . . . τὰ χιτώνια**: 'hitch up your tunics.' Many of the women (74 n.) have not yet donned himatia (275) or shoes (269). The diminutive χιτώνιον seems not to imply shortness (whatever may be true of other places, as *Pl.* 984), for ἀναστέλλεσθε is then pointless. In the plays it is specifically used of *women's* dresses (374, *Ra.* 411): but fineness of material (Abrahams, 70) is not necessarily connoted (it seems improbable in *Ra.* loc. cit.). Affectionate familiarity perhaps explains Praxagora's use here.

269–71 τὰς Λακωνικάς: 74 n.　**ἐθεᾶσθ'**: the imperfect is well explained by V. Coulon ('Observations philologiques sur divers passages d'Aristophane', *REG* l [1937], 30 n. 6): the days when *men* will leave the house to attend the Assembly are now over. (ἄνδρα θεᾶσθ' ΛMu1.)　**εἰς ἐκκλησίαν**: so always without article (289, 352), ἐξ ἐκκλησίας (376). See also 135, 243 nn.　**θύραζ'**: as monuments indicate, neither men nor women (though see *Lys.* 229) would wear shoes very often in the house.

272–3 ταῦτα . . . ἔχῃ καλῶς: 219 n.　**περιδεῖσθε**: only the speakers donned their beards at 118, and Woman *A* probably removed hers (144–6 n.) immediately after.

273–6 δέ γε: merely continuative (contrast 261), *Th.* 987.　**ἀκριβώσητε**: 'fit exactly', 'adjust to a nicety'. There is no need for change here (ἀκριβῶς ἦτε, Bisschop): E. *Hipp.* 468 οὐδὲ στέγην γὰρ ἦ κατηρεφεῖς δόμοι | καλῶς ἀκριβώσαις ἄν (Barrett).　**ἅπερ γ'**: 'those same ones that you stole'. (Her implication is, the time is now at hand to put them to the use for which you stole them.) Cf. E. *El.* 909 οὔποτ' ἐξελίμπανον |

θρυλοῦσ᾽ ἅ γ᾽ εἰπεῖν ἤθελον κατ᾽ ὄμμα σόν (and now the time has come for me to say them). γ᾽ (A: other manuscripts have τ᾽, a common error, 473, 780) is usually read after ἀνδρεῖα. But its force in that position is not clear.   ἐπαναβάλησθε: J. D. Denniston (*CR* xlvii [1933], 215). *Suda* -βάλεσθε (for MSS.' unmetrical -βάλλεσθε). But καὶ . . . γε is then difficult to parallel ('throw on your husbands' cloaks *as well*?) in spite of Coulon's efforts to defend it (art. cit. [269 n.], 31). The order, 'throw up on (your shoulder)', side unspecified, suggests that no one style of draping the himation was currently *de rigueur* for their men-folk. This is supported by the evidence of monuments: it may be, however, that a draping to the right-hand side was seen as a mark of better breeding. Cf. *Av.* 1567 οὗτος τί δρᾷς; ἐπ᾽ ἀριστέρ᾽ οὕτως ἀμπέχει; | οὐ μεταβαλεῖς θοἰμάτιον ὧδ᾽ ἐπιδέξια; Pl. *Tht.* 175 e ἀναβάλλεσθαι δὲ οὐκ ἐπισταμένου ἐπιδέξια ἐλευθερίως. For discussion see M. M. (Lady) Evans, *Chapters on Greek Dress* (1893), 49 ff.

276-9 κᾆτα: the καί is 'apodotic', i.e. introducing the main clause (*GP* 308).   ταῖς βακτηρίαις | ἐπερειδόμεναι: by *leaning* on their sticks (74 n.) they will look like older men (278). Cf. in general 150.   ᾄδουσαι . . . ἀγροίκων: it would seem that old men and country-folk were given to singing in the streets. So the aged jurors (*V.* 219) will make their way towards the court-house λύχνους ἔχοντες καὶ μινυρίζοντες μέλη | ἀρχαῖα μελισιδωνοφρυνιχήρατα. The learning of old national songs and music was part of the ἀρχαία παιδεία which the Just Cause applauds (*Nu.* 966). Types of country (and other) songs are listed and described by Athenaeus (618 c-620 a).

279-81 ἡμεῖς: i.e. the actors, as αὐτῶν (280) is the chorus, to whom Praxagora's orders were addressed. So the scholiast interprets (rightly). Praxagora and the two women (fully dressed, apart from beards, from the beginning) are ready to start before the others. I attribute these words to Woman *A*: the preceding εὖ λέγεις seems better to suit the coryphaeus (Händel, 27 n. 16).   δέ γε: continuative (273 n.).   καὶ γὰρ ἑτέρας: 'for others too' (cf. 340). These other women from the country (300 n.) do not appear.   ἄντικρυς: 'straight to the meeting' (without joining their sisters from the town, and seemingly not needing a rehearsal), *Lys.* 1069 ἀλλὰ χωρεῖν ἄντικρυς | ὥσπερ οἴκαδ᾽ εἰς ἑαυτῶν. The words are seen by C. Anti (who believes 'il rigore di verisimiglianza topografica che . . . appare caratteristica delle commedie di Aristofane') as a proof (496, 1152 nn.) that the play was produced in the Lenaeum (*Teatri Greci Arcaici da Minosse a Pericle* [Padua, 1947], 227). Cf. C. F. Russo, 'I due teatri di Aristofane', *RAL* Ser. 8ª xi (1956), 14-27, id. *Aristofane Autore di Teatro* (Florence, 1962), 3-18, who postulates (on dramaturgical criteria) a Dionysian theatre with permanent equipment, and a Lenaean 'teatro di fortuna'.

282–4 Praxagora's last orders to the chorus as she and the two others hurry off. They leave by the right passageway, conventionally used for movements to or from parts of the town (M. Bieber, 'The Entrances and Exits of Actor and Chorus in Greek Plays', *AJA* lviii [1954], 277–84). **εἴωθ':** 'it is the custom'. The impersonal use with dative and infinitive is not to be found again in Greek, on which grounds many editors reject it (as does Jackson, 99). It seems, however, wholly natural: cf. the analogous use and construction of παρέχει (E. *El.* 1080). V. Coulon refers to Th. ii. 64. 2 ταῦτα γὰρ ἐν ἔθει τῆδε τῇ πόλει πρότερον ἦν (*RhM* c [1957], 196). **ἐκεῖ:** 100 n. But here (unless taken, unconvincingly, with εἴωθ') its meaning is ἐκεῖσε (168). So τοὺς ἐκεῖ καταπεφευγότας (Th. iii. 71. 2). **παροῦσιν... ἐς τὴν πύκνα:** cf. *Eq.* 751 χρὴ παρεῖν' ἐς τὴν πύκνα. There is no need to suppose these words mistakenly repeated from 281 (van Leeuwen, Jackson): on the contrary, Praxagora deliberately echoes Woman *A*'s words to emphasize her own. **ὀρθρίοις:** 20, 526 nn. **ὑπαποτρέχειν:** 'slip back home' (ὑπο-, 15 n.), cf. *Av.* 1011 κἀμοὶ πιθόμενος ὑπαποκίνει τῆς ὁδοῦ. **ἔχουσι μηδὲ πάτταλον:** 'without even a clothes-peg' ('sans même un clou', H. Van Daele), as Chremes has to come back (381). Her words are explained further (292 n.). The saying (τὸ δὴ λεγόμενον) is found again in Lucian, *Jud. Voc.* 9 ὡς ... μηδὲ πασσαλόν μοι καταλιπεῖν. Similarly used is οὐδὲ πασπάλην (i.e. 'not a grain'), *V.* 91: many other examples in O. Lottich, *De sermone vulgari Atticorum maxime ex Aristophanis fabulis cognoscendo* (Halle, 1881), 24. The expression here suggests (cf. 1020) that a *double entendre* is intended.

285–310 *Parodos.* After the actors' departure the chorus complete their preparations. They split into two groups, the first one more concerned with establishing their new male role securely (there is no suggestion in their words that they regard themselves as representing people from the *city*), the second group more specifically acting (300 n.) as dwellers in the country. *Both groups* (contrast, for example, H. Rosenbusch, *Quaestiones de parodi in comoedia Atticorum antiquissima compositione* [Marburg, 1892], 51) give a comic imitation (fulfilling their instructions, 278 n.) of the voice and gauche demeanour of the rustic. The leader, addressing them as ἄνδρες (285) reminds them to be similarly careful: and the first group take his words up (289) as they start to move round the orchestra, towards the exit (282 n.) on the right.

This is technically the πάροδος: the point at which the chorus file into the orchestra along the side passageways (πάροδοι). But in this play (see 41 n.) a formal πάροδος is dispensed with, and the following choric passages are sung as the women *leave*, not *enter*, the orchestra. For the exit of a chorus in the course of a performance cf. A. *Eu.* 234.

285–8 Metre: iambic tetrameters catalectic, i.e. with final syllable suppressed (cf. *Lys.* 254–5).

```
  --υ-   --υ-   --υ-   υ--
  --υ-   υ-υ-   --υ-   υ--
  --υ-   --υ-   υ-υ-   υ-υ
    --υυ-υ-υ-   --υ-   υ-υ
```

285–7 ὥρα προβαίνειν: 30, 352.   **τοῦτο:** i.e. the word ἄνδρες.   **ἐξ-ολίσθῃ:** sc. τὴν μνήμην, *Eq.* 491 (below) or τῆς μνήμης, *Lys.* 678, Alciphr. ii. 8. 2 δαιμόνων ὀνόματα, ὧν διὰ τὸ πλῆθος ἀπώλισθέ μου τῆς μνήμης τὰ πλείονα.   **ἡμᾶς:** best taken with χρὴ λέγειν (as Rogers) since its construction after ἐξολίσθη is not to be upheld by *Eq.* loc. cit., ἵν' ἐξολισθάνειν δύνῃ τὰς διαβολάς.

287–8 οὐχὶ μικρός: litotes (71 n.).   **ἐνδυόμεναι:** Le Febvre, i.e. 'putting on (cf. 332) such daring'. The metaphorical use of the compound is unparalleled in classical Greek (see LSJ). But compare Homeric δύω ἀλκήν (*Il.* ix. 231) and the lyric ἀνάγκας ἔδυ λέπαδνον (A. *A.* 218). The coryphaeus uses lofty language in accord with her conception of their mission and its danger. For the anapaest thus introduced (not uniquely, despite J. W. White, *The Verse of Greek Comedy* [1912], 63) cf. (for example) *Ra.* 948. ἐνδούμεναι, MSS., not 'binding . . . on ourselves' (as Homeric ἐδήσατο πέδιλα), but 'binding ourselves in . . . ' (cf. *Ach.* 905) with dative (ἱκέτευε μή μιν ἀναγκαίη ἐνδέειν, Hdt. i. 11. 3). **κατὰ σκότον:** 'in darkness', i.e. secretly (no reference to night-time is intended). Similarly, S. *Ph.* 578 τί με κατὰ σκότον ποτὲ | διεμπολᾷ λόγοισι πρός σ' ὁ ναυβάτης; cf. E. *Ion* 1522 (θέλω) καὶ περικαλύψαι τοῖσι πράγμασι σκότον.   **τόλμημα τηλικοῦτον:** 106.

289–99 Metre: two iambic dimeters (the second 'syncopated', i.e. with a short syllable suppressed: D. S. Raven, *Greek Metre²* [1968], § 44) followed by a series of acephalous glyconics and acephalous glyconics catalectic (acephalous pherecrateans).

In the following metrical analysis note (*a*) that the passage falls into five divisions (separated by a catalectic verse), (*b*) that in 1–3 the *first* verse, in 4–5 the *last* verse, is the long one.

```
289/90       --υ-      --υ- ⎫
             ·-υ-      --υ- ⎬  cf. Lys. 286
                              ⎭
291a         υ-υυ-υ-
             --υυ-υ-
291b         --υυ-υ-
292a         --υυ--        (acephalous pherecratean)

292b         υ-υυ-υ-
             --υυ-υυ
293a         --υυ-υ-
293b         --υυ-υ-
294          υ-υυ--

295a         --υυ-υ-
             --υυ-υ-
```

```
295b      - - ∪∪ - -
─────────
296       ∪ - ∪∪ - ∪ -
297       ∪ - ∪∪ - ∪ -
          ∪ - ∪∪ - ∪ -
          - - ∪∪ - ∪
─────────
298       ∪ - ∪∪ - ∪ -
299       - - ∪∪ - ∪ -
          - - ∪∪ - ∪ -
          - - ∪∪ - -
```

289–91b εἰς ἐκκλησίαν: 270 n.   ὤνδρες: they are exercising great caution (285), but falter for a moment, 299.   ὁ θεσμοθέτης: the six junior archons were officially so called. Their widely ranging powers in legal matters are described in *Ath. Pol.* 59. 1, though nothing in that catalogue exactly corresponds to the situation represented here. They seem to have exercised a similar authority (μὴ δώσειν τὸ τρι-ώβολον, 292b) over jurors (*V.* 774), κἂν ἔγρῃ μεσημβρινός, | οὐδείς σ᾽ ἀποκλήσει θεσμοθέτης τῇ κιγκλίδι.   ὃς ἂν: such relative clauses may represent antecedents in *any* case (here αὐτῷ): cf. *Pax* 371, Thphr. *Char.* 18. 6 καὶ τὸ ἱμάτιον δὲ ἐκδοῦναι δεινὸς οὐχ ὃς ἂν βέλτιστα ἐργάσηται. **πρῷ πάνυ τοῦ κνέφους:** cf. *V.* 104, 124 (of early arrival at the law-courts) ὁ δ᾽ ἀνεφάνη κνεφαῖος ἐπὶ τῇ κιγκλίδι.   **κεκονιμένος:** 'dusty', i.e. having hurried on the way (ἐγκονεῖν, 'to hasten', 489). Cf. 1177 n., Lucian, *Tim.* 45 πανταχόθεν συνθέουσι κεκονιμένοι καὶ πνευστιῶντες. The point is, presumably, that those who came too late would not receive their tickets (296 n.).

292a στέργων σκοροδάλμῃ: 'content with brine and garlic' (Cratin. fr. 143. 3, cf. *Eq.* 199 Neil). The words seem to indicate another mark of haste, i.e. eating the bare minimum for 'breakfast' (though a country-man's meal was unlikely to be sumptuous at any time, cf. *Nu.* 421). Alternatively, but not (I think) so good, 'content to bring a simple dinner with them' (306 n.), prepared to spend the whole day on the Pnyx. Garlic was especially popular with country-folk (cf. *Ach.* 164): the ἄγροικος (Thphr. *Char.* 4. 1) comes reeking of it into the Assembly. στέργω, constructed with dative of the *thing* (E. *Supp.* 257), accusative of the *person* (897).

292b βλέπων ὑπότριμμα: 'with a keen expression', as befits those who are called on to carry out important public duties, ἀντὶ τοῦ δριμύ (as the scholiast explains)· οἱ γὰρ δικάζοντες ὀφείλουσι δριμεῖς εἶναι. Cf. Pl. *R.* 519 a ἢ οὔπω ἐννενόηκας . . . ὡς δριμὺ μὲν βλέπει τὸ ψυχάριον καὶ ὀξέως διορᾷ ταῦτα . . . Similar expressions, Lottich, 24. ὑπότριμμα, suggested perhaps by σκοροδάλμῃ, was a pungent mixture (no doubt including garlic, cf. *V.* 679) in which fish was sometimes cooked and served (1170, Antiph. fr. 222. 3, Nicostr. Com. fr. 1. 3). The usual translation is thus 'surly'. But this has no meaning in the context.

τὸ τριώβολον: the current fee for attending the Assembly (309, 380, 392) as for service in the law-courts (*V.* 690, with which this whole place may be compared). Ecclesiasts were unpaid to begin with (305*b*), then given an obol (302*b*). But this rate failed to encourage their attendance (183, 303*a*): till Agyrrhius raised it (184 n.) and in consequence they now crowd and jostle (303*b*). Laments for the loss of the three obols (392) and the hurry not to lose them (282) betray, however used for comic purposes, real underlying poverty and need (cf. 353, 408 nn.). The money would have purchased a ἑκτεύς of wheat at current prices (547 n.). Aristotle criticizes State pay for ecclesiasts (*Pol.* 1293ᵃ5).

293a–4 They use some common *men's* names: they are anxious to avoid 'wrong notes' in their performance (295). For the naming of individuals cf. *V.* 230, *Lys.* 254, 321. T. B. L. Webster discerns a rule 'in satyr-play' (cf. *S. Ichn.* 177 ff.) 'and comedy that when the chorus name one another in the vocative, four is the maximum of names used together, and if the names are put together they are connected by "and"' (*The Greek Chorus*, 1970, 69). **Χαριτιμίδη**: Bentley (see apparatus criticus), Ctes. 688 F 14. 36. **Σμίκυθε**: cf. Σμικυθίων (46 n.), Σμικύθης (*Eq.* 969). **Δράκης**: *Lys.* 254 χώρει Δράκης, ἡγοῦ βάδην. **ἕπου**: for the singular forms see 483.

295a–b σαυτῷ προσέχων: sc. τὸν νοῦν, 'watching yourself', 'being on your guard'. Cf. (for construction) X. *Mem.* iii. 7. 9 διατείνου μᾶλλον πρὸς τὸ σεαυτῷ προσέχειν. But the sense here seems not to recur before St. Luke, προσέχετε ἑαυτοῖς ἀπὸ τῆς ζύμης τῶν Φαρισαίων (12: 1). **παραχορδιεῖς**: the verb occurs here only. For the sense of 'aberration' ('strike a *wrong* note') cf., for example, παράμουσος, 'out of tune' (E. *Ph.* 785), παραφρονεῖν (250). **ὧν . . . ἀποδεῖξαι**: 'in the show you must put on'. We might have expected rather ἐπι-, which is regularly used of a 'performance' (Pl. *Phdr.* 235 a) and would suit the metaphor in παραχορδιεῖς.

296–9 τὸ σύμβολον | λαβόντες: 'after we get the ticket', which presumably entitled them (see *Pl.* 278, of jurors) to claim the three obols for their service. Of the system at this time we know nothing: but later (in 341) three prytaneis appear to have distributed the tickets (*IG* ii. 872 B. 2 ἐπεμελήθησαν τῆς συλλογῆς τοῦ δήμου καὶ τῆς δ[ι]α-δόσεως τῶν συμβόλων). Types of ticket (for the theatre) are seen in Pickard-Cambridge, *DFA* 270, fig. 140. On symbola see further A. L. Boegehold in *Hesperia*, xxix (1960), 393–401, Margaret Crosby in *The Athenian Agora*, x (Princeton, N.J., 1964), 76, pls. 19–32. **πλησίοι καθεδούμεθ'**: 101 n., cf. *Il.* iv. 21 πλησίαι αἵ γ' ἥσθην. For construction with ὅπως see 82, 300. **ἅπανθ' . . . φίλας**: possibly sc. χειροτονεῖν, 'anything our friends find they must vote for'. But grammar and meaning are both a little strange: rather, after 'striking a wrong note' with their 'φίλας', the chorus interrupt themselves with *καίτοι* (E. *Ion* 1385).   **γάρ**: note the position as first word in the line (913, S. *OT* 1103). Similarly, *μέν* in 302a (n.).

The first group now moves out towards the Pnyx: the second, before following, gives voice to its contempt for a concept of service to the city (310 n.) which equates it with the lowest forms of labour. For their general theme cf. Isoc. vii. 24–5.

300–10 Metre: see on 289–99.

300/1	∪ − ∪ − − − ∪ − ⎫
	· − ∪ − − − ∪ − ⎭
302a	− − ∪∪ − ∪ −
	∪ − ∪∪ − ∪ −
302b	− − ∪∪ − ∪ −
303a	∪ − ∪∪ − ∪
———	
303b	− − ∪∪ − ∪ −
	− − ∪∪ − ∪ −
304a	− − ∪∪ − ∪ −
304b	∪ − ∪∪ − ∪ −
305a	− − ∪∪ − −
———	
305b	∪ − ∪∪ − ∪ −
	− − ∪∪ − ∪ −
306	− − ∪∪ − ∪
———	
307	∪ − ∪∪ − ∪ −
308	∪ − ∪∪ − ∪ −
	− − ∪∪ − ∪ −
	− − ∪∪ − −
———	
309	− − ∪∪ − ∪ −
310	− − ∪∪ − ∪ −
	− − ∪∪ − ∪ −
	− − ∪∪ − −

300–1 ὅρα δ' ὅπως ὠθήσομεν: i.e. when we get to the Assembly. Speaking as (pretended, contrast Rogers) country-people, they mean to assert themselves by jostling these newly eager people from the town (for the contrast *ἄγροικοι, οἱ ἐξ ἄστεως* cf. *Ach.* 1185). Such jockeying for places is described by Dicaeopolis, *Ach.* 24–6 (cf., of the prytaneis, 42). **τούσδε** anticipates (contemptuously, 873) their neighbours at the meeting: they speak as if already on the Pnyx. A cleavage between town and country in Assembly is hinted at again in 432 (n.). Cf. (for construction) 82 n., (for the use of a future form *ὠθήσω*) E. *Cyc.* 592.

302a–3b μέν: the position (cf. *γάρ*, 299 n.) is 'remarkable' (*GP* 373). For antithesis *πρὸ τοῦ μέν* . . . *νυνὶ δ'* (303) cf. *Pax* 690–2.   **ἡνίκ'** . . . **ὀβολὸν μόνον**: 183 n.   **λαλοῦντες | ἐν τοῖς στεφανώμασιν**: 'chatting in the garland-market' (cf. *ἐν τοῖς ἰχθύσι*, *V.* 789), in spite of attempts to round them up. So, in *Ach.* 21, οἱ δ' ἐν ἀγορᾷ λαλοῦσι κἄνω καὶ κάτω | τὸ σχοινίον φεύγουσι τὸ μεμιλτωμένον (378 n.). The garland-market (like the myrrh-shop, the barber's, and the shoe-maker's, Lys. xxiv. 20) was a centre of social life and gossip. Cf. Pherecr. fr. 2 λουσάμενοι δὲ πρὸ λαμπρᾶς | ἡμέρας ἐν τοῖς στεφανώμασιν, οἱ δ' ἐν τῷ μύρῳ | λαλεῖτε περὶ σισυμβρίων κοσμοσανδάλου τε. **ἐνοχλοῦσ'**: 'they make themselves a nuisance' (*Ra.* 709) by crowding the meetings (ὄχλος, 383), whereas before they never came at all. Cf. *Pl.* 329 δεινὸν γὰρ εἰ τριωβόλου μὲν οὔνεκα | ὡστιζόμεσθ' ἑκάστοτ' ἐν τῇκκλησίᾳ, *Pl.* 171.

304α-4b Μυρωνίδης: the word used to describe him is a term of highest praise (γεννάδας ὢν καὶ μεγαλόψυχος, Arist. *EN* 1100ᵇ32). It marks him out as, in every sense, a 'gentle' man (χρηστὸς . . . καὶ γεν-νάδας, *Ra.* 179, γεννάδας καὶ πρᾶος, *Pl. Phdr.* 243 c). But Myronides at the same time was a tough man towards his enemies (*Lys.* 801-4): a type in fact of the old Athenian general (ἦρχεν of military service: at least we do not hear of him as archon). He defeated the Boeotian army, in 456 B.C., at Oenophyta (Th. i. 108. 3), a year after his unorthodox success against the Corinthians at Megara (ibid. 105. 3). We are not to connect this long-past victory (as van Leeuwen tries to in his note) with current Athenian–Corinthian relations, or Aristophanes' views upon them ('comico minime plaudente'). He is harking back to 'the good old days' of men like the Μαραθωνομάχαι (cf. *Nu.* 986). For this common theme of Old Comedy (and popular oratory, Burckhardt, 23) see A. Meder, *Der athenische Demos zur Zeit des Peloponnesischen Krieges im Lichte zeitgenössischer Quellen* (Munich, 1938), 15, W. Kassies, *Aristophanes Traditionalisme* (Amsterdam, 1964), 48-62.

305b τὰ τῆς πόλεως διοικεῖν: cf. Th. viii. 21.   **ἀργύριον φέρων**: 'and take pay', *Ach.* 66 μισθὸν φέροντας δύο δραχμὰς τῆς ἡμέρας.

306-8 ἀλλ' . . . ἐλάας: formerly they gave their public services for nothing, and moreover brought their dinners with them, prepared to sit for long enough if need be (as they did in the theatre, Pickard-Cambridge, *DFA* 272). So Dicaeopolis brought garlic and a pie (*Ach.* 164, 174). The provisions mentioned (with cheese, *Ra.* 559) are staple articles of common diet (cf. for example *Nu.* 1383, *Ra.* 654, 988). Athenian taste in food was simple (Eub. frs. 10, 12): see further B. A. Sparkes, 'The Greek Kitchen', *JHS* lxxxii (1962), 123. **φέρων | πιεῖν**: i.e. bringing something for drinking. Cf. Cratin. fr. 124, X. *Cyr.* i. 3. 9 καλῶς σοι πιεῖν ἐγκέας. **αὑτῷ**: von Velsen (αὑ R, αὖ ΛΜu1). The word well suits the old-time independence: each brought his own and did not 'sponge' on others. Other editors give αὖον (Reiske). **ἂν**: of regular habit, cf. *V.* 268 ἀλλὰ πρῶτος ἡμῶν | ἡγεῖτ' ἂν ᾄδων Φρυνίχου.

309-10 τριώβολον... λαβεῖν: 292b n., 380. **πράττωσί τι κοινὸν**: 'per-form some public service' (104, 208). So οἱ τὰ κοινὰ πράττοντες (distinguished from οἱ ἰδιῶται), Arist. *Pol.* 1324ᵇ1. **πηλοφοροῦντες**:

'builders' labourers' (carriers of clay, or mortar), cf. *Av.* 1142. They are clearly intended as the lowest class of citizen: there is no need to regard them (Ehrenberg, 174) as slaves. Olive-gatherers replace them in the similar remarks (*V.* 712) on modern juries: νῦν ὥσπερ ἐλαολόγοι χωρεῖθ' ἅμα τῷ τὸν μισθὸν ἔχοντι.

311–26 The second semi-chorus have moved off to the Pnyx (by the right-hand *parodos*, 282 n.), and thus leave the orchestra briefly empty (cf. A. *Eu.* 234, E. *Alc.* 746): empty of people, that is, for Woman *B* has presumably abandoned her ideas (88) and left behind her wool, wool-cards, and baskets. The garlands have been cast aside as well. Praxagora's lamp, too, must at some time have been discarded (perhaps, as Robert thinks, at 28). As the stage-hands (509 n.) are picking up these remnants, Praxagora's house-door opens once again. This must be her husband: and although of course we knew that Praxagora had made off with his cloak (see 26) we are still astonished and delighted by the sight of him in women's white shoes (319 n.) and saffron chiton (the colour gives the pretext for a typical sally, 329). The face on the mask is an old man's (323: so *that* was how his wife got out so early, compared with Women *B*, 39), his dress perhaps is scarcely decent (318 n.), and the high boots (346) are doubtless pinching. He is writhing in agony and looking for a spot (preferably nearer to a neighbour's than his own house) where no one will see him (322). His caution is needless (it is still dark, 321): but to make sure, he withdraws—towards the front of the orchestra, where the whole house can have him in its view.

311–13 τί τὸ πρᾶγμα; 'what's the matter?', *Lys.* 23, see 394. **φρούδη** 'στί: prodelision, 40 n., 341. **μοι:** probably not possessive dative (353) but dative of disadvantage, 'where has she gone off on me?' (*Ra.* 81). **πρὸς ἕω:** 20 n. **κατάκειμαι:** 'I've been lying down' (in bed), as 541. **χεζητιῶν:** exactly the type of 'customary' joke forbidden to Xanthias (*Ra.* 8). But even there Aristophanes *does* mention it: in deploring the low-level humour of his rivals (*Nu.* 537, *V.* 1015, *Pax* 739) he may mean only that he himself does these things rather better, or at least that he possesses *other* humorous resources in addition. This old man—identified as ἀνήρ τις βλέπυρος in ΛΜυι—certainly does not try to cover up (like the comic πρεσβύτης condemned in *Nu.* 542) his πονηρὰ σκώμματα: but he differs little as a laughter-raising figure from Eubulus' type (fr. 53. 4): ὡς χεζητιῶν | μακρὰν βαδίζων πολλὰ δὲ στένων ἀνὴρ | δάκνων τὰ χείλη, παγγέλοιός ἐστ' ἰδεῖν. At any rate, such contradictions need not trouble us: 'one misses the largeness of Aristophanes unless one appreciates his gift for self-contradiction' (Cedric H. Whitman, *Aristophanes and the Comic Hero*, [Cambridge, Mass.], 1964, 24).

314–15 τὰς ἐμβάδας: 47 n., further defined as Λακωνικαί (345). Praxagora was wearing them as she came out from the house at the begin-

ning. Does Blepyrus (not named till 327) have only *one* pair? (353 n.).
ἐν τῷ σκότῳ: she had also removed the bedside lamp.   θοἰμάτιον:
40. Does the article (cf. 341) again imply that he possesses only *one*?
If so, it may stand as another indication of current poverty (see 292 n.).
The ἀνελεύθερος and αἰσχροκερδής have similar deficiencies of wardrobe
(Thphr. *Char.* 22. 9, 30. 10) : presumably, however, the explanation
there is not so much poverty as meanness.

315–17 ὅτ' δὴ δ': 'but when I *couldn't* find it', 195 n. Probably he used it
as a blanket (536 n.) and expected to find it on the bed : beneath the
foot of which, perhaps he kept his shoes, like the sick man depicted on
the marble (A. Hirt, *Bilderbuch für Myth. Archäolog. u. Kunst* [Berlin,
1805], i, pl. xi. 3). A similar difficulty keeps Myrrhine late (*Lys.* 72),
μόλις γὰρ ηὗρον ἐν σκότῳ τὸ ζώνιον.   ψηλαφῶν: sc. ἐν τῷ σκότῳ (314),
cf. *Pax* 691.   τὴν θύραν | ἐπεῖχε κρούων: 'kept on knocking at the
door'. Cf. παῖ' αὐτὸν ἐπέχων (*Pax* 1121), 361, 990 nn.   ὁ κοπρεαῖος:
'the dung-man' (360). So R*Λ*Mu1 : change is needless. Aristophanes
plays elsewhere (*Eq.* 899) on the Attic deme-name Κόπρος (a similar
play in 362): cf. Ξενοκλῆς Κόπρειος (Is. iii. 2 Wyse), *IG* i². 301. 39.
And Copreus is a personal name in Homer (*Il.* xv. 639) and in inscriptions (as *CIG* 3014, from Teos), D. W. S. Hunt, *JHS* lxvii (1947),
76. But neither personal nor deme-name (ὅδε Κοπρεῖος, Lenting)
should find accommodation in the text. For the island deme of
Copros, off the south-west coast of Attica, see A. Milchhoefer, 'Unter-
suchungen über die Demenordnung des Cleisthenes' *APAW* (1892),
Phil.-hist. Abhand. (Anhang), i. 33, 47 (and map).

317–19 λαμβάνω . . . ἡμιδιπλοίδιον: the garment was presumably lying
on (or near) the bed where Praxagora had cast it the last time it was
worn (536 n.). A ἡμιδιπλοίδιον is not named elsewhere : but is clearly
synonymous here with κροκωτίδιον (332 n.) and χιτώνιον (374). For
illustrations of such dresses with an 'overfall' see Bieber, *GK*, pl. XV.
The diminutives *need* not suggest that the garment on Blepyrus is short
(see 268 n.), but his costume almost certainly is phallic (Introduction
§ IV).   τὰς . . . Περσικὰς: sc. ἐμβάδας (74 n.). These women's shoes
(*Th.* 734, cf. *Lys.* 229–30), possibly white (Poll. vii. 92) are referred
to as κόθορνοι (346). The latter were high boots (Hdt. vi. 125. 4) and
could easily be pulled on (ὑφέλκομαι) in darkness since they did not
distinguish right and left (X. *HG* ii. 3. 31). See Bieber, *GK*, pl. LXIV.

320–2 ἐν . . . τύχοι; Theban houses, like Egyptian (Hdt. ii. 35. 3) are
said (in jest?) to have boasted private privies (Eub. fr. 53. 1) : μετὰ
ταῦτα Θήβας ἦλθον, οὗ τὴν νύχθ' ὅλην | τήν θ' ἡμέραν δειπνοῦσι καὶ
κοπρῶν' ἔχει | ἐπὶ ταῖς θύραις ἕκαστος, οὗ πλήρει βροτῶν | οὐκ ἔστι μεῖζον
ἀγαθόν (cf. fr. 66. 3). But many Athenians rising in the night-time
(like the Theophrastan ἀναίσθητος, *Char.* 14. 5) were obliged to make
use of either a public convenience or the street. For the public privy
(κοπρών, λαύρα, θᾶκος) see *Pax* 99, 158, *Th.* 485, Thphr. *Char.* loc. cit.,

for the use of the street (as here) *Pax* 164 (Trygaeus observing from his beetle) ἄνθρωπε τί δρᾷς, οὗτος ὁ χέζων | ἐν Πειραιεῖ παρὰ ταῖς πόρναις; cf. *Ach.* 1170. *Nu.* 1385. A chamber-pot is not, of course, excluded: but Blepyrus, although he knows the word (371 n.) does not appear to have possessed one. Cf. Eup. fr. 224 ἐμοὶ γὰρ οὐκ ἔστ' οὐδὲ λάσανον οὗ χέσω. **ἐν καθαρῷ** may mean simply 'in the open' (Pl. *R.* 520 d), but possibly rather 'in a free place' (clear of people, ἐν ἐρημίᾳ, as scholiast explains: cf. 321–2, S. *OC* 1575). It is obvious that even at this early hour (see 20 n.) some citizens will be about their business. Similarly used is Latin 'purus' (Horace, *Epistles*, ii. 2. 71). Cf. (in general) *Th.* 292 ποῦ ποῦ καθίζωμ' ἐν καλῷ ('in a suitable spot', see 321) τῶν ῥητόρων | ἵν' ἐξακούω ; **τοι:** 'or is anywhere perhaps . . . ?' For the particle in asides and soliloquies see *GP* 538, which refers to 'a homeliness and *naïveté*' in this use. It is not very common in questions (*GP* 545) and might here be read as in a statement. But Blepyrus (I think) goes on to answer his own question '(Yes) for . . .': the γ' after χέζοντα will then serve to express 'and that's the main point'. Note the double negative: cf. the very similar 325.

323–6 οἴμοι κακοδαίμων: the words seem sometimes (as perhaps in 1093) to be used for comic heightening of lines parodying tragic diction (Neil on *Eq.* 1243). But in tragedy κακοδαίμων occurs only once (in anapaests, E. *Hipp.* 1362). **γέρων . . . ἠγόμην:** presumably undeterred by Euripides' monitory dictum (*Th.* 410): πρὸς τοὺς γέροντάς θ' οἳ πρὸ τοῦ τὰς μείρακας | ἤγοντο διαβέβληκεν, ὥστ' οὐδεὶς γέρων | γαμεῖν ἐθέλει γυναῖκα διὰ τοὔπος τοδὶ | "δέσποινα γὰρ γέροντι νυμφίῳ γυνή." Praxagora must have been, comparatively speaking, a μεῖραξ at the time of her marriage (cf. 243, 427 nn.), Ischomachus' wife was not fifteen, X. *Oec.* vii. 5 and οὐ . . . σύμφορόν ἐστι γυνὴ νέα ἀνδρὶ γέροντι (Thgn. 457, cf. fr. 600). But see *Lys.* 595. Cf. in general Strepsiades' feelings (*Nu.* 41–55): though he need not have been an old man when he married, and the inequality is not of age. On the characterization of old men in Aristophanes see Kassies, 63 ff., 104. **ἠγόμην:** 'I was for marrying' (Latin 'duco'). The force of the imperfect here (cf. 219, 826) is paralleled in *Nu.* 57, *Th.* loc. cit. **ὑγιὲς οὐδὲν:** 'no good'. Blepyrus shares in the suspicions (225 n.) engendered by Euripides' slanders, *Th.* 394 (καλῶν sc. Euripides) τὰς οὐδὲν ὑγιές, τὰς μέγ' ἀνδράσιν κακόν. See also 338, 350. He fears that his young wife may have found 'another harbour' (Thgn. 460). **ὅμως δ' οὖν:** 'but all the same' (i.e. forgetting about that) 'I must slip round the corner' (351 n., perhaps a substitution here for καρτερητέον, *TGF²* 849). Similarly, *Th.* 611 Μν. ἔασον οὐρῆσαί μ'. Κλ. ἀναίσχυντός ⟨τις⟩ εἶ. | σὺ δ' οὖν ποίει τοῦτ'· ἀναμενῶ γὰρ ἐνθάδε.

327–71 Blepyrus has just settled down about his business when from next door (see 33) comes Woman *B*'s husband (nameless, but a Salaminian, and maybe so distinguished, 38 n.); his lamp reveals his neighbour Blepyrus as the source of the strange sounds that have brought him out of doors, dressed only in his chiton and barefooted. His intention is to make for the Assembly, if he manages to find his missing cloak (the lack of shoes seems not to worry him, despite what he says in 342). He goes back in to look for it (the two men having meantime compared notes on the absence of their wives), but Blepyrus' business still detains him, its rate of progress being hampered by the constipating action of a pear. His efforts (and a scene of the highest-class scatology) end with Chremes' arrival from the Pnyx.

327 The manuscripts in this play (particularly R) are very careless in indicating names and changes of speaker (41 n.). See Lowe, 27 ff., Introduction § IV. Here they give simply ἀνήρ (R*Λ*Mu1). Blepyrus' name is not repeated, but presumably Βλέπυρος ('guardalgrano', D. Comparetti, in A. Franchetti, *Le Donne a Parlamento di Aristofane* [Città di Castello, 1901], xviii): a similar rhythm, 318.   **οὐ δήπου**: in incredulous questions, cf. *Ach.* 122 ὁδὶ δὲ τίς ποτ' ἐστίν; οὐ δήπου Στράτων;

328–31 δῆτ': in affirmative responses, often (as here) strengthened by an oath, cf. *Ra.* 552 νὴ Δία | ἐκεῖνος αὐτὸς δῆτα.   **τοῦτο . . . τὸ πυρρόν**: the light of his lamp picks out the saffron (see below) of Blepyrus' attire. Has Cinesias (he asks) been at his tricks? πυρρόν, as a comic term for excrement (1061 n.) could seemingly cover other shades of ordure. Cinesias had been a butt of Aristophanes as far back as the *Birds* in 414. He was chosen to represent the dithyrambic poets on an embassy to Hades (fr. 149. 10): and his thinness (*Ra.* 1437) was a by-word. Blepyrus' neighbour is thinking of his comic reputation, perhaps based (cf. 647 n.) on a single, but notorious, misdemeanour: ἢ κατατιλᾷ τῶν Ἑκαταίων κυκλίοισι χοροῖσιν ὑπᾴδων (*Ra.* 366, as scholiasts explain it). Cf. Lys. fr. 53 (Thalheim), where Cinesias' excesses are represented as an annual target for the comic poets (like Strattis, who devoted a whole play to him, Ath. 551 c).   **οὔτι που**: in incredulous questions, 372. Cf. δήπου (327 n.).   **ποθεν**: 'from somewhere or other', sc. ἄνωθεν, cf. *V.* 204 ἴσως ἄνωθεν μῦς ἐνέβαλέ σοί ποθεν. This literal use well suits κατατιλῶ, and the concept need hardly give us pause. Cinesias is pictured (with a side-glance at the 'airiness' of dithyrambic poets) as a bird in flight (*Av.* 1373 ff., cf. *Ra.* 1437) and acts in character (*Av.* 1054): μέμνησ' ὅτε τῆς στήλης κατετίλας ἑσπέρας; But the word perhaps means little more than 'somehow'. R has a double point, and *Λ*Mu1 Βλέπυρος πόθεν; a division which some editors have favoured. But (*a*) R's authority in this regard (cf. 327 n.) is small: it tends to mark a change of speaker with words of this nature (95), (*b*) πόθεν; οὐκ seems unidiomatic: Aristophanes at least has no examples, (*c*) the simple οὐκ is more in keeping: to Blepyrus the question is a perfectly straightforward one, though the answer this time happens to be 'no'.

331–2 ἐξελήλυθα: 48 n.   **τὸ κροκωτίδιον:** 'the little yellow dress'; a favourite woman's colour (879 n.). In men it would normally be thought of as effeminate: Agathon possesses (with his razor, 65 n.) a κροκωτὸς and other women's garments (*Th.* 138, 253). Cf. Arar. fr. 4 παρθένος δ' εἶναι δοκεῖ | φορῶν κροκωτοὺς (v.l. κροσωτοὺς) καὶ γυναικείαν στολήν.   **ἀμπισχόμενος:** most often used of *outside* garments (540, *Lys.* 1156). But this need not mean that Blepyrus (see next note) is wearing the dress round his shoulders. The verb has the general idea of 'put on' (540, *V.* 1153): and here means ἠμφιεσμένος (879, *Th.* 92). **οὑνδύεται:** i.e. ὃ ἐνδύεται (crasis, cf. οὑγώ, 341).

333–5 δ': 'and where's your cloak?', δέ asking for further information (72 n.). He does not mean (as Rogers sees) 'why are you wearing your wife's dress round your shoulders like a cloak?'   **εἶτ' . . . φράσαι:** Athenian women were expected to take charge of the wardrobe of their men-folk: Strepsiades' wife failed to please (*Nu.* 53). εἶτα, 'in that case' (535).

336–7 οὐ γὰρ: '(no) for . . .', 1026, cf. *V.* 1126 μὰ τὸν Δί' οὐ γὰρ οὐδαμῶς μοι ξύμφορον.   **ἔνδον:** 'in the house', see 225.   **ἐκτετρύπηκεν . . . ἔνδοθεν:** 'slipped out of the house' (as through a hole, τρύπημα). The verb (here only) means ἐξελθεῖν λεληθότως (Hsch. s.v., a fair deduction). Cf. εἰστρυπᾶν, which the *Suda* explains as 'enter by stealth' (παρεισέρχεσθαι).

338 ὃ καὶ . . . νεώτερον: perhaps a quotation (as van Leeuwen thinks) from tragedy. Cf. E. *Ph.* 263 ὃ καὶ δέδοικα μή με δικτύων ἔσω | λαβόντες οὐκ ἐκφρῶσ' ἀναίμακτον χρόα. ὅ, i.e. δι' ὅ (cf. ταῦτα = διὰ ταῦτα, *Nu.* 319, *Av.* 486): καί 'emphasizes the fact that the relative clause contains an addition to the information contained in the main clause' (*GP* 294). See also the usage in 350.   **νεώτερον:** as often, euphemistically used instead of κακόν, which manuscripts actually offer as a variant in E. *Med.* 37 δέδοικα δ' αὐτὴν μή τι βουλεύσῃ νέον. Cf. *Ba.* 362 and (for comparative) Th. i. 132. 5 οὐδ' ἠξίωσαν νεώτερόν τι ποιεῖν ἐς αὐτόν.

339–43 ταὐτὰ . . . ἄντικρυς: 'absolutely the same', cf. ἄντικρυς μηδὲν (*Th.* 442). Hess (107) sees the oath by Poseidon as suiting a Salaminian (38): cf. however 451 n.   **τοίνυν:** 'if that's the case', cf. *Nu.* 1406. The postponed position (second word is normal) is because of the oath's being thought of as a unit (cf. *Pl.* 863). The line recalls (irrelevantly, probably) E. *IT* 658 Πυλάδη, πέπονθας ταὐτὸ πρὸς θεῶν ἐμοί;   **καὶ γὰρ:** 'for she too . . .', cf. 280.   **ἦ ξύνειμ' ἐγὼ:** 38. **φρούδη 'στ':** 311.   **οὑγὼ:** 332.   **τὰς ἐμβάδας:** 47 n., sc. φρούδη 'στ' ἔχουσα, 'she's gone off with my shoes as well.' Philocleon shouts for his (*V.* 103) when setting out for duty in the law-courts.   **οὔκουν . . . γ' . . . οὐδαμοῦ:** 'at any rate, I couldn't find them anywhere.' Similarly, 350, 926.

344–7 οὐδ' . . . γὰρ: for this combination of particles in answers cf. *Lys.* 130.   **Λακωνικάς:** 74 n.   **τὼ κοθόρνω:** 319 n.   **σισύραν:** a rough cloak (cf. *Ra.* 1459) of skin (ps.-Plato, *Erx.* 400 e, Poll. vii. 70) which could also be used as rug or blanket: 840, cf. *Av.* 122, *Nu.* 10 ἐν πέντε σισύραις ἐγκεκορδυλημένος. **φανή**: 'newly laundered', *Ach.* 845 χλαῖναν δ' ἔχων φανὴν δίει.

348–9 τί δῆτ' ἂν εἴη; Blepyrus' words recall exactly those of his wife in 24. The similarity of these two places prompts one to attribute the speakers' parts as here. R has a paragraphus at 350, but this (327 n.) means little. And if (as Rogers, Coulon) Blepyrus speaks 350, he now thinks more highly of Praxagora than in 325, 338. **μῶν ἐπ' ἄριστον . . . κέκληκεν**: if such social morning calls were common, Athenian women's life was rather freer than one is sometimes given to believe. But clearly it was normally expected that a wife would be at home to prepare her husband's morning meal (469, cf. *V.* 610). 'Breakfast' time elsewhere comes closer to our 'lunch' (cf. *Av.* 788). But of course, on the mornings of Assembly (291 n.) or the theatre (Philoch. 328 F 171) one might well want a meal before departing. καλέω is often used of invitations: cf. 1146. μῶν, 'num forte' (see 976). **γυνὴ . . . τῶν φίλων**: for this use of the genitive (partitive? of definition?) cf. 1023, *Eq.* 425 εἶπ' ἀνὴρ τῶν ῥητόρων. The construction need not be regarded as elliptical: see J. W. Poultney, *The Syntax of the Genitive Case in Aristophanes* (Baltimore, Md., 1936), 75. He unnecessarily qualifies the statement by supposing 'that the indefinite τις was in the speaker's mind'. **γνώμην γ' ἐμήν**: 'I should imagine so.' Cf. (though not in answers) *V.* 983, *Pax* 232 ἀλλ' εἰμι· καὶ γὰρ ἐξιέναι γνώμην ἐμὴν | μέλλει.

350–3 οὔκουν . . . γ': 'at any rate she's not a bad one', 343.   **ὅ τι κἄμ' εἰδέναι**: 'as far as I know', *Th.* 34 μὰ τὸν Δί' οὔτοι γ' ὥστε καί μέ γ' εἰδέναι (*GP* 295). **ἱμονιάν . . . ἀποπατεῖς**: 'you are paying out a cable' (Rogers). The verb denotes (*a*) literally 'going to the privy' ('turning off the road', see 326 n.), (*b*) the process carried on there (354). Cf. εἰς ἄφοδον, 1059. The *transitive* use does not recur.   **τιν'**: 'a kind of', 'a cable, as you might say', 355, *Th.* 647 ἰσθμόν τιν' ἔχεις, ὦνθρωπ'. Similarly, 1056. For δ' as a line-ending cf. *Av.* 1716. **ὥρα βαδίζειν**: 30. The neighbour cannot wait until Blepyrus feels ready to rise (373).   **εἰς ἐκκλησίαν**: 270 n.   **ὅπερ ἦν . . . μόνον**: perhaps another indication of current difficulties (292 n.). But of course the lack of spare clothes is essential to the humour of the scene.

355 ἀχράς τις: the wild pear (like the cultivated ἄπιος, Thphr. *HP* i. 4. 1) a poor man's food (Alexis fr. 162. 13), was known (in its raw state) as a constipating agent, ἀχράδες χειμέριοι πέπειροι διαχωρέουσι, καὶ τῆς κοιλίης καθαρτικαί· αἱ δὲ ὠμαὶ στάσιμον (Hp. *Salubr.* ii. 55): also, from ancient times (as Rogers notes) its thorny branches served for fencing, ἐθρίγκωσεν ἀχέρδῳ (362 n.), *Od.* xiv. 10. Cf. the condition attributed to cresses (*Th.* 616). But as τις (see last note) shows, Blepyrus is not literal (cf. French 'poire d'angoisse', old English 'choke-pear'): the

word is an excuse for a contemporary reference (356) and a pun (362).
ἐγκλῇσασ' . . . ἔχει: either 'keeps on blocking' (i.e. prevents its
passage), 957, or 'keeps it shut up', *Av.* 1082, S. *Ant.* 180 ἀλλ' ἐκ φόβου
του γλῶσσαν ἐγκλῄσας ἔχει.   τὰ σιτία: 'food', *Pax* 138 νῦν δ' ἅττ' ἂν
αὐτὸς καταφάγω τὰ σιτία. Cf. of soldiers' rations, 234 n.

356 μῶν . . . Λακωνικοῖς; the neighbour's 'curtain' as he goes into his
house. I cannot believe (see Introduction§ III) that he speaks throughout this passage from his window. But his last words are exceedingly
obscure. They hardly mean (as the scholiast explains) that Thrasybulus put forward an illness brought about by eating pears to excuse
himself—the Spartans having bribed him—from opposing proposals
for a treaty (cf. *V.* 946–8): a similar story is told about Demosthenes
(Gell. xi. 9. 1). The reference may be (as van Leeuwen) to some
threat that Thrasybulus made of a 'blockade': it may be that he made
this suggestion after Cnidus, but had it rejected (203 n.). See further
Introduction § II. If so, take **εἶπε** as 'proposed in the Assembly'
(*Th.* 375, D. iii. 12, and in inscriptions): the dative (of disad-
vantage) then means 'against the Spartans' (ἐπεὰν . . . ἀλλήλοισι
πόλεμον προείπωσι, Hdt. vii. 9. 2 β), and construction is not as 22.
Λακωνικοῖς, a form used by Blepyrus, not in contempt (cf. scholiast,
Pax 215, C. W. Peppler, 'The termination -κός, as used by Aristophanes for comic effect', *AJP* xxxi, [1910], 443), but simply as the
normal one in comedy (*Pax* 212, *Nu.* 186, with Dover).

357–8 νὴ τὸν Διόνυσον . . . σφόδρα: 'it may very well be the same
"blockade": at any rate' (cf. 773) 'it's got me blockaded fairly tightly.'
ἐνέχεται: no comparable usage can be cited, but the scholiast is probably correct, οἷον ἐπίκειται καὶ θλίβει.   **γοῦν:** 73 n. This line is
flung after the neighbour: Blepyrus then turns (ἀτάρ, cf. in general *V.*
147, *Th.* 87) to contemplation of his plight. He thinks at first of
calling in a specialist: but ends with a prayer to the goddess of childbirth (Eilithyia) for delivery from labour.   **τί δράσω;** aorist subjunctive (not future indicative), deliberative, 'what am I to do?' Cf. *Ach.*
466, E. *Or.* 1610.

358–62 καὶ γὰρ: 148 n.   **οὐδὲ τοῦτο . . . μόνον:** not just his present
discomfort, but the thought of what will happen if he goes on eating
(ὅταν φάγω with ὅποι βαδιεῖται). For Blepyrus likes his food (469, 717).
van Leeuwen (supplementing needlessly) says oddly 'τοῦτο non habet
quo referatur.'   **οὗτος . . . ἀχραδούσιος:** 'this chap from Achras', as if
ἀχράς (like its synonym ἄχερδος) formed a genuine deme-name: *Com.
Adesp.* 1277 μοχθηρὸς ὢν καὶ τὴν γνώμην Ἀχερδούσιος (τοὺς τροποὺς
Ἀχραδούσιος, Edmonds), Aeschin. i. 110. See Milchhoefer (317 n.), 33.
Such plays are common: cf. (for example) 317, 979 nn.   **βεβαλάνωκε:** 370. The verb means 'bolted with a bolt shaped like a βάλανος'
(an acorn), *V.* 155, 200. How little the initial sense is felt is shown
clearly by the fact that in the present context the βάλανος is (so to

speak) an ἀχράς.   τὴν θύραν: 316.   ὅστις ποτ' ἔσθ': 'whoever he is', A. A. 160 Ζεύς, ὅστις ποτ' ἐστίν.

363–4 τίς ἂν οὖν: recalling such tragic question-forms as S. El. 1103 τίς οὖν ἂν ὑμῶν τοῖς ἔσω φράσειεν ἂν | . . . ; For the double interrogative cf. (for example) S. OT 1164 τίνος πολιτῶν τῶνδε κἀκ ποίας στέγης; for the query introduced by τίς in two successive lines, E. HF 143. Notice ἰᾱτρόν (short iota), cf. Pl. 406: but the normal ἰατρός (Av. 584). μετέλθοι: 'fetch', Nu. 801 ἀτὰρ μέτειμί γ' αὐτόν.   τῶν καταπρώκτων: RΛMuι correctly. Blepyrus' question is not 'who are the specialists in anal affairs?' (τὰ κατὰ πρωκτόν, cf. τὰ κατὰ νηδύν, Hdt. ii. 84), but 'which of these anal experts (κατάπρωκτοι, i.e. καταπύγονες, Ach. 79) will know most about my present trouble?' He then proceeds to two suggestions: Amynon (365), who according to the scholiast was ῥήτωρ ἡταιρικώς, οὐκ ἰατρός (as indeed we should never have supposed him) and Antisthenes (366), whose knowledge of Blepyrus' complaint is attested in 806–8. Amynon is not known elsewhere: Antisthenes, if not (as is unlikely) the philosopher (p. xx n. 4, cf. A. Weiher, Philosophen und Philosophenspott in der attischen Komödie [Munich, 1913], 25) is perhaps the choregus of X. Mem. iii. 4. 3 (cf. IG ii². 1138. 27). But to carry this guess further (as van Leeuwen would be rash: 'ridetur homo qui nuper in certamine musico chorum suum victum inique tulerat et alta voce fuerat conquestus.' The choice of name may have been helped by its suggestion of 'colui che si oppone con forza' (Cantarella).   τὴν τέχνην: i.e. the skill that the present trouble calls for.

365–6 ἆρ' οἶδ' Ἀμύνων; 'does Amynon know?' inviting a reaction (cf. 22 n.) from the house. The reading in R (see apparatus criticus) does not require to be altered, nor should these words (since Blepyrus is clearly on his own) be given, as by C. Frick, to the neighbour (WKP xiii [1912], 365–6).   ἴσως ἀρνήσεται: either (a) 'perhaps he will deny it' (the point then is that denial will be difficult in face of the crowd's expressed opinion) or, better, (b) 'perhaps he will refuse' (ἴσως ironical: Amynon has never refused any similar assignment). πάσῃ τέχνῃ: 'at any cost', 534, Th. 65 Ἀγάθωνά μοι δεῦρ' ἐκκάλεσον πάσῃ τέχνῃ. The choice of expression has possibly been influenced by τέχνην in 364.

367–8 ἕνεκά γε στεναγμάτων: 'as far as groans go', 'if groans are a criterion'. Cf. 170, Nu. 420 ἀλλ' οὕνεκά γε ψυχῆς στερρᾶς δυσκολοκοίτου τε μερίμνης . . . | ἀμέλει θαρρῶν οὕνεκα τούτων ἐπιχαλκεύειν παρέχοιμ' ἄν.   τί βούλεται: 'the meaning of', 'what it implies'. Cf. 753, Men. Dys. 431 τουτὶ τὸ κακὸν τί βούλεται; and the similar use in French of 'vouloir dire'.

369–71 ὦ πότνι' Εἰλείθυια: cf. Lys. 742 (where the prayer reverses this one), ὦ πότνι' Εἰλείθυι' ἐπίσχες τοῦ τόκου. The prosody of πότνι' shows (despite Rau, 206) that the style of address is paratragic (see Dover on Nu. 1468): cf. (for example) A. Th. 152 ὦ πότνι' Ἥρα.

'Ιλείθυια, Coulon (with the explanation 'tituli') : cf. *IG* ii. 3, 1590. 1. But the *Εἰ*- form of MSS. is also found in inscriptions (as ibid. 1586. 9). **μή...περιίδης**: 'don't look on with indifference', 'look on without taking any action'. Cf. 1054, *V.* 438 ὦ Κέκροψ ἥρως . . . περιορᾷς οὕτω μ' ὑπ' ἀνδρῶν βαρβάρων χειρούμενον; for μὴ . . . μηδέ (where μηδέ = καί) cf. (for example) *Eq.* 580 μὴ φθονεῖθ' ἡμῖν κομῶσι μηδ' ἀπεστλεγγισμένοις. **διαρραγέντα . . . βεβαλανωμένον**: 'bursting' (as after eating, X. *Cyr.* viii. 2. 21) and 'barricaded' (361 n.). **ἵνα . . . κωμῳδικῇ**: he has no wish to make himself (like those he has just mentioned) a target for Aristophanic humour, to be mocked as ἡ σκωραμίς (only here, 'commode'), an (unemptied) receptacle for σκῶρ. The scholiast explains ἀμὶς μέν, ἐν ᾧ οὐροῦσι (cf. *V.* 807), σκωραμὶς δέ, ἐν ᾧ ἀποπατοῦσιν. There is a σκωραμίς surviving from Olynthus (*Excavations* viii. 205, pl. 55. 1).

372–477 Blepyrus is just rising (his prayer for safe delivery unanswered) when another old man (465) arrives back from the Pnyx (he enters the orchestra from the right). Chremes (477) was too late to receive his three obols for attendance : an unprecedented mob of pale-faced citizens had crowded to join a debate about 'salvation'. He describes the reaction of the 'House' when Neoclides (who could not save himself) rose to address it, and outlines the suggestions of Euaeon for a winter relief scheme (408). Finally, 'a pale, handsome youth' (427) denounced the iniquities of men, proposed the handing over of Athens to the women, and—despite some initial opposition from the countrymen—succeeded in carrying his motion (455). After a brief preliminary survey of the likely implications of the measure, and a prayer to the gods for its success, the two old men depart into the houses.

372–5 The speaker's name is found only (327 n.) in *Λ*Μυι (ἀνὴρ χρέμης ἀπὸ ἐκκλησίας, Χρε. R in 476). **οὗτος**: 'hello, you', 'you there', 753. Similarly αὕτη, 520. **οὔτι που**: 329 n. **οὐ δῆτ'**: in emphatic denial, 856. **ἀνίσταμαι**: *Ra.* 490 ἐγὼ δ' ἀνέστην καὶ προσέτ' ἀπεψησάμην. Blepyrus, however, has not a sponge to hand, and in fact (despite his efforts) has 'done' nothing. He simply now forgets about his trouble. **δ'**: for the position, 49. **ἀμπέχει χιτώνιον**: 332, 268 nn. **γάρ**: '(yes), for . . .' 539, see 336 n.

376–7 ἀτάρ: 'but (to change the subject) . . .', 394, *V.* 815. **ἐτεόν**: in Aristophanes only in questions (literally 'truly', i.e. 'tell me'). Cf. (for example) *Eq.* 32 (below), *V.* 184 τίς εἶ ποτ' ὦνθρωπ' ἐτεόν; **ἐξ ἐκκλησίας**: 270 n. **ἤδη . . . γάρ**: 'what, has it risen already?' For γάρ in questions, of surprise or incredulity (and standing as *third* word in its sentence) cf. *Eq.* 32 ἐτεὸν ἡγεῖ γὰρ θεούς; λύω, of dismissing the Assembly, *Ach.* 173 οἱ γὰρ πρυτάνεις λύουσι τὴν ἐκκλησίαν. **ὄρθριον μὲν οὖν**: not only risen, but risen since the dawn (which has broken in the time since 321). For this use of μὲν οὖν (agreeing with but strengthening a previous remark) see 765, 1102 nn.

378–9 καὶ δῆτα: 'and in fact', 385. The use is very much like that of καὶ δή καί, but is 'more lively and picturesque' (*GP* 278).   **ἡ μίλτος**
. . . **κύκλῳ:** before payment was introduced for attendance at meetings of the Assembly (183 n.) the citizens had sometimes to be rounded up (by the Scythian archers, 258 n., Poll. viii. 104) and forced to carry out their public duty. This was done by a rope smeared with ver-milion (ἡ μίλτος), *Ach.* 19–22 ὁπότ' οὔσης κυρίας ἐκκλησίας | ἑωθινῆς ἔρημος ἡ πνὺξ αὑτηί, | οἱ δ' ἐν ἀγορᾷ λαλοῦσι κἄνω καὶ κάτω | τὸ σχοινίον φεύγουσι τὸ μεμιλτωμένον. Those who got smeared with the ver-milion were fined (Poll. loc. cit., scholiast ad loc.). But here there is no question of reluctance: on the contrary, the meeting is over (377) before it was scheduled to begin. It is thus best (with van Leeuwen and Coulon) to suppose that the archers use the paint to exclude those who (though coming early, 390 n.) arrive to discover the 'House' full. But it must be doubted whether such a situation would ever (outside comedy) arise.   **ὦ Ζεῦ φίλτατε:** cf. *Eq.* 1270 καὶ γὰρ οὗτος ὦ φίλ' Ἄπολλον ⟨ἀεὶ⟩ πεινῇ.   **γέλων παρέσχεν:** *Th.* 941 ἵνα μὴ . . . γέλωτα παρέχω.   **προσέρραινον κύκλῳ:** 'sprinkled around', cf. 1110 (not, as Coulon, 'autour de l'enceinte').

380–2 τὸ τριώβολον: 292*b* n.   **δῆτ':** 24 n.   **εἰ γὰρ ὤφελον:** 'I only wish I had', Pl. *Cri.* 44 d εἰ γὰρ ὤφελον . . . οἷοί τ' εἶναι οἱ πολλοὶ τὰ μέγιστα κακὰ ἐργάζεσθαι.   **ὕστερος:** too late to get the ticket (296 n.). Philocleon, as a juryman, avoided this disaster by sleeping all night before the court-house (*V.* 103–5).   **νῦν:** either 'as things are' (992 n.) or 'to-day', 'on this occasion' (*Lys.* 1236). R has νὴ δί', but this is (*a*) unmetrical (ἦλθον, νὴ Δί', Reiske), (*b*) peculiar with following μὰ τὸν Δί': unless we think Chremes incensed by his misfortune, postu-late a lacuna (as van Leeuwen), or attribute (as is done here) 382 to Blepyrus. Chr. 'I got there too late and am ashamed' (*Pax* 1215, cf. 680). Bl. 'You *needn't* feel ashamed before anyone except your meal-bag' (which will suffer). Cf. *V.* 300 ἀπὸ γὰρ τοῦδέ με τοῦ μισθαρίου (i.e. jury-pay) | τρίτον αὐτὸν ἔχειν ἄλφιτα δεῖ, and Blepyrus' own question to Praxagora (547–8). This solution follows partly Coulon, partly Jackson (48).   For **θύλακος,** cf. *Pl.* 763 ὡς ἄλφιτ' οὐκ ἔνεστιν ἐν τῷ θυλάκῳ, for αἰσχύνομαι ('feel shame in face of') E. *Ion* 934 αἰσχύνομαι μέν σ', ὦ γέρον, λέξω δ' ὅμως.   οὐδὲν ἄλλο (B, γ' Brunck), sc. ἔλαβον (as Blaydes) is close to nonsense.

383–5 τὸ δ' αἴτιον τί; cf. *Ach.* 607.   **ἦλθ' ἀθρόος:** 'came in a body', 'came en masse'. So (again of the Assembly) *Ach.* 26, cf. *V.* 1334 ἀθρόοι γὰρ ἥξομέν σε προσκαλούμενοι.   **καὶ δῆτα:** 378.   **πάντας:** R, correctly. This was the biggest crowd yet seen in the Assembly and they looked like shoemakers to a man. For a (weak) defence of πάντες (ΓΛΜυιVbιB, cf. 688) see B. Marzullo in *Miscellanea Critica*, i (Leipzig, 1964), 135.   **σκυτοτόμοις:** see 432. The point here is their pallor, from their indoor (because of a warm climate?)

occupation ('pervigilat noctes totas, tum autem interdius | quasi
claudus sutor domi sedet totos dies', Plaut. *Aul.* 72). It became
the subject of a proverb (scholiast *Pax* 1310), οὐδὲν λευκῶν ἀνδρῶν
ἔργον εἰ μὴ σκυτοτομεῖν: hence the reaction to Praxagora (νεανίας
λευκός τις, 427) and her equally pale-faced friends (see 64 n.). But a
feeling of contempt may be implicit: for though shoemakers and other
'rude mechanicals' might properly be heard in the Assembly (as
Plato explains, *Prt.* 319 d), in general their stock stood very low. Cf.
id. *Tht.* 180 d ἵνα καὶ οἱ σκυτοτόμοι αὐτῶν τὴν σοφίαν μάθωσιν ἀκούσαντες,
Eq. 738–40 τοὺς μὲν καλούς τε κἀγαθοὺς οὐ προσδέχει, | σαυτὸν δὲ
λυχνοπώλαισι καὶ νευρορράφοις | καὶ σκυτοτόμοις καὶ βυρσοπώλαισιν δίδως.

386–7 οὐ γὰρ ἀλλ': 'for really', cf. *Ra.* 58 μὴ σκῶπτέ μ' ὦδελφ'· οὐ γὰρ
ἀλλ' ἔχω κακῶς. **ὑπερφυῶς | ὡς λευκοπληθὴς:** 'it's wonderful the
number of white faces . . .', Pl. *Phd.* 66 a ὑπερφυῶς . . . ὡς ἀληθῆ
λέγεις. The adjective (here only) is probably intended to glance at
tragic epithets in *-πληθής*: as (specially relevant here) γυναικοπληθής
(A. *Pers.* 122, E. *Alc.* 952). And the tone of the whole passage recalls
the tragic ῥῆσις: cf. (for example) E. *Rh.* 309 στρατοῦ δὲ πλῆθος οὐδ' ἂν
ἐν ψήφου λόγῳ | θέσθαι δυναίμην, ὡς ἄπλατον ἦν ἰδεῖν.

389–91 πόθεν; 'don't be silly' (see 976 n.). **οὐδ' εἰ . . . ἐφθέγγετ':**
Chremes is exaggerating slightly (31 n.). The cock is of course 'the
bird of dawning' (*Nu.* 4, Ath. 374 d) : for its *second* crowing as a herald
of the day cf. *Ev.Marc.* 14 : 72. So Juv. 9. 107 (of the swiftness of rumour
in the city) : 'quod tamen ad cantum galli facit ille secundi | proximus
ante diem caupo sciet, audiet et quae | finxerunt pariter librarius
archimagiri | carptores.'

391–3 οἴμοι δείλαιος: 1051. His subsequent lament is from the *Myrmi-
dons* of Aeschylus (fr. 227 Mette) : for (to quote van Leeuwen) 'tantus
luctus nisi Aeschyli lingua apte exprimi nequit.' Achilles there grieves
for Patroclus (τοῦ τεθνηκότος) : τριωβόλου is substituted here. For
Antilochus as the bearer of bad news to Achilles see *Il.* xviii. 2. There
is little doubt that **τἀμὰ γὰρ διοίχεται** is meant to stand as part of the
quotation (cf. E. *Med.* 739 τἀμὰ μὲν γὰρ ἀσθενῇ) : the reversion to
Blepyrus' own words is marked by ἀτάρ (376 n.). For **διοίχεται**,
'destroyed', 'completely done for', see *Th.* 609.

394–5 ἀτὰρ τί τὸ πρᾶγμ' ἦν: 1071. **τοσοῦτον χρῆμ' ὄχλου:** 'such
a whopping crowd', a common colloquial use of χρῆμα. Cf. (for example) *Ra.* 1278 ὦ Ζεῦ βασιλεῦ τὸ χρῆμα τῶν κόπων ὅσον, i.e. 'what an
awful lot of blows', Hdt. i. 36. 1 ὑὸς χρῆμα μέγα. The connotation of
the idiom is *wonder*, most often elicited by *size*. A similar idiom (expressing *smallness*) is the Irish country phrase 'a weethin' of' (i.e. 'a wee
thing . . .', 'a small amount of'). **οὕτως ἐν ὥρᾳ:** 'in such good time',
V. 689.

395–7 δ' . . . γ': 32 n. For the set phrase τί δ' ἄλλο γ' ἢ ('what else but?',
i.e. 'just that') see 771, *Av.* 25. **τοῖς πρυτάνεσι:** the prytaneis, among

their other duties (87 n.), would put down the business for the day
(*Ath. Pol.* 43. 3). This function (**γνώμας καθεῖναι**, 'to enter on the
order-paper', as it were) is distinct from that of bringing a resolution
forward and inviting the views of the Assembly (*γνώμας προθεῖναι*, Th.
vi. 14 *καὶ σύ, ὦ πρύτανι, ταῦτα . . . ἐπιψήφιζε καὶ γνώμας προτίθει αὖθις
Ἀθηναίοις*). Cf. D. xxix. 46 *τοῦτον τὸν λόγον καθεῖκεν*, 'he put this plea
down to be considered.' Although *προτίθημι* may be used in both
these senses (Aeschin. ii. 66 *λόγον γὰρ μὴ προτιθέντων εἰς τὴν ὑστέραν
ἐκκλησίαν τῶν προέδρων*) we need not read *προθεῖναι* (Schoemann)
here. Cf. in general *Ra.* 1435 *ἀλλ' ἔτι μίαν γνώμην ἑκάτερος εἴπατον |
περὶ τῆς πόλεως ἥντιν' ἔχετον σωτηρίαν.*

398 Νεοκλείδης ὁ γλάμων: 254 n.   **παρείρπυσεν**: 'crept forward to
speak', see 511. But the sense of *stealth* there (226 n.) is irrelevant
to Neoclides here: he *has* to creep because of his bad eyesight. The
verb is thus a comic substitution for *παρῆλθε* (the *vox propria*, see
409 n.).

399–402 ἀναβοᾷ: 'shouts out loud' (vivid present), *Ra.* 779 *μὰ Δί' ἀλλ' ὁ
δῆμος ἀνεβόα κρίσιν ποιεῖν.* Cf. *ἀνακράζω* (431). Neoclides the prospective interrupter (254 n.) is himself denied a hearing.   **πόσον
δοκεῖς**: 'for all they are worth', a question ('how much do you
think?') become an adverb, as commonly *πῶς δοκεῖς* (*Ach.* 24), *πῶς
οἴει* (*Ra.* 54). Cf. the use of *πόσ' ἄττ' οἴει* ('countless'), *Pax* 704.
οὐ δεινά: 'isn't it a fine thing?', *V.* 1368 *οὐ δεινὰ τωθάζειν σε τὴν
αὐλητρίδα | τῶν συμποτῶν κλέψαντα*; cf. *Ra.* 610.   **τουτονί**: 27 n.
δημηγορεῖν: 111 n.   **καὶ ταῦτα . . . προκειμένου**: 'and that too' (137,
V. 718) 'when the topic of discussion' (*τὸ προκείμενον*, Pl. *La.* 184 c)
'is safety'. For the genitive absolute with subject unexpressed (impersonal here) see 185 n. *προκείμενον* (Blaydes), accusative absolute
(cf. 1003) is facile.   **ὃς αὐτὸς . . . οὐκ ἐσώσατο**: cf. (for expression)
Eq. 1223 *αὐτὸς δ' ἑαυτῷ παρετίθει τὰ μείζονα*, (for the taunt) *Ev.Matt.*
27: 42 *ἄλλους ἔσωσεν, ἑαυτὸν οὐ δύναται σῶσαι.* For a similar view see
Aeschin. i. 30 (politicians should be competent to help themselves
before they attempt to help the State).   **βλεφαρίδ'**: probably not
'eyelash' (*Eq.* 373), although conjunctivitis could affect it, but rather
'eyelid' (*βλέφαρον*, 406 n.). For this use of the word see Arist. *HA*
504ᵃ29. The singular in either sense is odd, but may refer to some
proverb or colloquial expression: cf. our 'he didn't bat an eyelid.'

403–4 ἀναβοήσας: to match his opponents (399).   **περιβλέψας**: he
looks around him (*περιβλέψας δὲ πρὸς τοὺς παρόντας*, ps.-Pl. *Erx.*
395 c) so that all can *see* the trouble they are making, before shouting,
'Well, how can I help it?' *χρῆν*, ΛΜυι (E. *Or.* 551) destroys the
vivid impact of his question. Cf. 978, *Av.* 1640 *τί δαὶ ποιῶμεν;*

404–7 Blepyrus, thus called on for advice, would have prescribed a
plaster composed of pungent herbs (contrast his wife's idea, 255). His
excellent exemplar is Aesculapius himself (*Pl.* 716–22). Blepyrus, if

not quite so sadistic, would doubtless mean his remedy to sting. Both
physicians include garlic (σκόροδον) and bitter fig-juice (ὀπός, *Pax*
1184): for the latter's medicinal powers see Thphr. *HP* ix. 8. 2. Blepyrus adds spurge (τιθύμαλλος, Cratin. fr. 212A), particularly specifying
Spartan. This (despite Blaydes) has no significance except that the
Spartan type was famous (scholiast, ἦν διαβόητος).   τοῦ Λακωνικοῦ:
'of the Spartan kind', for which see Thphr. *HP* ix. 15. 6. Genitive *plural* is common in such contexts (θύμον . . . τῶν Ὑμηττίων, Eub.
fr. 19. 4), but the singular appears to be unique. (Cf. the fuller phrase
Av. 833 ὄρνις ἀφ' ἡμῶν τοῦ γένους τοῦ Περσικοῦ.) Should we perhaps
translate 'of Sparta' (τὸ Λακωνικόν, Hdt. vii. 235. 3)? The genitive is
then one of origin (cf. *Ra.* 472 Κωκυτοῦ . . . περίδρομοι κύνες): it
should not, in any case, be classified as partitive (Poultney, 76).
σαυτοῦ: ΓΛΜυιVbιB have σαυτῶ, but the genitive is regular (*Pl.*
721).   παραλείφειν τὰ βλέφαρα: 'smear along the eyelids'. Cf. in a
similar context *Pl.* 721, Gal. xiv. 343 (Kühn) καταχρίομεν τὰ βλέφαρα.
τῆς ἑσπέρας: no doubt representing (as indeed does the whole passage)
the language of a medical prescription. Cf. 251, 1057 nn.

408–21 Neoclides is followed—we are not told if in fact he succeeded in
putting his proposals—by a speaker named (unsuitably) Euaeon.
A pauper, he doubtless represents the situation of many in the Athens
of his day: and σωτηρία to him means clothes and blankets. He suggests (*a*) that the fullers should provide warm cloaks for those who ask
them in the winter, (*b*) that the tanners should open up their premises
for sleepers, or incur a heavy fine.

408–10 Εὐαίων ὁ δεξιώτατος: his appearance (see below) belies his
name (that of a son of Aeschylus, *PA* 5255). The epithet implies 'who
really knows what he's about', a capable man (*Ra.* 71) in his profession.
Euaeon is well versed in all the tricks of poverty, and also a good
speaker (241). He is not (like Demus) δεξιώτατος at home, but
tongue-tied on the Pnyx (*Eq.* 752). It is this forwardness, and not his
poverty, that Ar. is mocking: cf. the boastful paupers Theogenes and
Aeschines (*Av.* 821–3). There is nothing (despite Hess, 57) to connect
him with his namesake in D. xxi. 71, who had killed a certain Boeotus
at a banquet.   παρῆλθε: 'came forward to speak'. Cf. D. xviii. 170
ἠρώτα μὲν ὁ κῆρυξ τίς ἀγορεύειν βούλεται; παρῄει δ' οὐδείς (130).
γυμνός: 'without a cloak', Aeschin. i. 60 ὁ Πιττάλακος ἔρχεται γυμνὸς
εἰς τὴν ἀγοράν.   ὡς ἐδόκει: because his cloak was full of holes and
threadbare (ὀπὰς γὰρ εἶχεν οὐκ ὀλίγας μὰ τὸν Δία, *Pl.* 715). The cold
on a winter morning (416 n., 539) would be keen: he thus makes very
practical proposals. Isocrates speaks (vii. 54) of paupers χορεύοντας μὲν
ἐν χρυσοῖς ἱματίοις, χειμάζοντας δ' ἐν τοιούτοις ἐν οἷς οὐ βούλομαι λέγειν.
Cf. (of the informer's cloak) *Av.* 1417 δεῖσθαι δ' ἔοικεν οὐκ ὀλίγων
χελιδόνων, i.e. it is only for warm weather. Praxagora foresees that
under women (566, 605) this kind of poverty will vanish.   γε μέντοι:

the common adversative use (see 1008 n.), cf. *Eq.* 885. For the crasis (μέντοι ἔφασκεν, 650 n.) cf. μεντουγώ (*Ra.* 971).

411–14 δημοτικωτάτους λόγους: 'popular' words (see 631) in every sense, cf. *Nu.* 205 τὸ γὰρ σόφισμα δημοτικὸν καὶ χρήσιμον. **ὁρᾶτε μέν . . . καὐτόν:** I *myself* require saving: all the same, I will show you how to save the city. Cf. E. *Heracl.* 11 σῴζω τάδ' (sc. τὰ τέκνα αὐτὸς δεόμενος σωτηρίας. In his subsequent suggestions the interests of Athens and Euaeon turn out to be the same: for the price of safety is apparently the price of a cloak (four staters, 413). For μέν used in parody of speeches cf. 151, 504. **τετραστατήρου:** probably not adjectival (i.e. 'costing four staters', LSJ) but rather genitive of price (*Nu.* 876). The four-stater piece (Arist. fr. 529, Rose) is taken to equal sixteen drachmae (cf. Hsch. s.v. στατήρ). If so, Euaeon contemplates a cheaper garment than that referred to, *Pl.* 982: ἀλλ' ἀργυρίου δραχμὰς ἂν ἤτησ' εἴκοσιν | εἰς ἱμάτιον. Cf. Eup. fr. 252. **ἀλλ' ὅμως:** answering μέν (*Ra.* 602).

415–17 οἱ κναφῆς: these, as well as cleaners (*V.* 1128) were seemingly also manufacturers of clothes, or at least retailers (ἱματιοπῶλαι). So too the tanners (420). **χλαίνας:** men's cloaks (507, *Th.* 142) distinguished (cf. *Ra.* 1459) from σισύρας (421) by smoother texture (*V.* 738, *Av.* 493). They were *winter* wear, exchanged for a lighter garb in summer (*Av.* 714, 1090): and their use distinguished the free man from the slave (*Lys.* 1156). Bieber's illustration (*GK* pl. XLIV. 3) oddly uses a *woman* as a model. **ἐπειδὰν . . . τραπῇ:** 'right in the middle of winter', when the sun 'turns' from Capricorn back to the Equator (scholiast, εἰς χειμερινὴν . . . τροπήν). The solstice meant is shown by the context: cf. Th. viii. 39. 1 περὶ ἡλίου τροπάς (sc. τὰς χειμερινάς). Explicitly, Pl. *Lg.* 915 d (of summer), X. *Mem.* iv. 3. 8 ἐπειδὰν ἐν χειμῶνι (sc. ὁ ἥλιος) τράπηται. Euaeon's heartfelt proposals may suggest that he is in fact speaking in the winter (cf. *Eq.* 881–3). If so, the play may have been produced at the Lenaea, not at the Dionysia in spring: though no doubt even then the dawn was chilly. This point, incidentally, may tell against the likelihood of actors performing in the nude (see 1138 n.). **πλευρῖτις . . . οὐδέν' ἂν λάβοι:** since the biting wind would be excluded. Cf. Alciphr. iii. 6. 2 . . . λάβρως ἐπαιγίζων ὁ βορρᾶς δίεισί μοι τῶν πλευρῶν ὥσπερ βέλος. The verb is used both of the complaint (ἤ που πρὸς ὄρθρον σπασμὸς ὑμᾶς λαμβάνει; *Lys.* 1089) and of the sufferer (χίμετλον οὐδὲν λήψομαι, *V.* 1167), depending on the nature of the ailment.

418–20 κλίνη . . . στρώματα: *Ach.* 1090, though the sense there is not 'bed', but 'dining-couch' (840). Those who have no beds or bed-clothes are to go ('after washing') to the tanners'. **ἀπονενιμμένους** might mean 'after supper' (for the custom of washing then see *V.* 1217) and the joke lie in supposing that a pauper has a *supper* when he hasn't a *couch* (κλίνη, *Ach.* loc. cit.). But the meaning (I think) is 'after visiting the bath-house': where paupers gathered, not indeed to *wash* (the word is jesting) but rather for free heat from the furnace (*Pl.* 535, 953), till forcibly ejected by the bath-man (*Pl.* 955). It is after this (Euaeon is proposing) that the tanners should offer them a bed. ἐς τῶν σκυλοδεψῶν: the local noun (as frequently) omitted, *Th.* 89 ἐς Θεσμοφόροιν ἐλθεῖν, 443. The σκυλοδέψαι (tanners) are included (with the ἀλφιταμοιβοί, 424) in the list of city tradesmen (*Av.* 490). If Cleon, their most famous representative, is typical (*Eq.* 316–18) they were also retailers (415 n.).

420–1 ἦν δ'... ὀφειλέτω: sc. τις τῶν σκυλοδεψῶν. The words are typical of legal language. (*a*) Notice the change to the third person singular (cf. the law in D. xxiv. 63); (*b*) cf. the law of Solon (Lys. x. 17) "Οστις δὲ ἀπίλλει τῇ θύρᾳ, ἔνδον τοῦ κλέπτου ὄντος. Τὸ ἀπίλλειν τοῦτο ἀποκλήειν νομίζεται, καὶ μηδὲν διὰ τοῦτο διαφέρου. For the dative, see Lys. loc. cit., *V.* 333 τίς γάρ ἐσθ' ὁ ταῦτά σ' εἴργων | κἀποκλῄων τῇ θύρᾳ; for the genitive (which B gives here) *Lys.* 423, Timocl. fr. 23. 4 τῆς θύρας | ἀπεκλειόμην. **χειμῶνος ὄντος:** *Eq.* 883, *V.* 445. **σισύρας:** 347 n.

422–6 χρηστά γ': 70 n., cf. 241. **τοὺς ἀλφιταμοιβοὺς:** the sellers of barley-meal (*Av.* 491) whose shady dealings (*Nu.* 640) made Strepsiades keen to learn his measures: ὑπ' ἀλφιταμοιβοῦ παρεκόπην διχοινίκῳ. Ehrenberg believes that this form (for ἀλφιτοπώλης, 686 n.) in fact connotes a swindler (119 n. 6). But similar compounds do not support that view (χρυσαμοιβός, A. *A.* 437, Pl. *Plt.* 289 e). **τοῖς ἀπόροις τρεῖς χοίνικας:** sc. ἀλφίτων (fr. 465). A promise of dole for the poor was not a novelty, *Av.* 580, *Eq.* 1104 ἀλλ' ἄλφιτ' ἤδη σοι ποριῶ 'σκευασμένα. But demagogues' promises were not the same as practice: they would offer Euboea (*V.* 715) and end with a grudging dole of barley. A rate of a quart (χοῖνιξ, 45) per man per day was evidently thought of as the standard (Hdt. vii. 187. 2, Heraclid. Lemb. *FHG* iii. 169): so Blepyrus is doubtless justified in his belief that the new scheme would have met no opposition. It is specially aimed at Nausicydes, who presumably gave very close measure (cf. Thphr. *Char.* 30. 11) with the flour by which he made his fortune (X. *Mem.* ii. 7. 6). Cf. in general *Pax* 1144, 1217 δοίην ἂν αὐτοῖν ἰσχάδων τρεῖς χοίνικας. **ἢ κλάειν μακρά:** 'or be damned', *Eq.* 433 κλάειν σε μακρὰ κελεύσας. **ἵνα ... τἀγαθόν:** 'in which event' (ἵνα, 152 n.) 'they would have got this benefit from Nausicydes' (i.e. either his meal or his damnation).

With this whole passage (408–26) compare the list of the 'benefits' of Poverty (*Pl.* 540–7).

427–57 Praxagora's speech reported: its reception and result. She seems (as Chremes reports her) to have given more detailed criticism of the men (this would, of course, be the part he best remembered) than she did in her rehearsal (169). But the positive qualities of women (214) were repeated (435, 453), and she made her main points (210, 441 nn.). Aristophanes could hardly be expected to rewrite her first speech indirectly.

427–30 τοίνυν: 'well, to continue' (after interruption), cf. *Pl.* 563. **εὐπρεπὴς νεανίας:** Praxagora is a good deal younger than her husband (cf. 243, 323 nn.), and is handsome in a feminine way, naturally (λευκός, 387, 64 nn.). She thus recalls such effeminates as Nicias: cf. *Th.* 191 (of Agathon) σὺ δ᾽ εὐπρόσωπος λευκὸς ἐξυρημένος | γυναικόφωνος ἁπαλὸς εὐπρεπὴς ἰδεῖν. Perhaps this also explains (see 101 n.) why her feminine voice appears to pass unnoticed (though of course it would be fatal if it were). The Nicias meant may be the grandson of the general (*PA* 10809). **ἀνεπήδησ᾽:** 'sprang to his feet', Δημοσθένης . . . ἀναπηδήσας ἐν τῇ ἐκκλησίᾳ (Aeschin. iii. 149). Praxagora had been waiting with impatience for her opportunity to speak. Cf. in general Ephipp. fr. 14 ἔπειτ᾽ ἀναστὰς εὔστοχος νεανίας . . . ἔλεξεν. **δημηγορήσων:** 111, 400. **κἀπεχείρησεν λέγειν:** 'and attempted to say' (in face of opposition, 432), Pl. *Prt.* 319 c ἕως ἂν . . . αὐτὸς ἀποστῇ ὁ ἐπιχείρων λέγειν καταθορυβηθείς, unless the sense is simply 'she began' (*Lys.* 674). **ὡς χρὴ . . . τὴν πόλιν:** 210.

431–3 ἐθορύβησαν: the *mot juste* for 'kicking up a din' in the Assembly: *Eq.* 666, D. xxi. 194 βλέπων εἰς τὸν ἀεὶ θορυβοῦντα τόπον τῆς ἐκκλησίας (cf. Pl. *Prt.* 319 c above). So also θόρυβος (519 n.). **κἀνέκραγον** . . . **λέγοι:** 399 n., X. *An.* v. 1. 3 ταῦτα ἀκούσαντες οἱ στρατιῶται ἀνεθορύβησαν, ὡς εὖ λέγοι. **τὸ σκυτοτομικὸν πλῆθος:** 385 n. The πλῆθος is seen as composed of individuals, hence the preceding plural verbs (cf. Th. i. 125. 1 καὶ τὸ πλῆθος ἐψηφίσαντο πολεμεῖν). The fashionable -κός termination (441) *may* mark contempt (356, 385 nn., Peppler, 439). More likely, the phrase is the normal adjectival equivalent of οἱ σκυτοτόμοι: contempt would be expressed by voice alone. **οἱ δ᾽ ἐκ τῶν ἀγρῶν | ἀνεβορβόρυξαν:** 'they rumbled loudly' (399 n.), the compound verb (a coinage) only here. βορβορύζω, of intestinal rumbling (Hp., *Int.* 6): medicine still uses (id. *Prog.* 11) 'borborygmi'.

The countrymen, as one would expect, are more conservative (and incidentally, must have risen very early to claim their seats on the Pnyx on this occasion). There is evidence here (since cobbling is an urban occupation) of friction (see 300) between the country-dwellers and the townsmen. Cf. *Pax* 1185. On this question of country-town relationships see Ehrenberg, 82–9. Blepyrus, himself not long in Athens (243 n.) is at first sympathetic to the country, and can only hope that this folly, as he sees it, will turn out for the best (473). But after Praxagora's explanations, he becomes her keen supporter (710, 725).

433 γὰρ: '(doubtless they did) for . . .', 603, *Ra.* 916 Δι. ἐγὼ δ᾽ ἔχαιρον τῇ σιωπῇ . . . Εὐ. ἠλίθιος γὰρ ἦσθα. Both there and here some editors read ἄρ᾽ (see 558 n.). Cf. in general *Av.* 1371 νοῦν ἄρ᾽ ἕξεις νὴ Δία.

434–6 ὁ δὲ . . . τῇ βοῇ: 'he came off best in the shouting', bawled the opposition down (as Cleon promises, *Eq.* 286 καταβοήσομαι βοῶν σε).

The same play (276) provides the closest parallel: ἀλλ' ἐὰν μέντοι γε νικᾷς τῇ βοῇ, τήνελλος εἶ. For κατέχω see Thgn. 262 ἄλλος ἀνὴρ κατέχει πολλὸν ἐμοῦ κακίων. Others prefer to regard the verb as transitive, translating either 'he mastered (them)' or else 'he filled (the Assembly) with his shouting' (cf. Th. iii. 62. 4, S. *Ph.* 10). On any view, the speaker appears to have been strong-voiced for a woman.   πόλλ' ἀγαθὰ λέγων: 214–38.   σέ: i.e. as a typical male (see 455 n.), who has mismanaged matters up to now. Blepyrus, taking the pronoun to himself, will not believe himself the *sole* offender: and Chremes at last confirms that *all* the men (440) came under Praxagora's attack. πολλὰ κακά: she denounced men in politics (see under) as πανοῦργοι (a compliment, *Lys.* 12, men also paid to women), κλέπται (a stock charge against Cleon in *Eq.*), and συκοφάνται (the most typical product of Athens, 452 n., *Ach.* 904, *Av.* 1410). For these attributes in combination (all of Cleon) see *V.* 1227, *Pax* 652. Cf. fr. 40 καὶ νὴ Δί' εἰ Πάμφιλόν γε φαίης | κλέπτειν τὰ κοίν' ἅμα τε συκοφαντεῖν, and the reason Th. gives (v. 16) for Cleon's opposition to a peace . . . γενομένης ἡσυχίας καταφανέστερος νομίζων ἂν εἶναι κακουργῶν καὶ ἀπιστότερος διαβάλλων.

436–7 πρῶτον μέν: answered by κἄπειτα (438), see 60 n. above. Blepyrus' reaction is almost automatic: 'and what' (he asks) 'did he call *you*?'   μή πω τοῦτ' ἔρῃ: S. *OT* 740 Οι. μήπω μ' ἐρώτα· τὸν δὲ Λάιον . . . φράζε. Similarly, *Av.* 323 μήπω φοβηθῇς τὸν λόγον (i.e. let me finish with my news first).

438–40 καὶ νὴ Δία | καὶ συκοφάντην: the first καί implies 'and moreover' (more often in such contexts reinforced by γε, cf. 140, 445 n.), the second 'as well' (*Nu.* 663). *Lys.* 24 (corrupt) perhaps conceals the same construction: cf. E. Fraenkel, *Kleine Beiträge zur klassischen Philologie* (Rome, 1964), i. 442.   τωνδὶ τὸ πλῆθος: with a gesture (27 n.) towards the audience (cf. 167–8). As Praxagora was criticizing *men*, we may assume, perhaps, that its membership was male (see 165 n.). For similar humorous condemnation of the audience cf. (for example) *Ra.* 274 Δι. κατεῖδες οὖν που τοὺς πατραλοίας αὐτόθι | καὶ τοὺς ἐπιόρκους, οὓς ἔλεγεν ἡμῖν ; Ξα. σὺ δ' οὔ ; τίς . . . λέγει; 'but who's denying *this*?' this is a different story from your σέ. Cf. *Ra.* 1140, Hdt. vi. 124. 2 καὶ τοῦτο οὐκ ἔστι ἄλλως εἰπεῖν.

441–2 πρᾶγμ' . . . νουβυστικόν: 'a thing stuffed (βύω) with intelligence (νοῦς)', as it were νόῳ βεβυσμένον (see *Th.* 506). πρᾶγμα is perhaps preferred to χρῆμα (ἱππικώτατον γάρ ἐστι χρῆμα κάποχον γυνή, *Lys.* 677) because of χρηματοποιόν (236 n.). Cf. Men. *Mon.* 734 ὑπερήφανον πρᾶγμ' ἐστὶν ὡραία γυνή. Cf. for the -κός ending 432 n.

442–3 κοὔτε τἀπόρρητ' . . . ἐκφέρειν: 'don't divulge the mysteries' of the Thesmophoria (223 n.). See *Th.* 356 ὁπόσαι δ' | . . . τἀπόρρητα . . . τοῖσιν ἐ-|χθροῖς τοῖς ἡμετέροις λέγουσ' . . . ἀσεβοῦσιν ἀδικοῦσίν τε τὴν πόλιν. The secret nature of the rites is intimated, *Th.* 472 αὐταὶ γάρ

ἐσμεν, κοὐδεμί' ἔκφορος λόγου, a passage which also illustrates the use
of ἐκφέρειν, cf. Hdt. iii. 74. 2 ἢ μὲν ἕξειν παρ' ἑωυτῷ μηδ' ἐξοίσειν
μηδενὶ ἀνθρώπων τὴν ἀπὸ σφέων ἀπάτην ἐς Πέρσας γεγονυῖαν. For οὔτε
. . . δέ, cf. E. *HF* 1281 οὔτ' ἐμαῖς φίλαις | Θήβαις ἐνοικεῖν ὅσιον· ἦν
δὲ καὶ μένω, | ἐς ποῖον ἱερὸν ἢ πανήγυριν φίλων | εἶμ'; This responsion
is used mostly when the second clause expresses a contrast to the first
(*GP* 511).   ἐκ Θεσμοφοροῖν: 420 n. τὼ Θεσμοφόρω (*Th.* 1230) are
Demeter and Persephone (*Th.* 296, cf. τὼ θεώ, 155 n.), as originating
civil customs (θεσμοί, θέσμια), Call. *Cer.* 17 μὴ μὴ ταῦτα λέγωμες ἃ
δάκρυον ἤγαγε Δηοῖ· | κάλλιον, ὡς πολίεσσιν ἑαδότα τέθμια δῶκε.

444-5 σὲ δὲ κᾀμὲ . . . ἀεί: sc. ἐκφέρειν ἀπόρρητα (of state secrets, *Eq.* 647,
Lys. xii. 69 τῶν πολεμίων ἕνεκα τἀπόρρητα ποιοῦνται). Men can't
keep the secrets of the boule.   βουλεύοντε, see apparatus criticus,
'when serving as members of the boule' (cf. *Eq.* 774). This committee
of five hundred (ἡ βουλὴ οἱ πεντακόσιοι, Aeschin. iii. 20) arranged the
times of meeting (four in any prytany, 87 n., *Ath. Pol.* 43. 3) and the
business for debate in the Assembly: 'ἔδοξε τῇ βουλῇ τάδε | τῇ τῶν
γυναικῶν . . . to hold an assembly at dawn in the middle of the Thesmo-
phoria . . . and to deliberate first of all about the punishment due to
Euripides . . .' (*Th.* 372). Its own steering committee of fifty was the
prytaneis (87, 396 nn.) and its membership, like theirs, would not be
constant: ἡ βουλὴ . . . ἡ ἀεὶ (i.e. 'for the time being') βουλεύουσα, And.
i. 91. But we need not assume (from σὲ κᾀμέ: 436 n.) that either
Chremes or Blepyrus had ever been in fact a member. For the boule
as recipients of secret information see *Eq.* 647, Lys. xiii. 21, And. ii. 3.
20, and for part of a list of fourth-century bouleutai see S. Chari-
tonides, *Hesperia*, xxx (1961), 30–57.   καὶ . . . γ': 'yes, and what's
more . . .', in answers, 816. For position of γε in 445 (140 n.) cf. *Eq.*
423. With Blepyrus' ready admission of his guilt, cf. *Lys.* 11–12 Αυ.
παρὰ μὲν τοῖς ἀνδράσιν νενομίσμεθα | εἶναι πανοῦργοι— Κα. καὶ γάρ
ἐσμεν νὴ Δία.

446-8 συμβάλλειν πρὸς ἀλλήλας: 'they lend one another'. Cf. (for
the meaning of συμβάλλειν) Isoc. xxi. 13 ἐξῆν ἅ τ' ἔλαβεν ἀποστερεῖν
(449) καὶ οἷς μὴ συνέβαλεν ἐγκαλεῖν, (for construction) Pl. *Alc. I* 125 d
κοινωνούντων . . . πολιτείας καὶ συμβαλλόντων πρὸς ἀλλήλους. For
borrowing and lending among neighbours cf. *Ra.* 1158 νὴ τὸν Δί'
ὥσπερ γ' εἴ τις εἴποι γείτονι, | "χρῆσον σὺ μάκτραν, εἰ δὲ βούλει, κάρ-
δοπον." Even men would hardly insist on having witnesses (448) for
such informal dealings. But when *money* (ἀργύριον) was lent (at least
by usurers, cf. *Nu.* 1152), some witnesses would normally be present
(D. xxxiv. 28). Their presence at repayment could also be insisted on
(ibid. 30, cf. Thphr. *Char.* 14. 8). Women are both more trusting and
more trustworthy (449). For the other borrowings mentioned cf. *Th.*
250 ἀλλ' ἱμάτιον γοῦν χρῆσον (to the womanly Agathon) ἡμῖν τουτωί,
Thphr. *Char.* 18. 7 καὶ ὅταν ἥκῃ τις αἰτησόμενος ἐκπώματα (there is an

interesting reference to drinking-bowls of glass, *Ach.* 74). **χρυσία** are
women's golden trinkets (*Lys.* 1190, D. xxvii. 10).   **μόνας μόναις**: cf.
V. 1272, D. xxxiv. 32 σὺ δὲ μόνος μόνῳ φῄς δοῦναι τῷ ναυκλήρῳ τὸ χρυσίον.
For lending or repayment without witnesses see also Isoc. xvii. 2, Is. fr.
28. 2 (Thalheim) οὐ παρεχομένων αὐτῶν μάρτυρας, ὧν ἐναντίον (451)
ἡμῖν ἀποδοῦναί φασιν. Praxagora's case, of course, is overstated: for
formal contracts entered into by women were limited by law (1024 n.).
The new regime would change this.

449–50 ἀποφέρειν: 'to give back', of a loan or a deposit, Hdt. i. 196. 4
ἀποφέρειν τὸ χρυσίον ἔκειτο νόμος.   **ἀποστερεῖν:** 'keep someone out of'
his money or belongings, 'withhold' repayment of one's debts. Cf.
Isoc. xxi. 13 (446 n.), *Nu.* 1303 ὁ γὰρ γέρων ὅδ' ἐρασθεὶς | ἀποστερῆσαι
βούλεται | τὰ χρήμαθ' ἁδανείσατο.   **ἡμῶν δὲ τοὺς πολλοὺς:** she might
have found an example in Strepsiades, whose inclination τοῦτο δρᾶν
(i.e. ἀποστερεῖν) is innate, and who seeks to help 'natura' by 'doctrina',
Nu. 487, 116 ἦν οὖν μάθῃς μοι τὸν ἄδικον τοῦτον λόγον, | ἃ νῦν ὀφείλω διὰ
σέ, τούτων τῶν χρεῶν | οὐκ ἂν ἀποδοίην οὐδ' ἂν ὀβολὸν οὐδενί. For
men's delight in putting off repayments see *Av.* 114–16.

451 νὴ τὸν Ποσειδῶ . . . ἐναντίον: 'even when witnesses are present' men
are ready to deny their debts (ὀφείλων ἐξαρνεῖν, 660, see below).
Hence the elaborate precautions of Theophrastus' ἄπιστος (*Char.* 18.
5): καὶ τοὺς ὀφείλοντας αὐτῷ ἀργύριον μετὰ μαρτύρων ἀπαιτεῖν τοὺς
τόκους, ὅπως μὴ δύναιντο ἔξαρνοι γενέσθαι. Cf. in general *Eq.* 298
κἀπιορκῶ γε βλεπόντων. Blepyrus' proficiency in oaths is worth a mention (422, 445, 662): see *Nu.* 1232–5.   **γ'** with preceding oath, 422,
748, cf. *Eq.* 1035 νὴ τὸν Ποσειδῶ πολύ γ' ἄμεινον, ὦ Γλάνι. The choice
of oath here (as 445) is not significant: see H. Müller-Strübing, 'Zu
Aristophanes', *FJCP* xi (1878), 755.

454 ἕτερα . . . ηὐλόγει: I read this line (454) here, with O. Bachmann,
Conjecturarum Observationumque Aristophanearum Specimen I (Göttingen,
1878), 32.   In its manuscript context it can only be explained by
placing a full stop at κἀγαθά (Blaydes) or assuming a lacuna (Bergk).
For ἀλλὰ πολλὰ κἀγαθὰ | ἕτερά τε πλεῖστα . . . ηὐλόγει, while just
conceivable, must certainly be reckoned odd: Van Daele translates,
'Mais il leur attribuait mille qualités et ne tarissait pas d'éloges sur
d'autres mérites des femmes.' Transposition mitigates the harshness
of supplying (*a*) αὐτὰς ἔφασκε (443, 450), (*b*) (with Blaydes's punctuation) δρᾶν. The infinitives (452–3) are then dependent on the notion
of saying in ηὐλόγει: and Blepyrus ends his catalogue (in 453) with
ἄλλα (see apparatus criticus) (τε?) πολλὰ κἀγαθά, cf. ἄλλων τε πολλῶν
κἀγαθῶν (as Trygaeus ends his list), *Pax* 538, D. xix. 228 . . . ἔλεος, φθόνος,
ὀργή, χαρίσασθαι τῷ δεηθέντι, ἄλλα μυρία.

452–3 οὐ συκοφαντεῖν: 436 n. Women do not act as informers (439),
and under them the practice (to Blepyrus' dismay, 562–3) will disappear. Solon had given any citizen (τῷ βουλομένῳ) the right to

bring criminal proceedings (Plu. *Sol.* 18. 5). But the system was open to serious abuses, for private enmity could make use of informers, and their services in fact were often purchased (D. xxi. 103, lviii. 65). Not infrequently they profited by blackmail (Telecl. fr. 41, see 563 n.). The Thirty at first seemed ready to counteract this danger, but no permanent protection was afforded (*Ath. Pol.* 35. 3). For violent denunciation of their practice see D. xxv. 52, lviii. 63.   **οὐ διώκειν:** 'prosecute', 'bring to court' (*Eq.* 368). A play on the two meanings (Scots 'pursue'), *Ach.* 699 εἶτα Μαραθῶνι μὲν ὅτ᾽ ἦμεν ἐδιώκομεν, | νῦν δ᾽ ὑπ᾽ ἀνδρῶν πονηρῶν σφόδρα διωκόμεθα. Athenian φιλοδικία is neatly satirized in Strepsiades' comic disbelief—he has just been shown Athens on a map, but is sceptical, for he sees no dicasts sitting (*Nu.* 207–8). See *Pax* 505, *Eq.* 1317. The *permanent* closure of law-courts will bring down the new regime, Blepyrus alleges (657).   **τὸν | δῆμον καταλύειν:** 'try to put down the democracy', Th. iii. 81. 4 τοῖς τὸν δῆμον καταλύουσιν, cf. *Pl.* 948. This is a more serious offence in men than some of the others that she mentioned, and punishable by death (And. i. 95). For οὐ . . . οὐ . . . οὐδέ cf. fr. 317, for τὸν | δῆμον S. *Ant.* 409 τὸν | νέκυν.

455–7 τί . . . ἔδοξεν; sc. τῷ δήμῳ, 'what was the decision of the meeting?' The words ἔδοξεν τῷ δήμῳ were the preface to published decrees of the Assembly (96 n., 1015).   **δῆτ᾽:** 24 n.   **ἐπιτρέπειν γε:** RΓΛMu1Vb1 have σε, which is superficially attractive not just because of 435 (n.), but because of Blepyrus' reaction. His following questions (460, 462) are concerned with the effect upon himself. But (*a*) the Assembly did *not* of course decree that he *personally* should hand over and (*b*) the jest from Chremes in this place is improbable (his σε joke clearly ended at 440). For the γε/σε variation cf. 571, *V.* 1450 (where the *Suda*'s σε is likewise out of keeping).   **ἐδόκει . . . γεγενῆσθαι:** 'they thought this the one thing not yet tried.' The words need not satirize the city's love of novelty, or her citizens' swift changes of opinion (220, 474, 584 nn.). They may very well express the poet's disillusionment, belief that *any* change is for the better. But they do not, of course, suggest a serious belief in salvation through the 'regiment of women'. For here or elsewhere (571 n.) we are not to confuse the comic poet with the political theorist or thinker. So far, one must agree with E. Barry, 'The *Ecclesiazusae* as a Political Satire' (University of Chicago dissertation, 1942), 42, 'None of the ideas presented in the play . . . contains a shade of philosophy.' See Introduction § III.

457 καὶ δέδοκται; the perfect indicates a completed state, i.e. has the measure been agreed on? See S. *OC* 1431 Αν. οὕτως ἄρ᾽, ὦ παῖ, ταῦτά σοι δεδογμένα; ('you've quite made up your mind, then?').   **καί** here expresses surprise or incredulity, cf. *Av.* 325 καὶ δέδρακας τοῦτο τοὔργον;   **φήμ᾽ ἐγώ:** 'yes indeed', 717. Cf. colloquial 'I'll say.'

458–77 The two old men discuss the implications of the change (its very far-reaching implications, as outlined by Praxagora, 590, they could hardly be expected to foresee). Blepyrus fears (465) that women will use force, but ends (473) in resignation: Chremes emerges as the law-abiding citizen (471) we later see in practice (730–45).

458–9 ἅπαντα ... προστεταγμένα: cf. *Lys.* 177 ταῖς πρεσβυτάταις γὰρ προστέτακται τοῦτο δρᾶν. ἃ ... ἔμελεν: and which in future ταῖσιν ἀσταῖσι (*Th.* 541) μελήσει. See 463, *Lys.* 520, 538, *Il.* vi. 492 πόλεμος δ' ἄνδρεσσι μελήσει | πᾶσι. οὕτω ταῦτ' ἔχει: 'quite so', 'that's the situation' (834), cf. *Nu.* 829 ἴσθι τοῦθ' οὕτως ἔχον.

460–1 ἐς δικαστήριον: for omission of the article in this phrase (cf. 62 n.), see Pl. *Phdr.* 273 b. ἀλλ' ἡ γυνή; Blepyrus of course does not suspect that the new government will do away with lawsuits (657): he merely assumes (as Chremes understands him, 461) that his wife will be the bread-winner in future. The three-obol payment (292*b* n.) for jurymen gave citizens an extra source of income: cf. Philocleon (*V.* 550). But the duties (like most Greek jobs, see 20 n.) involved some early rising (462 n.): Blepyrus looks forward to their ending. For the late position of ἄρ' (cf. ἄρα, 462 n.) after interrogative see 91 n. οὓς ἔχεις: 'those whom you have in your keeping', 'your dependants'. Cf. *Th.* 1140 (of Pallas as tutelary goddess) ἥ πόλιν ἡμετέραν ἔχει. One's closest dependants, of course, are wife (cf. ὁ ἔχων of a husband, Semonides fr. 7 D.² 68) and children (*Th.* 1205): Dicaeopolis is careful to include them in his private truce (*Ach.* 132). Blepyrus' family, if any, are not mentioned (cf. 1138 n.).

462 στένειν τὸν ὄρθρον: the sense is not 'bewail the dawn' (van Leeuwen) but 'groan *at dawn*' (Hdt. iv. 181. 3 ὕδωρ ... τὸ τὸν ... ὄρθρον γίνεται χλιαρόν) at the thought of 'crawling from his bed' (see *V.* 550, 290 n.) to carry out his duties in the law-courts. As one of the γέροντες ἡλιασταί, φράτερες τριωβόλου (*Eq.* 255) he has to be in time (see 381 n.) to get the money. πρᾶγμ' ... μοι: either (*a*) 'it won't be my business any longer' (τουτὶ μέν, ἄνδρες, οὐδὲν ἡμῖν πρᾶγμά πω, *Pax* 244) or (*b*) 'I won't have any further trouble' (ἀλλ' οὐκ ἔτ' οὐδὲν πρᾶγμά σοι, *Th.* 244). In this sense the plural is more common: cf. *V.* 313 (which also illustrates the general context and construction) ἵν' ἐμοὶ πράγματα βόσκειν παρέχῃς (a father referring to his son). See 670. ἄρά: Kuster's metrically necessary change (ἄρα MSS.: for the confusion, cf. 479, 1102). The particle's position varies greatly, from first (479, 1102) to second last (as here, 672).

463–4 μὰ Δί' ἀλλὰ: 'by Zeus, no, but ...', 158, 550. ταῖς γυναιξὶ ... μέλει: *Lys.* 538 (see 459). ἀστενακτὶ: taking up στένειν (462). The adverb occurs in A. fr. 613. 2 Mette and is thus perhaps 'incongruous' within a comic context (cf. 868, 1102 nn.). But cf. ἀμυστί (Pherecr. fr. 202) and ἀσκαρδαμυκτί, a variant reading (*EM*) in *Eq.* 292. περδόμενος ... μενεῖς: like Phidippides (*Nu.* 8–10). Dover

remarks on the 'lively insouciance' (cf. *Pax* 335) implied in farting.
For the further implication here of laziness cf. *Ach.* 256.

465-7 ἐκεῖνο δεινὸν . . . μή: '*that*'s the danger . . . , that . . .' cf. Hdt. vii.
157. 2 τοῦτο δὲ ἤδη δεινὸν γίνεται μὴ πέσῃ πᾶσα ἡ Ἑλλάς. **τοῖσιν
ἡλίκοισι νῷν:** 'men of the age that we are' (i.e. old men). Cf. *Ach.*
703 . . . ἄνδρα κυφὸν ἡλίκον Θουκυδίδην, X. *HG* ii. 3. 25 ἡμεῖς δὲ γνόντες
μὲν τοῖς οἴοις ἡμῖν τε καὶ ὑμῖν χαλεπὴν πολιτείαν εἶναι δημοκρατίαν. νώ
(Dobree) is possible (*Ach.* 601) but the text does not require alteration.
παραλαβοῦσαι . . . τὰς ἡνίας: 107 n., Pl. *Plt.* 266 e παραδοῦναι τὰς τῆς
πόλεως ἡνίας. Cf. *Eq.* 1109.   **τί δρᾶν;** a formula of interruption, 789.
Cf. E. *Hel.* 1242, *IT* 1217.

468-72 κινεῖν: *sensu obscaeno*, i.e. βινεῖν, *Nu.* 1371. The confusion of these
two words in manuscripts (as 706) is very common: see further G.
Pascucci, '*KINHTIAN*', *A&R* iv (1959), 102-5.   **ἢν δὲ μὴ δυνώμεθα;**
cf. 799-800.   **ἄριστον οὐ δώσουσι:** 348 n. Notice the change of
construction: Blepyrus' fear (μὴ ἀναγκάζωσι) of compulsion has turned
into a certainty of sanctions.   **δέ γε:** 32 n.   **δρᾶ ταῦθ', ἵν' . . . ἅμα:**
if eating is going to depend on making love, you must do your duty
and combine them.   **τὸ πρὸς βίαν δεινότατον:** so (but with reference to men who force a woman) *Lys.* 163 οὐ γὰρ ἔνι τούτοις ἡδονὴ τοῖς
πρὸς βίαν.   **ξυνοίσει:** 'help' (see 17 n.).   **πάντ' ἄνδρα:** cf. *V.* 1113
πάντα γὰρ κεντοῦμεν ἄνδρα . . . Possibly here the sense is 'every *true* man'
(cf. *Eq.* 333) : πολλοὶ μὲν ἄνθρωποι, ὀλίγοι δὲ ἄνδρες (Hdt. vii. 210. 2.).
Chremes is a type of the good citizen, obedient to the city and its laws
(728 n., 762). This patriotic sentiment is echoed by others, for less
patriotic ends (861, 944).

473-5 λόγος . . . τῶν γεραιτέρων: *Lys.* 1126 τοὺς δ' ἐκ πατρός τε καὶ
γεραιτέρων λόγους . . . Blepyrus, still unconvinced, seeks comfort in
recalling a saying prevalent among the elders. There *may* be a reference (as the scholiast suggests) to a *story* that Athenian ill counsel was
a curse imposed upon them by Poseidon: a curse which Athene (their
patron goddess) negatived, by making all happen for the best. But
the mention of Pallas (476) seems natural, without the need of any
such assumption. For this tradition of Athenian δυσβουλία see *Nu.*
587-9: 'for they say that δυσβουλία attaches to this city; the gods,
however, turn all these errors of ours ἐπὶ τὸ βέλτιον', *Eq.* 1055 Κεκρο-
πίδη κακόβουλε, E. *Supp.* 321. Cf. the praise of 'Eubule', who is set in
contrast to the out-going bouleutai (*Th.* 807). **γέ τοι:** 'certainly,
there *is* a saying' (if that counts for anything in these circumstances),
76 n.   **ἀνόηθ' . . . μῶρα:** see apparatus criticus, ἀνόητον καὶ κενόν
(*Ra.* 530). The Athenians (politically speaking) are elsewhere described
as ἀνόητοι (*Ra.* 734, 1503) : especially in their love of καιναὶ γνῶμαι (*Nu.*
898, see 456 n.). Cf. Woman *A*'s opinion (137) of the measures that are
passed by the Assembly.   **ἐπὶ τὸ βέλτιον . . . ξυμφέρειν:** 'turn out
for the best', *Nu.* 594 ἐπὶ τὸ βέλτιον τὸ πρᾶγμα τῇ πόλει συνοίσεται.

476-7 καὶ ξυμφέροι γ': 'and *may* they turn out, too' (i.e. as well as being said to). For this use of καὶ... γε see *Ra.* 164 below. **ὦ... Παλλὰς καὶ θεοί:** ὦ Ζεῦ καὶ θεοί (*Pl.* 1). Pallas of course is preferred here as guardian (she is πολιοῦχος, *Eq.* 581) of Athens, taking precedence over Zeus (as she does in the oaths, *Pax* 218). Cf. in general *Pl.* 438, Alex. fr. 245. 14 μὰ τὴν Ἀθηνᾶν καὶ θεούς. **σὺ δ' ὑγίαινε:** for this verb used as an alternative to χαῖρε cf. *Ra.* 164 (which also illustrates the use of καὶ... γε) *Hp.* καὶ χαῖρε πόλλ' ὦδελφε. Δι. νὴ Δία καὶ σύ γε | ὑγίαινε.

478-82 Metre: catalectic iambic tetrameters (285 n.), with introductory anapaestic metron (478) and a single iambic metron (480). **ἔμβα χώρει:** the words are spoken off stage, either (*a*) by the whole chorus or (*b*) (as is assumed here) by the coryphaeus only. So ὅρμα χώρει, *Th.* 953. For ἔμβα introducing 'marching orders' see *Lys.* 1303. Cf. *Ra.* 378, with J. A. Haldane, *CQ* n.s. xiv. 2 (1964), 208.

479-81 ἆρ' ἔστι... ἐπακολουθεῖ; the women urge suitable precautions, while falling in with his command. They cannot afford to bluster like Philocleon: κλαύσεταί τις τῶν ὄπισθεν | (cf. 482) ἐπακολουθόντων ἐμοί (*V.* 1327). **στρέφου... ἀσφαλῶς:** their words and attitude recall some tragic passages. Cf. (with other places quoted under) E. *IT* 67 Ορ. ὅρα, φυλάσσου μή τις ἐν στίβῳ βροτῶν. Πυ. ὁρῶ, σκοποῦμαι δ' ὅμμα πανταχῇ στρέφων, *Or.* 1295 Χο. ἀμείβω κέλευθον σκοποῦσα πάντῃ. Similarly, *Th.* 659-67.

481-2 πολλοὶ... οἱ πανοῦργοι: Praxagora (437) had collectively so classified the men: there may (as Rogers thinks) be a glance here (cf. 440 n.) at the spectators. The women mean footpads (see below). **μή... καταφυλάξῃ:** 'in case perhaps' (S. *El.* 897 καὶ περισκοπῶ | μή πού τις ἡμῖν ἐγγὺς ἐγχρίμπτει βροτῶν) 'somebody behind us is keeping a sharp eye on our bearing'. The following words explain her meaning: we are *dressed* like men, we must *walk* like them as well, both to escape detection and deter would-be assailants (545 n.). Cf. *V.* 1170 ἰδού. θεῶ τὸ σχῆμα, καὶ σκέψαι μ' ὅτῳ | μάλιστ' ἔοικα τὴν βάδισιν τῶν πλουσίων. καταφυλάσσω (not found elsewhere) is presumably intensive (κατα-) from φυλάσσω in the sense of 626 (n.). The whole recalls precautionary military practice (X. *An.* iv. 1. 6).

483-92 Metre: catalectic iambic tetrameters (as 479-82) with two iambic dimeters (− − ∪ − − − ∪ −, 484, 487), and an acatalectic tetrameter (486). The chorus, while chanting in strophe and antistrophe, no longer purports (as 300-10) to represent a town or country faction. They are solely concerned to get back to where they started from (Praxagora's street-door, 491) and resume their own appearance (499).

483-5 ἀλλ'... βάδιζε: as men (note the masculine -ῶν form, 31 n., 293) they clump with their heavy 'Spartan' shoes. So Praxagora walked (see 545) in imitation of her husband: cf. *Pl.* 758 ἐκτυπεῖτο δὲ | ἐμβὰς γερόντων εὐρύθμοις προβήμασιν. **ἡμῖν δ'... ἐλεγχθέν:** 'for' (84 n.)

'the exposure of this business would bring us all into disgrace' not 'among the men' (*Lys.* 11) but rather 'with our husbands' (*Th.* 394). No doubt the men-folk would in general resent a trick aimed at ousting them from office: but here the women have in mind more the discovery of individual wives' participation. Their reputation in the male world did not (says Lysistrata) stand high: and doubtless individuals (like Blepyrus, 529) would like to be informed of their wives' movements. παρὰ τοῖς ἀνδράσιν: 582. τὸ πρᾶγμα . . . ἐλεγχθέν: i.e. if we are caught red-handed. Cf. A. *A.* 1350 ἐμοὶ δ' ὅπως τάχιστά γ' ἐμπεσεῖν δοκεῖ | καὶ πρᾶγμ' ἐλέγχειν σὺν νεορρύτῳ ξίφει. Similarly, fr. 246.

486–8 συστέλλου σεαυτὴν: the usual translation (cf. 99) is 'wrap your cloak around you tightly', E. *Tr.* 378 πέπλοις συνεστάλησαν (of the dead). It perhaps means rather 'keep in close formation', 'contract yourself' to form a compact body. This military meaning (cf. 478, 482 nn.) recurs *V.* 424 ξυσταλεὶς εὔτακτος. Cf. E. *IT* 295. ⟨ ἄθρει κύκλῳ ⟩ : some such supplement is needed to satisfy both construction and metre (though A. M. Dale, *The Lyric Metres of Greek Drama*² [1968], 207 n. 1, sees the omission of a metron as 'approximate responsion' cf. e.g. *Ra.* 592). The present suggestion (see apparatus criticus) is based on *Av.* 1196 ἄθρει δὲ πᾶς κύκλῳ σκοπῶν and Pl. *Tht.* 155 e ἄθρει δὴ περισκοπῶν μή τις τῶν ἀμυήτων ἐπακούῃ, a passage illustrating our construction. Cf. S. *El.* 897 (482 n.) and (for future indicative) 495. κἀκεῖσε καὶ | τἀκ δεξιᾶς: cf. E. *Ph.* 265 ὧν οὕνεκ' ὄμμα πανταχῇ διοιστέον | κἀκεῖσε καὶ τὸ δεῦρο (illustrating, incidentally, the needlessness of Le Febvre's alteration to τἀκεῖσε). But the chorus's words may here be pointed: there are only two sources from which they fear detection, the audience (168, 440 nn.) and the right-hand πάροδος, leading from the Pnyx. For καί as a line-ending cf. *Ra.* 392 and (in iambic dialogue) *Pl.* 752. συμφορά . . . πρᾶγμα: cf. E. *Or.* 138 ἀλλ' ἐμοὶ | τόνδ' ἐξεγείραι συμφορὰ γενήσεται. The indicative expresses more vivid apprehension: that it actually *will be* a disaster.

489–92 ἀλλ' ἐγκονῶμεν: a similar exhortation to the chorus, *V.* 240, cf. *Ach.* 1088. For the literal meaning ('make the dust fly') cf. κεκονιμένος (291*b* n.). ὅθενπερ . . . ἦμεν: we may either (*a*) relate εἰς ἐκκλησίαν to *both* verbs (εἰς ἀγῶνα . . . ὁρμᾷ, E. *Ph.* 259), the so-called construction ἀπὸ κοινοῦ, or (*b*) assume some dislocation (169 n.) of the natural order of the words. For the second (and better) course see *Av.* 1418 τίς ὁ πτερῶν δεῦρ' ἐστὶ τοὺς ἀφικνουμένους; ὅθενπερ . . . ἔσθ': cf. *Eq.* 333 ἀλλ' ὦ τραφεὶς ὅθενπέρ εἰσιν ἄνδρες οἵπερ εἰσίν. ἡ στρατηγὸς: Praxagora has already, in their own minds, been appointed to the office that they promised (246). They are thinking, of course, of her *political* abilities, and do not consider her potential for *military* service in the field. ὃ νῦν ἔδοξε: which they have now voted in favour of (197 n.).

493–503 Metre: as 483–92. Their first concern is to be finished with the beards, which have caused them much discomfort (145): besides, they are all the time more fearful of detection (notice the emphasis on hurry, 493, 500, 501). Their last words (502–3) are obscure: on the reading suggested (see under) they return to the theme of their discomfort.

493–5 ἐπαναμενούσας . . . ἐξηρτημένας: 'waiting any longer with our beards on'. Cf. 790, Aeschin. iii. 164 τὰς ἐπιστολὰς ἃς ἐξηρτημένος ἐκ τῶν δακτύλων περιῄεις. **μὴ καί τις . . . κατείπῃ:** 'in case some one actually (29 n.) should denounce us'. For κατεῖπον, 'speak against', 'inform on', cf. *Pax* 377. MSS.' ὄψεθ᾽ ἡμᾶς is unmetrical: ἡμᾶς ὄψεται (Hermann). But ἡμᾶς . . . ἡμῶν is an ugly repetition, and I follow A. von Blumenthal (ἡμέρας, 'bei Licht'), *Hermes*, lxxi (1936), 455–6. Cf. S. fr. 65. 1 (Pearson) τὰ πολλὰ τῶν δεινῶν, ὄναρ | πνεύσαντα νυκτός, ἡμέρας μαλάσσεται. For indicative (488 n.) *and* subjunctive (482), see E. *Ph.* 93 μή τις πολιτῶν ἐν τρίβῳ φαντάζεται, | κἀμοὶ μὲν ἔλθῃ φαῦλος ὡς δούλῳ ψόγος, | σοὶ δ᾽ ὡς ἀνάσσῃ, W. W. Goodwin, *Syntax of Greek Moods and Tenses* (1889), 369.

496–8 ἐπὶ σκιᾶς: i.e. 'in the direction of the shade'. **πρὸς τὸ τειχίον:** the wall of Praxagora's house. The word is used (like τοῖχος) for walls of private properties, distinguished from the city walls (τὰ τείχη): of a court-room, *V.* 1109. There is no allusion to a southern wall of the acting area in the Lenaeum (Anti, 242). See 281, 1152 nn. **παραβλέπουσα θατέρῳ:** 'keeping an eye out' (sc. ὀφθαλμῷ) 'looking out of the corner of your eye', ἡ λαχανόπωλις παραβλέψασά φησι θατέρῳ (*V.* 497), cf. *Ra.* 409. παρα-, of a 'side' glance (226, 250).

499 μετασκεύαζε σαυτὴν: 'change yourself', i.e. your clothing (σκευή), μετα-, of change, as in similar verbs like μεθυποδοῦμαι (544). They have, in fact, just time to get their beards off, before Praxagora's arrival. **ἥπερ ἦσθα:** as before you 'became a man' (see 121). The construction may be seen as a somewhat harsh extension of that (as 290 n.) where antecedent is omitted. Or perhaps it merely fuses two ideas: 'change yourself' and 'change back (by a change of dress) to the person you originally were.' ἥπερ (Σᴿ), ἀντὶ τοῦ ὡς ἦσθα: but though that is undoubtedly the meaning, the adverb (in the context) will not bear it.

500–2 καὶ δή: marking a new arrival (like καὶ μήν, 41 n.). Cf. for both meaning and position in the sentence, *Lys.* 65 ἀτὰρ αἴδε καὶ δή σοι προσέρχονταί τινες. The chorus, of course, have eyes only for the general: but it seems clear she *is* entering alone. We hear no more of Women A and B (509 n.), with whom she had gone off (279). **ἐξ ἐκκλησίας:** 270 n. **μίσει . . . ἔχουσα:** construction with infinitive would certainly be commoner (συγγελᾶν . . . μίσει, E. fr. 362. 22). 'The choice of expression shows a degree of eccentricity' (Jackson, 160). Possibly: though the meaning (I think) is not quite μίσει . . .

ἔχειν (cf. *Pl.* 645) but rather μίσει σάκον, ὅν ... ἔχεις. Cf. E. *Supp.*
1108 ὦ δυσπάλαιστον γῆρας, ὡς μισῶ σ᾽ ἔχων, S. *Ph.* 410 ἀλλ᾽ εἰ
παρὼν | Αἴας ὁ μείζων ταῦθ᾽ ὁρῶν ἠνείχετο. And indeed μισεῖν here
(both in sense and construction) is used as if μὴ ἀνέχεσθαι (cf. *Eq.*
1102). μὴ θεῖ, 'do not run about', J. A. Nairn, *CR* xii (1898), 163.
σάκον, 'beard', from its resemblance to coarse hair-cloth (as used for
bags, *Ach.* 822). Hence σακεσφόρος, 'rough-bearded', of Epicrates
(71 n.).

503 χαῦται ... ἔχουσιν: 'for these in fact' (148 n., but with καί ... γάρ
the καί adheres more closely to the following word, *GP* 110) 'have
long had this disguise' (σχῆμα, of *deceptive* outside appearance, E. fr.
25. 2 γέροντες οὐδέν ἐσμεν ἄλλο πλὴν ψόφος | καὶ σχῆμ᾽, ὀνείρων δ᾽
ἕρπομεν μιμήματα) 'against their will'. The text is tentative (see
apparatus criticus) : cf. in general 948. On this view αὗται has reference to γναθοῖν (as Palmer, reading ἀλγοῦσιν, suggested) and not to
Praxagora and others (*Pax* 612, if ἄκουσ᾽ is correct, will parallel the
personification). That interpretation in itself is not impossible : the
chorus's interest is centred on Praxagora, and their words in 500 need
not exclude the presence of at least one other woman, to whom 509
(n.) is addressed. But χαῦται γάρ then comes in very oddly, and the
line still requires emendation. To translate 'they have come back,
having long since changed their costume', is difficult as Greek (τὸ
σχῆμα τοῦτ᾽ is forced) and also nonsense. The women were to come
back to the rendezvous for changing : where did these other women
find an opportunity not open to the members of the chorus? And
(although we ought not to press this question, see below), what of
their husbands' clothes? Did they discard them? It seems clear (511,
540 n.) that Praxagora is still, apart from the beard, in full disguise :
and I cannot agree with Coulon (*RhM* c [1957], 197) that she enters,
accompanied by Women *A* and *B*, all three changed and carrying
their men's wear.

504–13 Praxagora enters, tearing off her beard. She briefly refers to the
plan's success, and urges the women to discard their men's dress
quickly. Her own intention is to slip into the house, and leave back the
things which she has borrowed. Metre and style (though note ταυτί,
504) are quasi-tragic.

504–5 ταυτὶ μὲν: a good oratorical beginning (151, 412 nn., *GP* 383),
perhaps with a gesture (27 n.). Cf. (for the tragic manner) S. *Tr.* 672
τοιοῦτον ἐκβέβηκεν, οἷον, ἦν φράσω, | γυναῖκες, ὑμῖν θαῦμ᾽ ἀνέλπιστον
μαθεῖν. **τὰ πράγματ᾽** ... **ἀβουλεύσαμεν:** S. *Ant.* 266 τῳ συνειδέναι |
τὸ πρᾶγμα βουλεύσαντι.

506–7 ἀλλ᾽ ὡς τάχιστα: E. *Andr.* 989, *Rh.* 70. ἀλλ᾽ answers μέν (*Av.*
1119), cf. 412 n., S. *OT* 998 εὐτύχως μέν, ἀλλ᾽ ὅμως ...   τιν᾽
ἀνθρώπων: S. *OC* 1522 τοῦτον δὲ φράζε μήποτ᾽ ἀνθρώπων τινί, E. *Hel.* 152
φεῦγε πρίν σε παῖδα Πρωτέως | ἰδεῖν. Similarly 511. Perhaps in the

present passage also τιν' ἀνθρώπων means merely τινά: but ἀνθρώπων (apart from the parody of tragedy) is possibly synonymous with ἀνδρῶν, and may express (despite their anxiety) superiority, if not contempt ('some of the fellows', 811 n.).   ῥιπτεῖτε χλαίναϛ: 416 n. ῥίπτω, of discarding clothes, 850, Lys. iii. 35 τὸ μειράκιον ... ῥῖψαν θοἰμάτιον, and the passages quoted 409 n. The form in -εω (present and imperfect, cf. διαρριπτοῦντε, V. 59) is guaranteed here by the metre.   ἐμβάϛ: 47 n.   ἐκποδὼν ἴτω: cf. E. Ph. 521, Or. 1447 οὐκ ἐκποδὼν ἴτ'; There is no doubt a glance at ἐκ ποδῶν (so Rogers). ἐκποδὼν πώγων ἴτω, Th. Colardeau, effecting 'inverse symmetry' with 269–75 (AUG xxiii [1911], 47–57).

508-9 χάλα ... ἡνίαϛ: singular, probably quotation or a parody (though this is denied by Willems, 328). Cf. E. fr. 409 μήτ' εὐτυχοῦσα πᾶσαν ἡνίαν χάλα. ἡνίαι, in the tragic models 'reins' (see 466) are here the Spartan (74 n.) shoe thongs. For the χάλα / συναπτούϛ antithesis, cf. S. Aj. 1317 εἰ μὴ ξυνάψων, ἀλλὰ συλλύσων πάρει.   βακτηρίαϛ ἄφεσθε: 74 n.

509-13 καὶ μέντοι: this collocation (distinguish from καί ... μέντοι, 969) is not found in Aristophanes elsewhere. μέντοι gives 'liveliness and force' to the addition introduced by καί (GP 413) and is rightly retained by V. Coulon (RhM c, 197) against Μελιτοῖ (Jackson, 123) and his own earlier preference for κἀνταυθοῖ (REG xxxvi [1923], 381). σὺ μὲν: she may be addressing this order to a woman who has entered with her (see above). This is the view of Coulon (503 n., cf. REG loc. cit.) and Wilamowitz, 211: who further turns these women into servants and makes use of them (similarly Robert, 337) to carry off the men's things when discarded. But the link-boys (V. 408) are not a proper parallel: it seems much more likely that the garments are removed (311–26 n., Pax 729) by stage-attendants, and the person addressed here is not a new arrival, but rather the leader of the chorus (Robert, wrongly reading ταυτί, 510, regards him as above such menial duties). The chorus, while Praxagora is speaking, have been eagerly divesting themselves of cloaks and shoes: he must now get his 'troops' back into order. εὐτρεπίζω and its compounds are not applied to persons elsewhere, but the use here is like that of κατατάσσω (X. Cyr. iii. 3. 11), τὴν στρατιάν ... κατέταξεν.   παρερπύσασα: 'creeping furtively, by stealth' (see 226 n.). Contrast the sense in 398. καταθέσθαι θοἰμάτιον: cf. Pl. 926 κατάθου ταχέως θοἰμάτιον. ἀξηνεγκάμην: 'that I brought out of the house', 76 n.

514-19 The chorus, quickly changed, announce that they are ready to carry out Praxagora's further orders. She asks them, in view of their great services, to 'stay around' and act as her advisers.

Metre: catalectic anapaestic tetrameters, known by Hephaestion (8. 2) as τὸ Ἀριστοφάνειον, from its frequent occurrence in the playwright. Cf. Ra. 354–71. Notice the frequency of dactyls (permissible in 1, 2, 3, and 5) and the heavily spondaic 518.

```
  ⏤ ⏤ ⏤ ⏤    ⏜ ⏜ ⏑ ⏤ ⏤    ⏤ ⏤ ⏤ ⏤      ⏑ ⏑ ⏤ ⏤
⏜ ⏜ ⏤ ⏤ ⏤    ⏤ ⏜ ⏑ ⏤ ⏤    ⏤ ⏜ ⏑ ⏤ ⏤    ⏑ ⏑ ⏤ ⏤
  ⏤ ⏜ ⏑ ⏤ ⏤    ⏤ ⏜ ⏑ ⏤ ⏤    ⏤ ⏤ ⏤ ⏤      ⏑ ⏑ ⏤ ⏑
518. ⏤ ⏤ ⏤ ⏤    ⏤ ⏤ ⏤ ⏤    ⏤ ⏤ ⏤ ⏤      ⏑ ⏑ ⏤ ⏤
```

514–16 κεῖται ⟨καὶ⟩ δή: i.e. there they all are, on the ground. Cf.850, *Ach.* 583 *Δι. παράθες νυν ὑπτίαν αὐτὴν ἐμοί.* | *Λα. κεῖται. καὶ δή* points to the fulfilment of an order: cf. (in a similar context) *Th.* 214 *Εὐ. ἀπόδυθι τουτὶ θοἰμάτιον. Μν. καὶ δὴ χαμαί, Pax* 327. From now on the women of the chorus will be seen in their chitons and barefooted.

ὅ τι . . . ὑπακούειν: literally, 'doing what of benefit in your eyes (σοι) we will seem to be giving you true service'. σοι is constructed *ἀπὸ κοινοῦ* with both ξύμφορον and ὑπακούειν. Cf. in general Th. v. 98 *ὥσπερ ὑμεῖς . . . ἡμᾶς . . . τῷ ὑμετέρῳ συμφόρῳ ὑπακούειν πείθετε.* **οὐδεμιᾷ γὰρ . . . γυναικί:** their wonder now exceeds Woman *A*'s (245 n.). But the chorus's praise here is more general: they refer to the whole conduct of the plan. Cf. *Lys.* 1108.   **ξυμμείξασ᾽ οἶδα:** 'I know I have encountered . . .': cf. Hdt. iv. 151. 2 *συμμίσγουσι ἀνδρὶ πορφυρέϊ.*

517–19 ἦν . . . κεχειροτόνημαι: 264 n. There has of course been no election. The men's votes are in any case abolished: Praxagora holds office (491 n.) by reason of the previous agreement. For the use of the cognate accusative, see Aeschin. iii. 24 *ἀνάγνωθι, ἐπὶ τίνος ἄρχοντος . . . ἐχειροτονήθη Δημοσθένης τὴν ἀρχήν . . .* **ξυμβούλοισιν:** with genitive *τῆς ἀρχῆς* ('in the office'), cf. A. *Pers.* 170 *σύμβουλοι λόγου* | *τοῦδέ μοι γένεσθε.* Her words are more polite than realistic (572 n.).   **καὶ γὰρ:** 211 n.   **ἐκεῖ:** 100 n.   **τῷ θορύβῳ:** the general din in the Assembly (431 n.), Aeschin. i. 83.   **ἀνδρειόταται γεγένησθε:** 'you have been very manly' (not without a pun). The chorus conversely hail Lysistrata as *πασῶν ἀνδρειοτάτη* (*Lys.* 1108).

520–70 Attendants clear away the surplus clothing: Praxagora makes towards the house to change. As ill luck will have it Blepyrus (who has now found his tunic in the daylight, but is probably barefooted, 271 n.) emerges at the same time and confronts her. The scene that follows is a short and brilliant dialogue, with Chremes intervening (564 n.). Praxagora went out (she says) to help a friend at childbirth: she took the cloak, for it was cold (and she is fragile) and took the shoes and stick to save the cloak (Athenian streets were dangerous at night-time). Blepyrus shows anger at having lost his payment through failure to appear upon the Pnyx (although of course the absence of his cloak was not by any means the only reason) but tells her of the outcome of the meeting. Praxagora sees great prospects here, and offers (569) to substantiate her feelings.

520–1 αὕτη: 1049, 372 n.   **ὦ μέλε:** 120 n. Praxagora takes strong objection to the tone of Blepyrus' address. For *τί σοι τοῦθ᾽;* ('is that any of *your* business?') cf. *Eq.* 1198.   **ὡς εὐηθικῶς:** 'that's cool' (Rogers), literally 'with what simplicity!' (cf. *Nu.* 1258), sc. *λέγεις.*

522–3 οὖτοι . . . γε: adding force to the negation, S. *El.* 772 *Πα. μάτην ἄρ' ἡμεῖς, ὡς ἔοικεν, ἥκομεν* | *Κλ. οὖτοι μάτην γε.* Cf. *V.* 1122. Aristophanes' common use of *οὖτοι* is in oaths (*GP* 543). Praxagora speaks up strongly: attack is the best means of defence. **τοῦ μοιχοῦ**: *the* lover (whom you of course assume I have). The article suggests a relationship as commonplace as that described by *τἀνδρός* (48, 243). Blepyrus is the typically suspicious Athenian husband (225 n.) : he answers as if Praxagora had said (what editors attribute to her) *τον.* The latter raises questions of word-order (see Dover on *Nu.* 37). For *τοῦ/τον* confusion (as alternative interpretations of manuscripts' *TOY*) cf. *Pl.* 674.

523–4 καὶ μὴν . . . ἔξεστι: 'all right, then, you can test it', *V.* 537 *καὶ μὴν ὅσ' ἂν λέξῃ γ' ἁπλῶς μνημόσυνα γράψομαι 'γώ.* A similar usage, 583. **εἰ . . . μύρου**: scent is included (with the razor, 64 n.) and cosmetics (878 n.) in the long list of feminine equipment (fr. 320. 4). For its use as a man-bait (fr. 666 *αἱ τῶν γυναικῶν παγίδες*) see *Lys.* 46–8. Like Praxagora here (526) Myrrhine is unwilling to have intercourse without it (*Lys.* 938), though that is, of course, delaying tactics : and Cinesias no more appreciates the perfume than Strepsiades did (*Nu.* 51). Women eat garlic when returning from a lover (*Th.* 494), no doubt to conceal the smell of perfume *ἵν' ὀσφρόμενος ἀνὴρ ἀπὸ τείχους εἰσιὼν* | *μηδὲν κακὸν δρᾶν ὑποτόπηται.* For the double genitive (denoting (*a*) the type of the smell and (*b*) its source) cf. *Ach.* 852 *ὄζων κακὸν τῶν μασχαλῶν* | *πατρὸς Τραγασαίου.*

525–6 τί δ'; 135 n. **οὐ δὴ τάλαιν' ἔγωγε**: 'not *I*, more's the pity' (see above). Praxagora regrets her own preference for perfume, which perhaps she only seldom can afford. Cf. Myrrhine (after bringing the *wrong* perfume), *Lys.* 944 *τάλαιν' ἐγὼ τὸ 'Ρόδιον ἤνεγκον μύρον.* The words could imply at the same time (as Professor Dover has suggested) a certain dissatisfaction with Blepyrus' ardour as a husband. *δή* is rarely used to reinforce a negative (*Th.* 567) : but *δῆτα τάλαν* (Reiske: 373, 124 nn.) misunderstands the point of her reply.

526 ὄρθριον: 377. *ὀρθρία* (Cobet), 283, *Lys.* 59 *ἀλλ' ἐκεῖναί γ' οἶδ' ὅτι* | *ἐπὶ τῶν κελήτων διαβεβήκασ' ὄρθριαι.* Blepyrus seems illogical : a faithless wife (one might expect) would be returning, not just setting out, at dawn (*Th.* 494, Lys. i. 14). But (*a*) dawn and sex are, in comedy, connected, *Lys.* loc. cit. and 966, (*b*) Praxagora's tale gives no full proof of innocence: the time required to assist a friend at childbirth would be adequate for a meeting with a lover.

528–9 γυνή . . . ὠδίνουσα: cf. Alciphr. ii. 7 (a wholesale repetition of the passage) *'Ωδίνουσά με ἀρτίως ἥκειν ἐς ἑαυτὴν ἡ τοῦ γείτονος μετέπεμψε γυνή.* Such contingencies presumably were common, and Praxagora's a plausible excuse: so Lycaenium in Longus 3. 15 *τότε δὲ ἐξ ἑωθινοῦ σκηψαμένη πρὸς Χρόμιν ὡς παρὰ τίκτουσαν ἄπεισι γείτονα* . . . The wife in Lysias (i. 14) explains her absence by the need to get a lamp re-

kindled at a neighbour's. For ἑταίρα of a woman-friend cum neighbour,
cf. *Lys.* 701 τὴν ἑταίραν ἐκάλεσ' ἐκ τῶν γειτόνων.

529-31 κἂτ' ... **ἦν** ... **φράσασαν:** 'and could you not have told me,
in that case' (εἶτα, 335, 535). κἆτα expresses indignation: cf. (for
example) *Nu.* 1292. ἦν, i.e. παρῆν, most commonly (see 561) with
negative, as here. Cf. *Lys.* 1-3 Ἀλλ' εἴ τις ἐς βακχεῖον αὐτὰς ἐκάλεσεν ...
οὐδ' ἂν διελθεῖν ἦν ἂν ὑπὸ τῶν τυμπάνων. **τῆς λεχοῦς:** i.e. 'the new
mother'. Praxagora speaks (see 549) in retrospect: we need not
interpret (with the scholiast) of labour, a sense in which the word is
unexampled. Cf. E. *El.* 652 λεχώ μ' ἀπάγγελλ' οὖσαν ἄρσενος τόκῳ.
οὐ φροντίσαι: cf. *Nu.* 125 ἀλλ' εἴσειμι, σοῦ δ' οὐ φροντιῶ, E. *Ba.* 637.
εἰποῦσάν γέ μοι: the particle implies both assent and limitation, 'I
wouldn't have minded, but you might at least have told me' (*GP* 135).

532-4 μὰ τὼ θεώ: Praxagora, though still dressed as a man, can now feel
free again to use this woman's oath (155 n., 558).   **ὥσπερ εἶχον:**
i.e. 'dropping everything', 'straight off', Hdt. i. 114. 5 ὁ δὲ Ἀρτεμβάρης
ὀργῇ ὡς εἶχε ἐλθὼν ... Blepyrus' answer (535) means: 'if you went as
you were' (*Lys.* 610) 'what are you doing with my cloak on?'   **ἥπερ
μεθῆκέ μ':** 'she who came for me', 'the messenger', cf. *Eq.* 937 ἔπειτα
πρὶν φαγεῖν ἀνὴρ μεθήκοι.   **πάσῃ τέχνῃ:** 366 n.

535-8 Blepyrus complains that she had left him to all intents and purposes a corpse.   **εἶτ':** 'in that case' (529 n.).   **ἔμ' ἀποδύσασ':**
'having stripped me', i.e. having robbed me of my cloak (see 668).
ἐπιβαλοῦσα τοὐγκυκλον: 'you threw your wrap on top of me', replacing the cloak which he was using as a coverlet (cf. on σισύρα, 347).
ἔγκυκλον, a woman's *outer* garment (see *Th.* 261), is clearly not the
same thing (see fr. 320. 8) as the tunic Blepyrus got his hand on in the
darkness (318, 332, 374). But only a pedant will stress this inconsistency: the yellow dress (see 329) gave greater scope for humour at the
time. And it may well have lain (if not likewise on the bed) on some
chair conveniently beside it (cf. Hdt. i. 9. 2, *Th.* loc. cit.). The point
that Blepyrus wants to stress here is Praxagora's cool deliberation.
καταλιποῦσ' ... **προκείμενον:** 'abandoning me' (*Th.* 1134) 'like a
corpse laid out for burial' (*Av.* 474, *Lys.* 611). The ritual of 'laying
out', or πρόθεσις (including the garlands and oil flasks, 538) is
described 1030 ff. (see notes). Blepyrus exaggerates immensely: he is
lying on his back and covered with a garment (E. *Tr.* 1143: not
necessarily a *white* one, Pl. *Lg.* 947 b, *IG* xii. 5. 593. 2) but these are
the sole points of resemblance. Of course he means only in effect 'as
good as dead' (cf. his wife's answer, 541).   **ἐπιθεῖσα:** 'placing beside
me', 1032. On the funeral λήκυθοι see 996 n.

539 λεπτὴ κἀσθενής: this place has been taken as 'strong evidence' for
comic actors' use of padding, T. B. L. Webster, *CQ* N.S. v (1955), 94.
There is, in other words, a comic incongruity between the woman's
words and her appearance. Praxagora, still in men's clothes (see

under) will look like the figure on the Leningrad oenochoe (M. Bieber, *A History of the Greek and Roman Theater*² [1961], fig. 184, Webster, art. cit. 95). That this is inconsistent with Chremes' description (427) is possibly not of much importance, W. Beare, *CQ* N.S. iv (1954), 74. But I tend to agree with Beare that padding was not an inviolable rule: in this play the women's dress (see Introduction § IV) is that of ordinary life.

540–2 ἔπειθ': 'and so', 'accordingly', S. *E.* 345 ἔπειθ' ἑλοῦ γε θάτερ'... **ἵν' ἀλεαίνοιμι ... κατέλιπον**: i.e. in providing for her own warmth, she did not neglect to see to his. She turns his verb (537 n.) against him. **τοῦτ' ἠμπεσχόμην**: there is no noun for τοῦτο to refer to, though no doubt 'your cloak' is implicit in the context. But the natural sense is 'this (that I am wearing)'. ἠμπεσχόμην, see 332 n. **ἐν ἀλέᾳ ... καὶ στρώμασιν**: i.e. 'in warm coverings', hendiadys, cf. *Av.* 1182 ῥύμῃ τε καὶ πτεροῖσι καὶ ῥοιζήμασιν | αἰθὴρ δονεῖται. For ἀλέα opposed to ψῦχος, see ps.-Pl. *Erx.* 401 d.

542–3 αἱ ... Λακωνικαί: 74 n.   **δὲ δή**: in emphatic questions, cf. *Av.* 155 οὗτος δὲ δὴ τίς ἔσθ' ὁ μετ' ὀρνίθων βίος;   **κατὰ τί**; 'for what purpose?', οἱ δὲ ξένοι καὶ ὁ ἄλλος ὄχλος κατὰ θέαν ἧκεν (Th. vi. 31. 1). Cf. *Pax* 192. A different use, 559, 604.   **ἡ βακτηρία**: 74 n.

544–6 ἵνα ... σώσαιμι: that is, from λωποδύται, 'footpads' especially clothes thieves (λῶπος, δύω). Euelpides is clubbed and has his cloak removed by one such, *Av.* 496–8. Praxagora put on the heavy shoes and took the stick in the hope that the noise made would deter them. Men are denounced as such marauders by the women (*Th.* 817), and Praxagora affirms that under *their* rule, this class of citizen will disappear (565, 668). The prevalence of night assaults in Athens is attested in many passages, and Orestes was particularly noted (cf. *Av.* 1491): the crane's migration warns him (*Av.* 712) to wrap up well (like Praxagora) for the night-time, ἵνα μὴ ῥιγῶν ἀποδύῃ. Cf. *Ach.* 1165: and for *daylight* robbery *Ach.* 257.   **μεθυπεδησάμην**: 'I changed' (μετα-, 499 n.) 'my shoes' (i.e. for yours).   **μιμουμένη ... τοῖν ποδοῖν**: 483 n.   **τοὺς λίθους παίουσα**: the city streets were paved loosely, if at all. Their muddy condition is referred to, *V.* 248, 257: and cf. especially *V.* 246, where the fear is specifically mentioned of a stone's tripping one up in the dark.

547–8 Blepyrus blames his wife (unjustly) for the loss of the three obols (292*b* n.) which could have bought them eight quarts (χοίνικας, 424) of wheat, ἐκτεὺς δέ γ' ἐστὶν ὀκταχοίνικον μέτρον (fr. 640 Edmonds): cf. *Nu.* 644–5. He is living up to his name (see 327 n.). The standard corn measure, the μέδιμνος (1025), consisting of six ἑκτεῖς, was thus at this time selling for three drachmae. In Solon's time a *medimnus* of grain (at any rate for sacrificial purposes) is said to have been valued at a drachma (Plu. *Sol.* 23. 3). Between this play and *c.* 335—except for a period of shortage, when the price rose to sixteen—wheat sold at five drachmae the *medimnus* (D. xxxiv. 39). And a few years later (in 329/8) the official state selling-price was six (*CIA* iv. 2, 834b 70 ff.). See further Wyse on Is. x. 10. 2. For a calculation of the annual consumption and cost of grain in Athens, see R. Thomsen, *Eisphora* (Copenhagen, 1964), 160.   ἐξ ἐκκλησίας: 270 n.   εἰληφέναι: probably not simply 'got', but 'gained', Thphr. *Char.* 23. 2 ὅσα εἴληφε καὶ ἀπολώλεκε.

549-50 μὴ φροντίσῃς: that is, in effect, 'forget about it', cf. *Th.* 247. ἄρρεν παιδίον: *Lys.* 748. The birth of a *male* child is especially a reason for rejoicing: except to the Theophrastan μεμψίμοιρος (*Char.* 17. 7) who sees it as a drain upon his income.   ἠκκλησία; Blepyrus' intelligence (or his wit) is rather on the level of Strepsiades' κατὰ δάκτυλον; (*Nu.* 649–52). But it should be said, in fairness, that Strepsiades is faced with a technical term of the metricians.   μὰ Δἰ' ἀλλ': 'by Zeus, no, but . . .' (158, 463).   ἐφ' ἣν ἐγᾠχόμην: cf. 948, *Ra.* 478 ἐφ' ἃς ἐγὼ δρομαῖον ὁρμήσω πόδα. For the crasis (ἐγὼ ᾠχόμην) cf. *Av.* 86 χὡ κολοιός μοίχεται.

551-3 ἀτὰρ γεγένηται: 85. Praxagora now innocently switches (ἀτάρ, cf. 358) to the meeting she herself has just attended.   οὐκ ᾔδησθα; 'did you not know?' (by remembering), 814.   χθές: if Praxagora really only knew the day before, she must have gone into action quickly. This seemingly was, indeed, a σύγκλητος ἐκκλησία (i.e. one specially summoned, D. xviii. 73) and not a *stated* meeting (κυρία ἐκκλησία, cf. *Ach.* 19): if so the notice might be short. But no doubt Praxagora would hear from other sources before Blepyrus mentioned it at home. ἄρτι γ': 'I'm only now remembering' (40 n.).   ἄρα: inferential, as 460.   τὰ δόξαντ': 'the decisions', 455 n., D. iii. 14.

554-5 κάθησο . . . μασωμένη: apart from the fact that it clearly is not literal (contrast κάθησθε τοίνυν, 57, ἀλλ' ἔντραγε | τὴν σηπίαν τηνδὶ λαβοῦσα, Theopomp. Com. fr. 6) Blepyrus' meaning is obscure. οἷον ἐντρυφῶσα διὰ τὴν ἐξουσίαν, as scholiast and editors (*Suda* s.v. σηπία, Taillardat, *Images* 321) explain it, is very far from carrying conviction. For fried cuttle-fish (though regarded as expensive, Eriph. fr. 3. 3, three a drachma, Alex. fr. 187. 1) are a standard dish in peacetime (*Ach.* 1041) and familiar to ordinary women (126). Further references in D'Arcy W. Thompson, *A Glossary of Greek Fishes* (1947), 233. The same objection will apply to C. Kock's suggested parallel in German, 'sich gebratene Tauben in den Mund fliegen lassen' (*FJCP*, Supp. Bd. iii [1857–60], 275). Moreover, Blepyrus' thought is much less (cf. 460, 462) for his wife's future comfort than his own. Nor is he (I think) 'glorying in his superior knowledge' (Rogers) : 'Sit you down and chew cuttle fish with your gossips.' Perhaps 'well, now (you can) play the master' (Dover). I prefer, however, to interpret (without being able to bring evidence) 'Go on with what you're doing at the moment' (the proverb being based on some old and long-forgotten story). It is, in fact, a formula to use when introducing some unexpected news, as here. Blepyrus, about to make astounding revelations, begins with 'Now then, don't let this disturb you—but they say *you women* have been given charge of Athens.' Possessing his big news, he is willing to discuss the Assembly with his wife as men seldom were (at least if one believes Lysistrata, *Lys.* 510–20). His use of a popular saying recalls the style of Epicharmus (frs. 168, 229–35 Kaibel).

556–8 Praxagora at first affects a comic incredulity (can women manage anything but wool?) but further thought enables her to see future blessings in the project. **ὑφαίνειν;** women's customary work (see 89 n.), which they will in fact continue (654). **ἀπαξαπάντων:** 'absolutely all' (see 217). **τῶν κατὰ πόλιν πραγμάτων:** cf. *τῶν κατ' ἀγορὰν πραγμάτων* (fr. 387. 3). **νὴ τὴν Ἀφροδίτην:** Praxagora feels free again (cf. 532) to answer like a woman (189 n.). **μακαρία γ' ἄρ':** 'happy indeed, then' (70, 460), cf. *Lys.* 31 (in manuscripts) *ἐπ' ὀλίγου γ' ἄρ' εἴχετο.*

559–61 In reply to Blepyrus Praxagora describes the evils that she pictures disappearing. She is broadly repeating her remarks in the Assembly (as Chremes reports her, 452). **κατὰ τί;** 'according to what?', i.e. 'how do you make that out?', as 604 (see also 543 n.). **πολλῶν οὕνεκα:** 'on many counts', 659, cf. *Nu.* 6. **τοῖς τολμῶσιν . . . αἰσχρὰ δρᾶν | ἔσται:** sc. *δρᾶν ταῦτα* (*ἔσται* for *παρέσται*, 529 n.). Cf. *Pl.* 415 *ὦ θερμὸν ἔργον . . . | τολμῶντε δρᾶν.* Or *τοῖς τολμῶσιν* may be absolute, 'for villains', E. *Ph.* 726 *ἴσον φέρει νύξ, τοῖς δὲ τολμῶσιν πλέον.*

561–2 **οὐδαμοῦ . . . συκοφαντεῖν:** I punctuate with a strong stop after *λοιπόν* (*Λ*Mu1 : cf. 559, 822) without resort to emendation (*οὐδάμ'*, *οὐδὲ* Blaydes). Praxagora, whose syntax may in any case be hindered by mounting excitement, is proceeding to say that these doings will be 'nowhere' (i.e. 'despised', 'of no account', S. *Ant.* 183), when Blepyrus interrupts her with his plea (modelled on that of Philoctetes, S. *Ph.* 933 *πρὸς θεῶν πατρῴων, τὸν βίον με μὴ ἀφέλῃς*). **μαρτυρεῖν,** of giving evidence in law-courts for reward, a practice which will naturally vanish when courts are abolished (657). Cf. fr. 437 *ἦν γὰρ ἔν' ἄνδρ' ἄδικον σὺ διώκῃς, ἀντιμαρτυροῦσι | δώδεκα τοῖς ἑτέροις ἐπισίτιοι.* For the 'framing' of inoffensive citizens by producing witnesses against them, see *V.* 1037–42. Hence the Sausage-seller's proclamation (*Eq.* 1316) *χρὴ . . . μαρτυριῶν ἀπέχεσθαι, | καὶ τὰ δικαστήρια συγκλῄειν οἷς ἡ πόλις ἥδε γέγηθεν.* Praxagora may also have in mind the abolition (already in force among the women, 448) of witnesses for borrowing and lending (who are ineffective anyway, 451). **οὐ συκοφαντεῖν:** 452 n.

562–3 **μηδαμῶς . . . τὸν βίον:** see above. The god-fearing Chremylus, his own means of livelihood (*βίον*, *Pl.* 34) exhausted, and seeing informers growing wealthy, thought of turning his son into a rascal. For the profits available from blackmail, see Telecl. fr. 41, 'Charicles paid a *mina* so that he [an informer] wouldn't tell he was his mother's first-born changeling.' Informing is humorously spoken of as a family tradition in *Av.* 1451 *Σv. τὸ γένος οὐ καταισχυνῶ.* | *παππῷος ὁ βίος συκοφαντεῖν ἐστί μοι.* The prevalence of the practice is suggested (despite the joke) in 439–40.

564 The manuscripts, as often in this play (327 n.), give no indication of the speaker (see apparatus criticus for details). But clearly a *third* character has joined the discussion: apparently remaining (cf. *σφῶν,* 710) to take part in the dialogue ensuing. He is Chremes (as Rogers rightly saw). Re-emerging (see 477), whatever the pretext, from his house, he overhears and has his interest awakened by Praxagora's remarks about the future, though he scarcely can believe it (568). Hence his questions to Praxagora (583 n.). He has, of course, heard similar sentiments (452 ff.) in the Assembly; but he does not recognize, in the present speaker, the 'handsome, pale-faced youth' (427) who spoke on that occasion. Willems (226) believes the neighbour (Woman *B*) re-entering (500, 509 nn.) remains to intervene in the debate. **ὦ δαιμόνι' ἀνδρῶν:** Chremes employs the same form of remonstrance (though with rather less good humour) 784 (n.). He is here a kind of mediator, like Dionysus in *Ra.* 1227, 835 *ὦ δαιμόνι' ἀνδρῶν μὴ μεγάλα λίαν λέγε.*

565–7 μὴ λωποδυτῆσαι: 544 n. The interruptions have further spoiled her syntax: she proceeds (influenced by Blepyrus' *μηδαμῶς,* 562) as if she had said *ἀπορρηθήσεται* instead of *ἔσται* (561). **μὴ φθονεῖν τοῖς πλησίον:** 'envy the next man' (see 16 n.). But envy (says Pericles) is unknown only to the dead, Th. ii. 45. 1. **γυμνὸν . . . πένητα:** like Euaeon (408 n.). **μὴ λοιδορεῖσθαι:** 142 n. **μὴ 'νεχυραζόμενον φέρειν:** it is not quite clear if she is speaking of the ending of distraint on goods for debt, or merely of an end to 'harrying' (*φέρειν*) the debtor. The Utopian context is in favour of the former: the participle will then be neuter, and synonymous with *ἐνέχυρον* (a pledge to be taken as security by creditors), Antiphon vi. 11 *οὔτε ἐνέχυρα βίᾳ φέρων.* But language parallels support the second meaning: the participle is then masculine, cf. Strepsiades, *Nu.* 241 *ἄγομαι φέρομαι, τὰ χρήματ' ἐνεχυράζομαι,* and Praxagora means only that none will be 'harried' by an over-swift claim for repayment, and the consequent removal of his goods. The difference is not of much importance, since either way she is saying indirectly that debts will be unknown (660).

568–70 μεγάλα γ': 70 n. **εἰ μὴ ψεύσεται:** 'if she doesn't turn out to be a liar'. Cf. 667, *Nu.* 261 *μὰ τὸν Δί' οὐ ψεύσει γέ με* (i.e. 'you will prove not to have deceived me') and (for absolute use) *V.* 966 *νὴ Δί', ἀλλὰ ψεύδεται.* **ἀποφανῶ τουθ':** 'I'll explain this' (i.e. what I've been saying). Cf. *Nu.* 368 *τουτὶ γὰρ ἔμοιγ' ἀποφῆναι πρῶτον ἁπάντων.* **ὥστε σε . . . μαρτυρεῖν:** 'so that you' (Chremes) 'will side with me, and himself here' (her husband) 'say nothing against me' (as he showed signs of doing, 562). Cf. S. *Tr.* 899 πεύσῃ δ', ὥστε μαρτυρεῖν ἐμοί. ἐμοί, MSS. (see apparatus criticus), and surely the emphatic word may stand. *She* is the master now.

571–729 Praxagora in both senses casts off her disguise, and appears both as woman and strategos. As she hands her husband back his cloak and stick and shoes (he had come out barefooted, 520 n.), the chorus invite her to present them straight away with some bright new project for the city. The theatre audience dislikes the old stale topics: they also like a play to move on quickly. Praxagora's answer is to outline a nakedly communistic programme, whose interest is increased by its resemblance to Plato's in Book V of the *Republic*. The relationship between the two is dealt with in Introduction § I: the commentary confines itself to noting the parallels of thought and language as they crop up in the course of the discussion.

571–80 Metre: dactylo-epitritic. The cola are formed from basic sequences of − ∪ − (e) and − ∪ ∪ − ∪ ∪ − (D) (the notation of P. Maas, *Greek Metre*, tr. H. Lloyd-Jones, 1962), normally separated by ≍. Great freedom, however, is permitted in their grouping. See Maas, 40, 55 (confined to Pindar and Bacchylides), Dale, 184–8, Raven, § 71. Resolution (as 571, 577) is rare: but spondees (i.e. syncopated cretics) are admissible (571, 576, 577, cf. Dale, 182), and the dactylo-epitrites of drama sometimes end in varied clausulae (here ithyphallic, 580, cf. *Eq.* 1273, E. *Med.* 420, Dale, 180).

(1) 571.   − −   − ∪∪ − ∪∪ −   ∪   ∪∪∪∪ −   −
                     − ∪∪ − ∪∪ −
(2)   − ∪∪ − ∪∪ −   −
(3)   −   − ∪∪ − ∪∪ −   ∪
(4)   − ∪ −   −   − ∪∪ − ∪∪ −   −
(5) 575.   − ∪∪ − ∪∪ −   ∪
(6)   − ∪ −   ∪   − ∪∪ − ∪∪ −   −   − ∪∪ − ∪∪ −   − −
(7)   − − − −   ∪   − ∪∪ −   −   − ∪∪ − ∪∪ −   −
(8)   − ∪∪ − ∪∪ −
(9)   − ∪∪ − ∪∪ −   −   − ∪∪ − ∪∪ −
(10) 580.   −   − ∪∪ − ∪∪ −   ∪   − ∪ − ∪ − −

Notation: (1) sp D ∪ resolved choriamb (see (7)) – D (2) D – (3) – D ∪ (4) e – D – (5) D ∪ (6) e ∪ D – D sp (7) 2 sp ∪ d¹ (choriamb, cf. S. *OT* 1086) – D – (8) D (9) D – D (10) – D ∪ ithyph.

571–2 νῦν δὴ ... ἐγείρειν: 'now you must summon up . . .', the time we have been waiting for has come. Similarly, *V.* 526 *Xo.* νῦν δὴ τὸν ἐκ θἠμετέρου | γυμνασίου δεῖ τι λέγειν | καινόν . . .   **πυκνὴν φρένα:** 'a shrewd intelligence', E. *IA* 67. Euripides himself is made to use the same phrase, *Ach.* 445 δώσω· πυκνῇ γὰρ λεπτὰ μηχανᾷ φρενί. And might there be here a thought of πνύξ? Cf. the play on πυκνότης and πυκνί (*Eq.* 1132, 1137).   **φιλόσοφον ... φροντίδ':** this is one of the

three places (cf. 647, 995 nn.) where some of the older commentators
detected a reference to Plato. Of the three, only here would it be
likely. The chorus, of course, are not demanding a harangue on
philosophy, political or other (and they do not get it, 456 n.) : the
words merely mean 'a bright idea' (τοῖς περιδεξίοισι | λόγοισι καὶ
φροντίσι, *Nu.* 949). But the thoughts of some *readers* at least (for a
spectator might well miss the reference completely) could turn, in
retrospect, to earlier discussions of the communistic programme here
suggested (a comic dramatist had readers as well as spectators in his
view). If so, however, the philosopher recalled is someone of transient
importance, not Plato (Introduction § I). **ἐπισταμένην . . . ἀμύνειν:**
it was they who were to act as advisers to Praxagora, but that was
merely courtesy (516 n.). It is she who is the brain behind the venture.
Contrast E. *HF* 346 σῴζειν δὲ τοὺς σοὺς οὐκ ἐπίστασαι φίλους.

573–6 κοινῇ . . . βίου: 'for the inventive power of your tongue' (γλώττης
ἐπίνοια, cf. *Eq.* 89–96), 'to our common prosperity' (κοινῇ . . . ἐπ᾽
εὐτυχίαισιν, cf. *Ra.* 1482–90) 'will gladden the citizen people with
countless benefits of life'. ἐπίνοια might mean 'plan' (as 589): hence
καινή (Blaydes), *V.* 346 ζητεῖν καινὴν ἐπίνοιαν. But ἐπίνοια γλώττης is
then difficult (γνώμης, Markland: cf. *Ra.* 355), and the meaning (I
think) is rather this: 'we have heard your powers of eloquence : they
have brought the γυναικοκρατία to birth, and the city will benefit, we
know. But now is the time to show just what they *can* do, for we need
some clear new scheme' (ἐξεύρημα, 577). **κοινῇ,** Mu1 : other manuscripts have κοινή (for which with ἐπίνοια see Plb. vi. 5. 2). **ἐπ᾽
εὐτυχίαισιν,** a phrase recurring, with different meanings, *Eq.* 1318, *Nu.*
1205. **ἔρχεται . . . ἐπαγλαΐοῦσα:** 'is going to gladden', cf. Pl.
Euthphr. 2 c ἔρχεται κατηγορήσων μου. **πολίτην δῆμον:** cf. θεοὶ
πολῖται (A. *Th.* 253), λίθος πολίτης in a fragmentary epigram from a
papyrus of third century B.C. (Hugh Lloyd-Jones, *CR* N.S. xv. 3 [1965],
246). For the πόλις/δῆμος conjunction cf. (for example) *Ach.* 631.

576–7 ὅ τί περ δύναται: sc. γλώττης ἐπίνοια, 'just what your inventive
tongue can do'. δύνασαι, Blaydes: but this is needless. **γάρ τοι:**
'for the city needs, you know . . .' (see 35 n.). R has τοί γε (an unknown combination, *GP* 152): perhaps γε was added to produce a
catalectic anapaestic tetrameter (581). **σοφοῦ . . . ἐξευρήματος:**
'some wise scheme', cf. E. *IT* 1029 ἔχειν δοκῶ μοι καινὸν ἐξεύρημά τι, *V.*
1053.

578–80 ἀλλὰ πέραινε . . . πρότερον: i.e. only make sure that your
suggestions are for measures never carried out or spoken of before.
πέραινε, 'go right through to the end', 'relate in full', E. *Or.* 1118 τὸ
πρᾶγμα δῆλου καὶ πέραιν᾽, ὅπως λέγεις (haste is also connoted, 581).
They mean, of course, in the theatre (580) : for communism, in theory
or practice, was not new at this time to the Greeks. See Introduction
§ I. For the rupture of dramatic illusion by the chorus cf. 1142, 1154,

Nu. 1115, *Ra.* 386, (by an actor, *Pax* 173). The poet will be 'opening a new vein', 586 : where Blepyrus corroborates the chorus's remark that audiences hate the repetition of the old stale topics of the drama. Aristophanes prides himself not only on departing from the customary jokes (see 313 n.), but also on his own new themes (*Nu.* 547) : and if audiences now disliked the old plots, it was not always so (*V.* 1051). **θεῶνται**: of the theatre audience, as often (888). There is also a hint, though, at the fondness for novelty in general (583 n.) : cf. Kassies, 59.

581–2 The coryphaeus introduces the debate in the metre in which it will continue (catalectic anapaestic tetrameters, 513 n.). This is a recurring formal feature (cf. *Nu.* 959, *V.* 546).   **ἅπτεσθαι . . . ταῖς διανοίαις**: if the text is correct, the verb is absolute, 'set to', i.e. begin the *agon* (583 n.), 'with the high thoughts' i.e. that we expect (*a*) in Praxagora, (*b*) in Aristophanes the playwright. Cf. his self-praise, *Pax* 750, 'he made the art great and built it tower-like' ἔπεσιν μεγάλοις καὶ διανοίαις καὶ σκώμμασιν οὐκ ἀγοραίοις. See also *V.* 1044. The absolute use is unparalleled. I prefer it, however, to the common alteration to τῆς διανοίας (Le Febvre). This regularizes the construction, but makes for an unconvincing meaning ('mets-toi à ton projet', Van Daele).   **καὶ δὴ**: 'here and now' (ἤδη), 786. See *GP* 252.   **τὸ ταχύνειν**: the quality that certain Roman critics found in Plautus (Hor. *Ep.* ii. 1. 58), '(dicitur) Plautus ad exemplar Siculi properare Epicharmi.'   **χαρίτων μετέχει πλεῖστον**: 'finds the greatest favour', cf. *Ra.* 332 τιμάν, | χαρίτων πλεῖστον ἔχουσαν μέρος.   **παρὰ τοῖσι θεαταῖς**: 485 n.

583–729 The *agon* (*V.* 533, *Ra.* 883) : regarded by T. Geltzer, *Der epirrhematische Agon bei Aristophanes* (Munich, 1960), 56, as dramatically inappropriate (but see K. J. Dover, *Gnomon*, xxxiii [1961], 122). A series of questions and answers elicits Praxagora's full scheme. The manuscripts (see 41 n.) are no help in distributing the speakers : in the present arrangement, Chremes (as the genuinely interested citizen, 564 n.) is given larger share in the discussion. Blepyrus plays the βωμολόχος, or buffoon : interrupting with questions and remarks that aim to reduce the conversation to his own limited level of intelligence and humour (cf. Arist. *EN* 1128ᵃ4). A similar role is played by Euelpides (*Av.* 462–626).

583–600 Praxagora states the basis of her scheme. Inequalities of wealth will disappear : land and money will be owned by the community, and the women will manage things (600).

583–5 καὶ μὴν: 'well, then' (since you ask me to speak). So often, in response to invitations from the chorus. Cf. *Nu.* 1031 *Xo.* δεῖ σε λέγειν τι καινόν . . . *Aδ.* καὶ μὴν πάλαι γ' ἐπινιγόμην τὰ σπλάγχνα κἀπεθύμουν | ἅπαντα ταῦτ' . . . συνταράξαι. Somewhat similarly, 523.   **εἰ . . . ἐθελήσουσιν (δέδοικα)**: so (for example) E. *Med.* 184 δράσω τάδ'· ἀτὰρ φόβος εἰ πείσω | δέσποιναν ἐμήν. Praxagora's fear is ironical (as Blepyrus of course fails to understand) ; for however conservative in

matters of the theatre (579 n., cf. *Ra.* 1), the Athenian fondness for
novelty (political or other) is several times referred to (474 n.).
Silenus expresses an Athenian-like sentiment, E. *Cyc.* 250 τὰ καινά γ'
ἐκ τῶν ἠθάδων, ὦ δέσποτα, | ἥδιόν' ἐστίν. **καινοτομεῖν**, a metaphor
from mining (X. *Vect.* iv. 27) is to 'open a new vein', 'make innovations'. Cf. *V.* 876, Arist. *Pol.* 1266ᵃ36.

586-7 μὲν τοίνυν: 'have no fear of innovations—on the contrary . . .'
The combination (only here in Aristophanes) differs little from μὲν
οὖν (111 n.). **μὴ δείσῃς· τοῦτο γὰρ**: Blepyrus' failure to understand
her irony permits a clearer statement of the point. His next words
play on ἀρχή and ἀρχαῖα: we prefer doing this (καινοτομεῖν) to anything that smacks at all of ἀρχή. Whatever may be true of other places
(for example, *Eq.* 1387) we should not read into the present pun the
poet's conservative opinions. **ἀντ' ἄλλης ἀρχῆς**: 'in preference to'
(925 n.) 'any ἀρχή', cf. *Ra.* 1163, 'the man with a share in a fatherland
may "come" (ἐλθεῖν) to a country, for he comes χωρὶς ἄλλης συμφορᾶς.'

588-9 μή . . . ὑποκρούσῃ: she addresses the audience (ὑμῶν) not just
(cf. σφῶν, 710) her two companions. It is before them that her views
(like those of the Just and Unjust Logos, *Nu.* 889) will be debated. So
Dicaeopolis (*Ach.* 496) and Hermes (*Pax* 664). Such addresses, of
course, are common from the *chorus* in parabases (cf. for example *Nu.*
575 ὦ σοφώτατοι θεαταὶ δεῦρο τὸν νοῦν προσέχετε). Praxagora here
again puts into practice the style she learnt (244) on the Pnyx: cf. D. v.
3 ἂν ἐθελήσητε τοῦ θορυβεῖν καὶ φιλονικεῖν ἀποστάντες ἀκούειν, ibid. 15
καί μοι μὴ θορυβήσῃ μηδεὶς πρὶν ἀκοῦσαι (where, however, the plea
seems to come *after* interruptions). **ὑποκρούσῃ**: 256 n. **τὴν
ἐπίνοιαν**: here 'the scheme' (574 n.). **τοῦ φράζοντος**: 'the one
who is explaining'. Cf. *Ra.* 1054 τοῖς μὲν γὰρ παιδαρίοισιν | ἔστι
διδάσκαλος ὅστις φράζει. Praxagora makes the *masculine* and *general*
expression refer specifically to herself.

590-610 Her first proposal: *community of goods.* Cf. Pl. *R.* 416 d–
417 b. Plato, of course, is legislating for his Guardians, not (like
Praxagora) for the people. Hers is a startling programme (even more
radical than γῆς ἀναδασμός: for which see Pl. *Lg.* 684 e) to be introduced by women, who are praised (214 ff.) precisely for their love of
τὰ ἀρχαῖα (584). For its problems in practice see Arist. *Pol.* 1262ᵇ38.

590-2 κοινωνεῖν . . . ζῆν: cf. *R.* 416 d, 'to begin with, no one will have
any private property, unless it is absolutely necessary.' **κἀκ ταὐτοῦ
ζῆν**, cf. D. lvii. 36 τοὺς ἐργάζεσθαι καὶ ζῆν ἐκ τοῦ δικαίου προαιρουμένους.
τὸν μὲν πλουτεῖν, τὸν δ' ἄθλιον εἶναι: her words indicate, and simul-
taneously protest against, the normal situation in the world. In Athens
the imbalance seems later to have worsened, if one may treat as serious
evidence Isoc. viii. 69, vii. 83: 'At that time no citizen stood in want
of the necessities, and did not bring disgrace upon the city by begging
from those casually met with, whereas now the needy are more

numerous.' For equality of wealth, this was effected (says Isocrates, for what his declaration may be worth) under Solon and Clisthenes (vii. 35). **μηδὲ γεωργεῖν τὸν μὲν πολλήν:** sc. *γῆν* (cf. 651). Land too will be common (as with Plato, 597 n.) and worked by slaves while citizens dine in comfort (an idea, 651 n., of which Plato would not have approved). **τῷ δ' εἶναι μηδὲ ταφῆναι:** cf. *Pl.* 555 (the words addressed to Poverty) *ὡς μακαρίτην, ὦ Δάματερ, τὸν βίον αὐτοῦ κατέλεξας* | *εἰ . . . καταλείψει μηδὲ ταφῆναι.* But the reference here (as Rogers notes) is to the ground, not the money, required for the burial: cf. Aeschin. i. 99, 'his mother begged him to let be and not to sell, or, if nothing else, *ἐνταφῆναί γ' ὑπολιπεῖν αὐτῇ.* But he did not keep his hands off even this spot.'

593–4 ἀνδραπόδοις τὸν μὲν χρῆσθαι πολλοῖς: like Nicias, who was said to have a thousand in the silver-mines, whom he hired out to Sosias the Thracian (X. *Vect.* iv. 14). **οὐδ' ἀκολούθῳ:** not even the single attendant (cf. *Av.* 73) that respectability demanded 'you saw fit to expel these, your daughter's children, out of their own house *οὐ μετὰ ἀκολούθου*' (Lys. xxxii. 16). The Theophrastan *ἀνελεύθερος* will merely hire one for the occasion (*Char.* 22. 10) : the other extreme is the ostentatious Midias, who *τρεῖς ἀκολούθους ἢ τέτταρας αὐτὸς ἔχων διὰ τῆς ἀγορᾶς σοβεῖ* (D. xxi. 158). The present passage—though Praxagora perhaps exaggerates to press her point more firmly—implies that many citizens (like the cripple in Lys. xxiv. 6) found the upkeep of a single slave beyond them. See W. L. Westermann, 'Athenaeus and the Slaves of Athens', *HSPh* Suppl. I (1941), 469 : reprinted in M. I. Finley *Slavery in Classical Antiquity* (1960), 91. Finley himself believes 'strongly' (58) that many such did none the less employ them: certainly Chremes has two servants (867) and Praxagora (but this is in the *new* regime, 1113 n.) has a maid. **καὶ τοῦτον ὅμοιον:** cf. *Eq.* 1079 *ἐγὼ πορίω* (sc. *μισθόν*), *καὶ τοῦτον ἡμερῶν τριῶν.*

595–6 Blepyrus breaks in with a question which Praxagora was just about to answer, and is treated (cf. 520) with some sharpness : 'you will eat human ordure' (*πέλεθον, Ach.* 1170) 'before I do.' This is not (I think) abusive, or a threat, but simply the statement of a fact: 'you're very keen to anticipate', she tells him, 'even if I eat dung you'll be before me' (a case where few others would rush in). The phrase—if it is not Praxagora's own—may have its origin in some ancient fable (554 n.) or traditional popular joke. Blepyrus, buffoonlike, takes up the literal meaning and asks if 'the dungs' are to be common. **μὰ Δί' ἀλλ':** 550 n. **ἔφθης μ' ὑποκρούσας:** '(as I asked people not to)', 588.

597–600 τὴν γῆν . . . καὶ τἀργύριον: Guardians are not to be landowners (Pl. *R.* 417 a), for with land and houses and money of their own, 'they will be businessmen and farmers, not Guardians, and will become the hated masters, not the allies, of the other citizens.' They are not (see

quotation) to have money of their own, or have any gold or silver
whatsoever, 'for many impious deeds are done for the common
currency but in *their* souls the coin is untarnished' (*R.* loc. cit.).
ταμιευόμεναι . . . προσέχουσαι: carrying on, in fact, as usual (211 n.).
γνώμην προσέχουσαι, only here in Aristophanes for the very common
προσέχειν (τὸν) νοῦν. Cf. Th. v. 26. 5 αἰσθανόμενος . . . καὶ προσέχων τὴν
γνώμην.

601–2 Chremes can understand the plan as far as land goes: but what
about 'invisible' wealth, money? (ἀργύριον is here more strictly silver).
πῶς οὖν ὅστις: i.e. πῶς εἴ τις (642 n., 655). For position of ἡμῶν, 44 n.
Chremes' question is pointed by Lys. xxxii. 4 ἀδελφοὶ ἦσαν . . . καὶ τὴν
μὲν ἀφανῆ οὐσίαν ἐνείμαντο, τῆς δὲ φανερᾶς ἐκοινώνουν: which also
illustrates the use of ἀφανής for personal opposed to real (φανερός,
ἐμφανής) estate. But the terms are more elastic than appears from
Harpocration, ἀφανὴς (οὐσία) μὲν ἡ ἐν χρήμασι καὶ σώμασι καὶ σκεύεσι,
φανερὰ δὲ ἡ ἔγγειος, and Rogers's note could be misleading (Is. vi. 30.
3, with Wyse). See further And. *On the Mysteries* ed. Douglas Mac-
Dowell (1962), 146. Chremes may be thinking too of money that is
kept, as it were, beneath the floor-boards, cf. Men. *Dys.* 811, 'a friend
you can see (ἐμφανής) is far better than πλοῦτος ἀφανής, which you
keep buried.' The habit of concealing wealth in tax returns is very
frequently referred to (as ps.-Lys. xx. 23): see G. E. M. de Ste
Croix, 'Demosthenes' Τίμημα and the Athenian Εἰσφορά in the Fourth
Century', *C&M* xiv (1953), 34 n. 17.   **Δαρεικοί:** sc. στατῆρες (Hdt.
vii. 28. 2) were Persian gold coins current throughout Greece, called
after a Darius (cf. Ἀλεξάνδρειοι, Φιλίππειοι). The name was probably attached to the new refined gold coinage of Darius the Great,
father of Xerxes (Hdt. iv. 166. 2), cf. B. V. Head, *Historia Numorum*²
(1911, repr. 1963), 825, though Harpocration (s.v.) derives it (oddly)
'from some other older king'. Their Attic equivalent was twenty
drachmae (X. *An.* i. 7. 18). Plato (597 n.) denies gold and silver to his
rulers, *R.* 416 e: 'we must tell them that they have always in their soul
the divine gold and silver that the gods give, and have no need of the
human in addition.'

602–3 Individuals, Praxagora explains, will have no use for it, and all
must be donated ἐς τὸ μέσον.   **ἐς τὸ μέσον καταθήσει:** 'he will lay it
in the common pool.' Both literal and figurative meanings are
exemplified, E. *Cyc.* 547 κάτθες αὐτὸν (τὸν κρατῆρα) ἐς μέσον, 'in the
middle (for anyone to use it)'.   **ψευδορκήσει:** 'he will be a perjurer',
by swearing that he has not the money which all know him to have
'hidden' (601–2 n.).   **κἀκτήσατο . . . τοῦτο:** '(doubtless he will)'
433 n., 'for that was how he got it' (as false witness or informer, 561 n.).

604–5 ἀλλ' . . . αὐτῷ: 'but in any case' (πάντως, 704) 'it won't be any
use to him, you know' (τοι, 35 n.).   **κατὰ . . . τί;** 559 n.   **δὴ,**
emphasizing interrogatives, 791, 858.   **οὐδεὶς . . . δράσει:** 'no one

will get up to any mischief', *Th.* 398 δρᾶσαι δ' ἔθ' ἡμῖν (as women) οὐδὲν
ὥσπερ καὶ πρὸ τοῦ | ἔξεστι. (A different connotation, 704.) Praxagora
is thinking (as Chremes, 608, confirms) of theft.   For Poverty as an
inspirer of crime, see E. *El.* 375 ἀλλ' ἔχει νόσον | πενία, διδάσκει δ' ἄνδρα
τῇ χρείᾳ κακόν. And faced with her claim (*Pl.* 564) that 'κοσμιότης
dwells with me', Chremylus feels constrained to answer 'yes, of *course*
it's κόσμιον to steal and dig through house-walls.'

606–7 ἄρτους . . . ἐρεβίνθους: there is, of course, in comedy, much
emphasis on food (for example, *Eq.* 1166). Blepyrus likes his (see
359 n.), and Praxagora is well aware where punishment is likely to hit
hardest (666). But her promise that 'all men will have all things' does
not mean 'a glutton's Paradise' (Ehrenberg, 320): rather, that all will
have necessities of life (she mentions not only food but clothing) that
Poverty has denied to many so far. For what *she* offers, among other
things, is this: 'to eat, instead of bread, shoots of mallow, and instead
of cake, tops of withered radish' (*Pl.* 543–4). *Praxagora's* offer is a
remedy, not a complete switch from poverty to wealth (as seen in *Pl.*
803–20): 'for to a hungry man barley-cake is worth more than gold
and ivory' (Achae. fr. 25). Of the eatables mentioned here, the μᾶζαι
(i.e. barley-cakes) and τεμάχη (slices of salt-fish) are features of the
later public banquet, along with the garlands and the wine (834–52
nn.).   **χλαίνας:** 416 n., **ἐρεβίνθους** (chick-peas), 45 n.   **σὺ . . .
ἀπόδειξον:** cf. *Nu.* 737 αὐτὸς ὅ τι βούλει πρῶτος ἐξευρὼν λέγε.   **γὰρ:**
'(I ask this) for . . .', 717, 133 n.

608–10 Chremes cannot see that a rise in living standards is going to help
bring down the crime rate. The best off are the greatest thieves at
present. His reference is not made more specific, but he no doubt has
in mind the leading public figures in the city. Bdelycleon points out
(*V.* 663) that jurors' pay accounts for a mere tenth of the state revenue,
and on Philocleon's asking where the rest goes, replies (666) ἐς
τούτους τοὺς "οὐχὶ προδώσω τὸν Ἀθηναίων κολοσυρτόν, | ἀλλὰ μαχοῦμαι
περὶ τοῦ πλήθους ἀεί". They grow rich from the public purse (*Pl.* 569)
and (more specifically) steal the tribute (*V.* 1100). Cf. (with Rogers)
X. *An.* iv. 6. 16 (Cheirisophus answering Xenophon), 'I hear that you
Athenians are clever at stealing public funds . . . and particularly
your biggest men . . .'   **ὠταῖρ':** cf. *V.* 1238. The form of address
(ὦ τὰν, B) leads some editors (attributing 608 to Blepyrus) to give the
succeeding line to Chremes. But the repetition of her question (607,
610) makes it certain that Praxagora is speaking: and her tone towards
Chremes arises from the fact that she senses his support (see 564 n.).
διεχρώμεθα: δια- compounds are much favoured in old Attic (particularly by Thucydides, cf. Wilamowitz, 214 n. 3).   **γὰρ:** antici-
patory and parenthetical (38 n.).

611–13 Blepyrus sees *one* cause for holding back one's property: no girl
will grant her favours without presents. **ἢν . . . ἐπιθυμήσῃ:** sc. τις,

618, 633. Cf. S. *OC* 1225 τὸ δ', ἐπεὶ φανῇ, | βῆναι κεῖσ' ὁπόθεν περ
ἥ-|κει . . . **μείρακ'**: 'a lass' (696) with no reflection on her charac-
ter, whatever of 1138 (n.). **ἐπιθυμήσῃ**: of sexual desire, 618, 1016.
σκαλαθῦραι: i.e. βινεῖν (σκάλλω, 'poke', ἀθύρω, 'play'). Cf. σκαλεύω,
Pax 440 ἔχονθ' ἑταίραν καὶ σκαλεύοντ' ἄνθρακας. **τούτων**: i.e. τῶν μὴ
κατατεθέντων, depending by an appropriate construction ἀπὸ κοινοῦ
both on ἀφελών and ἕξει ('he will have some') : though the verb may
rather mean 'he will be able'. **τῶν ἐκ κοινοῦ . . . ξυγκαταδαρθών**:
i.e. having had his wishes granted, he'll have all the 'communism'
that he wants. **τῶν ἐκ κοινοῦ**: at first sight 'common property'.
But Blepyrus does not yet know that μείρακες will be so : he simply
means that the man he has in mind will be sharing common pleasures
with his girl-friend. The meaning has been needlessly perplexed.

613-43 Blepyrus' question introduces Praxagora's second proposition :
community of women and of children. Cf. Pl. *R.* 423 e, 457 c–466 d. See
also Introduction § I.

613-15 **προῖκ'**: 'free of charge', without the lady's asking for any kind of
payment in return. Cf. *Pax* 1203 ἀλλ' ὦ Τρυγαῖε, τῶν δρεπάνων τε
λάμβανε | καὶ τῶνδ' ὅ τι βούλει προῖκα. **καὶ ταύτας . . . τῷ βουλομένῳ**:
cf. *R.* 457 c, with its proposal 'that all these women should be wives in
common to all these men' (i.e. the Guardians) 'and none of them have
any private partner: the children, again, should be common, and no
father know his own child nor any child its father' (635). **καὶ . . .
γὰρ**: 'for these, in fact' (see 503 n.). **τῷ βουλομένῳ**: Praxagora in
613-15 appears to be using legal language (987, 1019 nn.).

615-16 Blepyrus' question did not occur to Plato. But (*a*) when he
advocates the union of 'the best' we may take it that beauty is included (*R.* 459 d), (*b*) his unions also will be subject to controls
(460 a), like Praxagora's (below). **ἴασιν | ἐπὶ**: 'go in search of'
(625). **ἐρείδειν**: *sensu obscaeno*, *Th.* 488 εἶτ' ἠρειδόμην | παρὰ τὸν
Ἀγυιᾶ κὔβδ' ἐχομένη τῆς δάφνης.

617-18 These regulations *could* be read as a burlesque of Plato's proposed
selective breeding. See, however, Introduction § I. Praxagora means
to see that the less attractive *and* the lower classes get their rights.
Contrast the opinion of Nicocles (Isoc. iii. 42), 'I did not think I
should have some children from a woman of lower rank and others
from a woman of higher (ἐκ σεμνοτέρας).' **φαυλότεραι**: not only of
physical appearance (626, Hdt. vi. 61. 3) but also of *class*; 'if they
cannot win honour from the greater and σεμνότεροι, they are content
to be honoured by the lesser and φαυλότεροι' (*R.* 475 a). That passage
also illustrates the social sense of σεμνός (632, Isoc. loc. cit., *Nu.* 48, of
Megacles' niece) : the word (a *vox propria* of deity) connotes the grave
and handsome air of such high breeding (γυναῖκας . . . τὰς σεμνοτάτας καὶ
καλλίστας τῶν ἐν Θήβαις, X. *HG* v. 4. 4). For the φαῦλος/σεμνός
antithesis cf. *Lys.* 1109. **σιμότεραι**: the snub nose is regarded in

both sexes (cf. 705, Theoc. 3. 8) as a defect, though lovers were prepared to overlook it (*R.* 474 d), 'one lad, for his snub-nose, will be praised by you as charming, another with a hooked nose you call kingly.' ἤν . . . ἐπιθυμήσῃ: 611 n.   τὴν αἰσχρὰν: 'the ugly' (625) thus gets the precedence denied the αἰσχίονες παρθένοι of Babylon (Hdt. i. 196. 2).

619–20 καὶ πῶς κ.τ.λ.: Blepyrus' problem (from his different situation) also troubles the youth (cf. 1080).   ἡμᾶς τοὺς πρεσβύτας: general, with no reference to Chremes, though he clearly is an old man (465 n.). ἐπιλείψει: 'let us down', through impotence, a medical term? (see 251 n.).   ἐκεῖσ' οἱ φῂς: i.e. παρὰ τὰς σεμνάς (617). For the use of ἀφικέσθαι (1080) see Hp. *Aër.* 22 ἐπειδὰν ἀφίκωνται παρὰ γυναῖκας, καὶ μὴ οἷοί τε ἔωσι χρῆσθαί σφισιν . . .

621–2 Praxagora answers that her husband's fears are needless: for (*a*) even ugly women will not struggle to claim the service due to them from *him*, (*b*) he is impotent already. To punctuate reading περὶ σοῦ with θάρρει, not μαχοῦνται, would no doubt give the line a better balance, and also provide a better answer ('don't fear about yourself') to his distress. For θαρρῶ περί cf. Pl. *R.* 574 b Οὐ πάνυ, ἦ δ' ὅς, ἔγωγε θαρρῶ περὶ τῶν γονέων τοῦ τοιούτου. But (*a*) σου for σαυτοῦ, if not quite impossible, is odd, (*b*) normal Aristophanic usage suggests that θάρρει is independent. Cf. particularly Pl. 1091 θάρρει, μὴ φοβοῦ, and (for punctuation) Pl. 1076 Νε. ἐγὼ περὶ ταύτης οὐ μαχοῦμαί σοι. Χρ. τὸ τί; περὶ τοῦ; he affects not to understand her meaning, thus leading her to be still more explicit. 'And', she adds, 'such' (i.e. ἐπίλειψις τοῦ πέους) 'is your natural condition' (114 n.).

623–9 Blepyrus objects that her proposal is greatly in favour of the women. But what of the less handsome of the men? Are they not going to be victimized, if the women can pick and choose at random? Her reply is that the women, in the same way, will have to give the precedence to these.

623–5 τὸ μὲν ὑμέτερον . . . ἔχει: '*your* side of the question' (624 τὸ τῶν ἀνδρῶν) 'makes sense of a kind' (*V.* 64 λογίδιον γνώμην ἔχον, cf. *Ra.* 696). Similarly E. *Ph.* 994 καὶ συγγνωστὰ μὲν | γέροντι, τοὐμὸν δ' οὐχὶ συγγνώμην ἔχει.   προβεβούλευται: simply 'you have taken steps beforehand', Th. iii. 82. 5 προβουλεύσας . . . ὅπως μηδὲν αὐτῶν δεήσει. But there may be an underlying meaning: 'you women (as a βουλή) have framed a προβούλευμα, which we men (as an ἐκκλησία) may fail to ratify, if we dislike it.' Cf. the discussion on the trial of the generals (X. *HG* i. 7. 9) after hearing the proposals of the boule, (ibid. 7) τὴν δὲ βουλὴν προβουλεύσασαν . . . ὅτῳ τρόπῳ οἱ ἄνδρες κρίνοιντο. τρύπημα: a ship's oar-hole (*Pax* 1234), here 'cunnus' (cf. τρῆμα, 906). Similarly, Eup. fr. 354 (where the literal meaning is an 'axe-hole') οὐδὲν κενὸν τρύπημ' ⟨ἂν⟩ ἐν ταῖς οἰκίαις ἂν εὕροις.   τὸ δὲ τῶν ἀνδρῶν: Pl. *Chrm.* 154 c καὶ τὸ μὲν ἡμέτερον (cf. 623) τὸ τῶν ἀνδρῶν ἧττον

θαυμαστὸν ἦν.　τοὺς αἰσχίους: 618 n.　ἐπὶ . . . βαδιοῦνται: 616 n.
For position of δέ here cf. A. *A.* 1638 (with Fraenkel).

626–9 φυλάξουσ᾽: 'keep an eye on' (482 n.).　οἱ φαυλότεροι: 617 n.
ἀπιόντας | ἀπὸ τοῦ δείπνου: 694. Praxagora has in mind the common
meal that she will institute. She has not yet referred to it: but at
least one of her listeners is too absorbed with other points to notice.
Or possibly they understand their ordinary δεῖπνον (for the article cf.
675).　ἐπὶ τοῖσιν δημοσίοισιν: 'the public places' (scholiast, sc.
τόποις), and 'public buildings' (Hdt. vi. 52. 7), for example the agora
and baths. On these social centres see the words of the Just Logos (*Nu.*
990–1, 1052–4).　καὶ τοῖς μεγάλοις: Tyrwhitt's supplement (cf.
καὶ τοῖς μικροῖς, 629), replacing the otiose οἱ φαυλότεροι (RΛMᴜɪ)
in front of κοὐκ. Note the Greek (especially heroic, καλός τε μέγας τε,
Il. xxi. 108) equation of handsomeness with stature. Cf. Arist. *EN*
1123ᵇ7, 'greatness of soul depends on greatness, just as beauty depends
on a tall stature: small people may be elegant and charming, καλοὶ δ᾽
οὔ.　χαρίσωνται: *in re amatoria*, 'grant their favours', πολλῶν γὰρ δὴ
πειρασάντων αὐτὴν ὀλίγοις χαρίσασθαι (*Eq.* 517).

630–2 Lysicrates, with his small stature and snub nose (a fair inference
from the preceding: for a series of unflattering comments on noses and
their owners see *AP* xi. 196–204) will fare well in this new dispensation.
Elsewhere (736) he is said to dye his hair and (if this is the same
person, which is doubtful) to be open to bribes (*Av.* 513).　ἴσα . . .
φρονήσει; will it think (of itself, 937 n.) as the handsome do (of themselves), 'hold itself as high as anybody's'? (Rogers). I take this as a
question: for ἆρα with the future, of surprise or incredulity, cf. 668,
Ra. 795 τὸ χρῆμ᾽ ἆρ᾽ ἔσται; Praxagora's answer is then a strong affir-
mative (a man's oath, 160 n.), 'Yes, by Apollo. And what's more'
(καὶ . . . γε, 199 n.) 'the scheme is democratic' (411 n.). So Strepsiades (*Nu.* 388) in answer to Socrates' question, νὴ τὸν Ἀπόλλω, καὶ
δεινὰ ποιεῖ γ᾽ εὐθύς μοι.　καταχήνη . . . πολλὴ: a 'great laugh'
(καταγέλαστος, 125) 'in the face of the upper classes' (τῶν σεμνοτέρων,
617 n.). Cf. *V.* 575 ἆρ᾽ οὐ μεγάλη τοῦτ᾽ ἔστ᾽ ἀρχὴ καὶ τοῦ πλούτου
καταχήνη;　τῶν σφραγῖδας ἐχόντων: 'the wearers of signet-rings',
the foppish and the wealthy, Antiph. fr. 190 (from his Πλούσιοι),
'Euthynus with his sandals and signet-ring and perfume', cf. *Nu.* 332.
For illustrations of contemporary signet-rings see Richter, *Handbook*,
249.

633–4 ἔχων: sc. τις (as 611).　ἐμβάδ᾽: possibly ἐμβάδε (dual), cf.
κοθόρνω, 346. See, however, *Nu.* 719. The wearing of the ἐμβάς (47 n.)
here indicates the common male citizen of Athens, aspiring to neither
wealth nor fashion. So Cephisodotus before the judges ἐμβάδας καὶ
τρίβωνα φορεῖ (Is. v. 11. 9, cf. 850) in order to elicit their compassion
for a poor man (ibid. 11) of the people. Ἐμβαδίων, Heinsius: cf.
Ἐμβάδας, a name for Anytus, because he was a shoemaker

(Theopomp. Com. fr. 57). **πρότερος**: emboldened by the new law, he will speak first, as he would not to his social superiors before. **παραχώρει**: 'stand aside', *Ra.* 767. **ἐπιτήρει, | ὅταν**: 'watch out (for the time) when', 'wait until', cf. *Eq.* 1031 σ' ὁπόταν δειπνῇς ἐπιτηρῶν. **διαπραξάμενος**: 'having gained my objective' (Hdt. ix. 41. 2), 'having carried my job through (δια-) to completion'. **δευτεριάζειν**: 'for a second pressing' (as van Leeuwen). The verb (here only) is a metaphor *in re amatoria* from wine. δευτερίας was the poorer kind of wine (ὁ ἐλάσσων, *Ev.Jo.* 2 : 10) produced by such a second pressing (Poll. vi. 17 ὁ φαῦλος οἶνος) : and these 'seconds' (says the privileged admirer) are all the second lover will enjoy. So Chremylus (*Pl.* 1084) to a young man in a similar position : 'since you have seen fit to drink the wine, you must drink up the lees as well.'

635–50 How will a father recognize his children? This serious question (hence here ascribed to Chremes) is very similar to that of Glaucon (*R.* 461 c) : '(these are reasonable proposals) but how will they distinguish one another's fathers and daughters, and the other relations you were speaking of just now?' By family likenesses, says Arist. (*Pol.* 1262ᵃ14). But Praxagora's answer is, they *won't* know. Each one will think *every* older man his father, where difference in ages will allow it. Similarly, Socrates proposes (*R.* 461 d) that all children born in the tenth or seventh month after a man's wedding, will be spoken of by him as sons or daughters : while those born during the procreative lifetime of his parents will be known as brothers and sisters (cf. *Ti.* 18 d). None of Plato's Guardians can address a fellow Guardian as a stranger (*R.* 463 c), 'for in every one he meets he will think that he is meeting brother, sister, father, mother, son, or daughter . . .' Further, a younger man will not assault an elder (*R.* 465 a), prevented by the shame of laying hands upon his parents, and fear that the others (as sons, brothers, and fathers) will come to the injured man's assistance. So in Praxagora's new society (641–3).

636–7 τί δὲ δεῖ; any more than (for example) among the Gargarians, whose random mating Strabo mentions (xi. 5. 1) : ᾠκείωται δ' ἕκαστος πρὸς ἕκαστον, νομίζων υἱὸν διὰ τὴν ἄγνοιαν (639). Similarly, the Tyrrheni, who practise community of wives, rear 'the children who are born, without knowing what father each belongs to' (Theopomp. Hist. 115 F 204). Aristotle objects to such arrangements, which mean the rejection of the family relationships to which he himself attaches value (*Pol.* 1262ᵃ1, 7, 13). **τοῖσι χρόνοισιν**: i.e. provided that the difference in ages does not make the relationship absurd. Cf. Socrates' answer to Glaucon's inquiry (*R.* 461 d, above).

638–40 Young men notoriously ill-treat their fathers *now*: what will they do when they *don't* know them? **ἄγξουσ'**: Aristophanes had attacked the πατραλοῖαι (*Ra.* 274) in his play (*The Merchantmen*) of 423 : cf. *V.* 1037–9. And a father-beater seeks the kingdom of the

birds in the hope of finding freedom for his pastime, ὅτι καλὸν νομίζεται |
τὸν πατέρα τοῖς ὄρνισιν ἄγχειν καὶ δάκνειν (Av. 1347). Cf. Phidippides'
alleged treatment of Strepsiades (Nu. 1375), Arist. EN 1149ᵇ8.
εὖ καὶ χρηστῶς ἑξῆς: taking their time and doing a good job.
Similar phrases, 253 n.   **ἑξῆς**: not 'in his turn' (Van Daele) but
rather 'in an orderly fashion', 'step by step'. So, of an argument,
Pl. Plt. 257 b ἑξῆς . . . διέξελθε.   **ἀγνὼς ᾖ**: sc. ὁ πατήρ.
κἀπιχεσοῦνται: καί, 'too' (as well as strangling him), or 'even' (subject
him to a worse fate). Cf. 330, and the milder fate of Socrates, 'a lizard
dirtied on him (κατέχεσεν) at night-time from the roof' (Nu. 173). By
τότε he means 'when the new laws take effect': contrast Praxagora's
τότε (641 n.). Blepyrus, in his own style, here anticipates the Stagirite
(Pol. 1262ᵃ30), ἀλλὰ καὶ πλεῖον συμβαίνειν (i.e. αἰκίας κ.τ.λ.) ἀναγκαῖον
ἀγνοούντων ἢ γνωριζόντων.

641-3 Cf. Pl. R. 465 a ff. (635 n.).   **ἀλλ' . . . ἐπιτρέψει**: 'the by-
standers' (Th. 6) 'won't allow it' (Pl. 1078).   **τότε δ'**: 'for' (84 n.)
'before the new laws' (contrast 640).   **τῶν ἀλλοτρίων**: sc. πατέρων.
Anyone could beat his *own* father up till now without a bystander's
interfering (ὅστις, i.e. εἴ τις, 601 n.): cf. Nu. 1324. But now if a
passer-by hears someone being beaten he will fear that it may be *his*
own father (αὐτὸν ἐκεῖνον, 643) and tackle the thugs (τοῖς δρῶσιν
τοῦτο).   **ἀκούσῃ**: sc. τις τῶν παρεστώτων (420). For the double
ellipsis (τίς τινος) cf. 670 (τίς τινα).   **αὐτὸν ἐκεῖνον**: 'that very man'
(he immediately thinks about), his father, in contrast with πατὴρ
ἀλλότριος (ὁ ἐντυχών), cf. Pl. Alc. II 144 b οὐ γὰρ δήπου τὸν ἐντυχόντα,
ἀλλ' αὐτὸν ἐκεῖνον, ὃν ἠβούλου.   **τύπτει**: R, correctly, 'is at the
moment striking' (the subject, of course, is 'the assailant'—the prevalence of ellipsis in this passage does not prevent its meaning being
clear). Cf. Pl. Chrm. 163 a ὅρα μὴ ἐκεῖνον κωλύει, MT 369. Contrast
the subjunctive (of fear for the *future*) in 650, where manuscripts show
the same -η/-ει confusion.

644-5 Blepyrus, buffoonlike, lowers the tone of the discussion. He has
no wish to be addressed as 'Daddy' by Epicurus or Leucolophus (for
which name see Ra. 1513, Is. ii. 3), of whom we can say nothing
certain except (with the scholiast) οὗτοι αἰσχροί. πάππας is the form of
affectionate address used especially in asking for a favour, Pax 120,
ἡνίκ' ἂν αἰτίζητ' ἄρτον, πάππαν με καλοῦσαι. Cf. too V. 609.   **ἤδη
δεινὸν**: 'terrible already', even in prospect, cf. V. 426 τοῦτο μέντοι
δεινὸν ἤδη νὴ Δί', εἰ μαχούμεθα.

646-8 Praxagora can think of something worse—if *Aristyllus* should
claim him and treat him as *his* father. Aristyllus (says Blepyrus)
would regret it. And so (says Praxagora) would he! Bergk suggested
that Aristyllus here is Plato (571, 995 nn., cf. Weiher, 45). It is not
impossible that (a) Plato was (or at any rate was *believed* to be) a
pervert, (b) some one incident (cf. 330 n.) had given the comedian

a pretext, and (c) that Aristophanes should use it. But otherwise there are no grounds for equating Aristyllus (whose coprophilous nature is referred to again, see below) with Plato. It is true that Ἀρίστυλλος is attested as a hypocoristic form of Ἀριστοκλῆς (Eust. 989. 49, *EM* 142. 55): but did Plato *really* have the name of Aristocles (D.L. iii. 4)?   **φιλήσειεν**: 'kiss' (a) as a child looking for a present (*V.* 607 ff.), (b) as a lover (*Av.* 671).   **Ἀρίστυλλος**: for his coprophilia see *Pl.* 314. The chorus there threaten to smear Carion's nose with dung: σὺ δ' Ἀρίστυλλος ὑποχάσκων ἐρεῖς, | ἔπεσθε μητρὶ χοῖροι.   **οἰμώζοι γ' ἂν καὶ κωκύοι**: 942 n. The second verb (used normally of *women's* lamentations) seems to class him with Agyrrhius and Epigonus (103, 168), cf. *Ra.* 34 (of Dionysus). But Praxagora's answer (δέ γε, 32 n.) reverts to his love of μίνθος ('human ordure', Mnesim. fr. 4. 63) for the sake of the pun on (καλα)μίνθη, 'catmint' (Thphr. *CP* ii. 16. 4).

649–50 ἀλλ' ... φιλήσῃ: Praxagora turns from her twitting (646 ff.) to re-assure him: the decree will not be retrospective. The words should not be given to Chremes (Rogers).   **οὗτος μὲν**: 'he at least' (see 144 n.).   **οὐχὶ δεός μή**: cf. Th. iii. 33. 2, X. *Mem.* ii. 1. 25 οὐ φόβος μή σε ἀγάγω. For **φιλήσῃ** (B -ει) see 643 n.   **δεινὸν ... ἐπεπόνθειν**: 'he'd have *suffered* for it, if he had!' Similarly, *Ra.* 741 Αἰα. τὸ δὲ μὴ πατάξαι σ' ἐξελεγχθέντ' ἀντικρυς ... Ξα. ὤμωξε μέντἄν. For the Attic pluperfect 3rd person singular in ει(ν) cf. *Nu.* 1347 (Dawes), KB ii. 66. ἐπεπόνθη, *Suda*: there is similar confusion in pluperfect endings in 32 (n.).

651–2 Chremes brings the conversation back to her proposal (597) for community of land. Who will work it? The short and simple answer is, the slaves: who will not disappear as farm-hands (contrast *Pl.* 522) but play the role the helots did in Sparta (Plu. *Lyc.* 24. 3). Aristotle admits that this will make the scheme more workable (*Pol.* 1263ᵃ9). Plato, of course, does not object to slavery (*R.* 469 c): he *does*, though, object to farmers' sitting back in luxury and thereby ceasing to be farmers (*R.* 420 e): 'for we know that we might dress farmers up in robes and golden crowns, and bid them work the land at their own pleasure . . . but give us no such advice, for if we heed it, οὔτε ὁ γεωργὸς γεωργὸς ἔσται . . .' In general, slave-labour may be seen as complementing, not replacing the labour of the master (καὶ οἰκέτας μὲν οἱ δυνάμενοι ὠνοῦνται, ἵνα συνεργοὺς ἔχωσι, X. *Mem.* ii. 3. 3): Praxagora's scheme is 'Utopian dreaming' (Finley, 63 n. 155). Cf. however, the later plan of Xenophon, which provided for state maintenance of citizens from revenue derived from slaves' labour in the mines (*Vect.* iv. 17). On the whole question of slavery and its place in the economy of Athens see A. H. M. Jones, *Athenian Democracy* (1957, repr. 1960), 10 ff.

ὅταν ... στοιχεῖον: 'when the shadow (of a man) is ten feet long'. The gnomon (introduced from Babylon, Hdt. ii. 109. 3, 'invented' by Anaximander, D.L. ii. 1) is sometimes thought to be referred to here as determining the time of the evening meal (τὸ δεῖπνον). See, however, D. R. Dicks, 'Solstices, Equinoxes and the Presocratics', *JHS* lxxxvi (1966), 30, who believes that the instrument was not used to tell the time before the Hellenistic era. The time here (some half-hour before sunset) is that of a public feast in Ceos (*IG* xii. 5. 647. 16 ἀποδιδόναι δὲ τὸ δεῖπνον δέκα ποδῶν): but earlier (a seven-foot shadow, fr. 675) and later times are also mentioned, Eub. fr. 119. 5, (Philocrates) 'who, they say, was asked to dinner . . . when the shadow of the dial (τὸ στοιχεῖον) measured twenty feet. He measured it at dawn, when the sun had merely risen, and arrived' (with apologies for unpunctuality) 'when the shadow was still more than two feet longer' (i.e. over twenty-two feet, and therefore imperceptible, see Rogers). Cf. Men. fr. 364. **λιπαρὸν**: sleek and shining, as after bath and oiling, *Pl.* 615 λουσάμενος | λιπαρὸς χωρῶν ἐκ βαλανείου. It is tempting to read fr. 109 to make the adjective refer to the diner, not the food: εἰ γὰρ ἐμοὶ . . . λουσαμένῳ †διελκύσαι† | τῆς τρυγὸς ἄρτον λιπαρὸν καὶ ῥάφανον φαγόντι. σοὶ δὲ μελήσει, sc. τὸ λιπαρὸν (λιπαρῷ, Bentley) χωρεῖν ἐπὶ δεῖπνον.

653–4 περὶ δ᾽ ἱματίων . . . ἔσται; a serious question, for over-cloaks are scarce (not least with Blepyrus, 315 n.). And Chremes at the same time is twitting him, remembering the state he found him in (374). For the form of expression cf. *Pax* 124 καὶ τίς πόρος σοι τῆς ὁδοῦ γενήσεται; **καὶ . . . ἐρέσθαι**: 'for this too is a question one might ask' (ἔστιν = πάρεστιν, 529 n.). **πρῶτον**: notice this usage of the adverb 'solitarium', without an answering εἶτα (234) or ἔπειτα (438). Cf. 657, and (occurring in a passage very similar in structure to the present) *Pl.* 519, 522. **ἡμεῖς ὑφανοῦμεν**: 89 n., 556.

655–6 Chremes' final question: what of costs incurred in law-suits? To pay these from common funds would be unfair. **ἐν ἔτι ζητῶ**: a variation (*metri causa*) on ἐν ἔτι ποθῶ, cf. *V.* 818: ἐν ἔτι ποθῶ, τὰ δ᾽ ἄλλ᾽ ἀρέσκει μοι. He is almost convinced by her suggestions. **ὄφλῃ . . . δίκην**: 'incur costs in a law-suit', 'lose one's case', cf. *Av.* 1457. In certain private suits, a 'pursuer' (452 n.) had to carry one-fifth of the jury: otherwise he was liable for costs assessed at an obol in the drachma (technically called ἐπωβελία). Cf. D. xxvii. 67. **παρὰ τοῖς ἄρχουσι**: 'in front of the archons' who presided in the jury-courts, but whose duties were at this time merely formal: 'he did not expound the laws or direct the jury; questions of law as well as fact had to be decided by the dikasts, who had nothing to guide them but their own superficial knowledge of the law and the grounds put forward in the speeches delivered by the parties to the suit' (C. Hignett, *History of the Athenian Constitution* [1952], 223). But they did examine at preliminary hearings: προσεκαλεσάμην αὐτὸν πρὸς τὸν πολέμαρχον (Lys. xxiii. 2). **ἐκτείσει**: 'pay out', or 'pay in full' (of fines, 663 n.) Lys. loc. cit. 14. **τῶν κοινῶν**: supply ἐκ from πόθεν (i.e. ἐκ τίνος;) or the verb. But Jackson (154) reads ταῦτ'; οὐ γὰρ δὴ 'κ.

657–72 The question introduces her third main proposition: *the disappearance of the law-courts.* No debt (and hence no denying it) is possible, since no one will have private funds to lend. Assaults committed at a banquet (for example) will hurt the offender in his stomach, and efforts at gain (whether criminal or other, as by thieving and dicing) will be pointless.

657–8 ἀλλ' . . . ἔσονται: R. 464 d, 'Well, won't lawsuits and prosecutions vanish, more or less, if all they own in private is their body?' Actions for assault and battery (δίκαι βιαίων, αἰκείας, 663 n.) are mentioned as especially precluded.   **τουτὶ τοὔπος σ' ἐπιτρίψει:** 'this remark will finish you' (224 n.), cf. E. *Med.* 585 ἐν γὰρ ἐκτενεῖ σ' ἔπος. Apart from the money (292b n.) the Athenians will not give up their hobby (452 n.). The state of things which Praxagora envisages had actually come about in Sparta (Plu. *Lyc.* 24. 4) with the abolition of coinage (602). But Aristotle is far less optimistic of communism's influence on lawsuits (*Pol.* 1263ᵇ15).   **κἀγὼ . . . ἐθέμην:** his words may answer (a) Praxagora's (i.e. 'I support your proposition' cf. S. *Ph.* 1448), (b) Blepyrus' (i.e. 'that talk *will* ruin her'), the view which is (I think) to be preferred. Chremes for the first time feels misgivings. But he speaks in an aside, and Praxagora retorts upon her poor uncomprehending husband (τάλαν). The phrase is analogous to τίθεμαι τὴν ψῆφον, with which expression ταύτῃ ('on this side', 'in this sense') is more common: μηδαμῶς, ὦ βουλή, ταύτῃ θῆσθε τὴν ψῆφον (Lys. xxiv. 23). However, change here (ταύτῃ, Toup) is needless: οὐκ ἂν τιθείμην ταύτην τὴν ψῆφον (Pl. *Lg.* 674 a), cf. Thgn. 717. The ταύτῃ/ταύτην variation may be seen in manuscripts of Sophocles loc. cit.   **γὰρ:** 133 n.   **τάλαν:** 124 n. Her tone implies (a) confidence in the truth of her own statement ('Why will there be lawsuits? You tell *me*, then'), (b) exasperation at Blepyrus' obtuseness. Cf. her pointed repetition (661) of his confident δήπου (659 n.).

659–61 πολλῶν οὔνεκα: 'for many reasons', 559 n.   **νὴ τὸν Ἀπόλλω:** 631 n. Blepyrus is indiscriminate, however (451 n.), in his choice of deities to swear by.   **δήπου:** 'of course', in a tone connoting certainty, cf. *Pl.* 496 κᾆτα ποιήσει | πάντας χρηστοὺς . . . δήπου . . . ὀφείλων ἐξαρνῆται:** 'owes money and denies it' (451 n.). Strepsiades, behaving thus, is threatened by his creditors with legal action for repayment (*Nu.* 1254, 1277).   **δήπου:** 'your lender is a manifest thief of course' (retorting his own word on him, 659).

662–4 Chremes is lost in admiration of her argument (cf. Woman *A*, 213). But Blepyrus continues (τοίνυν, 427 n.) with his series of questions: what of assault? 'Well, then, let someone tell me this.' He cannot believe that serious civil law-suits (like proceedings for αἴκεια) will be stopped.   **φρασάτω:** sc. τις (as 611 n.).   **τῆς**

αἰκείας: sc. δίκην (656), Pl. *R*. 464 e. αἴκεια implies blows (as οἱ τύπτοντες indicates), D. liv. 18, cf. *Av*. 1671 τί δῆτ' ἄνω κέχηνας αἴκειαν βλέπων; (scholiast, ὡς τυπτήσων τινά). εὐωχηθέντες: 'après un bon dîner' (Van Daele). ἀπορήσειν: 'you will be on the spot there', 'left unable to reply'. Similarly, *Ra*. 1007.

665-6 Such offenders will pay for their excesses by losing their food allowance (μᾶζα). The word, which properly (as 606) means 'barley-cake', is here 'bread' as the staple human diet (equivalent to τροφή or τράπεζα) : cf. A. *A*. 1040 καὶ παῖδα γάρ τοι φασὶν Ἀλκμήνης ποτὲ | πραθέντα τλῆναι, δουλίας μάζης βίᾳ. On μᾶζα (μάσσω, literally 'kneaded thing') see L. A. Moritz, *Grain-Mills and Flour in Classical Antiquity* (1958), 150. Its preparation is possibly depicted on a red-figured pelike in Berkeley : D. A. Amyx, 'A New Pelike by the Geras Painter', *AJA* xlix (1945), 509, figs. 1, 3. ἧς σιτεῖται: sc. τις or ὁ τύπτων (663). Since σιτέομαι with genitive is a late use (LSJ) we must understand ἧς as the attraction of ἥν to the genitive preceding, cf. *Pl*. 1044 τάλαιν' ἐγὼ τῆς ὕβρεος ἧς ὑβρίζομαι. ταύτης . . . ἀφαιρῇ: 'diminishes' it, in forfeit for his crime. Cf. X. *Vect*. iv. 4 οὐδεὶς τοῦ πλήθους ἀφαιρεῖ. φαύλως οὕτως: 'so lightly, thoughtlessly', cf. *Av*. 961 ὦ δαιμόνιε τὰ θεῖα μὴ φαύλως φέρε.

667-71 No more thieves or marauders in the night-time? Of course not, for all will be share-holders in a common fund sufficient for their needs (cf. *Lys*. 1159, 'why then, when you have many benefits to hand, do you go on fighting and not cease from your badness?'). οὐδ' αὖ . . . ἔσται; 'again' (αὖ, 193 n.) 'will no one be a thief?' He is thinking of her words in 661. γάρ: '(no), for . . .', 672, 1026. κλέψει: 'turn out to be a thief', 568 n. μετὸν αὐτῷ: 'when he holds a share in the common property', 1003, fr. 381 οὐ μετὸν αὐτῷ. ἀποδύσουσ': 536, 544 nn. ἄρα: inferential, as 460, which also illustrates the late position. οὐκ . . . καθεύδῃς: 'not if you sleep at *home*'. For γε (limitative) with conditional conjunction see *GP* 142 : cf. 669, 670. It sounds as if Blepyrus' suspicions of his wife (see 523) may well have been assisted by some recollections of his *own* past. But of course a contemporary Athenian would have agreed that these things were different for *men*. ὑπάρξει: 'will exist', 'will be available', *Lys*. 1159 (above). ἢν δ' ἀποδύῃ γ': sc. τίς τινα (642 n.). αὐτὸς: of his own accord (ἑκών, as the scholiast explains), cf. *Ach*. 36. The subject of δώσει is, of course, 'the man attacked'. τί . . . πρᾶγμα μάχεσθαι; 'what need for him to fight?', 'why should he bother fighting?', 462 n.

672 No more dicing, to give rise to fights and lawsuits? If so (he perhaps thinks) it will ill suit φιλόκυβοι like Amynias (*V*. 75). Socrates regarded dice as one way of avoiding working for one's living (X. *Mem*. i. 2. 57). It is madman's business, which soon shows Wealth the door (*Pl*. 243) and a mark of ἀπόνοια (Thphr., *Char*. 6. 5). Three dice (κύβοι) were apparently employed, βέβληκ' Ἀχιλλεὺς δύο κύβω (i.e. 'aces') καὶ τέτταρα (E. fr. 888, *Ra.* 1400) and the highest throw (called *Κῷος*, ibid. 970 with scholiast) consisted in turning up three sixes (A. *A.* 33). See Fraenkel there for details of an ancient gaming-board, based on a model now in Copenhagen. An ivory die (with numbers one to six) is illustrated from Olynthus (*Excavations* x. 504, pl. CLXIV, 2570).   **ἆρ':** for the late position see 462 n.   **περὶ τοῦ:** 'for what stake?', since no one will have any private property. Cf. *Il.* xxii. 161, X. *HG* vi. 3. 16 περὶ διπλασίων κυβεύουσιν.   **ποιήσει:** sc. τις, ὁ κυβεύων (665 n.).

673–86 What will our style of life be? asks Blepyrus. The answer is her fourth and last proposal, which is twofold: *a common house and common meals*. All existing private dwellings will be knocked together into one, and citizens will intermingle freely. The public meals (ξυσσίτια, 715) will be set out in the porticoes and law-courts (which are now, of course, no longer needed): and one's eating-place will be decided by a lottery-ticket (682). These schemes again are reminiscent of Plato's *Republic* (see the notes).

673–5 δίαιταν: 'way of life', with special reference (in Blepyrus' mind, at least) to food. Cf. *Pax* 571 'remembering the old δίαιτα which she [Peace] once provided for us, the fig-cakes, figs and myrtles, and sweet new wine'.   **τὸ γὰρ ἄστυ . . . ποιήσειν:** Pl. *R.* 462 b ἢ μεῖζον ἀγαθὸν (ἔχομεν πόλει) τοῦ ὃ ἂν ξυνδῇ τε καὶ ποιῇ μίαν; Communal dwellings, ibid. 458 c, 'they will live together, with common houses and common meals (συσσίτια)': cf. 464 b, 416 d, 'nobody will have a dwelling-house or store-house . . . which any one who wishes may not enter' (675).   **συρρήξασ' εἰς ἓν ἅπαντα:** Plato (above) writes in terms of 'houses'. But Praxagora seems to think of alterations that will make a single dwelling for the people (thirty thousand, 1132 n.). For similar structural changes see Th. ii. 3. 3 'the Plataeans began to collect together, διορύσσοντες τοὺς κοινοὺς τοίχους.' Cf. 'the middle wall of partition' (τὸ μεσότοιχον τοῦ φραγμοῦ) which is broken down (Eph. 2: 14). The form of expression here recalls *Ra.* 1262 εἰς ἓν γὰρ αὐτοῦ πάντα τὰ μέλη ξυντεμῶ.

675 τὸ δὲ δεῖπνον: Blepyrus' chief interest (see above). The article (cf. 627 n.) implies 'the *customary* dinner': he assumes that *this* custom will continue (though evidently feeling some misgivings, cf. 688–9).   **παραθήσεις:** of setting a meal down *beside* one, cf. *Eq.* 778 ἁρπάζων γὰρ τοὺς ἄρτους σοι τοὺς ἀλλοτρίους παραθήσω.

676 τὰ δικαστήρια: diverted from their old use (657) they will still have some comfort to offer in their new one.   **τὰς στοιὰς:** the porticoes also will be free from former uses. ἡ βασίλειος (685 n.), for example, was the seat of the court of the king archon (Pl. *Euthphr.* 2 a), ἡ ἀλφιτόπωλις (686 n.) the scene of private trading now outmoded. στοιά is the form used *metri gratia* in anapaests (684, 686), cf. ῥοιά (*Pax*

1001). Similarly, ποία (in trochaics, *Eq.* 606).   ἀνδρῶνας: 'men's quarters', and then 'dining-halls', confined (at least in origin) to *male* citizens (A. *A.* 243, X. *Smp.* i. 4). For excavated androns see 686 n., *Excavations* viii. 173, Jones–Sackett–Graham, [14 n.], 109. So τὸ ἀνδρήιον, the public hall in Crete (*GDI* 4992a. ii. 9), τὰ ἀνδρεῖα, the Cretan and Spartan public meals: 'both [Cretans and Spartans] have συσσίτια (715), and the Spartans of old called them not φιδίτια but ἀνδρεῖα, just as the Cretans do' (Arist. *Pol.* 1272ᵃ2). Even in the public meals that they themselves will institute the women (693) will not be sharers: such a bold proposal was not to be put forward till the *Laws* (780 e ff., see Arist. op. cit. 1265ᵃ10). The original scheme (*R.* 416 e, cf. 458 c, 674 n.) was for the Guardians φοιτῶντας... εἰς συσσίτια ὥσπερ ἐστρατοπεδευμένους κοινῇ ζῆν. Some have supposed that Aristophanes is tilting at the *Spartan* meals (above): if so, cf. Antiph. fr. 44, 'you must follow the Spartan customs if in Sparta. Go into the φιδίτια to dine.' On ancient συσσίτια and ἀνδρεῖα see R. F. Willetts, *Aristocratic Society in Ancient Crete* (1955), 21.   πάντα: 'every one of them' (δικαστήρια καὶ στοιάς).

677–80 Blepyrus, well acquainted with the law-courts, wonders what use the platform can be put to. Praxagora explains that it will serve (*a*) for utensils, (*b*) for the children to recite on.

677–8 τὸ δὲ βῆμα: not here the well-known platform on the Pnyx (*Eq.* 77, 87 n.), but that (or rather *those*) on which participants in lawsuits (plaintiff and defendant) were seated. Cf. *Pl.* 382, Aeschin. iii. 207 τοὺς μὲν... ἥκειν πρὸς τὸ τοῦ κατηγόρου βῆμα, τοὺς δὲ... πρὸς τὸ τοῦ φεύγοντος.   τί... ἔσται; 'for what will it be useful?', cf. *Eq.* 1183 καὶ τί τούτοις χρήσομαι | τοῖς ἐντέροις;   κρατῆρας... καὶ... ὑδρίας: Richter and Milne, 6, 11 ff., figs. 43, 76 ff., E. Diehl, *Die Hydria* (Mainz, 1964), pls. 8, 13. Though women liked their wine neat (227 n.), the men would prefer it more diluted. Hermes, deprived of his divine rights, regrets his drink of 'equally mixed' wine, οἴμοι δὲ κύλικος ἴσον ἴσῳ κεκραμένης (*Pl.* 1132): three parts of water to two of wine are mentioned, *Eq.* 1187. But the heavy drinkers might mix it five and two (Nicoch. fr. 1) and a meal could end with the participants unfitted by drink to 'count the rafters' (Thphr. *Vert.* 12): cf. the query (fr. 72), πόσους ἔχει στρωτῆρας ἀνδρὼν οὑτοσί;

678–80 καὶ ῥαψῳδεῖν... παιδαρίοισιν: 'and (there) the children may celebrate...' (ἔσται for παρέσται, 561). Or (sc. τὸ βῆμα) 'it will serve for...', cf. *Pax* 1248 καὐτό σοι γενήσεται | τὰ σῦκ' ἐν ἀγρῷ τοῖς οἰκέταισιν ἱστάναι. For the custom, see *Pax* 1265–1304, where two boys practise epic verses in preparation for a banquet. An ancient meal was frequently concluded with such recitations, songs, or dances: Iphigenia entertained her father's guests (A. *A.* 243), Phidippides (to his father's great annoyance) chose Euripides when asked for a recital after dinner (*Nu.* 1371). See further in my note on Thphr. *Char.* 15.

10.   ἐν τῷ πολέμῳ: either (a) quite general, 'in warfare', or (b) 'in
the war' that is referred to in their verses, no doubt the Trojan War
(cf. ῥαψῳδεῖν). The listeners would be free to find their *own* deeds in
the *present* war reflected in 'the poet': and either pride themselves or
slink away abashed in the light of his praises or reproaches. That the
boys' verses deal with the *current* war directly (a theory implicit in van
Leeuwen) is possible, but very much less likely. The context here
recalls the songs of Sparta (Plu. *Lyc.* 21. 1) : 'for the most part they were
praises of those who had died for Sparta, portraying them as happy,
and reproach of the cowards, whose life they represented as painful and
ill-starred . . .'   εἴ τις: i.e. ὅστις, 601 n.   ἵνα . . . αἰσχυνόμενοι:
sc. οἱ δειλοί. Her idea appears to be that cowards, having heard *one* of
these proposed recitals, will choose to 'cut' the common meal in
future. Or she may intend to *preface* the meal with recitations, so
shaming the cowards from the table. Such reversal of ordinary
practice (see above) could symbolize the *governmental* changes.
αἰσχυνόμενοι: absolute, 381 n. The everyday Greek attitude to
cowardice is probably summed up in the proverb, δειλοῦ μήτηρ οὐ
κλαίει (*PG* ii. 155). Cf. *Th.* 836.
680–1 χάριέν γε: 'a fine idea!' (see 190 : not here ironical, however). But
what of the machines inside the law-courts ? Are you able to make any
use of those ?   τὰ δὲ κληρωτήρια: Pollux, listing σκεύη δικαστικά (x.
66) is very vague: he infers from Aristophanes ἐν τῷ Γήραι that
κληρωτήριον may mean 'the place', i.e. (cf. ix. 44) ἵνα οἱ κληρωταὶ
(συνεκαθίζοντο). But the word would also suit 'the urn' (ἀγγεῖον).
Ath. Pol. 63. 2 distinguishes urn (ὑδρία) and κληρωτήρια distinctly: the
latter have been commonly identified as rooms (two for each tribe, i.e.
twenty) where courts were allotted to the jurors, seemingly mere
kiosks which could readily be moved to the city centre and set up
there, though now for allocating *dining-centres*. For the true sense,
'allotment machines', with illustrations and description of their use,
see Sterling Dow, 'Aristotle, the Kleroteria, and the Courts', *HSPh* l.
(1939), 1.   ποῖ τρέψεις; 'to what use will you turn them ?', cf. *V.*
665 καὶ ποῖ τρέπεται δὴ 'πειτα τὰ χρήματα τἆλλα;
681–2 They will be set down by the tyrant-slayers' statue in the agora.
The citizens will draw lots (marked with letters of the alphabet) and
proceed to places similarly marked (this, as the procedure of the law-
courts, will afford no difficulty to Athenians) : marked where possible,
moreover, with their own initial letter (684). The courts were lettered
Λ–Ω (for reasons which *Ath. Pol.* 63 explains) but Praxagora is less
restricted (686 n.).   εἰς τὴν ἀγοράν: 759, see 62 n.   παρ' Ἁρμοδίῳ:
beside the statue of the saviour of Athens (Th. i. 20. 2, cf. *Eq.* 786) to
mark its *new* salvation through the women. And here too, in face of a
revival of the tyranny, the old men thought appropriate to muster
ἑξῆς Ἀριστογείτονι, *Lys.* 631–4). Harmodius, the subject of a cele-

brated scolion (quoted *Lys.* 632, cf. *Ach.* 980) was also honoured by
statuary groups, together with his friend Aristogeiton (Paus. i. 8. 5).
See R. E. Wycherley, *The Athenian Agora* iii (Princeton, N.J., 1957),
93–8, Gisela M. A. Richter, *The Sculpture and Sculptors of the Greeks*[4]
(New Haven, Conn., 1970), 154, figs. 609–15.   **κληρώσω πάντας**:
'I'll make them all draw lots' (see 836). Praxagora's procedure is much
simpler than the courts' (for details see *Ath. Pol.* 63, Dow, 27 ff.) and
her own role, unlike that of the θεσμοθέτης (*Ath. Pol.* 63. 5, 64. 1, see
291a) will be mainly supervisory (835).

682–3 ἕως . . . ἀπίῃ: *Ath. Pol.* 64. 4 ἵν' εἰς οἷον ἂν λάχῃ εἰσίῃ καὶ μὴ εἰς
οἷον ἂν βούληται. But where dinner is concerned he has *no* preference
in dining-rooms: and will go to that allotted gladly (χαίρων).   **ἐν
ὁποίῳ γράμματι**: i.e. in the hall marked with which letter. δειπνεῖν (as
the scholiast observes) in this new context replaces δικάζειν in the old,
cf. *Pl.* 277 ἐν τῇ σορῷ νυνὶ λαχὸν τὸ γράμμα σου δικάζειν. A similar
substitution, *Pl.* 972 ἀλλ' οὐ λαχοῦσ' ἔπινες (a παρὰ προσδοκίαν for
ἔκρινες) ἐν τῷ γράμματι; *Ath. Pol.* 63. 5 shows the reference: 'the
attendant takes and fixes on each court its allotted letter.'

684–5 She explains what she means by three examples.   **κηρύξει**: sc.
as commonly, ὁ κῆρυξ (or rather ἡ κηρύκαινα, 713), X. *An.* iii. 4. 36
ἐκήρυξε τοῖς Ἕλλησι συσκευάζεσθαι. For his presence here (though
different in function), cf. *Ath. Pol.* 64. 3 καλεῖ τοὺς εἰληχότας ὁ κῆρυξ.
τοὺς ἐκ τοῦ βῆτ': 'those in the B group' (τὸ βῆτα, cf. τὸ θῆτα, 685),
those, that is, who draw the letter B. (See the dicast's ticket, marked
with E, from Olynthus, *Excavations* x. 500, pl. CLXIV, 2562.) Now
there is (as it happens) a portico whose name begins with B: so thither
this group goes (676 n.). For details of the Stoa Basileios see Wycherley, 21–5.   **στοιὰν**: cf. 676.   **τὸ δὲ θῆτ'**: similarly this group will
be taken to a building beginning with that letter. The στοά of Zeus
Eleutherios is thus excluded from consideration (β' εἰσὶ στοαὶ παρ'
ἀλλήλας, ἥ τε τοῦ Ἐλευθερίου Διὸς καὶ ἡ βασίλειος, Harp. 71. 11, cf.
Wycherley, 22). But *behind* the στοὰ βασίλειος (and presumably
therefore παρὰ ταύτην) was a stoa whose mural decoration featured
Theseus, with Democratia and Demus (Paus. i. 3. 2). I follow van
Leeuwen in identifying this as the portico Praxagora means here (the
Poikile, Wycherley loc. cit.). And possibly this is what the scholiast
intended (although his εἰς τὸ Θησεῖον is patently mistaken or corrupt).
The στοὰ Θησεῖος would not need to be named: for even Blepyrus
(687) is aware of some point in the choice of her examples.

686 τοὺς δ' ἐκ τοῦ κάππ': since stoai and law-courts are limited in
number, the K's, and others, must naturally go to places unconnected
with the letter. If K represents the *last* group (as jurors were given
letters up to K, *Ath. Pol.* 63. 4), her plan involves *ten* centres altogether
(to seat three thousand each, 674 n.). Improbabilities do not count in
Aristophanes (think only of the whole plot of the play): but we need

not, in any case, believe she is thus limited, since K is pretty clearly chosen to accommodate her husband's little joke. Likewise, it is purely accidental (one imagines) that K's are furthest from their dinner. For the στοὰ ἀλφιτόπωλις in the Piraeus (see 14 n.) cf. *Ach.* 548 (with scholiast) στοᾶς στεναχούσης, σιτίων μετρουμένων. Others prefer to see a reference here to the 'Long Colonnade' ἐν Κεραμεικῷ (*IG* i². 968. 14, Wycherley, 193): while A. Raubitschek ('The Gates in the Agora', *AJA* lx [1956], 279–82) identifies the Stoa Alphitopolis with one excavated to reveal a row of dining-rooms (*Hesperia* xxiii [1954], 39–45, fig. 4, p. 44).

687 ἵνα κάπτωσιν; 'to guzzle' the *alphita*, as slaves would, when working at the mill, if unrestrained: παύσειν ἔοιχ' ἡ παυσικάπη κάπτοντά σε (fr. 302). The word suggests also an animal-like greediness (Arist. *HA* 595ª10, cf. *Av.* 579): but of course is used here primarily to introduce a pun on 'kappa'.   **μὰ Δί' ἀλλ'**: 158 n.

687–90 Blepyrus fears there will be *blank* lots: and that those who draw them will stand to lose a dinner, as jurors in the same case lose a fee. Praxagora reassures him: not with *them*.   **ὅτῳ . . . ἅπαντες**: a statement, as Hall and Geldart rightly print it. Blepyrus knows his fellow citizens. ὅτῳ, τούτους, in loose correlation, as commonly with ὅστις, E. *El.* 933 κἀκείνους στυγῶ | τοὺς παῖδας, ὅστις . . . For the general form of the construction, cf. (for example) *Pl.* 41. The meaning is, 'those unsuccessful in the lottery', οἱ ἀπολαγχάνοντες (*Ath. Pol.* 65. 3).   **'ξελκυσθῇ**: 40 n., cf. *Pax* 315.   **παρ' ἡμῖν**: 'with us', cf. *Nu.* 903.   **πᾶσι . . . παρέξομεν**: 1143.

691–709 She pictures the scene as the men, well fed and tipsy, make their way back from their various dining-centres. The older and less handsome women will allure them with offers of young and lovely lasses: the catch is, however, that the *law* must be complied with, and they themselves accorded first attention. (Something of the picture painted here is seen in practice, 877–1111.) And similarly, young good-looking lads must check their hurry in favour of their less well-favoured elders, and find themselves alternative amusement.

The metre (from 689) is anapaestic dimeters,

ᴗᴗ⏑⏑ ᴗᴗ⏑⏑   ᴗᴗ⏑⏑ ᴗᴗ⏑⏑

with single anapaestic metra (697, 701, 708), ending in a catalectic dimeter (paroemiac): cf. *Av.* 209–22.

691–2 ὥστε . . . λαβών: their drunken state (see Bieber, *HT* 38, fig. 134) and their equipment betoken revellers (κωμασταί). Such revels (κῶμοι) were common post-prandial amusements (cf. Antiphanes below). There is no mention here of the music-girls (Praxagora perhaps did not provide them) who would normally attend at *private* dinner-parties, and then go with the revellers in the streets (Pl. *Tht.* 173 d). But of course in the *new* polity, with its extension of the sexual rights of free Athenian women, the part played by slave-girls will be smaller (cf. 718–20 n.). Otherwise, compare (for drunkenness and garlands) Alcibiades, the celebrated comast, who 'stood in the doorway garlanded with a thick wreath of violets and ivy . . . and said "Good evening, gentlemen, are you willing to receive a fellow-drinker wildly drunk already?" ' (id. *Smp.* 212 d), (for garlands and a torch) Antiph. fr. 199, A. 'Shall we go to the revel just as we are?' B. 'Without taking torch and garlands?' A. Χαιρεφῶν οὕτως ⟨γέ πως⟩ | μεμάθηκε κωμάζειν ἄδειπνος, cf. T. B. L. Webster, *Monuments*, pl. IIId. Lights of course were a necessity for *anyone* abroad in Athens after dark (27, 546 n.); but probably such nocturnal travellers were few, and a torch (δᾱς) would most often mean a reveller: 'he looks as if he's going to a κῶμος.' 'He does: anyway, he's coming with a garland and a torch' (*Pl.* 1040).   αὐτῷ στεφάνῳ: 'garland and all' (*V.* 119), i.e. still wearing the garland he had put on for the drinking (131 n.).   τὴν δᾳδα: either just 'his', or else 'the *customary*' torch (cf. on 50). Lycurgus forbade it to the Spartans: 'after drinking moderately they go off home' (i.e. from the συσσίτια, cf. 626) 'without a torch. For they are not permitted to walk with a light, on this or other journeys, so that they may get used to proceeding, boldly and fearlessly, amid the darkness of the night' (Plu. *Lyc.* 12. 7).

693–6 αἱ δὲ γυναῖκες: excluded from the meal (676 n.). The women here (cf. 877) are free-born women standing on their rights: they are neither prostitutes (718) nor the bawds that (out of mischief) they pretend.   κατὰ τὰς διόδους: 'along their route(s)', *V.* 359 νῦν δὲ ξὺν ὅπλοις | ἄνδρες ὁπλῖται διαταξάμενοι | κατὰ τὰς διόδους σκοπιωροῦνται.   προσπίπτουσαι: 'falling on', 'waylaying' them (like brigands, Th. i. 5. 1). Cf. 881, 1020, Thphr. *Char.* 28. 3 αὗται αἱ γυναῖκες ἐκ τῆς ὁδοῦ τοὺς παριόντας συναρπάζουσι.   τοῖς ἀπὸ δείπνου: 627, 877, cf. Thphr. *Char.* 24. 2. The words are to be taken ἀπὸ κοινοῦ with προσπίπτουσαι and λέξουσιν.   δεῦρο παρ' ἡμᾶς: 'come to my place' (952, 689 n.). The revellers are to be invited in (Pl. *Smp.* 212 d).   μεῖραξ: 611 n.

697–701 "παρ' ἐμοὶ δ' ", ἑτέρα: preferable to "παρ' ἐμοὶ δ' ἑτέρα", which leaves φήσει τις very bald. Cf. *Lys.* 524.   ἄνωθ' ἐξ ὑπερῴου: 'from an upper storey', in which was situated the γυναικωνῖτις (women's quarters), reached by a ladder, Lys. i. 9. Cf. Men. *Sam.* 232 κατέβαιν' ἀφ' ὑπερῴου τις γυνὴ | ἄνωθεν. So καταδραμοῦσα (962 n.). For double-storeyed classical Greek houses see *Excavations*, ii. 37.   λευκοτάτη: her attractive pallor heightened (see 878 n.) by cosmetics.   πρότερον . . . αὐτῆς: i.e. πρότερον ἢ παρ' αὐτῇ. A similar combination, 925. The words here forecast in fact *are* used (1050), though not in the context she imagines.

702b–5 μειρακίοις: 'youths' (cf. μεῖραξ), 1146.   οἱ φαυλότεροι: 617 n.   οὗτος: 372 n.   πάντως: 'in any case' (604).   οὐδὲν δράσεις:

'you'll achieve nothing' (cf. *Pax* 481), possibly not without a feeling of the *literal* meaning (605). **σιμοῖς . . . αἰσχροῖς**: 617–18 nn.

707–9 The youths are to wait in the porch (*V.* 802), reduced by the law to masturbation. **θρῖα . . . διφόρου συκῆς**: 'leaves of the double fig-tree' (Antiph. fr. 198). Whatever its meaning ('twice-bearing'?) of the fig-tree, διφόρος here means 'bearing two' (sc. ὄρχεις). θρίω, of the two lobes of the brain (*Ra.* 134): here used metaphorically of the foreskin. Cf. ἀποθριάζω, 'circumcise' (*Ach.* 158). Figs are a symbol for the genitals, *Pax* 1344–50. **δέφεσθαι**: consoling themselves, that is, like Datis (*Pax* 290–1). More explicit allusions to the nature of the practice, *Eq.* 24, 29. This situation is a side-effect of the new law (sc. ἐψήφισται).

710–29 Her plans are given an enthusiastic welcome, and she moves off (closely followed by Blepyrus) to supervise their implementation. Chremes goes back into the house to make arrangements for bringing his belongings to the stores.

For the transition to iambic dialogue (710) after an anapaestic sequence cf. *Pax* 1016.

710 φέρε νυν φράσον: 28, *Nu.* 1088 φέρε δή μοι φράσον. This *may* be a loose use of the singular imperative (as editors in general explain it). Praxagora, however, by ταῦτ' means more explicitly the picture 705–9, aware of its attraction for Blepyrus: he clearly understands her in the same sense, and assumes that she wants confirmation (hence his πάνυ). Chremes also, no doubt, indicates approval. **σφῷν**: i.e. 'you two' (564 n.).

711–13 βαδιστέον τἄρ' ἐστὶν: 'in that case, then' (τοι ἄρα) i.e. since you're both happy. Cf. *Ra.* 656 βαδιστέον τἄρ' ἐστὶν ἐπὶ τονδὶ πάλιν. **εἰς ἀγορὰν**: 728, 62 n. **τὰ προσιόντα χρήματα**: 'the goods as they come in'. προσιέναι is the *vox propria* for tribute coming in to the exchequer: cf. *V.* 657, Lys. xxx. 19 (θύειν) ἃ . . . δυνησόμεθα δαπανᾶν ἐκ τῶν προσιόντων χρημάτων. **κηρύκαιναν**: we meet her later (834 n.). The word is an *ad hoc* coinage, like Σκύθαινα (*Lys.* 184). For the often derogatory sense of comic forms in -αινα see E. Fraenkel, 'Neues Griechisch in Graffiti', *Glotta*, xxxiv (1954–5), 44–5 (*Kleine Beiträge* i. 149–50). She is chosen for the *volume*, not the *beauty* of her voice ('Cleocritus, the herald of the initiates, μάλ' εὔφωνος ὤν, created a deep silence . . .' X. *HG* ii. 4. 20), in fact as a κῆρυξ Στεντόρειος (Arist. *Pol.* 1326ᵇ8): her immediate function is, presumably, to 'cry' the goods as they arrive, and then proclaim the first meal (834 n.).

714–17 ᾑρημένην | ἄρχειν: 246 n. **τὰ ξυσσίτια**: Pl. *R.* 416 e, Arist. *Pol.* 1272ᵃ2 (676 n.). **εὐωχῆσθε . . . τήμερον**: *all* the new laws are to take effect at once: Blepyrus is delighted, but incredulous (γάρ, cf. 786). The verb implies 'you *men*-folk' (693 n.). **φήμ' ἐγώ**: 457 n.

718–20 Her new law is to benefit free women: so a ban must be placed upon slave prostitutes, to stop them enticing the young men with their charms (cf. *Ach.* 524).   τὰς πόρνας: slaves (721), housed in brothels like that attributed (improbably) to Aspasia (*Ach.* 527, Plu. *Per.* 24. 3), they could either be visited (*V.* 500) or hired privately (*V.* 739) and for parties (*Ach.* 1091). The industry seems to have been centred on the Piraeus (cf. *Pax* 164–5).   καταπαῦσαι: 'put down *completely*' (κατα-intensive, 482), Hdt. vi. 43. 3 'Mardonius set up democracies . . . τοὺς . . . τυράννους . . . καταπαύσας πάντας.'   ἀπαξαπάσας: 217 n. ἵνα τί; sc. γένηται, And. iii. 26. Similarly 791 (n.).   τουτογί: 189 n., see apparatus criticus. Confusion of Γ and T is easy.   τῶν νέων . . . τὰς ἀκμάς: 'the young men, in their prime', cf. τὴν ἀκμὴν τῶν νέων, Demad. fr. 12. 6. The *plural* here thinks of the youths as individuals, X. *Lac.* i. 6 ἔταξεν ἐν ἀκμαῖς τῶν σωμάτων τοὺς γάμους ποιεῖσθαι.   αὗται: the chorus (510) representing the free women of the city. αὐταί (Scaliger) distinguishes the citizenesses from the slaves.

721–4 κοσμουμένας: 'dressed up' to attract (878 n.). Notice the present, i.e. '*keeping* dressing up', and hence appearing dressed on all occasions.   τὴν . . . Κύπριν: *Th.* 205 κλέπτειν ὑφαρπάζειν τε θήλειαν Κύπριν. Both these lines suggest a tragic origin (probably in Agathon, whose poetry and person are ridiculed in the early part of *Th.*).   ὑφαρπάζειν: 'snatch away secretly' (15 n.), or 'from under one's nose' (see 921).   κατωνάκην . . . ἀποτετιλμένας: their *pudenda* (*Th.* 538) shaved like a slave's rough sheep-skin chiton (*Lys.* 1155), i.e. depilated not at all. Slaves should not ape their betters (12 n.). For the idiom cf. *Av.* 806 σὺ δὲ κοψίχῳ γε σκάφιον ἀποτετιλμένῳ (ἔοικας), 'a blackbird with a bowl-cut'.

725–7 φέρε νυν . . . παρακολουθῶ: 28 n.   ἵν' ἀποβλέπωμαι: 'that folk may look at me', the verb implying their looking *away from* other objects. So the flatterer of his patron (Thphr. *Char.* 2. 2), ἐνθυμῇ, ὡς ἀποβλέπουσι πρὸς σὲ οἱ ἄνθρωποι; Blepyrus believes 'pulchrum est digito monstrari et dicier hic est' (Pers. 1. 28).   λέγωσιν . . . θαυμάζετε; his attitude is reminiscent of Theophrastus' ἄρεσκος, who comes late to public performances, allowing spectators to say to one another ὅτι τούτου ἐστὶν ἡ παλαίστρα (*Char.* 5. 10).   λέγωσιν ἐμὲ ταδί: see apparatus criticus. μοι (RΓVb1B) can only be interpreted (harshly) as a dative of advantage.   τὸν τῆς στρατηγοῦ: sc. ἄνδρα, cf. 46 n. Even common language must be altered in a context where men are known only through their wives (a reversal of things, see 41 n.). And στρατηγός must be *feminine* in future.

728–9 δ' . . . γε: the separated particles retain the force of δέ γε (a lively rejoinder, 32 n.).   εἰς ἀγοράν: 711, 62 n.   ἐξετάσω: 'review' my belongings (*a*) by sifting them mentally and (*b*) by passing them before me in procession (730–45). The audience, of course, will not expect the second meaning: but they must, all the same, have been delighted when the old man lined up his utensils (see below).

729 R here and 876 has χοροῦ. See Introduction § III.

730–45 Chremes, after a brief interval, is seen re-emerging from his house. Two slaves (867) bring out his household property, and line it up, on his instructions, in the order of a ritual procession (756–7). The procession parodied is illustrated by the Parthenon frieze (for details of Panathenaic rites see Deubner, 22–35). His sieve (κιναχύρα) is to act as the κανηφόρος (*Ach.* 242). A black pot (χύτρα) follows in the role of the διφροφόρος (like Pisthetaerus, 734 n.), and after her another attendant (ἡ κομμώτρια), represented by some article unnamed. Of the other objects mentioned (for details see the notes) only ἡ κιθαρῳδός (739) could cause misunderstanding. (The exact *part* the functionaries named played in *processions* remains, of course, extremely doubtful: it is also irrelevant to both the understanding and enjoyment of Chremes' charade.) The two slaves are not addressed directly till the main procession has been formed; when some accessories and oddments must be added before it can move—towards the agora, where the general will 'receive' it (cf. *Ath. Pol.* 18. 3).

730–3 κιναχύρα: only here, but clearly a 'sieve' (κινεῖν, ἄχυρα). In this place—whatever may be true of 539 (n.)—the joke rests in the choice of an ugly household article (for fragments of sieves see *Excavations*, x. 191, pl. XLIX) to represent the young and handsome maiden who led such processions with 'the basket': ἄγ' ὦ θύγατερ ὅπως τὸ κανοῦν καλὴ καλῶς | οἴσεις (*Ach.* 253). So the women (*Lys.* 646) look back to their glories of the past. The only likeness is that both are powdered (ἐντετριμμένη): *it* with flour acquired in sifting, *she* with cosmetics (904), cf. Hermipp. fr. 26 ὥσπερ αἱ κανηφόροι | λευκοῖσιν ἀλφίτοισιν ἐντετριμμένοι | ἔγωγ' ἐνέκαψα ⟨δια⟩λαθὼν τὴν διφροφόρον. καλὴ καλῶς is formulaic in such contexts (cf. *Ach.* loc. cit.). κάτω . . . στρέψασ': 'caused to capsize', as S. *Ant.* 716 ὑπτίοις κάτω | στρέψας (τὴν ναῦν) τὸ λοιπὸν σέλμασιν ναυτίλλεται. For the use of δή with temporal and local adverbs (*GP* 206) cf. S. *OT* 968 ὁ δὲ θανὼν | κεύθει κάτω δὴ γῆς. θυλάκους: 'meal-bags' (382 n.).

734 ἡ διφροφόρος: number two in the procession (Hermipp. loc. cit., cf. παρ' αὐτήν, 737) comes this attendant with a chair, καὶ τὸν δίφρον γε διφροφόρει τονδὶ λαβών (*Av.* 1552), cf. Cratin. fr. 30. See the Athenian terracotta statuette in G. M. A. Richter, *The Furniture of the Greeks, Etruscans and Romans* (1966), fig. 233. ἡ χύτρα: nominative for vocative (737, 739) as in speaking to a slave (see 833 n.). Cf., in a very similar passage, Crates Com. fr. 14. 8 τὴν χύτραν, χρὴ ⟨σ'⟩ ἐξεραν τὰ τεῦτλα. This often mentioned pot (1092) served as a saucepan for cooking porridge (*Pl.* 683), meat (fr. 591), soup (845): see further B. A. Sparkes, 'The Greek Kitchen', *JHS* lxxxii (1962), 130. Illustrations ibid. pl. VI. 1, B. A. Sparkes and L. Talcott, *Pots and Pans of Classical Athens* (Princeton, N.J., 1958), figs. 42, 62. ἔξιθι: i.e. from the house (48 n.).

735–6 μέλαινά γ'· . . . μελαίνεται: I punctuate with colon at γ' (see 422 : Chremes is abrupt throughout the passage) and suppose an aposio-pesis at μελαίνεται (sc. μελαντέρα εἴης). The break implies 'enough said', 'you all know what I mean' : and if this ellipsis seems harsh it is no more so than the change of οὐδ' to ὡς (Halbertsma). But μέλαινά γ'· οὐδὲν εἰ. (Jackson, cf. 144) is attractive. The pot's blackness (from much work in the kitchen, cf. V. 828 ἡ Θρᾶττα προσκαύσασα πρώην τὴν χύτραν) reminds him of Lysicrates, whose nose (630) appears to have been offset by a fine head of (dyed) black hair. From this play his name became a by-word, Λυσικράτης ἕτερος being used of black-haired persons (PG ii. 513). The ageing beauty (Hor. Carm. iv. 10) is attempting to conceal his greying hair. Cf. Nicol. Com. fr. 1. 33 'one steals from the years ἢ καὶ βάπτεται' (εἰ . . . βλάπτεται, Edmonds, wrongly, of facial depilation), 'because he wishes to be handsome.' And Kuster aptly cites Serenus, 'Quos pudet aetatis longae, quos sancta senectus Offendit, cupiunt properos abscondere canos Et nigrum crinem fuco simulare doloso' (Liber Medicinalis iv, CML ii. 3. 43). Cf. Mart. iii. 43.

737–8 παρ' αὐτήν: i.e. beside the κιναχύρα as κανηφόρος. Punctuate with colon after αὐτήν, since the order is best understood as to the χύτρα (διφροφόρος) and not the maid-in-waiting.   **κομμώτρια:** 'a lady's maid' (Pl. R. 373 c), was possibly, in actual processions, one of those who held up the parasols (cf. Av. 1550). The text gives no indication of the vessel that represents her here.   **ὑδρίαν:** 678 n. The sight of the hydria suggests the ὑδριαφόροι (the wives of metics, Poll. iii. 55), as that of the σκάφη (742 n.) does their husbands (ibid. σκαφηφόρος· οὕτω δὲ τοὺς μετοίκους ὠνόμαζον). For (male) hydriaphoroi see the north frieze of the Parthenon, and Bieber, HT 46, fig. 200.

739–41 ἡ κιθαρῳδός: what represented the processional musician? Most commentators, depending on the scholiast's wrong-headed explana-tion ἡ ἀλετρίς, explain that Chremes here brings out a hand-mill. Now, hand-mills did make a merry sound at morning (cf. Pherecr. fr. 10) and when struck sounded ὥσπερ ἐπὶ λύρας (Nicostr. περὶ γάμου, in Stob. iv. 102). But if this explanation is the true one, the description in terms proper only (see below) to a cock, is closer to absurdity than humour. The true fun—as Brunck saw—lies in Chremes' producing, among his pots and pans, a real live rooster. Cf. V. 815 ἀτὰρ τί τὸν ὄρνιν ὡς ἔμ' ἐξηνέγκατε; (744).   **ἀναστήσασά μ':** for this function of the cock see V. 100 (a complaint of its rousing a juryman too late). Similarly, Av. 489 (in 20 n.) : the same note illustrates the reference to dawn as the time of the Assembly.   **εἰς ἐκκλησίαν:** 270 n.   **ἀωρὶ νύκτωρ:** the second adverb elaborates the first, i.e. 'too early, while still night-time'. For the sense of his complaint see 462. Chremes is, doubtless, a type of the good citizen, bestowing all his goods upon the State: but note at the same time that his troublesome alarm-clock is

now no longer needed (463), nor is he bound to suffer any longer this
ἀωρόνυκτον ἀμβόαμα (A. *Ch.* 34). The State scheme provides an
alternative to Chares' (Heraclid. Com. fr. 2), who 'caught Philip's
rooster wandering and ἀωρὶ κοκκύζοντα and cut it up in pieces'. ΓVbιB
have νυκτῶν, but the article would be needed, ἀωρὶ . . . τῶν νυκτῶν
ἐξαναστάς (Lucian, *Dem. Enc.* 1).   **τὸν ὄρθριον νόμον**: 30, 390 nn.,
Av. 489 ὁπόταν μόνον (νόμον, Porson) ὄρθριον ᾄσῃ (of the cock). There
may also (as the scholiast suggests) be an allusion to the well-known
ὄρθιος νόμος (cf. *Eq.* 1279).

742–3 τὴν σκάφην: the bowl containing offerings of honeycombs
(τὰ κηρία), carried by metics in processions. Harp. s.v. σκαφηφόροι:
'Demetrius says the law ordered metics in processions themselves to
carry σκάφαι' (cf. Men. fr. 191), 'and their daughters ὑδρεῖα and
σκιάδεια'(contrast Pollux in 738 n.). The honeycombs, of course, are
only mentioned as forming the contents of the σκάφη (cf. Phot. s.v.
σκάφας) and no other eatables come forward. Apart from the fact that
the scene imposes limits, there was probably little in the larder.
τοὺς θαλλοὺς: carried in the Panathenaic procession by old men now
fit for nothing else (*V.* 540–545). There was mention of the custom
(says the scholiast ad loc.) in lost plays by Cratinus (fr. 31) and
Pherecrates (fr. 56).

744 τὼ τρίποδ᾽: 787. These articles, apart from their importance in the
kitchen, could of course be used in ritual as well (E. *Supp.* 1197, S. *Aj.*
1405). They were frequently used as dedications: Hes. *Op.* 658, Hdt.
i. 92. 1. Tripods of bronze (as E. loc. cit.) are described and illustrated
by S. Benton, 'Excavations in Ithaca III' and 'The Evolution of the
Tripod-Lebes', *ABSA* xxxv (1934–5), 45–130. But Chremes' would be
of terracotta (Sparkes, 123–4). Poll. (x. 80) quotes this passage in
support of τρίπους as 'table' (fr. 530).   **ἐξένεγκε**: 76 n., 754.   **τὴν
λήκυθον**: the flask (Richter and Milne, figs. 91–102) for the oil used in
religious and superstitious practices (996 n., Thphr. *Char.* 16. 5). But
ληκυθοφόροι did not take part in processions: at least Pollux (iii. 154)
so calls slaves in attendance at the baths.

745 τὰ χυτρίδι᾽ . . . ἀφίετε: the asyndeton (cf. 735) is in keeping with
Chremes' tone throughout the passage. His meaning is not 'never
mind about the *small* pots' (χυτρίδια, cf. *Pax* 202), for (*a*) Chremes
means to withhold *nothing*, (*b*) the use of ἤδη is then awkward. Rather
—he is speaking to slaves inside the house—'release the small stuff
now' to join the procession (the big pots are already in position). Cf.
Alex. fr. 62. 2 τέτταρας | περιστερὰς ἀφῆκεν.   **τὸν ὄχλον**: i.e. the
other bits and pieces, his miscellaneous collection. Similarly, X. *An.*
iv. 3. 15 τὰ δὲ ὑποζύγια καὶ τὸν ὄχλον ἐν μέσῳ τούτων διαβαίνειν. For
a slave with kitchen articles see Bieber, *HT* 41, fig. 159.

746–876 While Chremes is completing his arrangements (785) for
transporting his possessions, another person enters from the right. A

reader will not recognize him (he is unnamed, like many in the play), but the audience (as I understand, with Rogers) are seeing Woman B's husband, who earlier had stumbled on Blepyrus (327) and will now meet his *second* strange sight of the morning. He does not observe it as he enters (he is musing, 746, upon the new decree): but when he does, and understands the reason, he makes clear his refusal to comply. Athenians are more inclined to take things than to give them—like the gods who on their statues (779 ff.) hold their hands out. Besides, they often vote laws in a hurry, and go back on them later (798). Chremes continues tying up the goods, reminding him that that was when *men* were still in power. His slave has just raised the baggage-pole for their departure, when the heraldess arrives (834) to cry the public meal. The dissident citizen now brightens up, intending to make for the feast without delay. Restrained temporarily, he stays behind still musing on how to keep his goods and banquet too. He is, in fact, the proof of his own dictum that Athenians would rather get than give: an example of Praxagora's assertion (207) that everyone is out for his own pocket. But we must not see him as a peg to hang a thesis on: Aristophanes does *not* mean that plans for common owner-ship will founder through individuals' greed (Wilamowitz, 215, cf. Meder, 81, Händel, 326). The opposition of Woman B's husband is a mere foil to the loyalty of Chremes, and his plans—if he pursued them —come to nothing. At any rate he does not reappear.

746–7 ἐγώ . . . τἀμά; 'shall *I* (am *I* to) give up *my* goods?' The tense connotes resentment at the course which is proposed to one, cf. *Av.* 369 φεισόμεσθα γάρ τι τῶνδε μᾶλλον ἡμεῖς ἢ λύκων; **κακοδαίμων ἄρα . . . κεκτημένος:** 'I'll be finished, in that case, and a fool.' Cf. 760: 323, 460 nn. **νοῦν ὀλίγον κεκτημένος:** not like the sophists with their thriftiness that Strepsiades approves of (*Nu.* 834): μηδὲν εἴπῃς φλαῦρον ἄνδρας . . . | νοῦν ἔχοντας.

748–9 μὰ τὸν Ποσειδῶ γ': in such expressions (451 n.) γε more often attaches to the word stressed, not the oath, μὰ τὴν Ἀφροδίτην οὐδέποτέ γ' (*Lys.* 252). But change is needless (οὐδέποτέ γ', Porson, involving synizesis of -ω ου-), *Th.* 225 οὐ γὰρ μὰ τὴν Δήμητρά γ' ἐνταυθοῖ μενῶ. See J. Werres, *Die Beteuerungsformeln in der attischen Komödie* (Bonn, 1936), 20 n. 12, and (for fourth foot anapaest) 62. **αὐτά:** things in general, 'the situation'. The word seems natural enough, as repre-senting the matters in the man's head at the moment. Cf. the vague Thucydidean use of αὐτά, (for example) vi. 10. 5.

750–2 φειδωλίαν: 'thriftiness' (in good sense, cf. *Nu.* 835, representing the speaker's own opinion). Cf. φειδωλός, Lys. i. 7. But those who here denote the speaker as φειδωλός (following manuscripts, see apparatus criticus 746) presumably intend it to mean 'niggard' (*Pl.* 237, Plutus speaking): 'if I ever by chance entered the house of a φειδωλός, he immediately buried me deep down underground.'

182   COMMENTARY

οὐδὲν πρὸς ἔπος: 'for nothing' (literally, 'for no word'), without a
firm promise in exchange. For the connotation of ἔπος, see A. *Pr.*
1032 ψευδηγορεῖν γὰρ οὐκ ἐπίσταται στόμα | τὸ Δῖον, ἀλλὰ πᾶν ἔπος
τελεῖ. ἐκβαλῶ: 'throw *away*', *Lys.* 155 ὁ γῶν Μενέλαος . . . ἐξέβαλ'
. . . τὸ ξίφος. ἐκπύθωμαι: this compound verb seldom differs from
the simple. But perhaps here the prefix should be stressed, 'make *full*
inquiries', A. *Pers.* 955 οἰοιοῖ . . . πάντ' ἐκπεύθου.

753–5 οὗτος: 372 n.   τί . . . βούλεται; what do they mean?, 368 n.
τὰ σκευάρια ταυτὶ: 'these bits of pots and pans here' (27 n.), cf. *Pax* 201
τὰ λοιπὰ τηρῶ σκευάρια τὰ τῶν θεῶν, | χυτρίδια καὶ σανίδια κἀμφορείδια.
μετοικιζόμενος: 'flitting', 'changing house' (see 544 n.).   ἐξενήνοχας:
744 n.   ἐνέχυρα θήσων: 'to put them out to pledge' (see 567 n.), cf.
Pl. 450 ποῖον γὰρ οὐ θώρακα, ποίαν δ' ἀσπίδα | οὐκ ἐνέχυρον τίθησιν ἡ
μιαρωτάτη;

756–7 Then why this processional line-up? are they going to Hiero, for
auction?   τί δῆτ'; 24 n.   οὔ τι μὴν . . . πέμπετε; 'you're never
sending them to Hiero?' For οὐ μήν introducing an incredulous
alternative when an earlier suggestion is rejected see E. *Alc.* 518
(*GP* 334). There is no parallel for τι so placed in *questions*: cf. however
A. *A.* 1640, which also illustrates (see Fraenkel ad loc.) the common
confusion of μήν/μή. οὔ τι μὴ (the reading of all manuscripts here) is
not to be twisted into meaning (οὐ δεινὸν μὴ . . . πέμπετε, Hermann):
the text is a tentative correction. The scholiast explains the context
rightly: Κῆρυξ οὗτος (Hiero) ὅστις τὰ πιπρασκόμενα ἐκήρυττε, τὸ δὲ
πομπὴν ὅτι ὡς ἐν πομπῇ αὐτὰ ἐξάγει. Cf. Hdt. vi. 121. 2 'Callias alone
of the Athenians brought himself to buy up (Pisistratus') property,
when it was put up for auction by the State' (κηρυσσόμενα ὑπὸ τοῦ
δημοσίου), Lucian, *Am.* 39 ὡς δὲ ἐπὶ δημοτελοῦς πομπῆς ἄλλο τις ἄλλη
τῶν ὑπηρετουσῶν ἐγκεχείρισται, λεκανίδας ἀργυρᾶς καὶ προχόους . . .
κῆρυξ, 'praeco', cf. Hor. *Ars* 419 'ut praeco ad merces turbam qui
cogit emendas . . .'   πομπὴν πέμπετε; 'are you people' (i.e. Chremes
and the slaves)'arranging a procession?' So Dicaeopolis (at the
Rural Dionysia), τήνδε τὴν πομπὴν ἐμὲ | πέμψαντα (*Ach.* 248).

758–9 μὰ Δί' ἀλλ': 158 n.   ἀποφέρειν: 'carry them off' to the agora
(857, 859), but also (for Chremes) 'hand them over as required'. So
(for example) Hdt. iv. 64. 1 '[a Scythian] ἀποφέρει to the king the
heads of everyone he kills in the battle.'   τοὺς δεδογμένους νόμους:
763, 455 n.

760–1 The man is astounded: 'You're going to pay up?'   κακοδαίμων
. . . εἶ: 746 n. The *present* expresses his absolute conviction that
Chremes is already 'a dead duck'.   νὴ τὸν Δία τὸν σωτῆρα: the
choice of oath may be suggested by the feeling that Chremes (to *his*
mind) will *need* salvation. Cf. 79, 1045. There is also an implicit
prayer that he himself may be rescued from such a situation. It is
probably fortuitous that the attribute of Σωτήρ is confined to the plays

from 411 onwards: though Ehrenberg thinks that there may be a connection with 'the general deterioration of the political and economic conditions' (271 n. 2). **πῶς; . . . ῥᾳδίως:** Chremes' *πῶς;* (ambiguous, 524) could be interpreted (a) *πῶς κακοδαίμων;* (126), (b) *πῶς;* sc. *λέγεις* (*Pax* 698). Woman *B*'s husband answers question (a): *ῥᾳδίως*, 'you won't have any trouble' (cf. *Ra.* 642). The slight illogicality is readily explicable since *εἶ* (see above) in practice means 'you *will* be'. For the second *πῶς;* (not *ὅπως, V.* 48 and commonly) cf. *Nu.* 664 (in manuscripts), for the questioner's interrogative repeated by the questioned, *Ra.* 1424.

762–8 Chremes is prepared (like Socrates, Pl. *Cri.* 50 a ff.) to act in obedience to the laws: the other thinks such obedience folly. **τί δ';** in genuine surprise (see 135 n.). **οὐχὶ . . . δεῖ;** cf. his patriotic sentiments, 471–2. Similarly, Creon in E. *Ph.* 1648 *πῶς; τἀντεταλμέν' οὐ δίκαιον ἐκπονεῖν;* **ποίοισιν;** not that he doesn't know of them, but simply indicating his refusal to regard the laws as binding ('laws, indeed', cf. *Ra.* 529). There and elsewhere the noun used by the previous speaker is repeated. **ὦ δύστηνε:** 'my poor fellow', expressing the pity of contempt (*Lys.* 699). **τοῖς δεδογμένοις:** 759, 455 n. **ὡς . . . ἄρα:** '*what* a fool you are then' (as is plain to me now). Imperfect with *ἄρα* is thus used of a truth that has just been brought home to the speaker: cf. *V.* 451 *σὺ δ' ἀχάριστος ἦσθ' ἄρα* ('you have no sense of gratitude, I see'). **οὐ γάρ;** 'well, aren't you?' (sc. *ἀνόητος εἶ*), cf. *Av.* 1525 Pi. 'are there some other gods, barbarians, up above you?' Pr. '*οὐ γάρ εἰσι βάρβαροι*, since Execestides' ancestral god is from there?' **μὲν οὖν:** i.e. 'not just . . . but actually . . .' 377 n., cf. 1102. The meaning in 768 is 'on the contrary', 'the ool, you mean' (111 n.). **ἀπαξαπάντων:** 217 n. **τὸ ταττόμενον:** i.e. by law, cf. Pl. *La.* 199 *ἃ καὶ ὁ νόμος οὕτω τάττει.*

769–76 Chremes' innocence is further mocked. The people will bring their goods (they *say* so): the other will believe it when he sees it.

769–70 φυλάξομαι: 'I'll keep a look-out', i.e. 'be on my guard' (*Lys.* 631). The effective meaning is, 'I'll move with caution' (*δοκεῖ . . . βέλτιον εἶναι φυλαττομένους πορεύεσθαι, X. Cyr.* v. 2. 30), hence followed by *πρὶν ἄν* with the subjunctive. He explains his idea more fully, 788–90.

771–2 τί γὰρ ἄλλο γ' ἤ: 395 n. The *γάρ* expresses surprise (377) that any such question should arise. **ἰδὼν ἐπειθόμην:** he quotes directly a proverbial expression (Brunck's addition of *ἄν* is a mistake) to mean 'I'll believe it when I see it.' So Xanthias, ending Dionysus' heroics: *κᾆτ' ἔγωγ' ἐξηγρόμην (Ra.* 51). Cf. Theoc. 15. 25.

773–6 λέγουσι . . . ἐν ταῖς ὁδοῖς: he presumably had overheard discussions on his way back from the Pnyx (372 n.). **γοῦν:** 'at any rate' (357 n.), i.e. whatever may be true. **λέξουσι γάρ:** 'oh yes, they'll talk all right', 'assentient' *γάρ*, with a word from the previous speech repeated. The accumulation in this passage (cf. in general 221–8, which also parallels the assonance, 799–803) has suggested that parody is intended of a usage now coming into fashion (*GP* lxvii, 88). See Pl. *R.* 433 a, X. *Mem.* iii. 5. 11 οἳ δὴ καὶ λέγονται πολὺ διενεγκεῖν τῶν καθ' αὐτοὺς ἀνθρώπων. Λέγονται γάρ, ἔφη. **οἴσειν ἀράμενοι**: cf. *Ra.* 525 ἀλλ' ἀράμενος οἴσεις πάλιν τὰ στρώματα. **ἀπολεῖς**: 'you'll be the death of me', *Pl.* 390. The reply (if not intended as mere nonsense) may suggest 'the citizens, too, you'll find, will be distrustful.' **ὁ Ζεὺς . . . ἐπιτρίψειεν**: γ' is attracted to the pronoun (*GP* 122), but the emphasis is 'may Zeus *destroy* you.' Again, the answer is perhaps not quite nonsensical: the citizens will 'kill' the plan. The following line to some extent supports this.

777–83 To give in this way is not in nature, whether human (Athenian) or divine.

778–9 οὐ γὰρ . . . νὴ Δία: the thriftiness of the Athenian is caricatured, *Ra.* 980 ff. And an ancient proverb claims he holds his hand out (cf. 782) on his deathbed (*PG* i. 216). Cf. 185, 206. The point is spoiled by the attribution of ἀλλὰ . . . δεῖ to Chremes as a question, J. C. B. Lowe, *Hermes*, xcv (1967), 66–71: cf. H.-J. Newiger, *Hermes*, xcvi, (1968), 122, who remarks (*a*) on the double point at δεῖ (RΓΛMu1 Vb1), (*b*) the late position of νὴ Δία (which surely, however, emphasizes δεῖ, 'we *must* only take, if we want to do as gods do': and cf. *V.* 134, *Lys.* 777). But Newiger's further punctuation τίν'; (double point RΓΛMu1Vb1) in 777 is attractive (cf. *Pl.* 478). With the answer—which he sees as finally nonsensical—in 776 the pattern changes: Chremes now *replies* (twice) to the other man, till finally bested (779) by the clinching argument about the gods.

779–83 καὶ γὰρ οἱ θεοί: sc. λαμβάνουσι μόνον. Cf. *Eq.* 251 (for the ellipsis), ἀλλὰ παῖε . . . καὶ γὰρ ἡμεῖς . . . But there καί means 'also' (280), here is best translated 'even' (*Ra.* 797). The charge here laid against the gods in general is justified of Hermes in the *Plutus*: he is there portrayed as completely egocentric (*Pl.* 1118–19), with no thought but his personal advantage (πατρὶς γάρ ἐστι πᾶσ' ἵν' ἂν πράττῃ τις εὖ, ibid. 1151). Similarly in *Peace* he is greeted (*Pax* 193) as γλίσχρων, and himself admits to a softness for gold vessels (ibid. 425). **ὅταν . . . τἀγαθά**: *Th.* 310, X. *Mem.* i. 3. 2 καὶ εὔχετο δὲ πρὸς τοὺς θεοὺς ἁπλῶς τἀγαθὰ διδόναι. The article (as that passage indicates) implies 'their blessings, not the evils that they *could* give'. **ἐκτείνοντα τὴν χεῖρ' ὑπτίαν**: as the venal prytanis holds out his right hand (*Th.* 936) cf. *AP* xii. 212. 3, Tib. ii. 4. 14. Of the pose here attributed to deity, I have found no clear example extant: it is presupposed, however, in the words of Pisthetaerus (*Av.* 518), 'when in sacrificing one places the innards in their' (i.e. the gods') 'hand, as is the custom'. And cf. the marble statue of the goddess (*c.* 480 B.C.) from Tarentum (Richter, *Handbook*, 85, fig. 101). The power of gifts over gods and men was recognized in an old saying: δῶρα θεοὺς πείθει, δῶρ' αἰδοίους βασιλῆας (Pl. *R.* 390 e, cf. Hes. *Op.* 263–4). Plato's Guardians would not be taught it.

784–90 Chremes, impatient of such blasphemy, begs leave to complete his preparations. Woman *B*'s husband repeats his own belief in waiting for the others, and then—waiting.

784–5 ὦ δαιμόνι' ἀνδρῶν: the vocative here (see 564 n.) implies both remonstrance and entreaty, 'let me get on with *something*' (515). 'Socrates, with his Attic urbanity, makes use of this form of address in a dialogue with a rude opponent who is completely unworthy of him', E. Brunius-Nilsson, *Δαιμόνιε* (Uppsala, 1955), 143. Perhaps we may say the same of Chremes, but he seems to be only just holding himself in (804, 809, 833).   **ἔα:** one syllable, by synizesis (8 n.): cf. *Nu.* 932.   **τῶν προὔργου:** the things on hand, see *Pl.* 622 τι τῶν προὔργου ποιεῖν.   **ταυτὶ:** the line of utensils, which he points to (27 n.).   **ποῦ μοῦσθ' ἱμάς;** to a slave. μοῦσθ', i.e. μοί ἐστι (crasis), 1006, 1029.

786–90 ὄντως γὰρ οἴσεις; γάρ of incredulity (717), cf. *Pl.* 286 ὄντως γὰρ ἔστι πλουσίοις ἡμῖν ἅπασιν εἶναι; The answering μὲν οὖν ('yes, and more than that') is illustrated *Pl.* 287.   **καὶ δή:** 'here and now' (as 581 n.).   **τωδὶ . . . τὼ τρίποδε:** 785, 744.   **τῆς μωρίας:** genitive of exclamation ('oh, the folly'). The words τὸ μηδὲ . . . ἐπαναμένειν may be (*a*) explanatory of the folly, cf. *Nu.* 818, (*b*) themselves exclamatory ('to think of your not waiting') cf. *Ra.* 741.   **περιμείναντα:** 'hang around' (517) for the others to move first.   **ὅ τι | δράσουσιν:** cf. 259, 946.   **τηνικαῦτ' ἤδη:** 'then and only then' ('tum demum'), cf. Pl. *Alc. II* 150 e . . . δεῖν ἀπὸ τῆς ψυχῆς πρῶτον τὴν ἀχλὺν ἀφελόντα . . . τὸ τηνικαῦτ' ἤδη προσφέρειν δι' ὧν μέλλεις γνώσεσθαι ἡμὲν κακὸν ἠδὲ καὶ ἐσθλόν.   **τί δρᾶν;** 467 n.   **ἐπαναμένειν:** 'wait longer' (493), ἐπανέμειναν . . . διατρίβοντες, Hdt. viii. 141. 2. It is παρὰ προσδοκίαν for καταθεῖναι. Cf. 31 n., 155.   **διατρίβειν ἔτι:** '*still* put time in'. Cf. Hdt. loc. cit.

791–3 But *why* wait? asks Chremes. The question of a madman: might not some natural calamity or other ill omen supervene?   **ἵνα δὴ τί;** 719, 604 nn., cf. *Nu.* 1192.   **εἰ . . . πολλάκις:** 'si forte', cf. 1105, Pl. *Phd.* 60 e καὶ ἀφοσιούμενος εἰ ἄρα πολλάκις ταύτην τὴν μουσικήν μοι ἐπιτάττοι ποιεῖν. For an earth tremor (σεισμός) as an omen, see (among numerous examples) Th. vi. 95. 1 (causing the Spartans to turn back from Cleonae), for lightning (πῦρ ἀπότροπον) *Nu.* 583 (on Cleon's election as στρατηγός), for both in combination (warning off Agesipolis) X. *HG* iv. 7. 4 ff. (cf. Paus. iii. 5. 9). Had such things as these which the dissident now hopes for occurred while the Assembly was in session, the new law might never have been passed: they would certainly have led to an adjournment (Th. v. 45. 4). But he evidently feels that the bulk of the Athenians (like the Theophrastan δεισιδαίμων) could still be deterred by lesser omens, *Char.* 16. 3 (where see my note): 'if a polecat (924 n.) runs across the road (sc. τὴν ὁδὸν here with διάξειεν), he does not move forward till some (other) crosses over or he throws three stones across the roadway.' Cf. Origen *Cels.* 4. 93 (tr. H. Chadwick, 1953, p. 258 n. 4).   **παύσαιντ' ἂν ἐσφέροντες**: the literal sense of ἐσφέροντες ('bringing in', 866) here predominates (808 n.).   **ὡμβρόντητε σύ**: 'you head-case', Philem. fr. 44, 3. ἐμβρόντητος, literally 'thunder-struck', i.e. out of one's right mind: 'the claps of thunder made them ἔκφρονας' (Paus. loc. cit.).

794–6 Chremes says he would look a fine one if he waited and then arrived to find no room left. Woman *B*'s husband (from his knowledge of Athenians) reassures him.   **χαρίεντα γοῦν**: ironical (95 n.), E. *Ph.* 618 χαρτὰ γοῦν πάσχω, τέκνον.   **'χοιμ'**: 40 n.   **καταθείην**: Brunck, for MSS.' καταθείμην (-θοίμην Vb1). The middle is not impossible (cf. *Pax* 1207), but the sudden change from the active, which is used throughout the passage, is both unnecessary and unlikely. Possibly the μ became inserted by the scribe's eye moving forward to the μή.   **μὴ γὰρ . . . ὅποι;** interpretation starts from the assumption that the words are closely connected with what follows, i.e. they are a preface to his θάρρει. I consequently print a question-mark (with Glypheus), keep the optative (λάβῃς, Heindorf), and translate (sc. ἐδεδοίκεις, with Van Daele), 'You wouldn't find a *place*?' (Was *that* your fear?). He now understands, that is, the reason for the hurry (so far incomprehensible) of Chremes: and incredulously (γάρ, 786) takes his words up, with λάβοις as a substitute for ἔχοις (cf. 799). Others (in the light of 778) attempt to interpret 'take', 'receive'; but the words cannot be twisted into meaning.   **ἔνης**: there will still be room 'the day after tomorrow' (*Ach.* 172).   **τιή**; 'what do you mean?' 1086.

797–8 **χειροτονοῦντας . . . ἀρνουμένους**: Blepyrus spoke earlier (473) of the δυσβουλία of the Athenians. Here they are branded by Woman *B*'s husband as ταχύβουλοι and μετάβουλοι, as Aristophanes himself had found them, *Ach.* 630–2 (cf. Pl. Com. fr. 220, Isoc. viii. 52). Perhaps among his present audience (τούτους) were some of those same people he had thus addressed in 424. For their speediness in passing resolutions, and reluctance to follow them with action, see D. xiii. 32 'As a result, our public affairs are such that if anyone read out your resolutions, and then, after that, went through your actions, no one would believe that the same men were behind both the decrees and the performance.' For specific examples, 814.

799–806 Chremes still believes that the Athenians will co-operate: if any don't, the 'loyalists' will fight them. Goaded to rudeness by the other's taunting questions, he restates his determination firmly, his resolution strengthened by the sight of his neighbours bringing *their* goods.

799–801 οἴσουσιν, ὦ τᾶν: 'they'll bring them, friend' (Rogers) exactly
reproduces the dismissive and contemptuous tone of ὦ τᾶν (cf. 830,
858). **ἦν δὲ . . . τί;** cf. 468, 862–4 (where Chremes adopts the
technique of his opponent), and (in general) 221–8, 772–6. Note the
substitution of κομίζω for φέρω (cf. the similar substitution of λαμβάνω
for ἔχω, 795). **ἀμέλει:** 'don't worry about that.' So *Nu.* 877
ἀμέλει δίδασκε (i.e. 'just get on with the teaching'). This reply is un-
satisfactory; accordingly, the question is repeated (we should not
read κωλύωσι, Coulon).   **μαχούμεθ':** we, the patriotic citizens, who
will (he assumes) be the majority.

802 ἄπειμ' ἐάσας: 'I'll walk away and leave them.' Chremes (like the
chorus, 261) is not prepared to push things to the limit. *He* will have
done his patriotic duty by bringing his goods in as instructed. ἄπει
μ' ἐάσας; (Tyrwhitt: Μυι?) is neat, but needless. Some regard the
following question as mere nonsense: but surely it marks another
aspect of this man's beliefs about Athenians? They won't *contribute*
goods, they'd rather *get* them, or, at any rate, the non-subscribing
party will be *stronger*: and if Chremes *does* give *his* goods in, they'll *sell*
them (αὐτά, i.e. τὰ κατατεθέντα). In other words, like Cleon, they will
show no opposition to 'reaping another person's harvest' (*Eq.* 391–4).
Cf. (for general structure) 863.

803–4 διαρραγείης: 'damn you' (literally, 'may you burst', 370), cf. *Av.*
1257.   **καλῶς ποιήσεις:** 'you'll be doing me a good turn', cf. *Pl.* 863
νὴ Δία καλῶς τοίνυν ποιῶν ἀπόλλυται.

804–6 ἐπιθυμήσεις φέρειν; 'will you *really* want to bring them?', the
future expressing (cf. 746) both incredulity and indignation.   **ἔγωγε:**
60 n.   **καὶ γὰρ:** 148 n.   **γείτονας | ὁρῶ:** these neighbours,
of course, like the 'many other women' (52) do not appear in the
orchestra.

806–10 Antisthenes and Callimachus are no doubt very likely to contribute! The former would suffer excruciating pain first: the latter has
nothing that he *could* bring. He could bring more than Callias, says
Chremes.   **γ' ἂν οὖν:** ironical, cf. *Eq.* 344 καλῶς γ' ἂν οὖν σὺ πρᾶγμα
προσπεσόν σοι . . . μεταχειρίσαιο χρηστῶς.   **αὑτ':** loosely, 'his
belongings' (802).   **εἰσενέγκοι:** 'contribute' for the city's use (810,
Lys. 651). Cf. the use (more literal), 793.   **πολύ . . . ἐμμελέστερον:**
'it would suit his tune much better', though causing him much
suffering because of his chronic constipation (cf. 366–8). He would
not (even so) be rivalling the King (*Ach.* 81–2) who εἰς ἀπόπατον
ᾤχετο . . . κἄχεζεν ὀκτὼ μῆνας ἐπὶ χρυσῶν ὁρῶν.   **πλεῖν ἢ τριάκονθ'**
ἡμέρας: cf. *Ach.* 858, Men. fr. 118.   **οἴμωζε:** Chremes, unable to
deny that his opponent is right about Antisthenes, just curses (*Av.*
1572). See 648, 942 n. Of Callimachus we can say nothing, except
(with the scholiast) οὗτος πένης: perhaps he of Isoc. xviii? It is pure
conjecture that he served as 'chorus-trainer' (appointed συγκροτεῖν καὶ

διδάσκειν τὸν χορόν, D. xxi. 17) with Antisthenes as choregus (366 n.). **αὐτοῖσιν**: i.e. the authorities. **πλείω Καλλίου**: 'more than Callias' who was preyed on (*Av.* 284) for his riches, and whose own dissipation (*Ra.* 432) had reduced his inheritance from two hundred talents down to barely two (Lys. xix. 48). See further *PA* 7826.

811–33 Chremes will ruin himself if he persists: does he not remember the decrees concerning salt, copper coinage, and (property?) taxation? Indeed, yes, he suffered from the second: but that was when *men* were still in power. The other replies (831) with an obscenity, and Chremes, whose patience is finally exhausted, bids a slave make preparations for departure.

811–14 ἄνθρωπος οὗτος: he speaks half aside, like Bdelycleon, ἄνθρωπος οὗτος μέγα τι δρασείει κακόν (*V.* 168). **δεινά γε λέγεις**: 'that's putting it *strongly*', *Lys.* 499. **ὥσπερ οὐχ ὁρῶν**: sc. λέγεις. **τοιαῦτα . . . ψηφίσματα**: he proceeds (like D. xiii. 32 ff.) to give examples. **οἶσθ'**: know by remembering, 816. **οὕδοξε**: ὃ ἔδοξε (455 n.). The decree, like the others, is unknown. Salt was imported from Megara (cf. *Ach.* 521): the measure (says the scholiast) was meant to bring its price down, but never put into operation.

815–22 ἔγωγε: 60 n. **τοὺς χαλκοῦς δ' ἐκείνους**: the silver mines at Laurium had ceased working when the Spartans captured Decelea (cf. the advice of Alcibiades, Th. vi. 91. 7). The closure was not permanent (cf. X. *Vect.* vi. 4, and for fourth-century mining leases see Margaret Crosby in *Hesperia* xix [1950], 189–312). But the subsequent shortage of silver brought silver-plated bronze coins (bronze being used for very small denominations) into circulation (τὰ πονηρὰ χαλκία, *Ra.* 725). See Head, 375, Ehrenberg, pl. XVIII c. Some (as van Leeuwen) think this decree too distant for Aristophanes to mention here: though τὸ ἔναγχος, 823, (as Rogers notes) suggests that the other schemes were *not* so recent. The reference (I think) is the correct one, but we still know nothing of the swift change (822) back to silver. And a χαλκοῦς was certainly in use in the fourth century (D. xlii. 22, Alex. fr. 15. 2: cf. Eub. fr. 83). **ἤνίκα . . . οὐκ οἶσθα;** cf. *Lys.* 1150 οὐκ ἴσθ' ὅθ' ὑμᾶς οἱ Λάκωνες αὖθις αὖ | . . . ἀπώλεσαν; For the use of οἶδα here see 814. **καὶ . . . γε**: 140 n. **μεστὴν . . . ἔχων**: for the custom in general cf. *Av.* 503 (where Euelpides swallows inadvertently the obol he is holding in his mouth), Thphr. *Char.* 6. 9, for coins so carried by a 'fruiterer' Alex. fr. 128. 7 ὁ δ' ἐγκάψας τὸ κέρμ' εἰς τὴν γνάθον . . . **ἀπῆρα**: a verb much used of sailing (Th. viii. 100. 1): Rogers translates 'I steered away'. Or does English colloquial 'I pushed off' come nearer? **εἰς ἀγορὰν**: 62 n. **ἐπ' ἄλφιτα**: 'to get barley', *Ra.* 1418 κατῆλθον ἐπὶ ποιητήν. Chremes does the shopping: he perhaps cannot afford (see 62 n.) an ἀγοραστής (X. *Mem.* i. 5. 2, cf. Thphr. *Char.* 18. 2). To do one's own marketing was normally looked on with disfavour (for example, it marks the ἀνελεύθερος, ibid. 22. 7). **ὑπέχοντος . . .**

LINES 811–829   189

θύλακον: 'when I was just' (ἄρτι, cf. *Av.* 494) 'holding out my meal-bag' (382 n.).   ὑπέχοντος: 'holding *under*', to catch the meal: cf. *Ach.* 1063.   ἀνέκραγ': 431 n.

823–9 Then again there was that recent tax, a *great* thing when Euripides proposed it, but soon the cause of bitterness against him. Euripides (unknown, but perhaps the poet's son) appears (on the evidence of this passage) to have acted as one of the πορισταί (i.e. 'fiscal procurators', 825 n.), and in that capacity to have levied a tax of 2½ per cent (on property?) in order to raise five hundred talents. This seemed a reasonable levy at the time for a purpose (one assumes) they all agreed with: Euripides' 'budget' was acclaimed. But once it appeared that the sum was unobtainable—another miscalculation 'at the top'— they were ready to turn round and tar him.

823–6 τὸ δ' ἔναγχος: 'lately', cf. *Nu.* 639.   τῆς τετταρακοστῆς: sc. μοιρᾶς, cf. 1007. The genitive is one of origin—the city would raise five hundred talents from the tax. Euripides (says scholiast) ἔγραψε τεσσαρακοστὴν εἰσενεγκεῖν ἀπὸ τῆς οὐσίας εἰς τὸ κοινόν. Such direct taxes (εἰσφοραί, Jones, 23–30, de Ste Croix, 31) were levied to help meet emergency expenses: 'the Athenians needed money for the siege (of Mytilene), even though they had for the first time raised an ἐσφορά of two hundred talents' (Th. iii. 19. 1, cf. D. l. 8). Taxes of 1 and 2 per cent are mentioned: in 354 B.C., to raise five hundred talents, 8½ per cent would have been needed (D. xiv. 27). These taxes were repeatedly demanded in the course of the Corinthian War, and by this date two had been already levied (Isoc. xvii. 41). It is not clear, however, that *Euripides'* measure was an εἰσφορά: possibly it represented a novel form of indirect taxation. See Thomsen, 184. ἐπόρισ': 'raised as a ποριστής' (*Ra.* 1505). The earliest mention of the office of ποριστής is in Antiphon vi. 49: and it may have been in that capacity that Cleophon τὴν διωβελίαν ἐπόρισε πρῶτος (*Ath. Pol.* 28. 3). Cf. 236 n., D. xiv. 26 (below). For Euripides Bergk proposed Heurippides (*IG* ii². 145. 3). But cf. Diph. fr. 60. 1 (a possible reference to this passage) εὖ γ' ὁ κατάχρυσος εἶπε πόλλ' Εὐριπίδης.   κατεχρύσου: 'was for gilding' (cf. 219 n., 829), 'was loud in praise of him', cf. *Nu.* 912 χρυσῷ πάττων μ' οὐ γιγνώσκεις (i.e. when you call me πατραλοίας).

827–9 ὅτε δὴ δ': 'but when finally' (195 n.) 'they looked at the thing closely' (ἀνα-, cf. *Ra.* 978) 'and it seemed to be just the same old story . . .' i.e. the constant call for taxes, which as constantly turned out insufficient. For the folly of inadequate taxation, cf. D. xiv. 26 'all that you could raise' (πορίσαιτ' ἄν) 'at the moment would be more ridiculous than nothing.'   ὁ Διὸς Κόρινθος: of an oft-repeated cry, ἀλλ' ἦ Διὸς Κόρινθος ἐν τοῖς στρώμασιν (*Ra.* 443), 'it's always "baggage".' Corinthian ambassadors to Megara appear to have harped on this chauvinistic slogan (scholiast on Pi. *N.* 7. 105), from which time it passed into a proverb.   ἤρκεσεν (MSS.) gives good

190 COMMENTARY

sense (see 823–9 n.); ἤρεσεν (Scaliger, cf. Bauck, 57), i.e. they regretted their decision. **κατεπίττου**: 'was for tarring', 826. κατα- suggests 'from head to foot', 'all over', Cratin. fr. 189 ὄψῃ γὰρ αὐτὴν . . . καταπιττουμένην. For tarring as a punishment cf. 1109, Pl. *Grg.* 473 c.

830–3 ὦ τᾶν: 799 n. **μὴ κατουρήσωσι**: the κατα- compound is suggested by those in 826 and 829, the sentiment perhaps by talk of 'pitch', ἀλλ᾽ ἐς κάδον λαβών τιν᾽ οὔρει πίττινον (fr. 269). Such compounds have been regarded as examples of colloquialism (Lottich, 14). **οὐκ οἶδ᾽ ὅ τι ληρεῖς**: so frequently τί ληρεῖς; (*Nu.* 500), cf. (for expression) 989. **τἀνάφορον**: the pole used by a slave (cf. *Ra.* 8) to carry baggage. See Ehrenberg, pl. XIV c. **ὁ παῖς**: for vocative (see 734 n.), the article imparting an authoritative tone. Similarly *Ra.* 521.

834 Praxagora (as promised, 717) has set the public meal on foot already: her newly appointed 'heraldess' (713 n.) now enters to 'cry' it to the people. This she seems to do in imitation of tragic style and language (see below): the passage is omitted from the list in A. C. Schlesinger, 'Indications of Parody in Aristophanes', *TAPhA* lxvii (1936), 308. Manuscripts (see apparatus criticus) describe her (correctly, cf. 491) as κῆρυξ: we should not (with Le Febvre) introduce here Praxagora's coinage κηρύκαινα. Cf. *Th.* 295.

834–7 ὦ πάντες ἀστοί: *Lys.* 638. See S. *Ant.* 1183, E. *IT* 1422. For parody (as here) of tragic *rhesis* see Rau, 162 ff., 166. **νῦν γὰρ . . . ἔχει**: i.e. I say 'all you citizens' for (3 n.) you *all* of you *are* invited now. Before this (as Rogers explains, rightly) invitations to public banquets were an honour bestowed upon a few distinguished people: cf. the herald's proclamation (*Ach.* 124) τὸν βασιλέως ὀφθαλμὸν ἡ βουλὴ καλεῖ | ἐς τὸ πρυτανεῖον. **χωρεῖτ᾽, ἐπείγεσθ᾽**: cf. E. *Or.* 1258 χωρεῖτ᾽ ἐπειγώμεσθ᾽. So, in like circumstances Dicaeopolis is urged by a messenger to hurry (*Ach.* 1088). The whole of that passage may be quoted as relevant to 836–45: ἀλλ᾽ ἐγκόνει· δειπνεῖν κατακωλύεις πάλαι. | τὰ δ᾽ ἄλλα πάντ᾽ ἐστὶν παρεσκευασμένα, | κλῖναι τράπεζαι προσκεφάλαια στρώματα | στέφανοι μύρον τραγήμαθ᾽, αἱ πόρναι πάρα, | ἄμυλοι πλακοῦντες σησαμοῦντες ἴτρια, | ὀρχηστρίδες, τὰ φίλταθ᾽ Ἁρμοδίου, καλαί. | ἀλλ᾽ ὡς τάχιστα σπεῦδε. **εὐθὺ τῆς στρατηγίδος**: 'straight to the general', cf. fr. 161 ἦσαν εὐθὺ τοῦ Διονυσίου. ἡ στρατηγίς, 'la générale' (870). New conditions mean changes (see 727 n.) in language. The word is cited also from Pherecr. (fr. 141 Β). **κληρουμένοις**: 682 n. **ὅποι**: the use may be explained by the underlying sense of motion, 'where you will (go and) dine'. Cf. S. *OC* 23 ἔχεις διδάξαι δή μ᾽ ὅποι καθέσταμεν; But of course confusion of ὅποι/ὅπου (Β) is very easy: cf. *Ach.* 950.

838–40 ὡς αἱ τράπεζαί γ᾽ . . . παρεσκευασμέναι: *Ach.* 1089 (above). For the common idiomatic ὡς . . . γε (the particle retaining little force) cf. *Ach.* 346, *GP* 143. **ἐπινενησμέναι**, so Brunck, 'heaped high (with)', cf. *Nu.* 1203. Similarly, Pherecr. fr. 190 βριθομέν⟨ης πάντ⟩ων ἀγαθῶν ἐπί⟨μεστα⟩ τραπέζης. Manuscripts' ἐπινενασμέναι (cf. their νενασμέναι, 840) is (a) known only in Hesychius, ἐπινάξαι· ἐπιπακτῶσαι (i.e. 'shut to', fr. 721), (b) if this is its true meaning, inappropriate, (c) on the analogy of νάττω should properly refer to a container, ἔναττον οὖν οἱ παῖδες εἰς τὰς . . . σπυρίδας (Hippolochus, Ath. 130 b). κλῖναι . . . νενησμέναι: so Brunck (cf. 838) for manuscripts' νενασμέναι. The latter is not to be supported by Josephus' πᾶσα . . . ὁπλιτῶν οἰκία νένακτο (BJ i. 17. 6), a parallel late and specious (see above). κλῖναι: 'dining-couches', Ach. 1090 (contrast 418, 909). The ancient evidence on couches is surveyed by Pritchett, 'The Attic Stelai II', Hesperia xxv (1956), 226–33. They are often represented on the vases: see Ehrenberg, pl. VIII b, Richter [734 n.], 52 ff., figs. 290–340. σισυρῶν καὶ δαπίδων: see (for the former) 347 n., (for the latter, woollen 'rugs' or 'coverlets') Pl. 528, and further in Pritchett, 246.

For the homoeoteleuta (very common in the plays) in 838–40 cf. (for example) Ach. 547–9, 551–4.

841–2 κρατῆρας ἐγκιρνᾶσιν: so Dawes, for R's κρατῆρα συγκιρνᾶσιν (cf. his τίς οὐγκαλυμμός; for τίς ὁ συγκαλυμμός; Av. 1496). For this form of expression, 'they are mixing (wine in) bowls', see Eub. fr. 94. 1 τρεῖς γὰρ μόνους κρατῆρας ἐγκεραννύω, cf. Pi. N. 9. 50. συγκίρνημι is a late verb, and its cognate forms (as συγκεράννυμι) rarely literal (see LSJ s.v.). αἱ μυροπώλιδες: for scent as a concomitant of banquets, cf. Ach. 1091, X. Smp. ii. 3 (where, however, it seems to be regarded as an 'extra', and meets with Socrates' disapproval). These 'sales-staff' are on duty to facilitate the diners, since shopkeepers (including μυροπῶλαι such as Peron, Antiph. fr. 35) would presumably have closed for the occasion. But this may have been a normal service available to guests at a state banquet. ἑστᾶσ' ἐφεξῆς: cf. fr. 66 ἵστασθ' ἐφεξῆς πάντες ἐπὶ τρεῖς ἀσπίδας.

842–4 τὰ τεμάχη ῥιπίζεται: 'the fish-slices (606) are roasting' (scholiast, ἀντὶ τοῦ ὀπτᾶται), sc. on a fire 'fanned' to brightness. For ῥιπίς ('fan' or 'bellows') see Ach. 669, for ῥιπίζω (metaphorical) Ra. 360 (στάσιν) ἀνεγείρει καὶ ῥιπίζει. λαγῷ ἀναπηγνύασι: 'they are spitting hares', for which delicacy see 1174, Ach. 1006, 1110; for the process, Ach. 1007 'bring the spits, ἵν' ἀναπείρω τὰς κίχλας.' πόπανα πέττεται: women's work, Pl. R. 455 c, cf. 221, 223a nn. πόπανα, cakes often used in sacrifice (Th. 285, cf. Pl. 660, 680) were perhaps a kind of πλακοῦς (223b, Ach. 1092). στέφανοι πλέκονται: for the wearing of garlands at banquets and symposia see 133, 691 nn., Ach. 1091. The practice is often seen on vases (Ehrenberg, pl. VIII b) and their weaving could afford a modest living for such persons as the war-widow left with five small children (Th. 446). φρύγεται τραγήματα: cf. 221, Ra. 510 καὶ τραγήματα | ἔφρυγε. This term (Ach. 1091) denotes dessert dishes such as chick-peas, with which one sipped wine (see 45 n.): 'and we will set before them, I suppose, τραγήματα of figs and chick-peas and

On 893–5: Henderson p. 144

beans, and they will roast myrtle-berries and acorns at the fire, μετρίως ὑποπίνοντες' (Pl. *R.* 372 c).

845–7 χύτρας ἔτνους . . . αἱ νεώταται: pea-soup (ἔτνος) was a favourite with Heracles, at news of whose arrival (*Ra.* 505) Persephone ἧψε . . . χύτρας | . . . δύ' ἢ τρεῖς. 'The youngest girls' will entertain with it (cf. the chorus in *Lys.* 1058) a latter-day Ariphrades (but of whom we know nothing else) called Smoius (τρύβλια 252, *pudenda muliebria*). The point is that their guest will have a preference for meat soup (ζωμός) containing animal fat: which—in another meaning—προσπεσὼν ἐκλάψεται (*Pax* 885).   **ἱππικὴν στολὴν:** 'his riding-suit', with reference to ἱππ- forms used of intercourse, *V.* 502, Machon 362 (Gow), Hsch. s.vv. ἵππον, 'Ἱπποκλείδης.

848–52 Γέρων: Geron (a proper name, *SGDI* 5545. 27: we should not read Γέρης, 932 n.) had seemingly reached the age his name denoted, but now was acting like a young lad : hence the ironical ἑτέρου (849). He has cast aside the old man's shoe (ἐμβάς, 47 n.) and his sober if shabby cloak (τρίβων, *Ach.* 184) in favour of the 'younger' pumps (κονίποδα, στενὸν σανδάλιον, says the scholiast: cf. Bryant, 79, Pritchett, 208) and a gayer and finer mantle (χλανίς, *Av.* 1116). This latter seems to differ from the χλαῖνα (416 n.) as made of better wool (cf. Antiph. fr. 33. 2, where the χλανίς is 'dressy' in an old man) : for the change see *V.* 1131 'put off your τρίβων, and throw on this χλαῖνα . . .' Geron, of course, is not simply aping youthfulness (like the ὀψιμαθής of Thphr. *Char.* 27. 4) : he has taken a new lease of life in his transition from poverty (633 n.) to riches.   **κεῖται:** 'lies there', 'is discarded' (514 n.).   **ὁ . . . φέρων:** citizens are freed from public duties, but male *slaves*, of course, are to continue.   **τὴν μᾶζαν:** the staple food (615 n.) of which at least a man can now be certain.   **ἀλλὰ . . . διοίγνυτε:** cf. S. *Aj.* 344 ἀνὴρ φρονεῖν ἔοικεν. ἀλλ' ἀνοίγετε, 346 ἰδού, διοίγω ('open *wide*'). ἀλλά, in commands and exhortations (*GP* 13) 'expresses a transition from requests for action to a statement of the action required' : cf. 915, 993.

The 'heraldess' probably goes off here to re-enter as the servant-girl (1112). See Introduction § III.

853–62 Woman *B*'s husband can *now* see (cf. 861) his duty clearly : he must make for the dinner straight away. He *will* bring his goods (it is a matter of priorities) and others (he still believes) won't hurry.

853–4 οὐκοῦν: 'if that's how matters stand I'll *go* then.' With this particle, δῆτα appears to stand for δή (*GP* 279). ΓVb1 have οὔκουν (116 n.) : but that combination, though commoner (cf. 1144) is here much less suitable in meaning.   **ἕστηκ' ἔχων:** 'keep standing', 1151.   **ἐπειδὴ . . . δοκεῖ:** he now rivals Chremes in his patriotic sentiments (762–3).

855–7 καὶ ποῖ: καί, of incredulity (457) or indignation (529).   **μὴ καταθεὶς:** 603.   **οὐ δῆτ' . . . ἐνῇ:** 'oh no, you won't' (cf. 373), 'not,

LINES 845-871

193

at least, if they're in their senses' (ἐγὼ γυνὴ μέν εἰμι, νοῦς δ' ἔνεστί μοι, *Lys.* 1124). ἀπενέγκῃς: 758. ἀλλ' ἀποίσω: 'but I'll bring them', i.e. there's no need to get excited, cf. *Lys.* 1028-30 . . . *Xo.* ἀλλὰ δράσω ταῦτα.

858-62 οὐ τοὐμόν . . . ἔσται: 'the obstacle won't be on *my* side' (623 n.). ὦ τᾶν: 799 n. τί δή; 'what do you mean?', cf. Pl. *R.* 357 d. βαδιεῖ δὲ . . . ὅμως; 'and are you really for going, all the same?' δέ, of incredulity (cf. καί, 855), σὲ δὲ ταῦτ' ἀρέσκει; (*Ra.* 103). τί γὰρ πάθω; '(yes), for what am I to do?' (375). He has no choice, like the Sycophant (*Av.* 1432), τί γὰρ πάθω; σκάπτειν γὰρ οὐκ ἐπίσταμαι, and again supports his reasoning with sentiments recalling those of Chremes (471). τὰ δυνατὰ: 'in anything feasible' (like dining). Cf. (for sense) Th. v. 89 τὰ δυνατὰ . . . διαπράσσεσθαι, (for construction) X. *Cyr.* vii. 5. 49 εἰ ταῦτα προθύμως σοι συλλάβοιμι . . .

862-6 Suppose the women try to stop him? He will go for them. Suppose they whip him like a slave? They will be summoned. If they laugh at his threats? He'll *snatch* a dinner. For the series of questions (with the roles reversed) see 799-804. The *general* resemblance is noted by the scholiast (ἐξ ὧν πρώην αὐτὸς μὴ βουλόμενος τὴν οὐσίαν κατα-θεῖναι ἐπηρώτα) : we should not, however, alter manuscripts (see 800 n.) to introduce a *verbal* echo here. ὁμόσ' εἶμι κύψας: 'I'll lower my head and charge', using metaphors from warfare (ὁμόσε ἰέναι, 876, i.e. 'come to close quarters, come to grips with', cf. *Lys.* 451) and wrestling (*Pax* 33). ἢν . . . μαστιγῶσι: i.e. treat you as a disaffected slave. For the practice cf. *Eq.* 64. Chremes does not envisage that the women will proceed to such subsequent treatment as breaking on the wheel (*Pax* 452, cf. *Ra.* 618). They will simply laugh him down (κατα-, 125) when he utters his threat of legal action. καλούμεθ': 'summon' into court, the *middle* of a *plaintiff* (*Nu.* 1221), the *active* of the *judge* (*V.* 851). ἐπὶ ταῖς θύραις . . . τὰ σιτία: i.e. he will stand at the door-ways of the dining-halls and snatch food as people bring it in (ἐσφέρω, 793). The reference here is not to servants (sc. τὰς τραπέζας, cf. *V.* 1216, van Leeuwen) but to citizens contributing their food-supplies as part of their total surrender of possessions (cf. 597-600). For construction (ἁρπάζομαι with accusative and genitive) cf. *Pax* 1118 ἀλλ' ἁρπάσομαι σφῶν αὐτά. κεῖται δ' ἐν μέσῳ (exactly as the man might argue here); for τί δράσεις; (865), 467 n.

867-76 Chremes dismisses the man curtly with a quip, and this time (833) takes his departure (he leaves by the right-hand entrance, 282 n.). The other, left alone in meditation, soon arrives at a plan that pleases him (875 n.). But he does not reveal (or implement) it.

867-71 βάδιζε . . . ὕστερος: 'come after me, in that case' (339 n.), i.e. 'I don't want you stealing *my* food.' (The joke is helped rather than hindered by the fact that he *hasn't* much, 742.) But Chremes (870) is alive to other dangers too. Σίκων | καὶ Παρμένων: for these slave

O

names cf. Men., *Dysc.* 889 (with Handley), *Sam.* 281, for Sicon (an actor) A. D. Trendall, *Paestan Pottery* (1936), fig. 10; for slave masks Pickard-Cambridge, *DFA* 226.   **παμπησίαν**: 'the whole property', πᾶν, πέπαμαι ('I possess', in lyric parody *Av.* 943). Cf. E. *Ion* 1305. For the word's 'incongruity' see 464, 1102 nn.   **φέρε . . . ξυμφέρω**: 'come, let me help you' (28).   **μὴ μηδαμῶς**: 'please don't mention helping', cf. *Nu.* 83 *Φ. νὴ τὸν Ποσειδῶ τουτονὶ τὸν ἵππιον.* | *Στ. μὴ 'μοί γε τοῦτον μηδαμῶς τὸν ἵππιον.* Chremes fears the other will want also to 'assist' (in the French sense) when the goods are handed over, and claim them as *his* contribution too (scholiast, *μὴ προσποίῃ διαφέρειν*). For similar (political) opportunism see Aeschin. iii. 167.   **τῶν χρημάτων**: cf. Is. iv. 7. 6 *πόσοι συγγενεῖς . . . προσεποιήσαντο τῶν Νικοστράτου;*

872–6 δεῖ γοῦν . . . τινος: 'I need a plan then' (exclamatory *γοῦν*, *GP* 445). The implication is 'my ruse is unsuccessful' (he *had* hoped to slip in along with Chremes).   **τοῖσδέ τε**: see apparatus criticus (*γε/τε* confusion is common, 275). For *μέν . . . τε* cf. S. *Ph.* 1426 *Πάριν μὲν . . . νοσφιεῖς βίου,* | *πέρσεις τε Τροίαν.*   **τοῖσδε**, with contempt (cf. 300). The use of the deictic pronoun is not limited (ibid.) to persons at present on the scene.   **τῶν ματτομένων**: 'the baking' in general, cf. *V.* 614 *ἀλλ' ἦν μή μοι ταχὺ μάξῃ* (sc. *ὁ ταμίας*), but doubtless in practice mainly *μᾶζαι* (cf. *Eq.* 54–7).   **κοινῇ**: with *τοῖσδε*, *Lys.* 525 *κοινῇ* | *ταῖσι γυναιξίν.*   **ὀρθῶς, . . . φαίνεται**: 'I think I've got it.'   **ὀρθῶς**, which follows on a short pause for reflection, expresses his own approbation of whatever idea has just struck him. Cf. Pl. *Prt.* 359 e *Ἀληθῆ λέγεις, καὶ ἀεὶ ἔμοιγε δοκεῖ οὕτως. Ὀρθῶς γε, ἔφην ἐγώ.*

876 R here again has *χοροῦ* (729 n.).

877–1111 The two background houses, used already by Blepyrus, Woman *B* and her husband, and by Chremes, have now changed their occupants again. They are given over to two women, free Athenians (see 720, 878 nn.): the old hag anxious (944 n.) to profit by Praxagora's decree and force the girl's young lover (958 n.) to pay his first attentions to herself. For this purpose she has placed herself in readiness (878, 884 nn.) at her door. The girl is at her window (962 n.). (For fuller discussion of the staging of this 'episode' see Introduction § III.) Routed by her youthful rival's sally (1041 n.) the hag is replaced by two more hideous and even more legalistic crones (1049, 1065) who violently drag the young man off. For the characterization of these beldames cf. Oeri, 1–32.

This fine bawdy scene is the fulfilment of Praxagora's prediction (693 n.). We are not, however, to see it as a sermon on the evils of 'amor effrenatus' (E. Roos, 'De exodi Ecclesiazusarum fabulae ratione et consilio', *Eranos* xlix [1951], 9) : cf. on 746–876.

877 τί . . . οὐχ ἥκουσιν; i.e. *ἀπὸ δείπνου* (694). *ἥξουσι(ν)* (MSS.) is meaningless: for Brunck's correction cf. fr. 453 . . . *πῦρ ἔοιχ' ἥκειν*

(Herwerden, MSS. ἥξειν) ἄγων.   ὥρα . . . πάλαι: the meal, that is, should long since have been over (δ' i.e. γάρ, 84 n.). Cf. in general *PMG* fr. adesp. 58. 3 παρὰ δ' ἔρχεθ' ὥρα | ἐγὼ δὲ μόνα καθεύδω. See V. Longo, 'Aristofane e un'interpretazione di Saffo', *Maia* vi (1953), 220-3.

878-9 ἐγώ . . . ἕστηκα: i.e. at my door (Introduction § III).   καταπεπλασμένη ψιμυθίῳ: the preparation of ψιμύθιον ('white lead') is fully described by Theophrastus (*Lap.* 56). It appears in the list of feminine accessories (fr. 320. 3) : and younger women seem to have rubbed it in to lighten their already (64 n.) white complexions. Ischomachus warns his young wife against it (X. *Oec.* x. 2, cf. 7) 'seeing her ἐντετριμμένην (904) with much white lead, in order to seem whiter than she was: and again with much ἔγχουσα (929 n.), to appear redder than she was in truth'. He has in mind, perhaps, its over-use by common prostitutes (Alex. fr. 98. 17). This 'plastering' (μὴ τοίνυν τὸ πρόσωπον ἅπαν ψιμύθῳ κατάπλαττε, *AP* xi. 408. 3) the old hag has emulated here, in an all-out effort to look younger: cf. Chremylus on the similar attempt in *Pl.* 1065, 'if this white lead is washed off, you will see her face's tatters clearly.' Such excess (at least in married women) would in normal circumstances have been frowned on (Eub. fr. 98. 1) : and 'powdering' is in general inconsistent with (*a*) religious ceremonial (*IG* v. 1. 1390. 22), (*b*) a period of mourning (Lys. i. 14), ἔδοξε (implying a light rubbing, see above) . . . τὸ πρόσωπον ἐψιμυθιῶσθαι, though her brother's death was not yet thirty days past. The use of white lead as a cosmetic is confirmed by discovery of samples in small covered bowls, exclusively in graves of girls and women (E. R. Caley and J. F. C. Richards, *Theophrastus On Stones* [Ohio, 1956], 189).   κροκωτὸν ἠμφιεσμένη: 'with my yellow dress on', to add to her seductiveness. She is acting, in fact, very much like the slave prostitutes (721) now banned for her advantage. The colour, much favoured by Athenian women (332 n.), is to catch the men's attention. So Lysistrata (46) intends to use it (cf. *Lys.* 51, 219). For the wearing of this, one's most attractive dress, at festivals, see *Lys.* 645.

880 ἀργός: cf. *Pax* 256 (to an idle slave) ἕστηκας ἀργός; The word may have four separate (though closely linked) suggestions: (*a*) quite literally 'idle' (cf. *Nu.* 53), perhaps implying 'dressed up to no purpose': so Arist. *HA* 627ª14 αἱ δὲ (μέλισσαι) φαναὶ καὶ λαμπραί, ὥσπερ γυναῖκες ἀργαί (notice the later form of ending), (*b*) without a profession or trade' (i.e. having no takers for it at the moment), cf. Antiph. fr. 123. 3 ὅταν γὰρ ἀπορῆταί τις, ἂν μὲν ἀργὸς ᾖ, (*c*) 'neglected' (S. *OT* 287), (*d*) 'unworked', 'uncultivated' (X. *Cyr.* iii. 2. 19).

880-1 μινυρομένη . . . μέλος: cf. *V.* 219. The verb and its cognates are often used of bird-song (as *Av.* 1414) : here no doubt (though not in the old woman's *own* opinion) the cry of the eagle (Arist. *HA* 619ª3) rather than the nightingale (S. *OC* 671).   πρὸς ἐμαυτὴν: cf. 931,

Ra. 52 ἀναγιγνώσκοντί μοι | . . . πρὸς ἐμαυτόν . . . **παίζουσ' ὅπως ἂν:**
see apparatus criticus. But 'folâtrant' (Van Daele) misrepresents her
meaning, 'to see if I can get my sport and capture . . .' (ὅπως ἄν,
916 n.: after μινυρομένη, potential). For παίζω in contexts of hunting
(see below) cf. S. *El.* 567 (with Jebb's note) θεᾶς | παίζων κατ' ἄλσος
ἐξεκίνησεν ποδοῖν | . . . ἔλαφον. Dobree read παίζουσα. πῶς . . .; (a com-
mon way of expressing a wish, as *Eq.* 16). But the participle then is
very feeble: unless one might alter to παίζουσα (for confusion of ξ and
ζ see 2 n.), 'intending to have my amorous sport' (*Th.* 795). For the
active future form see Strat. *AP* xii. 211. 7.   **περιλάβοιμ':** (*a*) literal,
'embrace' (X. *Smp.* ix. 4 περιλαβὼν ἐφίλησεν αὐτήν), (*b*) 'catch', 'get
hold of' (*Pl.* 934). So Pl. *Sph.* 235 b (a metaphor from hunting, see
above) σχεδὸν . . . αὐτὸν (sc. 'the beast') περιειλήφαμεν. περιβάλοιμ'
(Dobree) is needless: for possible λαβ-/βαλ- confusion elsewhere cf.
Pl. 1053.

882–3 Μοῦσαι, δεῦρ' ἴτ' ἐπὶ . . . στόμα: the parodied prologue to a ὕμνος
κλητικός, as *Ra.* 875 (see Radermacher) ὦ . . . ἀγναὶ Μοῦσαι . . . ἔλθετ'
ἐποψόμεναι δύναμιν | δεινοτάτοιν στομάτοιν.   **μελύδριον . . . τι τῶν**
Ἰωνικῶν: cf. Pl. Com. fr. 69. 14 ἥ δ' ᾖδεν . . . μέλος Ἰωνικόν τι. For the
form of the diminutive of μέλος (880) see Theoc. 7. 51: cf. ἑλκύδριον
(*Eq.* 907).   **τῶν Ἰωνικῶν:** Ionia was a by-word for (*a*) luxury (τῶν
τρυφηλῶν, scholiast, cf. Hsch. s.v.), (*b*) wantonness (ὡς μαλακῶν
ἐκείνων ὄντων, scholiast at 918). Cf. (for (*a*)) Pl. Com. loc. cit., Antiph.
fr. 91 . . . τις Ἰώνων | τρυφεραμπεχόνων ἁβρὸς ἡδυπαθὴς | ὄχλος . . . ,
(for (*b*)) 890, 918 nn. For the sensuous Ionian variety of *music* see
Th. 163 διεκλῶντ' Ἰωνικῶς: cf. the voluptuous βαυκισμός (Ἰωνικὴ
ὄρχησις, Hsch. s.v.), Ath. 629 e. So too lewd *verses* were known as
Ἰωνικά: 'the *Ionicologus* recites the poems called *Ionic* of Sotades and
his predecessors . . . and other poets of that kind. He is also called
cinaedologus' (620 e).

884 μέν: (*a*) emphatic, Pi. *O.* 8. 65 νῦν μὲν αὐτῷ γέρας . . . , (but this use
is limited in Attic, *GP* 364), (*b*) 'solitarium' (109 n.): the unexpressed
contrasting thought is 'but later on I'll get in front of you.'   **παρα-**
κύψασα: 'peeping out' (slily, 924), perhaps ἐξ ὑπερῴου (698), cf. *Th.*
797. But (*a*) the present situation corresponds only roughly to
Praxagora's description (689–709) of the probable effects of her
decree, (*b*) other passages—as well as the whole tenor of 877–83—
suggest that she is speaking from the *door*. So, in particular, *Pax* 981
καὶ γὰρ ἐκεῖναι παρακλίνασαι | τῆς αὐλείας παρακύπτουσιν, cf. Theoc.
3. 6. To appear there was immodest (992). Thus *Pax* 979 ff., Lycurg.
40 (after news of Chaeronea) 'one might see free-born women at their
doors, a sight unworthy of themselves and of the city.' Cf. Prov. 9: 14.
See also *Th.* 792, men's anger at finding wives θύρασιν ('out of
doors', 997 n.).   **προὔφθης:** the girl speaks from an upper-storey
window (962). She means (in effect) 'you have managed to get

LINES 882–891   197

down and be looking out for lovers before me.' Notice the epic and
Attic form of aorist: 596, *Nu.* 1384.   **ὦ σαπρά**: 926, a term of abuse
for ageing women. So in the young man's description (1098): cf. *Lys.*
378, *Th.* 1024, Theopomp. Com. fr. 50 (943 n.). The term is sometimes merely factual: *Com. Adesp.* 1401a (Edmonds III A) σαπρὰν
γυναῖκα ⟨δ'⟩ ὁ τρόπος εὔμορφον ποιεῖ, cf. *Pax* 698. Phot. s.v. σαπρόν· οὐ
τὸ μοχθηρὸν καὶ φαῦλον, ἀλλὰ τὸ παλαιόν) : and the unpleasant stress on
putrefaction may be lessened if one thinks instead of the word as
applied to withered roses (D. xxii. 70). But to play down the full force
of the adjective is far from the intention of the speaker.

885–6 ᾧου δ' ἐρήμας . . . τρυγήσειν: sc. ἀμπέλους (accusative of that *off*
which the fruit is gathered), 'for' (δ', see 84 n.) 'you thought that you
would strip the unwatched vines.' The same proverbial expression
(Aristid. ii. 77 ἵνα μὴ μάτην ἡ παροιμία τὰς ἐρήμους τρυγᾶν ἀγορεύῃ)
occurs *V.* 634, where the scholiast explains 'of those who act fearlessly,
when no one is acting to oppose them'. For a similar ellipsis, see *Od.*
vii. 124 ἑτέρας δ' ἄρα τε τρυγόωσιν | ἄλλας δὲ τραπέουσι (where under-
stand σταφυλάς, 121). There may be a glance at another sense of
τρυγᾶν, cf. *Pax* 1338 τρυγήσομεν αὐτήν.   **ἐρήμας**, 'unguarded', as
often in Thucydides, for example ii. 4. 4 οἱ δὲ κατὰ πύλας ἐρήμους . . .
ἐξῆλθον. The sense here is clarified by οὐ παρούσης ἐμοῦ: cf. *Il.* v. 140
τὰ δ' ἐρῆμα (i.e. sheep without a shepherd) φοβεῖται (at the onset of a
lion).   **προσάξεσθαι**: (*a*) 'attract', 'win over', (*b*) 'embrace' (*Av.* 141).

888–9 δι' ὄχλου: 'tedious', 'boring', for the form cf. *Ra.* 1412 δι' ἔχθρας.
Note the self-depreciating reference to comic technique (cf. *Ra.* 1). Of
course neither poet—who does not 'half-audibly yawn' here, Norwood,
267—nor audience—who hate stale stage topics, 580 n.—expects the
women's ditties to be boring: no doubt (as Rogers explains) an
opportunity is given (888) for shouting 'No!' (So the speaker in *Lys.*
1217 defers to the low taste of spectators.) Cf. (for phraseology) *Th.*
i. 73. 2 'we must speak of the Persian war . . . εἰ καὶ δι' ὄχλου μᾶλλον
ἔσται ἀεὶ προβαλλομένοις . . .', a Thucydidean use of ὄχλος (i.e. ὄχλησις,
see Phot., Hsch. s.v.) noted by Dionysius of Halicarnassus (*Amm.* 2. 10).
τοῖς θεωμένοις: 'the audience' (as often). So (for example) *Ra.* 1475:
cf. 580 n., 583.   **ὅμως . . . κωμῳδικόν**: cf. Thgn. 1018 πτοιῶμαι δ'
ἐσορῶν ἄνθος ὁμηλικίης | τερπνὸν ὅμως καὶ καλόν, *Pl.* 424 βλέπει γέ τοι
μανικόν τι καὶ τραγῳδικόν.

890–1 τούτῳ διαλέγου: possibly she (*a*) points to her *pudenda* (so apparently the scholiast ἡ γραῦς τῷ αἰδοίῳ λέγει), in other words, the
girl is to be left (like the youths by *their* elders, 707) to find consolation
for herself, (*b*) tosses her an imitation penis (ὄλισβος, fr. 320. 13,
βαυβών, Herod. 6. 19), for which Ionian refinement cf. *Lys.* 108, fr.
969. 5, (*c*) offers her posterior (Bothe), which is probably closer to the
meaning (cf. the 'kiss my arse' posture of the kordax dancer, Bieber,
HT, fig. 180). The clue may lie in *Pl.* 1133, where, in answer to

Hermes' complaint about his drink, Carion ('lâchant un pet', Van Daele) recommends ταύτην ἐπιπιὼν ἀποτρέχων οὐκ ἂν φθάνοις. The sense is then 'stop talking to me' (cf. 930, Kock [554 n.], 283) : with (a) or (b) the usage is *in re amatoria*, recognized in Aristophanes (fr. 343) by Pollux (ii. 125). Cf. *Pl.* 1082. *Some* rude gesture is certainly intended : Coulon supposes (after Willems, 195 n. 1) that τούτῳ means τῷ δακτύλῳ (cf. Pers. 2. 33, Mart. vi. 70. 5). See *REG* xxxvi (1923), 389, *RhM* cv (1962), 20.   **φιλοττάριον αὐλητά:** 'my little piper love', apparently a coinage (cf. the affectionate diminutives νηττάριον, *Pl.* 1011, νεοττίον, Thphr. *Char.* 2. 6). We should not (as LSJ, cf. C. W. Peppler, *Comic Terminations in Aristophanes and the Comic Fragments* [Baltimore, Md., 1902], 18) refer it to the use of φιλότης in such apostrophes as Alciphr. iv. 19. 19 ὥστε πειρῶ μᾶλλον, ἐμὴ φιλότης, θᾶσσον εἰς ἄστυ παραγενέσθαι.

If *XOPOY* (876) is thought to represent (see 729 n.) choral dancing, the piper will have stayed in the orchestra. More probably, he left at 582 and now re-enters (cf. *Av.* 666) to play for the old woman, girl, and boy. The αὐλός is used in comedy in three ways : (a) as a solo instrument (cf. *Ra.* 312), (b) to accompany the chorus (cf. *Av.* 682), (c) as here, to accompany solo singers. Its suitability to the human voice is pointed out by Aristotle (*Pr.* 922[a]1). For the exhortation to the player to begin, see *Av.* 676–83 ; there he is (a) masked, like the chorus (for his costume see Handley on Men. *Dysc.* 880), (b) playing a *single* aulos for the anapaests of the parabasis. But playing on *two* auloi (891, Theoc. *Ep.* 5. 1) gave a more intricate and fuller background, whether to solo voices or—as shown on vases—to a chorus (Ehrenberg, pl. II). M. Okál tries to show that Aristophanes 's'entendait mieux avec la cithare qu'avec l'aulos' (*Charisteria F. Novotný* [Prague, 1962], 39).

892 ἄξιον . . . σοῦ: probably meaning nothing more than 'do your stuff', but she may imply 'a fine old ribald ditty' (classing the player with herself). **προσαύλησον μέλος:** Nicophon fr. 7 ἀλλ' ἴθι προσαύλησον σὺ νῶν πτισμόν τινα (with the notion of accompaniment, as here).

893–9 The hag's μελύδριον (ᾄδει ἡ γραῦς, scholiast) celebrates (for passing men's attention, 881) the value of *experience* in love. And *she* will also be *faithful*.

Metre : trochaic dimeters, interrupted by one trochaic trimeter (cf. 904, 909), with 'choriambic substitution' (Raven, §§ 43, 50) in its second metron (898). Note the frequency of anapaests and tribrachs.

– ∪ ∪∪ –	– ∪ – ∪	2 tr
– ∪ ∪∪ –	– ∪ – –	2 tr
– ∪ – ∪	– ∪ ∪∪∪	2 tr
– ∪ – –	– ∪ – –	2 tr
– ∪ – –	– ∪ ∪∪ –	2 tr
– ∪ – –	– ∪ ∪ –	– ∪ – –	3 tr
– ∪ ∪∪∪	– ∪ – ∪	2 tr

LINES 892–900   199

895–6 τὸ σοφόν: 'skill' in an art (*Ra.* 766), here the art of love. Her skill
is presumably more *practical*, however, than Cydias', who is praised as
an adviser, σοφώτατον . . . τὸν Κυδίαν τὰ ἐρωτικά, Pl. *Chrm.* 155 d. Cf.
(for ἔνεστιν) *Lys.* 544 αἷς . . . ἔνι . . . . σοφόν. **ταῖς πεπείροις:** the
metaphor ('ripe', cf. πεπείρους ἀχράδας, Eup. fr. 33) of course is self-
advertisement on her part. It means the maturity not of age, but
youth: 'they married their women . . . not when they were small and
ἀώρους for marriage, ἀλλὰ καὶ ἀκμαζούσας καὶ πεπείρους' (Plu. *Lyc.* 15.
3), and the hag, from the girl's point of view, is so far past it as to be
in fact σαπρά (884). For the sentiment see Lucian, *Am.* 25, 'the
experience (of older women) has something to say σοφώτερον than the
young' (E. *Ph.* 529), Goethe, *Faust,* II i. 6361–2 (quoted by V. Coulon,
RhM cvi [1963], 160), 'Müßt Euer Glück nicht auf die Jüngste setzen,
Die Angejahrten wissen Euch zu schätzen.' So, but from the opposite
view-point, Timocl. fr. 22. 1.

897–8 τοι: RΓΛMuiVbi. Translate 'you know', 'let me tell you'
(35 n.), addressed to her prospective clientele: supplying τις (S. *OC*
1225, X. *Smp.* v. 2), not ἡ νέα (Rogers, 895). The hag is not here
intending to compare herself (as Rogers, van Leeuwen) with the
μεῖραξ: she rates her quality against the world. τις is a variant in B
(and so most editors): cf. the same correction (Aristarchus) in *Il.* x.
341. **στέργειν:** with accusative of person (292a n.). The sense may
(as there) be 'rest content with', 'bear with': the hag will put up with
any lover, little fear of *her* deserting anyone she captures. But the verb
also indicates continuing affection (the two ideas are possibly com-
bined, E. *Andr.* 213 χρὴ γὰρ γυναῖκα, κἂν κακῷ πόσει δοθῇ, | στέργειν),
and it is this desirable quality, not a mere transient excitement, that
the old woman offers to a lover. **ᾧπερ ξυνείην:** 619 (but of *marriage*,
38, 340). Cf. fr. 583 ἵνα ξυνῶσιν ᾧπερ ἥδεσθον βίῳ.

899 πέτοιτο: of fickleness, *Av.* 169 ἄνθρωπος ὄρνις . . . πετόμενος, | . . . οὐδὲν
οὐδέποτ' ἐν ταὐτῷ μένων. This part of her 'advertisement' (897–9)
recalls the true ἐρασταί of Pl. *Smp.* 181 d, who mean to form a stable
partnership for life and not καταγελάσαντες οἰχήσεσθαι ἐπ' ἄλλον
ἀποτρέχοντες.

900–10 The girl's song opens with some counter-propaganda (ἀντᾴδει ἡ
νέα τῇ γραΐ, scholiast: cf. 885). She perhaps interrupts the other
quickly (since the acatalectic dimeter in 899 is exceptional as the
pause-end of a series, Dale, 87 n. 1). Young girls (she says) have τὸ
τρυφερόν to offer, as against τὸ σοφόν in the old. But she soon relapses
into personal abuse (cf. her first appearance, 884) which calls forth
a blistering reply.

900–5 Metre: trochaic dimeters, interrupted by a trimeter (904). The
seemingly choriambic 902, 905 (see *Th.* 955) are probably assimilated
to trochaic time (Dale, 91) as 'syncopated' (i.e. with a short syllable
suppressed, cf. in iambics 289) catalectic dimeters (the 'aristophaneus').

– ⏑ – –	– ⏑ – ⏑	2 tr
⏓ ⏑ ⏑ – ⏑	– ⏑ – ⏑	2 tr
– ⏑ ⏑ –	⏑ – –	ar
– ⏑ – – – ⏑ –		lekythion +
– ⏑ – –	⏑ ⏑ ⏑ – – – ⏑ – –	3 tr
– ⏑ ⏑ –	⏑ – –	ar

900–3 μὴ φθόνει: perhaps addressed (as 893) to passers-by. But the imperative's application (as elsewhere in lyrics) may be general (*Th.* 128). **ταῖσιν**: so R, *ταῖς* (Hermann). The change gives exact correspondence (906): but this is not vital (see below). **τὸ τρυφερὸν**: (*a*) literally 'softness', *Anacreont.* 16. 26 Preisendanz *τρυφεροῦ δ' ἔσω γενείου . . . | Χάριτες πέτοιντο πᾶσαι*, (*b*) with overtones of 'lewdness', Antiph. fr. 174. 5 *τῆς τρυφερᾶς ἀπὸ Λέσβου* (see 920), cf. on *τρυφή* (973*b*). **ἐμπέφυκε**: E. *Hipp.* 966 *τὸ μῶρον . . . γυναιξὶ . . . ἐμπέφυκεν.* **ἁπαλοῖσι**: especially of youth, *Pax* 351. The word, like *τρυφερός*, (*a*) means 'tender', 'soft', Archil. fr. 88 West *οὐκέθ' ὅμως θάλλεις ἁπαλὸν χρόα, κάρφεται γὰρ ἤδη | ὄγμοις*, (*b*) has overtones of 'sensuous', *Th.* 192, Sapph. fr. 126 (L–P) *δαύοις ἀπάλας ἐτάρας ἐν στήθεσιν.* On the use of the adjective in lyric see M. Treu, *Von Homer zur Lyrik* (Munich, 1955), 178. **κἀπὶ . . . ἐπανθεῖ**: cf. in general 12, 13 nn., *Nu.* 978. **μήλοις**: 'apples', metaphorically used of (*a*) the cheeks, Lucian, *Im.* 6 *τὰ μῆλα . . . καὶ ὅσα τῆς ὄψεως ἀντωπά*, (*b*) the breasts, *Lys.* 155 (scholiast, *τοὺς μαστοὺς μῆλά φησιν*).

904 παραλέλεξαι: 'you are plucked', either (*a*) in the general sense of *παρατίλλω* (see 13 n.) or (*b*) of the eyebrows in particular (Hsch., Phot. s.v. *παραλέγειν· τὰς ὑπερεχούσας ἐν ταῖς ὀφρύσι τρίχας ἐκλέγειν*), though Photius (s.v. *παρέλεξας*) says that some deny (*ἐκσύρουσι*) such a practice. The context (beside *ἐντέτριψαι*, see below) suggests that the second sense is better: we expect a reference to *visible* results of superfluous (*παρα-*) hair's removal. The scholiast's explanation is of plucking grey hairs from the head, but this would be expressed by *ἐκ-*, not *παρα-* (cf. *Eq.* 908): and the girl (apparently herself undepilated) is comparing her own smooth skin (*τὸ τρυφερόν*) with that of her hairy old opponent. **κἀντέτριψαι**: 'and your face is painted over', 732 n. The reason for such preparation (to arouse desire in their men-folk) is explained, *Lys.* 149.

905 τῷ θανάτῳ μέλημα: 'you death's delight', for only Death (cf. 994) could fancy *you*. *μέλημα*, an object of solicitude, a loved one (973*a*). Cf. Sapph. fr. 163 (L–P) *μέλημα τὦμον*, Pi. *P.* 10. 59 *νέαισιν . . . παρθένοισι μέλημα.* Similarly used is Latin 'cura' (Verg. *Ecl.* 10. 22, Hor. *Carm.* ii. 8. 8).

906–10 Metre: trochaic dimeters, in loose responsion (cf. Dale, 88) to 900–5. There is probably again assimilation (see note there) to trochaic time in the aristophaneans 908, 910.

(1) – ◡ –   – ◡ – ◡   cr+tr (cf. S. *El.* 1282, *Lys.* 1249)
(2) ◡◡◡ – ◡ ◡◡◡ –   lek
(3) – ◡◡ –   ◡ – –   ar ∼ 902
(4) – ◡ – –   – ◡ – ◡   – ◡ – ◡ 3 tr (cf. 897)
(5) – ◡◡ –   ◡ – –   ar ∼ 905

(3) and (5) correspond exactly to 902, 905. The other responsions are:
(1) cr+tr ∼ 2 tr (i.e. syncopated tr ∼ tr, cf. A. *Eu.* 526 ∼ 538,
Wilamowitz, *GV* 269) (2) lek ∼ 2 tr (i.e. catalectic tr dim. ∼ dim.,
cf. *Av.* 1560 as in MSS. ∼ 1701) (4) 3 tr ∼ lek+3 tr.

906–8 ἐκπέσοι . . . τὸ τρῆμα: the noun means (a) a perforation in a bed
(and was so explained here by Le Febvre), (b) τρύπημα (624 n.). The
second sense is certainly the right one (cf. *Lys.* 410): for a more
scientific use see Arist. *HA* 497ᵃ25. ἐκπέσοι with (a) will mean
'disintegrate' (scholiast, *Eq.* 532 ἐκπιπτούσων τῶν ἠλέκτρων), with (b)
'slip' (medical, Hp. *Art.* 8): probably a reference to ὑστερικὴ πρό-
πτωσις (Willems, 196 n. 1). For this Hippocratean meaning of ἐκπίπτω
cf. *Mul.* 153 αἱ ὑστέραι ἐκπίπτουσι.   τό τ' ἐπίκλιντρον ἀποβάλοις:
'may you throw away the head-rest of your couch in your desire, only
to find your lover disappointing' (Pritchett, 233). But the old woman's
wish is, of course, to stop her rival from successfully attracting men at
all: she does not look ahead to their performance. I suspect, then,
that the curse is parallel to the preceding (similar strong curses, *Ach.*
1156, Archil. fr. 79a D.³): that ἐπίκλιντρον has the (elsewhere un-
attested, see LSJ Supp.) meaning of *pudenda*: and the force of the curse
is 'may you lose . . .'

909–10 κἀπὶ τῆς κλίνης: 840 n.   ὄφιν προσελκύσαιο: the verb
means (a) 'attract', εἰς φιλότητα (Thgn. 372); the scholiast uses it in
explanation of προσάξεσθαι (886 n.), (b) 'draw towards oneself',
'embrace', Plu. *Moralia* 508 e προσελκόμενος ὡς φιλήσων. ὄφις, in
erotics, corresponds to Latin 'anguis' (i.e. 'penis languidus', P.
Pierrugues, *Glossarium Eroticum Linguae Latinae*, [Amsterdam, 1965],
52, cf. σαύρα, *AP* xi. 21). This would suit Pritchett's view (above).
But the hag's meaning is (I think) quite literal, 'may you look for a
man and find a snake as lover.' εὔροις of MSS. (see apparatus criticus)
is probably a gloss (cf. *Ach.* 949) but a correct one. Cf. Temple to
Boswell (22 November 1767) '. . . you may still be deceived and,
instead of an angel, wake with a serpent in your arms.'   φιλῆσαι:
the verb represents three stages (so to speak) in the history of an
affair (a) 'regard with affection' (992), (b) 'kiss' (647, Plu. loc cit.),
(c) 'have intercourse' (used rather of the male, Hsch. s.v. βαίνειν: cf.
Pl. *Phdr.* 250 e), sc. here τὸν σὸν ἐραστήν.

911–17 The girl laments a quickly passing and wasted opportunity for
love: her mother is out, no lovers come. But in answer to some ribald
comment (914 n.) from her rival, she moves from lamentation to
abuse.

Metre: syncopated iambic dimeters, 911, 912; syncopated iambic dimeter+, 913; an iambic trimeter, 914; aeolic cola (hipponactean, glyconic, hendecasyllable), 915–17. For the form of the hendeca-syllable see S. *Aj.* 629, *OC* 701, (in general) Dale, 141–43: cf. the scolion metra (938 n.).

$--\cup\cup\cup$	$-\cup-$	ia+cr
$---$	$---$	2 mo
$\cup--$	$--\cup-$	ba+ia+
$---$ $---$	$\cup--$	2 mo+ba (mo+ba = ar)
$--\cup-$ $-\cup\cup\cup-$	$\cup-\cup-$	3 ia
$---\cup\cup-\cup-\cup$		hippon
$-\cup-\cup\cup-\cup-$		gl
$---\cup\cup--\cup\cup-\cup$		hendec

912–14 μοὐταῖρος: i.e. μοι ἑταῖρος (Reiske, R μ' οντ' αἶρος), the counter-part here, almost, of ἑταίρα. Cf. μοὔγκώμιον (*Nu.* 1205), μοῦσθ' (785). **λείπομ':** for elision of the diphthong cf. *Lys.* 927 ἀλλ' οὐδὲ δέομ' ἔγωγε. **γάρ:** cf. for position 299 n. **καὶ . . . λέγειν:** metre (an iambic trimeter, 920) is restored by the addition of μ' and τὰ (Dobree): 'I need say no more, you know my meaning.' Perhaps the hag, by some obscene gesture, shows she *does* know, thus calling forth the subsequent suggestion.

915–17 ἀλλ': 852 n.   **ὦ μαῖ':** she uses, in irony, a deferential form employed in addressing older women (Hsch. s.v., προσφώνησις πρὸς πρεσβῦτιν τιμητική). **ἱκετεύομαι:** the middle form occurs here only (and in MSS. Herodotus iii. 48. 3). But this is no reason for Hermann's ἱκετεύομεν. With ἀντιβολῶ (917), as D. xxviii. 20 ἱκετεύω, ἀντιβολῶ πρὸς παίδων. **κάλει:** of summoning a lover, *Lys.* 871. **τὸν Ὀρθαγόραν:** (a) a comparatively rare name (*PA* 11486–8), but borne by a celebrated piper (Pl. *Prt.* 318 c) and a καλός (on an am-phora in Würzburg, Kretschmer [80 n.], 185), (b) an ὄλισβος (890 n.) personified. This explains the woman's answer (918). For ὀρθός ('arrectus') see *Lys.* 995. Cf. the Priapean deity Ὀρθάννης (Str. xiii. 1. 12), Phot. Hsch. s.v., . . . ἐντεταμένον ἔχων τὸ αἰδοῖον. **σαυτῆς ⟨ἄν⟩ κατόναι':** an aeolic hendecasyllable (923). Cf. Wilamowitz, *Griechische Verskunst*[2] (Darmstadt, 1958), 478. For ὅπως ἄν (of purpose) and opta-tive with a *primary* tense see 881 (cf. 346). **σαυτῆς:** 'enjoy *yourself*', you won't find any pleasure from a lover. The compound verb recurs in an inscription (Delphi, 2nd century B.C.): μήτε τέκνων μήτε σπορῶν μήτε καρπ[ῶν μή]τε οὐσίας κατόνασθαι ἐάσωσιν ἐμέ (*BCH* xxvii [1903], 107, 15).

918–23 The old woman's answer: she casts the girl's taunt back at her and throws in another for good measure. She will not be deprived of her enjoyment. It is not likely that (a) 918–23 (as Willems), (b) 921–3 (as Bergk) should be given to the girl. This avoids problems of responsion: but 924 (n.) hardly suits the hag.

Metre: two iambic dimeters, an iambic trimeter, and three aeolic
cola (hipponactean, glyconic, hendecasyllable).

(1) — — ∪∪∪ — ∪ —   ia+cr
(2) ∪ — ∪ —   ∪ — ∪ —   2 ia
(3) ∪ — ∪ —   — — ∪∪∪ — — ∪ —   3 ia
(4) — — — ∪∪ — ∪ — ∪   hippon
(5) — ∪ — ∪∪ — ∪ —   gl
(6) — — — ∪∪ — — ∪∪ — —   hendec

(1) and (3) correspond exactly to 911, 914, (4) (5) and (6) to 915, 916,
917. In (2) 2 ia ∽ 2 mo (cf. the double molossus in an iambic context, S.
Tr. 653, 661). There is no line corresponding (see 487, 920 nn.) to 913.

918–19 ἤδη . . . κνησιᾷς: i.e. your lust has already got the better of you,
hence your talk of Orthagoras (916). The ὄλισβος was Ionian (890 n.).
τάλαινα: in ironically patronizing sympathy for the girl who 'is itching'
('wants to scratch').   **κνησιᾷς:** the desiderative form, Pl. *Grg.* 494 c
ψωρῶντα καὶ κνησιῶντα, ἀφθόνως ἔχοντα τοῦ κνῆσθαι, used *in re amatoria*,
as ibid. 494 e. Similarly used (cf. 36 n.) are κνάω, κνίζω, κνήθω: cf.
Latin 'prurio' (as Mart. ix. 73. 6).

920 δοκεῖς δέ . . . Λεσβίους: sc. εἶναι, cf. X. *An.* vii. 1. 6 (λαβδᾶν, T. L.
Agar, *CQ* xiii [1919], 19) 'and further' (δέ) 'you seem to be a Λ also'
(καί), i.e. your itch is such you seem prepared to go to abnormal
lengths to gratify it. The old woman passes from Ionia to Lesbos: no
lacuna (Jackson, 109 ff.) ought to be postulated here. Her jibe against
the girl, in other words, is twofold: (a) 'you are ready to resort to
masturbation', (b) 'you are prepared for *cunnilinctus*' (assuming, of
course, that you *get* a man, which you *won't* if *I* can help it, 907 n.,
921–3).   **λάβδα:** standing perhaps (see Coulon) for λειχάζειν (a verb
not recorded by LSJ: λαικάζουσιν οἱ Λέσβιοι ἀπὸ τοῦ ἄρχοντος στοιχείου,
scholiast) i.e. λεσβίζειν (*V.* 1346), λεσβιάζειν (*Ra.* 1308). Cf. Latin
'lingere', Mart. xii. 55. 13, Aus. *Epigr.* 128. 8, 'cui ipse linguam cum
dedit suam, Λ est.' Labdace is a girl's name in *Priap.* 79. 5 (Müller):
though Labda the mother of Cypselus (Hdt. v. 92 β. 1) seems to have
no such associations. If λάβδα can indicate 'the legs stretched out and
wide apart', the reference will suit both (a) *and* (b), and the meaning of
920 then is '. . . a labda in the Lesbian sense as well'.   **κατὰ τοὺς
Λεσβίους:** i.e. 'in the manner of . . .', cf. fr. 326 καὶ κατ᾽ Ἀγάθων᾽
ἀντίθετον ἐξευρημένον, or perhaps 'as the Lesbians say', *Av.* 910 (V.
Coulon, *RhM* cv [1962], 28). Λεσβίσαι, μολῦναι τὸ στόμα (Phot.),
Λέσβιοι γὰρ διεβάλλοντο (though it may be that the word had a wider
application—cf. *V.* 1346—to *all* kinds of sexual deviation). This
Lesbian practice is not to be confused with that attributed (perhaps
unjustifiably) to Sappho, which gives the modern 'Lesbian' her name.
A contrasting picture of the womanhood of Lesbos, Agath., *AP* vii. 614.

921–3 ὑφαρπάσαιο: 'snatch from under my nose' (see 722 n.) 'for your
own enjoyment' (middle). For the middle form, which suits both

sense and metre, see Agath., *AP* ix. 619. 2 (of Aphrodite) τὴν πρὶν
Ἀλεξάνδρου ψῆφον ὑφαρπαμένη.   **τἀμὰ παίγνια:** (a) 'playthings', (b)
'favourites' ('deliciae'), cf. παίζουσα (881 n.). So Plu. *Ant.* 59. 4 . . .
παιγνίων . . . ἃ δηλίκια ʽΡωμαῖοι καλοῦσιν, Plaut. *Pers.* 204 'Paegnium,
deliciae pueri, salve.'   **τὴν δ' ἐμὴν ὥραν:** there are three possibilities, (a) 'my rightful time' (which Praxagora's new law, 618,
allots me). The closest parallels are in *NT*, e.g. *Ev. Jo.* 2 : 4 οὔπω ἥκει ἡ
ὥρα μου. On this view **ἀπολήψει** means 'recover' (as your own), X.
An. vii. 3. 31 πολλὴν χώραν . . . ἀπολήψει πατρῴαν οὖσαν: the precedence
with lovers which the young girl has enjoyed is now the legal right of
the old woman, (b) 'my youth' (with overtones of 'beauty'), cf.
ὡραῖος, 616, *Av.* 1724. But then ὥραν ἀπολεῖς is very difficult (whether
given to the hag or to the girl), and even in irony the hag would not
pretend to possession of either youth or beauty: her case rests on experience (895). The best explanation may accordingly be (c) 'my
right time of life', sc. παίγνια ἔχειν, παίζειν, cf. Is. ix. 28 ἐπειδὴ . . . ὥραν
εἶχον παιδεύεσθαι. She is thinking, that is, of her maturity (she has
reached, as it were, her ὥρα ἔτους, Th. ii. 52. 2, D. l. 23) which
gives her a definite advantage.

924 παράκυφθ': 884 n., presumably (as there) the words are to be given
to the girl. Allocation of speakers here is difficult: MSS. help little
(41 n.). The present text differs (see apparatus criticus) from other
editorial arrangements.   **ὥσπερ γαλῆ:** 128, 792. The ferret, or
domesticated polecat, as distinct from our domestic cat, αἴλουρος
(commoner and much esteemed in Egypt, Hdt. ii. 66, but given a
single passing mention in Aristophanes, *Ach.* 879) was used by
Athenians as a vermin-killing house-pet (cf. *Pax* 795) in spite of its
unpleasant odour (*Pl.* 693). It kept stealthy watch (as the hag here
with the girl) for its chance to snatch away a tasty morsel, and its
thieving habits (cf. *V.* 363) made it a symbol for rapacity (ἁρπακτι-
κώτεροι τῶν γαλῶν, Lucian, *Pisc.* 34). Praxinoa's γαλέαι perhaps are
rather mongooses (Theoc. 15. 28): see A. S. F. Gow, 'Mousers in
Egypt', *CQ* n.s. xvii (1967), 195-7.

925 γὰρ: '(yes, I will) for . . . .', cf. 433, 603.   **ὡς σὲ . . . εἴσεισ':** (a)
'will enter your house', cf. X. *Cyr.* 1. 3. 14 εἰσιέναι ὡς ἐμέ, (b) 'will go in
to as a lover', id. *Smp.* ix. 2. Both meanings may be glanced at, *V.* 500
κἀμέ γ' ἡ πόρνη . . . εἰσελθόντα . . . ἥρετ'.   **πρότερον . . . ἀντ':** as
Palmer at *Ra.* 76.

926-7 οὔκουν . . . γε: 'not for my funeral, at any rate' (343 n.). Cf. fr.
644b †ὅταν φίλοι παρῆσαν† ἐπὶ τὴν ἐκφοράν. In the similar context *Pl.*
1008 the sense of ἐπ' ἐκφοράν; is doubtful: it seems, however, to mean
'to get your money?' (τοῦ λαβεῖν . . . χάριν, *Pl.* 1009). So here the
scholiast and editors (with Bergk), attributing the words to the old
woman ('because lovers carry off old women's money'). This seems
impossible (see below).   **καινόν γ':** 'that's something new for

you', a quip you haven't heard before (. . . τι καινόν, ὧν πρὶν οὐκ ἀκήκοας S. *Ph.* 52) : cf. Pl. *R.* 328 a 'On horseback?', I said. καινόν γε τοῦτο. Or 'that was a surprise', a retort you weren't expecting, Hp. *Int.* 17. R here marks a change of speaker (a common context of exclamatory γε, 93, 213). But (a) ὦ σαπρά (cf. 884) can only be given to the girl, (b) οὔκουν . . . γε in the hag's mouth is then devoid of meaning. The scholiast, in keeping with his theory above, says καινόν, ὅτι οὐκ ἐπ' ἐκφοράν. Taken as a question (Rogers) the words seem irrelevant and weak.   οὐ δῆτα: in flat contradiction of a statement, 856.   γὰρ: '(no), for . . .', 336, 1026.

928–9 οὐ . . . γῆρας: 'it is not my old age' (γῆρας emphatic by position) 'that will hurt you', i.e. by depriving you of lovers. She means that her *experience* (896 n.) will be the lure. The girl wilfully misunderstands her: 'will it rather be your simulated youth?' For female old age emulating youth see *AP* ix. 139. 4.   ἀλλὰ τί; cf. *Ra.* 488. **ἤγχουσα:** ἡ ἔγχουσα (the Attic form, *EM* 313. 30 : otherwise ἄγχουσα, as Nic. *Ther.* 838), i.e. 'alkanet' or 'bugloss'. It was used (a) medicinally and as a dye (Hp. *Mul.* 32, Plin. *Nat.* xxii. 23), (b) as a cosmetic, 'rouge' (so here). Thus Hsch. ἔγχουσα· 'a root with which women make their cheeks red'. See *Lys.* 48 (with scholiast), fr. 320. 3. For its use with ψιμύθιον see X. *Oec.* x. 2 (878 n.), D.C. lxxix. 14 ψιμυθίῳ καὶ ἐγχούσῃ ἐχρίετο.

930–1 τί . . . διαλέγει; formulaic, 'stop talking to me' (890 n.), cf. *Ach.* 1113 ὦνθρωπε βούλει μὴ προσαγορεύειν ἐμέ;   τί διακύπτεις; the compound (a) echoes διαλέγει, (b) seems stronger than παρακύπτω (924 n.). It possibly suggests (as van Leeuwen says) an open, not furtive, appearance at the window (rather the *door*, see 884 n.). So Hdt. iii. 145. 1 διακύψας διὰ τῆς γοργύρης (i.e. 'putting his head out through the drain'), cf. *Th.* 644. But furtiveness *is* implicit elsewhere (as *Pax* 78), where the meaning, however, is 'look *in*'.   ᾄδω πρὸς ἐμαυτὴν: 880.   Ἐπιγένει . . . φίλῳ: 'to Epigenes my sweetheart', as if (a) she *had* a lover, (b) he were beside her as she sings. Blaydes interprets the dative 'in honorem': a sense, which, although elsewhere expressed by εἰς (κάεισω . . . | ἐς τὼς Ἀσαναίως, *Lys.* 1243), may find some support in the last words of Theramenes (X. *HG* ii. 3. 56) : 'and when . . . he drank the hemlock, they reported that he said, as he jerked the dregs out, Κριτίᾳ τοῦτ' ἔστω τῷ καλῷ.'

932–3 σοὶ . . . Γέρης: 'have *you* a sweetheart—apart, that is, from Geres?' (a suitable lover for a γραῦς). Despite the scholiast (οὗτος φαλακρὸς καὶ πένης) we are not to believe in his existence. The name recurs as that of a Boeotian in Ionia (Paus. vii. 3. 6). Cf. the personification of Γῆρας (Hes., *Th.* 225 with West) : interesting data and illustrations in B. E. Richardson, *Old Age among the Greeks* (Baltimore, Md., 1933). **δείξει γε καὶ σοί:** either (a) 'the event' (*Ra.* 1261, cf. *Lys.* 375) or (b) 'he (my lover) will show you'.   καὶ, either 'you too' (as he has shown me already) or 'even you' (despite your disbelief). Cf. S. *OT* 1294 δείξει δὲ καὶ σοί, where the subject is similarly doubtful.

934–5 ὁδὶ: 27 n.   **γὰρ:** translation depends on attribution of the line. If the old woman's, translate '(as you see) for . . .', if the girl's '(we'll see about that) for here he is himself.' The second is better: the hag's next words reply to the particle's suggestion ('he won't have any need of *you*'). Cf. 951, Alc. Com. fr. 22 ὁδὶ γὰρ αὐτός ἐστιν. **ὤλεθρε:** 'you pest' (ὦ ὄλεθρε), *Th.* 860. ὄλεθρος, abusive or contemptuous, Eup. fr. 376 ἄνεμος καὶ ὄλεθρος ἄνθρωπος. It is unjustifiable to give the words οὐ . . . οὐδέν to the girl. For even though ὤλεθρε might be taken as a pun (fr. 320. 3 ὄλεθρον τὸν βαθύν, apparently a feminine cosmetic, Hsch., Phot. s.v. ὄλεθρος), φθίνυλλα (see below) must be the hag. Cf. the similar abusive use of φθόρος (*Eq.* 1151).   **δεόμενος οὐδέν:** sexually speaking, as *Lys.* 875–6.

935–6 φθίνυλλα: from φθίνω, 'you old rotter' (cf. on σαπρά, 884 n.). Analogous proper names: Ξένυλλα (*Th.* 633), Σίβυλλα (*Pax* 1095). Cf. Ἀρίστυλλος (647).   **δείξει τάχ' αὐτός:** see above.   **ὡς ἔγωγ' ἀπέρχομαι:** i.e. from the window. We'll see (she means) if the young man will want anything from *you* (even with no other choice before him). But she does not really go (see 949).

937 ἵνα γνῷς ὡς . . . μεῖζον φρονῶ: i.e. you think very highly of yourself, but I think of *myself* much more highly (and therefore am willing to put matters to the test by likewise withdrawing from the door). Cf. Pl. *Phdr.* 257 e οἱ μέγιστον φρονοῦντες (sc. ἐφ' ἑαυτοῖς, Ath. 583 f) τῶν πολιτικῶν. Similarly (with that on which one prides oneself expressed by ἐπί with the dative) D. xx. 109 μεῖζον . . . Θηβαῖοι φρονοῦσιν ἐπ' ὠμότητι . . .

938–45 A youth enters, garlanded (691 n.) and carrying a torch (978). He chafes at the new law (617–18) which detains him from visiting his girl friend: and is antistrophically answered by the hag (who has not yet withdrawn from the doorway, 946) although of course he neither sees nor hears her.

938–41 Metre: a stanza of the form a a b c, reproducing the metre of the scolia (i.e. songs for convivial occasions, which the Theophrastan αὐθάδης, *Char.* 15. 10, declines to sing). The most celebrated (on Harmodius, *PMG* 893) is often referred to (682 n.). A scolion by Timocrates is parodied (*Ach.* 532) and parody may well be present here. Cf. (after Tyrwhitt) 938 with Ath. 694 d (*PMG* 889), εἴθ' ἐξῆν ὁποῖός τις ἦν ἕκαστος . . . This author (694 c–696 a) has numerous examples of the genre.

− − − ∪∪ − ∪ − ∪ − −	phalaecean (*V.* 1226, a scolion
− − − ∪∪ − ∪ − ∪ − −	quotation)
∪∪ − ∪ − − ∪∪ −	*Lys.* 345
− ∪∪ − ∪ − − ∪∪ − ∪ −	*V.* 1246

See Dale, 139 and 142, Raven, § 139.

LINES 934–951

939–41 μὴ 'δει: Elmsley (see apparatus criticus), with prodelision (40 n.).
πρότερον διασποδῆσαι: 113 n., 1016.　　　**ἀνάσιμον:** 'snub-nosed'
(617 n.), scholiast and *Suda* ἄμορφον.　　　**ἀνασχετόν . . . ἐλευθέρῳ:** cf.
Lamachus' exclamation (*Ach.* 618), ὦ δημοκρατία ταῦτα δῆτ' ἀνασχετά;
The old woman also (945) believes in her democratic rights, and
there may be some parodying echo here of typical scolion sentiments
(cf. 945 n.) on freedom.

942–5 Metre: as 938–41.

942–3 οἰμώζων ἄρα: 'to your sorrow, then', *Th.* 248 οἰμώξετἄρ' (i.e.
οἰμώξεται ἄρα). Cf. 648, 1027 nn.　　　**σποδήσεις:** sc. τὴν νέαν. She
means that the law will be enforced.　　　**τἀπὶ Χαριξένης:** 'the era of
Charixena' (a shadowy figure like Coesyra, *Nu.* 800). A musician and
composer of erotica (*EM* 367. 21), she had possibly persisted in
efforts to attract—despite her age—and thus become a by-word,
αὐλεῖ γὰρ σαπρὰ | αὕτη γε κρούμαθ' οἷα τἀπὶ Χαριξένης (Theopomp.
Com. fr. 50), cf. Hsch. ε 113. So Pericles to Elpinice, γραῦς εἶ, γραῦς εἶ,
ὡς πράγματα τηλικαῦτα πράσσειν (Plu. *Per.* 10. 5). If so, the hag means
that Charixena could not (as she, backed by legislation, can) afford to
ignore gibes at her folly. More probably and simply she is saying (in
the form of a proverb, Hsch. loc. cit., *App. Prov.* ii. 82) that 'times
have changed, a new law is in force' Cf. Cratin. fr. 135 οὐκ ἴδια τάδ'
οὐκέτ' ὄντα θ' οἷα τἀπὶ Χαριξένης. Similar expressions: τὰ ἐπὶ Κρόνου
καὶ 'Ρέας (Pl. *Cra.* 402 a), τὰ ἐπὶ Ἀννακοῦ (St. Byz. s.v. 'Ικόνιον).

944–5 κατὰ . . . νόμον: the hag's approach throughout this episode is
purely legalistic (see above).　　　**εἰ δημοκρατούμεθα:** cf. D. xxiv. 99 εἶτ'
ἔτι δημοκρατησόμεθα; Ath. 695 b (the Harmodius scolion, whose metre
has perhaps recalled its words) ὅτε τὸν τύραννον κτανέτην | ἰσονόμους τ'
Ἀθήνας ἐποιησάτην. The hag here (cf. 1055 n.) may be using the
language of the law-courts.

946 ἀλλ' εἶμι: she leaves only now (937 n.), the girl returning to the
window (949 n.).　　　**ὅ τι καὶ δράσεις ποτέ:**'what in the world you
will do' (see 259).　　　**καὶ:** 'actually', 'in fact', 29.　　　**δράσεις:**
R*Λ*Mu1, rightly: she is talking to herself. δράσει (Brunck), cf. *Nu.* 731
φέρε νυν ἀθρήσω πρῶτον ὅ τι δρᾷ τουτονί.

947–51 μόνην: 'alone', 'unattended' (48 n.) 'with her mother out' (913).
ἐφ' ἥν . . . ποθῶν: *Pl.* 675 ἐφ' ἥν ἐπεθύμουν δαιμονίως ἐφερπύσαι.
πεπωκὼς: in the false belief that wine is aphrodisiac (in another sense
he is μεθύων ἔρωτι, *PMG* 376. 2) : cf. Ion of Chios, fr. 2 D.³, 9 'he whom
a fair young mistress waits for will drink more deeply than the others'
(similarly id. fr. 8). The porter in *Macbeth* (II. i) knew better : 'Lechery,
sir, it [drink] provokes and it unprovokes; it provokes desire, but it
takes away the performance.' See also 1092.　　　**ἐξηπάτησα:** the girl
reappears at her window (962 n.).　　　**γράδιον:** 1000, 1003, diminutive (here contemptuous) of γραῦς. Cf. *Pl.* 1095.　　　**ἀλλ' . . . γὰρ:**
indicating a new character's arrival (new to the girl, that is, who has

not so far seen him), cf. καὶ μήν, 41 n. Cf. *Lys.* 1239 ἀλλ' οὑτοιὶ γὰρ αὖθις ἔρχονται πάλιν. **οὑτοσὶ ... αὐτός: 934** n. **'μεμνήμεθα: 40** n.

952a–75 This 'love-duet' (Bowra, *AJP* lxxix [1958], 376–91 : the notes here owe a good deal to his essay) is not exactly paralleled in Greek. Closest are (*a*) a tomb poem from Marisa, dated to 150 B.C. (J. U. Powell, *Coll. Alex.* [1925], 184, Wilamowitz, *GV* 344), (*b*) the (assumed) Greek original of Hor. *Carm.* iii. 9 (though each of these contains a *quarrel*), (*c*) (rather doubtfully) Arist. *Rh.* 1367ª9. Aristophanes here parodies (so Bowra) a certain type of low-life love-song: a type originating with κωμασταί (cf. Thgn. 1046, Eub. fr. 94. 8, X. *Smp.* ii. 1). The metrics of such popular forms are unfamiliar, and may well have allowed looser correspondence (cf. 906 ff., 918 ff. nn.). Abnormal responsion can be found even in tragedy (cf. Dale, 117) and in comedy such laxness can be 'startling' (ibid. 189) : 'responsion', in fact, may merely mean that 'corresponding' verses have the same number of syllables in each. Cf. *V.* 274 ff. ∼ 281*a* ff. and (in general) *Nu.* 1029 ff., 1311 ff., with Dover.

For these reasons the following 'strophe' (952*a*–9*b*) and 'antistrophe' (960–8*b*) are printed with a minimum of emendation of the text which the manuscripts transmit.

952a–9b Metre : trochaic and iambic dimeters, mainly syncopated and catalectic (for the close interrelationship of trochaic and iambic metra see Dale, 94, Raven, §§ 21, 41) with one anapaestic colon (954*b*).

	– ∪ – – ∪ –	2 cr
	∪∪∪ – – ∪ –	2 cr
	∪ – ∪ – ∪ – ∪ –	2 ia
954*a*	– – ∪ – ∪ – ∪ –	2 ia
954*b*	∪∪ – ∪∪ – ∪∪ –	3 an (cf. *Ach.* 285)
	– ∪ – – – ∪ –	lek
	∪∪ – – – – – – ∪∪	2 do
	– ∪∪∪ – – ∪ –	lek
	∪∪∪ – – ∪ –	2 cr
959*a*	– – ∪ – – – ∪ – –	2 tr
959*b*	– ∪ – ∪ – –	cr+ba (ithyphallic)

952a–4a δεῦρο δή: this refrain (960, cf. 958, 967, 971, 974) (*a*) indicates a popular basis for the song, (*b*) recalls like invitations elsewhere (695, *Pax* 709).   **δή:** imperatively, Pl. *Ly.* 203 b *Δεῦρο δή, ἦ δ' ὅς, εὐθὺ ἡμῶν* (*GP* 218). Cf. *δεῦτε δή* (Men. *Dys.* 866).   **φίλον ἐμόν:** the neuter of endearment (970, 1046). So τὰ φίλα, τὰ φίλτατα, one's 'dear ones' (E. *Ion* 613, S. *OT* 366).   **ξύνευνέ:** Bergk, for MSS. ξύνευνός, thereby restoring the iambic dimeter (cf. 954*a*) that we expect. For a similar attraction see S. *Ph.* 760. On balance I prefer this to the catalectic dimeter produced by omitting μοι (as Bothe). The word, here used of the *male* partner (A. *Pr.* 866) is somewhat more common of the *female*

(A. *A.* 1116, S. *Aj.* 1301).   ὅπως ἔσει: hortative-imperatival, 82 n.
Emendation *metri gratia* (ἐμὸς ὅπως τήνδ', Blaydes) is needless.

954b–7 This section of the girl's song adapts to the vernacular (cf. also
972 n.) imagery and ideas from lyric and tragic verse (Bowra, 384).
But folk-songs in primitive cultures may exhibit archaic and 'poetic'
vocabulary alien to that of the current spoken language: and this may
be the truer explanation of the 'high-flown' language of her ditty.
δονεῖ: 'agitates me', 'puts me in a whirl' (as wind does leaves, cf. B. 5.
65). Cf. Bion 6. 5 ἦν δὲ νόον τις "Ερωτι δονεύμενος ἁδὺ μελίσδῃ. The
phrase (in both places) echoes Sapph. fr. 130 (L–P) "Ερος δηὖτέ μ' ὁ
λυσιμέλης δόνει. βοστρύχων: 'clusters', 'curls' (*Nu.* 536).   ἄτοπος:
this word (not in Pindar, Aeschylus, or Sophocles) seems almost literally
'out of place'. But it illustrates the combination in 'song-language' of
the ordinary (*Av.* 1208) and 'poetic'.   ἔγκειται . . . πόθος: 'desire'
(*Th.* 481, cf. 966 n.) 'presses hard on me.' Cf. Archil. frs. 193, 196
West, E. fr. 816. 9 ἔρως βροτοῖσιν ἔγκειται βίου. There may also be
a hint at other uses: Ἀμφυταίῃ τῇ Μένωνος ἔγκεισαι; (Herod. 5. 3). See
apparatus criticus for (needless) suggested alterations.   διακναίσας
ἔχει: 'has me worn away' (355 n.). Cf. Pherecr. fr. 145. 19 ὁ δὲ Τιμόθεός
μ', ὦ φιλτάτη, | κατορώρυχεν | καὶ διακέκναιχ' ᾄσχιστα. The verb marks
(*a*) physical wasting, Hp. *Morb.* i. 13 ἡ ἀσιτίη διακναίει (cf. *Nu.* 120), (*b*)
anguish, physical (A. *Pr.* 93) or mental (E. *Heracl.* 295), (*c*) complete
overthrow, destruction (E. *Med.* 164, cf. *Pax* 251).

958–9b The refrain (a mark of folk-song) is repeated, 967–8b.   μέθες:
'release me' (i.e. from my πόθος), 'grant me the indulgence of my love.'
The idea of Love as a *tormentor* and of consummation as *release*, is
notably at variance with later traditions of 'romance' (*Daphnis and
Chloe, Romeo and Juliet*). The singer here, incidentally, may well be
merely Juliet's age (Introduction p. xxxvii, n. 3): she is anyway under
twenty (984), and her boy friend may be very little older.   ἱκνοῦμαί
σ': parenthetic, as S. *Ph.* 932.

960–8b Metre: trochaic dimeters, mainly syncopated and catalectic, with
a catalectic iambic dimeter (968b). For anapaests and dochmiacs (964,
965) and aeolic cola (966) in iambo-trochaic (963) contexts, see Raven,
§§ 95, 96, 131. There is only very loose response with 952a–9b (n.).

	(1)	−∪− −∪−	2 cr
	(2)	∪∪∪− −∪−	2 cr
	(3)	∪∪∪−∪−∪−	lek
	(4)	∪−− −−∪− ∪∪∪− −∪−	ba+ia+2 cr
	(5)	−−−− −∪−−−	an+hypodochmiac (E. *IT* 870)
965	(6)	−−−− ∪∪−−−	an+dochmiac (S. *OC* 118)
	(7)	∪∪∪−− −−∪∪−−	cr+reizianum
	(8)	∪∪∪− −∪−	2 cr
968a	(9)	−∪−− −∪−−	2 tr
968b	(10)	−∪− ∪−−	cr+ba (ithyph)

(1) and (2) correspond exactly to 952*a*, 952*b*, (8), (9), and (10) to 958, 959*a*, 959*b*. The other responsions are: (3) lek ∼ 2 ia (cf. A. *Pr.* 182 ∼ 163), (4) ba+ia+2 cr (cf. Wilamowitz's colometry in B. 17. 23 ff., *GV* 302) ∼ 2 ia, (5) an+hypo (cf. Pi. *I.* 7. 17) ∼ 3 an+lek (954*b*+955), (6) an+do (cf. A. *Pers.* 976) ∼ 2 do (for an ∼ do, see Dale, 54, on A. *Pers.* 908 ff.) (7) cr+reizianum (cf. latter part of Pi. *O.* 2. 20, 9. 11) ∼ lek.

960–3 δεῦρο δή: 952 n.   **φίλον ⟨ἐμόν⟩, καὶ σύ μοι**: Wilamowitz. Cf. 952 (n.). The manuscripts read φίλον in front of ἀλλ' in 964.   **καταδραμοῦσ'** . . . **ἄνοιξον**: 'run down and open' (the girl is upstairs, at her window, 884 n.). The verb may also connote 'hurry' (Plu. *Moralia* 512 e), though the use there may be otherwise explained.   **τήνδ'**: pointing to the girl's front door.   **καταπεσὼν κείσομαι**: the traditional gesture of the lover in despair, Theoc. 3. 52 οὐκέτ' ἀείδω, | κεισεῦμαι δὲ πεσών (cf. *Nu.* 126), Call. *Epigr.* 63. 1. See Pl. *Smp.* 183 a, 203 d: and cf. (for example) Hor. *Carm.* iii. 10. 2, Mart. x. 13. 7 'ad nocturna iaces fastosae limina moechae.' But the youth here is not a type of 'exclusus amator' (Lucr. iv. 1177), for the girl has no disinclination to admit him (indeed invites him, 952): and his song is not a παρακλαυσίθυρον (Plu. *Moralia* 753 b: cf. Rufin. *AP* v. 103. 1 μέχρι τίνος, Προδίκη, παρακλαύσομαι;) despite Headlam–Knox's comprehensive note on Herod. 2. 34. One may isolate it only by ignoring the obvious form of the duet.

965 πληκτίζεσθαι: this verb (or δια-) (*a*) means 'to come to blows with' (Plu. *Luc.* 31. 6), (*b*) is used of the 'skirmishing' of love. So Str. xi. 8. 5 πινόντων ἅμα καὶ πληκτιζομένων πρὸς ἀλλήλους ἅμα τε καὶ τὰς συμπινούσας γυναῖκας (though Headlam–Knox, Herod. 5. 29, explain it as there meaning 'bandy jests'), Plu. *Tim.* 14. 2. Similarly, πληκτισμός (Strat. *AP* xii. 209. 4).   **μετά**: perhaps here 'with the help of' (Pl. *Smp.* 179 a), Taillardat, *Images*, 102 n. 2. And does πυγή mean 'bottom parts', not simply 'bottom' (cf. *Pax* 868)?

966 Κύπρι: i.e. Aphrodite. She is sometimes seen as 'mother' of πόθος (956, which personified may thus be synonymous with Ἔρως), A. *Supp.* 1038. Scopas (Plin. *Nat.* xxxvi. 4. 13, cf. Paus. i. 43. 6) 'fecit Venerem et Pothon'. See also Phld. *AP* x. 21. 2 Κύπρι Πόθων μῆτερ ἀελλοπόδων, Babr. 32. 2. Cf. Hor. *Carm.* i. 19. 1, ibid. iv. 1. 5.   **ἐκμαίνεις ἐπὶ**: 'drive mad with love for', Ant. Lib. 34. 1 δεινὸς γὰρ αὐτὴν ἔρως ἐξέμηνεν ἐπὶ τῷ πατρί, cf. Theocr. 10. 31. For the question see *AP* xii. 89. 1 Κύπρι, τί μοι . . . ἤλασας ἰούς;

967–8*b* 958–9*b* nn., with the change of τόνδε into τήνδε.

969–75 (1) This whole passage may be given to the youth (R, and all editors before Hermann), (2) the first four lines may be given to the girl (Hermann, van Leeuwen, Hall and Geldart). The second course, continuing the form of the duet, appears superficially attractive: but (*a*) ἄνοιξον in the girl's mouth is unnatural (it seems unlikely, despite

Bowra, 381, that such inept use of conventional refrains is Aristophanes' target), (b) the impassioned repetition of his plea by the young man is effective and dramatic: his *cri de cœur* is answered by the hag (details and discussion in the notes).

969–72 Metre: aeolic and iambic.

$--\cup--\cup\cup- \quad --\cup-\cup--$	choriambic dimeter + catalectic iambic dimeter
$--\cup--\cup\cup- \quad -\cup\cup-\cup--$	choriambic dimeter + catalectic iambic dimeter with choriambic 'substitution' (898)
$\cup-\cup---\cup$	catalectic iambic dimeter
$\cup\cup-\cup\cup- \quad \cup-$	acephalous glyconic (telesillean)

969 καὶ . . . ἀνάγκην: and yet (καὶ . . . μέντοι, in spite of all I *have* said) my words have come nowhere near my feelings. The girl has not yet left the window (despite the scholiast at 959): so he ends (973a) with a long string of endearments, and a passionate plea (repeated) for admission. In *her* mouth, the words would mean 'this song too' (like my own) 'inadequately speaks of what I feel' (μέντοι emphasizing ταῦτα, as in comedy it often does a pronoun, cf. *V.* 426, *Av.* 661). ἀνάγκην: Pl. *R.* 458 d οὐ γεωμετρικαῖς . . . ἀλλ' ἐρωτικαῖς ἀνάγκαις (cf. *Nu.* 1075).

970–2 φίλτατον: 952 n.   **ὦ ἱκετεύω:** fused by synizesis. Or possibly ὦ is shortened by correption (*Lys.* 1304): when the dimeter will scan $-\cup\cup\cup\cup--$.   **ἄνοιξον:** sc. τὴν θύραν (962). Cf. A. *Ch.* 877 ἀλλ' ἀνοίξατε | ὅπως τάχιστα. The word in the girl's mouth is not literally apt (Hermann ἄρηξον, von Velsen ἄνελθε κἀσπάζου με): and though this, in an echo of 'conventional refrains', may not be a serious objection, it does strike an odd note in a context where there *is* a door of which she herself is on the *in*side.   **διά . . . ἔχω:** his choice of expression emphasizes the goddess-like powers commanded by his girlfriend, cf. E. *Cyc.* 1 ὦ Βρόμιε, διὰ σὲ μυρίους ἔχω πόνους.   **διά τοι σὲ:** 'it's because of you, you know' (35 n.).   **πόνους:** of the pains of love, as Strat. *AP* xii. 258. 2.

973a–5 Metre: as 969–72 (resolution in the iambic dimeter, 973a, | ∪ – ∪∪∪––). The language (a) parodies Ibycus and tragedy and generally lofty lyric style, (b) mocks the more pretentious element in certain types of ancient song (Bowra, 388).   **χρυσοδαίδαλτον:** E. *IA* 219 (applied to a horse with splendid trappings).   **ἐμὸν μέλημα:** 905 n. **Κύπριδος ἔρνος:** Pi. fr. 78. 1 (Bowra) Λατοῦς ἱμεροέστατον ἔρνος, E. *IA* 116 ὦ Λήδας ἔρνος.   **μέλιττα Μούσης:** a compliment to her song (952a–9b), as well as an endearment (ὦ μελίττιον, *V.* 367). The noun is used (a) of poets (as Phrynichus, *Av.* 748, Sophocles, *Vita* 20), B. 9. 10 (cf. Hor. *Carm.* iv. 2. 27), (b) of their poetry (Pi. *P.* 10. 54). Cf. τὸν Μουσῶν τέττιγα (i.e. the poet's soul), Posidipp. *AP* xii. 98. 1. **Χαρίτων θρέμμα:** θρέμματα . . . Νηρεΐδων, *PMG* 939. 9; σεμνᾶν Χαρίτων

μέλημα τερπνόν, Pi. fr. 85. 3 (Bowra). The noun recurs, *Lys.* 369.
Muses and Graces in conjunction: Hes. *Th.* 64, E. *HF* 673. **Τρυφῆς:**
personified again (as the name of wine) Alex. fr. 230. 3, a girl's name
(Mel. *AP* v. 154. 2). See *Lys.* 387 and (generally) 901 n. For the use
of πρόσωπον, Pi. *N.* v. 16, E. *IA* 1089 τὸ τᾶς Αἰδοῦς | ἢ τὸ τᾶς Ἀρετᾶς ... |
πρόσωπον. Cf. *Av.* 1321.

The whole passage echoes Ibyc. fr. 7 (*PMG* 288) Εὐρύαλε γλαυκέων
Χαρίτων θάλος ⟨   ⟩ | καλλικόμων μελέδημα, σὲ μὲν Κύπρις | ἅ τ'
ἀγανοβλέφαρος Πει-|θὼ ῥοδέοισιν ἐν ἄνθεσι θρέψαν. Agathon speaks
of 'the celebrated Ibycus' (*Th.* 161), bracketing him with Alcaeus
and Anacreon (cf. fr. 223) as a writer dressed to match his own
erotics.

976 The youth follows up his request in 961 with an impatient knocking
on her door. But before the girl (who has stayed beside the window to
hear the serenade to its conclusion) can come down to the doorway to
admit him, the hag rushes forward and accosts him (she has not been
far away, see 946). She pretends that she has heard a knock at *her*
door: which he strongly (and truthfully) denies. The passage does
not imply a *single* door as background (whatever may be true of other
places): see Introduction § III. **οὗτος:** 372 n. **τί κόπτεις;** sc. τὴν
θύραν (*Nu.* 132): cf. *Av.* 59 ποιήσεις ... με κόπτειν αὖθις ... The
word is neutral: the *manner* of his knocking is explained by ἤραττες
(below). For the 'vocabulary of knocking' see W. W. Mooney, *The
House-Door on the Ancient Stage* (Baltimore, Md., 1914), 20 ff. **μῶν
... ζητεῖς;** 'are you looking for me, by any chance?' ('num forte',
348 n.). The young man's reply is 'Don't be silly' (for which use of
πόθεν; see 389).

977 καὶ ... γ' ἤραττες: 'yes, and what's more (140) you *battered* on the
door', E. *Hec.* 1044 ἄρασσε, φείδου μηδέν, ἐκβάλλων πύλας, cf. *Eq.* 641.
τὴν θύραν: i.e. '*my* door' (cf. *Ra.* 38), not implying that the scene has
only one. **ἀποθάνοιμ' ἄρα:** 'I'm damned if I did' (ἄρα as commonly,
'in that case', cf. for example 942) sc. εἰ ἤραττον τὴν θύραν. Such
expressions are commoner with reference to future, νὴ Δί' ἀπολοίμην
ἄρα ('if I cheat you', *Lys.* 933) or present, ἀπολοίμην εἴ σε δέδοικα (*V.*
630).

978–81 τοῦ δαὶ δεόμενος; 'well, what *is* your business, then?' (if not
what one naturally thinks of, 934), since you come with a torch (see
692). Cf. *Ach.* 764 τί δαὶ φέρεις; i.e. if you haven't salt or garlic.
Ἀναφλύστιον ... ἄνθρωπον: 'some fellow from the deme of Anaphlys-
tus' (X. *Vect.* iv. 43: it was situated west of the Laurium hills,
C. W. J. Eliot, *Coastal Demes of Attika* [Toronto, 1962], 79–81, and
further W. K. Pritchett, *Studies in Ancient Greek Topography* i [Berkeley
and Los Angeles, Calif. 1965], 135–7) which lent itself to puns on
ἀναφλάω (i.e. δέφομαι, 709), 'but not the one *you*'re maybe looking out
for', i.e. Σεβῖνον ὅστις ἐστὶν ἀναφλύστιος (*Ra.* 427). Any person so

named (suggesting βινεῖν) would be liable (like Lamius, 77 n.) for wisecracks. The name here is probably a coinage: but cf. (for example) Posthalion (*SEG* xvii. 829. 3).   νὴ τὴν Ἀφροδίτην: 189, 999 nn. ἤν . . . μή: i.e. you're going to *get* Sebinus, whether you're wanting him or not. Cf. 1097, *Lys.* 1036.

982–4 He explains his position in the language of the law-courts: 'I'm not handling the "cases" (sc. δίκας) over sixty.' An εἰσαγωγεύς (*Ath. Pol.* 52. 2) was responsible for introducing cases which were due to be heard within a month: the youth has no wish for an appointment which will limit his chances of slipping out of 'acting'. He transfers to terms of *age* legal language which dealt in terms of *monetary value* (*Ath. Pol.* 53. 3), thereby (*a*) indicating the respective ages of the claimants, (*b*) satirizing (it may be) the slowness of judicial procedure (cf. the Court of Chancery in *Bleak House*). In another sense also (εἰσάγειν γυναῖκα, Hdt. v. 40. 2) he refuses to 'introduce' a woman over sixty, while quite prepared to sit it out and settle finally (οἱ ναυτοδίκαι οὐκ ἐξεδίκασαν, *Lys.* xvii. 5) a case which concerns one under twenty. ἀλλ' οὐχὶ νυνὶ: 'not just at the moment', 104 n., 991.   εἰσαῦθις ἀναβεβλήμεθα: 'we've put it off till some other occasion', E. fr. 11. 52 (*GLP* iii. 76) δ[έδοκται] μὴ ἀναβάλλεσθαι δίκην, Pl. *Smp.* 174 e εἰς αὖθις ἀναβαλοῦ. For position of γάρ cf. *Nu.* 1198.

985–6 The young man (she alleges) is living in the past if he thinks that that is how things happen now.   ἐπὶ τῆς προτέρας ἀρχῆς: when the men were in power (cf. 830).   ἐπὶ . . . ἀρχῆς γε . . . νυνὶ δέ (γε approximate to μέν), E. *Andr.* 5 ζηλωτὸς ἔν γε τῷ πρὶν . . . χρόνῳ, | νῦν δ' . . . δυστυχεστάτη γυνή.   ὦ γλύκων: cf. ὦ γλυκύτατον (1046). But the word here implies no real affection, and is rather indicative of triumph (she thinks that she has him where she wants him): 'that's not just at the moment' (taking up his own word), 'sweetie.'

987–8 τῷ βουλομένῳ γε . . . νόμον: she is clearly conversant with law and he can counter only feebly from the laws that govern πεττοί (a game that may be either 'draughts' or 'dicing', Page on E. *Med.* 68). He seems to be referring to some rule by which a player might εἰσάγειν (a third sense, as a special term in πεττοί?) or refuse to do so, at his pleasure (τῷ βουλομένῳ is formulaic in a law, cf. 615, 1019 n.). R*Λ*Mui and scholiast, who sees a pun on παίειν, read Παιτοῖς, a Thracian tribe referred to by Herodotus (vii. 110).   ἀλλ' οὐδὲ δειπνεῖς . . . νόμον: i.e. you don't raise quibbles about *eating* (he is, after all, just coming from the meal).

989–91 The young man, now running out of patience (cf. Chremes, 833) turns towards the girl's door to knock again. But the hag claims precedence for *her* 'door' (θύρα of *any* entrance or exit, 316, Apollod. Com. fr. 13. 9): whereupon he says he does not want a flour-sieve. τηνδεδί: sc. θύραν, as the woman's answer shows (the girl has by this time left the window, but does not appear till 1037). For the form

(27 n.) see *Av*. 18.   **κρουστέον**: 317, *sensu obscaeno* (*κρούματα*, 257) as elsewhere *ὑπο-* and *προκρούω* (256, 1017). Dover, however, thinks the *literal* sense is meant here and the *double entendre* picked up in 990 (*PCPhS* N.S. xii [1966], 15).   **ὅταν . . . θύραν**: the line must not, of course, be quoted to support one's theory of two doors in the back stage.   **ἀλλ' οὐχὶ νυνί**: 982.   **κρησέραν**: with punning reference to *κρούσῃς*, though the sense of the noun is not quite clear. The scholiast and *Suda* explain it as rough cloth for casing wicker baskets (cf. Moritz, 163 n. 2). More probably, the meaning is 'a flour sieve' (Poll. vi. 74, x. 114): cf. *κρησερίτης*, 'bread baked from sifted flour' (Diph. fr. 26), and the youth is comparing the hag's *θύρα* to the perforation in the sieve. A reference to her over-whitened face (van Leeuwen, 878, 1101 nn.) or white hair (Taillardat, *Images* 52, cf. 730–2) seems rather less appropriate in the context.

992–3 She pretends that she thinks *he* is pretending, and attributes his conduct to surprise. 'You can't believe it's me, the modest maiden' who would not, as a rule, be at her door. Cf. 884 n., E. fr. 521 'it behoves the *good* woman to be staying inside, the worthless one to be *θύρασι'* (below).   **νῦν**: 'as things are at the moment' (153).   **θύρασι**: i.e. *ἐπὶ ταῖς θύραις*, 1114. See also 997 n.   **ἀλλὰ πρόσαγε . . . στόμα**: cf. *Lys*. 893 and (for use of *ἀλλά*) 852 n.

994–7 He fears her lover ('the best of painters', Death) (*a*) for himself, because the hag will kill him (cf. 1030–3) if she manages to carry out her purpose, (*b*) for her, should Death find her thus immodest, and exact his revenge (see 1036). She should thus anticipate him by departing. Cf. the young girl's similar taunt against her aged rival (905) : so, to an old man with one foot in the grave (*Lys*. 372), 'Why have you come with fire, *τύμβε*; in order to set fire to *yourself*?'

994–5 ἀλλ', ὦ μέλ': 'but my dear woman, I'm in terror of your lover', remonstrance (see 120 n.) with heavy sarcasm overlaid.

995–7 τὸν . . . ἄριστον: the third place (571, 647 nn.) where critics (incredibly) find reference to Plato. Other candidates : Aristophanes the vase painter (Hauser, 100), more vaguely, 'the undertaker' (Rogers). But 'the finest of the painters' is surely Death himself, who 'paints' (i.e. causes to be painted) 'the funeral oil flasks for the dead'. A further (not quite convincing) explanation is suggested by J. H. Quincey, 'The Metaphorical Sense of *ΛΗΚΥΘΟΣ* and *AMPULLA*', *CQ* xliii (1949), 39–40. He thinks that *λήκυθοι* was colloquially used for cheeks (originally when inflated with blowing, from the shape of the spherical lekythos called aryballos, see Richter and Milne, 16, figs. 103, 104). 996 then has a secondary sense, 'the man who paints the cheeks of old women who have one foot in the grave' : a reference (*a*) to the hags' white lead and rouge (878, 904, 929, 1072), (*b*) to the colours (red and white) with which funeral lekythoi were painted. The youth's refusal to kiss the old woman is 'for fear of smearing the painter's work and daubing his own cheeks . . . in the process'. See also 1101, 1111 nn. Lekythoi, one-handled, narrow-necked vases, were used (*a*) in general, as oil jars (*Av.* 1589), (*b*) in particular, for offerings of oil and unguents to the dead (scholiast on Pl. *Hp. Mi.* 368 c). They were placed beside the body on the bier (538, 1032), and also (as is actually shown on surviving vases) by the tomb. See Richter and Milne, 14 ff., figs. 91–102.   ζωγράφει: 'decorates with figures' (ibid. 15, 18).   ἐπὶ θύραισιν: omission of the article may make the phrase more general, i.e. 'outside' (θύρασι, *Pax* 942, *Th.* 792) not 'at the door' (1114 n.). Cf. however Arist. *Rh.* 1363ᵃ7, 'the proverb, to break the pitcher ἐπὶ θύραις' ('on the doorstep', having carried it successfully thus far).

998–1001 Each understands the other's wishes, and the hag is determined that *hers* will be accomplished.

998 οἶδ' . . . βούλει: cf. *Ra.* 580.   καὶ γὰρ ἐγώ σε: sc. οἶδα, ὅ τι βούλει, as Rogers notes, a somewhat strange ellipsis. But that this is the meaning is confirmed by her reply, 'you're right, and I'll not let you escape me.'   καὶ γὰρ: 'yes, and . . .', *Eq.* 1092, E. *IA* 640 Ιφ. ὦ πάτερ, ἐσεῖδόν σ' ἀσμένη πολλῷ χρόνῳ. | Αγ. καὶ γὰρ πατὴρ σέ. But ἐγώ σέ (Blaydes) in the present passage would destroy the parallelism of the thought.

999–1000 μὰ τὴν Ἀφροδίτην . . . κληρουμένη: Aphrodite has favoured her, and hence her boastful claim of that mighty goddess as her δαίμων (Latin 'Iuno'), by whom she appropriately swears. Cf. Aristophanes' oath, *Nu.* 519. So too she feels it her duty to the goddess not to let slip opportunities for love (hence her firm μὴ 'γώ σ' ἀφήσω). The phraseology suggests the 'province' allotted to a deity: Παῖ 'Ρέας, ἅ τε πρυτανεία λέλογχας, Ἑστία (Pi. *N.* 11. 1). For belief in one's personal δαίμων see Men. fr. 534Α 2, 'a δαίμων attends every man at the moment of his birth, a good guide for his life'; for the allocation of souls to their own δαίμονες, Pl. *Phd.* 107 d; for the use of κληρόω Alciphr. iii. 13. 1 (perhaps a reminiscence of this passage) ὦ δαῖμον, ὅς με κεκλήρωσαι καὶ εἴληχας. And for her formula of resolution (cf. 1075, 1085) see *Lys.* 917.   παραφρονεῖς: 250 n.   ὦ γρᾴδιον: 949 n.

1001 ἄξω . . . στρώματα: we are not to assume (with Rogers) that at this point the hag lays violent hands upon the boy. On the contrary, she continues with persuasion and with argument (including the reading of the law, 1015) till driven to action by his taunt (1036) just as the girl at last emerges.

1002–4 Why do we bother buying hooks, when one could use a hag shaped like *this* for drawing water? So Sosipolis (*AP* xi. 199. 3) οὐ λίνον, οὐ κάλαμον προσάγων τῇ ῥινὶ δὲ προσθεὶς | ἄγκιστρον, σύρει πάντα τὰ νηχόμενα.   τί δῆτα . . . ; 24 n., 1151.   κρεάγρας: strictly, for lifting meat (κρέας) from a pot (*V.* 1155–6), but here regarded, in a broader sense, as implements for drawing up pots (κάδοι) from a well. Comparison with a κρεάγρα (Pritchett, 295) is invited by her skinny arms and fingers: it was 'shaped like a hand with the fingers slightly bent' (scholiast, *Eq.* 772), cf. the example from Olynthus (*Excavations*, x. 198, pl. l. 623). A figure holding a κρεάγρα is depicted on a red-figure stamnos in Berlin (P. Jacobsthal, *Ornamente griechischer Vasen* [Berlin, 1927], pl. 96a). For κάδοι as pots for drawing water see Men. *Dysc.* 190 'the nurse was drawing water, and let the κάδος fall into the well.' Their various shapes and sizes may be seen in D. A. Amyx, 'The Attic Stelai iii', *Hesperia* xxvii (1958), 186–90 (illustrations pl. 47).

The actor thus compared to a κρεάγρα—even if his exceptional skinniness of limb is more to be imagined than presented—was probably both himself thin by nature and (like Praxagora, 539 n.) unpadded. There are other references to thinness in the theatre: the chorus in *Wasps* (1071) are tightly corseted, and Poverty (*Pl.* 561) presumably resembles her adherents, who are spoken of as ἰσχνοί and σφηκώδεις.

1005–7 μὴ σκῶπτέ μ' . . . **ἀλλ'**: 'stop making fun of me, and . . .', 1074, cf. *Nu.* 1267 μὴ σκῶπτέ μ' ὦ τᾶν, ἀλλά . . . κέλευσον. But we need not substitute τᾶν (Bentley) here. **ὦ τάλαν:** 124 n. **δεῦρ':** into her house (1054). **μούστίν:** 785 n. **τὴν πεντακοσιοστὴν:** sc. μοῖραν (825 n.), but the point of the reference is doubtful. The sense seems to be, 'I am not compelled to follow you, unless you have paid the legal tax' (the article suggests a current levy—0·2 per cent on property, including slaves, transferred?). On that assumption (van Leeuwen) I interpret, 'I am not your legal property, unless . . .' (and so not bound to carry out your orders). **τῶν ἐμῶν:** almost ἐμοῦ (393). ἐτῶν (Tyrwhitt) is ingenious (cf. *Pl.* 1083) but needless.

1008–10 νὴ τὴν Ἀφροδίτην: still swearing by her 'Iuno' (999 n.). **γε μέντοι:** adversative (410 n.), here used almost as μὲν οὖν ('quite the contrary, you *must*'). She answers the boy's *legal* argument with one much more *personal*, thus risking the chance of a personal reply (δὲ . . . γε, in lively answers, 728 n.).

1011–20 The personal argument failing, she falls back upon the law: producing (τουτί, 27 n.) and reading a copy of Praxagora's decree. For a similar enactment ('nach dem die alten Männer nur junge Mädchen heiraten sollen, die Jünglinge aber—nur alte Weiber') see the Ukrainian folk-tale cited by B. Warnecke, *WS* li (1933), 140. The passage illustrates the style and language (987 n.) employed in ψηφίσματα and νόμοι. **τί ποτε κἄστι:** 'what in the world it *is*' (καί, 946 n.). He knows, of course, all too well already (938). **καὶ δή . . . λέγω:** 'I'm *telling* you' (in response to your request, see 514 n.), with that request repeated (cf. *Av.* 175). **ἔδοξε ταῖς γυναιξίν:** 455 n., *Th.* 373 ἔδοξε τῇ βουλῇ τάδε | τῇ τῶν γυναικῶν. **σποδεῖν:** 113, 939. **προκρούσῃ:** 256, 990, cf. Προκρούστης (1021 n.). **γυναιξίν . . .**

λαβομένας: so σοι . . . λαβόντα (*Eq.* 1394), see Poultney, *Syntax*, 369. ἔστω: in legal contexts, 'let it be permissible', [ἔ]σ[τ]ο ἀ[ποφέρε]σθαι τôι βολομένοι (*IG* i². 10. 7); equivalent, that is, to ἐξέστω: μὴ ἐξέστ[ω ταῖς] πόλεσιν εὐθύνας λαμβάνειν (*IG* iv².68. 75). Cf. also 1026.   ἕλκειν ἀνατεὶ: 'drag off' (259), 'manhandle with impunity' (a legal use, Pl. *Lg.* 871 d), as one could not (Aeschin. i. 35) the chairmen in the boule or Assembly.   τοῦ παττάλου: literally 'peg' (284), here τοῦ πέους (*AP* v. 129. 5). Cf. *Ach.* 1216, *Lys.* 1115–21.

1021–2 The youth will become a 'Procrustes', if the hag insists on the letter of the law. She does ('yes, for . . .', 375). Procrustes (cf. 1029 n.) was a celebrated brigand of Eleusis (in another version known as Procoptas, B. 17. 28), who stretched (προκρούω) his victims on a bed (D.S. iv. 59. 5). But the boy, of course, is punning on the sense of προκρούειν (1018). Similarly, *V.* 151.   τοῖς . . . νόμοις . . . πειστέον: her patriotism, though expressed in words like those of Chremes, resembles that of Woman *B*'s husband (762, 853).

1023–7 Suppose a demesman or a friend should bail him out? Impossible, since men are now restricted (as women used to be) to minor contracts. Can he not be excused on oath? No legal loop-holes now. Suppose he claims exemption from duty, as a merchant? If he does so, he will do it to his sorrow.

1023–4 ἀφαιρῆταί μ': 'go bail for me', *Lys.* xxiii. 10 (with synonymous use of ἐξαιρεῖσθαι) ἵν' εἰδείην τόν τ' ἐξαιρησόμενον αὐτὸν καὶ ὅ τι λέγων ἀφαιρήσοιτο (sc. εἰς ἐλευθερίαν, ibid. 11, D. lix. 40). Later, in desperation, the boy offers (1064 n.) to find two securities himself.   ἀνὴρ τῶν δημοτῶν: 348 n., 1115. Athenian youths were registered, at the age of eighteen, in their demes (*Ath. Pol.* 42. 1), and members of a deme would 'stick together' (*Ach.* 333, 675). The present passage implies that one could look to a fellow demesman for assistance (as in danger, *Lys.* 684) in putting up the necessary bail. *Entertainment* (ἑστίασις) of one's demesmen was an obligation on the wealthy (Thphr. *Char.* 10. 11): and Cimon not only discharged the common liturgies, but τῶν δημοτῶν ἔτρεφε πολλούς (*Ath. Pol.* 27. 3).

1024–5 κύριος | ὑπὲρ μέδιμνον: legally entitled (Arist. *Pol.* 1287ᵇ16) to enter into contracts where more than a μέδιμνος is involved. For this previous restriction upon *women* (446 n.) cf. Is. x. 10. 2 (with Wyse), 'for the law absolutely forbids the possibility of an infant's entering into contracts, or of a woman's doing so πέρα μεδίμνου κριθῶν.' At this time a μέδιμνος (six ἑκτῆς, approximately one and a half bushels) was selling for three drachmae (547 n.).

1026 ἐξωμοσία: literally, 'swearing' oneself 'out' (of public office), by putting forth excuses under oath (ἔστιν, legally possible, 1019 n.). Aeschines pleads ill health, with medical support (D. xix. 124), and the ὑπερήφανος his lack of leisure (Thphr. *Char.* 24. 5). 'To refuse an appointment on oath and give no reason was a strange thing and a

great cause of suspicion' (D., loc. cit.) : and the boy will not evade his
duties by a 'wriggle' (στροφή, a metaphor from wrestling, 259 n., cf.
Ra. 775; στρόφις, a 'twister', *Nu.* 450). Cf. in general *Pl.* 1154, and
for οὐ δεῖ (i.e. 'it's not a matter for . . .'), *Lys.* 432 οὐ γὰρ μοχλῶν δεῖ
μᾶλλον ἢ νοῦ . . .

1027 ἀλλ' ἔμπορος . . . σκήψομαι: merchants were exempted from
military service, and the youth (by posing as one) will claim exemption
from the dangerous conflict which now threatens. So the scholiast:
but perhaps the boy means rather 'as a merchant I shall get the law-
suit quashed.' In other words, he challenges the present court's
authority, for merchants were answerable only before a bench of
ναυτοδίκαι (Lys. xvii. 5). On either explanation cf. *Pl.* 904 Δι. ἀλλ'
ἔμπορος; Συ. ναί, σκήπτομαί γ', ὅταν τύχω. **κλάων γε σύ:** 'to your
sorrow', 'you'll regret it', *Ach.* 827 (similarly 942).

1028–33 What must he do then? She is firm in repetition of her earlier
command (1005). But the boy's former confidence (1006) has
vanished: his assertion has now become a question (and a question to
which he knows the answer). So he bids her prepare the bed—of
death. The preparations which follow are those requisite for ritually
laying out a corpse (cf. 537–8 nn.) : for prothesis and funeral scenes
on vases see W. Zschietzschmann, 'Die Darstellung der Prothesis
in der griechischen Kunst', *MDAI* liii (1928), 17–36, pls. VIII–
XVIII.

1028–9 τί . . . δρᾶν; with a note of resignation. The phrase (see 404) is
formulaic.   **Διομήδειά γε:** sc. ἀνάγκη, a seemingly proverbial
expression to indicate the ultimate compulsion (ἡ Διομηδεία λεγομένη
ἀνάγκη, Pl. *R.* 493 d). The scholiast *there* refers the proverb to a story
of Diomedes harried by Odysseus: the scholiast *here* accepts the version
of Clearchus (in Hsch., s.vv. Διομήδειος ἀνάγκη). In this, a lesser-
known Diomedes subjected passers-by to the compulsion of lying with
his daughters, who were harlots: a situation (whether or not it is
accepted as the true origin of the expression) akin to the boy's position
here. Διομήδειᾰ, as Θεσπιέπειᾰ (πέτρα, S. *OT* 463).

1030–1 ὑποστόρεσαι . . . ὀριγάνου: 'well (since there's no help) strew dittany beneath us', as the custom was (clearly) with a corpse: cf. (though
in unknown context) *PMG* 799 τεταμένον ὀρίγανα διὰ μυελοτρεφῆ. The
bier is appropriate—the youth has been compelled to play the role of
Death (see 994 n.).   **ὀριγάνου:** 'dittany', a pungent-smelling herb
(δριμυτάτην ὀρίγανον, Pl. Com. fr. 154). The same passage illustrates
the *feminine* declension (masculine, Anaxandr. fr. 50; neuter, *Ra.* 603),
cf. Alex. fr. 188. 1.   **κλήμαθ'** . . . **τέτταρα:** sc. ἀμπέλου, Pl. *R.*
353 a, i.e. a number (τέτταρα particular for general, cf. *Ra.* 915,
Men. *Dysc.* 390) of broken vine twigs. The twigs would serve, when
the laying-out was over, to kindle the body on the bier. Cf. *Th.*
728.

1032-3 ταινιῶσαι: 'decorate with ribbons'. The magistrate, bidden to
'go away and die' (*Lys.* 599), is presented (602-4) with fillets and
garlands (see 1034 n.).   **τὰς ληκύθους**: the *customary* oil flasks
(hence the article, as *τοὔστρακον* in 1033), cf. 538, 996 nn.   **ὕδατος
... θύρας**: a water jug (called technically *ὄστρακον*, Poll. viii. 66) was
placed in front of house-doors at a death. Its purpose (Pollux
says) was for visitors to sprinkle and purify themselves upon departure.
The custom is well known from E. *Alc.* 98 'I do not see . . . lustral
water from the spring as the custom is at the door of the departed'
(the queen, that is, cannot be dead). For archaeological evidence
of the funerary customs here see *Excavations*, xi (*Necrolynthia*),
184-7.

1034-6 The hag feigns to misunderstand his meaning. In his catalogue
of wedding preparations (cf. *Necrolynthia*, 184) he has left out a
garland (she reminds him): but he'll buy her a garland too (*καί*) yet.
He will, but a wax one (for her grave).

1034-5 ἦ μὴν: with future indicative, introducing (*GP* 350) 'a strong and
confident asseveration' (not here necessarily a threat). Similarly, *Pl.*
608 *ἦ μὴν ὑμεῖς γ' ἔτι μ' ἐνταυθοῖ | μεταπέμψεσθον*.   **στεφάνην**: a
wreath of wax (*τῶν κηρίνων*, sc. *στεφάνων*) appears to have been laid
(like a modern artificial one) beside the dead man's bier or on his
tomb. The use of wax is seen in reference to *κήρ* (Artem. i. 77),
'*στέφανοι κήρινοι* bode ill to all' (in dreams) 'but especially to people
who are sick, since the poets in fact call death *κήρ*' : and for imitative
work in this material (*κηροπλαστική*, Poll. vii. 165) cf. Eub. fr. 41.
This wreath is distinct from that of *real* flowers, which was evidently
placed upon the body (538, E. *Ph.* 1632) : and of course from the
bridal wreath, of which the hag is thinking (E. *IA* 905). See *Necrolynthia*, 17, 201-2. *στεφάνη*, for *στέφανος* (cf. *Eq.* 968).   **νὴ τὸν Δί'
... κηρίνων**: 'yes, by Zeus' (cf. 786) 'at any rate if it's one of . . .', *Eq.*
447 *τὸν πάππον εἶναι φημί σου | τῶν δορυφόρων*.   **γέ που**: like *γοῦν*
(357), cf. Pl. *Tht.* 200 e . . . 'knowledge is true opinion. *ἀναμάρτητόν
γέ πού ἐστιν τὸ δοξάζειν ἀληθῆ*.'

1036 διαπεσεῖσθαί σ': 'you will fall asunder' (*δια-*), cf. *Eq.* 695. She is
long and skinny (1002 n.). Similarly, Chremylus to the old woman,
οὐκ ἀλλὰ κατασέσηπας (cf. 884 n.), *ὥς γ' ἐμοὶ δοκεῖς* (*Pl.* 1035).

1037-42 The young girl now dashes from her doorway. She is just in
time to see her rival (now stung beyond endurance by his taunting)
lay violent hands upon the boy: and puts her to flight (breathing
vengeance, 1044) by suggesting possibilities of incest.

1037 τόνδ' ἐμαυτῆς εἰσάγω: 'this is my *own* "husband"' (727 n.), i.e.
don't you interfere, 'that I'm bringing home' (a reversal of the usual
procedure, 983 n.).

1041-2 εἰ καταστήσεσθε ... νόμον: 'if you (old women) put this law
into force', cf. E. *Or.* 892, *Nu.* 1400 *τῶν καθεστώτων νόμων*.   **τὴν**

γῆν . . . ἐμπλήσετε: you will set a precedent for incest between mothers and their sons, which was hardly Praxagora's intention. For presumably, just as (635 n.) all the young men will think every older man his father (where difference in ages makes it likely), so every old man and woman will think every younger man their son. And after all (the girl is pointing out) you *are* old enough to be his mother. This aspect of the law has not struck the hag, and horrified—as well as enraged at being cheated—she runs (like Jocasta, to whom, by implication, the girl's words in 1042 compare her) back into the house in agitation (S. *OT* 1072). The risk of incestuous relationships (between *males*) is seen by Aristotle as a consequence of Plato's communism (*Pol.* 1262ᵃ33).

1043–4 ὦ παμβδελυρά . . . ἐξηῦρες: 'you have thought up this pretext' (λόγον, Le Febvre, cf. S. *Ph.* 352) 'from envy.' νόμον (MSS., repeated perhaps from 1041) is scarcely credible as 'this (interpretation of) the law'. ἀλλ' . . . τιμωρήσομαι: we are not to look (as van Leeuwen, 1049 n.) for fulfilment of this threat in the play.

1045–8 The boy thanks his rescuer and promises reward. νὴ τὸν Δία τὸν σωτῆρα: the title is more obviously relevant here (to its context in the play) than it is elsewhere. Cf. however 761 n. κεχάρισαί γε: exclamatory γε, with oath (see 70), cf. *Ach.* 867 νεὶ τὸν Ἰόλαον ἐπεχαρίττα γ' ὦ ξένε. ὦ γλυκύτατον: more sincerely than the hag's ὦ γλύκων (985 n.). εἰς ἑσπέραν: 'at evening', as Chremylus too (*Pl.* 1201) promises the hag. For this idiom and its development see Wyse on Is. i. 14. 6. Its fixed use in amatory contexts (cf. *Pax* 966), reflecting a conventional connection perhaps of sexual activity with evening (though see 526 n.), may account for its loose use in the present, where it seems to be evening already: at any rate, the δεῖπνον is long over, and the boy enters carrying a torch (878, 978). μεγάλην . . . χάριν: cf. *Pl.* 1031 (the old hag has been saying that the youth ought to repay her) Χρ. οὔκουν καθ' ἑκάστην ἀπεδίδου τὴν νύκτα σοι; For the special reference of μέγας, παχύς, cf. *Ach.* 787. Similarly, *Pax* 1349, *Lys.* 23.

1049–64 His joy is short-lived, for another hag appears to challenge the girl for his possession. (We are not to connect her arrival with the first old woman's threat, 1044 n., though the actor who played Hag *A*, going off at that point, must certainly have changed masks very quickly to reappear five lines later as Hag *B*: see T. B. L. Webster, 'The Masks of Greek Comedy', *BJRL* xxxii [1949–50], 116). She resembles the frightening Empusa (1056 n.): and so far exceeds the first in ugliness and violence that fear makes the girl quite incapable of trying to save the boy again. *This* old woman, zealous (1049 n.) for the law, disregards the likely consequence (1060), rejecting the sureties he offers with firmness (1064) and contempt.

A. Körte (on the slim grounds of the notice γραῦς β 'in Höhe von V. 8') suspects a scene similar to this one in Pap. Brit. Mus. 404 D (*APF* x [1932], 61, 733).

1049–53 αὕτη σύ: 520, 372 n.   **ποῖ παραβᾶσα . . . ἕλκεις:** in spite of a certain superficial ambiguity, the manuscripts' word-order should be kept (τονδὶ παραβᾶσα, Bothe). See 105, 169, 490 nn. The hag is concerned first and foremost with the law (1055) and its *transgression* (παραβαίνω, Lysias in 1056 n.).   **τῶν γραμμάτων εἰρηκότων:** i.e. 'it is down in black and white.' For γράμματα of statutes, the 'letter' of the law, cf. Pl. *Plt.* 293 a ἐάντε ἑκόντων ἀντ' ἀκόντων ἄρχωσιν, ἐάντε κατὰ γράμματα ἐάντε ἄνευ γραμμμάτων. **οἴμοι δείλαιος:** 391.   **πόθεν ἐξέκυψας . . .;** 'where have you popped out from?', the probable sense also in *Th.* 790 κἀπαγορεύετε (you husbands) μήτ' ἐξελθεῖν μήτ' ἐκκύψασαν ἁλῶναι (though often there translated 'peeping out'). Cf. Ath. 455 e (of a snail) ὄμματά τ' ἐκκύπτοντα προμήκεα κεἰσκτύπτοντα.   **ὦ κάκιστ' ἀπολουμένη:** literally, 'destined to meet a dreadful end', a formula of vigorous abuse (cf. *Pl.* 456). Similarly, 1076.   **τοῦτο . . . ἐξωλέστερον:** 1070.

1054–6 βάδιζε δεῦρο: she lays hands upon the boy and starts to drag him towards the houses in the background (1005).   **μηδαμῶς . . . περίιδῃς:** 'don't watch me . . . (and do nothing about it)', 369 n. He is speaking to the girl, but she has seemingly departed, in terror, at 1048. In any event, she does not speak again: his next appeal is directed (1067) to a third old woman, just arrived.   **ἀλλ' οὐκ ἐγώ, | ἀλλ' ὁ νόμος:** 1049 n. For the formula (a type used in court by the defence, *Rh. Al.* 1442ᵇ8, cf. also 1011 n.) see Lys. i. 26 'I said, "It is not I, but the law of the city, that will kill you: the law that you transgressed (παραβαίνων) and thought less important than your pleasures" ' (a charge that the hag might here well have brought against the boy). Rogers cites *Measure for Measure* II. ii. 80: 'It is the law, not I, condemns your brother.'   **οὐκ ἐμέ γ':** his answer (to parallel οὐκ ἐγώ) means 'the law's not dragging *me*, what's dragging *me* is a bogey.' Similarly, 1066 n.

1056–7 Ἔμπουσά τις: 'a kind of Empusa', 351 n. He thinks that the hag must be some sort of Empusa (a bogey, fr. 500, identified with Hecate, ἐπιτύμβιος γραῦς, Alciphr. iii. 26. 3) in one of her numerous disguises (cf. *Ra.* 288–95). The blood-blisters (next note) give her face the fiery brightness that Xanthias (*Ra.* 293) thinks characteristic of the bogey. And she also (of course) shows an Empusa's noted lustfulness, Philostr. *V.A.* 4. 25.   **ἐξ αἵματος . . . ἠμφιεσμένη:** 'dressed in a blister', i.e. one big blister. So Bdelycleon tells Philocleon that he looks like 'a boil dressed up in garlic', Δοθιῆνι σκόροδον ἠμφιεσμένῳ (V. 1172).   **φλύκταιναν:** a term used by the doctors (251 n.): cf. Hp. *VM* 16.

1058–62 The hag continues to drag him towards the houses: if he's frightened, he can cheer himself inside.   **μαλακίων**: from μαλακός, explained as an endearment ('mignon', Van Daele, 'chickling', Rogers, 'a caressing effect', Peppler, *CT* 36). But this hag does not wheedle (985 n.) and her meaning is rather 'coward', 'faint-heart' (a charge the boy acknowledges, 1060). For μαλακός in this sense see Th. vi. 13. 1. Similarly formed is δειλακρίων (*Pax* 193, *Av.* 143).   **εἰς ἄφοδον**: like εἰς ἀπόπατον (*Ach.* 81), 351 n. Cf. Antiph. fr. 40. 5 εἰς ἄφοδον ἐλθὼν ὅμοιον πᾶσιν αὐτὸν ὄψεται. For a similar request, in an awkward situation, see *Th.* 611.   **θαρρῆσαι πρὸς ἐμαυτόν**: 'to act with self-confidence', cf. Pl. *Prt.* 350 b ἤδη δέ τινας ἑώρακας . . . θαρροῦντας . . . πρὸς ἕκαστα τούτων ;   **τι δρῶντα πυρρὸν . . . | ὑπὸ τοῦ δέους**: like Dionysus (*Ra.* 479), through fear of violence (*Ra.* 477) from women of the Attic deme of Teithras.   **πυρρόν**: 329 n., cf. *Ra.* 308 (as rightly interpreted by Stanford) ὁδὶ δὲ δείσας ὑπερεπυρρίασέ σου.

1062–5 **θάρρει . . . χεσεῖ**: referring back to his θαρρῆσαι. 'Be bold and come: you will be able to put yourself at ease inside.' Her house is unlike that of the rich man in the saying, τὸ δὴ λεγόμενον οὐκ ἔχεις ὅπο[ι χέσῃς | ὑπὸ τῶν ἀγαθῶν (Men. *Phasm.* 43).   **ἔνδον χεσεῖ**: for the facilities see 321, 371 nn. His answer (1063) expresses fear of being asked to do *more* (γ' best taken as emphatic) in *every* sense than he intended.   **ἐγγυητάς . . . | ἀξιόχρεως**: 'I'll produce two sureties of substance' (lega llanguage). Cf. *IG* ii². 111. 46 ἐξεῖναι αὐτοῖς ἐγγυητὰς καταστῆσαι . . ., ibid. 1183. 27 δανείζειν τοὺς ἱερέα[s] ἀξιοχρείωι ἐπ[ὶ χωρίω]ι, Pl. *Lg.* 914 e. See further And. *On the Mysteries*, ed. Douglas MacDowell (1962), 63.

1065–1111 As the old hag continues to drag him towards the houses another figure bursts upon the scene. The *tone* of the newcomer should have warned him: but the boy, by this time prepared to clutch at *any* straw, is ready to regard her as his saviour (that is, until he *sees* her, 1068). A tug-of-war (1076) ensues for his possession: till finally, with a paratragic utterance of farewell and instructions for the mode of his interment, the boy disappears between the two old women into one of the houses in the background.

1065–8 **ποῖ . . . ταύτης;** expressing rivalry towards the old hag in possession, not sympathy for the young man in her clutches. He corrects her verb ('*I'm* not going', if you're talking about *me*, cf. 1056), but blesses her for her timely intervention (cf. his plea to the girl in 1054). For the double interrogative cf. Men. *Sam.* 324.   **ἀτὰρ . . . γε**: 'but (all the same), *whoever* you are', cf. *Nu.* 801 ἀτὰρ μέτειμί γ' αὐτόν.   **πόλλ' . . . σοι**: *Pax* 453 ἡμῖν δ' ἀγαθὰ γένοιτ'.   **ἐπιτριβέντ'**: not with desire (224 n.).

1068–73 His hopes of safety disappear abruptly as he catches his first glimpse of the speaker: a white-leaded monkey or a ghost? (On the hags' masks see Introduction § IV.) He thinks of Heracles (who knew

all about monsters, but never encountered one like this), of the Panes
(who never inspired wilder panic than does the present ghastly appa-
rition), of the Corybants, the frenzied priests of Cybele (*Lys.* 558), who
symbolize the hags' sexual frenzy (is the third old woman dancing
wildly round him?), and of Castor and Pollux (more a prayer this)
who bring the traveller through dangers safely (E. *Hel.* 1664).

1069-73 Πᾶνες: generic plural, as *Σάτυροι, Σειληνοί* (Pl. *Lg.* 815 c). See
S. fr. 136 (with Pearson). **Διοσκόρω:** dual as often (*Pax* 285) of the
twin offspring of Zeus and Leda. **τοῦτ'** ... **ἐξωλέστερον:** 1053,
with *τούτου* (the second hag, still present) for *ἐκείνου* (the first hag,
who had vanished). **πίθηκος** ... **ψιμυθίου:** *πίθηκος* as an abusive
term, of *character*, is common (Cligenes, *Ra.* 708), but the use here is
clearly of *appearance* (she is one of *αἱ σιμότεραι*, 617). So Bito's nose is
'three times worse than a monkey's (*AP* xi. 196. 1). And a naturally
ill-favoured face is not improved by its plaster of white lead (878 n.),
ψιμυθίῳ πίθηκος ἐντετριμμένος (*Com. Adesp.* fr. 517, Edmonds III A,
434). **ἀνάπλεως:** 'chock-full' to the top, with the result that the
hair above the forehead looks quite grey, *ἐπὶ τῷ προσώπῳ* δ' *αἱ*
τρίχες φορούμεναι | *εἴξασι πολιαῖς, ἀνάπλεῳ ψιμυθίου* (Eub. fr. 98, 7).
γραῦς ... **τῶν πλειόνων:** 'an old woman risen from the dead', from
'the majority' ... *κεῦτ' ἂν ἵκηαι* | *ἐς πλεόνων* ... (*AP* xi. 42. 5). Simi-
larly, Plautus (translating from Philemon) *Trin.* 291 'quin priu' me
ad pluris penetravi?' Greek and Latin idiom perhaps here coincide,
cf. 'incurrere in pleores' (*Hymn of the Arval Brothers*, 4). See further in
Rogers and van Leeuwen.

1074-8 μὴ σκῶπτέ μ' ... **ἔπου:** 1005 n. **μὲν οὖν:** 'on the contrary',
111 n., 1084. They pull him violently in different directions (cf.
διασπάσεσθε, 1076). **ὡς** ... **οὐδέποτ':** sc. *ἴσθι*, E. *Ph.* 625 *ὡς τάχ'*
οὐκέθ' *αἱματηρὸν τοὐμὸν ἀργήσει ξίφος*. All the old women are determined (cf. 1000, 1085). **οὐδὲ μὴν ἐγώ:** 'nor will *Γ*', 1085, *Ra.* 263.
ὦ κακῶς ἀπολούμεναι: 1052 n. **γὰρ:** '(yes) for ...', 375 n. Hag *B*
is prepared to go on pulling. **σ' ἔδει:** so manuscripts, correctly, 'it
were right that you should follow *me*.' Cf. *Ra.* 37, *Pl.* 432 *ἀλλ' ἥτις εἶ*
λέγειν σ' ἐχρῆν (*σε χρῆν* R, *σε δεῖ* Cobet here), Hor. *Carm.* i. 37. 2
'nunc Saliaribus | ornare pulvinar deorum | tempus erat dapibus,
sodales.' **οὔκ** ... **φανῇ:** she has no false ideas of her beauty
(*αἰσχίων* as 618 n.).

1079-81 The law demands that he should deal with the old woman before
having access to the girl. But must he be *killed* before he gets there?
οὐ φροντὶς γρᾳδίῳ Γ. **ἐπ' ἐκείνην** ... **ἀφίξομαι;** 620 n. **αὐτὸς**
σκόπει σύ: 'that's *your* look-out' (Rogers). **τάδε** ... **ποιητέον:** we
are hardly to understand (van Leeuwen) 'quae in hocce meo libello
scripta exstant', even if (for which there is no evidence) Hag *Γ* (like
Hag *A*, 1013) has a copy to hand of the decree. The boy knows her
meaning well enough.

1082–8 He also knows that he is beaten. So which of the two to tackle first? His surrender leads to still more vigorous attempts to 'pull him asunder', and he comments that the hags would make rough ferrymen (1086). Hag *B* (1088) is not amused. **ποτέρας προτέρας**: cf. for the jingle *Nu.* 940 φέρε δὴ πότερος λέξει πρότερος; **οὖν**: in *third* position (as 1157), more often second (1079). **κατελάσας**: *sensu obscaeno*, *Pax* 711. Cf. 109, 1091. **δευρὶ μὲν οὖν**: 1074. **ἀλλ' οὐκ ἀφήσω**: cf. 1000, 1075. **οὐδὲ μὴν ἐγώ**: 1075. **χαλεπαί . . . πορθμῆς**: that is, even rougher than these gentlemen are normally in drawing away custom from their rivals: a truculent ferryman is implied in Arist. *Mete.* 356ᵇ16. For the tendency of boatmen to overload their vessels see Hor. *Sat.* i. 5. 12. **ἕλκοντε . . . ἀπεκναίετε**: 'you would wear away your passengers with pulling', cf. Pl. *R.* 406 a 'Herodicus, a trainer in gymnastic, fell ill, and by a mixture of gymnastic and medicine ἀπέκναισε first and especially himself, and then many others after him', a passage illustrating both the literal and (commoner) metaphorical senses of the verb. **σιγῇ . . . βάδιζε**: that's enough (she means) of trying to be funny, *not* 'come quietly' (offer no resistance). **μὰ Δί' ἀλλ'**: 'no, by Zeus, but . . .', 158, 463.

1089–90 The youth is a prisoner between two ghastly warders: who hold him fettered like a miscreant on trial (δεδεμένον ἀποδικεῖν, X. *HG* i. 7. 20) by the terms of Cannonus' decree. Xenophon (loc. cit.) puts the matter clearly: 'You all know, men of Athens, that Cannonus' decree is very stringent. It bids that all who injure the Athenian people be bound and meet the charge before the people.' So Hsch. s.vv. *Καννωνοῦ πανδοκεῖον*: 'this man introduced a decree ὥστε διειλημμένους τοὺς κρινομένους ἑκατέρωθεν ἀπολογεῖσθαι.' See G. Busolt–H. Swoboda, *Griechische Staatskunde*, ii [Munich, 1926], 1008 n. 6. **διαλελημμένον**: 'bound', 'fettered', Pl. *Phd.* 81 c διειλημμένην (sc. τὴν ψυχήν) γε οἶμαι ὑπὸ τοῦ σωματοειδοῦς. For the differing forms see 58 n.: the use of the rarer here may indicate the more formal language of the law.

1091–2 πῶς . . . δυνήσομαι; he expresses his 'dilemma' more exactly. **δικωπεῖν**: 'handle two oars at once', *sensu obscaeno*, 1082 n. For a δίκωπον σκάφος (of Charon) see E. *Alc.* 252. **βολβῶν χύτραν**: for 'bulbs' (Thphr. *HP* vii. 13. 8) as aphrodisiac (see 948 n.) cf. Alex. fr. 279 'pinnae, crayfish, bulbs . . . who ἐρῶν ἑταίρας would find other drugs of greater use than these?' Similarly, Pl. Com. frs. 173. 9, 174. 12, and other passages in Athenaeus (64 b, 356 e). The βολβός (modern Greek βορβός) is identified (see Willems, 247) with the tassel-hyacinth (*muscari comosum*).

1093–7 It is almost over, he is nearly at the door: and he utters a cry of lamentation. The next words, if addressed to him, are difficult: how can Hag *Γ*—the boy's answer shows that the speaker here is not she whose door is mentioned, 1093—understand him to see prospect of salvation? But she means to refer back (I think) to 1091 : 'you may think you're going to get out of handling *two* of us : but never mind, the door is not so narrow that *all* of us can't tumble in together.' And the boy's reply lends some credence to her view that this idea may indeed have struck him. (Others explain that ἀλλ' . . . σοῦ is addressed to Hag *B*, who is winning.)

This interpretation may be eased by punctuation after κακοδαίμων (*Ra*. 33), so that these words refer to 1092. If so, what alarms him is the prospect of swallowing down a pot of βολβοί: a dish 'by itself' (i.e. without the seasonings) 'bad and bitter' (Philem. fr. 122. 4).

1093–5 οἴμοι . . . εἰμ': not quite paratragic (Brunius–Nilsson, 95), but rather quasitragic (323 n.). It may, all the same, be justifiable to join ἑλκόμενος with εἰμί (i.e. ἕλκομαι), the so-called *schema Chalcidicum*, Χαλκιδι[α]κόν, ὡς τὸ "Σωκράτης ἀπολογούμενός ἐστιν" ἀντὶ τοῦ ἀπολογεῖται (Lesb. Gramm. 4 Müller) : otherwise, εἰμί goes with ἐγγύς. For the ambiguity cf. *Ra*. 35 ἐγγὺς τῆς θύρας | ἤδη βαδίζων εἰμί. Neither in that passage nor the present does the article imply a single stagedoor (34 n.). **ἀλλ' οὐδὲν . . . πλέον:** 'that won't help you at all', cf. Pl. *R*. 341 a Εὖ μὲν οὖν οἶδα, ἔφη· καὶ οὐδέν γέ σοι πλέον ἔσται. **ξυνεσπεσοῦμαι:** perhaps with some hint of its military meaning, of soldiers pursuing the besieged to their own gates and rushing along with them inside, καὶ αὐτοῖς ξυνέπεσον οἱ διώκοντες (Th. vi. 100. 2).

1096–7 ξυνέχεσθαι: three possible meanings, (*a*) 'to be afflicted' (φροντίς τις . . . ἧ συνειχόμην, E. *Heracl*. 634), (*b*) 'to engage in close combat' ('at first, it is said, they stood apart and shot at one another with their arrows: afterwards συμπεσόντας τῆσι αἰχμῆσί τε καὶ τοῖσι ἐγχειριδίοισι συνέχεσθαι', Hdt. i. 214. 2), (*c*) 'to have sexual intercourse' (ἀλλ' ὥσπερ ⟨κύνες⟩ αἱ γυναῖκες ἐν ταῖς ὁδοῖς συνέχονται, Thphr. *Char*. 28. 3). **νὴ τὴν Ἑκάτην . . . ἤν τε μή:** 70 n., 981.

1098 ff. The youth (in paratragic tone) laments his situation. He anticipates shipwreck (1106 n.) and appeals to the spectators (1105 n.) to see that he is buried on the spot. The uglier of the old hags, after treatment, will be placed as a funeral λήκυθος on his grave.

1098–1101 ὦ τρισκακοδαίμων: cf. 1112 n., 1129. **γυναῖκα . . . σαπρὰν:** 884 n. **Φρύνην . . . γνάθοις:** '1101 signifie à la fois: "une Phryné qui a un pot de fard sur les joues" et "un crapaud qui a une pustule sur les joues"' (J. Taillardat, 'Calembours sur des noms propres chez Aristophane', *REG* lxix [1956], viii–ix, cf. id. *Images*, 64). But (*a*) I do not think that λήκυθος (in view of 1111, 1032, and the boy's question 1073) can be other than the funeral oil flask (996 n.), (*b*) there is no evidence that it could be equated (despite a sense of 'swollen language', 'bombast' sometimes given to ληκύθιον in *Ra*. 1246) with φλύκταινα (1057). Quincey, 40, sees a reference (cf. 996 n.) to cosmetics superimposed on wrinkles. The meaning of the phrase is very doubtful: I take it, however, as an idiom expressing 'a whore who has got one foot in the grave'. Two prostitutes called Phryne are referred to by Athenaeus (591c): of the more celebrated one (from Thespiae, but later than our play) he has much to relate (590 e). φρύνην, Blaydes, i.e. 'a toad', which may be right: if so, cf. for his aversion Alciphr. iv. 12. 3 μετὰ φρύνου καθεύδειν ἂν εἱλόμην. But ἔχουσαν . . . γνάθοις then reads very oddly.

1102–4 μὲν οὖν: corrective, βαρυδαίμων (E. *Alc.* 865) being stronger in tone than κακοδαίμων. Similarly, 765. Another example (perhaps) of 'incongruity' (cf. 464, 868 nn.). νὴ τὸν Δία τὸν σωτῆρ': the irony can scarcely be deliberate (at least on the part of the young man), and clearly the oath here is a stock one, whatever may be true of other places (79, 761, 1045 nn.). Or is it a half-*prayer*, in a last (not hopeful) effort to achieve an eleventh-hour salvation? **θηρίοις συνείρξομαι**: compare the fate of the unfortunate Athenian girl whose father, discovering that she had been seduced, shut her up in an empty house with a horse ὑφ' οὗ προδήλως ἔμελλεν ἀπολεῖσθαι συγκαθειργμένη (Aeschin. i. 182), and for θήρια, of the old women, see *Lys.* 468. The boy fears (*a*) being mangled by the wild beasts, (*b*) being forced to perform his married duty, once shut up inside the marriage chamber: for which use of συνείργω cf. Pl. *R.* 461 b.

1105–11 Addressed to the audience (22 n.), not the chorus (1114). But we need not alter (see apparatus criticus): ὅμως (1105) means 'whatever my misfortune, I may get a decent burial at least.'

1105–6 ἐάν . . . πολλὰ πολλάκις: 'if (as is probable)', a stronger version of εἰ πολλάκις ('si forte'), 791. For the collocation of the adverbs see *Th.* 287. τι . . . πάθω: i.e. 'die', a common euphemism (cf. *V.* 385, below). ὑπὸ . . . κασαλβάδοιν: with ἐσπλέων, not πάθω, 'with these two whores' (fr. 478) 'as pilots'. ἐσπλέων: of sailing into harbour (Pl. *Criti.* 115 d). But here the entrance (ἐσβολή, E. *Med.* 1264) is narrow (1094 n.): should he fail, with his tugs, to navigate it, he wishes to be buried 'at the mouth' (cf. Th. iv. 49, Pl. *Criti.* loc. cit.). Willems (248) detects a reference here to Themistocles' (alleged) tomb in the Piraeus (Plu. *Them.* 32. 4).

1107–11 θάψαι: infinitive for imperative, 1111, *V.* 385 ἤν τι πάθω 'γώ, | . . . θεῖναί μ' ὑπὸ τοῖσι δρυφάκτοις. τήνδ': i.e. the third hag, whose connections with the grave (1101 n.) suggest her suitability to mark that of the boy she helps to kill. The reading is Bergler's alteration of manuscripts' τῶν (RΓΛMu1Vb1), τὴν (B). It is odd, perhaps that the boy has no prescription for the other old woman who torments him: but I cannot believe that τὴν ἄνωθεν can be taken (as Blaydes suggests) to mean 'the one above him', as though the young man were a sandwich, and the 'bottom' hag collapses (1036) to form his grave. Nor need we find a reference to σχήματα συνουσίας (*Lys.* 773). Rather, take ἄνωθεν ἐπιπολῆς together (cf. Hdt. iv. 201. 1 κατύπερθε δὲ ἐπιπολῆς τῶν ξύλων χοῦν γῆς ἐπεφόρησε), with ἄνω (1111) resumptive. She is to be tarred from head to foot as a punishment (Ath. 524 a), but also to make her water-proof and air-tight as a λήκυθος (Cratin. fr. 189, 829 n.). It is just conceivable that λήκυθος (cf. Taillardat in 1101 n., Quincey, 40) could refer at the same time to her *shape*. The molten lead poured round her ankles is to fix her securely in place upon the σῆμα: cf. E. *Andr.* 267, 'even if molten lead held you firmly round about' (i.e. fastened like a statue to its base). **'πιθεῖναι:** 1107, 40 nn. With the meaning of the compound here ('— on top of') contrast that ('— beside') in 538 n. **πρόφασιν ἀντὶ ληκύθου:** 'as a substitute for', 'in the role of a funeral λήκυθος' (996 n.). **πρόφασιν:** either (*a*) adverbial (cf. *Eq.* 466) or (*b*) with τήνδ' (cf. *Nu.* 55): and ἀντί may mean either 'instead of', or 'like', 'as if' (D. xvii. 3 δουλεύειν ἀντὶ τῶν ἀργυρωνήτων).

For the implications of Bergk's *XOPOY* (1111) see 729, 876 nn.

1112–83 The reluctant lover and his captors have now vanished (still furiously struggling) through a doorway: a tipsy figure reels in from the right. Praxagora's serving-girl has come to find her master, and call him, with her dancing-girl companions (1138 n.), to the banquet. The chorus sing a μέλος μελλοδειπνικόν, a pretext to make 'a small suggestion' to the judges on how they should set about their duties; describe a wondrous cooked dish (1169 n.) now in prospect; and finally, all exit dancing.

This brief summary makes assumptions discussed in Introduction § III.

1112–13 ὦ μακάριος ... δῆμος: not nominative for vocative (734), but predicative ('happy are the people'). I thus print ὤ (cf. 1098). Her slightly awkward syntax and repetitiveness (1112, 1116) suggest a recent indulgence in the Thasian and Chian wines she praises (1119, 1139). Emendation (see apparatus criticus) should certainly be resisted. It is the height of good cheer (says Σᴿ, *Pax* 537) when even the servant-girls get drunk: cf. the picture of τις βραχεῖσα προσπόλων in Men. *Dysc.* 950. **δέσποινα:** i.e. Praxagora. It is true that we hear nothing of this serving-girl before, but this is not a serious objection. She may, in fact, have been a recent acquisition: for slaves, of course, are not to be abolished, just distributed more fairly (592). The fact that she calls others—whether or not the women of the chorus—μείρακες (1138 n.) is no good reason for assuming that she herself is *old* (Oeri, 19 ff., cf. 120 n. ad fin.): she is probably the usual young slave-girl (Pickard-Cambridge, *DFA* 228), and identical with the 'heraldess' (834). See Introduction § III.

1114–17 ὑμεῖς ... ὅσαι: clearly the chorus (see 1125), whereas the boy (1105 n.) was appealing to the audience at large. **ἐπὶ ταῖσιν θύραις:** she probably means 'at our door' (i.e. that of Blepyrus), not a true plural (865 n.). The plural form need not always mean a *double* door

(Pritchett, 236). References to the 'door' or 'doors' in comedy give no clue to the number of stage houses (Introduction § III). On Greek doors see Pritchett, 236, Mooney, 17, *Excavations*, viii. 249.   οἱ ...
δημόται: 1023 n.   **ἡ διάκονος**: a comparatively rare word for a servant (cf. *Av.* 1253), here perhaps especially one who waits at table (as later, cf. Acts 6 : 1). Seemingly, she has been helping *herself* freely to the perfume (841 n.) and the wine—a true Athenian woman, though a servant.   **μεμύρισμαι ... μυρώμασιν**: cf. *μυρίοισιν μυρίσαι Pl.* 529.

1118–19 ὑπερπέπαικεν: literally, 'has over-struck', i.e. 'excels', 'surpasses', in perfect as here (but with accusative) D. l. 34 ἢ σὺ τοσοῦτον ... ὑπερπέπαικας ... τοὺς ἄλλους ...; Possibly, although of course (see under) her primary thought is of its fragrance, her choice of verb hints also (cf. 1120) at the potent effect of Thasian wine: it 'hits' one more (makes one more drunk) than others. Cf. Eub. fr. 138 ὄξει παίει πρὸς τὰ στήθη. Similarly, κρούω, id. fr. 49 ἀλλὰ παραλαβὼν ἀκράτῳ κροῦε καὶ δίδου πυκνάς, | καὶ βότρυς τρώγειν ἀνάγκαζ' αὐτὸν ἐξ οἴνου συχνούς.   **τὰ Θάσι' ἀμφορείδια**: 'the dear little jars of Thasian', diminutive of *ἀμφορεύς* (cf. *Pax* 202), here used in affection, not of size. For its celebrated bouquet cf. *Lys.* 206, *Pl.* 1021, obtained (says Theophrastus) by the placing of dough mixed with honey in the jar (*Od.* 51). It is often named (with Chian, 1139 n.) as one of the choicest wines of Greece.

1120–2 ἐν τῇ κεφαλῇ ... χρόνον: i.e. both the perfume *and* the wine, which exhilarates without a 'morning after'. 'I will provide . . . Chian . . . Thasian . . . so that no one has a hangover' (Philyll. fr. 24). For Thasian and Chian amphoras see Virginia Grace, *Amphoras and the Ancient Wine Trade* (Princeton, N.J., 1961), fig. 52, figs. 44–7.
ἀπανθήσαντα: 'lose their flower', i.e. their bouquet (οἶνος ἀνθοσμίας, *Pl.* 307), elsewhere of 'ageing' wine (compared to ageing man) ἀπανθήσαντα ... | σκληρὸν γενέσθαι (Alex. fr. 45).   **πάντ' ἀπέπτατο**: Cobet held *-επτόμην* the proper comic aorist, and many commentators here and elsewhere (as *Av.* 90) have altered the text to suit. But even if that view were demonstrably true, the girl might still be using tragic diction (cf. E. *HF* 69).   **ἐστὶ ... βέλτιστα**: i.e. τὰ Θάσι' ἀμφορείδια. The loose syntax would not worry a spectator who saw the drunk and mixed-up girl before him. But it may not be *intentional*: for the speech of drunken characters (cf. especially Philocleon, *V.* 1342 ff.) seems elsewhere not to be affected.   **πολὺ δῆτ'**: '*far* the best, I tell you', in repetition and endorsement (*GP* 277). So S. *El.* 1163 φίλταθ' ὥς μ' ἀπώλεσας | ἀπώλεσας δῆτ', ὦ κασίγνητον κάρα.
1123–4 κέρασον ἄκρατον: she likes her wine 'neat' (137, 227 nn.) and feeling 'on top of the world' she is addressing an imaginary servant of her own. For ἄκρατος (sc. οἶνος, *Ach.* 75), 'unmixed' wine, cf. *Eq.* 105. The word had perhaps even now become so common that its *literal*

sense was little felt (cf. Rev. 14: 10 τοῦ κεκρασμένου ἀκράτου . . .), but one must at least preserve a sense of humour: 'ἄκρατον κεράσαι quomodo sine vitio unquam potuerit dici non video' is an unhappy comment from van Leeuwen. εὐφρανεῖ . . . ἐκλεγομένας: sc. ἡμᾶς. The verb is used (as elsewhere) of 'wine that maketh glad the heart of man' (Ps. 104: 15), cf. Apolloph. fr. 6. ὅ τι . . . ὀσμὴν ἔχῃ: like the Thasian (1119 n.).

1125–7 She sobers and turns from her rhapsody on drinking to ask the chorus where to find her master. Notice that 'master' is identified more closely as 'the husband of my mistress': in the new state Blepyrus is a 'consort'. ἡ κεκτημένη (cf. Men. *Dysc.* 411), though no doubt in common use already as a slave's way of referring to his mistress (cf. of the owner of an animal, S. fr. 762. 2 Pearson), will from now on tend to oust (cf. 727 n.) ὁ κεκτημένος (*Pl.* 4). ἀλλ', ὦ γυναῖκες, φράσατέ μοι: for this type of question to the chorus cf. (for example) *Ra.* 435 ἔχοιτ' ἂν οὖν φράσαι νῷν | Πλούτων' ὅπου 'νθάδ' οἰκεῖ; Her question is necessary here because Blepyrus, though he left (at 727) with his wife, has been distracted in the meantime—even from thoughts of dining—by some dancers: Praxagora, who knows this (1138) but as head of state feels able to ignore it, has sent the servant (1137) to invite him *and* his girl-friends to the banquet. αὐτοῦ . . . δοκεῖς: the chorus know no more of his whereabouts than she does. But, standing at his house-door (Händel, 163, n. 8), they can tell her in effect 'if you stay *here*, he's bound to turn up sometime.' The line is paratragic (cf. Rau, 164): αὐτοῦ as first word is common in Euripides, who also often uses αὐτοῦ μένειν, cf. (for example) *Hel.* 1085.

1128–40 Blepyrus and the girls are seen approaching: the servant hails him as the happiest of men, explains her commission from her mistress, and tells him of the good wine still remaining.

1128–33 μάλισθ': 'you're right', cf. *Pl.* 826 Κα. δῆλον ὅτι τῶν χρηστῶν τις, ὡς ἔοικας, εἶ. Δι. μάλισθ'. ὁδὶ . . . ἔρχεται: 'for here he is' (cf. 934) 'on his way . . .' Note that Blepyrus is not coming from the *house*, in which sense ἐξέρχομαι is normal (331, 734). τρισόλβιε: cf. τρισκακοδαίμων (1098), *Av.* 1271–3. ἐγώ; σὺ μέντοι, νὴ Δί': 'yes, you, by Zeus', the particle assenting by taking up another's word or words (*GP* 401). Cf. (in general) *V.* 150 ἀτὰρ ἄθλιός γ' εἴμ' ὡς ἕτερός γ' οὐδεὶς ἀνήρ. τίς . . . μόνος; she indicates the nature of his bliss. He alone (out of thirty thousand citizens) has still got the feast's delights before him. The coryphaeus, misinterpreting her meaning, exclaims ironically (95 n.). For the language of her question cf. Solon in Hdt. i. 32. 5 οὐ γάρ τι ὁ μέγα πλούσιος μᾶλλον τοῦ ἐφ' ἡμέρην ἔχοντος ὀλβιώτερός ἐστι, for its paratragic flavour A. *Th.* 673 τίς ἄλλος μᾶλλον ἐνδικώτερος; E. *Hel.* 594.

The traditional figure of thirty thousand citizens was accepted by Herodotus (v. 97. 2), and R. Meiggs suggests that this was 'the real

230 COMMENTARY

total of Athenian adult males enrolled on the deme registers at the time of Cleisthenes' reforms' (*CR* n.s. xiv [1964], 2–3). Their true number at any time lay probably between the twenty thousand *poorer* ones (*V.* 709) and the more than thirty thousand *Greeks* who in the theatre (Pl. *Smp.* 175 e: the context invites exaggeration) were dazzled by the brilliant Agathon. The plague, of course, had its effect: in the fourth century, 'there are about twenty thousand Athenians in all' (D. xxv. 51). Cf. the twenty-one thousand of the census of Demetrius of Phalerum (Ctesicles 245 F 1), a figure which Jones (76 ff.) accepts.

1134 εὐδαιμονικόν γ' ἄνθρωπον: the -ικός ending may be merely *metri gratia*. But Peppler (438) detects its use in contexts (1153, *Pax* 856) where old ways or fortunes are brought into contrast with the new.

1135–8 ποῖ ποῖ βαδίζεις; at first sight it looks as if Blepyrus now starts running (for which implication of ποῖ ποῖ; see *Th.* 1093). But this ill suits (a) 1140 (μὴ βραδύνετε), (b) his continuing presence and his speech (1144–50), since nothing has been said that might have checked him. It is better to interpret as an ordinary question: her earlier words (in 1128) were naturally a mere assumption. Blepyrus, however, now confirms it—he *is* in fact making for the banquet. **νὴ τὴν Ἀφροδίτην:** 189 n. **ἐκέλευε:** 'was bidding me' (and that command still stands). For the idiomatic use of the imperfect cf. *Eq.* 1181 ἡ Γοργολόφα σ' ἐκέλευε τουτουὶ φαγεῖν | ἐλατῆρος. **συλλαβοῦσαν . . . τὰς μείρακας:** cf. Pl. 1079 νῦν δ' ἄπιθι χαίρων συλλαβὼν τὴν μείρακα. The μείρακες are not (as scholiast) the chorus: not because that term is inept for married women (E. Fraenkel in *Greek Poetry and Life* [1936], 268: V. Coulon is defending an undisputed thesis in stressing that the chorus may be *youthful*, *Ph.* xcv [1942], 41), but because the chorus (speaking 1151, n.) distinguish themselves from Blepyrus' companions. Still less are they 'the little daughters of Blepyrus and Praxagora' (as Rogers). I follow Fraenkel (270, after Bothe and H. Voss, cf. Russo, *Aristofane*, 344, who justifiably remarks on the word-order) in the view that they are dancers, forming (with the Chian wine and 'other good things') the 'apparatus convivii' of *Ach.* 1089–3; in fact, a παραχορήγημα, like the courtesans (*Ach.* 1199) or dancing-boys (*V.* 1501). See also Introduction § III. That the girls enter naked (cf. Wilamowitz, *Lysistrate*, 57) is unlikely, if only (415 n.) because of the coldness of the weather: see K. Holzinger in *SAWW* ccviii. 5 (1928), 38.

1139 οἶνος . . . Χῖος: the Chians were reputedly the first to plant the vine, an art acquired from their founder, Oenopion the son of Diony-sus (Theopomp. Hist. 115 F 276). Athenaeus calles Chian wine 'the pleasantest' (χαριέστατος, 32 f), describes sweet, dry, and medium varieties, and concludes that 'speaking generally' (κοινῶς) 'Chian is an aid to digestion and is nourishing: it creates good blood and is satisfying because of its richness of quality.' Its after-effects, like those of Thasian, were gentle (1120 n.), but 'blameless Chian' is placed first by the god of wine himself (Hermipp. fr. 82. 4).   περιλελειμ-μένος: 'left over' (περι-), 'still surviving', τοὺς περιλελειμμένους φίλων, E. *Hel.* 426.

1140–3 The girl urges haste and extends her invitation to take in the audience and judges—at least those well disposed towards the play. εἴ τις . . . τυγχάνει: ὤν, as fairly often, omitted. Porson (after Phrynichus) denied this use in Attic (proposing here κεἰ τῶν θεατῶν ὤν τις) and some apparent examples *are* uncertain, cf. *Av.* 760 (Blaydes), Pl. *R.* 369 b (ὤν perhaps lost by homoeoteleuta). But see S. *Aj.* 9, *El.* 313: and for fuller discussion W. L. Lorimer in *CQ* xx (1926), 195 ff.   καὶ τῶν κριτῶν . . . ἑτέρωσε βλέπει: 'doesn't turn his eyes elsewhere', doesn't favour Aristophanes' rivals. The chorus of course —no longer speaking as women of the city (cf. 578, 1154 nn.) but as choreutae involved in the success of the production—want the votes of *all* the audience and judges (cf. *Av.* 445). A majority of *one* vote (*Av.* 447 ἑνὶ κριτῇ νικᾶν μόνον) is thought fit punishment for broken pledges: though that expression, in the context, is a humorous παρὰ προσδοκίαν for πίπτειν (*Eq.* 540). Audience and judges (1154 n.) are mentioned together, since the former might sometimes (by a show of partisanship) exert a certain pressure on the latter (Pl. *Lg.* 659 a): and had allegedly tried (though without success) to do so for Aristophanes' *Clouds* (Ael. *VH* ii. 13. 24).   πάντα γὰρ παρέξομεν: i.e. we women, whether mistresses or slaves, cf. 690, 599.

1144–8 Blepyrus, full of *bonhomie* engendered by good fortune, both political and private, would go further: let *everyone* be brought without exception. They will find their dinner waiting—back at home! For this comprehensive invitation to the audience cf. *Pax* 1115, for the παρὰ προσδοκίαν conclusion (31 n.) *Lys.* 1063–71, 1203–15.

οὔκουν . . . καλεῖς . . . ; so Plautus' Simo, 'quin vocas spectatores simul?' (*Ps.* 1331). οὔκουν . . . δῆτα, in emphatic questions, *Eq.* 878 οὔκουν σε δῆτα ταῦτα δεινόν ἐστι πρωτοτηρεῖν . . .; οὐκοῦν (*ΔΜ*u1), 95 n.   γενναίως: i.e. 'like a lady'. So γενναῖος εἶ, 'you're a gentleman' (*Th.* 220), Μυρωνίδης . . . ὁ γεννάδας (304a). Similarly, ἐλευθέρως (1145) means not just 'freely', but 'like a free-born citizen', Men. fr. 857 ἐλευθέρως δούλευε, δοῦλος οὐκ ἔσῃ.   παραλείψεις: 'leave to one side' (παρα-), cf. 250.   καλεῖς: 'invite' for a meal, as 349. καλεῖν, *R*ΛΜu1: but passages of different construction (like *Ra.* 462, where R has γεῦσαι) lend no support to the harsh imperatival (1107) usage here. γέροντα, μειράκιον, παιδίσκον: this may mean 'everyone', as we might say, 'from sixteen up to sixty': perhaps by convention ladies were not mentioned (cf. Handley on Men. *Dysc.* 967). But the fact that his list contains no women (καὶ γραῦς καὶ γέρων καὶ παιδίον, Alex. fr. 125. 9) does suggest that none in fact was present at the play (cf. 167, 440 nn.) as does the all-male catalogue, *Pax* 50. Pl. Com. (fr. 206)

232 COMMENTARY

lists ἄνδρες, γέροντες, μειράκια, παλλάκια (the context, however, is unknown). For boys in the theatre (attested in these passages) see also *Nu.* 539, for the rare diminutive παιδίσκος X. *HG* v. 4. 32. ἀπαξάπασιν: 217 n.

1148 ἦν ... οἴκαδε: a type of stock joke in audience invitations in comedy both Old (above) and New (Plaut. *Rud.* 1418). It is not meant to imply the return from dreams to hard reality, after the extravagant promises of a state-supported life for all (Roos, 11) : to show that 'die bombastischen Versprechungen der kommunistischen Frauenrepublik als eitel Dunst erwiesen werden' (W. Süss, 'Scheinbare und wirkliche Inkongruenzen in den Dramen des Aristophanes', *RhM* xcvii [1954], 293).

1149–50 Blepyrus announces his intention of proceeding, without more ado, towards the banquet ('and luckily, you know, I have this torch here'). But possibly his 'torch' pre-occupies him (see below): he seems to be still around to join in the dancing (1166 n.). 'πεί-ξομαι: 40 n. ἔχω ... καλῶς: he is looking forward after dining to joining in a κῶμος (692 n.), and may have been carrying 'this torch here' (see 27 n.) from the beginning. But his form of expression, 'actually' (καί, 29 n.), 'you know' (τοι, 35 n.), 'fortunately' (καλῶς, cf. 2), suggests it is a recent acquisition. If so, he perhaps (as Rogers thinks) picks up the torch which the young man (978) discarded. But one may suspect (as van Leeuwen, cf. Süss, 294) that 'torch' here has other connotations: Philocleon makes one represent a music-girl (*V.* 1373). And was Δᾱς perhaps a nickname of some courtesan? Cf. Synoris, known as Λύχνος (Ath. 583 e). See also 50 n. ad fin. The 'little torch' is a hetaira in New Comedy (Webster, 'Masks', 106).

1151–2 R has a paragraphus, but gives no indication (cf. 327 n.) of speaker. It is clearly (I think) the coryphaeus (not the servant, as Robert, 345) : who begins by reproaching Blepyrus' time-wasting and urges him to take the girls and go. Meanwhile the chorus, while awaiting the feast that *they* anticipate, will sing. 1151–3 *could* be spoken by the servant (Wilamowitz) : if so, the song (1163 ff.) must also be given to her (id.). I prefer to assign them to the chorus (cf. *Pax* 729–33). There they begin on their 'path of words' immediately: here they break off (with δ', cf. E. *Cyc.* 597) to make their 'small suggestion' to the judges.

τί δῆτα ... ἔχων; 'why do you keep on wasting time, then?', 24, 853 nn., i.e. in dalliance with your 'torch'. τασδί: the μείρακες (1138 n.). On Wilamowitz's assumption (see above) the reference of course is to the chorus. καταβαίνεις: down to the agora (where the feast is being held) from the theatre sited on the hillside. Cf. ἀνάβαινε (*Eq.* 149), to the Sausage-seller, 'come up' (from the market). The meaning is *not* (as Blaydes, van Leeuwen, cf. L. Roussel, 'La Scène dans les théâtres grecs classiques', *Mélanges Charles Picard*, ii [1949],

894) 'down from the stage to the orchestra'. There was either no raised stage in Aristophanes' theatre (Bieber, *HT* 73) or else a low temporary structure (57–9 n., T. B. L. Webster, *Greek Theatre Production* [1956], 7, Roussel, 893, on *V.* 1341–4: but see also P. D. Arnott, *Greek Scenic Conventions in the Fifth Century B.C.* [1962], 34) : and in *V.* 1514 (sometimes quoted here) καταβαίνω means 'to enter on a contest', ἀτὰρ καταβατέον γ' ἐπ' αὐτούς μ', i.e. 'I am compelled to take them on.' Anti (228, cf. Russo, *Aristofane*, 12–13) sees the verb as further evidence (281, 496 nn.) of production of the play in the Lenaeum: but see W. J. W. Koster, *Mn.* xvii (1964), 399.

1153 ἐπᾴσομαι . . . μελλοδειπνικόν: 'I will add a song' (E. *El.* 864), 'a Lay of Lay-the-Dinner' (Rogers). The translation neatly turns the pun on μέλος, μελλο-, but one may doubt if any reference is meant to συγκλητικόν μέλος, a song sung to bid guests assemble for a banquet (Ael. *VH* viii. 7. 31). Rather, in view of their following appeal, we may take it as a 'song of expectation of the dinner' they will share when the judges give their verdict. For victorious choregi would commonly (though not as a statutory duty) entertain their chorus-members at a meal. Hence the fierce denunciation of Antimachus, 'who, as choregus at the Lenaea, sent me away without a dinner' (*Ach.* 1152).

1154–62 In the chorus leader's 'small suggestion' to the judges, he is joined by the rest of the choreutae, and all continue (1155) in trochaic tetrameters catalectic: i.e. four trochaic metra, the last being catalectic (285 n.), cf. *Ra.* 718–37. Their play is the first of the five to be presented: let this fact not prejudice its chances of success, and let the judges not betray their oath.

1154 σμικρὸν . . . βούλομαι: so the Clouds (*Nu.* 1115: 578, 1142 nn.) and Birds (*Av.* 1101), 'we want to say something to the judges about victory—all the blessings we will give them, if they judge us victors in the contest.' Both those addresses are accompanied by threats of revenge for an unfavourable verdict: the Clouds will destroy crops and roof-tiles, while the Birds will do their worst to new white cloaks. The second passage suggests strongly, in its sequel, that the festival judges might be venal, and Midias, standing by them as they swore (1160 n.), allegedly attempted (by threats, if not with money) to corrupt them (D. xxi. 17). Cf. *Ach.* 656 (Aristophanes' principles are outlined) ; 'he says he will teach you many good lessons, for your happiness, without fawning or bribery . . .' (though the reference here may be to paid 'claqueurs', 1141 n.). But whatever the loop-holes— a choregus, for example, might get a pledged supporter on the panel, Lys. iv. 3—the city went to considerable lengths to ensure that decisions were impartial. The verdict was given by five judges (scholiast, *Av.* 445) in the sense that five tablets (γραμματεῖα, Lys. loc. cit.) were drawn at random by the archon from those which all *ten* judges had to place, inscribed with their decisions, in an urn. The ten themselves were similarly chosen: the boule selected a preliminary list (Isoc. 17. 33) from the ten tribes (Plu. *Cim.* 8. 7), and the names from each tribe were segregated in one of ten urns, from which, brought sealed into the theatre, the archon drew ten names (one from each). The judges thus picked were put on oath (1160 n.) to carry out their duties without favour. Further details in Pickard-Cambridge, *DFA* 95–9 (on which the above account is based).

1155–7 Metre: trochaic tetrameters catalectic (1154–62 n.). **τοῖς σοφοῖς μὲν . . . τοῖς γελῶσι δ':** the judges (chosen as above) would, like the audience, be a mixture of 'intellectuals' (or at any rate, those of sound literary judgement, 'discriminating', *Nu.* 535) and others who looked merely for amusement. We are not to see in the lines 'explicit proof' (Ehrenberg, 67) that the communistic ideas in the play are introduced with serious intention. **κρίνειν ἐμέ:** sc. νικᾶν, 'judge *me*' (the chorus speaks for the poet, *Pax* 765 ff.) 'the victor', cf. *Av.* 1101 (quoted in 1154 n.), *Ra.* 1473 ἔκρινα νικᾶν Αἰσχύλον. **σχεδὸν ἅπαντας . . . ἐμέ:** 'so it's almost all of you I'm clearly bidding vote for me' (there may be one or two not covered by the two categories he has mentioned). **οὖν:** third word, as 1082. **δηλαδή:** *V.* 442. The particle (always coalescing very closely with δῆλος, *GP* 205) is fused with it completely in this adverb.

1158–9 μηδὲ τὸν κλῆρον . . . ὅτι προείληχ': these words provide our only evidence that the order of the plays was fixed by lot (and could not, by the way, have been inserted before the lots were drawn—fairly late? But variant versions, of course, could be rehearsed against all possible outcomes of the 'draw'). To be first 'on' could clearly be a drawback: the judges had four other comedies to witness (*Hypoth.* IV to *Pl.* names the poet's four competitors), and even if these were given in succession on one day (Pickard-Cambridge, *DFA* 64) the last one—unless incontestably inferior—would gain from being vividly remembered (1162; 'plerique mortales postrema meminere', Sal. *Cat.* 51. 15).

1160 μὴ 'πιορκεῖν: see 1149. For the judges' oath cf. D. xxi. 17, for the adjuration not to break it, Pherecr. fr. 96. And for repetition (fairly rare) of ἀλλά, cf. *V.* 371.

1163–7 The chorus break into a 'Cretan kind' of dancing, bidding Blepyrus (καὶ σύ, 1166) and his dancing-girl companions join in. The metre (trochaic tetrameters, above) is interrupted by 1163 (*extra metrum*) and an obvious lacuna (1166–8).

1163–6 ὥρα δή . . . ὑπανακινεῖν: cf. 30, *Th.* 1228 ὥσθ' ὥρα δή (emphatic) 'στι βαδίζειν . . . The -ανα- of the compound verb suggests a kind of dancing in which the leg is raised (1180, cf. 1167) and this recalls the movement ὕψι βιβάς (*h. Ap.* 516) in processional Minoan Cretan dancing—a movement illustrated by the 'Harvester' vase from Hagia Triada in Crete. This is what the chorus mean: hence Κρητικῶς ('in the Cretan manner', 1165), and we need not find a reference to 'cretics' (with the scholiast), much less engage in juggling to obtain them. For this explanation (and a detailed discussion of the passage) see Lillian B. Lawler, 'Krêtikôs in the Greek Dance', *TAPhA* lxxxii (1951), 62–70.   ὦ φίλαι γυναῖκες: self-apostrophe by the chorus, cf. (for example) *Lys.* 539: the words should not be given to the servant (Wilamowitz, 1151 n., cf. 1166) nor yet to a semi-chorus (R, cf. 1166). εἴπερ . . . τὸ χρῆμα δρᾶν: 'if we're going to do the thing' (vaguely, cf. 148).   Κρητικῶς . . . κίνει: see above. For a similar exhortation to a certain kind of dance see *Th.* 981, and for attempted reconstruction of Greek comic choreography Germaine Prudhommeau, *La Danse grecque antique* (Paris, 1965), i. 531.

1166–7 τοῦτο δρῶ: cf. *V.* 457.   καὶ τάσδε νῦν . . . τὸν ῥυθμόν: attributed to the servant (Wilamowitz) or a semi-chorus (R), see above. The lacuna gives wide scope for ingenious conjecture (see apparatus criticus for details).   λαγαρὰς: 'loose-limbed', 'agile', dancers in good training and condition. Cf. (of a horse) ὁ . . . αὐχὴν αὐτοῦ . . . λαγαρὸς . . . τὰ κατὰ τὴν συγκαμπήν (X. *Eq.* i. 8). We are not to suppose (with Coulon) that the chorus (to whom he refers the words) are 'lean and hungry' (cf. *Th.* 984). The diminutive σκελίσκος (here only) is exceptional as masculine derived from neuter (σκέλος). Cf. σανδαλίσκος (*Ra.* 405), Peppler, *CT* 23.   τὸν ῥυθμόν: cf. perhaps τὸν ῥυθμὸν σὺ τήρει (Men. *Dysc.* 910).

1168–83 A marvellous dish of fish and flesh and pickles—to name a few ingredients—awaits them. Blepyrus is bidden fetch a bowl and bring some porridge (a staple diet in ordinary times, but now a mere precautionary stand-by) and he, the chorus, the dancing-girls, and servant move high-stepping out of the orchestra, in a grand burlesque processional of victory—a type of comic exodus, the poet claims, first hit on by himself to close the *Wasps* (see *V.* 1536).

1168–76 τάχα . . . ἔπεισι: 'will soon be on the way' to the table. So ἐπιφέρειν, 'to bring to table', 'serve', ἐντεῦθεν εὐθὺς ἐπιφέρει τραγήματα | ἡμῖν ὁ παῖς μετὰ δεῖπνον (Mnesim. fr. 7. 5). This short line (metre doubtful, ∪ ∪ ∪ ∪ – ∪, but probably intended as dactylic) is succeeded by the great dactylic word, intended perhaps to be delivered in one breath (like a πνῖγος, *Ra.* 971 with Stanford): a feat pronounced by Eustathius impossible (1277. 49). πολυσύνθετοι λέξεις (he is saying) are affected by Attic comic writers (Blaydes's note offers numerous examples, as *Lys.* 457–8); and he speaks of a passage 'παρὰ τῷ κωμικῷ, in an unfamiliar play, so συχνοσύνθετον' (which certainly describes the present passage) 'that the person who sets out to read it . . . will not get through the whole in one breath'. Experiment shows Eustathius mistaken. The extreme πολυσύνθεσις (cf. Shakespeare's 'honorifacibilitudinitatibus', *Love's Labour's Lost* v. i. 40, and Rabelais's 'Antipericatametanaparbeugedamphicrationes', ii. 7) perhaps 'takes off' Philoxenus of Leucas, a poet of dithyramb renowned for innovations not only in words but also music (Antiph. fr. 209). The fragments of his celebrated Δεῖπνον (*PMG* 836) include a long gastronomic compound (ibid. (e) 13). No parody, however, seems intended (see next note) of Philoxenus' dactyls. Cf. Pl. Com. fr. 173. 6.

1169–76 Metre: dactylic tetrameters (four metra, each a dactyl) with resolution into tribrachs and proceleusmatics (see below). The second (∪∪∪∪) is very rare in dactyls (*Av.* 1752 is not perhaps a parallel, see Dale, 25 n. 2), the first (outside Homer) is unique. I venture, however, to let the scansion stand, for (*a*) a novel word excuses novel metre, (*b*) we may see here exaggerated parody (as elsewhere of *language*, cf. 973) of lyric *metre*, cf. Ibyc. (*PMG* 285. 3), ἄλικας ἰσοκεφάλους ἐνιγυίους, – ∪∪ ∪∪∪∪ – ∪∪ – –. 1169, of course, may also be regarded as proceleusmatic and a *trimeter* (Dale, loc. cit., White, 148).

> 1169 ∪∪∪ ∪∪∪ ∪∪∪ ∪∪∪
> 1171 – ∪∪∪ ∪∪∪∪ ∪∪∪∪ ∪∪∪∪

1169–75 Does the mighty mixture (cf. Suet. *Vit.* vii. 13. 2, and the German 'Saucissenkartoffelbreisauerkrautkrantzwurst', E. Deschanel, *Études sur Aristophane* [Paris, 1876], 216) include the saucepan (λοπάς) in which it is brought in piping hot? ('I would more gladly eat a tiny little lawsuit ἐν λοπάδι πεπνιγμένον', *V.* 510). For λοπάς shapes see Amyx (1002 n.), pl. 49e, Sparkes and Talcott (734 n.), figs. 39, 44. Or is λοπάς here (as later, Lucian, *Asin.* 47) 'limpet'? Certainly we start off with fish (see 56 n.) : slices of salt-fish (τεμάχη, 606 n.), shark (σέλαχος, medicinal, Eup. fr. 1), and dog-fish (γαλεοὺς . . . ὅσα τε . . . | ἐν ὀξυλιπάρῳ τρίμματι σκευάζεται, Timocl. fr. 3). On top of this are bits and pieces (λείψανα) of κράνιον ('head', unidentified, cf. κέφαλος, 'mullet', Arist. *HA* 543ᵇ16) in bitter pickling (ὑπότριμμα, 292*b* n.).

Birds now, thrush (κίχλη), an often mentioned favourite, to Dicaeopolis the summit of εὐωχία (*Ach.* 1011) 'on top of' (ἐπι-) blackbird (κόσσυφος), a delicacy (Ath. 136 d), various pigeons, φάττα, περιστερά, πέλεια (καλόν γε καὶ ξανθὸν τὸ τῆς φάττης κρέας, *Ach.* 1106), and finally cock and wagtail (κίγκλος), mentioned, like many of the other dainties here, in the long gastronomical catalogue, Anaxandr. fr. 41. The middle letters of 1173 (see apparatus criticus) are doubtful: presumably, however, they represent a *bird* (ὀπτὸκέφᾰλῐο, Coulon, 'roast mullet', see above), hence the text's οπτοπιφαλλι⟨δ⟩ο, 'roast lark' (Hsch. s.v. πιφαλλίς). With these are hare (843 n.) dipped in new wine boiled down (σιραιοβαφη), for the use of which sour relish (*V.* 878) see Alex. fr. 188. 4 σιραίῳ χρωματίσας καὶ σιλφίῳ | πυκνῷ πατάξας, and 'gristly wings' (? the sense again uncertain, τραγαλο, Blaydes, cf. *V.* 674). We need not probe this comic word too closely.

Poured all over (κατακεχυμενο) as seasonings (ἀρτύματα) are silphium and honey (Antiph. fr. 142), with 'oily dressings' (λιπαρο) cf. *Av.* 531, where birds are served up with grated cheese (hence Blaydes's

τυρο), olive-oil, silphium, and vinegar, and κατάχυσμ' ἕτερον γλυκὺ καὶ
λιπαρόν. Retention of παραο (R⁄Mυι) is barely possible (despite
επι, 1172) 'by the side of' (Rogers, following Le Febvre). Further
details of many of the birds and fishes mentioned may be found in
D'Arcy W. Thompson, *A Glossary of Greek Birds²* (1936) and *A Glossary
of Greek Fishes* (1947).

1175–6 σὺ δὲ: Blepyrus, as 1166.   ταχὺ καὶ ταχέως: perhaps a stock
colloquial expression (cf. for example 'well and good'). Most editors
ταχέως ταχέως (Meineke), cf. *Pl.* 644.   λαβὲ τρύβλιον: in two senses
(252, 847 nn.). Their next words are παρὰ προσδοκίαν (31 n.) : his
bowl is to be used for common porridge. Roos (12) detects here the
pricking of the bubble (cf. 1148 n.). But nothing suggests 'ein ganz
verdutzer, aus allen Wolken gefallener' Blepyrus (Süss [1148 n.], 297).

1177–9 Metre: catalectic trochaic dimeters with choriamb and tribrachs
(900, 893 nn.) and syncopation (900 n.).

$$- \cup \cup - \cup \quad - \cdot - $$
$$\cup \cup \cup \quad \cup \cup \cup \quad - \cdot - $$
$$- \cup - - \qquad - \cup - $$

εἶτα . . . ἐπιδειπνῇς: 'hurry' (291*b* n.) 'and bring porridge' (more
common fare, Alex. fr. 258, Pherecr. fr. 22 ἡ γυνὴ δ' ἡμῶν ἑκάστῳ
λέκιθον ἕψουσ' ἢ φακῆν | ἀναμένει) 'to make a *second* meal' (cf. Hp. *VM*
10) in case the banquet after all is slight.   ἀλλὰ . . . που: 'but'
(joking aside) 'they are stuffing it down, if I'm not mistaken' (111 n.),
i.e. it is time we were away. Hence the command 1180. The lines
should not be given to a semi-chorus (R, cf. 1163 n.), to Blepyrus
(most editors with Blaydes), or to the servant (Händel, 163 n. 8).
λαιμάττουσι: here only, but clearly in the sense of λαιμαργοῦσι (scholiast,
Nu. 1202), i.e. they are keeping their throats busy. Cf. (of a greedy
fish) λαίμαργος, Arist. *HA* 591ᵇ1. The verb may be coined on the analogy of κανάττω, *Eq.* 105 (C. W. Peppler, *AJP* xlii [1921], 154).

1180–3 All go off dancing (metre doubtful), the chorus with Bacchic
cries (becoming to the god of the festival) and confident of triumph
(εὐαί, ὡς ἐπὶ νίκῃ). They bid 'step high' (see 1165 n.) and boldly
proclaim 'we shall be dining'. They speak, in these last lines, as
choreutae (cf. 1154): their thoughts are not (as 1165) of Praxagora's
banquet, but of feasting as guests of the victorious choregus (cf.
1153 n.).

A similar ending, with triumphal shouts and dancing, *Lys.* 1291 :
ἀλαλαὶ ἰὴ παιήων | αἴρεσθ' ἄνω ἰαί, ὡς ἐπὶ νίκῃ ἰαί. | εὐοῖ, εὐαί, εὐαί.
For the exclamations see A. Schinck, *De interiectionum epiphonematumque
apud Aristophanem vi atque usu* (Halle, 1873), 20, 21.

ADDENDA

ix.   References to Menander, *Samia*, are from C. Austin, *Menandri Aspis et Samia*, i (Kleine Texte für Vorlesungen und Übungen 188a, Berlin, 1969).

xi.   Add: ROBERT, C., 'Aphoristische Bemerkungen zu den Ecclesiazusen des Aristophanes' (*Hermes*, lvii [1922], 321–56).

        DE STE CROIX, G. E. M., 'Demosthenes' τίμημα and the Athenian εἰσφορά in the Fourth Century B.C.' (*C &M* xiv [1953], 30–70).

        THOMSEN, R., *Eisphora. A Study of Direct Taxation in Ancient Athens* (Copenhagen, 1964).

xvi.   Plato. There are, of course, explicit references in comedy to Plato and his views: examples are cited in an interesting article by W. G. Arnott, 'From Aristophanes to Menander' (*G. & R.*, Second Series, xix [1972], 70–1).

xxviii. On the decline of the comic chorus: Arnott (xvi above) finds parallels in the entrance song of the chorus in Eubulus' *Stephanopolides* (frs. 104, 105) and 'that of Aristophanes' *Ecclesiazusae*' (art. cit. 68). I am grateful to Professor Arnott for permitting me a preview of his paper, though I find the parallels not entirely convincing, and to speak of an *entrance* song in this play (see 114) could be misleading.

xxx ff. Stage-doors. For the advantages of a *three*-door skene in this play see now K. J. Dover, *Aristophanic Comedy* (1971), 198.

xxxii.   Identification of 'master' with Blepyrus. See also G. Maurach, 'Interpretationen zur attischen Komödie' (*Acta Classica*, xi [1968], 2 n. 7a), who regards it as deliberate that 'der Mann der Initiatorin' gets nothing.

xxxviii. Phallic costume. J. F. Killeen, 'The Comic Costume Controversy' (*CQ* N.S. xxi [1971], 51–4), accepts Aristophanes' claim at its face value: the evidence of phallic costume on vase-paintings should not prevail against it (54). He is, however, 'not concerned to argue about later plays than the *Wasps*' (53).

ADDENDA   239

xliii n. 6. Arethas is the only Byzantine of whose private book collec-
             tions we have details. On institutional libraries see Nigel
             G. Wilson, 'The Libraries of the Byzantine World',
             GRBS viii (1967), 53–80.

xliv n. 7.   Callimachus. See further R. Pfeiffer, *History of Classical
             Scholarship* (1968), 125 ff.

xlvii n. 1. Performances. The play was performed in 1971 (in
             modern Greek) in Athens and in Oxford (adapted, as
             'A Diet of Women').

70.   Hymn/prayer parody. See further A. Kormornicka,
             'Quelques remarques sur la parodie dans les comédies
             d'Aristophane' (*QUCC* iii [1967], 72 ff.), and W. Horn,
             Gebet und Gebetsparodie in den Komödien des Aristophanes
             (Nuremberg, 1971).

74.   Σκίρα. Athena Skiras was honoured among the Salaminioi
             (Ferguson, 78 below, 18 ff.). Her cult involved dressing-
             up. See P. Vidal-Nacquet, 'The Black Hunter and the
             Origin of the Athenian Ephebeia' (*PCPhS* xiv [1968]
             49–64), and further S. F. MacMathúna, *Trickery in
             Aristophanes* (Cornell dissertation, 1971), 95. I am grateful
             to Dr. MacMathúna, whose work contains much of
             interest and value for this play, for allowing me to read
             his thesis.

77.   ἤ/ἦν variation. See (against Barrett) P. T. Stevens, Euripides
             Andromache (1971), 101.

78.   Σαλαμίνιος. For another possible meaning see W. S.
             Ferguson, 'The Salaminioi of Heptaphylai and Sounion'
             (*Hesperia*, vii [1938], 1–74).

88.   πληρουμένης: a *vox propria* of the Assembly (A. *Eu.* 570,
             E. *Andr.* 1097).

91.   ἡ μὴ 'μπειρία. For the philosophical use of μή to negative
             a concept see W. S. Barrett, Euripides *Hippolytos* (1964),
             198.

93.   τίς ἀγορεύειν βούλεται; For the general permission to speak
             (ἰσηγορία, cf. 385 n.) thus implied see G. T. Griffith,
             'Isegoria in the Assembly at Athens', in E. Badian (ed.),
             Ancient Society and Institutions (Oxford, 1966), 115–38.

104.   Women's accomplishments. For parallel lists see Stevens,
             Andromache, 104.

142.   ὑγίαινε/χαῖρε. Their alternative use was the basis of a
             fine pun by King Philip. Greeted by the half-crazed

'Menecrates called Zeus', who boasted of his skill in medicine' with the words Μενεκράτης Ζεὺς Φιλίππῳ χαίρειν,
the king answered Φίλιππος Μενεκράτει ὑγιαίνειν (Ath.
289 d–e).

155. Dramatic illusion: see D. N. Rudall, *The Function of
Inconsistency in the Plays of Aristophanes* (Cornell dissertation,
Ithaca, N.Y., 1968), 103–30. Its existence in the Greek
theatre is denied by G. M. Sifakis, *Parabasis and Animal
Choruses* (1971), 1 ff.

159. Δαρεικοί. See E. S. G. Robinson, 'The Beginnings of
Achaemenid Coinage' (*NC* Sixth Series, xviii [1958],
189–91). For an earlier Darius (if the record is authentic)
see Daniel 5:31.

165. ἤδη. Stevens (*Andromache*, 220) explains the use here as
'idiomatic . . . to mark a climax'.

166–7. Gnomon. See (against Dicks) Charles H. Kahn, 'On Early
Greek Astronomy' (*JHS* xc [1970], 112 ff.).

167. ἐπωβελία. See A. R. W. Harrison, *The Law of Athens*, i
(1968), 120 n. 4.

169. A. A. 1040. Add Hipponax 115. 8 (*Iambi et Elegi Graeci*,
ed. M. L. West, i, 1971), δούλιον ἄρτον ἔδων.

172. Allotment machines. See further J. D. Bishop, 'The
Cleroterium' (*JHS* xc [1970], 1–14).

173. Stoa Basileios. Its remains have been uncovered, and
identified with certainty, in the Agora excavations of
1970. See *Archaeological Reports for 1969–70*, 3, T. Leslie
Shear, Jnr., 'The Athenian Agora: Excavations of 1970'
(*Hesperia*, xl [1971], 243 ff., pls. 47–50).

181. Woman *B*'s husband. His characterization is fully discussed in the interesting essay by G. Maurach (xxxii
above). He shows that—unlike figures in the earlier
plays who enter at the same stage—this man is not a
single stereotype (cf., for example, Lamachus in *Acharnians*),
but a more complicated character whose traits are
gradually unfolded as he speaks. Thus he reveals himself
as first a niggard, then crafty, refractory, and a cynic.
Maurach points to parallel scenes in *Plutus* and Menander,
Dyscolus.
     On 'character' in Aristophanes see Maurach, 4 n. 10.

186. Athenian tardiness in action. Cf. (of Athenian women) *Lys.*
55–6.

ADDENDA 241

187. ὦ τᾶν. See G. J. de Vries, 'Remarks on a Greek Form of
     Address (ὦ τᾶν)' (*Mn.* N.S. xix [1966], 225–30).

189. Euripid(d)es. The man here mentioned is in fact identifi-
     able with an ambassador to Sicily in 393 B.C. (Arist.
     Rh. 1384ᵇ15). See further J. K. Davies, *Athenian Propertied
     Families* (1971), 202–4.

196. Women at door. Further passages in Stevens, *Andromache*,
     199.

197. ὄλισβος Ionian. The word is almost certain, however, in
     Sappho (D. L. Page, *Sappho and Alcaeus* [1955], 144–5
     n. 1).

203. Lesbos. Of course, 'Lesbianism', in the modern sense, was
     also attributed to the island. Cf. Anacreon, *PMG* 358. 6 ff.,
     Page, *Sappho and Alcaeus*, 143 ff.
     See also 845–7 n., V. Buchheit, *Studien zum Corpus Pria-
     peorum* (Munich, 1962), 86, 94–5.

204. Polecats as house-pets. Their incidence and suitability
     are questioned by Sylvia Benton, 'Pet Weasels: Theocritus
     xv. 28' (*CR* N.S. xix. 260–3).

207. τἀπὶ Χαριξένης. Cf. also ὁ ἐπὶ Κρόνου βίος (*Ath. Pol.* 16. 7).

211. διὰ σέ. This phrase (cf. *Nu.* 916, *Av.* 1546) is seen by E.
     Fraenkel ('Lyrische Daktylen', *Rh M* lxxii [1918] 178 =
     Kl. Beitr. i. 182 ff.) as a hymn formula, an idea rejected
     by Horn (70 above).

213. πεττοί. I accept that 'draughts' may be misleading.

214. Funeral lekythoi. See now D. Kurz and J. Boardman,
     Greek Burial Customs (1971), 102–5.

218. Prothesis: a duty allotted to women who were close rela-
     tions or (significantly, in the context of the play, see 982)
     to women over sixty years of age (D. xliii. 62). See Kurz
     and Boardman, 143, 360.

219. Water jug placed before the door. See Kurz and Board-
     man, 146, 360.

222–3. 1068 ff. The note treats Ἡράκλεις as vocative singular and
     πᾶνες as generic plural. But *both* may be plural, and seen
     as evidence for cults of duplicated deities: see Theodora H.
     Price, 'Double and Multiple Representations in Greek
     Art and Religious Thought' (*JHS* xci [1971], 531).

225. ληκύθιον in *Ra.* 1203. A *sensus obscaenus* (cf. ληκάω, αὐτο-
     λήκυθος) is now established by C. H. Whitman (*HSPh*

lxxiii [1969], 109–12) and J. G. Griffith (*HSPh* lxxiv [1970], 43–4).

232.   *Λύχνος*. Cf. Lampadion (Lucr. iv. 1165).

234.   1155–62. Sifakis (155 above), 67, sees these lines as 'an epirrhema ... that has been transposed to the exodos of the play' and 'a last relic of the parabasis'.

GENERAL INDEX

GREEK INDEX

252   GREEK INDEX